INVESTMENTS

Art or Science

An Overview, Fundamental Concepts, and Relevant Analysis in a Dynamic Environment (with useful Tables)

INVESTMENTS

Art or Science

An Overview, Fundamental Concepts, and Relevant Analysis in a Dynamic Environment (with useful Tables)

Sunil B. Kapadia

B.Com, MBA-Finance, CPFA

ISBN: 978-93-89583-07-6

Edition: 2019

Printed at: Shree Maitrey Printech Pvt. Ltd., Noida

Dedicated to

My Parents
and
My Teacher, Joshi Sir

Foreword

This book is a must for any person who invests for making money or planning for life and retirement. It is a comprehensive volume covering almost the entire gamut of investments – right from fundamental concepts of investments to the complexities of derivatives and the commodities markets. Normally, books focus on one segment of a financial sector, but this book is an encyclopedia for the reason that it covers a variety of investment options with simplified tables providing a useful guide for taking good investment decisions. Fundamental considerations for any investor are: safety, liquidity and returns. For the conservative investor, guidance is provided on debt market and, for an adventuresome there is guidance on stock and commodity markets. What is more! It gives useful clues on risk management.

I would strongly recommend this book for anyone who wants to secure his financial future, as it covers not only investment planning for oneself, but also for future generations through succession planning, and testamentary dispositions.

CA Mayur B. Nayak
Ex President
Bombay Chartered Accountants Society
Mumbai

Commendation

It is well said: your future is always more valuable than the present; the sooner you realize the better. And as a tax advisor – national as well as international – I have been associated with discussions on investment strategies, be it individuals or business houses. I generally talk about "financial freedom" that every investor must have. I also insist to bear the basic parameter in mind and, that is, let your money work for you, not vice versa.

This book aptly captures my vision of "financial freedom". The author Mr. Sunil Kapadia has critically diagnosed various symptoms of an investor as well as varied investments. The book touches every fundamental factor including psychological approaches of investor thinking. His discussion on individual/family risks versus available investments options, remarkably highlights and appropriately helps varied types of investors to check out as to what way one should ascertain the suitable kind of investment options amongst the many available in the market.

It needs to be taken seriously by new investors entering in the arena as well as those who claim to be "settled players" in this game. To all of them the topics such as "Fundamental Analysis and Technical Analysis" shall be an added advantage to gain insight therein. The chapter on "Commodity Markets" and "Foreign Exchange Market" along with regulatory guidelines under FEMA is worth reading so as to understand the importance of the very powerful investment segments though usually less explored by a common investor.

I am sure that every reader shall appraise himself on reading this book and shall very well recognize "the investor" in himself. My best wishes to Mr. Sunil Kapadia who has taken immense efforts in putting the strategies of investment planning in black and white – as he factually leads the results acting as an advisor on a day to day basis in world of reality as seen by me in close proximity.

I wish the readers get effective investment foresight and I also extend to Mr. Sunil Kapadia my warm wishes to pursue his fruitful future endeavours.

Regards,

CA Milind Kshirsagar
Pune

Preface

If you have more money than you need for current consumption, you are a potential investor. One of the probable decisions you may make is to sacrifice present savings to derive future benefits. Every investment decision therefore, will have three aspects to consider, namely: *Time horizon, Rate expectation* and *Attendant risk*.

Economic well-being of a person depends on how wisely he/she invests particularly for long term. Essentially, therefore, investment refers to committing funds to one or more assets that will be held over for some future time period. Two elements in investments are: *generation of income on a periodic basis*, and/or *growth in value over a period of time*.

We all work for money. Rather more importantly, we must ensure that money works for us. While investing we should manage our wealth effectively, obtaining the utmost from there. This obviously includes *growth in investments, protecting assets against inflation, taxes*, etc., to reduce risks.

Whether your money is invested in stocks, bonds, mutual funds, gold, real estate or certificate of deposits (CD), the end result is to create wealth for admission expenses to form a proportional college fees, marriage, retirement, vacations, and better standard of living or to pass on the legacy to the next generation. Further, it is exciting to review your investment returns and to see how they are multiplying exponentially.

Some fundamental rules of investments are:

Start early

Invest regularly

Ensure higher returns on your investments

Harness the power of compounding

Invest for long term or extended periods

So how does one improve his/her abilities in the field of investments? To answer this, a broad framework is provided in terms of the following parameters:

- Where are you now and where do you want to go?
- Environmental and regulatory aspects related to investments
- Investment objectives, asset allocation and portfolio diversification
- Spectrum of investment avenues

- Understanding of various risks and impact thereon for eventual returns
- Time horizon in investment management and time value of money
- Retirement planning and estate planning
- Different markets: Debt, equity, commodity, real estate, derivatives, foreign exchange and so on
- Fundamental and technical analysis, behavioral aspects of finance
- Provisions of income-tax for individuals and FEMA guidelines in Indian context
- Investigate, and Invest. Keep it simple. Learn from past mistakes.

Limitations

1. These investments and its findings are workable predominantly under Indian economic scenario for domestic investors. The same may not hold good for international/foreign investors.
2. Normally holds better for all investments except luxury investments.
3. Some or many conclusions may not hold in case of introduction of **EET** regime, i.e., exempt/exempt/tax regime.
4. It is suggested and recommended that an individual investor needs to be well informed and avail right, proper and timely advice from a qualified and experienced advisor/planner.
5. Although utmost care has been taken by providing updated (up to February, 2017) reference and table/(s), it is urged to refer to the prevailing/latest regulatory guidelines and policies in evaluating investment decision.
6. It is also urged to read different scheme information documents, terms and conditions, other relevant aspects so as to be well informed before making investment related decision.

Any limitations including flaws in table and the analysis due to circumstances beyond one's control is unintentional. The larger purpose and the greater interest of the book suggest how such limitations could be overcome in future.

Sunil B. Kapadia

Acknowledgements

I am grateful to M. S. Natarajan, (Rtd. Advocate, High Court, Mumbai) who has taken pain to review the entire book and provided valuable inputs.

I am also thankful to:

1. CA Mayur B. Nayak (FEMA consultant, Mumbai) for his valuable contribution on "FEMA guidelines chapter" and providing foreword to this book.
2. Professor (CA) Milind Kshirsagar (PuMBA, Pune University) for his motivation, reviewing book and providing commendations to book.
3. Professor (CA) Madhav Ganpule (Ganpule Classes, Pune) for his motivation and review of book.
4. Dr. Venu V. Madhav (Professor, KL University, and my guide for PhD) for his motivation and review of the book.

Last but not the least, I have always received very good support and encouragement from my family members, friends, colleagues, clients and well-wishers.

I would be happy to receive suggestions, inputs and feedback to make this book more useful and relevant to readers. Please share your feedback at: sk.sunil457@gmail.com

Sunil B. Kapadia

The Author

Since December, 2002 running consultancy services and advising clients in the matters of financial planning, wealth management and all related matter. The Ministry of Corporate Affairs had empanelled as '**Resource Person**' (2014 & 2016) to conduct Investor Awareness Program-**IEAP**.

Prior work experience (from August, 1993 to December, 2002) with Corporate include: lead a team in managing Industrial/Civil projects (worth INR: 3150 million) from finance and costs aspects. Arranged funds for working capital from banks, state financial corporation, coordinated for a Public-cum-Rights issue. Supervised Profit & Loss, Balance sheet, Internal audit, Budget, MIS, Cash-flow, etc.

Since 2009, evaluated and reviewed for Quality conduct, Performance Standards in assessing Business/Institutions. Provided feedback to - **Three** educational institutions, - **One** infrastructure, and **Three** manufacturing companies. Made contribution for Online Assessment for Process Improvement and Innovation for **Twelve** BFSI, **Seven** ITES (BPO/KPO), **Two** for Telecom, and **One** each for Logistics, Real Estate and Healthcare companies.

Presented **seven** papers at National and International Conferences in the area of: Economics, Investment and Consumer Protection.

Presented **nine** papers in the subject matter of Economics, Investments, Capital Markets, NPAs in Indian Banking system, Management Education, and Consumer Protection at National/International and Doctoral conferences/seminars in India. **Eight** of which got published in various journals (3 in Scopus and 4 in Google Scholar).

Certificate of Excellence: was awarded by **IMC-RBNQA**, for Performance assessment and Quality cycle as a Team member, Mumbai 2013.

Certificate of Merit: was awarded jointly by **Reliance** AMC and **Wellingkar Institute** for 3rd highest score in **CPFA** examination conducted by **NISM-SEBI**, Mumbai 2012.

Is associated with the Confederation of Indian Industry (**CII**-WR and NR), Indian Merchant Chambers, (**IMC**)-Mumbai and the Maratha Chamber of Commerce, Industry and Agriculture (**MCCIA**), Pune.

Hobby includes reading professional literature, and travelling.

Abbreviations

AIF	Alternate Investment Fund
AML	Anti Money Laundering
AD	Authorized Dealers
AMC	Asset Management Company
ADR	American Deposit Receipt
AMU	Asian Monetary Unit
ACU	Asian Clearing Unit
AFP	Actual Fair Price
ATM	At the Money
AMR	Active Management Return
AMP	Actual Market Price
APTM	Arbitrage Pricing Theory Model
BSE	Bombay Stock Exchange
BV	Book Value
CAGR	Compounded Annual Growth Rate
CD	Certificate of Deposit
CP	Commercial Paper
CBLO	Collateralized Borrowing and Lending Obligation
CAPM	Capital Asset Pricing Model
CAD	Current Account Deficit
CPI	Consumer Price Index
CMP	Current Market Price
CRR	Cash Reserve Ratio
CRISIL	Credit Rating Services of India Ltd.
CCI	Controller of Capital Issue
CDSL	Centralised Depository Services (India) Ltd.
CFO	Chief Financial Officer
CDD	Cooling Degree Days
CEO	Chief Executive Officer
CMO	Chief Marketing Officer
CIO	Chief Information Officer
CBDT	Central Board of Direct Taxes
CII	Cost Inflation Index
CTQ	Critical to Quality
DICGC	Deposit Insurance Credit Guarantee Corporation
DEMAT	Dematerialised
DB	Defined Benefit
DC	Defined Contribution
EOW	Economic Offences Wing
EOD	Economic Offence Division
ECGC	Export Credit Guarantee Corporation
ETF	Exchange Traded Fund
EPS	Earning per Share
EBIDT	Earning before Interest Depreciation & Tax

EAT	Earning after Tax
EBIT	Earning before Interest & Tax
EWP	Elliot Wave Principle
EMH	Efficient Market Hypothesis
EMU	European Monetary Union
ECAFE	Economic and Social Council for Asia Pacific
EP	Expected Price
EMP	Expected Market Price
E-I-C	Economic – Industry - Company
ELSS	Equity Linked Tax Savings Scheme
EPF	Employer/Employee Provident Fund
EMI	Equated Monthly Installment
FIU	Financial Intelligence Unit
FEMA	Foreign Exchange Management Act
FII	Foreign Institutional Investors
FMP	Fixed Maturity Plan
FMP	Fair Market Price
FPO	Follow-on Public Offering
FIFO	First in First out
FCCB	Foreign Currency Convertible Bond
FMC	Forward Markets Commission
FEDAI	Foreign Exchange Dealers Association of India
FERA	Foreign Exchange Regulations Act
FV	Future Value
FFP	Future Fair Price
FRA	Future Rate Agreements
GDS	Gross Domestic Savings
GNP	Gross National Product
G-Sec.	Government Securities
GM	Geometric Mean
GDR	Global Depository Receipt
GARP	Growth at Reasonable Price
GIC	General Insurance Corporation
GDP	Gross Development Product
HDD	Heating Degree Days
HLV	Human Life Value
HNI	High Net-worth Individual
IRR	Internal Rate of Return
IRDA	Insurance Regulatory Development Authority of India
IEPF	Investor Education Protection Fund
IGMS	Integrated Grievance Management System
IPR	Intellectual Property Rights
INT.	Interest
IPO	Initial Public Offering
IV	Intrinsic Value
IIP	Index of Industrial Production
IM	Information Memorandum
IRP	Interest Rate Parity
IFE	International Fisher Effect
ITM	In the Money
ITA	Income Tax Act
ISC	Investor Services Centre
KPI	Key Performance Indicator
KPIV	Key Performance Indicator Variable
KPOV	Key Performance Outcome Variable
LIFO	Last in First out
LIBOR	London Interbank Offer Rate
LTCG	Long Term Capital Gain

LAF	Liquidity Adjustment Facility
MCA	Ministry of Corporate Affairs
MOF	Ministry of Finance
MCX	Multi Commodity Exchange
MP	Market Price
MACD	Moving Average Convergence/Divergence
MF	Mutual Fund
MTM	Marked to Market
MIBOR	Mumbai Interbank Offer Rate
NPV	Net Present Value
NSE	National Stock Exchange
NBFC	Non Banking Financial Company
NHAI	National Highway Authority of India
NSC	National Savings Certificate
NSDL	National Securities Depository Ltd.
NCDEX	National Commodity and Derivatives Exchange Ltd.
NBT	National Board of Trade
NMCE	National Multi Commodity Exchange
NPS	National Pension Scheme
NHB	National Housing Bank
NRI	Non Resident Indian
NISM	National Institute of Securities Market
NCAER	National Council of Applied Economic Research
NDS	Negotiated Dealing System
OTC	Over the Counter
OMO	Open Market Operation
OTM	Out of Money
PFRDA	Pension Fund Regulatory and Development Authority
PMLA	Prevention of Money Laundering Act
PSU	Public Sector Unit
P/E	Price Earning
PTC	Pass through Certificate
PMS	Portfolio Management Services
PV	Present Value
PPF	Public Provident Fund
PAT	Profit after Tax
PPT	Purchasing Power Parity
P-Notes	Participatory Notes
PE	Private Equity
PF	Provident Fund
PA	Personal Accident
PRAN	Pension Registration Account Number
POA	Power of Attorney
QIB	Qualified Institutional Buyer
RBI	Reserve Bank of India
ROC	Registrar of Companies
REC	Rural Electrification Corporation
ROI	Return on Investment
R&D	Research & Development
REPO	Repurchase Obligations
ROE	Return on Equity
REIT	Real Estate Investment Trust
RGESS	Rahul Gandhi Equity Tax Savings Scheme
RPF	Recognized Provident Fund
RML	Reverse Mortgage Lender

SEBI	Securities and Exchange Board of India
SCORES	SEBI Complaints Redress System
SRO	Self Regulatory Organization
SML	Security Market Line
SCRA	Securities Contracts (Regulation) Act
S&P	Standard & Poor
SD	Standard Deviation
SMA	Simple Moving Average
SLR	Statutory Liquid Ratio
SAT	Securities Appellate Tribunal
SHCIL	Stock Holding Corporation of India Ltd.
Sec.	Section
STT	Securities Transaction Tax
STCG	Short Term Capital Gain
T-Bills	Treasury Bills
TWRR	Time Weighted Rate of Return
TDS	Tax Deducted at Source
ULIP	Unit Linked Insurance Plan
VC	Venture Capital
VAR	Variance
WDM	Wholesale Debt Segment
WPI	Wholesale Price Index
YTM	Yield to Maturity

Contents

UNIT-I

1 CHAPTER

What Investment is All About?

Investment involves making a sacrifice in the present with the hope of deriving future benefits. Some also define it as "postponed consumption". As benefit which is likely to accrue in the future, the two determinants of investment process are: *expected return* and *risk* associated with it. Thus, investment refers to a commitment of funds today to one or more assets that will be held over some future time period. It also means a *measurable asset* retained so as to increase one's personal wealth.

We all invest to improve our future welfare. Funds to be invested come from assets already owned, savings and/or foregone consumption. Anticipated future earning can be used for future consumption, such as *children's education, provision for retirement*, etc.

Investment decisions are premised on the assumption that investors are *rational* and hence prefer certainty. Generally, risk aversion is assumed if only an adequate compensation is expected. An investor usually postpones current consumption in anticipation to a rate of return suitably adjusted for inflation and associated risks. An investor looks for well thought-out solutions to complex financial situations while taking advantage of the investment opportunities.

Investment decisions are a part of economic life. Everybody makes such decisions in varied contexts at different times. Some are able to reap more profits through them; while others simply lose their investments. Attempts should, therefore, be made to understand how sound investment decisions can be made in order to enhance profit through them. Thus, investment decision-making is an important attribute.

Unfortunately, for too long, investment decision-making was regarded as an act. As an *art* it is personal/subjective, however, it was difficult to provide a general framework within which one could operate. Only recently, it was considered a *science* with the result that a body of literature has been developed so as to help us understand the way investment decisions can be driven. Recognizing its art content, this body of literature focuses on the thought such that a general framework can be suggested to be followed by those involved in investment decisions, which can be modified according to requirements. It has, therefore, been recognized that investment decision-making is both an *art* as well as a *science*.

1.1 SOME CONCERNS OF INVESTORS

- How do I scan investment opportunities and what, when and where to look for?
- How can I grow and protect my total wealth?
- How can I pay and manage my debt?
- How much should I save and invest so as to be able to pay for my children's education?
- How can I maximize tax benefits which can be availed?
- How can I save and invest in order to retire and maintain current lifestyle?
- How can I maximize what my heirs may inherit?
- How can I manage investment risks?
- When and how often do I review my investments to ensure that projected goals are achieved?

1.2 SOME USEFUL ASPECTS FOR INVESTMENT AND FINANCIAL PLANNING

- Identify all the financial needs of a person/family
- Translate the needs into measurable monetary goals
- Goals may be short term, medium term and long term
- Plan financial investments for achievement of goals.

Investment/financial planning is a *dynamic process*. You review your goals and objectives periodically and accordingly revise your financial plan, that is to say, if your circumstances change, e.g., in case of a marriage, birth/death, divorce, change of job, or any unforseen event. A plan would take into account the investor's profile, age/ sex, family size, income (quantum as well as periodicity of earnings), social/financial liability, goals, savings, cash flow, emergency needs, protection, different products, risk-return parameters, diversification amongst asset classes and tax matters, yielding both value and benefit.

1.3 IMPORTANT CONCEPTS USED IN INVESTMENTS

(a) Risk, return and investor outlook
(b) Risk appetite and optimal portfolio allocation
(c) Time value of money, e.g., Net Present Value (NPV)
(d) Annuities and their types
(e) Diversification by asset class, time maturity, geographical aspects
(f) Compounded Annual Growth Rate (CAGR) and Internal Rate of Return (IRR)
(g) Using derivative instruments for hedging portfolios
(h) Types of capital gains and tax based returns

A typical investment decision undergoes a process that is the basis of an investment. These are:

1. Determination of the investment **objectives** and **policy**.
2. Undertaking a security analysis and constructing a portfolio.
3. Reviewing and evaluating the performance of the portfolio on a regular basis.

1.4 INVESTMENT OBJECTIVES AND POLICY

An investor will have to work out his/her objectives first and then evolve a policy with the amount of investible wealth at his/her command. Important investment objectives of an individual investor include:

- Safety of the principal amount
- Liquidity at short notice
- To generate regular returns through interest or dividends
- To ensure that there is adequate capital appreciation, particularly during the times of inflation.

1.5 RISK PREFERENCES OF INVESTORS

The investment should take into account risk preferences of the investor. The risk preference is, in turn, decided by the willingness and ability to take risks.
Following are the factors to be considered for risk preferences by investors.

Personal Factors: Personal factors like age, income level, family commitments, time available for review and study of the investment portfolio are important in any invetment. Tax considerations, the effective marginal rate of income tax, wealth tax implications, capital gains, etc., have to be carefully examined.

One needs to remember that the pursuit of *large money* is not possible without the risk of *large losses*. Hence, the objectives of an investor must be defined in terms of risk and return.

Thus, investment management has to be custom-built to suit the needs of the individual and, of course, institutional investors. There is no single magic investment programme which suits everyone.

Security Analysis: This step consists of examining the risk-return characteristics of an individual security or group of securities identified. The purpose here is to know if it is worthwhile to acquire these securities for the portfolio. Now, this would depend upon the extent to which it is 'mispriced.' There are two broad approaches for finding out the 'mispriced' status of securities.

The first is known as *technical analysis* which studies past movements in prices of securities, the trends and patterns that repeat themselves, and the volume traded on stock exchanges. The second approach is known as *fundamental analysis* wherein a true or intrinsic value of a security is worked out to be compared with its current market price.

Portfolio Construction: This consists of identifying the specific asset/security in which to invest and determining the proportion of wealth to be invested in each. The investor will use security analysis approaches for this. Then, he must determine the timing of investments which is to observe the forecast price movements of equity share or debenture at the macro level. Finally, he will make all possible efforts to minimize the portfolio risk for a given expected level of average return. Thus, portfolio construction would address itself to three major problems, viz., security, timing, and diversification.

Portfolio Revision: As time passes, the investor would discover that securities which were once very attractive have ceased to be so. Also, new securities with promises of high returns and relatively low risk have emerged. In view of such developments, it would be necessary for him to review the portfolio. It must be kept in mind that transaction costs involved and the extent of improvement expected in the future in respect to the new assets/securities would prevail while revising the given portfolio.

Portfolio Performance Evaluation: A rational investor would constantly examine his/her chosen portfolio both for average return and risk. Measures, for doing so, must be developed. Also, the calculated risk-return position must be compared with benchmark yardsticks or norms. Such investment process would thus, acquire considerable significance since the tasks involved are quantitative measurement of actual risk and return evaluation against the objective norms.

2 Environmental and Regulatory Aspects Related to Investment

CHAPTER

Economic Legislation

For proper economic growth, it is essential to have reasonably sound rules and regulations in the form of economic legislation. This calls for review to ensure *continuing relevance* of such legislation periodically. Unfortunately, most of our economic legislation remains patterned on the British model, being out of tune with the changing circumstances.

The emergence of appropriate structure to provide *freedom* to savers and users of funds thus ensuring that banks operate in a competitive environment. Following are a few important needs to be taken care of while making any investment:

- Protection of savers' interest
- Create mechanisms to provide liquidity
- Create environment for facilitating direct investor/borrower interaction
- Freedom to save to align with risk-return
- Provide regulation and supervision to ensure compliance.

2.1 REGULATORY ENVIRONMENT AND ETHICAL ISSUES

(a) Need for regulation and investor protection/redressed mechanism
(b) Framework of regulatory system-Government and self-regulation
(c) Role of Ministry of Finance (MoF) & Ministry of Corporate Affairs (MCA) and its agencies
(d) Roles of regulators: RBI, SEBI, IRDA, PFRDA
(e) Securities Contracts (Regulation) Act & Securities Contracts (Regulation) Rules
(f) Companies Act, 1956 and 2012
(g) Registrar of Companies
(h) Indian Contracts Act, 1872
(i) Economic Offences Wing (EOW)
(j) Financial Intelligence Unit (FIU)

(k) Prevention of Money Laundering Act (PMLA), 2002

(l) Ethical issues in providing financial advice

MCA's Role: Investor Education and Protection Fund (IEPF)

The **IEPF** is a fund created by the Ministry of Corporate Affairs (MCA) for promoting *investors' awareness* and protecting their interests. The fund is created out of contributions from the central government, state government, companies and other related institutions.

Apart from the above, the fund also includes: unpaid dividends, matured debentures and deposits, application and call money due for refund and interest thereon provided such money remained unpaid and unclaimed for a period of seven years from the date when they fell due for payment.

The fund shall conduct investor education programs through media and seminars. It will fund investor education projects of institutions and organizations engaged in the same and which applies for resources to conduct such programs.

2.2 FRAMEWORK OF THE REGULATORY SYSTEM

It is important to ensure that investors make informed decisions about their financial transactions on the basis of a fair understanding of various markets which are engaged in such financial transactions. This implies that the entities issuing securities and units ought to furnish *adequate disclosures* on all relevant facts and the *intermediaries* selling/advising/distributing such products execute the financial transactions in the most efficient and ethical manner, while charging a fair and appropriate fee for transactions.

There are many issues which warrant regulations, e.g., deliberately engineered speculative activities in the stock market or insider trading is undesirable as they can hurt investors. Similarly, some mutual funds may take excessive risks, while some issuers of debt securities may not care to provide adequate collateral. There are many instances of unethical activities which can be *detrimental* to investors. These, if allowed unchecked, will lead to a drying up of investment activity, which is the lifeblood of capital formation in any economy.

The central government has created separate entities to regulate different sectors of the financial system. For instance, the Reserve Bank of India (**RBI**) regulates commercial banks, the Securities and Exchange Board of India (**SEBI**) regulates securities markets, the Insurance and Regulatory Development Authority (**IRDA**) regulates insurance companies (both life and non-life), while the Forward Markets Commission (**FMC**) regulates the commodities future sector. The central government exercises oversight at a certain level on these and other similar regulatory institutions.

Additionally, intermediaries representing some segment of the securities market may form a self-regulatory organization (**SRO**). For recognition as an SRO by SEBI, certain conditions have to be met with as spelt out under SEBI (Self-Regulatory Organizations) Regulations, 2004. Ideally, an SRO will seek to uphold investors' interest by laying and maintaining ethical/professional standards of conduct and encouraging *best practices* among its members.

The ruling given by a regulator may be challenged by petitioning the prescribed authority. In the case of SEBI, for example, the appellate authority is the Securities Appellate Tribunal (**SAT**). Rulings of the SAT can be challenged in the Supreme Court of India. Importantly, no civil court shall entertain any suit or proceeding relating to a matter which an adjudicating officer appointed under the SEBI Act, or under a duly constituted SAT, is empowered under the said Act to decide upon. Further, no *injunction* can be granted by any court or any other authority with regard to any action taken or to be taken pursuant to any power conferred by the SEBI Act.

2.2.1 Reserve Bank of India (RBI)

RBI is the central bank of the country and is vested with the responsibility of administering the *monetary policy*. Therefore, its key concern is to ensure adequate growth of money supply in the economy so that economic growth and financial transactions are facilitated, but not so rapidly which may precipitate inflationary trends. This is borne out in its Preamble, in which the basic functions of the Bank are thus defined: "... to regulate the issue of Bank Notes and keeping of reserves with a view to securing monetary stability in India and generally to operate the currency and credit system of the country to its advantage." In addition to the primary responsibility of administering India's monetary policy, RBI has other onerous responsibilities, such as financial supervision, etc.

RBI's functions are governed by the Reserve Bank of India Act, 1934, whereas the financial sector is governed by the Banking Regulations Act, 1949. The main functions of RBI are:

1. **As the Monetary Authority:** To formulate, implement and monitor the monetary policy in a manner as to maintain price stability while ensuring an adequate flow of credit to productive sectors of the economy.
2. **As the Regulator and Supervisor of the Financial System:** To prescribe broad parameters of banking operations within which India's banking and financial system functions. The objective here is to maintain public confidence in the system, protect depositor's interest and facilitate cost-effective banking services to the public.
3. **As the Manager of Foreign Exchange:** To administer the Foreign Exchange Management Act (FEMA), 1999 in a manner as to facilitate external trade and payment, and promote orderly development and maintenance of the foreign exchange market in India.
4. **As the Issuer of Currency:** To issue currency and coins and to exchange or destroy the same when not fit for circulation. The objective that guides RBI is to ensure supply for circulation of an adequate quantity of currency notes and coins of good quality.
5. **Developmental Role:** To perform a wide range of promotional functions to support national objectives.

6. **Banking functions:**
   (a) It acts as a banker to the government and manages issuances of central and state government securities.
   (b) It acts as a banker to the banks by maintaining the banking accounts of all the scheduled banks.

The general superintendence and direction of RBI's affairs are looked after by a Central Board of Directors appointed by the Government of India. Further, each of the four regions in the country is served by a *Local Board* which advises the Central Board on local issues and represents territorial and economic interests of local cooperative and indigenous banks. The Local Boards also perform other functions as delegated by the Central Board.

RBI performs the important function of financial supervision under the guidance of the Board of Financial Supervision (**BFS**) which was constituted in 1994 as a committee of the Central Board of Directors. The primary objective of the BSF is to carry out *consolidated supervision* of the financial sector consisting of commercial banks, financial institutions and non-banking finance companies. The BFS oversees the functioning of the Department of Banking Supervision and Financial Institutions Division and issues directions on regulatory and supervisory issues. Some of the initiatives undertaken by the BFS are:

- Restructuring of the system of bank inspections
- Introduction of offsite surveillance
- Strengthening the role of statutory auditors
- Strengthening the internal defenses of supervised institutions.

Currently, the BFS focuses on:

- Supervision of financial institutions
- Consolidated accounting
- Legal issues in bank frauds
- Divergence in assessment of non-performing assets
- Supervisory rating model for banks.

Redressal in Banking

Reserve Bank of India has set up the "Banking Codes and Standards Board of India (**BCSBI**)" as an independent autonomous watchdog to ensure that customers get fair treatment in their dealings with banks. The BCSBI has published the *Code of Banks Commitment to Customers* which sets minimum standards of banking practice and benchmarks in customer service for banks to follow.

Most banks are members of the BCSBI and have thus voluntarily adopted the Code as their Fair Practice Code in dealings with customers. The complete Code is available at http://www.bcsbi.org.in/Code_of-Banks.html

Each bank has a customer redressal department that handles issues that customers have against the bank. Customers can file complaints with this department. If the customer is not satisfied with the response, he/she can approach banking ombudsmen, appointed by the Reserve Bank of India in various locations across the country.

2.2.2 Foreign Exchange Management Act (FEMA), 1999

The Foreign Exchange Management Act (**FEMA**), 1999 consolidates and amends the law relating to *foreign exchange, external trade* and payments for promoting the orderly development and maintenance of *foreign exchange market* in India. As a result of this enactment, its predecessor, the Foreign Exchange Regulation Act (**FERA**), 1973 was repealed. FEMA extends to the whole of India and applies to all branches, offices and agencies outside India, owned or controlled by a person resident in India and also to any violation committed outside India by any person covered by FEMA. For illustrative purposes, some sections of the Act are discussed below:

Section 3 states that except as provided in FEMA and allied rules and regulations or under permission of RBI, no person shall

(a) deal in or transfer any foreign exchange or foreign security to any person not being an authorized person;

(b) make any payment to or for the credit of any person (resident/outside India) in any manner;

(c) receive otherwise through an authorized person, any payment by order or on behalf of any person (resident/outside India) in any manner; and

(d) enter into any financial transaction in India, as consideration for or in association with the acquisition or creation or transfer of a right to acquire any asset outside India by any person.

Section 4 lays down that except as otherwise provided in FEMA, no person resident in India shall acquire, hold, own, possess or transfer any foreign exchange, foreign security or any immovable property situated outside India.

Section 5 relates to Current Account transactions.

Section 6 pertains to Capital Account transactions.

Section 10 empowers RBI to authorize any person, or any application made to it, to deal in foreign exchange or in foreign securities as an authorized dealer, money exchange or offshore banking unit or in any other manner as it considers fit.

FEMA empowers the Central Government to appoint Adjudicating Authorities, Special Directors (Appeals) and an Appellate Tribunal. The latter two shall have for the purposes of discharging their functions under the Act, the same powers as are vested in a civil court under the Code of Civil Procedure, 1908 while trying a suit. Examples of some powers are:

(a) Summoning and enforcing the attendance of any person and examining him on oath.

(b) Requiring the discovery and production of documents.

(c) Receiving evidence on affidavits.
(d) Subject to the provisions of Sections 123 and 124 of the Indian Evidence Act, 1872, requisitioning any public record or document or copy of such record or document from any office.
(e) Issuing commissions for the examination of witnesses or documents.

2.2.3 Securities and Exchange Board of India (SEBI)

The Securities and Exchange Board of India (**SEBI**) is the apex regulatory and development agency of the *capital market* and *stock exchanges* in India. It was in the 1980s that India witnessed phenomenal growth and development of the securities market. For the first time it showed a potential not only to mobilize savings of the household sector, but also to allocate it with some degree of efficiency for industrial development.

Several companies came in the early 1980s and raised large resources from the market especially through debt instruments, which further sustained investor interest. During that phase, India was entering into the period of liberalization and decontrol so as to accelerate and gather momentum in the 1990s. These are some of the factors which spurred the growth of the capital market.

In order to sustain this growth and form growing awareness into a committed and discerning group of investors, it was necessary to remove the *trading malpractices* and *inadequacies* prevailing in the market. It was also found necessary to provide the investors with an organized and well regulated marketplace.

As seen earlier, the liberalized milieu does require regulation, but of a different kind. The practice of regulation of banking and the capital market have taken an entirely new look. Obviously, the new models have to draw some lessons from the *weaknesses* witnessed in the past. These lessons are:

- The regulatory function should have a sharp objective of fostering fair competition and correcting market deficiencies and irregularities with a view to bringing about healthy growth of the sector and the protection of participants.
- The regulatory body should be autonomous and, fragmentation of regulating agencies and laws should be avoided.
- While enactments empowering a regulatory body are important, the practice of regulations as well as the organization of the regulatory body are much more.
- No amount of regulation can be a substitute for efficient and honest management of the regulated entities and for an internal system of checks and balances. It is important to take a look at the entire gamut of changes taking place in the securities market regulation in India against this background.

Keeping in mind these necessities, the Government of India felt the need for setting up an apex body exclusively for the protection of the investors' potential, existing and prospective. And thus the Securities and Exchange Board of India (SEBI) was introduced on April 12, 1988, through an administrative resolution as an interim body under the overall administrative control of the Union Ministry of Finance, as a precursor to the statutory board.

Subsequent to the enactment of the SEBI Act, 1992, which is administered by SEBI, it lays down objectives, its powers and functions. Subsequent to the repeal of the Capital Issues (Control) Act, 1947, SEBI separately issued Disclosure and Investor Protection Guidelines in 1992 which laid down the framework for issue of capital by certain categories of companies. Through the SEBI Act and subsequent notifications issued by the Central Government, certain critical sections of the Act can now be administered by the regulatory body.

The objective of the SEBI Act is "… to protect the interests of investors in securities and to promote the development of and regulate the securities market and also for matters connected therewith or incidental thereto." Further, SEBI is also empowered to enforce disclosure of information or to furnish information to agencies as may be deemed necessary.

It aims at regulating business in stock exchanges and any other securities market, registering and monitoring the working of stock brokers, sub-brokers, share transfer agents, bankers to an issue, merchant bankers, underwriters, depositories, custodians, etc., and working of collective investment schemes including mutual funds. It also promotes self-regulatory organizations, prohibits fraudulent and unfair trade practices in the securities market and encourages investor's education. Other functions extend to regulating substantial acquisition of share and takeovers, calling for information, undertaking inspection, conducting enquiries and audits of stock exchanges and intermediaries, etc.

The existence of an efficient and stable financial system is essential to make the securities market vibrant, far reaching and effective. An efficient capital market ensures that resources are priced and allocated correctly. Institutions and mechanisms that enable this must be supported by regulatory structures that will streamline and enable the proper functioning of the securities markets. The purpose of securities regulation should be to develop markets that are *fair*, *transparent* and *efficient*, and ensure protection of the investors' interests.

The SEBI Act entrusts the SEBI the responsibility of inspection, investigation and enforcement of the activities, systems and mechanisms of the institutions and intermediaries of the securities market. SEBI has been assigned the powers of recognizing and regulating the functions of a stock market under the Securities Contract Regulation Act (**SCRA**). An integrated surveillance mechanism which tracks the activities of various participants in the securities market aim at timely identification of fraudulent activities. SEBI and the Central Government have riding-over powers under the SCRA in all matters relating to the stock markets.

The role of a regulatory body for the securities market in a country is determined by the stage of development of the securities market in the country. In the Indian context, with regard to the emerging nature of the market, the regulatory body must necessarily have the twin role of development and regulation. SEBI's efforts have always been to create an *effective surveillance mechanism* for the securities market, and encourage responsible and accountable autonomy on the part of all players in the market, who should discipline themselves and observe the rules of the game.

Evaluation of the Working of SEBI

Notwithstanding the fact that SEBI's functioning has come under severe criticism, it is able to make a dent into the jungle of stock market. In spite of hesitant attitude of the government in tackling the situation, SEBI started its activity on a firm note. The constituents, who enjoyed a degree of freedom more than the permitted levels, would normally be unwilling to curtail their activities. Even the stock exchanges have come into conflict with SEBI regarding the exercise of powers relating to calling for periodical returns, prescribing maintenance of certain documents, approving bylaws and licensing of dealers in securities in certain areas. As a matter of fact, the Central Government has the authority to exercise these powers under the Securities Contract Regulation Act, 1956. These are now sought to be transferred to SEBI through a new legislation.

SEBI keeps on *reviewing* its policies and *exploring* the scope for further *reforms* in the primary market. It is also carrying out significant and wide ranging reforms in the financial disclosures, issue procedures and allotment process and has also issued a consultative paper proposing these reforms to seek the views of market participants.

Although reforms have been carried out in a number of areas, SEBI is aware of the scope and need for further reforms in the secondary market. The exchanges are yet to be fully automated and they have to go a long way to introduce screen-based trading. There is also a need to *link* 21 stock exchanges across the country. Moreover, the stock exchanges have to be brought *close to* the investors and *access to* the stock exchanges made easy. The settlement cycles would have to be further shortened for ensuring efficient and faster settlement of trade transactions. SEBI is also moving in the direction of setting up the systems for derivatives trading.

SEBI has been constantly trying to look into methods of *investor protection*. However, it has been receiving investor complaints directly since its inception. To handle the ever increasing complaints, SEBI has introduced an automated complaints handling system. To create awareness among the issuers and intermediaries of the need to redress investor grievances quickly, SEBI has been issuing fortnightly press releases including the names of the companies against whom maximum number of complaints have been received.

Guidelines to Investors

1. Deal with a registered member of the stock exchange. If you are dealing with a sub-broker, make sure that all bills and contracts are made in the name of a registered broker.
2. Give specific orders to buy or sell within the fixed price limits and/or time periods within which orders have to be executed.
3. Insist on contract notes to be passed on to you on the dates when the orders are executed.
4. Make sure that your deal is registered with the stock exchange in the trade (*souda*) block book. In the case of a dispute, this will help trace the details of the deal easily.

5. Collect a settlement table from the stock exchange mentioning the pay-in and pay-out days. Each stock exchange has its own trading periods which are called *settlements*. All transactions within this period are settled at the end of it. All payments for shares bought and their deliveries take place on the pay-in day. An awareness of pay-in and pay-out days is useful when a broker tries to make excuses.
6. Insist on delivery. If the company returns your papers and shares with objections, contact your broker immediately.
7. Ensure that shares bought are transferred in your name before the company's book closure date. This is necessary to make sure that you receive benefits like dividend, interest and bonus shares. All companies have a book closure date on which the list of shareholders in the company is finalized.
8. Complain if the broker does not deliver the shares bought in your name. Proceed to contact another broker with the bill/contract given to you by the earlier broker, and the Exchange authorities and the latter will purchase the shares on your behalf. In such an event, the first broker will have to pay the difference in price (if any).
9. Do not take delays or harassment lying down. You have to complain to the grievance cell of the stock exchange or the SEBI in case of delay or harassment.

If one realizes the fact that the regulation of stock market activity is challenging, the proceedings turn out to be always tough. Even in its limited span of existence, it was able to make its presence felt by every constituent of the capital market. It is true that SEBI has had tussle with almost every participating institution in the capital market in respect to one or the other issue. Instead of taking up entire work with such a great speed, it should have implemented its policies in a sequential manner, allowing the participant institutions to learn the art of compliance. More so, SEBI should have taken at least public financial institutions and governing boards of stock exchanges into confidence, while formulating the guidelines for different issues, instead of throwing the responsibility to them unilaterally.

SEBI has laid down regulations to prevent insider trading and unfair trade practices which are detrimental to the interests of the investor. *Insider trading* refers to the dealing of securities by persons connected with a company having material information that is not available to the public at large. If an insider's charges are proved pursuant to SEBI's investigation, the penalties include monetary penalties, criminal prosecution, prohibiting persons/companies from securities markets and declaring transactions as void.

While creating the SEBI, the government seems to have been influenced by the legislative developments in USA. Parallel to SEBI in USA is Securities and Exchange Commission (SEC), created under Securities Exchange Act, 1934. Unlike SEBI, the SEC was given wide ranging powers for the purpose of protecting the investors' interests. Significant among them include:

1. monitoring the working of stock exchanges;
2. insisting on the companies for supply of extensive information on a regular basis;

3. penalizing members of stock exchanges who violate securities laws;
4. debarring the wrong-doers from any activity in the stock market and impose on them civil penalties and initiate criminal proceedings;
5. making rules about dealing with and managing the manipulative practices;
6. moving court for checking insider trading; and
7. prosecuting the company and its directors on its own, even without receiving complaints by an aggrieved investor in respect of supplying inadequate, incomplete and incorrect information.

Limitations in the Functioning of SEBI

The principal drawbacks in the functioning of SEBI are as follows:

1. Limited transparency
2. Bureaucratic administration
3. Lack of professionalism
4. Long and complex procedures
5. Lack of serious approach to investors' needs
6. Counterproductive regulations
7. Lack of adequate powers
8. Weak legislation
9. Mechanical procedures
10. Minimum accountability
11. Lack of confidence of all players in the capital market including investors, especially the small investors.

Way Forward, More Work is to be Done

Despite the importance of regulatory independence as a component of good regulatory governance, current practice in many countries falls short of the *ideal*. Much work needs to be done to strengthen the independence of regulatory agencies around the world and improve the *quality* of regulatory governance.

In the interest of financial stability, much attention should be given to ensuring the *independence* of the supervisory agencies as has been given to ensuring central bank independence. The current trends towards the unification of supervisory agencies provide an opportunity not only to harmonize independence arrangements among sector supervisors but also to raise them to a higher level.

Effective independence cannot be achieved without support from the broader political environment; however, vested political interests in the financial system remain strong in many parts of the world, and the cost of overriding regulators is often low. Nevertheless, the need to pursue goal of independent and accountable regulators and supervisors in the interest of long-term *financial stability* is as great as ever. Politicians must be convinced of this view.

Redressal in Capital Market

SEBI, as regulator of the capital market, has taken various measures for investor protection. Delegated redressal mechanisms have been put in place. For instance, investors having a grievance related to a transaction in stock exchange can approach the Investor Services Centre (**ISC**) of the stock exchange. Complaints can be filed online or physically. The ISC resolves queries of investors. The arbitration mechanism of the stock exchange is also available, for quasi-judicial settlement of disputes. These investor facilities are available at various centres across the country.

Similarly, for mutual fund investment, the Board of Trustees of the mutual fund can be approached, if the investor finds that queries are not resolved by the asset management company. In extreme cases, SEBI does not permit the mutual fund to launch new schemes.

If the specific company or intermediary against whom the investor has a complaint does not respond, or if the response is unsatisfactory, the investor can call SEBI's toll free numbers (currently, these are **1800 266 7575** or **1800 22 7575**) for assistance.

SEBI Complaints Redress System (**SCORES**) offers an online facility (www.sebi.gov.in) for investors to file their complaints against any listed company (issue or transfer of securities or non-payment of dividend) or intermediary registered with SEBI. Besides the investor details, the system captures details of complaints up to 1000 words. A pdf file up to 1 MB can also be attached as supporting document.

However, the following complaints are not registered in SCORES:

1. Complaints that are incomplete or not specific.
2. Allegations without supporting documents.
3. Offering suggestions or seeking guidance/explanation.
4. Seeking explanation for non-trading of shares or illiquidity of shares.
5. Not satisfied with trading price of the shares of companies.
6. Non-listing of shares of private offer.
7. Disputes arising out of private agreement with companies/intermediaries.

Further, SEBI does not deal with the following complaints:

- Complaints against unlisted/delisted/wound up/liquidated/sick companies.
- Complaints that are subjudice (relating to cases which are under consideration by court of law, quasi-judicial proceedings, etc.).
- Complaints falling under the purview of other regulatory bodies.

SEBI examines the complaints to confirm if they fall within its purview. It then forwards the same to the concerned entity which is required to respond with an Action Taken Report within 30 days. Investor can check the status of the complaint online.

Regulation Relating to Alternate Investment Funds Schemes (AIF)

Investment in all three categories of *alternative investment funds* shall be subject to the following conditions:

- The AIF may raise funds from any investor whether Indian, foreign or non-resident Indians (NRIs) by way of issue of units.
- Each scheme of the AIF shall have corpus of at least twenty crore.
- The manager or sponsor shall disclose their investment in the AIF to the investors of the AIF.
- No scheme of the AIF shall have more than one thousand investors.
- The fund shall not solicit or collect funds except by way of "private placement".
- The manager or sponsor shall have continuing interest in the AIF of not less than two and a half per cent of the corpus or five crore rupees, whichever is lower, in the form of investment in AIF and such interest shall not be through the waiver of management fees; provided that for Category III AIF, the continuing interest shall be not less than five per cent of the corpus or ten crore rupees, whichever is lower.
- The AIF shall not accept from an investor, an investment of value less than one crore rupees; provided that in case of investors who are employees or directors of the AIF or employees or directors of the manager, the minimum value of investment shall be twenty-five lakh rupees.

Units of close ended AIF may be listed on stock exchange subject to a minimum tradable lot of one crore rupees. Listing of AIF units shall be permitted only after final close of the fund or scheme (*i.e.* all committed subscriptions have been received in the fund). Each category of AIF has its set of investment parameters specified.

An AIF, by itself or through the manager or sponsor, shall lay down procedure for resolution of disputes between the investors, AIF, manager or sponsor through arbitration or any such mechanism as mutually decided between the investors and the AIF.

2.2.4 Self Regulatory Organizations (SRO)

In the developed world, it is common for market players to create self regulatory organizations, whose prime responsibility is to regulate their own members. Wherever SROs exist, the statutory regulatory bodies set up by the government (like SEBI in India) only lay down the broad policy framework, and leave micro-regulation to the SRO. For instance, the Institute of Chartered Accountants of India (**ICAI**) regulates its own members.

2.2.5 Insurance Regulatory and Development Authority (IRDA)

IRDA's mission is to regulate, promote and ensure orderly growth of the insurance sector, including the re-insurance business, while ensuring protection of the interests of insurance policy holders. IRDA was constituted by an Act of Parliament and according to Section 4 of the IRDA Act, 1999. The Authority comprises ten members who are all Central Government appointees. The powers and functions of the authority include:

1. Issuing a certificate of registration or renewing, modifying, withdrawing, suspending or cancelling such registration.
2. Protecting the interests of policy holders in matters relating to assignment of policy, nomination by policy holders, insurable interest, and settlement of insurance claims, surrender value of policy and other clauses of insurance contracts.
3. Spelling out the required qualifications, code of conduct and practical training for intermediaries including insurance intermediaries and agents.
4. Specifying the code of conduct for surveyors and loss assessors.
5. Seeking information, undertaking inspection, conducting inquiries and investigations including audit of the insurer, intermediaries and others.
6. Controling and regulating the rates and terms and conditions that may be offered by the insurers with regard to general insurance, which are not covered by the Tariff Advisory Committee.
7. Regulating the investment of funds by insurance companies.

Regulation Relating to Insurance

Any person or customer who is aggrieved by the service levels or a decision of an insurance company needs to first write to the insurance company. Insurance companies have *customer redressal forums* for the purpose.

If the insured is not happy with the response of the insurance company to the complaint lodged, the *insurance ombudsman* can be approached. IRDA appoints insurance ombudsmen for different geographical regions. This is an inexpensive avenue for the insurance buyer to have the complaint redressed.

IRDA also offers the facility of online registration of policy holders' complaints through its Integrated Grievance Management System (**IGMS**) in its website (www.irda.gov.in). The status of complaints can also be tracked online.

If the insurance buyer is not happy with the decision of the ombudsman, then the normal judicial process through courts as well as under the Consumer Protection Act, 1986 is also available.

2.2.6 Pension Fund Regulatory and Development Authority (PFRDA)

PFRDA was first constituted by the Government of India in October, 2003 and the Bill (2011) was passed in the Parliament and became as Act in September, 2013. The following are the two topmost responsibilities of PFRDA:

1. To promote *old age income security* by establishing, developing and regulating pension funds.
2. To *protect the interests of subscribers* to schemes of pension funds and related matters.

It is an interim body, under the administrative control of the Ministry of Finance, pending enactment of a comprehensive legislation. The authority consists of a chair-person and up to five members.

The new pension system will be based on defined contributions. It will also offer a menu of investment choices and fund managers. Though the new system is voluntary, it would be mandatory for new recruits to the Central Government, except the armed forces. It will also be available on a voluntary basis to all persons including self-employed professionals and others in the unorganized sector. However, mandatory programmes under the Employees Provident Fund Organization and other special provident funds will continue to operate according to the existing system, under the Employees Provident Fund and Miscellaneous Provisions Act, 1952 and other special acts governing these funds.

Subject to the overall directions and guidelines of the government, the PFRDA shall:

(a) deal with all matters relating to the promotion and orderly growth of the pension fund market;
(b) propose appropriate legislation for the purposes indicated above, and
(c) carry out such functions as may be delegated to the authority.

The PFRDA shall be free to determine its own procedures and will have powers to call for records and other materials relevant to its working, from official and non-official bodies and will also hold discussions with them. The PFRDA will also submit periodical reports to the government on various aspects of the pension sector and matters connected therewith.

Regulations relating to Pension Funds

Some of the changes incorporated in the recent legislation are as follows:

- The subscriber seeking minimum assured returns shall be allowed to opt for investing his/her funds in such a scheme providing minimum assured returns as may be notified by the authority;
- Withdrawals will be permitted from the individual pension account subject to conditions, such as, purpose, frequency and limits, as may be specified by the regulations (earlier withdrawals from Tier 1 accounts was restricted);
- Foreign investment in the pension sector is set at 26% or such percentage as may be approved for the insurance sector, whichever is higher (now increased to 49% in FY 2014-15);
- At least one of the pension fund managers shall be from the public sector;
- To establish a vibrant *Pension Advisory Committee* with representation from all major stakeholders to advise PFRDA on important matters such as framing of regulations under the PFRDA Act.

2.2.7 Companies Act, 1956

The Companies Act, 1956 is a legislation to consolidate and amend the law relating to companies and certain other associations. It came into force on April 1, 1956, but has undergone amendments by several subsequent enactments, some of which were warranted by events such as the establishment of depositories owing to dematerialization of shares.

This Act, for the first time, introduced a uniform law pertaining to companies across India. The legislation applies to all trading corporations and to those non-trading corporations whose objects extend to more than one state of India. Further, other entities not covered by the scope of the Act are corporations whose objects are confined to one state, universities, co-operative societies and unincorporated trading bodies, literary, scientific and other societies and associations mentioned in item 32 of the State List in the Seventh Schedule of the Constitution of India. With some exceptions relating to Jammu & Kashmir, Goa, Daman and Diu and Sikkim, the Act applies to the whole of India.

2.2.8 The Companies Act, 2013

The 2013 Act introduced several new concepts and has also tried to streamline many requirements by introducing new definitions. Herein, we have covered some of these new concepts and definitions in brief.

1. *Companies*

1.1 One-person company: The 2013 Act introduces a new type of entity to the existing list, i.e., apart from forming a public or private limited company, the 2013 Act enables the formation of a new entity called 'one-person company' (OPC). An OPC means a company with only one person as its member [Section 3(1) of 2013 Act].

1.2 Private company: The 2013 Act introduces a change in the definition for a private company, inter-alia, the new requirement increases the limit of the number of members from 50 to 200. [Section 2(68) of 2013 Act].

1.3 Small company: A small company has been defined as a company, other than a public company. It comprises:

(i) paid-up share capital of which does not exceed 50 lakh INR or such higher amount as may be prescribed which shall not be more than five crore INR, and

(ii) turnover of which as per its last profit-and-loss account does not exceed two crore INR or such higher amount as may be prescribed which shall not be more than 20 crore INR.

As set out in the 2013 Act, this section will not be applicable to the following:

- A holding company or a subsidiary company.
- A company registered under section 8.
- A company or body corporate governed by any special Act [Section 2(85) of 2013 Act].

1.4. Dormant company: The 2013 Act states that a company can be classified as dormant when it is formed and registered under this Act for a future project or to hold an asset or intellectual property and has no significant accounting transactions. Such a company or an inactive one may apply to the Registrar of

Companies (RoC) in such manner as may be prescribed for obtaining the status of a dormant company [Section 455 of 2013 Act].

2. *Roles and Responsibilities*

2.1 **Officer:** The definition of officer has been extended to include promoters and key managerial personnel [Section 2(59) of 2013 Act].

2.2 **Key Managerial Personnel:** The term 'key managerial personnel' has been defined in the 2013 Act and has been used in several sections, thus expanding the scope of persons covered by such sections [section 2(51) of 2013 Act].

2.3 **Promoter:** The term 'promoter' has been defined in the following ways:

(a) a person who has been named as such in a prospectus or is identified by the company in the annual return referred to in Section 92 of 2013 Act that deals with annual return; or

(b) who has control over the affairs of the company, directly or indirectly whether as a shareholder, director or otherwise; or

(c) in accordance with whose advice, directions or instructions the Board of Directors of the company is accustomed to act.

The proviso to this section states that sub-section (c) would not apply to a person who is acting merely in a professional capacity [Section 2(69) of 2013 Act].

2.4 **Independent Director:** The term 'Independent Director' has now been defined in the 2013 Act, along with several new requirements relating to their appointment, roles and responsibilities. Further, some of these requirements are not in line with the corresponding requirements under the equity listing agreement [Section 2(47), 149(5) of 2013 Act].

3. *Investments*

3.1 **Subsidiary:** The definition of subsidiary as included in the 2013 Act states that certain class or classes of holding company (as may be prescribed) shall not have layers of subsidiaries beyond such numbers as may be prescribed. With such a restrictive section, it appears that a holding company will no longer be able to hold subsidiaries beyond a specified number [Section 2(87) of 2013 Act].

4. *Financial Statements*

4.1 **Financial year:** It has been defined as the period ending on the 31st day of March every year, and where it has been incorporated on or after the 1st day of January of the period ending on the 31st day of March of the following year, in respect whereof financial statement of the company or body corporate is made up [Section 2(41) of 2013 Act]. While there are certain exceptions included, this section mandates a uniform accounting year for all companies and may create significant implementation issues.

4.2 **Consolidated Financial Statements:** The 2013 Act mandates consolidated financial statements (CFS) for any company having a subsidiary or an associate or a joint venture, to prepare and present consolidated financial statements in addition to standalone financial statements.

4.3 **Conflicting definitions:** There are several definitions in the 2013 Act divergent from those used in the notified accounting standards, such as a joint venture or an associate, etc., which may lead to hardships in compliance.

5. *Audit and Auditors*

5.1 **Mandatory auditor rotation and joint auditors:** The 2013 Act now mandates the rotation of auditors after a specified time period. The 2013 Act also includes an enabling provision for joint audits.

5.2 **Non-audit services:** The 2013 Act states that any services to be rendered by the auditor should be approved by the board of directors or the audit committee. Additionally, the auditor is also restricted from providing certain specific services.

5.3 **Auditing standards:** The standards on auditing have been accorded legal sanctity in the 2013 Act and would be subject to notification by the National Financial Reporting Authority (NFRA). Auditors are now mandatorily bound by the 2013 Act to ensure compliance with the standards on auditing.

5.4 **Cognizance to Indian Accounting Standards (In AS):** The 2013 Act, in several sections, has given cognizance to the Indian Accounting Standards, which are standards converged with International Financial Reporting Standards, in view of their becoming applicable in future. For example, the definition of a financial statement includes a 'statement of changes in equity' which would be required under In AS [Section 2(40) of 2013 Act].

5.5 **Secretarial audit for bigger companies:** In respect of listed companies and other class of companies as may be prescribed, the 2013 Act provides for a mandatory requirement to have secretarial audit. The draft rules make it applicable to every public company with paid-up share capital > Rs. 100 crore. As specified in the 2013 Act, such companies would be required to annex a secretarial audit report given by a Company Secretary in practice with its Board's report [Section 204 of 2013 Act].

5.6 **Secretarial Standards:** The 2013 Act requires every company to observe secretarial standards specified by the Institute of Company Secretaries of India with respect to general and board meetings [Section 118 (10) of 2013 Act], which were hitherto not given cognizance under the 1956 Act.

5.7 **Internal Audit:** The importance of internal audit has been well acknowledged in Companies (Auditor Report) Order, 2003 (the 'Order'), pursuant to which auditor of a company is required to comment on the fact that the internal audit system of the company is commensurate with the nature and size of the company's operations. However, the order did not mandate that an internal audit should be conducted by the internal auditor of the company. The order acknowledged that an internal audit can be conducted by an individual who is not in appointment by the company.

The 2013 Act moves a step forward and mandates the appointment of an internal auditor who shall either be a chartered accountant or a cost accountant, or such other professional as may be decided by the Board to conduct internal audit of the functions and activities of the company.

The class or classes of companies which shall be required to mandatorily appoint an internal auditor as per the draft rules are as follows:

- Every listed company.
- Every public company having paid-up share capital of more than 10 crore INR.
- Every other public company which has any outstanding loans or borrowings from banks or public financial institutions more than 25 crore INR or which has accepted deposits of more than 25 crore INR at any point of time during the last financial year.

5.8 **Audit of items of cost:** The central government may, by order, in respect of such class of companies engaged in the production of such goods or providing such services as may be prescribed, direct that particulars relating to the utilisation of material or labour or to other items of cost as may be prescribed shall also be included in the books of account kept by that class of companies. By virtue of this Section of the 2013 Act, the cost audit would be mandated for certain companies [Section 148 of 2013 Act]. It is pertinent to note that similar requirements have recently been notified by the central government.

6. *Other Regulators*

6.1 **National Company Law Tribunal (Tribunal or NCLT):** In accordance with the Supreme Court's (SC) judgement, on 11 May 2010, on the composition and constitution of the Tribunal, modifications relating to qualification and experience, etc., of the members of the Tribunal have been made. Appeals from the Tribunal shall lie with the NCLT. Chapter XXVII of the 2013 Act consisting of section 407 to 434 deals with NCLT and Appellate Tribunal.

6.2 **National Financial Reporting Authority (NFRA):** The 2013 Act requires the constitution of NFRA, which has been bestowed with significant powers not only in issuing the authoritative pronouncements, but also in regulating the audit profession.

6.3 **Serious Fraud Investigation Office (SFIO):** The 2013 Act has bestowed legal status to SFIO under Companies Act, 2013. One of the objectives is to redefine the role of auditors. As it was found that the regulatory system is weak, and also reporting of fraud and publication of fraud prevention policy are missing. Secondly, SFIO would enable and ensure prevention of corporate frauds that would reduce anxiety, improve corporate image and build-up confidence of investors at large which is very important and vital for financial markets.

Mergers and Acquisitions

The 2013 Act has streamlined as well as introduced concepts such as reverse mergers (merger of foreign companies with Indian companies) and squeezed out provisions, which are significant. The 2013 Act has also introduced the requirement for valuations in several cases, including mergers and acquisitions, by registered valuers.

Corporate Social Responsibility

The 2013 Act makes an effort to introduce the culture of corporate social responsibility (CSR) among Indian corporates by requiring companies to formulate a corporate social responsibility policy and at least incur a given minimum expenditure on social activities.

Class Action Suits

The 2013 Act introduces a new concept of class action suits which can be initiated by shareholders against the company and auditors.

Prohibition of Association or Partnership of Persons Exceeding a Certain Number

The 2013 Act puts a restriction on the number of partners that can be admitted to a partnership at 100. To be specific, the 2013 Act states that no association or partnership consisting of more than the given number of persons as may be prescribed shall be formed for the purpose of carrying out any business that has for its object the acquisition of gain by the association or partnership or by the individual members thereof, unless it is registered as a company under this 1956 Act or is formed under any other law for the time being in force.

As an exception, the aforesaid restriction would not apply to the following:

- a Hindu undivided family carrying out any business; or
- an association or partnership.

If it is formed by professionals who are governed by special acts like the Chartered Accountants Act, etc. [Section 464 of 2013 Act].

Power to Remove Difficulties

The central government will have the power to exempt or modify provisions of the 2013 Act for a class or classes of companies in public interest. Relevant notification shall be required to be laid in draft form in the Parliament for a period of 30 days. The 2013 Act further states that no such order shall be made after the expiry of a period of five years from the date of commencement of section 1 of the 2013 Act [Section 470 of 2013 Act].

Insider Trading and Prohibition on Forward Dealings

The 2013 Act for the first time defines 'insider trading and price-sensitive information and prohibits any person including the director or key managerial person from entering into insider trading [Section 195 of 2013 Act]. Further, the Act also prohibits directors and key managerial personnel from forward dealings in the company or its holding, subsidiary or associate company [Section 194 of 2013 Act].

2.2.9 Registrar of Companies

Pursuant to Section 609(1) of the Companies Act, 1956, the central government has appointed registrars at different places to discharge the function of registration of companies as provided in Section 33. Registrars of Companies (RoC) cover the various states and union territories and are vested with the primary duty of registering companies created in the respective states and the union territories and ensuring that such companies comply with relevant statutory requirements. These offices function as registry of records, relating to the companies registered with them, which are available for inspection by members of public on payment of the prescribed fee. The central government exercises administrative control over these offices through the respective regional directors.

The registrar also undertakes other important duties, some of which are given below:

Under Section 130, the Registrar is to maintain a register containing particulars of all charges in respect of each company. An example of a charge would be one created for the benefit of holders of debentures.

Under Section 139, the Registrar on being given satisfactory evidence with respect to any registered charges that:

(a) the debt for which the charge was created has been paid or satisfied wholly or partly; or
(b) the part of the property or undertaking charged for has been released from the charge or has ceased to form a part of the company's property or undertaking; the Registrar may enter in the Register of Charges a memorandum of satisfaction in whole or in part or about the fact that a part of the property or undertaking has been released from the charge or no longer forms a part of the company's property or undertaking as the case may be, even if no information is received by him from the company.

2.2.10 Securities Contracts (Regulation) Act, 1956

The Securities Contracts (Regulation) Act, 1956 is a legislation to prevent undesirable transactions in securities by regulating the business of securities dealing and trading. In pursuance of its objects, the Act covers a variety of issues, of which some are listed below:

1. Granting recognition to stock exchanges.
2. Corporatization and demutualization of stock exchanges.
3. The power of the central government to call for periodical returns from stock exchanges.
4. The power of SEBI to make or amend bylaws of recognized stock exchanges.
5. The power of the central government (exercisable by SEBI also) to supersede the governing body of a recognized stock exchange.

6. The power to suspend business of recognized stock exchanges.
7. The power to prohibit undesirable speculation.

2.2.11 Securities Contracts (Regulation) Rules, 1957

Section 30 of the Securities Contracts (Regulation) Act, 1956 empowers the central government to make rules for the purpose of implementing the objects of the said Act. Pursuant to which, the Securities Contracts (Regulation) Rules, 1957 were made. These rules contained specific information and directions on a variety of issues, as for example:

- Formalities to be completed including submission of application for recognition of a stock exchange.
- Qualification norms for membership of a recognized stock exchange.
- Mode of entering into contracts between members of a recognized stock exchange.
- Obligation of the governing body to take disciplinary action against a member, if so directed by SEBI.
- Audit of accounts of members.
- Maintaining and preserving books of accounts by every recognized stock exchange and by every member.
- Submission of the annual report and of periodical returns by every recognized stock exchange.
- Manner of publication of bylaws for criticism.
- Requirements with respect to listing of securities on a recognized stock exchange.
- Requirements with respect to the listing of units or any other instrument of a Collective Scheme on a recognized stock exchange.

2.2.12 Indian Contract Act, 1872

The Indian Contract Act came into force in September, 1872. It lays down general principles with regard to *contracts* and applies to the whole of India, except the state of Jammu & Kashmir.

The law of contracts represents the most important branch of *mercantile law* and rests as the foundation of trade and commerce. It is *pervasive* as it affects us in our daily lives, often without our realizing it. Whether it is buying a pouch of milk or a loaf of bread in the morning, or travelling by the suburban train to work or buying a ticket to watch a play or asking a tailor to stitch a shirt or even borrowing a book from our neighbour, we are entering into contracts that give rise to legal rights and obligations. Thus, the main purpose of the law is to impart *creditability* about the fulfilment of obligations in mercantile transactions. The contracts become *enforceable* through the courts of law.

The sections of the Act relate to matters such as:

1. Essentials of valid contract
2. Classification of contracts

3. Offer, acceptance and communication of offer
4. Capacities of the parties to contract
5. Free consent
6. Consideration
7. Legality of object and consideration
8. Performance of a contract
9. Remedies for breach of contract
10. Indemnity and guarantee
11. Bailment and pledge
12. Law of agency

From the perspective of the securities market, the law of agency is especially important and it governs the relationship between an investor (principal) and a broker (agent). The function of a broker is to establish privities of contract between two parties to a transaction for which he earns a commission, *i.e.* brokerage. When an agent engages in certain actions, it is as if the principal is doing so. Accordingly, Section 226 makes it clear that contracts entered into through an agent and the resulting obligations may be enforced in the same manner and will have the same legal consequences as if the contracts had been entered into and the acts performed by the principal in person.

2.2.13 Economic Offences Wing (EOW)

The **EOW** in the Central Bureau of Investigation (**CBI**) was created in 1994 to deal with offences under various sections of the Indian Penal Code and notified Special Acts mainly relating to serious frauds in banks, stock exchanges, financial institutions, joint stock companies, public limited companies, misappropriation of public funds, criminal breach of trust, violation of Customs Act, counterfeiting of currency, narcotics, drug trafficking, arms peddling and offences relating to adulteration, black-marketing and others.

Following the securities and the stock market scam of 1992, it was deemed desirable to strengthen and expand the EOW and accordingly, a full-fledged **Economic Offences Division (EOD)** was formed in 1994. The EOD has four zones of which one focuses exclusively on large and complicated security and bank frauds.

The areas currently covered by the EOD are:

1. Frauds relating to foreign trade
2. Banking frauds
3. Insurance frauds
4. Foreign exchange frauds
5. Frauds involving manipulation of share prices, insider trading and others
6. Smuggling of narcotics and psychotropic substances
7. Forgery of travel documents, identity papers and overseas job rackets

8. Counterfeit currency and fake government stamps and papers
9. Smuggling of antiques, arts and treasures
10. Cyber crimes
11. Violation of Intellectual Property Rights (IPR), audio and video piracy and software piracy
12. Wildlife and environmental offences.

2.2.14 Prevention of Money Laundering Act, 2002

Money laundering involves disguising financial assets so that they can be used without detection of the illegal activity that produced them. Through money laundering, the launderer transforms the monetary proceeds derived from criminal activities into funds with an apparently legal source.

The Prevention of Money Laundering Act (**PMLA**), 2002 forms the core of the legal framework put in place by India to combat money laundering. PMLA and the Rules notified thereunder came into force with effect from July 1, 2005. Director, FIU-IND and Director (Enforcement) have been conferred with exclusive and concurrent powers under relevant sections of the Act to implement its provisions.

The PMLA and rules notified thereunder impose obligations on banking companies, financial institutions and intermediaries to verify identity of clients, maintain records and furnish information to FIU-IND. PMLA defines money laundering offence and provides for the freezing, seizure and confiscation of the proceeds of crime.

The Prevention of Money Laundering Act, 2002 is an act to prevent money laundering and to provide for *confiscation of property* derived from, or involved in, money laundering and for related matters.

Unit II, Section 3 describes the offence of money laundering thus:

"Whoever directly or indirectly attempts to indulge, or knowingly assists or knowingly is a party or is actually involved, in any process or activity connected with the proceeds of crime and projecting it as untainted property shall be guilty of the offence of money laundering."

The offences are classified under Part A, Part B and Part C of the Schedule. Under Part A, offences include counterfeiting currency notes under the Indian Penal Code to punishment for unlawful activities under the Unlawful Activities (Prevention) Act, 1967.

Under Part B, offences are considered *money laundering* if the total value of such offences is Rs. 30 lakh or more. Such offences include dishonestly receiving stolen property under the Indian Penal Code to breaching of confidentiality and privacy under the Information Technology Act, 2000. Part C includes all offences under Part A and Part B (without the threshold) that has cross-border implications.

Section 6 of the PMLA confers powers on the central government to appoint Adjudicating Authorities to exercise jurisdiction, powers and authority conferred by or under the Act. According to Section 9, in the event of an order of confiscation being made by an adjudicating authority (**AA**) in respect of any property of a person, all the rights and title in such property shall vest absolutely in the central government without any encumbrances.

Section 11 of the Act makes it clear that the A A shall have the same powers as are vested in civil court under the Code of Civil Procedure while trying a suit, with regard to the following matters:

(a) Discovery and inspection.
(b) Enforcing the attendance of any person, including any officer of a banking company or a financial institution or a company and examining him on oath.
(c) Compelling the production of records.
(d) Receiving evidence on affidavits.
(e) Issuing commissions for examination of witnesses and documents.
(f) Any other matter which may be prescribed.

Sections 16 and 17 lay down the powers of the authorities to carry out surveys, searches and seizures. Section 24 makes it clear that when a person is accused of having engaged in money laundering, the burden of proving that the proceeds of the alleged crime are untainted shall be on the accused.

Sections 25 and 26 relate to the establishment of an appellate tribunal and the procedures for filing an appeal to the same. Section 42 deals with appeals against any decision or order of the appellate tribunal. Section 43 empowers the central government to designate courts of session as special courts for the trial of the offence of money laundering.

The offence of money laundering is punishable with rigorous imprisonment for a term which shall not be less than 3 years but which may extend to 7 years and shall also be liable to fine which may extend to Rs. 5 lakh.

Anti-Money Laundering (AML) Measures

There are several ways to check money laundering. Given below are some of the measures that a stock broking firm can adopt for anti-money laundering.

- Organizing training programmes on anti-money laundering for staff, especially personnel engaged in KYC, settlement, demat and account opening process.
- Verifying documents of clients during the account opening process.
- Personally interviewing clients who have declared wealth above Rs. 10 lakh or intend to trade (intraday) above Rs. 2 crore in a month or who have given initial margin of Rs. 4 to 5 lakh and above in the form of monies or securities.
- Interviewing clients who are NRIs or corporates/trusts who promote NRIs.
- Gauging the risk appetite of the client, as it helps in finding out any suspicious trading or transactions in the future.
- Scrutinizing documents including income documents of the employee involved in maintaining and updating official information about the transactions of the client and also of the employees who facilitate transactions of the clients like dealers, settlement officers.

2.2.15 Financial Intelligence Unit – India (FIU-I)

FIU-I was set up by the Government of India in 2004 as the central national agency responsible for receiving, processing, analyzing and disseminating information regarding *suspicious* financial transactions in order to support anti-money laundering efforts. FIU-I is an independent body reporting directly to the Economic Intelligence Council headed by the Finance Minister.

More specifically, the functions of FIU-I are to:

1. serve as the nerve centre for receiving reports on cash and other suspicious transactions;
2. analyze the information collected to trace patterns of transactions which could involve money laundering and other crimes;
3. share information on suspicious transactions with its counterparts and regulatory bodies in other countries;
4. establish and maintain a database on cash and suspicious transactions;
5. coordinate and strengthen collection and sharing of financial intelligence through an effective regional, national, and global network to fight money laundering and related crimes; and
6. undertake research and analysis in order to monitor and identify strategic areas on money laundering trends and other such developments.

Certain exclusive and concurrent powers under the PMLA are conferred on the Director, FIU-I, under Section 13(2) of the PMLA. The Director may impose a fine on any banking company, financial institution or intermediary for failing to comply with obligations of maintenance of records or in furnishing information or in verifying the identities of clients.

For the purposes of Section 13, the Director shall have the same powers as are vested in a civil court under the Code of Civil Procedure 1908, while trying a suit, such as discovery and inspection, compelling the production of records and so on. Under Section 66 of the PMLA, the Director of a specified authority may furnish or cause to be furnished any information received or obtained, to any officer, authority or body, if it is deemed to be in the public interest.

Investor Protection

Investors/Clients: Every intermediary shall make all efforts to protect the interests of investors and shall render the best possible advice to its clients having regard to the client's needs and the environments and his own professional skills.

High Standards of Service: An intermediary shall ensure that its key management personnel, employees, contractors and agents, shall in the conduct of their business, observe high standards of integrity, dignity, fairness, ethics and professionalism and all professional dealings shall be affected in a prompt, effective and efficient manner. An intermediary shall be responsible for the acts or omissions of its employees and agents in respect to the conduct of its business.

Exercise Due Diligence and No Collusion: An intermediary shall at all times render high standard of service, exercise due skills and diligence over persons employed or appointed by it; ensure proper care and exercise independent professional judgement and shall not at any time act in collusion with other intermediaries in a manner that is detrimental to the investor(s).

Fees: An intermediary shall not increase charges/fees for the services rendered without proper advance notice to its clients/investors.

Financial Intermediary – A Perspective

The main role of a financial intermediary is *channelizing* the domestic savings into various investment vehicles available. On the one hand the intermediary helps the issuer in mobilizing resources for development, implementation of projects while on the other hand, he helps the investor obtain a reasonable return on his investment.

The investor should be the *centre* of the activity and his interest should be uppermost in the minds of the advisors. It is important for the advisor/intermediary to nurture and take care of the financial well being of his clients to reap long term benefits.

Ethical Issues in Providing Financial Advice

The main problems/investor grievance areas in the advisory business can be highlighted as under:

1. Advisor's lack of focus on understanding client specific situations so as to provide appropriate advice.
2. Advisor's lack of information about the overall market conditions and other available financial products.
3. Adopting wrong practices like frequent switching from one product to another just for the sake of earning commissions.
4. Not enlightening, informing enough to the clients about risks, uncertainties about financial products that are recommended, while highlighting only good features of the product.
5. Poor after-sales service.

3 Structure of Markets in India

CHAPTER

The financial markets are in the *forefront* in developing economies. Efficient financial markets are a *sine quo non* for speedy economic development. The vibrant financial market enhances the efficiency of capital formation. It facilitates the flow of savings into investment *vis-à-vis* capital formation. It also tends to promote the development for financial structure. The role of financial markets in the financial system is quite unique. The relevance of financial markets in the financial system is not merely *quantitative* but also supportive. Thus, the financial markets bridge one set of financial intermediaries with another set of players. Well-developed financial markets *enlarge* the range of financial services. More importantly, under appropriate conditions, financial (capital) markets can provide long-term finance to government and private corporates.

3.1 DEVELOPMENT OF FINANCIAL MARKETS

Financial market development is a *complex* and *time-consuming* process. There are no short-cuts for developing well-functioning markets with *depth* and *liquidity*. Some of the pre-conditions for financial market reforms are:

- Macroeconomic stability, sound and efficient financial institutions and structure
- Prudential regulation and supervision
- Strong creditor rights and contract enforcement.

Measures to improve market infrastructure must be implemented at an early stage of reform alongside the appropriate legal framework. These conditions facilitate growth of financial transactions including *inter-bank transactions* and *active liquidity management*. At the same time, there are at least three major macroeconomic features which can inhibit reform of domestic financial markets.

1. Large government deficits crowd out financing of the private sector thereby inhibiting the growth of corporate debt markets.
2. High and variable inflation rates and unrealistic exchange rates also stifle the financial markets by raising uncertainties about the risks and returns to financial activity.

3. Financial repression policies such as high inflation, higher taxation, high reserve ratios, subsidized or direct credit programmes, credit rationing, and ceiling on deposit and loan interest rates also hinder financial market development.

3.2 STATE OF THE FINANCIAL MARKETS IN INDIA

The financial sector in India comprises financial institutions, financial markets and financial instruments. The various *segments* of the financial market in India are:

- Credit market
- Money market
- Government securities market
- Foreign exchange market
- Capital market
- Debt market
- Commodity market
- Insurance market
- Derivatives market
- Pension market.

While the money, government securities and foreign exchange markets are regulated by the Reserve Bank of India (RBI), the capital and derivatives market falls under the purview of Securities and Exchange Board of India (SEBI), the debt market is jointly monitored and supervised by both RBI and SEBI, the insurance market is regulated by the Insurance Regulatory and Development Authority (IRDA) and the pension market is regulated by Pension Fund Regulatory and Development Authority (PFRDA). Several measures have been taken by the Reserve Bank of India over the years and by SEBI and IRDA (during the 1990s) for developing these markets.

3.2.1 Unorganized Markets

In these markets there are a number of moneylenders, indigenous bankers, traders, etc., who lend money to the public. Indigenous bankers also collect deposits from the public. There are private finance companies, chit funds, etc., whose activities are not controlled by the RBI. Although of late, RBI has taken steps to bring private finance companies and chit funds under its strict control by issuing non-banking financial companies (Reserve Bank) directives, 1998. Thus, the RBI has taken some steps to bring the unorganized sector under the organized fold. However, the success rate is low. The regulations concerning their financial dealings are still inadequate and their financial instruments have not been standardized.

3.2.2 Organized Markets

In the organized markets, there are standardized rules and regulations governing their financial dealings. There is also a high degree of *institutionalization* and *instrumentalisation*. These markets are subject to strict supervision and control by the RBI and other regulatory bodies. These organized markets can be further classified into:

(a) Capital market and (b) Money market

Capital market facilitates free trading (buying and selling) in all securities. Capital markets deal with financial assets or securities. Securities will be fairly priced in the capital markets if they are efficient. Capital markets are considered to be efficient if the prices of securities reflect the available information on real time basis. Depending on the extent of the information being used in the security prices, capital markets may be efficient in all the three namely (a) weak, (b) semi-strong and (c) strong form, as the case may be.

The capital market is a market for financial assets which have a long or indefinite maturity. Generally, it deals with long-term securities which have a maturity period of above one year. Capital market may be further divided into:

- Industrial securities market
- Government securities market
- Long-term loans market.

Industrial Securities Market: It is a market for industrial securities namely: (i) *Equity shares* or ordinary shares, (ii) *preference shares*, and (iii) *debentures or bonds*. It is a market where industrial corporates raise their longterm capital or debt by issuing appropriate instruments. It can be further subdivided into two mutually supporting and indivisible segments: the **primary market** and the **secondary market**.

In the primary market, the companies issue new securities to raise funds. Hence, it is also referred to as **new issues market**. In the primary market, companies interact directly with investors and equity shares are issued to the members of public. A public offer is open to three categories of investors:

- **Qualified institutional buyers** (QIBs) which include foreign institutional investors (FIIs) and mutual funds; banks and financial institutions; pension funds and insurance funds and other institutional investors.
- **High net worth individuals** (HNIs) or non-institutional buyers (NIBs) who invest more than Rs. 2 lakh in an issue.
- **Retail individual investors** (including eligible NRIs and HUFs in the name of *karta*) who invest up to Rs. 2 lakh in an issue.

Primary issue of equity shares can be fresh issue of shares as *initial public offer* (IPO) or a *follow-up public offer* (FPO) where additional shares are offered to the public after the IPO or a rights issue where the shares are offered to existing investors (who may or may not be allowed to renounce their rights in favour of third parties). A primary market issuance can also be a private placement, where securities are issued to a defined group of investors. A private placement made by a listed company is called a *preferential allotment*. A preferential allotment made to qualified institutional buyers (**QIBs**) is called a *qualified institutional placement*.

Primary market offerings are subject to regulatory requirements laid down by Securities and Exchange Board of India (SEBI) in the SEBI Issue of Capital and Disclosure Requirements (**ICDR**) Regulations, 2009 and the provisions of the Companies Act, 2013 and the Companies Act, 1956, as applicable for disclosures and raising capital from the public. They are also subject to RBI regulations as regards issuance to non-resident investors (NRIs) and receipt of money from abroad.

The secondary market deals with the securities that have already been issued by companies that are listed on stock exchanges. Since the securities are listed and traded on the stock exchange, it is also called **stock market**. In the secondary market, investors interact mostly with themselves. In both primary and secondary markets, the capital market intermediaries (merchant bankers, stock brokers, bankers to the issue, registrars, etc.) play an important role.

The secondary market, based on all-available information, determines the price and the risk of the issued securities. Securities will be fairly priced in the capital markets if they are efficient. It provides useful signals to various stakeholders including listed companies, investors to act in the secondary markets.

The secondary market may also include the **over-the-counter** (OTC) **market** and the **derivatives market**. In the stock market, the share prices are determined by the demand and supply forces. On the other hand, in the OTC market, prices are negotiated between the buyer and the seller. The derivatives market deals in futures and options. In the derivatives market, securities or portfolios of securities (for example, a market index) are traded for future delivery.

Money market usually deals in very short tenure–mostly one day to few days, as such there is no relevant information for readers.

3.3 PRIMARY CAPITAL MARKET IN INDIA

We have seen that the primary capital market is a conduit for the sale of new securities. Private corporate sector in India did not show much enthusiasm to offer capital to the public till 1980, due to some of the following factors:

- Small size of operations and narrow capital base.
- Availability of loan capital on relatively easy terms from the term-lending institutions.
- Fear of losing control over the company.
- Highly regulated environment.

The decade of 1980s, however, witnessed a sea change in the funds mobilization efforts of companies through public issues of equity and debt, encouraged by the deregulation of capital markets and other economic reforms. As a result, the annual funds mobilization in the new issues market, which was only to the tune of about Rs. 700 million in 1960s and Rs. 900 million in 1970s, increased substantially to Rs. 43,120 million in 1990-91 (by private, corporate, non-government companies) which further increased to phenomenal level of Rs. 2,64,170 million in 1994-95. Thereafter, it started decreasing though. The public issues contributed to Rs. 1,88,060 million of funds in 1996-97 which further declined to Rs. 78,510 million in 2003-04. However, there was a spurt again in mobilization of funds through new issues during 2004-05 to 2007-08;

funds worth Rs. 3,23,820 million were raised in 2006-07. The funds mobilized in 1990-91 were 3.3 per cent of India's gross domestic savings (GDS), while it was 10.5 per cent in 1994-95 and much higher in 2006-07.

Table 3.1 Resource Mobilization by Corporate from Primary Market (1995-96 to 2016-17)

Year	Public Equity Issue	Debt Issue			Total Resources Mobilized	Private Placement (%)		Share of Debt (%)
		Public Issue	Private Placement	Total		Total Resources	Total Debt	
1	2	3	4	5	6	7	8	9
	(Rs. in millions)							
95-96	88820	29400	100350	129750	218570	45.91	77.34	59.36
96-97	46710	69770	183910	253680	300390	61.22	72.50	84.45
97-98	11320	19290	309830	329120	340450	91.01	94.14	96.67
98-99	5040	74070	387480	461550	466580	83.05	83.95	98.92
99-00	29750	46980	547010	593990	623740	87.70	92.09	95.23
00-01	24790	42390	524335	565725	590520	88.79	92.68	95.80
01-02	10820	53410	462200	515610	526430	87.80	89.64	97.94
02-03	10390	46930	484236	531166	541556	89.42	91.16	98.08
03-04	178210	43240	484279	527519	705729	68.62	91.80	74.75
04-05	214320	40950	551838	592788	807108	68.37	93.09	73.45
05-06	236760	0.00	818466	818466	1055226	77.56	100.00	77.56
06-07	249930	0.00	923552	923552	1173482	78.70	100.00	78.70
10-11	581050	94510	2187850	3132950	3714000	58.91	100.00	84.36
11-12	460903	356110	2612820	2968930	3429833	76.18	100.00	86.56
12-13	235100	169820	3614620	3784440	4019540	89.93	100.00	94.15
13-14	510750	423830	2760540	3184370	3695120	74.71	100.00	86.18
Apr-Dec 14	87320	73120	2692440	2866690	2954010	91.14	100.00	97.04
Apr-Dec 15	310220	187640						
15-16	901790	341120	4580730	4921850	5823640			
16-17	781750	293540	5550820	5844350	6626200			

Source: Prime Annual Report (2006-07) & SEBI Handbook Statistics & Bulletin, 2017

Note: Public Equity Issue for FY: 2015-16 and 2016-17 also includes amount raised through private placement.

3.4 SECONDARY MARKETS IN INDIA

Secondary capital markets deal in the issued and outstanding securities that are listed on the stock exchanges which facilitate both buyers and sellers to trade in an organized and transparent manner. A stock exchange provides the following useful economic functions:

- helps in determining fair prices based on demand and supply forces and all available information;
- provides easy marketability and liquidity for investors;
- facilitates in capital formation in primary market through pricing and trends in pricing; and
- enables investors to rebalance portfolios of securities in response to market developments.

Market Design for Secondary Markets

1. Corporate securities
2. Exchange management
3. Membership
4. Listing
5. Trading mechanism
6. Trading rules
7. Price band
8. Margin trading
9. Demat trading
10. Electronic trading
11. Charge
12. Trading cycle
13. Settlement calendar
14. Risk management
15. Government securities

Secondary market transactions by investors involve executing the trade and settling the obligations that arise from the transaction. The obligations involve transfer of funds and securities between the parties to the trade. The stock exchange mechanism provides the facility for conducting the trade on its trading platform and settlement of the transaction through clearing and settlement system of each stock exchange. The National Stock Exchange (NSE), the Bombay Stock Exchange (BSE) and the Multi Commodity Exchange-Stock Exchange (MCX-SX) are the leading stock exchanges in India.

Developments in Indian Stock Market

There has been impressive growth in the number of shareholders, number of listed companies, market capitalization and stock turnover in India over the last two-three decades. The number of shareholders is estimated to be about 40 million. Thus, India, after USA, has the second largest population of shareholders.

Let us look at the following table to gain more insights about some select indicators of Indian stock market operations.

Table 3.2

Year	Brokers Nos.	Listed Companies	Nifty	S & P Sensex	Market Cap (Rs. Millions)	M Cap (%)	Turover (Rs. Millions)
1995-96	8,476	9,100	985	3367	-	47.00	2,273,680
1996-97	8,867	9,890	969	3361	-	34.60	6,461,160
1997-98	9,005	9,833	1,117	3,893	-	37.70	9,086,810
1998-99	9,069	9,877	1,078	3,740	135,295	34.10	10,233,820
1999-00	9,192	9,871	1,528	5,001	273,410	84.70	20,670,310
2000-01	9,782	9,954	1,148	3,604	164,851	54.50	28,809,900
2001-02	9,687	9,644	1,130	3,469	153,534	36.36	8,958,180
2002-03	9,519	9,413	978	3,049	133,036	28.49	9,689,098
2003-04	9,368	-	1,772	5,591	303,940	52.25	16,209,326
2004-05	9,128	-	2,036	6,493	388,212	54.41	16,668,960
2005-06	9,335	-	3,403	11,280	677,469	85.58	23,901,030
2006-07	9,443	-	3,822	13,072	814,134	86.02	29,014,715
2010-11	9,235		5,584	18,605	13,541,700		46,824,370
2011-12	9,307	9,928	5,243	17,423	12,311,459		34,783,910
2012-13	10,128	8,062	5,257	18,202	10,580,918		32,570,530
2013-14	9,411	8,630	6,010	20,120	14,693016		24,623,820
Apr-Dec 2014	7,306	9,204	7,736	25,068	19,436,836		37,783,240
2015-16	6,167	5,911	7,738	25,342	20,794,120		49,772,780

Source: NSE, Indian Securities Market: A Review, Mumbai, NSE Vol. 2, 2002 & SEBI Handbook Statistics, 2014 & SEBI Annual Report 2015-16.

The above table is self-explanatory and explains how growth in all the above parameters has taken place from 1995-96 to 2006-07.

Equity Market Indicators

Equity Indices: A market index is a basket of equity shares whose price is weighted by market capitalization, and tracked for changes in price level of the stocks included therein. An index enables an overall understanding of the direction of equity markets. There are several indices that have been constructed to track equity markets.

1. **Narrow Bell Weathers:** These are indices made up of a few large shares, but serve as a quick barometer of market movement. They are often used as performance benchmarks. In India, the benchmark indices are S&P Sensex tracking 30 stocks, CNX Nifty tracking 50 stocks and SX40 tracking 40 stocks.
2. **Broad Indices:** These indices track a large basket of stocks; the S&P BSE 500, CNX 200 are broad indices.
3. **Sectoral Indices:** These are indices created to track various industry sectors such as technology, banking, metals, finance, real estate, consumer durables, pharma, capital goods, media and the like. Depending on the purpose on hand, various indices can be tracked to gauge market direction.

Government Securities Market: The private corporate debt market is yet to develop in India. The government debt/bond market constitutes about three-fourths of the debt market in India. Commercial banks and financial institutions in India own a large proportion of the government debt securities due to statutory liquidity and other investment requirements. The primary issues of the Central Government have increased manifold during the decade of 1990s and onwards.

In 2001-02, for the first time, turnover in the government securities was higher than the turnover of equities on all exchanges. The turnover of government securities increased from Rs. 56,229 crore in 1994-95 to Rs. 29,88,560 crore in 2002-03–an increase of more than 50 times. The turnover further increased to Rs. 35,83,337 crore in 2006-07.

NSE has developed the wholesale debt market WDM for government securities. The government debt securities have high level of liquidity. The turnover of the dated securities has been higher in recent years. The primary dealers offer two-way quotes for the active government securities.

Table 3.3 Growth of Turnover in Government Securities

Year	NSE WDM segment	SGL	Total turnover of government securities
1994-95	5,660	50,569	56,229
1995-96	9,988	127,179	137,167
1996-97	38,308	122,941	161,249
1997-98	103,585	185,708	289,293

1998-99	95,280	227,228	322,508
1999-2000	293,887	539,232	833,119
2000-01	414,096	698,121	1,112,217
2001-02	927,604	1,573,893	2,501,497
2002-03	1,032,829	1,955,731	2,988,560
2003-04	1,316,096	1,701,363	3,017,459
2004-05	887,293	1,260,867	2,148,160
2005-06	475,523	708,015	1,183,538
2006-07	219,106	398,299	617,045
2010-11	559,436		
2011-12	589,062		
2012-13	792,215		
2013-14	851,434		
Apr-Dec 2014	583,150		

(**Source:** NSE, Indian Securities Market: A Review, Mumbai, NSE-2002 & SEBI Handbook Statistics, 2014)

Table: 3.4 Turnover in Government Securities Market (Face Value) – in Rs. Billion

Week Ended	Central Government Dated Securities	State Government Dated Securities	91-day Treasury Bills	182-day Treasury Bills	364-day Treasury Bills
26-Jun-2015	4653.83	170.96	190.29	56.41	146.32
25-Sep-2015	2856.20	165.13	136.41	34.99	62.80
25-Dec-2015	2224.62	134.85	156.20	53.63	12.61
25-Mar-2016	2865.09	152.14	80.41	2.67	27.02
29-Apr-2016	5170.20	127.69	190.04	67.67	151.73
27-May-2016	3298.88	198.55	141.15	21.77	65.53
24-Jun-2016	4449.28	186.95	221.11	55.08	116.43
29-July-2016	9265.25	383.23	233.30	89.02	124.21

Source: RBI Handbook of Statistics on Indian Economy

Table 3.4.1 Trading in Corporate Bonds (In Rs. crore)

	BSE		NSE		FIMMDA**		Grand Total	
Date	No. of Trades*	Amount (Rs. cr)*	No. of Trades*	Amount (Rs. cr)*	No. of Trades*	Amount (Rs. cr)*	No. of Trades*	Amount (Rs. cr)*
Jan-07	2057	8090.56	0	0.00	0	0.00	2057	8090.56
Feb-07	1244	3611.83	0	0.00	0	0.00	1244	3611.83
Mar-07	1234	4233.85	123	1485.70	0	0.00	1357	5719.55
Total	4535	15936.24	123	1485.70	0	0.00	4658	17421.939
Data for 2007-08								
Total	11203	40957.56	3787	31453.14	4089	23479.01	19079	95889.706
Total	8327	37320.47	4902	49505.39	9501	61534.84	22683	148166.18
Data for 2009-2010								
Total	7408	53323.50	12522	151919.99	18300	195954.55	38230	401198.04
Data for 2010-11								
Total	4465	39581.09	8006	155951.23	31589	409741.92	44060	605274.24
Data for 2011-12								
Total	6424	49842	11973	193435	33136	350506	51533	593783
Data for 2012-13								
Total	8639	51622.40	21141	242105.11	36603	444904.15	66383	738631.66
Data for 2013-14								
Total	10187	103027.19	20809	275701.39	39891	592071.26	70887	970799.85
Total	10187	103027.19	20809	275701.39	39891	592071.26	70887	970799.85

Data For 2014-15								
	Bse		Nse		FIMMDA**		Grand Total	
Date	No. of Trades*	Amount (Rs. Cr)*	No. of Trades*	Amount (Rs. Cr)*	No. of Trades*	Amount (Rs. Cr)*	No. of Trades*	Amount (Rs. Cr)*
Apr-14	1171	14891.21	3670	60148.91	1	0.11	4842	75040.23
May-14	1298	14839.85	4459	79106.01	0	0.00	5757	93945.86
June-14	1378	13597.75	4176	54783.42	2	0.20	5556	68381.37
July-14	1422	16757.81	4290.00	66854.00	0	0.00	5712	83611.81

Aug-14	1211	10914.78	3843	57269.64	1	0.12	5055	68184.54
Sep-14	1866	22928.70	5807	94513.75	0	0.00	7673	117442.45
Oct-14	1662	19959.05	4706	72488.18	0	0.00	6368	92447.23
Nov-14	1791	19864.26	5400	86349.86	1	0.10	7192	106214.22
Dec-14	1609	17990.34	5694	85033.93	1	0.10	7304	103024.37
Jan-15	1587	23630.98	5706	95149.98	0	0.00	7293	118780.96
Total	14995	175374.73	47751	751697.69	6	0.63	62752	927073.05
2014-15	17710	204506.00	58073	886788.00				
2015-16	16900	207652.00	53223	814756.00				
2016-17	24372	292153.97	64123	1178508.55				

Source: SEBI website

** Comprises OTC trades and trades done on the exchange*

*** Trade Reporting on FIMMDA Reporting Platform w.e.f. September 01, 2007*

Table 3.4.2 Business Growth in Negotiated Platform

Year	Market Capitalisation (Rs. crores)	Trading Days	Number of Trades	Net Traded Value (Rs. crores)	Average Daily Value (Rs. crores)	Average Trade Size (Rs. crores)
2015-2016	5,745,074	82	4,921	198,484.30	2,420.54	40.33
2014-2015	5,739,272	237	18,789	772,369.06	3,258.94	41.11
2013-2014	5,128,733	243	21,143	851,433.62	3,503.84	40.27
2012-2013	4,928,331	242	26,974	792,213.78	3,273.61	29.37
2011-2012	4,272,736	239	23,447	633,179.45	2,649.29	27
2010-2011	3,594,877	248	20,383	559,446.77	2,255.83	27.45
2009-2010	3,165,929	239	24,069	563,815.95	2,359.06	23.42
2008-2009	2,848,315	238	16,129	335,951.52	1,411.56	20.83
2007-2008	2,123,346	248	16,179	282,317.02	1,138.38	17.45
2006-2007	1,784,801	244	19,575	219,106.47	897.98	11.19
2005-2006	1,567,574	271	61,891	475,523.48	1,754.70	7.68
2004-2005	1,461,734	293	124,308	887,293.66	3,028.31	7.14
2003-2004	1,215,864	294	189,518	1,316,096.24	4,476.52	6.94

Contd.

2002-2003	864,481	297	167,778	1,068,701.54	3,598.32	6.37
2001-2002	756,794	289	144,851	947,191.22	3,277.48	6.54
2000-2001	580,835	289	64,470	428,581.51	1,482.98	6.65
1999-2000	494,033	294	46,987	304,216.24	1,034.75	6.47
1998-1999	411,470	289	16,092	105,469.13	364.95	6.55
1997-1998	343,191	289	16,821	111,263.28	384.99	6.61
1996-1997	292,772	291	7,804	42,277.59	145.28	5.42
1995-1996	207,783	291	2,991	11,867.68	40.78	3.97
1994-1995	158,181	223	1,021	6,781.15	30.41	6.64

Source: NSE - Trade Statistics/Turnover/Business Growth (Debt) - July, 2015

Long-term Loans Market

Development banks and commercial banks play a significant role in this market by supplying long-term loans to corporates. It may be further classified into:

- Term loans market
- Mortgages market
- Financial guarantees market

Term Loans Market

In India, many industrial financial institutions have been created by the government both at the national and regional levels to supply long-term and medium-term loans to corporates directly as well as indirectly. These development banks dominate the industrial finance in India. Institutions like IDBI, IFCI, ICICI, and other state financial corporations come under this category. These institutions meet the growing and varied long-term financial requirements of industries by supplying long-term loans. They also help in identifying investment opportunities, encourage new entrepreneurs and support modernization efforts.

Mortgages Market

It refers to those centres which supply mortgage loan mainly to individual customers. A mortgage loan is a loan against the security of immovable property like real estate. The transfer of interest in a specific immovable property to secure a loan is called *mortgage*. This mortgage may be equitable or legal. Again it may be the first charge or second charge. *Equitable mortgage* is created by a mere deposit of title deeds to properties as security, whereas in the case of *legal mortgage*, the title in the property is legally transferred to the lender by the borrower. Legal mortgage is less risky comparatively.

Similarly, in the first charge, the mortgager transfers his interest in the specific property to the mortgagee as security. When the property in question is already mortgaged once to another creditor, it becomes the second charge when it is subsequently mortgaged to somebody else. The mortgagee can also further transfer his interest in the mortgaged property to another. In such a case, it is called *sub-mortgage*.

The mortgage market may have a primary market as well as secondary market. The *primary market* consists of original extension of credit and *secondary market* has sales and re-sales of existing mortgages at prevailing prices.

In India, residential mortgages are the most common ones. The Housing Development Finance Company (HDFC Limited), Housing and Urban Development Corporation (HUDCO), ICICI Bank Home Finance and the LIC play a dominant role in financing residential projects. Besides, Land Development Banks provide cheap mortgage loans for the development of lands, purchase of equipment etc. These development banks raise finance through the sale of debentures which are treated as trustee securities.

Financial Guarantees Market

A guarantee market is a centre where finance is provided against the guarantee of reputed persons in the financial circles. *Guarantee* is a contract to discharge the liability of the third party in case of his default. Guarantee acts as a security from the creditor's point of view. In case the borrower fails to repay the loan, the liability falls on the shoulders of the guarantor. Hence, the guarantor must be known to both the borrower and the lender and he must have the means to discharge his liability.

Though there are many types of guarantees, the common forms are: (i) performance guarantee and (ii) financial guarantee. *Performance guarantees* cover the payment of earnest money, retention money, advance payments, non-completion of contracts, and so on.

On the other hand, *financial guarantees* cover only financial contracts. In India, the market for financial guarantees is well organized. The financial guarantees in India relate to:

- deferred payments for imports and exports;
- medium-and long-term loans raised abroad; and
- loans advanced by banks and other financial institutions.

These guarantees are provided mainly by commercial banks, development banks, both central and state governments and other specialized guarantee institutions like ECGC (Export Credit Guarantee Corporation) and DICGC (Deposit Insurance Credit Guarantee Corporation). This guarantee financial service is available to both individual and corporate customers. For a smooth functioning of any financial system, this guarantee service is imperative.

Money Market

Money market is the most important segment of the financial system as it provides the fulcrum for equilibrating short-term demand for the supply of funds, thereby facilitating the conduct of monetary policy. It is a market for short-term funds with a maturity up to one year and includes financial instruments that are close substitutes for money. The money market is generally expected to perform three broad functions:

(i) It provides an equilibrating mechanism to even out demand for and supply of short-term funds.

(ii) It also represents a focal point for central bank intervention for influencing liquidity and general level of interest rates in the economy.

(iii) It provides reasonable access to providers and users of short-term funds to fulfill their borrowing and investment requirements at an efficient market clearing price.

The Indian money market during the pre-reforms period was characterized by *paucity of instruments, lack of depth* and *dichotomy* in the market structure. The inter-bank call money market was the core of the Indian money market.

The money market during the 1970s and 1980s was also characterized by poor liquidity, paucity of instruments and limited number of participants. The volume of business was low. However, in the 1980s, new instruments like treasury bills, bill rediscounting, certificate of deposits (CD), commercial paper (CP), and inter-bank participation certificates were introduced.

The money market in India witnessed significant progress since the post-reforms period. Following the various initiatives taken by the Reserve Bank of India over the years, the depth and liquidity in the money market has increased significantly.

Foreign Exchange Market

During the past seven decades, the foreign exchange market in India has witnessed a significant transformation from a highly controlled to a liberal regime. The forex market basically comprises authorized dealers (ADs) which are mostly banks, exporters and importers, individuals and the RBI. The forex market in India has acquired increasing depth with the transition to a market determined exchange rate system in March, 1993 and the gradual liberalization of restrictions on various external transactions.

Derivatives Market

Trading in derivatives of securities commenced in June 2000 with the enactment of enabling legislation in early 2000. Derivatives are formally defined to include:

- a security derived from a debt instrument, share, loan whether secured or unsecured, risk instrument or contract for difference or any other form of security, and
- a contract which derives its value from the prices, or index of prices, or underlying securities.

Derivatives are securities derived from other securities (called *underlying assets*) like equity, debt, or any other type of asset. They also include contracts that derive their values from prices or index of prices. In India, the OTC derivatives are not allowed. The legal derivatives must trade on recognized stock exchanges only. Derivatives trading in India began with SEBI approving trading in **index futures contracts**, based on S & P BSE's SENSEX index and NSE's Nifty index. Immediately after this, approval for trading in options in these two indices and some individual shares followed in July 2001. In June 2003, SEBI/RBI approved the trading on interest rate derivative instruments.

Table 3.5 Turnover of Government Securities – Index Futures and Index Options

Particulars	NSE	BSE				
	Dec-16	Jan-17	Percentage Change Over Month	Dec-16	Jan-17	Percentage Change Over Month
1	2	3	4	5	6	7
A. Turnover (₹ crore)						
(i) Index Futures	3,38,543	3,24,469	-4.2	0	0	-100.0
(ii) Options on Index						
Put	29,89,680	31,37,877	5.0	0	0	NA
Call	33,95,122	33,37,204	-1.7	0	0	NA
(iii) Stock Futures	7,81,055	9,63,574	23.4	9	7	-15.5
(iv) Options on Stock						
Put	1,47,317	1,77,441	20.4	0	0	NA
Call	2,72,871	3,64,053	33.4	0	0	NA
Total	**79,24,589**	**83,04,619**	**4.8**	**9**	**7**	**-16.8**
B. No. of Contracts						
(i) Index Futures	51,99,107	47,92,429	-7.8	2	0	-100.0
(ii) Options on Index						
Put	4,56,96,616	4,59,51,150	0.6	0	0	NA
Call	5,00,88,087	4,68,99,629	-6.4	0	0	NA
(iii) Stock Futures	1,22,69,473	1,45,12,081	18.3	115	97	-15.7
(iv) Options on Stock						
Put	22,58,375	26,89,907	19.1	0	0	NA
Call	33,15,699	51,61,359	55.7	0	0	NA
Total	**11,88,27,357**	**12,00,06,555**	**1.0**	**117**	**97**	**-17.1**

Contd.

C. Open Interest in terms of Value (₹ crore)						
(i) Index Futures	18,711	21,837	16.7	0	0	NA
(ii) Options on Index						
Put	69,548	65,074	-6.4	0	0	NA
Call	64,645	68,369	5.8	0	0	NA
(iii) Stock Futures	66,437	77,930	17.3	1	1	-35.8
(iv) Options on Stock						
Put	8,125	6,424	-20.9	0	0	NA
Call	13,260	11,630	-12.3	0	0	NA
Total	2,40,726	2,51,264	4.4	1	1	-35.8
D. Open Interest in terms of No. of Contracts						
(i) Index Futures	2,95,421	3,29,432	11.5	0	0	NA
(ii) Options on Index						
Put	8,92,132	9,82,705	10.2	0	0	NA
Call	8,50,463	10,27,463	20.8	0	0	NA
(iii) Stock Futures	11,02,412	12,05,320	9.3	16	10	-37.5
(iv) Options on Stock						
Put	60,655	95,805	58.0	0	0	NA
Call	91,486	1,74,555	90.8	0	0	NA
Total	32,92,569	38,15,280	15.9	16	10	-37.5

Source: SEBI Bulletin

Table 3.5.1 Day-Wise Turnover Debt Future Contracts Aug. 2015

Trade Date	Underlying	Total Contracts	Total Value (Rs. cr)	Open Interest
31-Aug-15	772GS2025	51103	1,017.98	138618
31-Aug-15	788GS2030	9581	191.03	11340
31-Aug-15	827GS2020	342	6.94	988
31-Aug-15	840GS2024	3861	79.44	57772
31-Aug-15	91DTB	0	0	0
21-Aug-15	772GS2025	56182	1,119.88	153081

21-Aug-15	788GS2030	6844	136.36	17001
21-Aug-15	827GS2020	3011	61.09	27323
21-Aug-15	840GS2024	16046	330.67	76063
21-Aug-15	91DTB	0	0	0
12-Aug-15	772GS2025	58595	1,165.64	121688
12-Aug-15	788GS2030	5577	110.69	13251
12-Aug-15	827GS2020	2229	45.15	16034
12-Aug-15	840GS2024	11455	235.37	77409
12-Aug-15	91DTB	0	0	0
3-Aug-15	772GS2025	33097	658.74	123070
3-Aug-15	788GS2030	3808	75.67	7347
3-Aug-15	827GS2020	806	16.35	860
3-Aug-15	840GS2024	14227	292.5	78850
3-Aug-15	91DTB	0	0	0

Source: NSC Statistics

Trading in derivatives mostly takes place on NSE, accounting for the large volume share of the country and traded value. As indicated in ISMR (2007), Index Futures and Options were first traded on the benchmark index Nifty 50. Nifty 50 constituted 99.64% of the total number of index contracts traded on NSE, with 76.05% of the contract trades in Index Futures and 23.59% in Index Options during the period 2006-07.

3.5 INTEGRATING FINANCIAL MARKETS

A segmented financial system complicates the conduct of monetary policy and adversely affects resource allocation and growth. To illustrate, suppose that interest ceilings are set at higher levels for non-bank financial institutions than for banks. A policy of credit restraint would then encourage the outflow of funds from the banking system. The *income velocity* (that is, ratio of GNP to money) of broad money (currency and demand deposits plus savings and time deposits) may increase, while that of narrow money (currency and demand deposits), which is used to reserve asset of non-bank financial institutions, may fall.

A redefinition of monetary and credit targets for purposes of financial management cannot sufficiently counteract the possible negative impact on the intermediation capacity of a financial system that is segmented by excessive and inappropriate regulations. A long-term solution is to reform the domestic regulatory framework to eliminate the major causes of segmentation, such as inadequate licensing regulations, burdensome reserve requirements and portfolio restrictions, unrealistic interest rate ceilings, and the operating inefficiencies of the regulated markets.

Dimensions of Financial Market Integration

Broadly, financial market integration occurs in three dimensions, nationally, regionally and globally. From an alternative perspective, financial market integration could take place horizontally and vertically. The *horizontal integration*, inter-linkages occur among domestic financial market segments, while *vertical integration* occurs between domestic markets and regional/international financial markets.

Domestic financial market integration entails horizontal linkages of various segments, reflecting portfolio diversification by savers, investors and intermediaries. Under horizontal integration, market interest rate typically revolves around a basic reference rate, which is defined as the *price of a short-term low-risk financial instrument* in a competitive and liquid market. It typically provides the basic liquidity for the formal financial system and central banks often use it to gauge the tightness of monetary policy. Domestic markets may be closely integrated because intermediaries operate simultaneously in various market segments; for instance, commercial banks operate in both the saving (deposit) and loan markets.

Global integration refers to the opening up of domestic markets and institutions to the free cross-border flow of capital and financial services by removing barriers such as capital controls and withholding taxes. A deeper dimension of global integration entails removing obstacles to movement of people, technology and market participants across the border. Global integration is promoted through harmonization of national standards and laws, either through the adoption of commonly agreed minimum standards or mutual recognition of standards.

Regional financial integration occurs due to ties between a given region and major financial centre serving that region. *Economic integration* might be easier to achieve at a regional level due to network externalities and the tendency of market makers to concentrate in certain geographic centres. Gravity models, which take into account the economic sizes and distance between two countries, explain bilateral trade and investment flows. Furthermore, *regional financial integration* can be an important means of developing local financial markets, for instance, through peer pressure to strengthen institutions and upgrade local practices.

4 Approaches to Investment Decision Making

CHAPTER

Financial goals of a family are an estimate of the money required to fulfill an "aspiration". Investors need to know and use various parameters to assess their financial position. The following are well known practices when approaching financial planning with respect to investments:

- Set measurable goals
- Understand the effect your investment decisions would have on other related financial issues.
- Re-evaluate your financial plan periodically.
- **Start now.** Do not assume that financial planning and making investments is only when you are older. It may be wise to invest as little as you can, since consistency of investment is indeed an important hallmark for growth and progress.
- Invest with what you have. Do not assume that financial planning is for the wealthy only.
- Take charge, look at the bigger picture.
- Financial planning is the most important in investment, retirement and tax planning.
- Do not expect unrealistic returns on your investments.
- Do not wait for a "money crisis" to provoke you to financial planning.

4.1 IMPORTANT STEPS IN FINANCIAL PLANNING PROCESS FOR INVESTMENTS

1. Analyze your Present Financial Position

One needs to understand his/her current financial position through the following considerations:

(a) Cash flow: Sources of income and heads of expenditure must be identified correctly. Determining current position is crucial since it will indicate the monthly/annual surplus that can be invested.

(b) Net worth: Determination of current net worth will indicate a starting point for the planning process. It is only that once the current position is examined, future goals can be worked out.

(c) Employee benefits and pension plans: Details of provident fund contributions and other pension plans that you may be entitled to should be recorded. This will becomes the starting point for retirement planning.

(d) Insurance: All current insurance policies must be listed to find out if your current financial position is secure and whether you are over- or under-insured.

(e) Tax: It is necessary to examine your tax status, tax liability from various sources of income and declaring/filing of tax returns.

(f) Will: A valid will is needed so that you are able to pass on your wealth to the people you want to benefit after you are gone. If there is no valid will, the relevant succession Acts would come into play and your assets may be distributed in a manner you may not like.

2. Determine your Investment/Financial Needs and Objectives

How does your investment/financial life look like? Do you know what you are saving for or how that goal of early retirement is going to be achieved?

One needs to set financial goals in order to fix the financial destination. Putting goals in a timeframe will allow you to walk back to begin allocating resources for the desired event. For a set of goals to be achievable, they must be: identified, quantified in a timeframe, prioritized, attainable, non-conflicting, actionable, reviewed, etc.

3. Examine Development, and Implementation, Review Your Investment/ Financial Plan Periodically and Analyze Resources of an Investor

(a) *Balance Sheet*: A personal balance sheet summarizes the value of your assets, liabilities and marks out your net worth on a particular date.

(b) *Income and Expenditure Statement*: This statement summarizes income received and expenses incurred over a fixed period.

(c) *Budget*: A budget is a summary of projected income and expense statement.

The wide range of investment approaches followed by investors with differing beliefs and convictions in the equity market may be summed up as under:

- Fundamental approach or fundamental analysis
- Psychological approach (behavioural aspects)
- Technical analysis

Life cycle of the investor and financial planning:

Risk/return tradeoffs for investors:

1. Accumulation (early career) - higher return – higher risks
2. Consolidation (mid to late career) - low to medium return – low risks
3. Spending stage and gifting stage - lower return – lower risks.

Life Cycle Identification: Investment goals of a client naturally emerge from the financial planning process. Goals of an individual will change over time, as the client emerges through various stages of his/her life. Thus, the investment objectives will also change over time.

Financial Planning and the Time Horizon

Short-term investors have a clear focus on total return as a measure of success of their investment strategy. Long-term investors, particularly individual investors, often focus on the same metric, which of course, is wrong. For example, it is common for individuals to have a target for accumulated savings before they feel comfortable to retire. Over short periods, an amount that was broadly appropriate can become inadequate if long-term interest rates fall.

The key is not the absolute amount of savings, but the ability of that amount, if cautiously invested, to support the intended level of retirement income. This leads to a focus on shortfall risk rather than the risk of generating a negative return. The benchmark for measuring shortfall is the performance of appropriate safety strategy, and so shortfall risk is the risk of underperforming that strategy.

It is widely believed that long-term bonds are inappropriate as investments for cautious private investors for whom the emphasis should, it is argued, be on controlling *absolute volatility* and *short-term capital preservation*. In fact, this is the appropriate focus only for cautious short-term investors. An error that often accompanies failure to design risk-taking strategies appropriate to an investor's time horizon is to confuse this time horizon with risk tolerance. There are cautious long-term investors and there are aggressive short-term investors.

This focus on controlling volatility often involves restricting interest rate exposure in investment portfolios. Bond market developments in recent years show how this approach can put at risk the spending power of long-term investors. The flip side of succession of profitable opportunities to refinance fixed-rate mortgages around the turn of the century was the much less publicized but more important phenomenon for retirement saving: the sequence of increases in the cost of purchasing continuing flows of income whether in the form of government bonds or life annuities from insurance companies.

Meanwhile, the cost of buying inflation-proof income through inflation-linked government bonds has also increased. For an endowment, or for a family wishing to transfer an unchanged level of real wealth to the next generation, this represents more than a halving in the level of "real" income that can, with full confidence, be supported by that fixed level of wealth. *Wealth planning* should not target wealth accumulation and would better be renamed "income planning". This is not a trivial distinction for any long-term investor, whether an individual planning for retirement or the best endowed foundation is planning its support for philanthropy.

Contingency Planning

Investors need to be aware of and prepare for various contingencies that might arise. The risks associated here need to be factored in by each family in their plan. Following are some of the contingencies to be provided for:

- *Income dependency*–adequate life cover for earning member/(s) must be bought to protect family if anything happens to sole or either earning member.
- *Healthcare costs* could also pose a financial risk. Proper, comprehensive medical insurance becomes necessary to address this risk.
- *Liquidity* is important and crucial to protect family against unwarranted contingency. In practice, generally 6 months expense needs are to be held as liquid assets. Through this, investor will have time to restore the income stream.
- *Healthy distribution* of the names in family's assets are to be carefully utilized both for operational aspects and to ensure wealth remains within family and its members.

4.2 BUDGETING PROCESS

It is important for every family to understand their household budget. Preparing a household budget entails an understanding of the sources from which the family receives income and cash flow, and the applications to which this money is put in a month. The budgeting process involves the following steps:

1. Calculate cash flow
2. Determine net worth
3. Define financial objectives
4. Determine type of investment–statutory (for tax saving purpose); committed (say LIP, annuity based etc); forced (bank requirements, business requirements); and luxury (investments made just to beat inflationary trends)
5. Create a spending plan
6. Check progress
7. Make adjustments when and where necessary.

A budget will assist you in determining whether:

- You are living within your income.
- Your current spending patterns are satisfactory.
- You are saving and investing sufficient amount to satisfy your financial needs.
- You need to make changes in order to satisfy your financial goals.

Setting Budget Goals: Like any other goals in life, your budget goals help you turn your "**wish list**" into an action plan. With clear goals in sight, you can chart your course of action which will also provide for deviation if and when needed. It is important to:

1. List your goals
2. Categorize your goals
3. Estimate the cost of each goal
4. Project the future cost
5. Calculate the monthly deposit
6. Prioritize your goals
7. Create a schedule
8. Implement
9. Review and make appropriate changes.

Estimating Financial Goals: Many aspirations of a family face a financial implication. For example, buying a car, providing for child's educational needs, purchase of residential space, and long vacation outside the country and so on. All these require money to realize. Thus, it becomes important for investors to quantify each of his/her aspirations within a timeframe. Following are some of the estimates for future financial goals that require inputs:

- What would be the cost if an expense were to be incurred today?
- When (after how many years) the expense would be incurred?
- How inflation would rise and impact these expenses?
- For a foreign vacation, how exchange rate changes will impact total costs?

An investor needs to ensure while making a financial plan that his/her family has enough to fulfill non-negotiable and important financial goals. Sometimes investors may have to make tradeoffs. However, clarity is essential to prioritize goals and aspirations for its effective implementation.

Types of Goals:

- Short-term high priority goals
- Long-term high priority goals
- Low priority goals

Since each financial goal has an implication, an investor needs to be aware of the following:

1. **Ensure adequate focus on retirement plan:** To save enough during the earning years for a comfortable retired life.
2. **Differentiate between investment and consumption expenditure:** An investor needs to be prudent while allocating money for various expenditures and savings. This will help avoid wrong decisions which might affect chances of fulfilling some goals.

3. **Allocation to various and important categories of goals:** It is advisable for an investor to clearly set limits on various outflows. Some thumb rules as per lifestyle and goals are to be adhered to.

4. **Windfalls:** Occasionally upon earning/receiving a windfall (say, high bonus, winning from lottery, etc.), an investor must carefully evaluate various options before selecting an investment decision.

4.3 DEVELOPING A MODEL PORTFOLIO

Since investors' aspiration level, life stage, lifestyle and risk appetite vary, some useful model portfolio would be a better choice as single portfolio cannot meet various needs. While choosing or selecting from the list of model portfolios, investor need to understand and provide for asset allocation mix suitable and appropriate to his/her goals and risk appetite. It is important to:

- Develop long-term goals,
- Define investment avenues, time horizon, risk and return,
- Determine asset allocation,
- Allocate under broad asset classes,
- Select specific fund schemes/products for investment,
- Compare products and choose actual funds to invest.

Jacob's Model Portfolio

- **Accumulation phase**
  - Diversified equity: 65 - 80%
  - Income and gilt funds: 15 - 30%
  - Liquid funds: 5%
- **Distribution phase**
  - Diversified equity: 15 - 30%
  - Income and gilt funds: 65 - 80%
  - Liquid funds: 5%

4.4 INVESTMENT OBJECTIVES AND INVESTMENT CONSTRAINTS

Investment Objectives: After specifying life-cycles and goals of investors, the investment objectives become easier to identify and consequently, the goals of the portfolio in tandem with their fundamental needs. Investment objectives can be further classified into four types: capital preservation; capital appreciation; current income; and total return.

Investment Constraints: Once investment objectives are identified, it is equally important to bear in mind the various constraints, viz., practical aspects which can have significant bearing on investments. Some of the constraints are: liquidity needs, time horizon, tax concerns, risk tolerance, and macroeconomic factors.

Strategies for Investors

(a) Active and passive strategies
(b) Types of asset allocation
(c) Strategic asset allocation
(d) Tactical asset allocation
(e) Fixed and flexible allocation
(f) Rebalancing strategies

These strategies are recommended based on each investor's financial plan, time horizon and risk profile. Accordingly, asset allocation and style of investment portfolio is implemented and reviewed on a periodic basis.

5 Spectrum (Various Choices) of Investment Avenues for Investors

CHAPTER

In India, the concept of saving is well understood by most people, however very few understand the *concept of investing*. We all save money to cater to our future needs. In order to get the best out of saved money, we must understand:

1. Our possible future requirements, needs and aspirations.
2. Various avenues/vehicles available for investing this saved money.
3. Pros and cons of these investment vehicles.
4. Various concerns and how to address these concerns.

Having understood the options available for investments, the next step is to match, align the products for achieving desired financial goals.

Generally, investment concerns are: growth, periodical returns, capital protection, inflation, taxation, liquidity, divisibility, trust, convenience, and so on.

Broadly, investments can be classified between assets: financial and non-financial (physical or real).

5.1 FINANCIAL ASSETS

5.1.1 Fixed Rate Securities

The key to developing a sound portfolio is striking the right balance between potential reward, risk, and your future financial needs. Fixed-income securities can be an excellent way to diversify your portfolio. They are also crucial for your tax planning. The main benefit of fixed income is low risk, i.e., relative safety of principal and predictable rate of return (yield).

- The coupon (the amount of interest the issuer has agreed to pay) is set for issuance and remains the same until maturity, thus, the term "fixed-income".
- Different fixed-income vehicles in the market allow you to choose from a range of credit ratings and maturity (one day to 30 years), diversifying and reducing risk.
- Fixed-income securities provide the flexibility and liquidity needed to structure a portfolio tailored to your specific investment objective.

A portion of your investments should be in fixed-income securities based on your risk tolerance and risk capacity for a predictable stream of income.

Small Savings Instruments

Post office investments

- Public Provident Fund
- National Savings Certificate
- Post Office Monthly Income Scheme
- Post Office Term Deposit Scheme
- Senior Citizen Saving Scheme
- Kisan Vikas Patra

Government Securities

- 10, 15, 20, 30 years GOI bonds (issued and managed by RBI on behalf of GOI (usually known as **G-Sec**).

  The long-term nominal risk-free rate of interest. This rate of interest is subject to the risk of unexpectedly high inflation.
- **Treasury bills:** 90 - 180 – 364 days (short-term, below 1 year)

  The short term (less than 1 year) has risk-free rate of interest.

Corporate Deposits

Terms could be for 1, 2, 3, and 5 years.

Bank Deposits

Same as corporate deposits i.e. terms could be for 1, 2, 3 and 5 years.

Other Fixed Rate/Debt Market Products

➢ **Certificates of Deposits (CDs):** Predominantly issued by banks, to meet short-term requirement of funds. They can be issued for maturities up to 364 days. These are between the bank (issuer) and the customer (generally institutional investor like Mutual Funds).

  Rates on CDs are similar to bank deposit rates of the same tenure.

➢ **Commercial Papers (CPs):** These are issued by corporate companies to meet their short-term funding needs. They can be issued for maturities between a minimum of 7 days and a maximum of 364 days. However, 90-day CP is most commonly issued. Issuer must obtain a credit rating and the rating must not be below an 'A3' rating, according to the rating symbols prescribed by SEBI. They are required to be compulsorily dematerialised. Stamp duties apply on issuance. The yield on a CP depends on the credit rating of the issuer. Higher the rating, lower the offered rate. Non-banking Financial Companies (NBFCs) are large issuers of CPs.

- **Collateralised Borrowing and Lending Obligation (CBLO):** CBLO is a short-term instrument used to lend or borrow for periods ranging from overnight to 14 days against the collateral of eligible debt securities (mostly G-Secs and T-bills). Mutual funds are among the biggest lenders in the CBLO segment. Rates in CBLO markets are closely aligned to repo rates; and slightly lower than call rates.

- **Securitised Instruments:** Here mostly primary lenders are usually finance companies and banks who receive repayment of loans such as: car, home, truck and others in the form of equated monthly instalments (EMIs). These monthly cash flows are a trickle compared to their need for lump sum funds to undertake further lending transactions. They, therefore, agree to securitize these receivables. A *special purpose vehicle* (usually a trust) is created, which takes over the loans, and issues securities against them. They are called PTCs (pass through certificates) because they pass the EMIs through to the buyer. PTCs are compulsorily credit rated. In March 2011, SEBI permitted listing of securitised paper with the objective of increasing retail participation and facilitating secondary market activity.

- **Inflation Indexed Bonds** are a category of government securities issued by the RBI which provides inflation protected returns to the investors. These bonds have a *fixed real coupon rate* which is applied to the inflation adjusted principal on each interest payment date. On maturity, higher of the face value and inflation adjusted principal is paid out to the investor. The WPI is the inflation measure that is considered for the calculation of the index ratio for these bonds.

- **Capital Gains Bonds (54 EC):** These are specified bonds that are issued by National Highway Authority of India (NHAI) and Rural Electrification Board (REC) usually for 3 years (lock-in) period. Investments in such bonds allow investors to save tax on long-term capital gains under Section 54 EC of the Indian Income Tax Act.

- **Corporate Bonds:** The market for long-term corporate debt is made up of two components:

- **Bonds issued by public sector units (PSUs),** including public financial institutions. These bonds are further classified into *taxable* and *tax-free* bonds. Tax-free bonds are mainly issued by PSUs in the infrastructure sector.

- **Bonds issued by private corporate sector with embedded options:** floating-rate interest, conversion options and a variety of structured obligations are issued in the market.

5.1.2 Market Rate Securities

Market Risk Premium: The compensation that any rational saver should seek in return for putting money or future income at risk of loss. The market provides this reward for bearing "market risk". This is most obviously reflected in the equity risk premium (the amount by which equities are expected to outperform bonds/debts or cash) and the credit risk premium (the extra yield paid on corporate bonds to compensate for the risk that a company might default). Less obviously, market risk premiums appear systematically to be offered in return for accepting various types of insurance risk and for different types of equity risk (for example, small company risk to be viewed separately from equity market risk).

Mutual Fund Products

Key features:

- Pool investor's money and deploy it in various assets
- Each mutual fund product has a defined objective
- Investors buy units (invest in) of a mutual fund product to participate in the portfolio
- Mutual funds are professionally managed and the trustee oversees its operations
- Mutual funds are subject to SEBI Regulations
- **Types:**
  (a) Generic (equity growth funds, income funds, balanced funds, liquid funds, index funds, ETFs, FMPs, etc.)
  (b) Specific (thematic and sectoral funds, arbitrage funds, etc.)
  (c) Overseas opportunities
  (d) Short-term funds for parking liquidity mutual funds are portfolios that are created and managed according to stated investment objectives. There are a variety of schemes focusing on different market segments and investment styles for investors to choose from. Performances of mutual fund schemes are benchmarked to market indices that reflect the objectives of the portfolio. Investors can easily evaluate how the fund has performed over different time horizons.

Equity

Blue-chip, Growth, Cyclical, Speculative, etc. are identified as different stock in capital market.

Types of shares: Dividend yield, EPS, P/E, etc.

Successful investing in equity markets requires adequate research in identifying and valuing stocks for investment. The investment portfolio has to be diversified to manage risks and needs to be periodically reviewed and rebalanced to reflect performance of sectors and companies. The process of equity investing involves time, costs and taxes and the returns to the investor can be significantly impacted by them. Efficient equity investment must bear these aspects. The options available to investors for participation in equity markets are: (i) direct investment, and (ii) investment through Portfolio Management Services (PMS).

An investor has to choose between primary and secondary markets to invest in stocks/equities.

Primary Market: Certain eligible companies may tap the capital market for their capital requirements. Eligibility criteria have been laid down by SEBI, the capital market regulator. The company may be entering the capital market for the first time whereupon its shares are to be listed on the stock exchanges – such an issue is called "Initial Public Offering (IPO)". An existing listed company may come out with a subsequent issue to raise capital which is called "Follow on Public Offering (FPO)."

Secondary Market: An investor can invest in shares through the secondary market. He/she can invest in a stock which is already listed in one of the stock exchanges. The two most important stock exchanges are, viz., National Stock Exchange (NSE) and the Bombay Stock Exchange (BSE).

(a) Convertible debentures: A company may choose to issue debentures which could be converted partly or fully into equity shares at a later date. These securities are also listed and traded on stock exchanges.

(b) Warrants are essentially issued to share holders and holders of the warrant will be able to exercise his/her right to purchase shares of the company at a future date till the prescribed date for exercising the rights to additional shares such as warrants are also traded on the stock exchanges.

(c) Preference shares can also be issued by a company. This is not a popular instrument with the stock market investors because this is essentially a fixed income instrument with no scope for capital appreciation.

(d) Bonus shares: Companies reward shareholders by issuing bonus *shares*. Bonus shares are shares distributed free by the company to its shareholders, as on a given date, in a proportion which is decided by its board and approved by the shareholders and subject to certain limits, as prescribed by SEBI in this regard.

(e) Rights shares: Issue of additional shares to existing shareholders is called rights issue. The price could be market related or discounted to the market price of the stock.

Alternate Investment Schemes

With a view to regulate other funds (apart from mutual funds), SEBI introduced the Securities and Exchange Board of India (Alternate Investment Funds) Regulations, 2012. Under the regulations, "Alternate Investment Fund" (AIF) means any fund established or incorporated in India in the form of a trust or a company or a limited liability partnership or a body corporate which:

(i) is a privately pooled investment vehicle which collects funds from investors, whether Indian or foreign, for investing in accordance with a defined investment policy for the benefit of its investors; and

(ii) is not covered under the Securities and Exchange Board of India (Mutual Funds) Regulation, 1996, Securities and Exchange Board of India (Collective Investment Scheme) Regulations, 1999 or any other regulations of the Board to regulate fund management activities.

The regulations provide for three categories of AIFs as follows:

- *"Category I Alternative Investment Fund"* which invests in start-ups or early stage ventures or social ventures or SMEs of infrastructure or other sectors or areas which the government or regulator considers as socially and economically desirable and shall include venture capital funds, SME Funds, social venture funds, infrastructure funds and such other "Alternate Investment Funds" as may be specified;
- *"Category II Alternative Investment Fund"* which does not fall in category I and III and which does not undertake leverage or borrowing other than to meet day-to-day operational requirements and as permitted in these regulations;
- *"Category III Alternative Investment Fund"* which employs diverse or complex trading strategies and may employ leverage including through investment in listed or unlisted derivatives.

5.2 NON-FINANCIAL ASSETS

1. Paintings, Antiques, Arts, and Collectibles
2. Other Financial Investments: Venture capital, private equity, structured products, participatory notes (as distinct from Corporate Promissory Notes)
3. Derivatives: These are basically risk management leveraged instruments, which derive their value from the underlying assets. These are extensively used by *hedgers, speculators* and *arbitragers*. Speculations in derivative markets can be risky, whereas if used with proper knowledge as risk management instruments, these could help to protect the returns of the underlying asset (for investors).

Various derivative products in use are:

(i) Forwards, (ii) Futures, (iii) Calls, (iv) Puts, (v) Swaps, (vi) Warrants, and (vii) Leaps

4. Physical Assets

1. Real Estate: Forms of real estate investment, financing real estate, cost of buying and maintaining, loans and financing.

2. Commodities: will include permitted items (e.g. Crude) as per guidelines directives by both regulator and stock exchanges for trading purpose.

5.3 INVESTMENT ATTRIBUTES

For evaluating investment avenues, the following attributes are relevant:

- Rate of return– plain, integrated
- Risk – lock-in period v/s inflation beating capability

- Capital protection
- Marketability
- Tax shelter
- Divisibility
- Convenience

1. **The rate of return** on an investment for a period (usually a year) is defined as: Annual income + (Ending price-beginning price)/Beginning price
   10 + (110-100)/100 = 0.10 or ten per cent.

Compounded Annual Growth Rate (CAGR)

The standard that is used in the financial markets for computing returns is not the simple return, but the compounded return, or the CAGR. Here, it is assumed that re-investment of return will happen every year and therefore, compute return after accounting for such compounding. We would therefore say that Rs. 10.50 grew at some CAGR to become Rs. 12.25 at the end of 15 months. 10.50 (1+r) ^n period = 12.25.

Table 5.1 The Effect of Compounding Described

Compounding Period	No. of times in a Year	Effective Interest Rate
Yearly	1	10%
Bi-annual/half yearly	2	10.25%
Quarterly	4	10.38129%
Monthly	12	10.47131%

Therefore, compounding can change the effective yield dramatically.

Rolling Return

Sometimes an investor may ask, what was average yearly return from an equity fund? (May not be interested in knowing return from one point to another) The answer will vary depending on which yearly period, and can obviously be very different from what the investor can expect.

As we create returns for every year, the CAGR that we will get is the *rolling return*. Using a worksheet application like MS Excel can help in storing the data and doing these computations efficiently, without error. Rolling returns provide a guide to investors on what to expect for a specified holding period, given the history of the fund's returns.

2. **Risk:** In the context of investments "risk" refers not only to the chance that a person may lose the capital, but more importantly, to the chance that the investor may not get the desired return on an investment instrument. The notion of risk

is integral, and therefore a primary concept in understanding investments as a whole.

Each of the investment assets has its own associated risk and return/reward, which every investor must understand before investing. The *risk of an investment* refers to the variability of its rate of return, i.e., to consider the possibilities of unexpected outcomes, namely, how much do individual outcomes deviate from the anticipated value?

It is, therefore, necessary to get explanation on risk that can be perceived, defined and handled in multiple ways. One way to handle risk is to avoid it. Another way to handle risk is to transfer it, say, resort to insurance, etc.

(a) **Risk Avoidance:** Risk avoidance occurs when one chooses to completely avoid the activity because of the risk associated therewith. In the investment world, avoidance of some risk is deemed to be possible notionally through the act of investing in "risk-free" investments. Short-term government bonds, Treasury bills of a certain term, about 90-360 days are a few illustrations.

(b) **Risk Transfer (through insurance mechanism):** An easy to understand example of risk transfer is the concept of insurance. Following are the areas that need to be insured:

Your Life: It is the most important (seldomly recognized) to be protected as it brings income into the dependant household to members against premature death. This insurance actually protects the living standard of dependants of chief breadwinner of a home and ensures they continue to live in the same way, even after chief income earner is no more.

Yourself against disability: While an untoward accident can take a life away, it can also cause temporary or permanent disability. Disability insurance assures you a source of income in case you are temporarily or permanently disabled and unfit to work to earn an income.

Yourself and your family against medical emergencies: A large expenditure, such as treatment of a heart disease or an operation after an accident, need large sums of money that may not be available from current resources and if taken from savings, will leave financial disaster in its place. Such medical situations need the protective umbrella of medical insurance.

Your assets: Home and its contents, vehicles, any other property, valuables, gold, jewellery, and any other asset. You will insure your assets against theft, fire or other damages that may be seen as a threat.

Insurance Planning

(a) Objective of risk management
(b) Law of large numbers
(c) Personal risk management, risk control and risk financing
(d) Insurance of liabilities

(e) Term insurance

(f) Life insurance

- Human life approach
- Needs approach
- Multiple approaches
- Capital needs analysis approach

(g) Types of life and health insurance products and their features

Risk Transfer (through prudent use of some derivative instruments)

A risk transfer can be made by purchasing a put option on a stock or on market index which allows a person to put to or sell to someone his stock or index at a set price, regardless of how low the stock or index may drop/go down on payment of certain nominal fee.

A simple measure of dispersion in the range of values is simply the difference of values between the highest and the lowest. Other measures commonly used in finance and investments are:

• **Variance:** This is the mean of the squares of deviations of individual returns around their average value.

• **Standard deviation:** This is the square root of variance. It is computed on the basis of a past series of return. It measures the total risk in an investment, without reference to any scope to reduce the risk through diversification. Therefore, it is a more appropriate measure of return of a single investment or a single-asset portfolio.

• **Beta:** This reflects how volatile the return is from an investment in response to market swings. Beta is a measure of the systematic risk of a security that cannot be avoided through diversification. Beta is a relative measure of risk–the risk of an individual stock relative to market portfolio of all stocks. Beta is useful for comparing the relative systematic risk of different stocks and in practice, is used by investors to judge a stock's risk. Beta is the slope of the regression line. The steeper the slope, the more the systematic risk; the shallower the slope, the less exposed the company is to market fluctuations.

3. Capital Protection: Protecting the investor's capital is the most important aspect of any investment. By nature, majority of Indians are risk averse.

4. Marketability: An investment is highly marketable if (i) it can be transferred quickly, i.e., a substantial portion of it can be withdrawn without significant loss; (ii) transaction cost is lower; and (iii) price changes between two successive transactions are negligible.

5. Tax shelter: Tax benefits are of three kinds: (i) an *initial* tax benefit refers to tax relief/benefit at the time of making investments; (ii) a *continuing* tax benefit represents the tax shield associated with periodic returns from the investment; and (iii) *terminal* tax benefit, refers to relief from taxation when an investment is realized or liquidated. These three are called **3-E**s, exempt while investing, exempt while it grows, exempt at its withdrawal.

6. **Divisibility:** This is the ability to convert part of the investment asset into cash, without liquidating whole of the asset. Divisibility may be an important consideration for many investors, while choosing an investment vehicle.
7. **Convenience:** It refers to the ease with which the investment can be made and looked after. The degree of convenience associated with different investment avenues varies vastly.

   Comparison of investment products on the basis of return, safety, volatility, and liquidity.

Table 5.2

Category	Return	Safety	Volatility	Liquidity
Equity	High	Low	High	High
Mutual Funds	High	Moderate	Moderate	High
Fin. Institution Bonds	Moderate	High	Moderate	Moderate
Corporate Debentures	Moderate	Moderate	Moderate	Low
Company Fixed Deposits	Moderate	Low	Low	Low
Bank Deposits	Low	High	Low	High
PPF	Moderate	High	Low	Moderate
Life Insurance	Low	High	Low	Low
Gold	Moderate	High	Moderate	Moderate
Real Estate	High	Moderate	High	Low

Table 5.3 Products in Debt Market

Issuer	Instruments	Maturity *
Central Government	Dated securities	2 – 30 years
Central Government	T – Bills	91/364 days
State Government	State development loan	5 -10 years
PSUs	Bonds, structured obligations	5 – 10 years
Private Corporate	Debentures, Bonds	1 – 12 years
Private Corporate	Commercial Papers	15 days to 1 year
Scheduled Commercial Banks	Certificates of Deposits	3 months to 5 years

* Maturity as mentioned in most cases. The same may be different in certain cases.

The forgoing discussion has clearly articulated the importance of each and every asset class that plays an important role in every investor's portfolio in line with the stated objectives/need/requirements.

6 CHAPTER

Concept of Value and Return (Measuring Investment Returns)

The human being is credited with discovery of money for various purposes and needs. Until the advent of money, all transactions took place under the barter system. However, with the passage of time, the barter system was found inconvenient and man came up with a better and simpler system, namely, the system of money. This remarkable breakthrough rests on the fact that anything can be treated as money so long as people are willing to associate a certain value with that thing. The value of money is an interesting concept carrying multifaceted meanings and interpretations.

Here we will talk about different types of returns and measure them. The discussion will help us grasp the connotation of ability and willingness to risk with optimal asset allocation. We will also go through the basics of finance in the form of time value of the money concept.

Let us discuss now the more important dimensions of the value of money.

Nominal Value

The value which is printed on currency notes and coins is called nominal value. As an example, the 500-rupee currency notes carry a nominal value of Rs. 500 each.

Real Value

The concept of 'real' value of money stems from the fact that the nominal value needs to be suitably adjusted for inflation, and/or deflation.

The real value of the Rs. 500 note in 1986 was different from that in 2000 and in 2010 because of the inflation during the period between: 1986-2000 and 1986-2010; the value depreciated and went down substantially.

A contrasting example is the one rupee silver coins issued before 1947. Due to their high silver content and the rise in silver prices, those old one-rupee coins fetched you many more rupees based on their intrinsic value.

Exchange Value

When a transaction is carried out in two different currencies, say rupees and sterling or Pounds, there is exchange value built into the transaction.

For example, if an investor had borrowed 1 million pound sterling in 1985, he/she would have got Rs. 20 million. Repaying in 1990 would require Rs. 35 million, excluding interest, due to a fall in the exchange value of rupee vis-à-vis the pound.

Tax Value

Since incomes and profits are subject to tax at rates varying for individuals and companies, the pre-tax and post-tax value of money vary greatly.

Book Value and Market Value

Book value is what an asset costs at the time of acquisition, less depreciation for wear and tear. *Market value* is what that asset can fetch when it is sold. Usually, there is a disparity between the two values.

Management decisions are typically taken on basis of the market values rather than book values. Understanding the significance of different dimensions of the value of money is very important in the study of finance and investments.

Most investment decisions, such as purchase of residential property or investing into any asset class, affect the cash flow of the investor in different time periods. The absolute cash flows, which differ in *timing* and *risk*, are not directly comparable. Cash flows become logically comparable when they are appropriately adjusted for their differences in timing and risk.

6.1 TIME PREFERENCE FOR MONEY

If an individual behaves rationally, he or she would not value the opportunity equally to receive a specific amount of money now, with the opportunity to have the same amount at some future date. *Time preference for money* is an individual's preference for possession of a given amount of money now, rather than the same amount at some future date. Three reasons may be attributed to the individual's time preference for money:

- Risk (uncertainty of return/cash inflows)
- Preference for consumption (subjective)
- Investment opportunities available

In order to overcome this time preference, the investor must be suitably rewarded. This reward is known by the various names like, *interest, cost of capital, required rate of return* or *cost of financing*. An explicit consideration of interest rate helps the investor to translate different amounts offered at different time periods to their equivalent value at present. An understanding of mathematics of interest is therefore important to appreciate most financial transactions for an investor which involve cash flows over a period of time.

Interest rate (time preference rate) gives money its value, and facilitates the comparison of cash flows occurring at different time periods. A 'risk premium' is usually demanded by an investor over and above the *risk-free rate* as compensation for time, to account for the uncertainty of cash inflows, which is the required rate one expects from risky investments.

Time Value of Money: Interest is cost of money. Impact depends upon: (a) the amount of money; (b) the rate of interest; (c) the period of investment; and (d) frequency of cash flows.

1. **Future Value:** It is the value receivable or payable in future once the rate of return is determined. Consider National Savings Certificate (NSC) where Rs. 100 deposited today is paid back as Rs. 160 in six years, rate of interest is 8% p.a. compounded half yearly. Future value can be calculated as:

$$FV = PV * (1 + r/100) \wedge n$$

   where r is interest rate per annum; n is maturity time in years; and PV is sum being deposited today.

   Compounded interest is the interest that is received on the original (principal) amount as well as on any interest earned but not withdrawn during earlier periods. Future value is therefore affected by the rate of return or interest, time available to maturity and the frequency of compounding. The process of finding future value is called **compounding**, a process by which money grows over time to a larger amount.

Table 6.1 Compound Value Factor of a Lump Sum of Re. 1 (at various interest rates)

Period	5%	10%	15%
1	1.050	1.100	1.150
2	1.103	1.210	1.323
3	1.158	1.331	1.521
4	1.216	1.464	1.749
5	1.276	1.611	2.011
6	1.340	1.772	2.313
7	1.407	1.949	2.660
8	1.477	2.144	3.059
9	1.551	2.358	3.518
10	1.629	2.594	4.046

2. **Present Value:** Today's value of an amount receivable or payable in future. Present value of a future cash flow (inflow or outflow) is the amount of current cash that is of equivalent value to the decision maker. The process of

determining/calculating the present value is called discounting. The *compound* interest rate used for discounting cash flows is also called the *discount* rate. Discounting is calculated as:

$$PV = FV/(1 + r/100) \wedge n$$

where r is interest rate per annum; n is maturity time in years; and FV is sum of money that will become due.

Let's consider a corporate deposit scheme that promises to pay Rs. 10,000 at the end of three years, whereas interest rate is 10% per annum. What amount needs to be deposited today?

Applying the formulae, the answer we get is Rs. 7,513.

Table 6.2 Present Value Factor of a Lump Sum of Re. 1 (at various interest rates)

Period	5%	10%	15%
1	0.952	0.909	0.870
2	0.907	0.826	0.756
3	0.864	0.751	0.658
4	0.823	0.683	0.572
5	0.784	0.621	0.497
6	0.746	0.564	0.432
7	0.711	0.513	0.376
8	0.677	0.467	0.327
9	0.645	0.424	0.284
10	0.614	0.386	0.247

There are general principles that can be summarized from the above discussion:

- Discounting and compounding are reciprocal.
- Higher the rate of compounding, greater the future value. Higher the rate of discounting, lower the present value.
- Longer the period, greater the impact of compounding or discounting.
- Compounding and discounting may occur at frequencies that are greater than once a year.

Net Present Value (NPV): *Net Present Value* is the return of an investment based on a discount rate and a series of future payments (negative values) and income (positive value).

Net present value is found by subtracting the required initial investment from the present value of the expected cash flows. Net present value of an investment decision is the difference between the present value of cash inflows and the present value of cash outflows. Suppose an investor has Rs. 2,00,000. He wants to invest this money in an asset, say land, which can fetch Rs. 2,45,000 after one year when he/she sells it. An investor will undertake this investment if the present value of the expected Rs. 2,45,000 after a year is greater than the investment outlay of Rs. 2,00,000 today.

How much should one invest to obtain Rs. 2,45,000 after a year? In other words, if ones' opportunity cost of capital (for investment) is 15 per cent, what is the present value (*PV*) of Rs. 2,45,000 if he/she decides to invest in land?

$$P = A * \text{PVF}n, i$$

where PVF A = present value factor

n = period (no. of years)

r = rate of interest

Using the above formula,

$$PV = 2{,}45{,}000 * (\text{PVF } 1, 0.15)$$
$$= 2{,}45{,}000 * 0.870$$
$$= 2{,}13{,}150$$

The land is worth Rs. 2,13,150 today, but that does not mean that one's wealth will increase by Rs. 2,13,150. One needs to commit Rs. 2,00,000, and therefore, the net increase in his/her wealth or net present value is Rs. 2,13,150 – Rs. 2,00,000 = Rs. 13,150. Hence, it is worth investing in land.

Time diversification:

- Volatility of common stock may be an enemy in the short run, but it is a friend in the long run.
- Portfolio diversification is attained by creating a basket of securities.
- Time diversification is obtained by creating a basket of securities.
- This idea is particularly important in equity investment.

Impact of Compounding

Compound interest arises when interest is added to the principal. The opportunity to reinvest the interest and earn more interest on interest is known as *compounding*. Compounding is referred to as the eighth wonder of the world and rightly so if we understand the impact of this calculation which all of us were taught in our 5th grade/standard. The formula of compounding is:

$$FV = PV (1 + r/100) \wedge n$$

where FV = Future value

PV = Present value

r = rate of return for each compounding period

n = number of compounding periods

The following table will demonstrate difference between time periods and the impact of compounding. It is assumed that an investor invests Rs. 2,000 p.m., systematically in different investment plans which yield 8%, 10%, 12% and 15% p.a. (over a time horizon of 5, 10, 15, 20, 25, and 30 years).

It is evident that a higher rate of return over lon[illegible] of time can make a "**world of a difference**" to the capital at the end of the term.

Table 6.3

For (years)	Maturity value @ 8% p.a.	Maturity value @ 10% p.a.	Maturity value @ 12% p.a.	Maturity value @ 15% p.a.
5	₹ 146,954	₹ 154,874	₹ 163,339	₹ 177,149
10	₹ 365,892	₹ 409,690	₹ 460,077	₹ 550,434
15	₹ 692,076	₹ 828,941	₹ 999,160	₹ 1,337,014
20	₹ 1,178,041	₹ 1,518,738	₹ 1,978,511	₹ 2,994,479
25	₹ 1,902,053	₹ 2,653,667	₹ 3,757,693	₹ 6,487,059
30	₹ 2,980,719	₹ 4,520,976	₹ 6,989,928	₹ 13,846,559

The objective of investors is to maximize expected returns subject to constraints, primarily risk. Return is the motivating force in investment process. Return on a typical investment consists of two components:

(i) Yield: The distinguishing feature of periodic cash flows (or income) on investment, is either interest or dividends, that issuer makes payment to the holder. Yield measures relate these cash flows to a price for security, such as the purchase price or the current market price.

(ii) Capital Gain/Loss: The second component is for (usually) long-term bonds or long-term physical assets. This component is appreciation (or depreciation) in price of the asset, commonly called capital gain/loss. It is the difference between purchase and sale price.

Total Return: Given the two components of a security's return, we need to add them together to form total return, which is defined as: Total return = Yield + Price change where yield can be positive or nil. Price change component can be nil, positive or negative.

Measurement of Total return: Total return = (Cash payments received + Price change over the period)/purchase price of the asset. The price change over the period = end price – open price (can be negative).

6.2 NOTION OF RETURN / DEFINING RETURN

When one invests in a stock (for that matter in any asset), he/she would like to know how much rate of return could be earned. Here a person can make intuitive judgements by himself/herself or can make use of past rates of return as an indicator of the future. Many prefer the latter since it is more objective.

Simply defin... ...come received on an investment plus any change in market price, usual... ...essed as a per cent of the beginning market price of the investment.

$$R = \frac{D_t + [Pt - (Pt - 1)]}{Pt - 1}$$

Computation of Returns

There are several ways in which returns can be computed, each of which would lead to a different result.

Types of Returns:

1. **Nominal Rate of Return:** It is simply the return that one earns on an investment, e.g. a bond that promises to pay 8 per cent per year on Rs. 100 investment, will yield Rs. 108 after one year. Here 8 is nominal return (without considering inflation or taxes, etc).

Arithmetic Mean: The return here can be considered the simple average of the annual rates of return. Such simple average return is also known as arithmetic mean. In the following example, the return from the first security, Tata Motors, is 20% [(18 + 22 + 20 + 17 + 23)/5]. The return from the second security Maruti is 18% [(15 + 18 + 22 + 25 + 10)/5]. Mathematically, this can be expressed as $[(R_1 + R_2 \ldots + R_n)/N]$.

Table 6.4

	Returns %				
Year	1	2	3	4	5
Tata Motors	18	22	20	17	23
Maruti	15	18	22	25	10

Effective vis-a-vis Nominal Return

Let us generalize this on an annual time span, taking 'per annum' rate of interest. Let us divide the period of one year in 'p' sub-periods and let the nominal rate of interest over one-year period be '$i(p)$' per annum.

In effect, $i(p)$ is the nominal rate of interest per annum payable (or reinvested) 'p' times over the year. In such a case, an investment of C for a period of length '$1/p$' will produce a return of $C * i(p)/p$. Thus, '$i(p)/p$ is the effective rate of interest over the sub-period '$1/p$'.

The relationship between a nominal rate of interest $i(p)$ and effective rate of interest i is:

$$1 + i = [1 + i(p)/p] \text{ \^{}} p$$

A nominal of 12% p.a. compounded quarterly will have an equivalent annual effective rate of interest of

$$i = [1 + (0.12/4)\ \text{^}4] - 1$$
$$= [(1.03)\ \text{^}4] - 1$$
$$= 1.125509 - 1$$
$$= 0.125509 \text{ or } 12.55\%$$

2. **Required Rate of Return:** While assessing an investment opportunity, investor gauges attractiveness of investment and would analyse two factors – the *risk* and *expected return*. The expectation of the return could be a combination of: risk-free (like Treasury bill) and some premium (additional compensation) in case of securities that might possibly default on obligations. The same can be explained as follows:

   Required Rate of Return = Risk-free Return + Risk Premium

3. **Real Rate of Return:** The decision to invest is to forego consumption. Alternatively, an investment decision that implies a *postponement* of current consumption. Let's look at one example of an investor who is considering to park with:
   - A bank offers 3 per cent on its savings account on Rs. 100 (nominal rate of return for a year to its customers) or
   - To buy a watch (due to general increase in the price level, i.e. inflation the price becomes Rs. 104).

   Here an investor decides to invest only when he/she is rewarded by a higher earning rate (higher than 4 per cent of inflation rate) for postponing the consumption. Therefore, another bank who offers 6 per cent, the additional 2 per cent would be real rate of return. The approximate relationship can be expressed as: Nominal rate = Real rate + Inflation rate; and

   $$\text{Real rate} = [(1 + \text{Nominal rate})/(1 + \text{Inflation rate})] - 1$$

   Therefore, real rate of return is the rate at which the purchasing power of an investment increases.

4. **Tax Adjusted (post-tax) Rate of Return:** Many returns that investors earn are not tax-free. Short-term capital gains are taxed at the investor's marginal tax rate. Taxes are relevant to all, particularly to high income-tax brackets, owing to being affected by post-tax returns. The formula here is:

$$r = (R)(1 - t) - I,$$

where r = post-tax return
R = Nominal rate of return
t = Tax rate (on which the investment will be taxed)
I = Inflation rate for the period

If the nominal rate (R) of a security is yielding 9 per cent, the individual's tax rate (t) is 30 per cent, and the inflation rate (I) is 4 per cent, applying formula,

$$r = (0.09)(1 - 0.30) - 0.04 = \mathbf{2.30\%}$$

Incorporating the notion of before- and after-tax investment returns is an important concept. Because laws change, tax planning becomes a challenging effort. Tax consideration and goals should be spelt out in investment policy to assist investors in quantifying tax consequences.

5. **Risk Adjusted Return:** It is a percentage return that an investor expects to earn for a given level of risk. **Risk premium** will be different for each investment product and its time horizon, and that all investments have different risk profiles and different expected returns. If **risk-free rate** is 8% (RBI Treasury bills), an investor might expect a rate of return of 17 to 18% (addition of 9 to 10% for risk-premium) on equity/common stock.

6. **Holding Period Return:** It takes interim cash flows during the period of investing along with the initial investment, i.e. the principal into account. We can look at return from another angle. Suppose in the above example of Tata Motors and Maruti, both began with a market price of Rs. 100 five years ago. Today, Tata Motors would be quoting 100 * 1.18 * 1.22 * 1.20 * 1.17 * 1.23 = Rs. 249 whereas Maruti would be quoting 100 * 1.15 * 1.18 * 1.22 * 1.25 * 1.10 = Rs. 228. The first one has given a return of 149% [(249-100)/100] over 5 years and the second has given a return of 128% [(228-100)/100] over 5 years. Such a period is referred to as **holding period return**. Mathematically, this can be expressed as $(1 + R_1) * (1 + R_2) * \ldots (1 + R_n)$.

   Annual Simple Return: We can convert the holding period return to an annual return. Mathematically, it would be holding period return divided by the number of years. In our example, Tata Motors would clock a return of 29.8% (149/5) and Maruti would clock a return of 25.6% (128/5).

Compounded Annual Growth Rate (CAGR)

We can also compute the CAGR inbuilt in the holding period return. This involves computing the internal rate of return (IRR). For instance, if Rs. 100 were to grow to Rs. 200 in 5 years the IRR would be 14%.

Time Weighted Rate of Return and Rupee Weighted Rate of Return

Time weighted rate of return (TWRR) is also called *geometric mean* (GM) and it assigns equal weights to the results achieved in each time period and does not account for each cash flows pattern. GM is considered a superior measure of returns as compared with rupee weighted rate of return also referred to as *internal rate of return* (IRR).

Geometric mean and *Compounded Annualized Growth Rate* (CAGR) are one and the same. On one hand, internal rate of return is the discount rate at which the investment's NPV equals zero. It is the net yield from an investment which is also useful in measuring the total return (experience) of the investment, reflecting investment performance as well as cash flows. GM or CAGR on the other hand, gives year on year return numbers. Let us understand the same with an investment.

Table 6.5

Investment details	Period 0	EOY 1	EOY 2	EOY 3
Rate of return	10%	20%	30%	
Stock/fund XYZ				
1. Initial investment	10000	11000	13200	17160
2. Cash flows	-	-	(17160)	
3. Actual investment	10000	11000	13200	-
4. EOY value	11000	13200	17160	-
Stock/fund ABC				
1. Initial investment	10000	11000	4800	6240
2. Cash flows	(7000)	-	(6240)	
3. Actual investment	10000	4000	4800	-
4. EOY value	11000	4800	6240	

In XYZ fund, Rs 10,000 invested for three years grows to Rs. 17,160 and has zero cash flows.

$$\text{IRR} = \text{NPV} = \text{FV}/(1 + r)\ \hat{}3$$
$$10000 = 17160/(1 + r)\ \hat{}3 = 19.72\%$$

In ABC fund, investment of Rs. 10,000 yields a cash flow of Rs. 7000 and Rs. 6240 respectively at the end of year 1 and year 3.

$$\text{IRR} = 10000 = (7000/1 + r) + (0/1 + r)\ \hat{}2 + (6240/1 + r)\ \hat{}3$$
$$= 16.20\%$$

IRR assumes that cash flows are reinvested at the internal rate. Calculating IRR is the process of applying a discount rate that equals the PV of future cash flows to zero.

Some Important Points

1. NPV is an absolute number.
2. IRR is expressed in % terms.
3. NPV calculates additional wealth.
4. IRR reflects investment performance as well as cash flows.
5. Use of IRR facilitates comparison.
6. Both NPV and IRR are discounted cash flow models.
7. Since NPV is a direct measure of increase in wealth, it is preferred over IRR in case of conflict in mutually exclusive investments (where we have to select only one investment). In case of a scenario like: A's NPV is high and B's IRR is high, always go with the higher NPV option.

In financial and investment management, the CARG is considered the most accurate representation of return. However, despite the superiority of CARG and the limitations of arithmetic mean, the portfolio theory bases its conclusions on arithmetic mean. This is because:

- Standard deviation, which is a measure of risk, is a deviation from arithmetic mean and not from CARG.
- An investor need not be a "buy-wait-and-sell-after-5 years" investor. Meaning he/she has the opportunity to enter and exit (buy and sell) at the end of each year; hence each year's return should be considered.
- Stock market returns are supposed to represent a pattern which corresponds to the normal distribution as understood in statistics.

6.3 MEASUREMENT OF RETURN IN RELATION TO RISK

In examining the performance of fund managers, the return measure commonly used is excess returns. Though the term, **excess return,** has many definitions, the one most commonly used is the total return on a portfolio (capital appreciation plus dividends) minus risk-free rate:

$$\text{Excess returns} = \text{Total portfolio return} - \text{Risk-free rate}$$

We look at three different approaches in comparing excess returns: the **Sharpe approach**; the **Treynor approach**; and the **Jensen approach.**

1. **Sharpe Approach:** In this, the excess returns on a portfolio are compared with the portfolio standard deviation. Also known as *reward to variability ratio,* it indicates the excess return per unit of risk associated with the excess return as derived from Capital Market Line in Capital Asset Pricing Model (CAPM).

$$\textbf{Sharpe measure} = \frac{\text{Total portfolio return} - \text{Risk-free rate}}{\text{Portfolio standard deviation}}$$

   This measure can be compared with other portfolios or with the market in general to assess performance. This ratio measures the effectiveness of a manager in diversifying the total risk, i.e., standard deviation. Positive and higher Sharpe ratio would represent a superior performance.

2. **Treynor Approach:** In this, the excess returns on a portfolio are compared with the *Portfolio Beta*. This measure indicates the excess return generated per unit vis-a-vis risk associated with it. However, here systematic risk is used instead of total risk.

$$\textbf{Treynor measure} = \frac{\text{Total portfolio return} - \text{Risk-free rate}}{\text{Portfolio Beta}}$$

   The only difference between Sharpe and Treynor is in the denominator. While Sharpe uses the portfolio standard deviation, Treynor uses the portfolio Beta.

This measure can be compared with other portfolios or with the market in general to determine whether there is a superior performance in terms of return per unit of risk. Here, too, positive and higher Treynor ratio would indeed represent a superior performance.

3. **Jensen Approach:** Jensen ratio is also called *Alpha* denoted as σ, or *portfolio alpha*, measures the fund manager's performance. Jensen measures the average return of the portfolio over and above that predicted by the Capital Asset Pricing Model (CAPM), given portfolio beta and the average market returns.

In other words, positive alpha means that the fund manager has done his job of identifying sectors/stocks with prospect of premium return. Negative alpha means the performance of the fund manager is below the benchmark. The calculation of return is as follows:

Jensen Ratio (S) = R (actual portfolio return) – SML (expected return)

Returns are the actual portfolio return and SML, is the expected return according to CAPM.

$$SML = R_f + \sigma (R_m - R_f)$$

where R_f is risk free return (generally rate of T-Bill is considered), β is portfolio beta and R_m is the market return.

For portfolio ABC the following data is given:

Return = 12.8%; Treasury bills = 4%; Standard deviation = 3%; Beta = 0.8

$$\begin{aligned}(SML) &= 4 + 0.8(12 - 8.4) \\ &= 4 + 7.04 = 11.04\end{aligned}$$

Sharpe ratio for ABC portfolio = (12.8 – 4)/3 = 2.93
Treynor ratio for ABC portfolio = (12.8 – 4)/0.8 = 11
Jensen ratio for ABC portfolio = (12.8 – 11.04) = 1.76

Jensen emphasizes using certain aspects of capital asset pricing model to evaluate portfolio managers. It compares their actual excess returns (total portfolio return – risk-free rate) with the required in market, based on portfolio Beta.

The expected portfolio excess returns should be equal to market excess returns. If the market return is 9 per cent and the risk-free rate is 6 per cent, the market excess return is 3 per cent. A portfolio with a Beta of 1 should expect to the market rate of excess returns, equal to 3 per cent (in this example).

Time Tested Valid 90:10 Rule

- We spend 90% of our time in stock selection and market timing.
- It accounts for less than 10% in investment performance.
- We spend less than 10% of our time in asset allocation.
- It accounts for over 90% of investment performance.

Management of Risk

Following are the ways in which risk can be managed effectively

Time horizon in Investment:

- Time is the least understood factor in investment.
- Always match the duration of the investment with liquidity requirements.
- Most long-term investments do not involve/state specific future needs.
- In long-term investment, equity becomes attractive and perhaps the unavoidable part of the portfolio.

The value of money has to be understood in all its dimensions. There is nothing like one given absolute value of money, valid at all times. It changes from time to time due to economic factors such as inflation, business conditions, political factors, international scenario, geopolitical situation, and so on.

In the final analysis, the value of money is what one is willing to pay for it.

7 Risk and Return (Tradeoff) – Measuring Total Risk

CHAPTER

Investor's Dilemma: Two-fold objective

- Returns to be high – *Maximize returns*
- Returns to be as certain as possible – *Minimize uncertainty (risks)*

Risk and *return* are the two most important concepts in investments and finance. These are basic to understanding of valuation assets or securities. The expected rate of return on a security is the sum of the products of possible rates of return and their probabilities. The expected rate of return is an average rate of return, which may deviate from the possible outcomes (rates of return). Therefore, risk and return, in fact, are the foundation of the modern finance theory.

After all, one can earn higher return by taking higher risk. Hence, it is necessary to be able to compute risk. At times it is possible to spot risk intuitively; more often it will have to be computed specifically.

We shall discuss in the following paragraphs and make an attempt to answer the below mentioned questions.

- What is risk and how it is measured?
- What is return and how it is measured?
- How do investors make their investment decisions?

Risk is *uncertainty*. Neither dividend nor capital gains are certain. Variance of actual return from expected return is risk and is quantified by *standard deviation*.

Risk is Volatility: Volatility depends on company fundamentals like

- Leverage – financial as well as operational
- Uncertainty surrounding expected cash flows
- Uncertainty surrounding discount (interest) rates
- Market psychology
- Random or sociological factors

- Speculative bubbles
- Trading activity
- Derivatives expiration
- Market volumes

Unlike natural science, medicine, law and economics, investing lies somewhere between an art and science. Certain aspects of investing lend themselves to a scientific approach. The creation of computer skills has undoubtedly accelerated the use of scientific methods.

Whether investing will ever be classified as a science is doubtful, but research, training and experience have developed investing into a discipline. *Discipline* means a structured, consistent and orderly process without rigidity either in concept or methods.

The risk/return tradeoff could easily be called the "ability-to-sleep-at-night test." While some people can handle the equivalent of financial skydiving without batting an eye, others are terrified to climb the financial ladder without a secure harness. Deciding what amount of risk you can take while remaining comfortable with your investments is very important.

The investor can minimize his risk on the portfolio. Risk avoidance and risk minimization are the important objectives of portfolio management.

Analyze Risk First, Expect Return Later

7.1 THINK ABOUT RISK BEFORE IT HITS YOU

Risk relates to the danger of failing to meet particular objectives or it can be defined as the probability that the expected return may not materialize. But risk is also the chance of anything happening at intermediate periods which undermine the investor's confidence in that future objective not fulfilled. Risk is about bad outcome. It is determined by each investor. It varies from investor to investor and from investment to investment.

If an investor is saving for a pension, or to pay off a mortgage, or to fund a child's education, the bad outcome that matters is the risk of a shortfall from the investment objectives. This is vastly different from the risk of a negative return.

The nature of risk and its relation with the investment return becomes relevant, to answer questions like why and how a particular investment decision is taken. Whenever more than one outcome is likely from an investment, there is always some amount of risk involved, except that the level of risk is different.

Risk and return go hand in hand, for higher the return higher the risk, or vice versa. So, while investing, return expectation should be based on the level of risk the investor can bear. It is important, if return expectations are not matching with your risk profile, in the long run it can make a big difference to your total wealth. The general literature on investment looks at the following types of investment risks classified into two: systematic and unsystematic.

1. **Unsystematic Risk** (can be controlled): This is part of the total risk that is specific to industry, a firm or a security. It is also called **unique risk** which arises from the unique uncertainties of individual securities and is independent of the general market movement. Industry specific factors like product life cycle, technology, etc., and the firm specific factors like management change, capital structure, labour unrest, etc., form a part of unsystematic risk. Many of these uncertainties are diversifiable if a large number of securities from different business cycles/industries are combined to form a well diversified portfolio. Unsystematic risk is also known as *diversifiable risk.*

Following are some important types of unsystematic risk.

(a) **Business risk** is associated with business cycles and uncertainties of business. The risk of doing business in a particular industry or environment with continued operation. The risk associated with changes in a firm's abilities to measure up to expectations is known as business risk. As a holder of corporate securities (equity shares/debentures), one is exposed to risk of poor business performance. This may be caused by a variety of factors like heightened competition, emergence of new technologies, and development of substitute products. Shifts in consumer preferences, inadequate supply of essential inputs, emergence of substitute product, new competition in business, and changes in governmental policies, and so on.

(b) **Financial risk** arises due to the way asset financing is done, the protection of debt in the capital structure of a firm. Presence of debt will cause a firm to pay regular interest to the debt providers; this affects shareholders who are recipient of residual earnings. Debt-free firm has no financial risk.

2. **Systematic Risk** (cannot be controlled): Risk could be systematic in future, depending upon its source. This is part of the total risk that is market specific, external and broad in its effect arising on account of the economy-wide uncertainties and tendency of individual securities which move together with changes in the market. It is also known as **market risk** or **beta.** Following are some important types of systematic risk:

(a) **Inflation Risk:** The risk arising from the decline in purchasing power on account of inflation is referred to as inflation risk. It is a risk that arises from the decline in the value of security's cash flows due to inflation, which is measured in terms of purchasing power. If inflation in the country is positive, purchasing power of the investor reduces. This is especially important to investment decisions where financial securities being utilized are interest-sensitive such as bonds, e.g., rate of an investment on a particular bond is 10% and the inflation rate is 7%, then effective rate of return would be = (1+10%)/(1+7%)-1 is equal to 2.804%. Inflation is cumulative and hence has a cascading effect over long periods. Someone planning for a lifetime should consider inflation as the biggest risk.

Table 7.1 Impact of Inflation on Nominal Rates

Inflation rate	Nominal 8%	Nominal 9%	Nominal 10%	Nominal 12%
5%	2.86%	3.81%	4.76%	6.67%
5.50%	2.37%	3.32%	4.27%	6.16%
6%	1.89%	2.83%	3.77%	5.66%
6.50%	1.41%	2.35%	3.29%	5.16%
7%	0.93%	1.87%	2.80%	4.67%

For reference: The above table narrates cost of inflation index (as per income-tax department).

(b) Interest Rate Risk: The variability in a security's return resulting from changes in the level of interest rates is referred to as interest rate risk. Interest rates may change owing to changes in the economic situation. Such changes generally affect securities inversely; that is, other things being equal, security prices move inversely to interest rates. The changes in interest rate have a bearing on the welfare of investors. As interest rate goes up, for other similar bonds or in the economy, market price of existing fixed income securities falls, fixed income investor suffers loss; vice versa when interest rate falls, bond prices rise, fixed income investor make gains. That is, when interest rates change, bond prices change in opposite direction.

(c) Market Risk: A market is a place where goods and services are traded. Events occur within the market which affects all the goods traded therein. In price fluctuations of equity shares (may be due to several reasons); one of the causes is the changing psychology of investors. There are periods when investors become bullish; their investment horizons lengthen and their optimism drives shares to greater heights. The buoyancy created is pervasive, affecting almost all shares. On the other hand, when a wave of pessimism (which is an exaggerated response to some unfavourable political or economic development) sweeps through the market, investors turn bearish. Prices of almost all equity shares register decline owing to pervasive fear and uncertainty. The market risk of a security represents that portion of its total risk which is attributable to fluctuations in the market as a whole.

(d) Reinvestment Risk: It is the risk that proceeds received in the form of interest and principal from fixed income securities may or may not be able to earn the same interest as the original interest rate. It explains how to seek opportunity or ability to reinvest corpus, periodic payments at the same prevailing rates (at least equal to) for fairly longer periods. If interest rate rises, reinvestment risk reduces, or is eliminated. However, if interest rate falls, reinvestment risk increases. Put differently, not being able to get desired return yield to maturity (YTM) is referred to as *investment risk*. YTM calculation assumes that investor reinvests all coupons received from a bond at a rate equal to computed YTM on that bond, thereby earning interest on interest until the bond matures. This significantly affects potential total return.

(e) **Default Risk:** It is defined as the risk that the issuer will fail to honour the terms of the obligation with respect to periodic payment of coupon and/or principal on maturity. In other words, whether the payment will be received by the investor on schedule is a function of willingness and ability of the borrower – issuer of the debt instrument. Any failure on the part of the issuer exposes the investor to a risk of loss. The level of default risk can be assessed through credit rating. There are agencies that carry out a detailed analysis of the issuer's financial ability to honour the payments on time. Higher the credit rating, lower the default risk and lower the credit rating, higher the default risk.

(f) **Liquidity Risk:** It is the risk that the investor may not be able to sell his/her investment when desired, or it has to be sold below its intrinsic value. Liquidity in investments is being able to sell and realize cash with least possible loss of time and money plus the likelihood of obtaining loan against the principal during lock-in-period of investment. While converting value of an asset into cash wherefore any event/condition that affects it, then it is called liquidity risk. *Illiquid security* has higher bid and ask spread – and hence higher liquidity risk, whereas *liquid security* has lower bid and ask spread and hence lower liquidity risk.

(g) **Exchange Rate Risk/Forex Risk:** It is incurred due to change in the value of domestic currency relative to foreign currency. Investor faces this risk, when investment is done in assets of different countries. When an investor purchases a security in a foreign country, it must be paid for in foreign currency. At the time of purchase, the value of the foreign security is derived from the current, or spot, exchange rate. The exchange rate that may prevail when the investor sells the security in the future cannot be predicted with any amount of certainty is known as exchange rate risk. There are two conditions in which exchange rate risk is observed: (i) if foreign currency depreciates (decreases in value) against domestic currency, the value of foreign asset goes down in terms of domestic currency; (ii) if foreign currency appreciates (increases in value) against domestic currency, the value of foreign asset goes up in terms of domestic currency.

(h) **Regulatory Risk:** It is a type of risk which arises due to changes in regulation of a country which is beyond the control of the investor. Most often, in personal finances, this risk arises when there are changes in tax laws.

(i) **Investment Manager (Alpha) Risk:** The return of a portfolio depend on the fund manager's skills to take correct decisions and, in turn, translate the portfolio return in capital gain over the period. *Alpha* is a measure of excess return over a benchmark and is positive when portfolio outperforms the benchmark and negative when portfolio underperforms the benchmark.

Since the portfolio can underperform the benchmark, investor is exposed to risk.

(j) **Socio-political Risk:** The risks of government change, change of social attitudes, *e.g.* urban land ceilings, ceilings on agricultural holdings, rent control laws and so on.

(k) **Event Risk:** A risk which arises from an event which is sudden, dramatic and unexpected. E.g. Natural disaster and the like.

(l) **Timing or Call Risk:** In some bond offerings, the issuer keeps an option to exercise call/redeem it before the expiry of usual tenure of the instrument. E.g. a seven year fixed rate bond is being redeemed at the end of three years by exercising call option. Here some investors may find it difficult to reinvest immediately the principal amount at the same or better rate of return (as planned earlier).

Ups and downs in the exchange rate affect investments done in other economies and flow of fund in the economy. It affects for example, share price of a firm predominately exporting its produce.

Therefore, losing money cannot be a general measure of risk. In fact the measure of total risk is called *standard deviation*. This means we need to be cautious in the use we make of common metrics such as the standard deviation or volatility of investment returns. However, measuring the volatility of performance, as a check on what the statistical models say is likely, can be helpful in coming to an independent assessment of risk. But it will always be based on a smaller sample of data. Thus we can attempt to measure only perceived risks. Risks that exist but that we do not have the imagination to perceive will always escape our attention.

Risk Computation

Intuitively one can compare two similar returns from two different securities and say one carries a lower risk because its return varied a lot less than that of other one. In statistical language, its probable outcomes were less disbursed. But what happens when one cannot intuitively measure this variability? That's where the statistical measure of "standard deviation" steps in. Standard deviation is the deviation which is recorded as arithmetic mean, a measure of total risk.

7.2 MEASUREMENT OF RISK

This is an important aspect to be understood and how important aspects like variance, standard deviation, co-variance, correlation coefficient and beta aid in the measurement of risk. Along with the calculation, their interpretation is also of great consequence in taking a financial decision. Understanding different products (with different features) available in the market and their risk-return aspects should not be ignored.

Volatility: Of all the ways to describe risk, the simplest and possibly the most accurate is "uncertainty of future outcome". The simple fact that dominates investing is that the realized return on an asset with any risk attached thereto may be different from what was expected.

Volatility may be described as the range of movement (or price fluctuation) from the expected level of return. Since wide range price swings create more uncertainty of an eventual outcome, increased volatility can be equated with increased risk. Being able to measure and determine the past volatility of a security is important in that it provides some insight into the riskiness of that security as an investment.

Standard Deviation: It is the square root of variance. It is used to calculate total risk associated with the expected return. This is a measure of the spread or dispersion in probability distribution; that is, a measurement of the dispersion of a random variable around its mean. One needs to be aware that larger this dispersion, the larger will be the standard deviation or variance. Consequently, larger the standard deviation, the more uncertain will be the outcome.

The standard deviation of a set of numbers is simply the square root of the mean of the square of deviations around the arithmetic average. Calculating a standard deviation using probability distribution involves making subjective estimates of the probabilities and the likely returns. However, we cannot avoid such estimates because future returns are uncertain. The prices of securities are based on investors' expectations about the future.

Although standard deviation based on realized returns are often used as proxies for *ex ante* standard deviation, investors should remember that the past cannot always be extrapolated into the future without modifications. One important point about the estimation of standard deviation is the distinction between individual securities and portfolios. Standard deviation for well-diversified portfolios is reasonably steady across time, and therefore historical calculations may be fairly reliable in projecting the future.

Something very important to remember about standard deviation is that it is a measure of the total risk of an asset or a portfolio, including, therefore, both systematic and unsystematic risks. It captures the total variability in the asset's or portfolio's return, whatever are the sources of that variability. In summary, the standard deviation of return measures the total risk of one security or the total risk of a portfolio of securities. The standard deviation, combined with normal distribution, can provide some useful information about the dispersion or variation in returns.

Steps in Computing Standard Deviation

1. Compute expected return using the formula
2. Compute deviation of each possible outcome from expected return ($d = r - \bar{r}$)
3. Square the deviation (d ^ 2)
4. Multiply probability with the squared deviation (pd ^ 2)
5. Summate the result to get variance [Σpd ^ 2]
6. Standard deviation is the square root of variance.

The following example will explain how standard deviation and variance are calculated in respect of a sample security.

Probability	Return expected
0.3	12%
0.4	14%
0.3	10%

Expected return in respect of the above scenario is: (0.3*12 + 0.4*14 + 0.3*10)
= 3.6 + 5.6 + 3 = 12.2%

Table 7.2 Calculation of Standard Deviation

Probability	Return	Return–expected return	(Return-expected return) squared	Probability*(Return-expected return) squared
0.3	12%	-0.2	0.04	0.012
0.4	14%	1.8	3.24	2.296
0.3	10%	-2.2	4.84	1.452

Standard deviation = square root of variance = square root of 2.76 = 1.661

A standard deviation is a measure of total risk which should be as low as possible. It shows how much variation there is from the average (mean). A low standard deviation indicates that the data points tend to be very close to the mean whereas a high standard deviation indicates that the data points are spread out over a large range of values.

Variance is a measure of variance of possible rates of return of the investment from the expected rate of return. It is the degree to which the return on an investment varies unpredictably. Formula for calculating variance of a single security:

Variance (σ^2) = Σ (Probability) * (Possible Return – Expected Return) ^2
= Σ (P_i) [R_i – $E(R_i)$] ^2

The higher the variances for an expected rate of return, the greater the dispersion of expected returns and greater uncertainty, or risk, of the investment.

In the above example, Variance = (0.012 + 1.296 + 1.452) = 2.76

Beta is a measure of the systematic or market risk of a security that cannot be avoided through diversification. Beta is a relative measure of the risk of an individual stock relative to the market portfolio of all stocks. It is important to note that beta measures a security's volatility, or fluctuation in price, relative to the market portfolio of all stocks.

Stocks having a Beta of less than 1.0 would be considered *conservative investments* (low risk), and stocks having a Beta of more than 1.0 would be considered *aggressive investments* (high risk). Beta is useful for comparing the relative systematic risk of different stocks and, in practice, is used by investors to judge a stock's riskiness.

Beta can be calculated in many ways; the commonly used formulae are:

1. Beta $\frac{(\beta) = \text{Cov}\,(i, m)}{\sigma_m \wedge 2}$

   where Cov (i, m) is the correlation between security i and the market m, and σ_m is standard deviation of the market.

2. Beta $\frac{(\beta) = r\,(i, m)}{\sigma_m} * \sigma_i$

   where $r(i, m)$ is the correlation between security i and the market m, σ_i is the standard deviation of the security and σ_m is the standard deviation of the market.

3. Beta of a portfolio = $\Sigma(W_n * \beta_n)$

   where W_n is weight of n number of securities and β_n is the Beta of n number of securities.

Correlation coefficient is a standardized measure of the relationship between two variables that ranges from −1.00 to +1.00. To obtain a relative measure of a given relationship, we use the correlation coefficient (r_{ij}), which is a measure of the relationship:

$$r_{ij} = \frac{\text{Cov } ij}{\sigma_i \sigma_j}$$

where

$$\sigma i = \sqrt{\frac{\sum (i - i) \wedge 2}{N}}$$

If the two series move together, then the co-variance would equal $\sigma_i \sigma_j$ and the correlation coefficient would equal one in this case, and we would say the two series are perfectly correlated.

Correlation: The magnitude of covariance depends on the magnitude of the individual securities' standard deviations and the relationship between their co-movements. The *covariance* is an absolute measure and is measured in return units squared.

Covariance can be standardized by dividing the product of the standard deviation of the two securities being compared. This standardized measure of co-movement is called *correlation* and is computed as:

$$P_1, 2 = \frac{\text{Cov } 1, 2}{\sigma_1 \sigma_2}$$

or

$$\text{Cov } 1, 2 = P_{1,2}\, \sigma_1 \sigma_2$$

The term $P_{1,2}$ is called the *correlation coefficient* between the returns of securities 1 and 2. The correlation coefficient has no unit. It is a pure measure of the co-movement of the two securities and bounded by −1 and +1.

Interpretation of correlation coefficient

- Correlation coefficients of +1 means that return always changes proportionally in the same direction. They are perfectly correlated positively.
- Correlation coefficients of –1 means that return always moves proportionally in the opposite direction. They are perfectly correlated negatively.
- A correlation coefficient of 0 means that there is no linear relationship between the two securities' returns, i.e., they are uncorrelated. One way to interpret a correlation (or covariance) of zero is that, in any period, knowing the actual value of one variable tells you nothing about the other.

Example: Computing correlation covariance between the stocks is 0.0510. The standard deviation for stocks 1 & 2 are 0.2041 and 0.2944 respectively. Calculate the correlation between the two stocks.

Solution: Correlation = 0.0510/(0.2041 * 0.2944) = 0.8488

The returns from the two stocks are positively correlated, meaning they tend to move in the same direction at the same time.

Significance of Correlation

As correlation between the two assets decreases, the benefits of diversification increase. That's because, as the correlation decreases, the tendency is less for stock returns to move together. The separate movements of each stock serve to reduce the volatility of the portfolio to a level that is less than that of its individual components.

7.3 RISK AND EXPECTED RETURN

Risk and expected return are the two key determinants of an investment decision. Risk, in simple terms, is associated with the variability of the rates of return from an investment, i.e., how much individual outcomes deviate from the expected value. Statistically, risk is measured by any one of the measures of dispersion such as coefficient of range, variance, standard deviation, etc.

The risk involved in investment depends on various factors such as:

(i) *Length of the maturity period* – longer maturity periods impart greater risk to investments.

(ii) *Credit-worthiness of the issuer of securities* – the ability of the borrower to make periodical interest payments and pay back the principal amount imparts safety to the investment and thus reduces the risk.

(iii) The *nature of the instrument or security* also determines the risk. The relative ranking of instruments by risk is once again connected to the safety of the investment.

(iv) *Equity shares* are considered to be the most risky investment on account of variability of rates of return and also because of the residual risk of bankruptcy to be borne by the equity holders.

(v) *Liquidity of an instrument* also determines the risk involved in that investment. Liquidity of an asset refers to its quick salability without a loss or with a minimum of loss.

(vi) In addition to aforesaid factors, there are also various others such as the economic, industry and firm specific factors that affect the risk to an investment.

Another major factor determining the investment decision is the *rate of return expected by the investor*. The rate of return expected by the investor consists of the yield and capital appreciation. If the investment is made in capital assets (other than government obligations) then such assets would carry a degree of risk that is idiosyncratic to the investment. For an individual, to invest in such assets, an additional compensation, called the *risk premium* will have to be paid over and above the nominal rate of return.

Three major determinants of the rate of return are:

(a) The time preference risk-free real rate

(b) The expected rate of inflation

(c) The risk associated with the investment, which is unique to the investment.

Hence, required return = Risk-free real rate + Inflation rate + Risk premium

7.4 RISK-RETURN RELATIONSHIP

The most fundamental tenet of finance literature is that there is a tradeoff between risk and return. The risk-return relationship requires that the return on a security should be commensurate with its inherent risks. If the capital markets are operationally efficient, then all investment assets should provide a rate or return that is consistent with the risks associated therewith. The risk and return are directly variable, *i.e.*, an investment with higher risk should produce higher return.

Low levels of uncertainty (low risk) are associated with low potential returns. High levels of uncertainty (high risk) are associated with high potential returns. The *risk-return tradeoff* is the balance between the desire for the lowest possible risk and the highest possible return. A higher standard deviation means a higher risk and higher possible return.

A common misconception is that higher risk equals higher return. The risk-return tradeoff tells us that higher risk gives us the possibility of higher returns. But there are no guarantees. Just as risk means higher potential returns, it also means higher potential losses.

The common question arises: who wants to earn 6% when index fund gives an average of 12% per year in the long run? The answer to this is that even the entire market (represented by the index fund) carries risk. The return on index funds is not 12% every year, but rather 8% one year, 22% for next year, and so on. An investor still faces substantially higher risk and volatility to receive an overall return that is higher than a predictable government security. This additional return is called the *risk premium*.

Determining what risk level is most appropriate for an individual investor is not an easy task. Risk tolerance differs from person to person. The decision an investor takes will depend among others on his/her goals, income and personal situation, time horizon, and the investment environment.

What then is the relationship between market risk (which is measured by Beta) and the expected rate of return? According to *capital asset pricing model* (which is an extension of the portfolio theory), risk and return are related as follows:

Expected rate of return = Risk-free rate of return + Risk premium

The risk-free return is the return on treasury bills. So then what is the risk premium? It is equal to the following product:

(Beta of the security) (Rate of return on market portfolio – Risk-free rate of return)

For example, if the Beta of a security is 1.20, the rate of return on market portfolio is 15 per cent, and the risk-free rate of return is 10 per cent, the risk premium on the security will be:

(1.20) (15 – 10) = 6.00 per cent

Adding this risk premium to the risk-free rate of return of 10 per cent, we find that the expected rate of return on the security works out to:

10 per cent + 6 per cent = 16 per cent

Ability and Willingness to Take Risk

How much risk should one take is a function of the ability and willingness to take risks. At the same time, the advisor must consider the investor's need to take risks.

1. **Ability:** Financial capacity to take risk.
2. **Willingness:** Attitude towards risk taking.
3. **Need:** If financial goals are fulfilled and there is adequate capital, there is no need to take risks. On the other hand, someone with limited resources may have to take higher risks.

Based on these factors and risk profiling, an investor can be broadly classified as:

1. Aggressive investor
2. Conservative investor
3. Moderate investor

Return on a Single Asset

Suppose an investor bought 100 shares of 'A' company at a market price of Rs. 225 at the beginning of a year. Assume that the company pays dividend at 25 per cent (on Rs. 10/face value). Further, suppose the price of this 'A' share at the end of the year turns out to be Rs. 267.50

Total investment made = 225 * 100 = Rs. 22,500

Dividend earned = Rs. 2.50 (per share) * 100 (number of shares)
= Rs. 250

Capital gain/(loss) = (Selling price – Buying price) * number of shares
= (Rs. 267.50 – Rs. 225) * 100
= Rs. 4,250

Total return = Rs. 250 + Rs. 4250 = Rs. 4500

Cash flow at the year-end = Dividend received + Value of shares sold
= Rs. 250 + (Rs. 267.50 * 100) = Rs. 27,000

Return made = Cash inflow at the year end – Cash outflow at the beginning of the year
= Rs. 27,000 – Rs. 22,500
= Rs. 4500

Return in percentage = Rs. 22,500 = 0.20 or 20%

7.5 RISK MANAGEMENT

Broadly, risk can be categorized as – systematic and unsystematic as already discussed. Unsystematic risk can be managed whereas systematic risk cannot be managed. Risk can be managed in two ways: (i) Diversification (ii) Hedging.

Diversification: Before credit cards came into vogue, when you travelled you put some money in your wallet, some in your suitcase and some in the handbag. The idea being in case you lost your wallet you still had some money to reach your destination.

Types of Diversification

(a) Horizontal Diversification: Diversifying investment across different securities within same asset class.

(b) Vertical Diversification: Diversifying assets across asset classes.

(c) Geographical Diversification: Diversifying across borders. Due to low correlation adding global securities in domestic portfolio, will help increase risk-adjusted return of the portfolio.

Portfolio Diversification and Risk

In an efficient capital market, the important principle to consider is that, investors should not hold all their *eggs* in one basket; investor should hold a well-diversified portfolio. In order to understand portfolio diversification, one must understand correlation which is a statistical measure that indicates the relationship, if any, between two securities. If two securities move together, they are positively correlated; and if they move in opposite direction, they are negatively correlated, combining which the overall variability of returns or risk can be reduced.

Illustration

The possible outcomes of two securities/alternatives A and B, depending on the state of economy, are as follows:

State of economy	Possible Outcomes (in Rs.)	
Normal	A 100	B 100
Boom	A 110	B 200

If we assume that the three states of the economy are equally likely, then expected value for each security/alternative is Rs. 100.

- A risk-seeker is one who, given a choice between more or less risky alternatives with identical expected values, prefers the riskier alternative, i.e., B.
- A risk-aversive person would select the less risky alternative, i.e., A
- A person who is indifferent to risk (risk neutral) would be indifferent to both alternatives A and B, because they have similar expected values.

The empirical evidence shows that a majority of investors are risk-averse. Some generalizations concerning the general shape of the utility functions are possible. People usually regard money as a desirable commodity, and the utility of a large sum is usually greater than the utility of a smaller sum. For a risk-averse decision maker, the expected utility of a function is less than the utility of the expected monetary value. It is also possible for the decision-maker to be risk preferring, at least over some range of the utility function.

Beta, a product of academic research, was initially viewed with disdain and suspicion by the investment community. Gradually, however, it was accepted as the initial empirical evidence supported it. The earlier resistance turned into enthusiasm. Beta indeed became very fashionable in the 1970s and the investment industry in the U.S. began manufacturing and supplying Beta on a large scale.

A lead story in the *Institutional Investor*, prestigious magazine of the investment community, noted that money managers with a meager background in mathematics were "tossing Betas around with abandoning Ph.D.s in statistical theory." As Burton Malkiel, the author of "A Random Walk Down Wall Street" observed: "The Beta boosters in the street oversold their product with an abandon that would have shocked even the most enthusiastic scribblers intent on spreading the Beta cult."

Along with the spread of the Beta cult, the capital asset pricing model and its various extensions were subject to more rigorous and comprehensive scrutiny and testing. Several issues have been raised:

- Can the capital asset pricing model be adequately tested?
- How stable are Betas?
- Is the relationship between risks (as measured by Beta) and return as stipulated by the capital asset pricing model? What factors, besides Betas, have a bearing on return?

While categorical answers to the above questions are not available as of now, the extensive research undertaken till date suggests the following:

1. There is a fundamental problem in testing the capital asset pricing model. Richard Roll, the author of "A Critique of the Asset Pricing Theory's Tests: Part-I" (March, 1977) has argued persuasively that since the "true" market portfolio (which in principle must include all assets – financial, real as well as human – and not just equity stocks) cannot be measured, the capital asset pricing model cannot be tested adequately.
2. While Betas of individual stocks are fickle, Betas of folios (consisting of 10 to 15 stocks) are fairly stable.
3. The actual relationship between risk (as measured by Beta) and return is flatter than what the capital asset pricing model says. This means that low Beta stocks earn rate of return higher than what the capital asset pricing model stipulates, whereas high Beta stocks earn a rate of return lower than what the capital asset pricing model suggests.
4. In addition to Beta, some other factors (like standard deviation of historical returns and company size) too, have bearing on the realized rate of return.

To sum up, while the Beta has an important bearing on returns, the basic capital asset pricing model does not fully capture the asset pricing process. As James Lorie, Peter Dodd, and Mary Kimpton said: "Beta, however, remains a valuable concept, and the capital asset pricing model remains one of the most powerful developments in modern finance." [The Stock Market: Theories and Evidence, 2nd edition.]

Investment Implications

We have learnt about the component of risk, consequences of diversification, and the relationship between risk and return. The investment implications of our discussion are as follows:

(i) Diversification is important. Owning a portfolio dominated by a small number of stocks is a risky proposition.

(ii) While diversification is desirable, an excess of it is not. There is hardly any gain in extending diversification beyond 16 to 18 stocks.

(iii) The performance of a well diversified portfolio more or less mirrors the performance of the market as a whole.

(iv) In a well ordered market, investors are compensated primarily for bearing market risk, but not unique risk. To earn a higher expected rate of return, one has to bear a higher degree of market risk.

Hedging

Hedging is an investment strategy where investment is made in order to reduce the risk of adverse price movement in an asset, by taking an offsetting position in related security such as option on underlying asset or a short sale of index, etc. Hedging simply can be called *insurance*. Investors can hedge their portfolio with the use of various derivative contracts known as Futures, Options, Swaps, and so on.

"It has become appallingly obvious that our technology has exceeded our humanity." – Albert Einstein

UNIT-II

8 Fundamental Analysis (Macroeconomic View & Analysis)

CHAPTER

Fundamental analysis is about understanding the *quantitative* and *qualitative* factors that impact earnings of a company and make an estimate of future earnings based on this analysis. Analysts follow two broad approaches to fundamental analysis – top down and bottom up. If the factors to consider are **economic (E), industry (I) and company (C)** factors, beginning at company-specific factors and moving up to the macro factors that impact the performance of the company is called the *bottom-up approach*. Scanning the economic scenario first and then identifying industries to choose from and zeroing in on companies, is the *top-down approach*.

Usually, investment decision-maker scans the opportunities to decide which securities or assets should be bought or held or sold by him/her. A very simple rule is to buy a security which has lowest risk per unit or return that has highest bought, held or sold security volume. And, sell the security, which does not satisfy the above rule. Though, this seems to be simple, it is very difficult to apply both risk and return rule in practice.

This is because there are a large number of factors, which affect both risk and return. Thus, a security or an asset that had the highest return per unit of risk at one point of time and was considered to be a good buy might turn into a less attractive proposition and could be considered later as a option for disinvestment. Such a situation might arise due to change in the company's management or changes in government policy concerning the economy, making it less attractive.

Investment decision-making being continuous in nature should be attempted systematically. Three approaches are suggested in the literature fundamental analysis, technical/economic analysis and behavioural approach.

8.1 FUNDAMENTAL APPROACH

In the fundamental approach, the investor attempts to look at fundamental factors that affect risk return characteristics of the security/asset. The effort here is to identify those securities that one perceives as mispriced in the stock market. The basic tenets of the fundamental approach, which perhaps most commonly employed by investment professionals, are:

(i) There is an intrinsic value of a security and that depends upon underlying economic (fundamental) factors. It is established by penetrating analysis of the fundamental factors relating to the company (and its management), industry, competitive environment, and economy (the major ones) of the country/entity.

(ii) At any point of time, market price of some securities would differ from intrinsic value. Sooner or later, the market price, of course, would fall in line with the intrinsic value.

(iii) The decision rule under fundamental approach is: If the price of a security at the marketplace is higher than the one, which is justified by the security fundamentals, sell that security. This is because, it is expected that the market will sooner or later realize its mistake and price the security properly. The price prevailing in the market is called "market price (**MP**)" and the one justified by its fundamentals is called "intrinsic value (**IV**)" of trading rules/recommendations.

if **IV** > **MP**, buy the security;
if **IV** < **MP**, sell the security; and
if **IV** = **MP**, no action (remain neutral)

The fundamental factors mentioned above may relate to the economy or industry or company or all of these. Thus, economy fundamentals, industry fundamentals and company fundamentals are considered while pricing the securities for taking investment decisions. In fact, the economy-industry-company framework forms an integral part of this approach. This framework can be properly utilized by making suitable adjustments contextual.

A word of caution: Please remember, the use of any analytical framework does not guarantee an actual decision. However, it provides an opportunity to remain informed and consider investment decision, which would hopefully be better as it is based on relevant and crucial information.

Fundamental Analysis and Efficient Market

Before elaborating in depth on the economy-industry-company framework, it is pertinent to mention that doubts are expressed about the utility of this approach in the context of efficient stock market setup.

Briefly, the market efficiency relates to the speed with which the stock market incorporates the information about the economy, industry and company, in the share price, rather instantaneously. This view about share market efficiency implies that no one would be able to make abnormal profits given such a setup. Some research studies in the literature also support this view. Majority of the practitioners, however, do not agree with such conclusions of an empirical nature.

Fundamental Analysis and Chemistry of Earnings

The logic for fundamental analysis becomes clear once we understand the chemistry of earnings and micro and macro factors which influence future earnings.

Table 8.1 Factors Affecting Distributable Earnings

Broad Source/Form of earnings	Company Specific Factors	Industry Factors	Macroeconomic Factors
Sales	Competitive strength	Industry demand/supply	National income, monetary policy, credit, savings, price level, export-import policies, population
Less cost of sales	Operating efficiency	Industry wage levels, industrial infrastructure, import-export policy	National wage policy, price levels, economic infrastructure, raw materials production
Earnings before Interest, Depreciation and Taxes (EBIDT) less interest	Capital structure/financial leverage policy	Industry cost of capital	Interest rates in the economy, capital conditions
Less depreciation	Operational leverage policy	Industry practices	Capital goods import
Less tax	Tax planning and management	Industry lobby	Fiscal policy
Net earnings after tax (EAT/PAT)			
Less percentage dividend	Capital structure policy	Industry practices	Interest rate structure, capital conditions
Distributable earnings less equity dividend	Dividend policy	Industry practices	Fiscal policy, credit, capital market conditions
Retained earnings			
Capital structure policy	Capital structure policy	Industry practices	Interest rate structure, capital conditions

The analysis of economy, industry and company fundamentals as mentioned above is the main ingredient of the fundamental approach. The analyst/decision-maker should take into account all the three constituents that form different but logical steps. These can be looked at different stages in the investment decision-making. Operationally, to base the investment decision on various fundamentals, all the three stages must be taken into account.

8.2 ECONOMY ANALYSIS

Economic analysis is essentially relevant in an economic system. There are basically three economic systems in the world:

1. Free enterprise system also known as *capitalist system* as prevalent in the USA, the UK, Germany, Japan, France, Australia, Canada, South Korea, Hong Kong, Taiwan, Singapore, etc.
2. State enterprise system also known as the *communist/socialist system* as in the USSR (now Russia), China, Albania, Cuba, etc.
3. The system of mixed economy, which is a hybrid of both systems, as prevalent in India, Malaysia, Thailand, etc.

In practice, one must have noticed that investment decisions of individuals and the institutions are made in the economic setup of a particular country. It becomes essential, therefore, to understand the state of economy of that country at the macro level. The analysis of the state of economy at the macro level incorporates the performance of the economy in the past, how it is performing in the present, and how it is expected to perform in the future. Also relevant is to know how various sectors of the economy are poised to grow over some future period of time.

Macroeconomic Analysis

Before we talk about macroeconomic analysis, let us first understand macroeconomics. Macroeconomics deals with the big picture, aspects like economic system, national income, business cycles, monetary policy, fiscal policy, etc. Since a business firm operates in a given macroeconomic environment, a broad understanding of these macroeconomic dimensions will go a long way in obtaining the right perspective.

The economic cycle has an impact on the performance of companies. A slowdown in Gross Domestic Product (GDP) growth rates can impact investment and consumption oriented businesses. Revival in economic indicators is tracked by looking at the index of industrial production (IIP), lead indicators such as auto sales, movement in consumer durables, capital goods imports, purchasing power manager's index (HSBC PMI), consumer confidence index, and the like. As the momentum returns concurrent and lag indicators such as changes in GDP, interest rates and wages are monitored.

Economic policy has an impact on the performance of most businesses. Direct and indirect tax rates, tax concessions and tax holidays impact business decisions on location, production and pricing. *Fiscal policy* impacts government and private spending patterns and market borrowing. *Monetary policy* impacts expectations for interest rates, liquidity in the system and inflation. *External policy* impacts relative competitiveness of exports and imports and the currency rates. Tracking policy stance is a critical part of economic analysis.

The analysis of the following factors indicates the trends in macroeconomic changes that affect the risk and return on investment. Broadly they are:

Table 8.2

Money supply (M1 and M3) and growth in M3	Industrial production (IIP)	Unemployment	Foreign trade	Stock prices
Institutional lending	Capacity utilization	Inflation (influencing factors)	Balance of payment position	Trends in capital markets
Credit/deposit ratio	Productivity of factors of production	Composition and growth in GDP	Foreign investments	Prices and asset valuation
Loans outstanding	Stock of food grains and essential commodities	Status of political and economic stability	Foreign exchange reserves	
Debt recovery	Industrial wages	Fiscal deficit	Current account deficits (CAD)	
Interest rates	Technological innovations	Cost of living index, WPI and CPI		
Government finances	Infrastructural facilities	Economic and industrial policies of the government		
	Stage of the business cycle			
	Aggregate demand			

The Global Economy

In a globalised business environment, the top-down analysis of the prospects of a firm must begin with the global economy. The global economy has a bearing on the export prospects of the firm, the competition it faces from international competitors, and the profitability of its overseas investors.

Traditionally, the focus was mainly on fiscal and monetary policies, the two major tools of demand-side of economics. From the 1980s onwards, however, supply-side of economics has received a lot of attention.

Fiscal Policy

Fiscal policy is concerned with the spending and tax initiatives of the government. It refers to taxation policy and budgetary policy of managing the surplus or deficit. It is the most direct tool to stimulate or dampen the economy.

An increase in government spending stimulates the demand for goods and services, whereas a decrease deflates the demand for goods and services. By the same token, a decrease in tax rates increases the consumption of goods and services and an increase in tax rates decreases the consumption of goods and services.

The budgets of the government are rarely balanced. They usually end up in deficits which are partly made up through additional resource mobilization, by way of fresh taxes and loans. An uncovered deficit is likely to lead to inflation, because it results in increased money supply without corresponding asset creation.

A financial analyst usually keeps in mind the type of fiscal policy being followed by the government and develops suitable investment and tax planning strategies.

Monetary Policy

Monetary policy refers to the management of money supply and encompasses credit policy and interest rate policy. Monetary policy is concerned with the manipulation of money supply in the economy. Monetary policy affects the economy mainly through its impact on interest rates.

When an economy is expanding, lack of adequate money supply may impede the process of recovery. On the other hand, excessive money supply in the economy may lead to inflation. The supply of and demand for money should be properly balanced by using the interest rate mechanism; the interest rates have to be suitably adjusted from time to time to match the demand and supply of money. The Reserve Bank of India plays this important role of monetary management.

A financial analyst always keeps himself/herself aware of the monetary policy being followed by the central bank as it has a direct bearing on the money markets, bank finance for working capital, large projects funding, etc.

The main tools of monetary policy are:

- Open market operation
- Bank rate
- Reserve requirements
- Direct credit controls

National Income

National income is the barometer of a nation's economic well-being and is measured in terms of per capita Gross National Product (GNP). The objective of economic development is to improve the GNP, improving the people's quality of life and narrowing the disparities of income and wealth.

Once the per capita income starts rising, all consumer goods and services will then be in great demand, leading the domestic market to grow at an exponential rate.

Business Cycle

The economy is not always in a steady state. It either grows as in a boom or keeps shrinking as in a recession due to a variety of economic, natural, national and international factors.

The business cycle mechanism is a self-regulating aspect of a market-oriented economy. An economy adjusts itself from time to time through these periodic corrections. Some economists, notably J.M. Keynes, suggested that if the government intervenes through a public spending programme at the recessionary phase, the economy can be revived without it having to go through the horrors of a great slump. Accordingly, they prescribe surplus budgets during times of boom and deficit during recessionary times.

It is important for a financial analyst and investor to be aware of the phase of the business cycle through which the economy is passing at any time for several strategic and operating reasons.

8.3 INVESTMENT MAKING PROCESS

Each of the sectors shows signs of stagnation and degradation in the economy. This, we can examine and understand by studying historical performance of various sectors of the economy in the past, their performance at present and then projecting the expectation about their performance in the future. It is through this systematic process that one would be able to realize various relevant investment opportunities as they arise.

The rationale of the above type of analysis depends on economic considerations, too. The way people earn and the way they spend their earnings would in the ultimate analysis, decide which industry or bunch of industries would grow in the future. Such spending affects corporate profits, dividends and prices of shares.

It must be clear by now that analysis of historical performance of the economy is a starting point; albeit an important step. But, for the analyst/investor to decide whether to invest or not, expected future performance of the overall economy along with its various segments is most relevant. Thus, all efforts should be made to forecast the performance of the economy so that the decision to invest or to disinvest the securities can be beneficial. A healthy outlook about the economy goes a long way in boosting the investment climate in general and investment in securities, in particular.

Economic Forecasting

At this stage, it is necessary to have proper understanding that economic forecasting is a must for making investment decisions. The fortunes of specific industry and the firm depend upon how the economy looks like in the future, both short-term and long-term. Accordingly, forecasting techniques can also be divided and categorized into: short-term intermediate and long-term techniques. *Short-term* refers to a period up to three years. Sometimes, it can also refer to a much shorter period, say, a quarter or a few quarters. *Intermediate period* refers to a period of three to five years. *Long-term* refers to the forecast made for more than five years. This may also mean a period of ten years or even more.

Forecasting Techniques

- Economic indicators
- Diffusion index

- Surveys
- Economic model building

At the very outset, the central theme of economic forecasting is to forecast national income with its various components. This is because it summarizes the receipts and expenditure of all segments of the economy, be the government, private business or households. These macroeconomic accounts describe the economic activities over a period of time. Not surprisingly, therefore, all the techniques focus on forecasting national income and its various components, particularly, those components that have a bearing on particular industry and/or the company to be analyzed.

Gross National Product (GNP) is a measure to quantify national income and its total value of the final output of goods and services produced in the economy. It is an important indicator of the level and rate of growth in the economy, and is of central concern to analysts/investors for forecasting overall as well as various components during a certain period. Following is a technique of short-term economic forecasting.

Anticipatory Surveys

This is a simple method through which investors can form their opinion/expectations with respect to the future state of the economy. As is generally understood, this is a survey of expert opinions of those prominent in the government, private business, trade and industry. So long as people plan and budget their expenditure and implement their plans accordingly, such surveys should provide valuable input, as a starting point.

Despite the valuable inputs provided by this method, care must be exercised in using the information obtained through this method. Precautions are needed because:

1. Survey results cannot be regarded as forecasts per se. A consensus of opinion must be used by an investor in forming his own forecasts.
2. There is no guarantee that the surveyed outcomes would certainly materialize. To this extent, they cannot rely solely on these.

Despite the above limitations, surveys are very popular and used for short-term forecast. Such surveys need continuous monitoring.

8.4 BEROMETRIC OR INDIAN APPROACH

In this approach, various types of indicators are studied to find out how the economy is likely to behave in the future. For meaningful interpretations, these indicators are roughly classified into leading, lagging and coincidental approach.

Leading Indicators

As the name suggests, these are indicators that lead the economic activity in their outcome. That is, these are those time series data of the variables that reach their high points as well as low points in advance of the economic activity contemplated.

Lagging Indicators

These are time series data of the variables that lag behind in their consequences vis-à-vis the economy. That is, they reach their turning points after the economy has already reached its own level.

In developed countries, data relating to various indicators are published at short intervals. For example, the Department of Commerce publishes data regarding various indicators in each of the following categories:

Leading Indicators

- Average weekly hours of manufacturing production workers
- Average weekly initial unemployment claims
- Contracts and orders for plant and machinery
- Index of S&P 500 stock prices
- Money supply (M2)
- Change in sensitive material prices
- Change in manufacturers' unified orders (durable goods industries)
- Index of consumer expectation

Lagging Indicators

- Average duration of unemployment
- Ratio of manufacturing and trade inventories to sales
- Average prime rate
- Outstanding commercial and industrial loans

Coincidental Indicators

- Index of industrial production
- Manufacturing and trade sales
- Employees on non-agricultural payrolls
- Personal income less transfer payment

The above list is not exhaustive. It is only illustrative of various indicators used by investors. A word of caution will not be out of place here as forecasting based solely on leading indicators is a hazardous business. One has to be quite careful in using them. There is always a time lag in which interpretation can be erroneous, if it is not done well in advance. Interpretation even if performed meticulously, cannot be fruitfully utilized. Further, problems with regard to their interpretation remain. The various measures may emit conflicting signals about the future direction of the economy; the use of diffusion index or composite index has, thus, been suggested.

This deals with the problem by combining several indicators into one index in order to measure the strength or weaknesses of a particular kind of indicator. Care has to be exercised even in this case as diffusion indices also face problems. Apart from the fact that its computations are difficult, it does not eliminate the varying factors in the series. Despite these limitations, indicator approach/diffusion index can be a useful tool in the armoury of a skilful forecaster.

Money Supply and Stock Markets

Analysts have recognized that money supply in the economy plays a crucial part in the investment decision per se. The rate of change in the money supply in the economy affects the GNP, corporate profits, interest rates and prices. Accordingly, monetarists argue that total money supply in the economy and its rate of change has an important influence on the stock prices as a hedge against inflation, and increases stock prices some times.

Diffusion Index

- It is an indicator of extensiveness or spread of an expansion or contraction.
- It has been developed by the National Bureau of Economic Research, USA.

There are two main categories of Diffusion Index:

1. **Composite or Consensus Index**: It combines several indicators into one single measure, in order to measure the strength or weakness in the movement of these particular time series data. For example, there are ten leading indicators; out of which four are moving up and others are not. How do we interpret it?

   Diffusion Index = Total no. of members in the set

   In the example, diffusion index = 4/10 = 0.4

   Next month, if the index moved to 0.6, it certainly is a strong confirmation of economic advancement.

2. **Component Evaluation Index**: This is a narrow type of index, one that examines a particular series taking into consideration its components. It measures the breadth of the movement within a particular series.

8.5 GEOMETRIC MODEL BUILDING APPROACH

This is an approach to determine precise relationship between the dependent and the independent variables. In fact, *econometrics* is a discipline wherein application of mathematics and statistical techniques is a part of economic theory. It presupposes the precise and clear relationship between the dependent and independent variables and the onus of such well-defined relationship with its attendant assumption rests with the analyst. Thus, by geometric model, the analyst is able to forecast a variable more precisely than by any other approach. But this derived approach would be as good as the data inputs used and assumptions made.

Static model building or GNP model building or sectoral analysis is frequently used in particular in the methods discussed earlier. These use national accounting framework in making short-term forecasts. The various steps while using this approach are:

1. Hypothesize the total demand in the economy as measured by its total income (GNP), based on likely conditions in the country like war, peace, political instability, economic changes, level and rate of inflation, etc.
2. Forecast the GNP figure by estimating the levels of its various components like:
   - Consumption expenditure
   - Private investment
   - Government purchases of goods and services
   - Net exports
3. Forecasting the individual components of GNP, the analysis then adds them up to obtain a figure of the GNP.
4. The analyst compares the total of GNP and arrives at an independent estimate appropriately. The forecast of GNP is an overall forecast of internal consistency. This is to ensure that both his total forecast and permanent forecast make sense and link together in a reasonable manner.
5. Thus, the GNP building model involves all the details described above with a considerable amount of judgement.
6. What has accounted for this suddenly revived economy? One likely answer is definitely a cut in custom duty and a corresponding reduction in excise duty, which helped reduce the cost structure of a number of products. This has made a number of products cheaper in the domestic market and consequently expanded the demand for them.

The foregoing discussion on macroeconomic analysis is always helpful and very important while analyzing investment decision in a particular country/state or a particular industry/sector from a top-down approach.

9 CHAPTER Industry Analysis

After conducting an analysis of the economy and identifying the direction it is likely to take in the short, interim and long term, the investor/analyst must look into various sectors of the economy in respect of different industries. Factors which are specific to an industry impact revenue, costs, margins and growth plans of companies. It is necessary to group these industries on some widely accepted basis of which some useful clarifications are:

Growth Industry: This industry is expected to grow consistently and its growth may exceed the average growth of the economy.

Cyclical Industry: In this industry, firms included are those that move closely with the rate of industrial growth of the economy and fluctuate cyclically as the economy fluctuates.

Defensive Industry: In this industry, firms move steadily with the economy but less than average growth rate and decline, in a cyclical downturn.

Regulation: For example, banking industry in India is subject to regulation that restricts acquisition of Indian banks by foreign banks to some extent. Inorganic and organic growth of banks is subject to several approvals and regulations. The analysis of growth prospects and expansion has to consider these constraints.

Entry Barriers: For example, telecom business in India can operate only if spectrum is allotted in a particular circle. There are restrictions on who can bid for spectrum and how much would be allotted. There are limitations to overall spectrum availability as well. Thus, industry factor may create entry barriers for new players.

Cost: For example, production of aluminium requires proximity to bauxite ore deposits and is highly energy-intensive. Aluminium producers have to bear the cost of captive power if located near the mines; or higher transport cost if located in a power-surplus location. Cement industry incurs huge costs for transporting the bulk of its produce owing to geographical dispersion of its markets. Regional costs per bag can vary depending on where the cement is coming from. Similarly, raw material costs hit automobile manufacturers.

Seasonal Factors: For example, sugarcane crushing is a seasonal activity. The industry works at high capacity in the crushing season, and holds the stocks for the rest of the season. Articles demanded during specific seasons, such as umbrellas, raincoats, woollens coolers, festival accessories, are all subject to seasonal fluctuations.

Another useful criterion to classify industries is the various stages of their development. Different stages of their life cycle development exhibit different characteristics. Each development is quite unique. Grouping of firms with similar characteristics of development helps investors to properly identify different investment opportunities. Based on the stage in the life cycle, industries are classified into:

1. Pioneering Stage

This is the first stage in the life cycle of a new industry. In this, technology and its products are relatively new and have not reached a stage of perfection and there is a long way to go for penetration. There is an experimental order both in product and technology. However, there is a demand for its products in market; profit opportunities are plenty. This is the stage where venture capitalists take a lot of interest, enter the industry and sometimes organize the business. At this stage, risk commences in this industry and hence, mortality rate is very high. If an industry withstands them, the investors would reap the substantial rewards or else substantial risk of investment would result.

2. Fast Growing Stage

This is the second stage when chaotic competition and growth which marked the first stage is more or less over. The surviving large firms now dominate the industry. The demand of their product still grows faster, leading to increasing amount of profits the company can reap. This is a stage where companies grow rapidly. These companies provide good investment opportunities.

3. Security and Stabilization Stage

In the third stage, industries grow roughly at the rate of the economy, develop and reach a stage of stabilization. Looked at differently, this is a stage where the ability of the industry appears to have more or less saturated. As compared to the competitive industries, the industry at this stage faces the problem of what Grodinsky ["The Ebb and Flow of Investment Values", June, 1941] called *latent obsolescence*, a term used for a stage where earliest signs of decline have emerged. Investors have to be very cautious to recognise those signs before it is too late.

4. Relative Decline Stage

The fourth stage of industrial life cycle development is the relative decline stage. The industry has grown old. New products, new technologies have entered the market. Customers have new habits, styles, likes, etc. The company's/industry's products are not much in demand as were in the earliest stage. Still, it continues to exist for some more time. Consequently, the industry's growth would decline vis-à-vis the economy during the best of times. But as is expected, the industry's decline is much faster than the decline of the economy in the worst of times.

Table 9.1 Characteristics of the Stages in the Life Cycle

Characteristics	Pioneering Low Sales	Growth Rapidly Rising	Maturity Peak Sales	Decline Declining Sales
Costs	High cost per customer	Average cost	Low cost per customer	Low cost per customer
Profits	Negative	Rising profits	High profits	Declining profits
Customers	Innovators	Early adapters	Middle majority	Laggards
Competitors	Few	Growing numbers	Stable number beginning to decline	Declining numbers

The characteristics of different stages of life cycle development of industries have a number of implications for decisions. It would be quite prudent on the investor's part to look for companies that are in the second stage, i.e., faster growth. This probably explains the prevalent higher stock prices of the companies in this industry.

From the investment point of view, selection of industries at the third stage of development is quite crucial. It is the growth of the industry that is relevant and not its past performance. Having discussed various investment implications, it may be pointed out that one should be careful while classifying them. This is because the above discussion assumes that the investor would be able to identify the industrial life cycle. In practice, it is difficult to detect which stage of the industry is passing through.

Needless to say, it is only a general framework that is presented here. One can modify this analysis with suitable changes. In order to strengthen the analysis further, it is essential to outline the features of the industry in depth. Due to its unique characteristic, unless the specific industry is analyzed properly, it will be difficult to form an opinion for profitable investment opportunities.

Some aspects to be kept in mind while carrying out industry analysis are:

1. There is competition among domestic and foreign firms, both in the domestic and foreign markets. How do firms perform here?
2. Many types of products are manufactured in this industry. What is the nature and prospect of demand for the industry? Are these homogeneous in nature or highly heterogeneous?
3. This may also incorporate the analysis of the markets for its products, customer-wise and geographical area-wise, identifying various determinants of this type of industry: growth, cyclical, defensive or relative decline.

9.1 IMPORTANCE OF INDUSTRY ANALYSIS

Why should a security analyst carry out an industry analysis?

To answer this question, logically two arguments are presented:

(i) Firms in each different industry typically experience similar levels of risk and similar rates of return. As such, industry analysis will be useful for knowing the investment-worthiness of a firm.

(ii) Mediocre stocks in a growth industry usually outperform the best stocks in a stagnant industry. This would point out the need for knowing not only the company prospects but also the industry prospects.

Risk-return pattern: Economic theory points out that a competitive firm in an industry tries to maximize its profits by adopting fairly similar policies with respect to the following:

1. The labour-capital ratio utilized by each firm
2. Mark ups, profit margins and selling prices
3. Advertising and promotional programmes
4. Research and development expenditure
5. Protective measures of the government

As such, they have the same risk level as well as rates of return, on an average. Empirical evidence shown by research supports this argument.

Growth Factor: All industries do not have equally good or equally bad experiences and expectations; for their fortunes keep on changing. It implies that the past is not a good indicator for the future.

This view is well supported by research. Researchers have ranked the performance of different industries over a period of one year and then ranked their performance over subsequent periods of years. They compared the ranking and obtained near zero correlations. It implies that an industry that was good during one period of time cannot continue to be good in all periods.

Another observation is that every industry passes through four distinct phases of the life cycle. The stages may be termed as pioneering, expansion, stagnation and decline. Different industries may be in different stages. Consequently, their prospects vary. As such, separate industry analysis is essential.

Classification of Industries

There are different ways of classifying industrial enterprises.

(i) **Classification by Reporting Agencies:** In India, the Reserve Bank of India has classified industries into 32 groups. Stock exchanges have made a broad classification of industries into 10 groups. Business media have their own classification. *The Economic Times* classifies industries into 10 groups and the *Financial Express* into 19 groups. The groups are further subdivided.

(ii) Classification by Business Cycle: The general classification in this framework is: growth industry, cyclical industry, defensive industry and cyclical growth.

Growth industries are characterized by high rate of earnings, expansion, often independent of business cycles. These industries are pioneers of a major change in the state of the art, i.e., innovation diffusing concerns. The ongoing revolution in the electronics industry and communication equipment are examples of this kind.

Cyclical industries are closely related to business cycles. Prosperity provides consumers purchasing power and boom to industry whereas depression adversely affects them. Consumer durables are subject to these kinds of changes.

Defensive industries are those the products of which have relatively inelastic demand. Food processing, pharmaceutical industries are example of this kind.

Cyclical growth industries are those that are greatly influenced by technological and economic changes. The airline industry, companies belonging to broad infrastructure projects can be cited as examples.

Key Indicators in Analysis: The analyst/investor is free to choose his or her own indicators for analyzing the prospects of an industry. However, many generally adopt the following:

(A) Performance factors

- Past sales
- Past earnings

(B) Environment factors

- Attitude of government
- Labour conditions
- Competitive conditions
- Technological progress

(C) Outcome factors

- Industry share prices
- Price earnings multiply with reference to these key factors
- Strengths and weaknesses
- Opportunities and threats

Some relevant questions that may be asked in this connection are given here. They are only illustrative and not exhaustive.

1. Are the sales of industry growing in relation to the growth in Gross National Product (GNP)?
2. What is overall return on investment (ROI)?
3. What is the cost structure of the industry?
4. Is the industry in a stable position? Does the success or failure of the industry depend upon any single critical factor?
5. What is the impact of taxation upon the industry?
6. Are there any statutory controls in matters of raw materials allotment, prices, distribution etc? Are they protective or crippling?
7. What is the industrial relations scenario of the industry?
8. Is the industry highly competitive? Is it dominated by one or two major companies? Are they Indian or foreign? Is there sufficient export potential? Are international prices comparable with domestic prices?
9. How does the stock market evaluate the industry? How are the leading scrips in the industry evaluated by the stock market?
10. Is the industry highly technology based? At what pace technological advancements are taking place?

Implications to the Investor: This approach is useful to the analyst as it gives insights, not apparent merits and demerits of investments in a given industry at a given time. What the investor has to do is to,

(i) collect relevant data to identify the industry life cycle stage;
(ii) forecast the probable life period of the stage; and
(iii) decide whether to buy, hold or sell.

Another analysis can be done periodically to evaluate strengths and weaknesses either by inside company executives or outside consultants. This can be done by using a form such as the one shown in Table A below. For each factor, minor or major weakness is displayed. Of course, not all factors are equally important for succeeding in business. Therefore, it is necessary to rate the importance of each factor – high, medium or low. When combining performance and importance levels, four possibilities emerge. These are illustrated in Table B.

Table A

		Performance	
		Low	High
	High	A. Concentrate here	B. Keeping the good work
Importance	Low	C. Take enough care	D. If overkill, divert

Table B

	Factor	Performance	Importance
	Major Minor Neutral	Minor Major	High Medium
MARKETING			
1. Popularity and regard			
2. Relative market share			
3. Quality image			
4. Service reputation			
5. Distribution costs			
6. Sales force			
7. Market location			
FINANCE			
1. Cost of capital			
2. Funds availability			
3. Financial stability			
4. Profitability			
MANUFACTURING			
1. Facilities			
2. Economies of scale			
3. Capacity utilization			
4. Labour productivity			
5. Manufacturing costs			
6. Raw material availability			
7 Technology of process			
HUMAN RESOURCES			
1. Leadership			
2. Management capabilities			
3. Worker attitudes			
4. Entrepreneurial competence			
5. Skill development			
6. Structural flexibility			
7. Adaptation			
8. Industrial relations			

9.2 FORECASTING METHODS

The techniques for analyzing information about industry within a timeframe are briefly explained.

1. The Market Profile

A market profile consists of those endogenous characteristics that have a significant bearing on demand or the way in which it can be developed.

Its basic elements are:

- Number of establishments
- Geographical location of establishment
- Number of employees
- Value of sales
- Value addition by manufacturing
- Capital expenditure
- Degree to which establishments are specialized
- Importance of their output in the national total

The trend of these elements when analyzed, reveal vital information about the position and progress of the industry.

2. Cumulative Methods

These are based either on market surveys or statistical measurements:

(a) Surveys: Surveys are carried out by research agencies, consultants, industry association and the research bureau of media. These surveys generally study the current facilities and demand, future demand and proposed investment, and thereby expansion prospects vis-à-vis demand gap. Other factors like, strengths and weaknesses of the organization, environmental factors are also brought into focus to evaluate the future of the industry. Surveys adopt the methodology of inquiry, through questionnaires and interviews. The subjects will be either manufacturers or dealers/end users.

(b) Correlation and Regression Analysis: Statistical methods like correlation and regression analysis can be of much help in demand measurement. The following steps have general application.

(i) Determine the total requirement for the type of product in question by the present customers in each industry classification. This can be done by asking the customer or obtaining the estimate from the salesmen, or by comparing with other customers of the same size and class.

(ii) Correlation of product requirement of customer established with a variable for output for which accurate published data are available. Generally, employment is the most useful variable.

The correlation can be observed by preparing a scatter diagram, or calculating mathematically, using the formula given below:

$$\text{Degree of relationship, } r = \frac{N\Sigma(xy) - (\Sigma x)(\Sigma y)}{[n\Sigma x - (\Sigma x)][N\Sigma x - (\Sigma y)]}$$

where x = number of employees
y = number of product items
n = number of observations

The nearer the correlation coefficient is to +1 or –1, the closer is the relationship between the two variables under study.

The significance of the relationship can be determined using hypothesis testing procedure.

(iii) Apply the relationship to estimate demand. If the degree of correlation between purchases of a given product by present customers and their employment size is considered significant, the demand estimation can be done as follows:

- Computing the average number of items purchased per employee and applying the ratio to the total employment.
- Formulating and estimating the equation through the regression model.

$$\Sigma y = Na + b\Sigma x$$
$$x\Sigma y = a\Sigma x + b\Sigma b$$

where, *a* equals number of products purchased when employment is zero and *b* equals the amount of change in the number of products purchased with every change in total employment.

The latter method is more accurate because it is more sensitive to the influence of independent variable on dependent variable.

Multiple regression analysis facilitates the study of impact of more than one independent variable on the dependent variable.

$$Y = a + bx + cx + dx + ex + fx$$

where Y = yearly sales in lakhs of rupees
x = yearly sales (lagged one year) in lakhs of rupees
x = yearly advertising expenditure in lakhs of rupees
x = a dummy variable
x = year
x = disposable personal income in lakhs of current rupees

(c) Time series analysis: Time series analysis consists of decomposing the original sales series over a period of time. The elements derived are:

Trend (T): It is the result of basic developments in population, capital formation, and technology. It is found by fitting a straight or curved line through past sales.

Cycle (C): It captures the wave-like movement of sales. Many sales are affected by swings in general economic activity, which tends to be somewhat periodic. The cyclical component can be useful in intermediate range forecasting.

Season (S): It refers to a consistent pattern of sales movements within the year. The term season describes any recurrent sales pattern. The seasonal component may be related to weather factors, holidays, and trade customs. The seasonal pattern provides a norm for forecasting short-range sales.

Erratic Events (E): It refers to the unpredictable sales caused by unforeseen events like strikes, riots, war scares, floods and other disturbances.

Another time series technique is *exponential smoothing*. For industries with several items in product line. This technique is useful for efficient and economical short-run forecast. It requires only three pieces of information.

- This period's actual sales (Q)
- This period's smoothed sales (Q)
- A smoothing parameter (a), where

Sales forecast for the next period $(Q + 1) = Q + (1 - a)\,Q$

The initial level of smoothed sales can simply be the average sales for the last few periods. The smoothing constant is derived by trial and error testing of different smoothing constants between zero and one, to find the constant that produces the best fit of past sales.

3. Technology and Research

Due to increasing competition in general, technology and research play a crucial part in the growth and survival of a particular industry. However, technology itself is subject to change; sometimes, very fast, and can lead to obsolescence. Thus, only those industries, which update themselves in the field of technology, can attain competitive edge over others in terms of quality, pricing of products, etc.

The relevant questions to be probed further by the analyst/investor in this respect include the following:

- What is the nature and type of technology used in the industry?
- Are there any expected changes in the technology in terms of offering new products in the market to increase sales?
- What has been the relationship of capital expenditure and the sales over time?
- Whether more capital expenditure has led to increase in sales?
- What has been the amount of money spent in the research and development activities of the firm? Did the amount on the research and development in the industry relate to its redundancy or otherwise?
- What is the assessment of this industry in terms of its sales and profitability in the short, intermediate and long run? What is the return on capital employed in the industry? (Return refers to EBIT)

- What is critical cost component? Whether industry has control over that component?
- Who are the players? Are there any bigger names of some players? What is the prospect of industry?
- What is the export potential of the industry? How big is the opportunity for its products/services in the global market?

The impact of all these factors has to be finally translated in terms of profitability – their level and expected rate of change during short, intermediate and long run.

9.3 INDUSTRY ANALYSIS FACTORS

The securities analyst will take into consideration the following for assessing the industry for making investments:

- Post-sales and earnings performance
- Government's attitude towards industry
- Labour conditions
- Competitive conditions
- Performance of the industry
- Industry share prices relative to industry earnings
- Stage of the industry life cycle
- Industry trade cycle
- Inventories build-up in the industry
- Investors' preference over the industry
- Technological innovations

Techniques of Industry Analysis

So far, we have discussed various factors that are to be taken into account while considering industry analysis. Now, we turn our attention towards various techniques that help us evaluate the factors mentioned above.

End Use and Regression Analysis

It is the process whereby the analyst or investor attempts to deal with the factor that determines demand for the output of the industry. This is also known as *end-use demand analysis*. In this process, the investor hopes to uncover the factors that explain the demand. Some of the factors are found to be powerful in explaining the demand for the product, like disposable income, per capita consumption, price elasticity of demand and per capita income. In order to identify the factors that affect demand, statistical techniques like regression analysis and correlation are used. These help identify the important factors/variables. However, one should be aware of their limitations.

Input Output Analysis

This analysis helps us understand demand analysis in greater detail. *Input analysis* is an useful technique that reflects the flow of goods and services through the economy, including intermediate steps in the production process as the goods proceed from the raw material stage to finished goods for ultimate consumption. This information of the input-output table reflects the pattern of consumption at all stages, and not at the stage of consumption of finished goods. This is done to detect any changing patterns. It might also indicate the growth or decline of industries.

One also needs to do a SWOT analysis of the industry. It involves identifying the strengths, weaknesses, opportunities and threats associated with the industry. This is done with regard to industry environment in Table 9.2.

Table 9.2

STRENGTHS	WEAKNESSES
1. Latest technology	1. Loose controls
2. Least diversified cost	2. Untrained labour force
3. Established products	3. Strained cash flows
4. Committed manpower	4. Poor product quality
5. Advantageous location	5. Family feuds
6. Strong finances	6. Poor public image
7. Well known brand names	

OPPORTUNITIES	THREATS
1. Growing domestic demand	1. Price wars
2. Expanding export market	2. Intense competition
3. Access to low manpower costs	3. Undependable suppliers
4. Booming capital market	4. Infrastructure bottlenecks
5. Low interest rates	

Identifying key factors, life cycle, industry key drivers, and doing a SWOT analysis is the heart of industry analysis.

10 CHAPTER Company Analysis

Having gone through the relevance of economic and industry analysis, we will now discuss company level analysis. In order to provide a proper perspective to this analysis, let us begin by discussing the way investor makes investment decisions given his maximization goal.

- Buy the share at a low price
- Sell the share at a high price

The above decision rule is simple to understand, but difficult to apply in practice. Huge efforts are made to operationalise it by using a proper formal and analytical framework. To begin with, problems faced by the investors are:

- How to find out whether the price of a company's share is high or low?
- What is the benchmark used to compare the price of the share?

The first question becomes easier if some benefits are agreed upon with which the prevailing market price can be compared. In this respect, fundamental analysis provides the investor a real benchmark in terms of intrinsic value. This value depends on industry and company fundamentals.

Out of the three, company level analysis provides a direct link to investor's action and his investment goal in operational terms. This is because the investor buys an equivalent of a company's share and not that of the industry and economy. This framework indeed provides him/her with a proper background, with which he/she buys the shares of a particular company. A careful examination of the company's quantitative and qualitative fundamentals is, therefore, essential.

As Fischer and Jordan have aptly stated: "If the economic outlook suggests investment to be made, then industry analysis will aid the investor in selection of proper industry to invest in. Nonetheless, when to invest and in which industry is not enough. It is also necessary to know which companies should be selected.

The real test of an analyst's competence lies in his ability to see not only the forest but also the trees. Superior judgement is an outcome of intelligence, and synthesis of inference. That is why, besides economic and industry, individual company analysis is important.

10.1 FRAMEWORK OF COMPANY ANALYSIS

The two major components of company analysis are:

(i) Financial
(ii) Non-financial

A good analyst gives proper weightage to both these aspects and tries to make an appropriate judgement. In the process of evaluating the investment-worthiness of a company's securities, the analyst/investor will be concerned with two broad categories of information: (a) internal and (b) external. *Internal* information consists of data and events related to the enterprise which are published by them. *External* information comprises the reports and analysis made by sources outside the company, viz., media, research agencies, and the like.

Non-financial Aspects

A general impressionistic view is also important for evaluating the worth of a company for investing in securities. This could be obtained by gathering and analyzing relevant information about companies published in the media, the stock exchange directory, annual reports and prospectus.

❖ **Company Factors:**

1. History and business of the company (Images)
2. Ownership structure
3. Top management team, strategy, quality and leadership attributes
4. Track record of promoters
5. Collaboration agreements
6. Investment rationale
7. Capital expenditure
8. Product range/segments (marketing mix)
9. Future plans of expansion/diversification
10. Commitment to R & D
11. Market standing – competition, market share and growth rates
12. Competitive environment
13. Corporate social responsibility
14. Industrial relation scenario

15. Corporate image
16. Financial history and prospects
17. Estimates for growth, margins and earnings
18. Risk factors to revenue and earnings
19. Valuation of the shares
20. Market price movement on stock exchange (statistics), etc.

Several commercial databases track information about companies and provide fairly accurate information to subscribers. Company analysis involves both quantitative and qualitative analysis. The objective is to present an investment or disinvestment recommendation on the stock proper.

Financial Analysis

❖ Detailed financial analysis of a company involves understanding of the following:

(a) Order books and growth in revenue
(b) Cost structure and operating margin
(c) Asset base and utilization
(d) Capacity expansion and funding plans
(e) Mix of debt and equity and costs
(f) Interest, depreciation, tax burden
(g) Cash generated by the business
(h) Pre- and post-tax margin
(i) Earnings defined variously – earnings before interest and tax (EBIT), earnings before interest, depreciation, tax and amortization (EBIDTA), profit after tax (PAT), and earnings per share (EPS) and so on.
(j) Comparison of earning estimates with revenue, capital, equity, assets, investments, market price and such other variables.

Besides these internal factors, the external environment related to the company's survival and image includes:

1. Statutory controls
2. Government policy
3. Industry life cycle stage
4. Business cycle stage
5. Environmentalism
6. Consumerism

A financial analyst or an investor interested in making investments in equity of a company is concerned with the prospects of rise in value of the firm. For equity valuation purpose, the relevant financial measures are:

1. Earnings per share: $\dfrac{\text{Profit after tax}}{\text{Number of outstanding equity shares}}$

2. Book value per share: $\dfrac{\text{Net worth}}{\text{Number of outstanding equity shares}}$

3. Yield: $\dfrac{\text{Dividend + Price change}}{\text{Initial price}}$

4. Price-earnings ratio: $\dfrac{\text{Average of market high and low}}{\text{Earnings per share}}$

5. Retention ratio: $\dfrac{\text{Retained earnings}}{\text{Profit after tax}}$

6. Earning power: $\dfrac{\text{Earnings before interest and tax}}{\text{Total Assets}}$

7. Return on equity: $\dfrac{\text{Profit after tax}}{\text{Net worth}}$

8. Debt-equity ratio: $\dfrac{\text{Total Debt}}{\text{Net worth}}$

9. Price volatility index: $\dfrac{\text{Market high in the year} - \text{Market low in the year}}{\text{Average market price in the year}}$

A few more financial measures include:

(a) Gross profit margin
(b) Operating profit margin
(c) Net profit margin
(d) Stock Beta
(e) Overall Beta

10.2 ASSET VALUE VS EARNINGS VALUE

The asset value of a security is determined by estimating the liquidating value of the firm, deducting the claims of firm's creditors and allocating the remaining net asset value of the firm over the outstanding shares of stock. The asset value is usually estimated in consultation with a specialist who appraises asset values and/or an accountant who gives book value.

This method is suitable only for companies heading towards bankruptcy. For them, the firm's income and dividends will be declining and discontinuous. Hence, they will have negligible value. On the other hand, for going concerns, the intrinsic value far exceeds the value of the firm's physical assets. There is generally a definite lack of relationship between book value and real value, in the case of prosperous firms.

Therefore, investment analysts/investors focus their attention on the trends of earnings and the related factors like dividends, bonus issues, rights shares, and appreciation of the market value of the shares. It is believed that the appropriate indices for a company's performance are current market price per share (CMPs) and earnings per share (EPS).

To determine the appropriate earnings multiplier (from the dividend payout ratio) an analyst/investor must consider the following:

- The earnings of the security
- The risk of the security
- The growth rate of the dividend stream
- The duration of the expected growth and
- The dividend payout ratio

Earnings Analysis

As seen earlier, to value common stocks or other risky assets, the present value model is employed. The true economic value or intrinsic value of a share of a company is equal to present value of all cash flows from the asset.

$$P_{io} = \frac{d_{it}}{k - g}$$

where P_{io} = Value of share i
d_{it} = Dividends of share i in the tth period
k_1 = Equity capitalization rate
G_{it} = Growth rate of dividends of share I(a constant)

The present value model gives rise to two questions:

1. How does the investor measure the income from the common stocks?
2. What discount or capitalization rate should be used?

The income question is discussed here.

Income concepts: Accountants and economists have provided two different concepts of income. Accountant's income is the revenue over and above all costs incurred. Economists define the income of a firm as the maximum amount, which can be consumed by the owners of the firm in any period without decreasing future consumption opportunities.

Adjusting for economic income: Since income, which is very important for determining the value of a security, is vaguely reported by accountants, it is necessary to adjust or normalize it in a consistent manner.

The fundamental analyst finds it necessary to significantly alter the income statements, so as to obtain estimates for two reasons:

(i) the accountant has used an accounting procedure, which is inappropriate for the relevant economic transaction; and/or

(ii) the accountant, perhaps under the pressure of top management, has adopted a procedure to minimize the firm's income taxes or window dress the firm's financial statements.

We will now discuss four differences in the accounting procedures. These are only illustrative of the controversy in reporting incomes.

1. Sales–Revenue Recognition Principle

Sales can be either cash sales or credit sales. Sales can be recognized as early as the date of the sale invoice is signed. However, in the case of long-term construction contracts the sale may not be recognized until as late as the day cash is fully received. Between these two extremes, the accountant may choose a suitable time point to recognize the sales revenue in the financial statements. He may do it either in an attempt to improve current income or because he is confident about the collectability. In the case of credit sales, companies may factor their accounts receivable and realize cash proceeds. One firm may recognize this immediately, whereas another may wait until the customer's final cash payment is actually received.

2. Inventory

Inventory valuation, generally is done based on two methods:

FIFO – First in, first out method

LIFO – Last in, first out method

3. Depreciation

Several depreciation methods may be used in financial statements:

(i) Straight line method

(ii) Sum-of-digit method

(iii) Double declining balance method

(iv) Units of production method

(v) Written down value method

The second and third methods are accelerated methods of depreciation. The second method may be used to accelerate depreciation during a period of rapid production.

Accounting Income Effect on Balance Sheet

A *balance sheet* is a summary of account balance carried after the appropriate closing of the books. Income statements deal with flows, whereas balance sheet deals with stocks. Since stocks are accumulation of flows, vagaries that undermine the estimates of accounting income are cumulated in certain balance sheet items.

For instance, the impact of inflation should be considered to make the balance sheet items realistic. Measures suggested are:

(a) Assets Side

1. Report marketable securities at current value.
2. Inventory should be valued at replacement costs.
3. Land and natural resources to be shown at net realizable value (current market price-future development, selling or interest costs).
4. Plant and machinery at replacement cost.
5. Goodwill.
6. R & D expenses.

(b) Liabilities Side

1. Debt. In future, at the time of maturity if repaid in cheaper money units (rupees) it is a gain to shareholders.
2. Deferred taxes
3. Retained earnings

Forecasting Earnings

It is necessary to estimate a stock's future income because the value of the share is the present value of its future income. This can be done by focusing on:

(a) identification of variables which will have impact on income; and
(b) determining the extent of change in income due to change in the identified variables, by employing appropriate method of forecasting.

Identification of Variables: Basically changes in income result from changes in:

(i) operations of business; and
(ii) financing of the business

(i) *Operations and Earnings:* The operating cycle of a firm starts with cash converted into inventory. Inventory turns into sale and accounts receivables, which finally become cash. Return on Investment (ROI) is the measure of the firm's operating result:

$$ROI = \frac{EBIT}{Investment} = \frac{EBIT}{Sales} * \frac{Sales}{Investment}$$

There are two products: (a) profit margins on sale and (b) turnover of assets

(ii) *Financing and Earnings:* The two main sources of financing an enterprise are:

(a) Borrowing (b) Issue of new shares

Debt financing provides leverage to common shareholders. It raises earning per share but also risk. Equity financing is advisable where new shares can be sold at a price in excess of asset value per share, as it improves EPS. This is possible only when the company management can maintain a reasonably higher ROI.

From the above, it is clear that EPS and changes in earnings are functions of:

(i) Turnover on investment
(ii) Margin on sales
(iii) Effective interest rate (cost of borrowed funds)
(iv) Debt equity ratio
(v) Equity base
(vi) Effective tax rate

Determining the extent of change method: Different methods of forecasting earnings are available. The two categories into which the methods fall are given below with a brief list of some of the methods.

1. Earlier methods

- Earnings methods
- Market share/profit margin approach (breakeven analysis)

2. Modern techniques

- Regression and correlation analysis
- Trend analysis (time series analysis)
- Decision trees
- Simulation

Determining Earnings

A. *Multiplier (P/E) Ratio*

So far, the focus has been on determining earnings per Share (EPS). This is to be translated into market price per share (MPS). As such, most of the fundamental security analysis work centres on determining the appropriate multiplier.

B. *Dividend Discount Model of Valuation*

In determination of the P/E ratio, the factors to be considered are:

- Capitalization rate (K)
- Growth rate of dividend stream (g)
- Dividend pay-out ratio (d/e)

(a) Capitalization rate (K): Capitalization rates vary with the firm's risk class and the prevailing market conditions. Three risk classes may be considered for analysis—high, medium and negligible. Based on market level and directions of change, markets can be classified as:

(i) *Normal market:* In which most securities prices are experiencing slow and steady growth and the average price-earnings ratio is the low mid terms (say around 12-16 times).

(ii) *Bear market:* When average earnings multiplier drop below 13 times, many market prices are deflated.

(iii) *Bull market:* When average earnings multiplier rise above approximately 18, many stocks are overpriced.

Since future expectations are influenced by past experience, a good way to estimate a firm's risk-class is to examine its historical data. Capital Asset Pricing Model (CAPM) or Security Market Line (SML) depicts the risk-return relationships based on historical data. It illustrates the positive relationship between assets, undiversifiable risk (as mentioned ROR) of the asset. A fundamental analyst can measure the risk of the company in recent periods, adjust it for anticipated changes and then use these forecasted risk statistics to obtain capitalization rates. Also adjustment upward or downward is to be made in earnings multipliers in line with the prevailing conditions, i.e., depressed or inflated.

(b) Growth rate (g): The next step is determination of growth rates of earnings. If payout ratio is constant, the multiplier is influenced by growth rate (g) conditions, *viz.*, zero growth, perpetual growth and temporary growth.

(c) Payout ratio (d/e): The effects of changes in dividend payout ratio (d/e) are direct and proportional, as can be observed from the P/E model. The EPS and DPS are not equal, for the reason that some companies prefer a stable dividend policy and some others retain earnings and maintain low dividend payout ratios. It implies that analysts have to study the history of dividends announcements by the firm to make proper prediction of future payout ratios.

Empirical studies have produced the following findings:

1. Companies seem to have predetermined payout ratio that they appear to adhere to in the long run.
2. Dividends are raised only if corporate management feels that a new higher level of earnings can be supported in the future.
3. Managements are extremely reluctant to cut the absolute monetary amount of the cash dividends.
4. It gives price earnings ratios or various risk classes and various rates of dividends or earnings growth in normal market along with formulae for comparing value of stocks.

C. Comparative P/E Approach

Comparative or relative valuation makes use of the P/E ratio of the market or industry to determine the P/E for an individual stock. The procedure is as follows:

(i) Determine the market P/E using dividend discount model.
(ii) Determine the market payback period based on earnings growth rate of market. (How many years it takes to obtain market P/E at a given growth factor?)
(iii) Assign P/E to the stock based on its growth rate and market payback period.
(iv) Make adjustments for dividend payout ratio and earnings volatility.
(v) Find volume of stock by multiplying normal earnings with the determined P/E.

10.3 GROWTH STOCKS

Investors are interested not only in current dividends but also future earnings through dividends and capital gains.

The following features help identify growth stocks.

(i) Substantial and steady growth in EPS
(ii) Low current DPS, because retained earnings are high and reinvested
(iii) High returns on book value
(iv) Emphasis on R & D
(v) Diversification plans for strategic competitive advantage
(vi) Marketing competence and edge.

Benefits: Investment in growth stocks would benefit investors in many ways.

1. The market value goes up at a rate much faster than the rate of inflation.
2. Higher capital gains.
3. Long range tension-free holding without any need for sell and buy operations and associated problems.

Valuation: The investor interested in growth shares can either employ (a) comparative P/E ratios approach or (b) dividend discount model for valuation of the stocks.

Estimation of Future Price

Before attempting to discuss the approach that can be adopted for company level analysis, let us talk about the objective of investor and how it can be quantified. It is also to reiterate the proposition that an investor looks for increasing his returns from the investment. Returns are composed of capital gains and a stream of income in the form of dividends. Assuming he has equity shares for a period of one year (known as holding period), i.e., he sells it at the end of the year; the total returns obtained by him would be equal to the capital gains plus dividends received at the end of the year.

$$R_t = (P_t - P_{t-1}) + D_t$$

where P_t = Price of the share at the end of the year

P_{t-1} = Price of the share at the beginning of the year

D_t = Dividend received at the end of the year
R_t = Return for the holding period, t

In order to calculate the return received by him on his original investment (i.e., purchase price), the total returns should be divided by P_{t-1}. These are expressed in percentage terms and known as *holding period yield*. Thus,

$$\text{HRY (\%)} = \frac{(P_t - P_1 - 1) + D_t}{P_{t-1}}$$

The above computation is quite simple as long as the value of the variables is available. In reality, however, the investor would know the original price of the share (called *purchase price*) as this is the price paid to buy the shares, but the price at the end of the year (i.e., selling price) as well as dividend income received would have to be estimated. The challenge lies in estimating the future price of the share as well as dividends. The time series data relating to dividend paid by companies provide us useful clues in estimating the dividends likely to be declared by companies. There is, it seems, a dividend policy followed by most corporates in general. Thus, an investor would be able to estimate dividend for the year with reasonable degree of accuracy under normal circumstances.

Estimation of the future price of the share that contributes a major portion in the total returns of the investor is invariably problematic. In order to estimate future price of share, an investor may adopt two approaches, namely, *quantitative analysis* and *attractive analysis*. ("The Cross-Section of Expected Stock Returns", Fama and French, June, 1992) Let us evaluate the two approaches.

Quantitative Analysis

This approach helps us to provide a measure of the future value of equity share based on quantitative factors. The methods commonly used under this approach are:

1. Dividend discounted method
2. Price-earnings ratio method

Dividend Discounted Method

It is based on the premises that the value of an investment is the present value, whereas return on investment is future value. The present value (*PV*) is calculated by discounting the future returns, which are divided in the following formula,

$$\text{PV} = \frac{D_1}{(1+K)} + \frac{D_2}{(1+K)} + \frac{D_3}{(1+K)} + \dots \frac{D_t}{(1+K)}$$

Under the constant growth assumption, this boils down to

$$\text{PV} = \frac{D_1}{K-g}$$

where K = discount rate; g = growth rate

DPS = EPS * (1 – b)

b = Proportion of earnings retained such that (1 – b) is the dividend payout

Substituting the above in the formula, it becomes

$$\frac{\text{EPS}\,(1-b)}{K-g}$$

On the basis of the above model, the following inferences can be drawn:

1. Higher the EPS, other things like b, K, g, remaining the same, higher would be the value of the share.
2. Higher the b, retention rate, or lower the $1 - b$, i.e., g remaining the same, higher would be the value of the share.
3. Higher the K, i.e., discount rate, other things like b, g remaining the same, higher would be the value of an equity.
4. Higher the growth rate, other things like EPS, b, K remaining constant, higher would be the value of the share.

Looking at the above methods, it is not uncommon to find that investor prefers shares of companies with higher P/E multiple.

You will appreciate that the usefulness of the above model lies in understanding the various factors determining the P/E ratio,

- Dividend payout
- Growth
- Risk-free rate
- Business risk
- Financial risk

Thus, other things remaining the same,

1. Higher would be the P/E ratio, if higher is the growth rate or dividend or both.
2. Lower would be the P/E ratio, if higher is risk-free rate, business risk and financial risk.

The foregoing presentation helps us provide a quantitative measure of the value of equity share. However, there remains the problem of estimating earning per share, which has been used in both the methods discussed. This is a key number, which is being quoted, reported and used most often by company management analysts, financial press, etc. It is this number everybody is attempting to forecast. The starting point to earning per share, however, is to understand the chemistry of earnings.

We describe various approaches to forecast earnings per share in the following sections.

10.4 FORECASTING EARNINGS PER SHARE

The most important, indeed the principal object is getting information about the earnings of the company's financial statements. The investor must remember that there is more to the financial statements than what meets his eyes. Out of the two statements, *balance sheet* and *income statement*, it is the income statement that is more often used in order to gauge the future state of the firm. Research studies have indicated the significance of this number in influencing prices and dividends. The research study conducted by *Niederhoffer and Regan*, "Earnings changes analysts' forecasts and stock prices" (CFA Journal, 1972) for example, found that the prices are strongly dependent on the changes in the earnings, both absolute and relative to the analysis.

The above study and some others indicate the importance of the forecast of earnings as the most important variable to work on in the investment decision-making process. The critical aspects of the earnings are its *level*, *trend* and *stability*.

There are various methods employed to assess the future outlook of the revenue, expenses and the earnings from the forecast of economic and industry outlook. These methods can be broadly classified into two categories, traditional and modern. Under the traditional approach, the forecaster obtains the estimate of the single value variable. While in the case of modern approach, he obtains the range of values with the probability of each of them. Let us discuss these two approaches in detail.

Traditional Methods of Forecasting EPS

Under the traditional approach, the following methods of forecasting are adopted:

1. ROI approach
2. Market share approach
3. Independent estimates approach

Beginning the discussion on the forecasting techniques, it will not be out of place to briefly mention that the earnings per share are measured from the financial statement. This will provide an understanding of its changes. Broadly, changes in earnings are affected by operating and financing decisions. Both these decisions are, however, interdependent. Various companies do this by presenting the information in the income statement reflecting both types of decisions. Given below is the format, which analyses:

Income statement for the period ended _ _ _ _ _

1. Sales revenue
2. Less operational expenses
3. Earnings before interest and tax (EBIT)
4. Less interest expenses
5. Earnings before tax (EBT)
6. Less taxes paid/provided
7. Earnings after tax (EAT)
8. Number of shares outstanding
9. EPS = EAT/number of shares outstanding

Let us now explain the ROI approach to forecast earnings per share.

ROI Approach

Under this approach, attempts are made to relate the productivity of assets with the earnings. That is, returns on the total investments (assets) are calculated and estimates made regarding per share.

Return on assets = EBIT/Assets

Return on assets is a function of the two important variables, viz., turnover of assets, and margin of profit.

Return on assets = Assets turnover * Profit margin

Ratio Analysis

Based on the financial data available in income statement and balance sheet, relevant ratios may be calculated and analyzed to appraise the financial soundness of a company.

An investor must decide the intrinsic price of a particular company's share on the bases of foregoing discussion. That is, what is the price that you would be willing to pay for the share? Remember, there is no readymade formula to decide the attractiveness of a company. Analysis is more an art than science. One can improve with experience and by having the guts to back one's judgement with investment.

Table 10.1

S. No.	Indicator	Ratios
A	Technical solvency	Current rato Liquidity ratio Net income to debt service ratio
B	Actual solvency	Debt-equity ratio Return on investment Profit margin Fixed assets to total assets
C	Profitability	Gross profit margin Net profit margin Return on investment Earnings per share Dividend yield ratio P/E ratio
D	Efficiency	Operating ratio Expense ratio Current assets turnover Inventory turnover Credit collection period

11 CHAPTER Technical Analysis

Technical analysis takes a completely different approach; it doesn't care about the 'value' of a company or a commodity. Technicians (sometimes called *chartists*) are only interested in the price movements in the market. In this approach, investors study the chart of share prices and buy those shares whose charts give "buy" signals and sell those shares whose charts give "sell" signals.

Technical analysis is concerned with the study of internal market data, with a view to develop trading rules aimed at profit-making. It assumes that there are certain persistent and recurring patterns of price movements which can be discerned by analyzing market data. Some tools used are: bar chart, moving average analysis, Elliot-wave, Japanese candlestick, etc.

Technical analysis attempts to explain and forecast changes in security prices by studying only the market data rather than information about a company or its prospects as is done by fundamental analysts.

John Magee, whose book *Technical Analysis of Stock Trends* is considered a classic for technical analysis, says: "The technician has elected to study, not the mass of fundamentals, but certain abstractions, namely, the market data alone. But this technical view provides a simplified and more comprehensible picture of what is happening to the price of a stock. It is like a shadow or reflection in which can be seen the broad outline of the whole situation. Furthermore, it works."

The technical analysts believe that the price of a stock depends on supply and demand in the marketplace and has little relationship to value, if any such concept ever exists. Price is governed by basic economic and psychological inputs so numerous and complex that no individual can hope to understand and measure them correctly. The technicians think that the only important information to work from is the picture given by price and volume statistics.

The technician uses the market, disregarding minor changes, moving in discernible trends, which continue for significant periods. A trend is believed to continue until there is definite information of a change. The past performance of a stock can then be harnessed to predict the future. It is not necessary that the future patterns should be in line with the past trends. The direction of price change is as important as the relative size of the change. With his previous charts, the technician attempts to correctly catch changes in the trend and take advantage of them.

11.1 TECHNICAL ANALYSIS

Technical analysis is the organized and systematic study of a pictorial representation (chart) of the past price actions of a particular item with a view to ascertaining its expected future behaviour.

Technical analysis is a method of evaluating securities by analyzing the statistics generated by market activity, such as past prices and volume. Technical analysis does not attempt to measure a security's intrinsic value, but instead use charts and other tools to identify patterns that can suggest future activity.

Just as there are many investment styles on the fundamental side, there are also many different types of technical traders. Some rely on chart patterns, others use technical indicators and oscillators, and most of them use a combination of the two. In any case, technical analysts' exclusive use of historical price and volume data is what separates them from their fundamental counterparts. Unlike fundamental analysis, technical analysis does not worry whether a stock is undervalued — the only thing that matters is a security's past trading data and what information this data can provide about where the security might move in the future.

Basic Technical Assumptions

Let us review the basic and necessary assumptions regarding the technical analysis.

1. The Market Discounts Everything

A major criticism of technical analysis is that it only considers price movement, ignoring the fundamental factors of the company. However, technical analysis assumes that, at any given time, a stock's price reflects everything that has or could affect the company – including fundamental factors. Technical analysis believes that the company's fundamentals, along with broader economic factors and market psychology, are all built into the stock, removing the need to actually consider these factors separately. This only leaves the analysis of price movement, which technical theory views as a product of the supply and demand for a particular stock in the market. Both rational and irrational factors can affect demand and supply.

2. Trends in Price Movement

In technical analysis, barring minor deviations, stock prices tend to move in fairly persistent trends. Shifts in demand and supply bring about changes in trends and can be tracked with the help of charts and similar tools. This means that after a trend has been established, the future price movement is more likely to be in the same direction as the trend. Most technical trading strategies are based on this assumption.

3. History Tends to Repeat Itself

Another important aspect in technical analysis is that history tends to repeat itself, mainly in terms of price movement. The repetitive nature of price movements is attributed to market psychology; in other words, a market participant tends to provide a consistent reaction to similar market stimuli over time. Irrespective of why they occur, shifts in demand and supply can be detected with the help of charts of market action. Technical analysts use chart patterns to analyze market movements and understand the trends. Because of the persistence of trends and patterns, analysis of past market data can be used to predict future price behaviour. Although many of their charts have been used for more than 100 years, they are still believed to be relevant because they illustrate patterns in price movements that often repeat themselves.

Following are some of the points technicians consider as part of technical analysis.

A. Technicians believe that behind the fundamentals are important factors

At any given time, some investors have gains in the stock, and some usually have losses. Those with gains want to safeguard them and if possible, build them higher, hence they will hold the stocks.

Those with losses will adopt different tactics; some will cut their losses short by selling when the stock price begins to decline; others will sell when a minor rally has moved the stock up to its cost price; and still others will hold on doggedly until there is a turnaround.

Each of these decisions points can be spotted on charts: current configuration to show the action of the past week or so; intermediate and long-term patterns to find the previous important price levels at which selling is likely; and interim and long-term high points from which the stock started to move down in the past.

In this method of analysis, a vital factor is *volume*. Volume is favorable on the upside when the number of shares traded is greater than before and on the downside when the number of shares traded dwindles. Volume is unfavourable when volume dips as prices rise or increases when there is a decline. None of these indicators is concerned with the fundamentals of the corporation.

B. Technicians act on what and not on the why

Technicians recognize that formations and patterns signify changes in real value as a result of investor expectations, hopes, fears, industry developments and so on. They are not as impressed with fundamental value of any security as they are with the current and prospective values reflected by market action.

C. Technicians are not committed to a buy-and-hold policy

As long as the trend is up, they will hold a stock. This may be for months or even years. But if there is a reversal, they will sell within hours of purchase. They recognize that, to achieve the greatest gains, they must never let sentiment or emotion override facts (as shown by technical indicators) and should always get out of a situation which, on available evidence, is no longer profitable.

D. Technicians do not separate income from capital gains

They look for total returns, that is, the realized price less the price paid plus dividend received. This is in sharp contrast to most long-term investors who buy a high-dividend paying stock and hold it for years, through up-and-down fluctuations. To the technicians, such strategy is not wise. A stock may continue to pay liberally but lose 50% of its value. If a stock is to be judged solely on its income, a non-dividend payer would have no value at all.

E. Technicians act more quickly to make commitments and to take profits and losses

They are not concerned with maintaining a position in any market, any industry or any stock. As a result, they are willing to take smaller gains in an up-market and accept quick losses in a down-market. Traders/technicians want to keep their money working at maximum efficiency.

Technicians know that there is no real value to any stock and that price reflects only supply and demand, which are governed by hundreds of factors, rational and irrational. No one can grasp and weigh them all, but to a surprising degree, the market does so automatically.

F. Technicians recognize that the more experience one has with the technical indicators, the more alert one becomes to pitfalls and failure of investing

To be rewarding, technical analysis requires attention and discipline, with quality stocks held for long term. The duration can make up for timing mistakes. With technical approaches, the errors become clear quickly.

G. Technicians insist that the market always repeats

What has happened before will probably be repeated again; therefore, current movements can be used for future projection.

With all markets and almost all securities, there are cycles and trends which will occur again and again. Technical analyses, especially charts, provide the best and most convenient method of comparison.

H. Technicians believe that breakouts from previous trends are important signals

They indicate a shift in important supply and demand. When confirmed, breakouts are almost always accurate signals to buy or sell.

I. Technicians recognize that the securities of a strong company are often weak and those of a weak company may be strong

Technical analysis can quickly show when such situations occur. These indicators always delineate between the company and the stock.

J. Technicians use charts to confirm fundamentals

When both agree, the odds are favourable for profitable movement, if the trend of the overall stock market is also favourable.

11.2 EVALUATION OF TECHNICAL ANALYSIS

Technical analysis appears to be a highly controversial approach to security analysis. It has its ardent votaries; it has its severe critics. The advocates of technical analysis offer the following interrelated arguments in support of their position.

(a) Under the influence of crowd psychology, trends persist for quite some time. Tools of technical analysis that help in identifying these trends early are helpful aids in investment decision making.
(b) Shifts in demand and supply are gradual rather than instantaneous. Technical analysis helps in detecting these shifts rather early and hence provides clues to future price movements.
(c) Fundamental information about a company is absorbed and assimilated by the market over a period of time. Hence, the price movement tends to continue in more or less the same direction till the information is fully assimilated in the stock price.

Old Puzzles and New Developments

Fibonacci Numbers

Fibonacci numbers have intrigued mathematicians and scientists for hundreds of years. Leonardo Fibonacci (1170-1240) was a medieval mathematician who discovered the series of numbers while studying the reproductive behaviour of rabbits. The beginning of the Fibonacci series is shown here: 1, 2, 3, 5, 8, 13, 21, 34, 55, 89, 144, 233 ....

The remarkable thing about the numbers is the frequency with which they appear in the environment. Sunflowers have seeds spiraling around the centre of the plant. Some spirals contain seeds leaning counterclockwise, with other spirals going the other way. On most sunflowers, the numbers of clockwise and counter-clockwise spirals are adjacent Fibonacci numbers. A blossom might have 34 counter-clockwise spirals and 55 clockwise spirals. The structure of pine cones, the number of chambers in a nautilus seashell, the topology of spiraling galaxies, and the ancestry of bees all reveal Fibonacci numbers. There is even a professional journal, the *Fibonacci Quarterly*, which is devoted to the study of this series.

Elliot Wave Principle

One theory that attempts to develop a rationale for a long-term pattern in the stock price movements is the *Elliot Wave Principle* (EWP), established in the 1930s by R.N. Elliot and later popularized by Hamilton Bolton. The EWP states that major moves take place in the successive steps resembling tidal waves.

Basic foundation of Elliot Wave theory:

- Wave structure
- Rules for impulse waves

- ❖ Corrections
- ❖ Fibonacci sequence

Brief elements:

- In a major bull market, the first move is upward; the second downward; the third upward; the fourth downward; and the fifth and final upward phase.
- The waves have a reverse flow in a bear market.
- Rule of alternation, especially in impulse waves, warns us not to expect the same thing again. Alternatively, it also helps us to expect what can follow.
- Corrections take place in three waves.
- Simple corrections are of two types: 5-3-5 and 3-3-5.
- Triangles are usually placed in the position of the 4th wave.
- The "Fibonacci sequence" is the mathematical basis of the Elliot wave theory.
- Fibonacci ratios and retracements are used to determine price objectives.
- Theory is primarily used for ***market indices*** and is not meant for use on individual scrips.
- A large public following is a must for effective use of the theory.

Kondratev Wave Theory

Nikolay Kondratev was a Russian economist and statistician born in 1892. He helped develop the first Soviet Five-Year Plan. From 1920 to 1928, he was the Director of the Study of Business Activity at the Timiriazev Agricultural Academy. While there, he devoted his attention to the study of Western capitalist economies. In the economies of Great Britain and the United States, he identified long-term business cycles with a period of 50-60 years. He became well-known after the US market crash of 1929, which Kondratev predicted would follow the US crash of 1870. His hypothesis of a long-term business cycle is called the *Kondratev Wave Theory*.

Note that the market crash for 1987 occurred 58 years after the crash of 1929, a period consistent with Kondratev's theory. Some modern economists believe that Kondratev's theory has merits. Many others believe that significant macroeconomic changes, such as floating exchange rates, the elimination of the gold standard, and the reduction of barriers to free trade, make the decision cycle less predictable. Still, many market analysts consider Kondratev's work in their assessment of the stock market and its risks.

Chaos Theory

At a recent finance conference, a few researchers have presented papers on the chaos theory and its application to the stock market. In physics, chaos theory is a growing field of study examining instances in which apparently random behaviour is, in fact, quite systematic or even deterministic. Scientists apply this theory to weather prediction, population growth estimates, and fisheries biology.

Investment analysts have sought a pattern in stock market behaviour since the origin of the exchanges. Many remain unknown about how security prices are determined and chaos theory may eventually provide some potential answers. If the apparent randomness of security price changes, can be known to be non-random, much of the theory of finance would need revision.

Neutral Networks

A neutral network is a trading system in which a forecasting model is trained to find desired output from past trading data. By repeatedly cycling through the data, the neutral network eventually learns the pattern that produces the desired output. If the desired output remains elusive, more data is included until a pattern is found. Neutral networks may also include a feedback mechanism whereby experience gained from past errors, is taken into account.

This topic is becoming popular in the investment community. National conferences have been organized dealing exclusively with this topic, and the trade literature publishes many articles on this. A problem with the concept of a neutral network is that the stock market is seldom deterministic. Situations constantly change, and what may have been true a few years ago need not necessarily prevail tomorrow. Financial academics are especially leery of back-tests, or research that tests a hypothesis using past data. Mining the data will almost always result in some apparent cause and effect between past events and stock market performance. Research that tests a hypothesis using the subsequent data is much more useful. An article in the popular press describes Wall Street's response to the criticism.

No matter whose field of study, technicians are interested in the search for a better mousetrap. Essentially, what security analysts seek to do is to find improvements in their methodology for security selection.

11.3 TOOLS FOR TECHNICAL ANALYSIS

The technician must (1) identify the trend, and (2) recognize when one trend comes to an end and prices set off in the opposite direction. His central problem is to distinguish between reversals within a trend and real changes in the trend itself. This problem of sorting out price changes is critical, since prices do not change in a smooth, uninterrupted fashion.

The two variables concerning groups of stocks or individual stocks are:

1. Behaviour of prices, and
2. Volume of trading contributing to and is influenced by changing prices.

The use of technical 'indicators' to measure direction of overall market should precede any technical analysis of individual stocks, because of systematic influence of the general market on stock prices. In addition, some technicians feel that forecasting aggregates are more reliable, as individual errors can always be filtered out.

First, we will examine the seminal theory from which much of the substances of technical analysis have been developed – the *Dow Theory* – after which the key indicators, viz., price and volume relating to entire market and individual stock performance as shown in following table will be examined.

Table 11.1 Tools of Technical Analysis

Category	Market Indicators	Market and indivdual stock indicators
Price indicators	Dow Theory - Breadth of market indicators	Line, bar and point and figure charts, Moving averages. Relative strength
	- Plurality	
	- Market breadth index	
	- Advance - Declines	
	- New highs and new lows	
	- The lost active list	
	- Confidence indicator	
	(Display index)	
Volume indicators	New York and American Exchange	Resistance and support charts
	Volume Contrary Opinion Theories	Price volume bar charts
	- Short selling	
	- Odd Lot trading	
Other indicators	Mutual fund activity	
	Credit balance theory	

Dow Theory

The Dow Theory is one of the oldest and most popular technical tools. It was originated by Charles Dow, who founded the Dow Jones Company and was editor of The Wall Street Journal.

The Dow Theory was developed by W.P. Hamilton and Robert Rhea from the editorial written by Dow during 1900-02. Numerous writers have altered, extended and in some cases abridged the original Dow theory. It is the basis for many other techniques used by technical analysts.

The Dow theory is credited with having forecast the Great Crash of 1929. On October 23, 1929 The *Wall Street Journal* published a still famous editorial, "A twin in the tide" which correctly stated that the bull market was then over and a bear market had started. The horrendous market crash which followed the forecast drew much favourable attention to the Dow Theory. Greiner and Whitecombe ["The Dow Theory and the seventy-year Forecast Record: Larchmont Investors Intelligence" (1969)] assert that "the Dow theory provides a time-tested method of reading the stock market barometer."

Basic Tenets of Dow Theory

- ❖ Averages discount everything
- ❖ Market has three trends
- ❖ Markets go through three phases
- ❖ Averages must confirm each other
- ❖ Volume must confirm the trend
- ❖ A trend is in effect until it gives definite signals of reversal

There are many versions of this theory, but essentially it consists of three types of market movements:

- ***major market trend***, which can often last a year or more;
- ***secondary intermediate trend***, which can move against the primary trend for one to several months; and
- ***minor movements*** lasting only for a few hours to few days.

The determination of the major market trend is the most important decision for the Dow theory.

The Theory: According to Dow, "The market is always considered as having three movements, all going at the same time. The first is narrow movement from day to day. The second is short swing running from two weeks to a month or more; the third is the main movement covering at least four years in duration." These movements are called:

- daily fluctuations (minor trends),
- secondary movements (trends), and
- primary trends.

Primary trends are long-range cycles that carry the entire market up or down (bull or bear markets). The primary trend is regarded as *bullish* when the high point of each rally is higher than the high point of the preceding rally and the low point of each decline is higher than the low point of the preceding decline. Likewise, a primary trend is considered *bearish* when the high point of each rally is lower than the high point of the preceding rally and the low points of each decline are lower than the low points of the preceding decline.

The secondary trend acts as a restraining force on the primary trend. It ends to correct deviations from its general boundaries. The minor trends have little analytical value, because of their short duration and variations in amplitude. The Dow theory is built upon the assertion that measures of stock prices tend to move together. It employs two of the Dow Jones' averages:

(i) Dow-Jones Industrial Average (DJIA)

(ii) Dow-Jones Transportation Average (DJTA)

Bull market – if both the averages are rising

Bear market – if both the averages are falling

If the Dow Jones industrial average is rising, then the transportation average should also be rising. Such simultaneous price movements suggest a strong bull market. Conversely, a decline in both the industrial and transportation averages suggests a strong bear market, both moves in opposite directions; the market is uncertain as to the direction of future stock prices.

If one of the averages starts to decline after a period of rising stock prices, then the two are at odds. For example, the industrial average may be rising, while the transportation average is falling. This suggests that the industries may not continue to rise but may soon begin to fall. Hence, the market investor will use this signal to sell securities and convert them to cash.

The converse occurs when after a period of falling security prices, one of the averages starts to rise while the other continues to fall. According to the Dow theory, this divergence suggests that this phase is over and that security prices in general will soon start to rise. The astute investor will then purchase securities in anticipation of the price increase.

Although Charles Dow believed in fundamental analysis, the Dow theory has evolved into a primary technical approach to the stock market. It asserts that the stock prices demonstrate patterns over four to five years and these patterns are mirrored by indices of stock prices. The Dow theory employs two of the Dow Jones' averages, the industrial average and the transportation average. The utility average is generally ignored.

Criticism of Dow Theory

1. It is not a theory but an interpretation of data. A theory should be able to explain why a phenomenon occurs. No attempt was made by Dow or his followers to explain why the two averages should be able to forecast future stock prices.
2. It is not an acceptable forecast. There was considerable lag between the actual turning points and those indicated by the forecast.
3. It has poor predictive power. According to Rosenberg ["An Empirical Investigation of the Arbitrage Pricing Theory" (1980)], the Dow Theory could not forecast the bull market which had preceded the 1929 crash. It gave bearish indication in early 1926. The three and a half years followed the forecast of Hamilton's editorials for a 26–year period, from 1904 to 1929. Of the 90 recommendations Hamilton made for a change in attitude towards the market (55% were bullish, 18% bearish and 29% doubtful), only 45 were correct. Such a result an investor may get by flipping a coin.

Types of Trend

There are three types of trend: (i) uptrend, (ii) downtrend, (iii) sideways/horizontal trend.

As the names imply, when each successive peak and trough is higher, it's referred to as an *upward trend*. If the peaks and troughs are getting lower, it's a *downward trend*. When there is little movement up or down in the peaks and troughs, it's a *sideways* or *horizontal trend*. If you want to get really technical, you might even say that a sideways trend is actually not a trend on its own, but a lack of a well-defined trend in either direction. In any case, the market can really only move in these three directions: up, down or nowhere.

Trend Lengths

Along with these three trend directions, there are three trend classifications. A trend of any direction can be classified as a long-term trend, intermediate trend or a short-term trend. In terms of the stock market, a *major trend* is generally categorized as one lasting longer than a year. An *intermediate trend* is considered to last between one and three months and a *near-term trend* is anything less than a month. A long-term trend is composed of several intermediate trends, which often move against the direction of the major trend. If the major trend is upward and there is downward correction in price movement followed by a continuation of the uptrend, the correction is considered to be an intermediate trend. The short-term trends are components of both major and intermediate trends.

When analyzing trends, it is important that the chart is constructed to best reflect the type of trend being analyzed. To help identify long-term trends, weekly charts or daily charts spanning a five-year period are used by chartists to get a better idea of the long-term trend. Daily data charts are best used when analyzing both intermediate and short-term trends. It is also important to remember that longer the trend, the more important it is: for example, a one-month trend is not as significant as a five-year trend.

Trend Lines

A trend line is a simple charting technique that adds a line to a chart to represent the trend in the market or a stock. Drawing a trend line is as simple as drawing a straight line that follows a general trend. These lines are used to clearly show the trend and are also used in the identification of trend reversals.

Volume and Chart Patterns

The other use of volume is to confirm chart patterns. Patterns such as head and shoulders, triangles, flags and other price patterns can be confirmed with volume. In most chart patterns, there are several pivotal points that are vital to what the chart is able to convey to chartists. Basically, if the volume is not there to confirm the pivotal moments of a chart pattern, the quality of the signal formed by the pattern is weakened.

Volume Precedes Price

Another important aspect in technical analysis is that price is preceded by volume. Volume is closely monitored by technicians and chartists to form ideas on upcoming trend reversals. If volume starts decreasing in an uptrend, it is usually a sign that the upward run is about to end.

Now that we have a better understanding of some of the important factors of technical analysis, we can move on to charts, which help to identify trading opportunities in price movements.

11.4 TECHNICAL ANALYSIS: CHART TYPES

One school of though led by William L. Jiler developed a comprehensive technique called "Chart Reading". Charts provide visual assistance detecting the emerging and changing patterns of price behaviour. The basic concepts underlying chart analysis are:

(a) persistence of trends;
(b) relationship between volume and trend; and
(c) resistance and support levels.

Technical analysts use four basic types of charts:
(i) Line charts, (ii) Bar charts, (iii) Japanese candlestick charts, (iv) Point and figure charts.

Line Charts: The most basic of the four charts is the line chart because it represents only the closing prices over a set period of time. The line is formed by connecting the closing prices over a time frame. Line charts do not provide visual information of the trading range for the individual points such as the high, low and opening prices. However, the closing price is often considered the most important price in stock data compared to the high and low for the day and this is why it is the only value used in line charts.

Bar Charts: Most investors interested in charting use bar charts – primarily because they have meanings familiar to a technical analyst, but also because these charts are easy to draw. The procedure for preparing a vertical line or bar chart is simple. Suppose an investor is to draw on graph or logarithmic paper a series of vertical lines, each line representing the price movements for a time period – a day, a week, or even a year. The vertical dimension of the line represents price; the horizontal dimension indicates the time involved by the chart as a whole. In a daily chart, for example, each vertical line represents the range of each day's price activity, and the chart as a whole may extend for a month. For this, extend the line on the graph paper from the highest transaction of each day drawn to the lowest and make a cross mark to indicate the closing price.

Japanese Candlestick Charts: The candlestick chart is similar to a bar chart, but it differs in the way that is visually constructed. Similar to the bar chart, the candlestick chart also has a thin vertical line showing the period's trading range. The difference comes in the formation of a wide bar on the vertical line, which illustrates the difference between the open and the close. And, like bar charts, candlestick chart also relies heavily on the use of colours to explain what has happened during the trading period.

A major problem with the candlestick colour configuration, however, is that different sites use different standards; therefore it is important to understand the candlestick configuration used at the chart site you are working with. There are two colour constructs for days when price goes up and one for days when the price falls. When the price of the stock is up and closes above the opening trend, the candlestick will usually be white or clear. If the stock has traded down for the period, then the candlestick will usually be red or black, depending on the site. If the stock's price has closed above the previous day's close but below the day's open, the candlestick will be black or filled with the colour that is used to indicate an up day.

Point-and-Figure Charts: Bar chartists count on discovering certain buying and selling forces in the market, on the basis of which they predict future price trends. These forces consist of three factors – time, volume and price. Members of another school, known as point-and-figure chartists, question the usefulness of the first two factors. They argue that the way to predict future price fluctuations is to analyze price changes only. Consequently, they assert, no volume action need be recorded, and the time dimension (day, week, or month) should also be ignored. If only significant price changes are important, then one needs to capture only (say one point or more, ignoring all fluctuations) significant price changes in a stock, no matter how long it takes for the stock to register the change.

Charts are one of the most fundamental aspects of technical analysis. It is important that one clearly understands what is being shown on a chart and the information it provides. Now we will move on to the different types of chart patterns.

11.5 TECHNICAL ANALYSIS: CHART PATTERNS

A chart pattern is a distinct formation on a stock chart that creates a trading signal, or a sign of future price movements. Chartists use these patterns to identify current trends and trend reversals and to trigger buy and sell signals. Following are the **major reversal** patterns:

- Head and shoulders
- Double/triple bottom
- Double top
- Rounding bottom/saucer
- Island reversal
- Diamond

Head and Shoulders

This is one of the most popular and reliable chart patterns in technical analysis. Head and shoulders are a reversal chart pattern that when formed, signals that the security is likely to move against the previous trend. Head and shoulders top is a chart pattern that is formed at the high of an upward movement and signals that the upward trend is about to end.

Cup and Handle

A cup and handle chart is a bullish continuation pattern in which the upward trend has passed but will continue in an upward direction once the pattern is confirmed. The handle follows the cup formation and is formed by a generally downward/

sideways movement in the security's price. Once the price movement pushes upward the resistance lines formed in the handle, the upward trend can continue. There is a wide-ranging time frame for this type of pattern, with the span ranging from several months to more than a year.

Double Tops and Bottoms

This is another well-known pattern that signals a trend reversal – it is considered to be one of the most reliable and commonly used. These patterns are formed after a sustained trend and signal to chartists that the trend is about to reverse. The pattern is created when a price movement tests support or resistance levels twice and is unable to break through. This pattern is often used to signal intermediate and long-term trend reversals.

The following are Trendline based patterns:

- Trendline
- Trend channel
- Triangles
- Pennants
- Wedges
- Flags

Flag and Pennant

These two short-term chart patterns are continuation patterns that are formed when there is a sharp price movement followed by a generally sideways price movement. This pattern is then completed upon another sharp price movement in the same direction as the move that started the trend. The patterns are generally thought to last from one to three weeks.

In a pennant, the middle section is characterized by converging trend lines, much like what is seen in a symmetrical triangle. The middle section on the flag pattern, on the other hand, shows a channel pattern, with no convergence between the trend lines. In both cases, the trend is expected to continue when the price moves above the upper trend line.

Triangles

Triangles are some of the most well-known chart patterns used in technical analysis. The three types of triangles, which vary in construct and implication, are the symmetrical triangle, ascending and descending triangle. These chart patterns are considered to last anywhere from a couple of weeks to several months.

The symmetrical triangle is a pattern in which two trend lines converge towards each other. This pattern is neutral in that a breakout to the upside or downside is a confirmation of a trend in that direction. In an ascending triangle, the upper trend line is flat, while the bottom trend line is sloping upward. This is generally thought of as a bullish pattern in which chartists look for an upside breakout. In a descending triangle, the lower trend line is flat and the upper trend line is descending. This is generally seen as a bearish pattern where chartists look for a downside breakout.

Wedge

The wedge chart pattern can be either a continuation or reversal pattern. It is similar to a symmetrical triangle except that the wedge pattern slants in an upward or downward direction, while the symmetrical triangle generally shows a sideways movement. The other difference is that wedges tend to form over longer periods, usually between three and six months.

Rounding Bottom

A rounding bottom, also referred to as a *saucer bottom*, is a long-term reversal pattern that signals a shift from a downward trend to an upward trend. This pattern is traditionally thought to last anywhere from several months to several years.

A rounding bottom chart pattern looks similar to a cup and handle pattern but without the handle. The long-term nature of this pattern and the lack of a confirmation trigger, such as the cup and handle, make it a difficult pattern to trade.

Gaps

A gap in a chart is an empty space between a trading period and the following trading period. This occurs when there is a large difference in prices between two sequential trading periods.

Triple Tops and Bottoms

Triple tops and triple bottoms are another type of reversal chart pattern in chart analysis. These are not as prevalent in charts as head and shoulders and double tops and bottoms, but they act in a similar fashion. These two chart patterns are formed when the price movement tests a level of support or resistance, three times and is unable to breakthrough; this signals a reversal of the price trend.

Confusion can arise with triple tops and bottoms during the formation of the pattern because they may look similar to other chart patterns. After the first two support/resistance tests are formed in the price movement, the pattern will look like a double top or bottom, which could lead a chartist to enter a reversal position too soon.

Limitations of Charts

The technical analyst may have charts of all the principal shares in the market. But what is necessary is a proper interpretation of charts. Interpretation of charts is very much like a personal offer. In a way, it is like an abstract art. Take an abstract painting and show it to ten people and you will get at least eight different interpretations of what is seen. Take one set of chart figures and show it to ten chartists and you are liable to get almost as many interpretations as to which way the stock is going.

The trouble with most chart patterns is that they cause their followers to change their option quite frequently. Most chart services change like the wind. One day they put out a strong buy signal, two weeks later, they see a change in the pattern and tell their clients to sell, then two weeks later, they tell them to buy again. The result is that these patterns force their followers in and out of the market time and again. Though this is great for broker's commission, but not so great for investor.

Another disadvantage which exists in charting is that decisions are almost always made on the basis of the chart alone. Most buyers under this method have no idea why they are buying a company's stock. They rely alone on a stock's action, assuming that the people who have caused or are currently causing the action really know something about the company. This is generally negative thinking – simply because, as more and more chartists are attracted to a stock, there are simply more and more owners who know little or nothing about the company.

11.6 TECHNICAL ANALYSIS: MOVING AVERAGES

Most chart patterns show a lot of variation in price movement. This can make it difficult for traders to get an idea of a security's overall trend. One simple method traders use to combat this is to apply moving averages.

A moving average is the average price of a security over a set period of time. By plotting a security's average price, the price movement is smoothed out. Once the day-to-day fluctuations are removed, traders are able to identify the true trend and increase the probability that it will work in their favour.

Types of Moving Averages

(i) Simple Moving Average (SMA): This is the most common method used to calculate the moving average of prices. It simply takes the sum of all the past closing prices over a time period and divides the result by the number of prices used in the calculation.

For an instance, in a 5-day moving average, the last 5 closing prices are added together and then divided by 5. Thus, a trader is able to make the average less responsive to changing prices by increasing the number of periods used in the calculation. Increasing the number of time periods in the calculation is one of the best ways to gauge the strength of the long-term trend and the likelihood when it will reverse.

To illustrate its calculation, consider the closing price of a stock on 10 successive trading days.

Table 11.2

Trading day	Closing price	Sum of the most recent closing prices	Moving average
1	25.0		
2	26.0		
3	25.5		
4	24.5		
5	26.0	127.0	25.4
6	26.0	128.0	25.6
7	26.5	128.5	25.7
8	26.5	129.5	25.9
9	26.0	131.0	26.0
10	27.0	132.0	26.4

To identify trends, technical analysts use moving average analysis:

- A 200-day moving average of daily prices (or alternatively, a 30-week moving average of prices) may be used to identify a long-term trend.
- A 60-day moving average of daily prices may be used to discern an intermediate term trend.
- A 10-day moving average of daily prices may be used to detect a short-term trend.

The buy and sell signals provided by the moving average analysis are as follows:

Buy signal	Sell signal
• Stock price line rises through the moving average line when the graph of the moving average line is flattening out.	• Stock price line falls through the moving average line when the graph of the moving average line is flattening out.
• Stock price line falls below the moving average line which is rising.	• Stock price line rises above the moving average line which is falling.
• Stock price line, which is above the moving average line, falls but begins to rise again before reaching the moving average line.	• Stock price line, which is below the moving average line, rises but begins to fall again before reaching the moving average line.

(ii) Exponential Moving Average (EMA)

This moving average calculation uses a smoothing factor to place a higher weight on recent data points and is regarded as more efficient than the linear weighted average. Having an understanding of the calculation is not generally required for most traders because most charting packages do the calculation for you. The most important thing to remember about the exponential moving average is that it is more responsive to new information relative to the simple moving average. This responsiveness is one of the key factors of why this is the moving average is the choice of many technical traders.

(iii) Linear Weighted Average

This moving average indicator is the least common out of the three and is used to address the problem of weighting. The linear weighted moving average is calculated by taking the sum of all the closing prices over a certain time period and multiplying them by the position of the data point and then dividing the sum by the number of periods.

For instance, in a five-day linear weighted average, today's closing price is multiplied by five; yesterday's by four and so on, until the first day in the period range is reached. These numbers are then added together and divided by the sum of the multipliers.

(iv) Moving Average Convergence/Divergence (MACD)

The *moving average convergence/divergence* (MACD) is one of the most well-known indicators used in technical analysis. This indicator comprises two exponential moving averages, which help to measure momentum in the security. The MACD is simply the difference between these two moving averages plotted against a centerline. The centerline is the point at which the two moving averages are equal. Along with the MACD and the centerline, an exponential moving average of the MACD itself is plotted on the chart. The idea behind this momentum indicator is to measure short-term momentum compared to the longer term momentum to help signal the current direction of momentum.

MACD = Shorter-term moving average – Longer-term moving average

When the MACD is positive, it signals that the shorter-term moving average is above the longer-term moving average and suggests upward momentum. The opposite holds true when the MACD is negative – this signals that the shorter-term is below the longer and suggests downward momentum. When the MACD line crosses over the centerline, it signals a crossing in the moving averages. The most common moving average values used in the calculation are the 26-day and 12-day exponential moving averages. The signal line is commonly created by using a nine-day exponential moving average of the MACD values. These values can be adjusted to meet the needs of the technician and the security. For more volatile securities, shorter-term averages are used, while less volatile securities should have longer averages.

Another aspect to the MACD indicator that is often found on charts is the MACD histogram. The histogram is plotted on the centerline and represented by bars. Each bar is the difference between the MACD and the signal line or, in most cases, the nine-day exponential moving average. The higher the bars are in either direction, the more momentum behind the direction in which the bars point.

Major Uses of Moving Averages

- Moving averages are used to identify current trends and trend reversals as well as to set up support and resistance levels.
- Moving averages can be used to quickly identify whether a security is moving in an uptrend or a downtrend depending on the direction of the moving average.

11.7 TECHNICAL ANALYSIS INDICATORS

Indicators are calculations based on the price and the volume of a security that measure such things as money flow, trends, volatility and momentum. Indicators are used as a secondary measure to the actual price movements and add additional information to the analysis of securities. Indicators are used in two main ways: to confirm price movement and the quality of chart patterns, and to form buy and sell signals (i.e., it uses the principle of divergence and confirmation).

There are two main types of indicators: leading and lagging.

- A *leading* indicator precedes price movements, giving them a predictive quality, while a *lagging* indicator is a confirmation tool because it follows price movement.
- A leading indicator is thought to be the strongest during periods of sideways or non-trending trading ranges, while the lagging indicators are useful during trending periods.

Most of the technical indicators make sense when examined individually but when one examines many technical indicators simultaneously, the interpretation of their collective meaning is often contradictory and confusing. One technical analyst issued the following report:

"The breadth of the market remains pretty bearish, but the odd-lot index is still in balance and is more bullish than bearish. While the short interest is not bearish, brokers' loans are at a dangerously high level. Business indices are beginning to turn sharply upward and most psychological indicators are generally uptrend. The index of 20 low-priced stocks remains in a general upward trend, but the confidence index still is in a long-term downtrend. The Canadian gold price index is still in a downtrend, which normally implies a higher stock market ahead. Professional and public opinion remains cautiously optimistic, which is also an indication of a higher stock market, but on a decline below 800, the Dow Jones industrial averages would emit a definite sell signal."

(i) Oscillators (Aroon Oscillator)

An expansion of the Aroon is the *Aroon Oscillator*, which simply plots the difference between the Aroon up and down lines by subtracting the two lines. This line is then plotted between a range of -100 and 100. The centerline is zero in the oscillator that is considered to be a major signal line determining the trend. The higher the value of the oscillator from the centerline point, the more upward strength there is in the security;

and lower the oscillator's value is from the centerline, the more downward is the pressure. (i.e., it uses the principle of overbought and oversold signals).

(ii) Relative Strength Index

The Relative Strength Index (RSI) is another well-known momentum indicator in technical analysis. RSI helps to signal overbought and oversold conditions in a security. The indicator is plotted in a range between zero and 100. A reading above 70 is used to suggest that a security is overbought, while a reading below 30 is used to suggest that it is oversold. This indicator helps traders to identify whether a security's price has been unreasonably pushed to current levels and whether a reversal may be on the way.

(iii) Confidence Index

It is the ratio of a group of lower-grade bonds to a group of higher-grade bonds. According to the theory underlying this index, when the ratio is high, investors' confidence is likewise high, as reflected by their purchase of relatively more of the lower-grade securities. When they buy relatively more of the higher-grade securities, this is taken as an indication that confidence is low, and is reflected in a low ratio.

(iv) Spreads

Large spreads between yields indicate low confidence and are bearish; the market appears to require a large compensation for business, financial and inflation risks. Small spreads indicate high confidence and are bullish. In short, the larger the spreads, lower the ratio and less confidence. The smaller the spreads, greater the ratio, indicating greater confidence.

(v) Advance-Decline Ratio

The index relating to advance to decline is called the decline ratio. When advances persistently outnumber declines, the ratio increases. A bullish condition is said to exist, and vice versa. Thus, an *advance-decline ratio* tries to capture the market's underlying strength by taking into account the number of advancing and declining issues.

(vi) Market Breadth Index

The market breadth index is a variant of the advance-decline ratio. To compute it:

1. In its simplest form, it is computed on a stock market by taking the ratio of the number of advancing stocks to declining stocks. For example, if in a given week 600 shares advanced, 200 shares declined, and 200 were unchanged, the breadth would be 2[(600-200)/200]. The figure of each week is added to previous week's figure. These data are then plotted to establish the pattern of advance and declines.
2. Obtain the breadth of the market by cumulative daily net advances/declines.

To gauge the state of the market, one may look at the breadth of the market. The purpose of the market breadth index is to indicate whether a confirmation of some index has occurred. If both the stock index and the market breadth index increase, the market is bullish; when the stock index increases but the breadth index does not, the market is bearish.

(vii) The Odd-Lot Ratio

Odd-lot transactions are measured by odd-lot changes in index. Odd-lots are stock transactions of less than, say, 100 shares. The odd-lot ratio is sometimes referred to as a *yardstick of uninformed sentiment* or an index of contrary opinion because the odd-lot theory assumes that small buyers or sellers are not very bright especially at tops and bottoms when they need to be the brightest. The *odd-lot short ratio theory* assumes that the odd-lot short sellers are even more likely to be wrong than odd-lotters in general. This indicator relates to odd-lot sales to purchase.

(viii) Insider Transactions

The hypothesis that insider activity may be indicative of future stock prices has received some support in academic literature. Since insiders may have the best picture of how the firm is faring, some believers of technical analysis feel that these inside transactions offer a clue, to future earnings, dividend and stock price performance. If the insiders are selling heavily, it is considered a bearish indicator and vice versa. Stockholders do not like to hear that the president of a company is selling large blocks of stock of the company. Although the president's reason for selling the stock may not be related to the future growth of the company, it is still considered bearish as investors figure the president, as an insider, must know something bad about the company that they, as outsiders, do not know.

11.8 CRITICISMS OF TECHNICAL ANALYSIS

Despite the assertions, technical analysis is not a sure-fire method. The various limitations of technical analysis pointed out by its critics are given as under:

(a) *Difficult to Interpret:* Technical analysis is not as simple as it appears to be. While the charts are fascinating to look at, interpreting them correctly is very difficult.

(b) *Frequent Changes:* With changes in the market, chart patterns keep on changing. Accordingly, technical analysts change their options about a particular investment very frequently.

(c) *Unreliable Changes:* Changes in market behaviour observed and studied by technical analysts may not always be reliable owing to ignorance or intelligence or manipulative tendencies of some participants.

A false piece of information or wrong judgement may result in trade at a price lower than the market price. If the technicians fail to wait for confirmation, they incur losses.

(d) *Unpredictable Changes:* Technicians expect changes to take place in a known and gradual fashion.

(i) History does not repeat itself: One of the major limitations of technical analysis is that the entire data is based on the past. It is presumed that future resembles the past. Further, contingency or unexpected events like a change of government, a violent agitation or a natural calamity may produce a different pattern of behaviour.

(ii) No Gradual Shifts: It is presumed that shifts in supply and demand occur gradually rather than instantaneously. Since these shifts are expected to continue as the price gradually reacts to new or other factors, the price change pattern is extrapolated to predict further price changes. However, economists assert that this is a wrong proposition. Their random walk theory has shaken the conceptual foundation of technical analysis. They believe that securities price changes are a series of random numbers, which occur in reaction to the random arrival of news.

(e) *Less Precise Tools:* The greatest limitation of technical analysis is perhaps the mechanical precision it gives to the entire exercise of investment in equity shares. However, the tools are subject to errors, breakdown and misinterpretation.

(f) *False Signals Can Occur:* Technical analysis is a signaling device. Like a thermometer, it may give a false indication when there is no alarm, but when there is cause for alarm, the signal will almost invariably be flashed.

(g) *No One Indicator is Infallible:* Technical analysis includes many approaches, most requiring a good deal of subjective judgement in application. A number of tests have been conducted to obtain statistically reliable estimates of the worth of various technical trading strategies. The results have been inconclusive because of different findings by different researchers using different procedures and different samples.

The crux of the problem as it applies to indicators is that while they may be crystal clear in definition and theory, they often break down in practice. Each one of them at some particular time has been ineffective, outweighted by a number of other indicators.

Because of this, technicians seldom rely upon a single indicator; they place reliance upon reinforcement provided by groups of indicators.

In conclusion, it can be said that technical analysis is essentially an imperfect science and an art. It helps those who have good skills, of course, not always.

The Future of Technical Analysis

Although there is much in finance that we do not completely understand, technical analysis has been around for more than hundred years, and it is not likely to disappear from the investment scene anytime soon. Improved quantitative methods coupled with improved behavioural research will continue to generate ideas for analysts to test. The well-known financial behaviourist Warner De Bont ["Anomalies: A Mean-Reverting Walk Down Wall Street" (1989)], for instance, recently reported substantial evidence that public expects the continuation of past price trends. That is, they are bullish in bull markets and pessimistic in bear markets.

Perhaps within a decade or more, the fragmentation of technical analysis into such a wide-ranging array of increasingly complex, widely differing formulae will cause a gradual movement away from the entire quasi-science back to some form of more fundamental evaluation, in a meaningful and practical manner.

"Since all human actions obey laws, as fixed as those of geometry, psychology should be studied in geometrical form, and with mathematical objectivity." **–Spinoza**

12 Efficient Market Theory

CHAPTER

In 1953, Maurice Kendall, a distinguished statistician, presented a somewhat unusual paper before the Royal Statistical Society in London. Kendall examined the behaviour of stock and commodity prices in search of regular cycles. Instead of discovering any regular price cycle, he found prices appeared to follow a random walk, implying that successive price changes are independent of one another. In 1959, two highly original and interesting papers supporting the random walk hypothesis were published.

In one paper, Harry Roberts showed that a series obtained by cumulating random numbers bore resemblance to a time series of stock prices. In the second paper, Osborne, an eminent physicist, examined whether stock price behaviour was similar to the movements of very small particles suspended in a liquid medium (such movement is referred to as the *Brownian motion*). He found a remarkable similarity between stock price movements and the Brownian motion.

Inspired by the works of Kendall, Roberts, and Osborne, and a number of researchers employed indigenous methods to test randomness of stock price behaviour. By and large, these tests have vindicated the random walk hypothesis. Indeed, in terms of empirical evidence, very few economic ideas can rival the random walk hypothesis.

12.1 SEARCH FOR THEORY

When the empirical evidence in favour of the ***random walk hypothesis*** seemed overwhelming, the more curious among the academic researchers asked themselves the question: what is the economic process that produces a random walk? They concluded that the randomness of stock prices was the result of an efficient market. Broadly, the key links in the argument are as follows:

1. Information is freely and instantaneously available to all the market participants. (location-independence) – stock prices reflect all the information.
2. Keen competition among market participants more or less ensures that market prices will reflect intrinsic values. This means that they will fully impound all the available information.

3. Prices change only in response to new information that, by definition, is unrelated to previous information (otherwise it will not be new information) and, therefore, unpredictable.
4. There is no benefit in examining the price series any more.
5. Since new information cannot be predicted in advance, price changes too cannot be forecast. Hence, prices behave like random walk, i.e., the share prices follow a probability distribution (generally a normal distribution) and every change is a drawing from that distribution.
6. Homogeneity – claim to future returns subject to risk.

Misconceptions about Efficient Market Theory

The efficient market theory has often been misunderstood. The common misconceptions about the efficient market theory are stated below along with answers meant to dispel them.

Misconceptions	Answers
Efficient market theory implies that the market has perfect forecasting abilities.	The efficient market theory merely implies that prices impound all the available information. This does not mean that the market has perfect forecasting abilities.
As prices tend to fluctuate, they cannot reflect fair value.	Unless prices fluctuate, they would not reflect fair value. Because the future is uncertain, the market is continually surprised. As prices reflect these surprises, they fluctuate.
Inability of institutional portfolio managers to achieve superior investment performance implies that they lack competence.	In an efficient market, it is ordinarily not possible to achieve superior investment performance. Market efficiency exists because portfolio managers are doing their job well in a competitive setting.
The random movement of stock prices suggests that the stock market is irrational.	Randomness and irrationality are two different matters. If investors are rational and competitive, price changes are bound to be random.

Recently, a new dimension has been added to the controversy because of the rapidly expanding research in behavioural finance that likewise has major implications regarding the concept of efficient capital markets. You need to understand the meaning of the terms efficient capital markets and efficient market hypothesis (EMH) because of its importance and controversy associated with it. You should understand the analysis performed to test the EMH and the results of studies that either support or contradict the hypothesis. Finally, you should be aware of the implications of these results when you analyze alternative investments and work to construct a portfolio.

EMH – Implication: Shares are so efficiently priced that the market can be beaten only for "good fortune".

12.2 NEED OF CAPITAL MARKETS TO BE EFFICIENT

As noted earlier, in an efficient capital market, security prices adjust rapidly to the infusion of new information, and, therefore, current security prices fully reflect all available information. To be absolutely correct, this is referred to as an *informational efficient market*. Although the idea of an efficient capital market is relatively straightforward, we often fail to consider why capital markets should be efficient. There is a set of assumptions that can be implied to an efficient capital market.

1. An initial and important premise of an efficient market requires that a large number of profit maximizing participants analyze and value securities, each independently of the others.
2. A second assumption is that new information regarding securities comes to the market in a random fashion, and the timing of one announcement is generally independent of others.
3. The third assumption is especially crucial; profit-maximizing investors adjust security prices rapidly to reflect the effect of new information. Although the price adjustment may be imperfect, it is unbiased. This means that sometimes the market will over-adjust and other times it will under-adjust, but you cannot predict which will occur at any given time.

Fair Price of Securities

How are the prices of securities determined? Are these prices fair? In the capital markets, hundred and thousands of investors make several deals a day. The screen-based trading makes these deals known to all in the capital market. Thus, a large number of buyers and sellers interact in the capital market. The demand and supply forces help in determining the prices. Since all information is publicly available, and no single investor is large enough to influence the security prices, the capital market provides a measure of fair price of securities.

A financial manager borrows and lends (invests) funds in the capital markets. Capital markets facilitate the allocation of funds between savers and borrowers. This allocation will be optimum if the capital markets have efficient pricing mechanism. What does capital market efficiency mean? Are capital markets efficient? *Capital market efficiency* is defined as the ability of securities to reflect and incorporate all relevant information, almost instantaneously, in their prices.

12.3 ARE CAPITAL MARKETS PERFECT?

We have seen that market efficiency refers to **information efficiency**. The degree of efficiency depends on the level of information disclosure and the speed with which information is processed by the market and incorporated in the share prices. Capital markets have been found to be fairly efficient in the advanced economies as well as in a number of emerging capital markets. Are these markets perfect as well? A **perfect capital market** envisions more stringent conditions. The following are important attributes of a perfect capital market:

(a) **No Entry Barriers (Free Trading):** Anyone can participate in the market. Thus, the suppliers or user of funds can enter the market and deal with each other. There should not be government restrictions on trading.

(b) **Large Number of Buyers and Sellers:** Perfect competition in the market is ensured by the presence of a large number of buyers and sellers of securities. No single market participant is large enough to be able to affect security prices.

(c) **Divisibility of Financial Assets:** Financial assets are divisible and therefore, affordable investments are made by all the participants.

(d) **Absence of Transaction Costs:** There are no transaction costs. Participants can buy and sell securities with ease and without much cost.

(e) **No Tax Difference:** Ideally, there are no taxes. There should not be any tax distortions; one set of investors should not be favoured over others.

A capital market which is otherwise reasonably efficient will have imperfection; to the extent it does not satisfy the conditions for the perfect capital market. There are three significant imperfections that may be found in different degrees.

- **Tax asymmetries:** Most economies have varieties of taxes and tax incentives which cause tax asymmetries. Tax asymmetries make security transactions more beneficial to some. A number of financial transactions may create additional wealth for some because of tax differences.
- **Information asymmetries:** Most financial information is published and is publicly available. But, sometimes, certain persons may have superior information than others. These persons may earn abnormal returns for some time in certain economies; the quality of disclosure of information is low. All information is not easily and timely available and it involves cost. Certain kinds of information provide signals to the market participants. In an efficient capital market, all information is speedily incorporated in the prices.
- **Transaction costs:** Transaction costs do not affect prices. But they can cause one transaction to be more profitable than the other. Transaction costs of two similar financial transactions may be different. Thus, investors would prefer one transaction over the other. Similarly, transaction costs of two persons to a transaction may be different.

12.4 ALTERNATIVE EFFICIENT MARKET HYPOTHESIS

Most of the early works related to efficient capital markets were based on the random walk hypothesis, which contended that changes in stock prices occurred randomly.

This early academic work contained extensive empirical analysis without much theory behind. An article by Fama attempted to formalize the theory and organize the growing empirical evidence. Fama presented the efficient market theory in terms of a fair game model, contending that investors can be confident that a current market price fully reflects all available information about a security and the expected return based upon this price is consistent with its risk. In his original article, Fama divided the overall *efficient market hypothesis* (EMH) and the empirical tests of the hypothesis into three sub-hypotheses depending on the information set involved:

(1) weak-form EMH,
(2) semi-strong-form EMH, and
(3) strong-form EMH

The **weak-form EMH** assumes that current stock prices fully reflect all security market information, including the historical sequence of prices, rates of return, trading volume data, and other market-generated information, such as odd-lot transactions, block trades, and transactions by exchange specialists. Because it assumes that current market prices already reflect all past returns and any other security market information, this hypothesis implies that past rates of return and other historical market data should have no relationship with future rates of return (that is, rates of return should be independent). Therefore, this hypothesis contends that you should gain little from using any trading rule that decides whether to buy or sell a security based on past rates of return or any other past market data.

The **semi strong-form EMH** asserts that security prices adjust rapidly to the release of all public information, that is, current security prices fully reflect all public information. The semi-strong hypothesis encompasses the weak-form hypothesis, because all the market information considered by the weak-form hypothesis, such as stock prices, rates of return, and trading volume, is public information.

Public information also includes all non-market information, such as earnings and dividend announcements, price-to-earnings (P/E) ratios, dividend-yield (D/P) ratios, market price to book value (CMP/BV) ratios, stock splits, bonus issues, takeovers, mergers, news about the economy, and of course political news. This hypothesis implies that investors who base their decisions on any important new information after it is made public should not derive above-average risk-adjusted profits from their transactions, considering the cost of trading because the security price already reflects all such new public information.

The **strong-form EMH** contends that stock prices fully reflect all information from public and private sources. This means that no group of investors has monopolistic process to information relevant to the formation of prices. Therefore, this hypothesis contends that no group of investors should be able to consistently derive above-average risk-adjusted rates of return (i.e., no one can consistently earn a profit higher than what could be earned by a naïve buyer and hold strategy by short-term trading).

The market price generally reflects all available information and the most ignorant investor buying at current prices gets the benefit of everyone else's thinking.

The strong-form EMH encompasses both the weak form and the semi-strong form EMH. Further, the strong-form EMH extends the assumption of efficient markets, in which all information is cost-free and available to everyone at the same time. However, strong form of EMH is not found to be quite acceptable. A few cases of monopolistic profit making are found which violate this hypothesis (e.g., specialists on the stock exchanges and insider trading).

Market hypothesis can be discussed through five major sections as follows:

1. The first section discusses why we should expect capital markets to be efficient and the factors that contribute to an efficient market where the prices of securities reflect available information. The efficient market hypothesis has been divided into three sub-hypotheses to facilitate testing.
2. The second section describes these three sub-hypotheses and the implications of each of them.
3. The third section is the largest section because it contains a discussion of the results of numerous studies. This review of the research reveals that a large body of evidence supports the EMH, but a growing number of other studies do not support the hypothesis.
4. In the fourth section, we discuss the concept of behavioural finance, the studies that have been done in this area related to efficient markets, and the conclusions as they relate to the EMH.
5. The final section discusses what these results imply for an investor who uses either technical analysis or fundamental analysis or what they mean for a portfolio manager who has access to superior or inferior analysis. We conclude with a brief discussion of the evidence of markets in foreign countries.

Efficient Frontier: Risk-Free and Risky Lending and Borrowing

We understand how the risk and return of investments may be characterized by measures of central tendency and measures of variation, i.e., mean and standard deviation. In fact, statistics are the foundations of modern finance, and virtually all the financial innovations of the past thirty (or so) years, broadly termed "*Modern Portfolio Theory*," have been based upon statistical models. Because of this, it is useful to review what statistics is, and how it relates to the investment problem.

For instance, the *average* is a single number that summarizes the typical "location" of a set of numbers. Statistics boil down a lot of information to a few useful numbers and as such, they ignore a great deal. Before the advent of modern portfolio theory, the decision about whether to include a security in a portfolio was based principally upon fundamental analysis of the firm, its financial statements and its dividend policy.

Finance professor, Harry Markowitz began a revolution by suggesting that the value of a security to an investor might best be evaluated by its mean, its standard deviation, and its correlation to other securities in the portfolio. This audacious suggestion amounted to ignoring a lot of information about the firm, its earnings, its dividend policy, its capital structure, its market, its competitors and calculating a few simple statistics. We shall now describe and follow Markowitz's study and see where the technology of modern portfolio theory takes us.

Risk and Return of Securities

Markowitz's great insight was that relevant information about securities could be summarized by three measures: the *mean return* (taken as arithmetic mean), *the standard deviation* and the *correlation with other assets' returns*. The mean and the standard deviation can be used to plot the relative risk and return of any selection of securities.

Markowitz and the First Efficient Frontier

The first efficient frontier was created by Harry Markowitz, using a handful of stocks from the New York Stock Exchange. Markowitz was interested in the effects of combining risky assets with a risk-free asset: cash. The state-of-art portfolio selection technology has some basic features to remember:

- A minimum variance portfolio exists.
- A maximum return portfolio is composed of a single asset.
- There are some critical points at which the set of assets used in the frontier changes, i.e., an asset drops out or comes in at these points.
- There are no assets to the northwest of the frontier. This is why it is called a frontier. It is the edge of feasible combination of risk and return.

The Efficient Frontier with the Risk-Free Asset

T-Bills are often taken to be risk-free assets, and their return is indicated as *Rf*, the risk-free rate. Once you allow the risk-free asset to be combined with a portfolio, the efficient frontier can change. Since it is risk-free, it has no correlation with other securities. Thus, it provides no diversification, per se. It does provide an opportunity to have a low-risk portfolio, however.

The Markowitz model was a brilliant innovation in the science of portfolio selection. With almost a disarming sleigh-of-hand, Markowitz showed that all the information needed to choose the best portfolio for any given level of risk is contained in three simple statistics: *mean, standard deviation* and *correlation*. It suddenly appeared that you didn't even need any fundamental information about the firm. The model required no information about dividend policy, earnings, market share, strategy, and quality of management – nothing about the myriad of things with which Wall Street analysts concern themselves! In short, Harry Markowitz fundamentally altered how investment decisions were made. Virtually, every major portfolio manager today consults an optimization programme. They may not follow its recommendations exactly, but they use it to evaluate basic risk and return tradeoffs.

Why doesn't everyone use the Markowitz model to solve his or her investment problems? The answer again lies in statistics. The historical mean return may be a poor estimate of the future mean return. As one increases the number of securities, one increases the number of correlations that one must estimate – and one must estimate them correctly to obtain the right answer. In fact, with more than 1500 stocks on NYSE, one is certain to find correlations that are widely inaccurate. Unfortunately, the model does not deal well with inaccurate inputs. That is why it is best applied to allocation decisions across asset classes, for which the number of correlations is low, and the summary statistics are well estimated.

12.5 BENEFITS OF AN EFFICIENT MARKET (INVESTOR'S UTILITY)

So far, arbitrageurs sound like vultures waiting to swoop in for the kill. They take risks to exploit new information at the expense of the less informed. The costs seem to be rewarding opportunism at the expense of other investors. Are there any benefits of having a market operate efficiently? Arguments in favour of efficient capital markets are:

(1) The market price will not stray too far from the true economic price if you allow arbitrageurs to exploit deviations. This will avoid sudden, nasty crashes in the future.

(2) An efficient market increases liquidity, because people believe that price incorporates all public information, and thus they are less concerned about paying way too much. Is the market for television sets efficient as the market for stocks? A lot less comparison-shopping would be needed.

(3) Arbitrageurs provide liquidity to investors who need to sell or buy securities for purposes other than "betting" on changes in expected returns.

Currently, China is seeking to limit access to global financial information in Shanghai (site of its major stock exchange). The government wishes to keep certain kinds of information (secret) from market participants. Is this desirable? Will this be possible?

12.6 EVIDENCE FOR MARKET EFFICIENCY

A simple test for *Strong Form Efficiency* is based upon price changes close to an event. Acts of nature may move prices, but if private information release does not, then we know that the information is already in the stock price. For example, consider a merger between two firms. Normally, a merger or an acquisition is known as an "inner circle" of lawyers, investment bankers and firm managers before public release of the information. When these insiders violate the law by trading on this private information, they may make money.

Unfortunately, stock prices typically move up before a merger, indicating that someone is acting dishonestly. An early move indicates that the market has a tendency towards strong-form efficiency, i.e., even private information is incorporated into prices. However, the public announcement of a merger is typically met with a large price response, suggesting that the market is not strong-form efficient. Leakage, even if illegal, does occur, but it is not fully impounded in stock price.

Evidence Based on Event Studies

❖ **Ball & Brown's Study on Earnings Announcements**

- 261 companies categorized as earnings increased or decreased with respect to previous year.
- Throughout the preceding twelve months of the announcements of earnings, the prices of shares moved in the same direction as that of the subsequent change of earnings.
- As much as 85 to 90% of the price movement was completed by the announcing date indicating that the market was a good forecaster of earnings.

❖ **Fama et al. Study of Stock Splits**

- Adjustment of share prices to reflect the potentially favourable results appeared to be sufficiently complete around the announcement date.

❖ **Dann, Mayers and Raab's Study on Large Block Trading**

- Block transactions did have an effect on price but to earn a return sufficient to cover transaction costs, investors have to react within five minutes of the event.

❖ **Peter Lynch: Beating the Street**

- Here's a tip from the prospectors of year-end anomalies.
- Act quickly.
- It doesn't take long for bargain hunters to find bargains in the stock market these days.
- By the time they're finished buying, the stocks aren't bargains anymore.

Conclusion: The market is not fooled by changes in reported earnings if they are not associated with corresponding changes in the underlying economic conditions.

12.7 IS THE STOCK MARKET SEMI-STRONG FORM EFFICIENT?

The most obvious indication that the market is not always and everywhere semi-strong form efficient is that money managers frequently use public information to take positions in stocks. While there is no evidence that they beat the market on a risk-adjusted basis, it is hard to believe that an entire industry of information production and analysis is for naught. It seems likely that there is value to publicly available information. However, there are probably degrees to which information really is public knowledge. What is surprising is that recent studies have shown some evidence that excess returns can be made by trading upon very sensitive inside information which is not generally available to public at large.

These tests usually take the form of 'back-testing' trading strategies. That is, you play a "what-if" game with past stock prices, and pretend you followed some rule, using information available only at the time of the pretended trade. One common rule that seems to perform well historically is to buy stocks when the dividend yield is high. This apparently has made money in the past, even though the information about which stocks have high yields and which have low yields is widely available. Another rule that generates positive excess returns in back-tests is to buy stocks when the earnings announcement is higher than expected. This seems simple, since current announcements and even forecast are widely available as well.

Does this mean that it is easy to become rich on Wall Street? Hardly! The profitability of these simple trading rules depends upon the liquidity of the stocks involved, and trading costs ("frictions"). Sometimes these costs overweigh the benefits. While many investment managers explain that they pursue a strategy of buying 'value' stocks (such as low P/E firms), a few of these managers have consistently superior track records.

The assumption of semi-strong form efficiency is a good, first approximation for a market with as many sharp traders and with as much publicly available information as in the US equity market.

12.8 IS THE STOCK MARKET WEAK-FORM EFFICIENCY

Weak-form efficiency should be the simplest type of efficiency to prove, and for a time it was widely accepted that the US stock market was at least weak-form efficient. Recall that weak-form efficiency only requires that you cannot make money using past price history of a stock (or index) to make excess profits. Recall the intuition that, if people know the price will rise tomorrow, then they will bid the price up today in order to capture the profit. Researchers have been testing weak-form efficiency using daily information since the 1950s and typically they have found some daily price patterns to make money.

Interestingly, as you increase the horizon of the return, there seems to be evidence of profits through trading. Buying stocks that went down over the last two weeks and shorting those that went up appears to have been profitable. When you really increase the horizons, stock returns look even more predictable. Eugene Fama and Ken French, for instance, found some evidence that 4-year returns tend to revert towards the mean. Unfortunately, this is a difficult rule to trade on with any confidence, since the cycles are so long. In fact, they are as long as the patterns conjectured by Charles Harry Dow some 100 years ago!

Does this all lend credence to the chartists, who look for cryptic patterns in security prices? Perhaps. But, in all likelihood there is no easy money in charting, either. Prices for widely traded securities are pretty close to a random walk, and if they were not, then they would quickly become so, as arbitrageurs move in to buy the stock when it is underpriced, and sell/short it when it is overpriced. But who knows?

The efficient market theory is a good first approximation for characterizing how prices in a liquid and free market react to the disclosure of information. In a word, 'quickly!' If they did not, then the market is lacking the opportunism we have come to expect from an economy with arbitrageurs constantly collecting, processing and trading upon information about individual firms. The fact that information is impounded quickly in stock prices and that windows of investment opportunity are fleeting is one of the best arguments for keeping the markets free of excessive trading costs, and for removing the penalties for honest speculation. Speculators keep market prices close to economic values, and this is good, not bad.

12.9 FORMS OF EFFICIENT MARKET HYPOTHESIS

Tests of market efficiency are essentially tests of whether the three general types of information – past prices, other public information and inside information – can be used to make above average returns on investments. In an efficient market, it is impossible to make above-average return regardless of the information available, unless abnormal risk is taken. Moreover, no investor or group of investors can consistently outperform other investors in such a market. These tests of market efficiency have also been termed *weak-form* (price information), *semi-strong form* (other public information) and *strong-form* (inside information) tests.

Weak-form and the Random Walk

This is the oldest statement of the hypothesis. It holds that present stock market prices reflect all known information with respect to past stock prices, trends, and volumes. Thus it is asserted, such past data cannot be used to predict future stock prices. Thus, if a sequence of closing prices for successive days for XYZ stock has been 43, 44, 45, 46, 47, it may be seen that tomorrow's closing price is more likely to be 48 than 46, but this is not so. The price of 47 fully reflects whatever information is implied by or contained in the price sequence preceding it.

In other words, the stock prices approximate a random walk. (That is why sometimes the terms Random Walk Hypothesis and Efficient Market Hypothesis are used interchangeably.) As time passes, prices wander or walk more or less randomly across the charts. Since the walk is random, knowledge of past price changes does nothing to inform the analyst about whether the price tomorrow, next week, or next year will be higher or lower than today's price.

The weak-form of EMH is summed up in the words of the pseudonymous "Adam Smith", author of *The Money Game*: "prices have no memory, and yesterday has nothing to do with tomorrow." It is an important property of such a market, so that one might do as well flipping a coin as spending time analyzing past price movements or patterns of past price levels.

Thus, if the ***random walk hypothesis*** is empirically confirmed, we may assert that the stock market is weak-form efficient. In this case, any work done by chartists based on past price patterns is worthless.

Random walk theory usually take as their starting point the model of a perfect securities market in which a relatively large number of investors, traders, and speculators compete in an attempt to predict the course of future prices. Moreover, it is further assumed that current information relevant to the decision-making process is readily available to all at little or no cost. If we 'idealize' these conditions and assume that the market is perfectly competitive, then equity prices at any given point of time would reflect the market's evaluation of all current available information that becomes known.

Unless the new information is distributed over time in a non-random fashion – and we have no reason to presume this – price movements in a perfect market will be statistically independent of one another. If stock price changes behave like a series of results obtained by flipping a coin, does this mean that on average stock price changes have zero mean? Not necessarily. Since stocks are risky, we actually expect to find a positive mean change in stock prices.

Testing Market Efficiency

There are several ways to test the EMH. Analysts have devised direct and indirect tests of market efficiency. *Direct tests* assess the success of specific investment strategies or trading rules. An example of direct test would be a test of accuracy of predictions by some specific technical indicator. *Indirect tests* are statistical tests of prices or returns. For example, if prices follow a random walk, the serial correlation of returns should be close to zero.

Establishing a Benchmark

Test of the EMH must usually establish some sort of benchmark. The most common benchmark is the so-called *buy-and-hold portfolio*.

The Time Factor

The time period(s) selected can, of course, always be criticized. A trading rule partisan may respond to a conclusion that the rule did not work by saying, "of course my trading rule didn't work over that period".

Kiss and Tell

Suppose that someone discovered an investment strategy that really worked and made a lot of money. Why would this person want to tell anyone? Suppose an analyst discovers that stocks beginning with the letter K rise on Wednesdays and fall on Fridays. He or she could try to make money writing a book or an investment newsletter describing the strategy, but it would probably generate more money if kept secret.

So, are the Markets Efficient?

Today, it is fashionable to discuss the pending demise of the old EMH. Well, we are not quite yet ready to bury it, but a considerable amount of evidence does contradict it, and more evidence seems to emerge daily. However, a considerable amount of evidence also supports the concept of market efficiency. And even if the markets are not efficient in an academic sense, they may be efficient in a more practical sense. In most parts of the world, the financial markets are well functioning, competitive institutions, in which consistent abnormal profits based on public or historical information are rare.

There is an often-repeated joke about a trader and a finance professor walking down the street. The trader notices a Rs. 500 note lying on the street and stops to pick it up. "Why bother?" the finance professor says, 'if it had really been a Rs. 500 more, someone would already have grabbed it."

In one sense, this joke sums up the debate over market efficiency. An unquestioning acceptance of the EMH, and subsequent rejection of all investment analysis and research as worthless, can leave a lot of money lying on the street for someone else.

12.10 CHALLENGES TO THE EFFICIENT MARKET THEORY

The advocates of the efficient market theory are matched by an equally eloquent opposing camp which argues that the stock market is neither competitive nor efficient. The critics contend that one or more of the following factors cast their shadow over the efficiency and competitiveness of the stock market.

1. **Information Inadequacy:** Information is neither freely available nor rapidly transmitted to all the participants in the stock market. In addition, there is a calculated attempt by many companies to circulate 'misinformation'.

2. **Limited Information Processing Capabilities:** Human information processing capabilities are sharply limited. As Nobel Laureate Herbert Simon observed: "Every human organism lives in an environment which generates millions of new bits of information every second, but the bottleneck of the perceptual apparatus certainly does not admit more than a thousand bits per second and possibly much less."

   Taking a dig at the experts who claim to have superior information processing capabilities, David Dreman said: "Under conditions of anxiety and uncertainty, with a vast interacting information grid the market can become a giant Rorschach test, allowing the investor to see any pattern he wishes ...experts can not only analyze information incorrectly, they can also find relationships that aren't there – a phenomenon called *illusory correlation*."

3. **Irrational Behaviour:** In theory, it is generally assumed that investor rationality will ensure a close correspondence between market prices and intrinsic values. In practice, this may not be true. As J.M. Keynes argued: "In point of fact, all sorts of considerations enter into market valuations which are in no way relevant to the prospective yield." A similar observation was made by L.C. Gupta [Stock Market Liquidity: How Much? For Whom? (Economic and Political Weekly, 1972)]: "Our findings suggest that the market's evaluation processes work haphazardly, almost like a blind man firing a gun .... The market seems to function largely on a *'hit-or-miss'* basis rather than on the basis of informed beliefs about the long-term prospects of individual enterprises."

4. **Monopolistic Influence:** In theory, the market is regarded as highly competitive. No single buyer or seller is supposed to have undue influence over prices. In practice, powerful institutions and big operators wield great influence over the market. The monopolistic power enjoyed by them diminishes the competitiveness of the market.

Investment Implications

We have examined the development of the efficient market theory, the results of empirical work, and the challenges posed by the critics of the efficient market theory. It is time now to hammer out the investment implications of what we have learnt so far. Let us now look at the investment implications of the observations – which are indeed of a mixed nature – made above.

(a) The substantial evidence in favour of the randomness of stock price behaviour suggests that *technical analysis* (which is based on the premise that stock prices follow certain patterns) represents useless market folklore. Burton Malkiel ("A Random Walk Down Wall Street") says:

"Being somewhat incautious, I will climb out on a limb and argue that no technical scheme whatsoever would work for any length of time."

Technical analysts, of course, vehemently dispute such an assertion and argue that the tests employed by the advocates of the random walk theory are too naïve to reveal the kinds of patterns and dependencies technical analysts perceive. Though there may be some merit in this rebuttal, the overwhelming evidence on randomness certainly suggests that technical analysis is of dubious value.

(b) *Routine and conventional fundamental analysis* is not of much help in identifying profitable courses of action, more so when you are looking actively at traded securities. We have a curious paradox here. The efficiency of the market place depends on the presence of numerous investors who make competent efforts to analyze information and take appropriate actions based on their analysis. If they abandon their work, the efficiency of the market would decline. Yet, the efficiency of the marketplace renders their efforts worthless. Though striking, this paradox is not different from the paradox of all efficient, competitive markets.

(c) The *key levers* for earning superior rates of return are:

- Early action on any new development
- Sensitivity to market's imperfections and anomalies
- Use of original, unconventional, and innovative modes of analysis
- Access to inside information and its sensible interpretation
- An independent judgement that is not affected by market psychology

To conclude, let us recall what Williams and Findlay said: "In some respects, we live in ideal times for the modern, well-versed analyst. Markets are not so perfect that all opportunities for better-than average returns are eliminated, and they are not imperfect so as to render impossible the task of making choices."

If we were to summarize:

Leading theories and assumptions on market efficiency have thrown a lot of light on the intricate aspects of USA market that remains worthy of mention here.

These are based on the mathematical models and have served the purpose during the period that they have been tested. However, this has not proved their efficiency for longer periods on empirical evidence.

The market efficiency theory is evolving and it will continue to evolve to meet the emerging developments in the corporate economy of USA. The idea is worthwhile contributions based on mathematical models for the benefit of investors and students at large.

CHAPTER 13 Behavioural Finance

During the classical period, economics had a close link with psychology. For example, Adam Smith wrote an important text describing psychological principles of individual behaviour, *The Theory of Moral Sentiments* and Jeremy Bentham wrote extensively on the psychological underpinnings of utility. Economists began to distance themselves from psychology during the development of neo-classical economics as they sought to reshape the discipline as a natural science, with explanations of economic behaviour deduced from assumptions about the nature of economic agents. The concept of *homo economics* was developed and the psychology of this entity was fundamentally rational. Nevertheless, psychological explanations continued to inform the analysis of many important figures in the development of neo-classical economics such as Francis Edgeworth, Vilfredo Pareto, Irving Fisher and John Maynard Keynes.

Psychology had largely disappeared from economic discussions by the mid-20th century. A number of factors contributed to the resurgence of its use and the development of behavioural economics. Expected utility and discounted utility models began to gain wide acceptance which generated testable hypothesis about decision-making under uncertainty and intertemporal consumption respectively, and a number of observed and repeatable anomalies challenged these hypotheses. Furthermore, during 1960s cognitive psychology began to describe the brain as an information processing device (in contrast to behaviourists' models). Psychologists in this field such as Edwards, Amos Tversky and Daniel Kahneman began to benchmark their cognitive models of decision-making under risk and uncertainty against economic models of rational behaviour.

Perhaps the most important paper in the development of the behavioural finance and economic fields was written by Kahneman and Tversky in 1979. This paper, *Prospect Theory: Decision-making under Risk* used cognitive psychological techniques to explain a number of documented anomalies in rational economic decision-making. Further, milestones in the development of the field include a well attended and diverse conference at the University of Chicago (see Hogarth & Reder, 1987), a special 1997 edition of the respected *Quarterly Journal of Economics* ('In Memory of Amos Tvesky') devoted to the topic of behavioural economics and award of the Noble Prize to Daniel Kahneman in 2002 "for having integrated insights from psychological research into economic science, especially concerning human judgement of decision-making under uncertainty".

Prospect theory is an example of generalized expected utility theory. Although not commonly included in discussions of the field of behavioural economics, generalized expected utility theory is similarly motivated by concerns about the descriptive inaccuracy of expected utility theory.

Behavioural economics has also been applied to problems of intertemporal choice. The most prominent idea is that of hyperbolic discounting, in which a high rate of discount is used between the present and the near future, and a lower rate between the near future and the far future. This pattern of discounting is dynamically inconsistent (or time-inconsistent), and therefore inconsistent with standard models of rational choice, since the rate of discount between time t and $t + 1$ will be low at time $t - 1$, when t is the near future, but high at time t when t is the present $t + 1$ the near future.

13.1 PSYCHOLOGICAL APPROACH

Very often decisions are influenced by behavioural biases in the decision maker, which leads to less than optimal choices being made. It is based on the premise that stock prices are guided by emotion, rather than reason. Stock prices are believed to be influenced by psychological mood. When greed sweeps the market, prices rise to dizzy heights. When fear and despair envelop the market, prices fall to abysmally low levels.

A good process can lead to more considered (and, hopefully, better) decision-making, but would also support stability and confidence in the existence of a "steady hand at the tiller". This should help control the potentially harmful effect of some of the biases that can influence investment decision making. One of the ways to manage the impact of these may be to draw attention to them and discuss their potential impact before important investment decisions are taken.

Investor Preferences

If investor biases are well managed, investor preferences should be respected and reflected in investment strategy, in so far as it is both feasible and sensible (after discussing the various issues).

There are two particular areas of investor preference that have been highlighted by behavioural finance. The first (perhaps not surprisingly) is *loss aversion*, which in behavioural finance fills the role of risk aversion in traditional finance. The second is *mental accounting*, which reflects the way in which the investor assigns sums of money to different actual or notional accounts for different purposes with varying degrees of risk tolerance depending upon the importance of achieving the particular objective. For example, an individual's summer vacation money will be in a different mental account (and probably a different actual account) from pension savings.

(a) Loss aversion

Much less convenient is the widespread evidence that rationally utility models (mathematical) do not reflect how people view the prospect of financial gains or losses. This has been reflected in prospect theory, which is built upon a wide range of experiments showing that people will take quite a large risk to have some chance of avoiding otherwise certain losses, but that they are quick to bank any winnings. The relationship between the disutility and dissatisfaction that comes from gains is captured in the so-called *coefficient of loss aversion*, which across a wide range of experiments has come out with a particular value. This highlights the need for investors to be educated as well as asked the appropriate questions, framed in an appropriate way.

(b) Mental Accounting and Behavioural Portfolio Theory

A division of investments between safety-first accounts or portfolios to meet basic needs and more aggressive "inspirational" accounts to meet more speculative, less critical, or simply more distant objectives is one of the predictions of the mental accounting framework of behavioural finance.

From the champion poker player, to the subsistence farmer, the individual investor in traded options, the central bank foreign exchange reserve manager, to the pension plan, each example will show a natural process of segmentation of risk taking, with separate allocation to different accounts, each with distinctive risk tolerances and time horizons dictated by particular objectives.

This mental accounting helps to discipline future behaviour by highlighting deviations from decisions that have already been taken. Mental accounting helps financial resources to be targeted for different purposes. Each person will have a different risk tolerance for achieving different objectives. Some goals are critical, but others are just nice. And decisions will be influenced by regulations that impinge on taxed and tax-exempt accounts, current-generation resources and trust or other tax-efficient accounts for future generations, and philanthropic accounts.

A more general example of mental accounting is quoted by Meir Statman and Vincent Wood in *Investment Temperament*, when they describe the pattern of responses to the following question in the Fidelity Investments Asset Allocation Planner:

If you could increase your chances of improving your returns by taking more risk, would you:

- Be willing to take a lot more risk with all your money?
- Be willing to take a lot more risk with some of your money?
- Be willing to take a little more risk with all your money?
- Be willing to take a little more risk with some of your money?

Overwhelmingly, the responses indicated a willingness to take either a lot or a little more risk of their money. This indicates a preference to segment or layer risk-taking. This is generally considered to be at odds with the traditional risk-return trade-off commonly presented to investors addressing the performance and risk of the total portfolio, which would presume taking either a little or a lot more risk with all of the money.

Consequently, four of the most prevalent seemingly irrational behaviours that individuals are prone to exhibit are:

First, individuals tend to separate their money into several *mental accounts* depending on the sources, magnitudes and purposes of such money.

Second, individuals exhibit *loss aversion*, which causes their decisions to depend on the context in which the problem is framed, rather than on the net effect of their decisions on their wealth.

Third, individuals are prone to a cognitive bias known as *representativeness*, whereby information that is easily available or has become known recently is given too much importance.

Fourth, people are subject to the *psychological tendencies* of limited self-control and procrastination.

13.2 EVOLUTION OF TRADITIONAL FINANCE AND BEHAVIOURAL FINANCE

In the past few years, steps have been taken towards synthesizing traditional finance with the insights from behavioural finance, but one needs to go further before an integrated approach is agreed upon which combines both the comprehensiveness of "traditional" finance with the more recent insights from behavioural finance.

It is important for investors and their advisors to benefit from the insights of behavioural finance in order to better understand the influences on their own behaviour and preferences. Advice and strategy can then be adapted to accommodate that. This does not provide an excuse for ignoring the fundamental principles of diversification, correlation between different investments or the need to tailor policies to the time horizon of investment objectives. Equally, it would be arrogant to suggest that it is always poor practice for individuals to purchase investment equivalent to lottery tickets, as this may be an efficient way of maximizing the chances of acquiring riches. Furthermore, behavioural finance helps advisors gain a better understanding of why investors' portfolios are structured as they are, how investors are likely to respond to any instance of disappointing performance and the nature of their strong preferences.

Against this background, the first most important step may be to start discussions of investment strategy with an assessment of whether an investor has sufficient wealth to guarantee survival. In other words, does the investor have sufficient resources to hedge against the risk of shortfall from critical objectives by investing in liability or objective-matching government bonds? If the answer is yes, the investor can choose between the objectives, and if so wished, pursue a high-risk strategy to have some chance, however remote, of achieving the least critical objectives.

It is important that we connect to a few tried-and-tested kernels of advice that financial professionals often give. One view is that a better understanding of the relevant psychological factors can only help as counsellors counsel, advisors advise, educators educate and planners plan on behalf of their clients. This may make it possible to move towards the ultimate goal, which is to nudge the client in direction what a well-informed, rational, emotionally neutral individual would opt for.

Behavioural principles come primarily from

- psychology,
- sociology, and
- anthropology.

Other behavioural principles are:

- prospect theory,
- regret and cognitive dissonance,
- anchoring,
- mental compartments,
- overconfidence,
- over- and under-reaction
- representativeness heuristic,
- the disjunction effect,
- gambling behaviour,
- speculation, perceived irrelevance of history,
- magical thinking,
- quasi-magical thinking,
- attention anomalies,
- the availability heuristic,
- culture and social contagion, and
- global culture

The field of modern financial economics assumes that people behave with extreme rationality, but they do not. Furthermore, people's deviations from rationality are often systematic.

Behavioural finance relaxes the traditional assumptions of financial economics by incorporating these observable, systematic, and very humane departures from rationality into standard models of financial markets.

Two common mistakes investors make are:

1. excessive trading, and
2. the tendency to disproportionately hold on to losing investments while selling winners.

It is argued that these systematic biases have their origin in human psychology. The tendency for human beings to be *overconfident* causes the first bias in the investors, and the human desire to avoid *regret* prompts the second.

13.3 INVESTOR BIASES

Economists frequently assume that people will learn from their past mistakes. Psychologists find that learning itself is a tricky process. Many of the *self-deception* biases tend to limit our ability to learn. For instance, we are prone to attribute good outcomes to our skill, and bad outcomes to the luck of the draw. This is *self-attribution* bias. When we suffer such a bias, we are not going to learn from our mistakes, simply because we don't see them as our mistakes.

Taxonomy of Biases

- Conservative bias
- Cognitive dissonance
- Hindsight bias
- Confirmation bias
- Self-attribution bias
- Overconfidence
- Over-optimism
- Illusion of control
- Illusion of knowledge
- Self-deception
- Limits to learning
- Loss aversion/prospect theory
- Cue competition
- Availability bias
- Anchoring/salience
- Categorization
- Framing
- Representativeness
- Heuristic simplification
- Information processing errors
- Regret theory
- Ambiguity aversion
- Self-control
- Hyperbolic discounting
- Mood
- Emotion/affect
- Cascades
- Contagion
- Imitation
- Social biases

The two most common biases are overoptimism and overconfidence.

For instance, when teachers ask a class who will finish in the top half, on average around 80% of the class think they will. Not only are people overly optimistic, but they are overconfident as well. People are surprised more often than they expect to be.

For instance, when you ask people to give a forecast, and provide estimates of 98% confidence intervals, the true answer only lies within the limits around 60-70% of the time! Over-optimism and over-confidence tend to stem from the illusion of knowledge. The illusion of the knowledge is the tendency for people to believe that the accuracy of their forecasts increases with more information.

Daniel Boorstin opined that the greatest obstacles to discovery is not ignorance. It is the illusion of knowledge. The simple truth is that more information is not necessarily better information; it is what you do with it, rather than how much you have that matters.

(i) Self-Attribution Bias: Self-attribution bias occurs when people attribute successful outcomes to their own skills but blame unsuccessful outcomes on bad luck.

(ii) Status Quo Bias: The example also illustrates what Samuelson and Zeckhauser ["Status quo bias in decision making" March, 1988] call a *status quo bias*, a preference for the current state that biases the economist against both buying and selling his wine." Richard Thaler (1992) [Anomalies: The Endowment Effect, Loss Aversion, and Status Quo Bias].

"One implication of loss aversion is that individuals have a strong tendency to remain at *status quo* because the disadvantages of leaving it loom larger than the advantages." Samuelson and Zeckhauser (1988) have demonstrated this effect, which they term *status quo bias*.

(iii) Cognitive Bias: Cognitive psychology is the psychological science that studies cognition, the mental processes that underlie behaviour, including thinking, reasoning, decision-making, and to some extent motivation and emotion. Cognitive psychology covers a broad range of research domains, examining questions about the working of memory, attention, perception, knowledge, representation, reasoning, creativity and problem solving.

(iv) Confirmation Bias: When trying to explain the occurrence of an event, humans have a tendency to seize upon any evidence, which may constitute an explanation. We believe that the subjective and judgement elements of reserving practice lead actuaries to be particularly vulnerable of this. Often they encounter an unexpected result for which it may not be easy to determine the cause – why numbers do not balance, why the best estimate changed so much, why loss ratios have increased – and proceed to brainstorm possible explanations. Humans are often satisfied with the first idea that explains the direction of anomaly, without regard for its feasibility.

(v) Optimism or Confidence Bias: Investors cultivate a belief that they have the ability to outperform the market based on some investing successes. Such winners are more often than not short term in nature and may be outcome of chances rather than skill.

(vi) Familiarity Bias: This bias leads investors to choose what they are comfortable with. Investors holding only a real estate portfolio or a stock portfolio concentrated in shares of a particular company or sector demonstrate this bias. Since other opportunities are avoided (mostly), the portfolio is likely to be underperforming.

(vii) Anchoring: Investors hold on to some information that may no longer be relevant, and make their decisions based on that. New information is labelled as incorrect or irrelevant and ignored in the decision making process. Investors who wait for the 'right price' to sell even when information indicates that the expected price is no longer appropriate, exhibit this bias.

(viii) Loss Aversion: The fear of losses leads to inaction. Studies show that the pain or loss is twice as strong as pleasure they felt at the gain of a similar magnitude. Investors prefer to do nothing despite information and analysis favouring a particular action that in the mind of the investor may lead to a loss.

(ix) Herd Mentality: This bias is an outcome of uncertainty and a belief that others may have better information, which leads investors to follow the investment choices that others make. Small investors keep watching other participants for confirmation and then end up entering when the market is overheated and poised for correction.

(x) Recency Bias: The impact of recent events on decision making can be very strong. This applies equally to positive and negative experiences. Investors tend to extrapolate the event into the future and expect a repeat. The recent experience overrides analysis in decision making.

(xi) Choice Paralysis:

The availability of too many options for investment can lead to a situation of not wanting to evaluate and make the decision. Too much information also leads to a similar outcome on taking action.

Sometimes actuaries tend to seize on a justification, and a few minutes later realize that the explanation actually indicates the opposite; the explanation then gets rejected and the search continues for another reason. Meanwhile, existence of the first idea should represent even greater concern. The confirmation bias is not only inaccurate, but also intellectually dishonest.

13.4 THREE MAIN THEMES OF BEHAVIOURAL FINANCE

The proponents of behavioural finance argue that a few psychological phenomena pervade the entire landscape of finance. Mental and emotional factors identified by Professor Shefrin as leading investors to make mistakes include the phenomena that are usually divided into three themes:

(a) Heuristic-driven Bias
(b) Frame dependence
(c) Inefficient markets

Heuristic-driven Biases

1. **Availability bias:** The tendency to have decisions on the most readily available information.
2. **Representativeness:** Projecting from stereotypes. It includes "the illusion of validity."
3. **Overconfidence:** Assuming more knowledge than one actually has. It includes "excessive optimism", "the illusion of control" and anchoring-and-adjustment. Too conservative extrapolation from current data and too slow readjustment of expectations based on changes. It also includes "hindsight bias", aversion to ambiguity and preference for the familiar over the unfamiliar.
4. **Self-attribution bias:** Ascribing successful outcomes to one's skill, but blaming failures on bad luck.

Frame Dependence

Loss aversion: The fact that losses are more painful than gains are pleasurable leads to a reluctance to realize losses.

- ❖ **Concurrent decisions:** Focusing on losses rather than netting gains and losses.
- ❖ **Hedonic editing:** Preferences for frames that obscure losses, e.g., a slim possibility of no loss often overweigh the taking of a sure but small loss.
- ❖ **Regret:** Focus on what might have been if not for one's past mistakes.
- ❖ **Money Illusion:** Valuing dollar amounts without regard to reduced value from inflation.

Other judgemental biases include:

- ❖ **Association Bias,** in which an individual tries to repeat past success by choosing strategies more related to the past situation than to the current set of circumstances.
- ❖ **Escalation Phenomena,** in which an individual finds it difficult to abandon a course of action and ignores feedback that the process is failing.
- ❖ **Self-serving Bias,** in which individuals take credit for successes which occur, but deny responsibilities for failures by blaming external issues or circumstances out of their control.

Promise of Behavioural Finance

Behavioural finance promises to make economic models better at explaining systematic (non-idiosyncratic) investor decisions, taking into consideration their emotions and errors and how these influence decision-making. Behavioural finance is not a branch of standard finance; it is replacement, offering a better model of humanity. It creates a long-term advantage by understanding the role of investor psychology. Human flaws pointed out by the analysis of investor psychology are: consistent and predictable, and that they offer investment opportunities.

UNIT-III

14

Analysis of Fixed Income Avenues

CHAPTER

Typically, the fixed income avenues (fixed deposits with banks and companies, debentures, provident funds, PPF, senior citizen post office schemes, and so on) represent a significant portion of individual financial portfolio. Fixed income avenues carry varying interest rates, maturities, and tax benefits associated with them. There are three most important aspects about fixed income avenues that need to be analysed, namely:

- basic concepts of time value of money;
- valuation of bonds; and
- how tax-sheltered fixed investment avenues should be analysed.

14.1 TIME VALUE OF MONEY

Money has time value. A rupee today is more valuable than a rupee a year hence. The reasons are:

(a) Individuals, in general, prefer current consumption to future consumption.

(b) Capital can be employed productively to generate positive returns. An investment of one rupee today would grow to $(1 + r)$ a year hence (r being the rate of return earned on investment).

(c) In an inflationary period, a rupee today represents greater real purchasing power than a rupee a year hence.

Financial investments typically involve cash flows occurring at different points of time over a period of several years. For evaluating such cash flows, an explicit consideration of the time value of money is required.

Compounding

Suppose an investor invests Rs. 10,000 today with a simple interest of 10 per cent. The amount would grow after three years to: Rs. 10,000 (1 + 3(0.10) = 10,000 + 3000 (13,000).

What happens if the investor earns compounded interest of 10 per cent per year? Compound interest means 'earning interest on interest'. Therefore, the amount will grow as:

$Cn = Co (1 + r)^n$
$= 10,000 (1 + 0.10)^3$
$= 13,310$

where Cn is the future value n years hence, Co is the amount invested today, *r* is the annual interest rate, and *n* is the period of investment.

Discounting

To translate a future cash flow into its present value, we resort to discounting, which is simply the inverse of compounding. Since the compounding factor is: $(1 + r)^n$, the discounting factor, being the inverse of it, is:

$$1/(1 + r)^n$$

Example: What is the present value of Rs. 1000 receivable 6 years hence if the discount rate is 10 per cent?

= Rs. 1,000 * 1/(1.10) ^6
= Rs. 1,000 (DF 10%, 6 years)
= Rs. 1,000 (0.565)
= Rs. 565

Private Placement

- Popular method of raising debt
- Minimum regulatory restrictions, therefore relatively fast process
- Information Memorandum (IM) need not be filed
- Green shoe option
- No minimum subscription rule
- Funds available fast
- Almost entirely Mumbai-based. Small contributions from Delhi, Kolkata and Chennai
- OTC marked through telephonic price discovery
- Investment grade and rating; listing on stock exchange
- Up to 49 investors; issued in Demat form
- Standard denomination – Rs. 1 million
- Primarily, a wholesale market with miniscule retail participation
- Participants in secondary markets: banks, mutual funds, financial institutions, primary dealers, insurance companies, private corporates, provident and pension funds, and so on.

Non-Government Bonds

- ❖ Prices quoted in terms of yields
- ❖ Active in view of mutual funds participation
- ❖ Compressing spreads have forced banks to participate

- ❖ Active primary dealers
- ❖ Settlement through demat $T + 1$
- ❖ Settlement risk shifted to seller

Bonds and debt instruments are an important financial asset class for almost every investor. The concepts of return and risk, as the determinants of value, are fundamental and valid to the valuation of all financial and physical assets. The concept of present value makes it clear to understand why some bonds are priced higher than others.

14.2 FEATURES OF A BOND

A *bond* is a long-term debt instrument or security. Bonds issued by the government generally do not have any risk of default. Bonds of the public sector companies in India are generally secured, but they are not free from the risk of default. The private sector companies also issue bonds, know as *debentures* in India. In the case of a bond or debenture, the rate of interest is generally fixed and known to investors. The principal of a redeemable bond is payable after a specified period, called *maturity period*.

The main features of a bond or debenture are as follows:

- **Face Value:** Face value is also called *par value*. A bond or debenture is generally issued at par with a value of Rs. 100 or Rs. 1000 for each, and interest is paid on face value.
- **Interest Rate:** Interest rate, also known as *'coupon rate'* is fixed. Interest paid on a bond/debenture is tax deductible for the issuer, while interest received by an investor is subject to income-tax, and tax rate is levied as per the prevailing rules.
- **Redemption Value:** The value that a bondholder will get on maturity is called redemption, or *maturity value*. A bond may be redeemed at par or at a premium (more than par value) or at a discount (less than par value).
- **Market Value:** A bond may be traded on a stock exchange. The price at which it is currently sold or bought is called the market value. Market value may be different from par value or redemption value.

Other Features of Bonds

Indenture: The indenture is a long, complicated legal instrument containing the restrictions, pledges and promises of the contract. Bond indenture involves three parties. The first party is the debtor corporation that borrows the money, promises to pay interest, and promises to repay the principal borrowed.

Maturities: Maturities vary widely. Bonds are usually grouped by their maturity classes.

Interest Payments: Bond interest is usually paid semi-annually, though annual payments are also popular. The method of payment depends upon whether the bond is a coupon (*bearer*) or a registered bond.

Call Feature: Most modern corporate bonds are callable at the direction of the issuer. This gives the issuing company the right to recall a bond before it reaches maturity.

Reasons for Issuing Bonds

(a) **To reduce the cost of capital:** Bonds are the cheapest source of financing.

(b) **To widen the sources of funds:** By issuing bonds, the corporation can attract fund from individual investors and especially from those investing institutions that are reluctant or not permitted to purchase equity shares.

(c) **To preserve control:** An increase in debt does not diminish the voting power of present owners, since bonds ordinarily carry no voting rights.

(d) **To gain the benefit of leverage:** The presence of debt and/or preference shares in the company's financial structure means that it is using financial leverage. When financial leverage is used, changes in earnings before interest and tax (EBIT) translate into the larger changes in earnings per share.

(e) **To effect tax savings:** Unlike dividends on taxes, the interest on bond is deductible in figuring up corporate income for tax purposes. Hence, the EPS increases if the financing is through bonds rather than with preference or equity shares.

14.3 TYPES OF BONDS

Convertible and Non-Convertible Bonds: Convertible bonds can be one of the finest holdings for the investor looking for both appreciation of investment and income of bond. A convertible bond is a cross between a bond and a stock. The holder can at his will, convert the bond into a predetermined number of shares of common stock at a predetermined price.

Whereas, non-convertible bonds cannot be converted into equity, in fact no option is available for investors. It usually gets redeemed after its specified term and money is returned to the investors.

Collateral Trust Bonds: Instead of being secured by a pledge of tangible property, as are mortgage bonds, collateral trust issues are secured by a pledge of intangibles, usually in the form of stocks and bonds of corporation.

Income Bonds: Income bonds are bonds on which the payment of interest is mandatory only to the extent of current earnings.

Redeemable and Irredeemable Bonds: A redeemable debenture is a bond, which has been issued for a certain period on the expiry of which its holder will be repaid the amount thereof, with or without premium.

A bond without the aforesaid redemption period is termed an irredeemable debenture. These may be repaid either in the event of the winding-up of the company or the happening of certain specified uncertain or contingent events.

Participating Bonds: Companies with poor credit positions issue participating bonds. These have a guaranteed rate of interest, but may also participate in the earnings up to an additional specified percentage.

Sinking Fund Bonds: Sinking fund bonds arise when the company decides to retire its bond issue systematically by setting aside a certain amount each year for the purpose. The payment, usually fixed annual amount or percentage instalment, is made to the sinking fund agent who is usually the trustee.

Serial Bonds: Like sinking fund bonds, serial bonds are not special types of bonds but just names given to describe the method of repayment. Thus, any bond can be a serial bond by merely specifying it in the indenture.

Mortgage or Secured Bonds: The term mortgage generally refers to a lien on real property or buildings. Mortgage bonds may be open-end, close-end, and limited open-end. An open-end mortgage means that a corporation under the mortgage may issue additional bonds. *But the open-end* mortgage indenture *usually provides* that the corporation *can issue more* bonds only if *the earnings* or additional *security obtained* by selling *the new securities* which *meet certain tests* of earnings *and asset coverage.*

Pure Discount Bonds: They do not carry an explicit rate of interest. They provide for the payment of a lump sum amount at a future date in exchange for the current price of the bonds. The difference between the face value of the bond and its purchase price gives the return or YTM to the investor.

Pure discount bonds are also called **deep-discount bonds** or **zero interest (coupon) bonds.** It is quite simple to find the value of a pure discount bond as it involves one single payment (face value) at maturity. The market interest rate is used as the discount rate. The present value of this amount is the bond value.

Consider the IDBI bond with a face value of Rs. 5,00,000 with a maturity of 30 years. Suppose the current market yield on similar bonds is 9 per cent. The value of the IDBI pure discount bond today would be as:

$$Bo = \frac{5,00,000}{(1.09)^\wedge 30} = \frac{5,00,000}{13.2677} = \text{Rs. } 37,685.51$$

Perpetual Bonds: Also called *consols,* they have an indefinite life and therefore, have no maturity value. These types of bonds are rarely found in practice. After the Napoleonic War, England issued these types of bonds to pay off many smaller issues that had been floated in prior years to pay for the war.

Suppose that a 10 per cent, Rs. 1000 bond will pay Rs. 100 annual interest into perpetuity. What would be its value if the market yield or interest rate were 15 per cent? The value of the bond is determined as under:

$$Bo = \frac{INT}{kd} = \frac{100}{0.15} = \text{Rs. } 667$$

The following table gives the value of a perpetual bond paying annual interest of Rs. 100 at different discount (market interest) rates.

Table 14.1

Discount Rate (%)	Value of Bond (Rs.)
5	2,000
10	1,000
15	667
20	500
25	400
30	333

14.4 VALUE OF A BOND

To understand how a bond may be valued, let us consider a debenture of Rs. 100 face value that carries an interest rate of 14 per cent and which is redeemable after 5 years, at a premium of 5 per cent. If an investor owns this debenture, he/she will enjoy the following benefits:

End of year	Interest income (Rs.)	Principal repayment (Rs.)
1	14	
2	14	
3	14	
4	14	
5	14	105

If required rate of return of investor is 14 per cent from this debenture, the present value will be:

Rs. 14 (PVAF 16%, 5 years) + Rs. 105 (DF 16%, 5 years)
= Rs. 14 (3.274) + Rs. 105 (0.476)
= Rs. 45.8 + Rs. 50.0
= Rs. 95.8

In general terms, the value of a bond may be expressed as follows:

$$V = I\ (\text{PVAF } k, n) + F(DF\ k, n)$$

Value of a bond = (Annual interest payable) (Present value annuity factor) + (Redemption value) (Discount factor)

Bond Price Theorems

Based on the above bond valuation model, the following results may be easily established:

1. When the required rate of return is:
   (a) lesser than the coupon rate, the value of the bond is greater than its par value;

(b) equal to the coupon rate, the value of the bond is equal to its par value; and

(c) greater than its coupon rate, the value of the bond is lesser than its par value.

2. As the maturity date of a bond approaches, the value of the bond converges to its par value.
3. The longer the maturity of a bond, the greater does its price change in response to a given change in the interest rate.

Macro Impact on Bond Pricing

- General economic activity/conditions
- Monetary and exchange rate policy
    - Money supply
    - Tools – CRR, SLR, Bank rate, LAF, OMO, speeches, side comments
    - Other internal/external developments
- Fiscal policy
    - Taxation
    - Government spending
    - Fiscal deficit
    - Government borrowing

Bond Pricing

- Returns are a combination of coupon accruals and capital gain/loss due to price changes.
- Price is equal to sum of present values of expected cash flows discounted at the appropriate yield.
- Price and yield are inversely functional.
- Sovereign yield curve – basis of pricing; bonds are priced at a spread over G-Sec yield.
- Spreads reflect the credit risk on the bond; they are largely a function of credit rating.
- The spreads change on a daily basis in the secondary market; they also depend on the supply of paper in the market.
- Within the same category different credits are priced differently.
- Coupon rate, yield and price
    - Coupon rate > required yield < > price > par (premium bond)
    - Coupon rate < required yield < > price < par (discount bond)
    - Coupon rate = required yield < > price = par
- Bond price and time
    - With no change in required yield, price of premium bond falls to par as time approaches maturity

  - With no change in required yield, price of discount bond rises to par as time approaches maturity
- Price yield relationship
  - Bow shaped downward slopping curve
  - Convex to the origin

Bond Price Volatility

Properties:

- Although prices of all bonds move in the opposite direction from the change in yield, the percentage price change is not the same for all bonds.
- For very small changes in yield, percentage price change for a given bond is roughly the same, whether the yield increases or decreases.
- For large changes in yield, percentage change is not the same for an increase in yield as it is for decrease in yield.
- For a given large change in yield, the percentage price increase is greater than the percentage price decrease.

Bond Valuation

Debt securities issued by governments and quasi-government organizations, and private business firms are fixed income securities. Bonds and debentures are the most common examples.

The intrinsic value of bond or debenture is equal to the present value of its expected cash flows. The coupon interest payments, and the principal repayment are known and the present value is determined by discounting these future payments from the issuer at an appropriate discount rate or market yield.

14.5 VALUATION PROCESS

Implicit in all rational buy-sell transactions relating to claims, goods, and services is the question: Is it good or real? The investor surrenders a cost (time of money) in exchange for promised benefits. Both cost and benefits have to face uncertainty since nothing appears certain in this world, except death and taxes. The basic valuation process, therefore, is a constant exercise in rationality with cost, benefits and uncertainty as important variables.

The question of the valuation process following a sequence has been widely examined in the literature and the industry performance, in turn, is linked to performance of the economy and the market in general.

The General Valuation Framework

Most investors look at price movements in security markets. They perceive opportunity of capital gains in movements. All wish that they could successfully predict movements and ensure their gains. A few, however, recognize that value determines both price and change randomly. It would be useful for an investor to be aware of this process. In the following section we will outline the evaluation of model, the relationship of value with price, and strategies of active and passive, finally the dynamic valuation model.

The Basic Valuation Model

Value of the security is a fundamental variable and depends on its promised return, risk and the discount rate. We can recall the basic understanding of present value concept with the mention of fundamental factors like sum and discount rate. In fact, the basic valuation model is none other than the present value procedure. Given an adjusted discounted rate and the future expected earnings flow of a security in the form of interest, dividend, earnings or cash flow, one can always determine the present value as follows:

$$PV = \frac{CF1}{1+r} + \frac{CF2}{(1+r)^{\wedge}2} + \frac{CF3}{(1+r)^{\wedge}3} + \ldots + \frac{CFn}{(1+r)^{\wedge}n}$$

PV = Present value

CF = Cash flow of interest or dividend, or earnings per time period up to n number of periods.

r = Risk-adjusted discount rate (generally the interest rate)

Expressed in the above manner, the model looks simple. But practical difficulties make the use of model complicated. For instance, it may be quite in the fitness of this that a single value is generated. Whosoever does the valuation job (a professional analyst or an intelligent investor); the safest course would be to work on the *margin of error*. The analyst will realize that market operations would become tedious with a range of values. Secondly, return risk and value would tend to change over time. Thus, security prices may rise or fall with buying and selling pressures respectively (assuming supply of securities does not change) and this may affect capital gains and hence returns expected.

Consequently, estimates of future income will have to be revised and values reworked. Similarly, the entire risk of the security may change over time. The firm may over borrow (and face operating risk) or engage in a venture (and face operating risk). An increase in risks would raise the discount rate and lower the value. It would seem to be a continuous exercise. Every new information will affect values and the buying and selling pressures, which keep prices in a continuous motion, and would drive them continuously closer to new values.

Value-Price Relationship

Investment strategies are known to be *passive* or *active*. Following this, investors and investment managers can also be broadly grouped into 'passive' and 'active' categories. One should note that buying and selling pressures predominantly originate with active investors. They follow certain rules of the game, which are:

Rule 1: Buy when value is more than price. This underlines the fact that securities are underpriced and it is deemed to be a bargain to buy while low and sell when prices move up towards value.

Rule 2: Sell when value is less than price. In a situation like this, securities would be overpriced and it would be advantageous to sell them now and avoid a loss when price later moves down to the level of the value.

Rule 3: Don't trade when value is equal to price. This is a state when the market price is in 'equilibrium' and is not expected to change.

14.6 VALUATION OF FIXED INCOME SECURITIES

A *debenture* is a legal document containing an acknowledgement of indebtedness by a company. It contains a promise to pay a stated rate of interest for a defined period and then to repay the principal at the maturity. In short, a debenture is a formal legal evidence of debt and is termed the *senior* (basic/committed) *security* of a company.

Unlike equity holders, the bond investor does not share in the growth of a company to any appreciable extent. Thus, although serious losses can accrue to bond holders if a company suffers financial reverses, they cannot profit to any significant degree by a spectacular improvement in the company's position. It is a case of heads they lose, and tails they cannot win. Therefore, their primary role in an investment portfolio is to provide continuity of income under all reasonably conceivable economic conditions.

Estimating Returns on Fixed Income Securities

Sovereign yield curve

- Government of India is sovereign borrower
- No possibility of default, therefore highest rating
- Sovereign risk is the benchmark for pricing

Several measures of returns on bonds are available. They are coupon rate, current yield and the yield to maturity. The *coupon rate* is specified at the time of issue and is all too obvious. The other two measures are here discussed

Current Yield

Current yield is the annual interest divided by the bond's current value. Current yield considers only the annual interest, and does not account for the capital gain or loss. Thus, bond's overall rate of return over a 5-year period would generally be more than the current yield. However, the current bond's price is less than its maturity value; its overall rate of return would be less than the current yield.

$$\textbf{Current yield} = \frac{\text{Stated (coupon) interest per year}}{\text{Current market price}}$$

Example: 15% Rs. 200 debenture is currently selling for Rs. 220, the annual current yield would be:

$$\frac{\text{Rs. } 30}{\text{Rs. } 220} = 13.64\%$$

Notice that the 15% debenture is currently selling for Rs. 220 because interest rates have subsequently declined and debenture/bond prices move inversely with interest rates. The current yield has declined to 13.64%. The coupon rate of 15% reflects this.

Current yield is a superior measure than coupon rate because it is based on the current market price. However, it does not account for the difference between the purchase price of the bond/debenture and its maturity value.

Yield-to-Maturity (YTM)

This is the most widely used measure of return on fixed income securities. It may be defined as the income (promised) that the compounded rate of return will receive from a bond purchased at the current market values and held to maturity. Compounding YTM involves equating the current market price of bond with the discount value of future interest payments and the terminal principal repayment. Thus, YTM equates two values, i.e., current value of the market price and the present value of future payments including the principal repayment. YTM is the measure of a bond's rate of return that considers both the interest income and any capital gain or loss.

Example: Assume that an investor purchased a 15% Rs. 500 fully secured non-convertible debenture at par five years ago. The current market price of the debenture is Rs. 400, which implies increase in market interest rates subsidy to the issue of the security. Five years remain to maturity and the debenture is repaid at par. What is required in this case is a value of YTM, which equates Rs. 400 with the sum of present value of Rs. 75 per year for 5 years and of Rs. 500 receivable at the end of the fifth year.

Solution: Several values of YTM can be tried till the equating value emerges. Trials can be started with the current rate and the next trial rate increased if the present value of the preceding trial exceeds the current market and vice versa. Thus, trying at 15%, the following present value of the right hand side cash flows is estimated.

PV15% = Rs. 75 per annum * PVIF 5 years 15% + Rs. 500 * PVIF 15% 5 years
= Rs. 75 * 3.3522 + Rs. 500 * .4972 = Rs. 251.42 + 248.60
= Rs. 500.08

Since the PV of Rs. 500.08 exceeds Rs. 400, a higher discount rate should be tried

PV20% = Rs. 75 * 2.9906 + Rs. 500 * .8333
= Rs. 224.295 + Rs. 200.95
= Rs. 425.245

Even the second trial has failed to equate the two values. Hence, one can go over to the third trial, say,

$$\begin{aligned} PV24\% &= \text{Rs. } 75 * 2.7454 + \text{Rs. } 500 * .3411 \\ &= \text{Rs. } 205.91 + \text{Rs. } 170.55 \\ &= \text{Rs. } 376.46 \end{aligned}$$

The third trial has lowered the present value to Rs. 376.46, which is less than Rs. 400. Hence, the required rate must lie between 20% and 24%. The estimate can be obtained by interpolating, thus:

$$YTM = \frac{20\% + 425.245 - 400.00 * (24\% - 20\%)}{425.245 - 346.46} = \frac{20\% + 25.245 * 4\%}{48.785}$$

$$= 20\% + 2.07\% = 22.07\%$$

An Approximation

Supposing an investor is not inclined to follow the trial-and-error method, he/she may employ the following formula to find the approximate YTM of a bond.

$$\frac{\text{Annual interest payment} + [\text{Redemption value} - \text{Present market price}]/\text{No. of years to maturity}}{[\text{Redemption value} + \text{Present market price}]/2}$$

To illustrate, consider the following bond:

Market price	: Rs. 90
Redemption value	: Rs. 100
Annual interest	: Rs. 14
Years to maturity	: 6 years

Using the approximation formula, the yield to maturity on the above bond works out to:

$$\frac{14 + (100 - 90)/6}{(100 + 90)/2} = 16.49 \text{ per cent}$$

It may be noted that YTM calculation is similar to calculating the internal rate of return. One may further note that the YTM is just a promised yield and the investor cannot earn it unless the bond/debenture is held to maturity. And if one has to hold the security till one cannot, at the same time, one should sell it. Thus, there would be no trading.

One significant implication of such a situation is that the investor simply buys and holds and assumes all intermediate cash flows in the form of interest, and the principal repayment to be reinvested at YTM. In other words, the YTM concept is a *compound interest* concept, i.e., the investor is earning interest-on-interest at YTM throughout the holding period till maturity. One should understand that intermediate cash flows are not reinvested at YTM. The realized yield actually earned will differ from the original coupon rate. The receipts are reinvested at different point in time at the prevailing rates.

Yield-to-Call

A number of companies issue bonds with buy-back or provision for call option. Thus, a bond can be redeemed or called before maturity. The procedure for calculating the *yield-to-call* is the same as for YTM. The call period would be different from the maturity period and the call (or redemption) value could be different from the maturity value.

Table 14.2 Illustration Showing Reinvestment Rate and the Realized Rate of Return

Coupon interest income (Rs.)	Assumed Reinvestment %	Interest on interest income (Rs.)	Total return (Rs.)	Realized return (%)
2000	0	0	2000	5.57
2000	5	1370	3370	7.51
2000	8	2751	4751	8.94
2000	9	3352	5352	9.46
2000	10	4040	6040	10.00
2000	11	4830	6830	10.56
2000	12	5738	7738	11.14

Consider the debenture to be a portfolio of three zero-coupon debentures:

Debenture	Duration	Value	Xi	Weighted Duration
1	1 Year	Rs. 9.82 *	10.06 per cent	0.1006 = (1 * 0.1006) = 10.06%
2	2 Year	Rs. 8.77 * *	8.99 per cent	0.1798 = (2 * 0.8999) = 17.98%
3	3 Year	Rs. 79.01 ***	8.95 per cent	2.4285 = (3 * 0.8095) = 24.29%
		Rs. 97.60	100.00	2.7087

*Rs. 11/1.12 = Rs. 9.82

**Rs. 11/1.122 = Rs. 8.77

***Rs. 111/1.123 = Rs. 97.01

Example: Calculation of the value and duration for the following bonds:

Bond	Years of Maturity	Annual Interest	Maturity Value
Wipro	10	Rs. 80	Rs. 1,000
SBI	15	Rs. 65	Rs. 1,000

Table 14.3

Bond	Wipro Bond	SBI Bond		
Bond value	Rs. 1000	Rs. 872		
Year	Interest (in Rs.)	PV of Interest (in Rs.)	Interest (in Rs.)	PV of Interest (in Rs.)
1	80	74	65	60
2	80	137	65	111
3	80	191	65	155
4	80	235	65	191
5	80	272	65	221
6	80	302	65	246
7	80	327	65	265
8	80	346	65	281
9	80	360	65	293
10	1080	5002	65	301
11			65	307
12			65	310
13			65	311
14			65	310
15			1065	5036
Sum of PV of Interest		Rs. 7247		Rs. 8398
Duration		7.25		9.63

Bond Value and Amortization of Principal

A bond (debenture) may be amortized every year, i.e., repayment of principal every year rather at maturity. Therefore, in that case, the principal will decline with annual payments and interest will be calculated on the balance outstanding amount. The cash flows of the bonds will be uneven. Let us illustrate with the following table.

Table 14.4

	Principal at beginning	Interest	Repayment	Total payments	Principal at the end
1	1000	80	200	280	800
2	800	64	200	264	600
3	600	36	200	236	400
4	400	24	200	224	200
5	200	12	200	212	0
PV=	NPV(0.08, 1:5)			1025.71	

14.7 VALUATION OF PREFERENCE SHARES

Preference shares are a hybrid security. They have some features of bonds and some of equity shares. Theoretically, preference shares are considered a perpetual security but there are convertible, callable, redeemable and having other similar features, which enable issuers to terminate them within a finite time horizon. In the case of redeemable preference shares, legal mandates require creation of redemption sinking funds and earmarked investments to ensure funds for repayments.

Preference dividends are like specified bonds. This has to be done because they rank prior to equity shares for dividends. However, specification does not imply obligation, failure to comply with which may amount to default. Several preference issues are cumulative where dividends accumulate over time and equity dividends need clearance of preference arrears first.

Preference shares are less risky than equity because their dividends are specified and all arrears must be paid before equity holders get dividends. They are, however, more risky than bonds because the latter earn priority in payment and in liquidation. Bonds are also secured and enjoy protection of the principal which is ordinarily not available to preference shares.

Investors' required return on preference shares are more than those on bond, but less than on equity shares. In exceptional circumstances when preference shares enjoy special tax-shares (like in the US, inter-corporate holdings of preference shares get exemption on 80% of preference dividends) required return on such shares may even be marginally below those on bonds.

The equation for valuing preference shares is,

$$V_p = \frac{D}{K_p}$$

where V_p = the value of a perpetuity today

K_p = the required rate of return appropriate for the perpetuity

D = preference dividend

One may note that D is perpetuity and is known and fixed forever. Perpetuity does not involve present value calculations and the equation provides for computing any of the three variables, viz., value of perpetuity (V), preference dividend (D) and required rate of return (K_p) only if the remaining two variables are known. Thus, the value of preference shares can be calculated if the dividend per share and the required rate of return are known. Similarly, the required rate of return (or yield) can be known if the value of the perpetuity and dividend per share are known.

14.8 RATING OF DEBT SECURITIES

The rate of return expected from a bond depends mainly on the risk associated with it. A detailed analysis is required to be made to assess such risks of a bond, which is an onerous task and very often it is beyond the scope of an ordinary investor to do so. In this context, the ratings provided by independent rating agencies are useful.

Rating for the debt securities first originated in the United States, where presently there are at least five firms offering such services. In recent years, rating agencies have been set up in several other countries. With the establishment of the **Credit Rating Information Services of India Limited** (CRISIL), India too has joined this league.

Debt rating essentially reflects the probability of timely repayment of the principal and interest by a borrower. As per Moody's definition, "Ratings are designed exclusively for the purpose of grading bonds according to their investment qualities."

Debt rating by an independent, professional rating firm offers a superior and more reliable source of information on credit risks for three interrelated reasons:

(a) An independent rating firm, unlike brokers and underwriters who have a vested interest in an issue, is likely to provide an unbiased opinion.

(b) Due to its professional resources, a rating firm has greater ability to assess risks.

(c) A rating firm has access to a lot of information that may not be publicly available.

Rating Methodology

Despite variations across individual rating agencies, the following features appear to be common in the rating methodology by different agencies:

- Two broad types of analysis are done: (i) industry and business analysis; and (ii) financial analysis.
- The key factors considered in industry and business analysis are: (i) growth rate and relationship with the economy; (ii) industry risk characteristics; (iii) structure of industry and nature of competition; (iv) competitive position of issuer; and (v) managerial capability of the issuer.
- The important factors considered in financial analysis are: (i) earning power; (ii) business and financial risks; (iii) asset protection; (iv) cash flow adequacy; (v) financial flexibility; and (vi) quality of accounting and disclosure practices.
- Subjective judgement seems to play an important role in the assessment of the issue/issuer on various factors.
- While each factor is normally scored separately, no mechanical formula is used for combining the scores on different factors to arrive at the rating conclusion. In the ultimate analysis, all variables are viewed as interdependent.
- The rating is expressed in alphabetic symbols. A typical example is the following set of rating symbols employed by CRISIL:

AAA : Highest safety
AA : High safety
A : Adequate safety
BBB : Low safety
BB : Inadequate safety
B : High risk
C : Substantial risk
D : In default

Industry risk characteristics are likely to set the upper limit on rating.

Table 14.5 Debt/Bond Market Indicators (Return in percentage – %)

Debt Indicators	6-Apr-17	30-Sep-16	31-Mar-16	31-Mar-15	28-Mar-14	28-Mar-13
Call Rate	5.80		6.40		10.50	8.00
3 M CP	6.90		8.23		8.86	9.35
10 Yr Gsec	6.65	7.15	7.42		8.80	7.95
Reverse Repo	6.00	5.75	5.75	6.50	7.00	6.50
Repo	6.25	6.75	6.75	7.50	8.00	7.50
Bank Rate	6.50	6.75	7.75	8.50	9.00	8.50
CRR	4.00	4.00	4.00	4.00	4.00	4.00
SLR	20.50	20.75	21.00	21.5	22.00	22.50

Source: RBI

Table 14.6 R.B.I. rates as per Monetary Policy Fixed Range Liquidity Adjustment Facility (LAF) Rates

Effective Date	Bank Rate	Repo	Reverse	CRR	MSF	SLR
06-Apr-17	**6.50**	**6.25**	**6.00**	**4.00**	**-**	**20.50**
30-Sep-16	**6.75**	**6.75**	**5.75**	**4.00**	**-**	**20.75**
05-Apr-16	**7.00**	**6.50**	**6.00**	**4.00**	**-**	**21.25**
29-Sep-15	7.75	6.75	5.75	4.00		21.50
27-Jun-15	-	-	-	4.00	-	-
02-Jun-15	8.25	7.25	6.25	-	8.25	-
04-Mar-15	8.50	7.50	6.50	-	8.25	-
07-Feb-15	-	-	-	-	-	21.50
15-Jan-15	8.75	7.75			8.75	-
09-Aug-14	-	-	-	-	-	22.00
14-Jun-14	-	-	-	-	-	22.50
28-Jan-14	9.0	8.0	7.0	-	9.0	-
29-Oct-13	8.75	7.75	6.75	-	8.75	-
07-Oct-13	9.00	-	-	-	9.00	-
20-Sep-13	9.50	7.50	6.50	-	9.50	-
15-Jul-13	10.25	-	-	-	10.25	-
03-May-13	8.25	7.25	6.25	-	8.25	-
09-Feb-13	-	-	-	4.00	-	-
29-Jan-13	8.75	7.75	6.75		8.75	-
03-Nov-12	-	-	-	4.25	-	-
22-Sep-12	-	-	-	4.50	-	-

Source: RBI Website

The Road Ahead

- Emergence of a benchmark yield curve – essentially an interest rate profile of specified key instruments across various maturities which broadly gets accepted by the market as authentic – this can happen if the market deepens to cover lower rated entities as well.
- This would lead to a strong hedge structure promoting a strong swap market which will find the right equivalence for converting fixed and floating interest rates into each other.

15 An Overview of the Indian Securities Market

CHAPTER

The process of industrial development requires, as one of its accompanying structural changes, the development of a capital market. Capital market is a place where people buy and sell financial instruments/securities, be it equity/stock or debt/bond. It is a mechanism to facilitate the exchange of financial assets. The capital market should be capable of meeting the requirements of credit and finance of the private entrepreneurs in particular. The capital market should also help in sustained national industrial development.

The capital market provides an alternative mechanism of reallocating resources; it channelizes household saving to the corporate sector and allocates funds among firms. As a result, the savers and investors are not constrained by their individual abilities, but by the economy's abilities to invest and save respectively, which invariably enhances savings and investments in the economy. In this process, it allows both corporate and households to share business risk. The capital market enables the valuation of firms on an almost continuous basis and it plays an important role in the governance of the corporate sector.

Sound development of various segments of the capital market is a prerequisite for a proper functioning financial system. The capital market in India has been modernised over some 19-20 years and is now comparable with the international markets. There has been a visible improvement in trading and settlement infrastructure, risk management systems and levels of transparency. These improvements have brought about a reduction in the transaction costs and led to an improvement in liquidity.

15.1 DIMENSION/PURPOSE OF CAPITAL MARKET

1. It helps in the capital formation of the country by mobilising national savings for economic development.
2. Mobilization and import of foreign capital and foreign investment capital plus skill to fill up the deficit in the required financial resources to maintain the expected rate of economic growth.
3. It maintains active trading.

4. It facilitates productive utilisation of resources
5. It increases liquidity of assets.
6. It also helps in price discovery process.
7. It enables directing the flow to funds of high yields and also strives for balanced and diversified industrialization.

Constituents of Capital Market

The constituents of capital market consist of development banks, specialised financial institutions, investment institutions, state level development banks, mutual funds, lease companies, financial service companies, commercial banks and other specialised institutions and regulatory bodies, notably, SEBI, SHCL, CRISIL, ICRA, I-Sec, AMC, OTCEI and the National Stock Exchange.

Special Features of the Indian Capital Market

The capital market in India has exhibited some special feasibility features in the recent years which are worth noting here:

- Greater reliance on debt instruments as against equity and in particular, borrowing from financial institutions.
- Issue of debentures, particularly convertible debentures with automatic or compulsory conversion into equity without the normal option given to investors.
- Floatation of mega issues for the purpose of takeover, amalgamation, etc., and avoidance of borrowing from amalgamations, and financial institutions for fear of their market discipline and conversion clause by bigger companies.
- Avoidance of underwriting by some companies to reduce the costs and avoid security by the financial institutions.
- Fast growth of mutual funds and subsidiaries of banks for financial services, leading to larger mobilisation of savings from the capital market.

Broad Classification

Primary Market: New issues are made for raising the long-term capital requirement of commercial organizations. New issues may be made in four ways, namely, public issue, rights issue, private issue and follow-up issue.

Secondary Market: Listed outstanding issues (shares) are traded. Here, a stock or bond issue (which has already been sold through initial public offer) is traded between current and potential owners.

Once new issues have been purchased by investors, they change hands in the stock market. There are two broad segments of capital markets: (i) organized stock exchanges, and (ii) over-the-counter (OTC) market. The primary middlemen in the stock market are *brokers* who act as agents, and dealers who act as principals in all transactions.

The securities which are traded in the secondary market on the basis of issuer may be classified as:

- industrial securities,
- government securities, and
- Financial intermediaries securities.

15.2 STOCK MARKET IN INDIA

From scattered and small beginnings in the 19th century, India's stock market has risen to great heights. In 1990, we had 19 stock exchanges in the country. There were around 6000 listed companies and the invested population stood around 15 million.

Origin and Growth

Organizations and institutions whether economic, social or political, are products of historical events and exigencies. They continually replace and/or reform the existing organizations, so as to make them relevant and operational in contemporary situations. It is, therefore, useful to briefly acquaint ourselves with the origin and growth of the stock market in India.

1800-1865: The East India Company and a few commercial banks floated shares sporadically through recognized brokers. The year 1850 marked a watershed. A wave of company floatation took over the market; the number of brokers spurted to 60. The backbone of industrial growth and the resulting boom in shares marked the general personality of the financial world (Premchand Rouchand).

Stock market created a unique history: The entire market was gripped by what is known as "share fever." The American Civil War created cotton famine. Indian cotton manufacturers exploited this situation and exported large quantities of cotton. The resulting increase in export earnings opened opportunities for share investments. New companies started to come up. Excessive speculation and reckless buying became the order. This mania lasted up to 1865. It marked the end of the first phase in Indian stock exchange history. With the cessation of Civil War, demand for Indian cotton slumped abruptly. Shares became a worthless paper. To be precise, on July 1, 1865 all shares ceased to exist because all time bargains which matured could not be fulfilled.

1866-1900: The mania effect haunted the stock exchange during these 25 years. Above everything else, it led to a foundation of regular market for securities. Since the market was established in Bombay, it soon became and still is the leading and the most organized stock exchange in India. A number of stock brokers who geared themselves, set up a voluntary organization in 1887, called *Native Share and Stockbrokers Association.* The brokers drew up codes of conduct for brokerage business and mobilized private funds for industrial growth. It also mobilized funds for government securities (gilt-edged securities), especially of the Bombay Port Trust and Bombay Municipality. A similar organization was started at Ahmedabad in 1894.

1901-1920: Political development gave a big fillip to share investment. The Swadeshi Movement led by Mahatma Gandhi encouraged indigenous trading and the business class to start industrial enterprises. As a result, Calcutta became another major centre of share trading. Trading was prompted by coal boom of 1904-1908. Thus, the third stock exchange was started by Calcutta stock brokers. During inter-war years, demand of industrial goods kept increasing due to British involvement in World War I. Existing enterprises in steel and cotton textiles, woollen textiles, tea and engineering goods expanded and new ventures were floated. Yet another stock exchange was started in Madras in 1920.

1930-1965: This period can be considered the period of development of the existing stock exchanges in India. In this period, industrial development planning played the pivotal role of expanding the industrial and commercial state of the independent seven stock exchanges that were functioning the country.

Between 1946 and 1990, 12 more stock exchanges were set up, trading in shares of 4843 additional listed companies. From 7 to 19 stock exchanges and from 1125 to 8290 were the numbers of stock issues made by companies. The paid-up capital of these issues also grew severalfold. From Rs. 270 crore in 1946 to Rs. 465 lakh crore in 1990.

In 1992, the number of stock exchanges had increased to 21 and number of listed companies to over 6500. It is equally important to note that the network of Indian stock exchanges is spread throughout the country. In addition to recognized stock exchanges, there are 36 collection centres. At these centres, licensed dealers are authorized to transact business in securities. Mumbai, Delhi, Ahmedabad, Kolkata and Chennai are linked by PTI stock-scan service.

15.3 FUNCTIONS OF STOCK EXCHANGE

The history of stock exchange in foreign countries as well as in India shows that the development of joint stock enterprise would have never reached its present stage but for the facilities which the stock exchanges provided for dealing in securities.

A stock exchange fulfils a vital function in the economic development of nation: its main function is to 'liquify' capital, enabling a person who has invested money in, say a factory or a railway, to convert it into cash by disposing of his shares in the enterprise to someone else. The stock exchange is really an imperative pillar of the private corporate sector of the economy. It discharges essential functions in the process of capital formation and in raising resources for growth in the corporate sector.

1. The stock exchange provides a marketplace for purchase and sale of securities, viz., shares, bonds, debentures, etc.
2. The stock exchange provides linkage between household savings and investment in the corporate sector.
3. Thirdly, it provides a market quotation for the prices of shares and bonds.

Stock Market Indices

Investors often ask the question, 'How is the market doing?' This interest in the broad market movement stems from the general observation that prices of most of the stocks tend to move together, a fact that has a fairly strong empirical underpinning. The general movement of the market is typically measured by indices representing the entire market or important segments thereof. Most of the stock market indices are of two types:

- **Type A:** An index reflecting the simple arithmetic average of the prices relative of the shares in a certain year (or month or week or on a particular day) with reference to a base year.
- **Type B:** An index reflecting the aggregate market capitalization of the sample shares in a certain year (or month or week or on a particular day) in relation to the same in the base year.

Having described how the stock market indices are constructed, let us look at the nature of the following stock market indices in India, which appear to be the more popular ones:

Table 15.1

Index	Base year	Sample	Type of Index
The Economic Times Index of Ordinary Share Prices	1984	72 actively traded shares	A
Financial Express Equity Index	1979	100 actively traded shares	B
Bombay Stock Exchange Sensitive Index	1978-79	30 sensitive shares	A
Bombay Stock Exchange National Index	1983-84	100 active traded shares	B
Reserve Bank of India Index of Ordinary Shares	1980-81	338 shares	Combination of un-weighted geometric mean and weighted arithmetic mean
National Stock Exchange Index Nifty	1992	50 (Nifty) shares	A

15.4 PRINCIPAL WEAKNESSES OF INDIAN STOCK MARKET

While in terms of number of stock exchanges, listed companies, daily turnover, market capitalization and investor population, the Indian stock market has witnessed impressive growth over the last four decades. But it still suffers from other forms of weaknesses, some of which are quite serious. Some of these are described below:

(a) **Rampant Speculation:** Indian stock exchanges have been witnessing spells of unprecedented booms and crashes. While the country has been experiencing generally a 6-8% of growth rate, share prices have shown high volatility. This only shows that the *speculative activities* are rampant.

(b) **Insider Trading:** Like speculation, insider trading is rampant in Indian stock exchanges. *Insider trading* means operation of information which is price sensitive and not available to the public. Insider trading is thus trading from a position of privilege in respect to price-sensitive information. Insider trading is decried because it violates the principle of level playing; a state where equal opportunity to information is available to all the participants in the market.

(c) **Limited Forward Trading:** There can be three types of transactions undertaken at the stock exchanges, namely, *spot delivery, hand delivery* and *forward delivery*. In 1981, government proceeded to permit the revival of limited volume of trading. This was done to revive the previous practice of trading in cleared securities, but by permitting carry forward contracts beyond days up to three months. The real problem however, still persisted. While a certain volume of forward trading is useful for providing liquidity and avoiding payment crisis, when speculation runs riot and the actual price transfer of securities lies far behind, there will inevitably be a payment crisis.

(d) **Problem of interface between primary and secondary markets:** The upsurge of the primary market at times creates serious problems of interfacing with the secondary market, viz. the stock exchanges which still, by and large, continue with the same old attitudes and ways which suited the very narrow base of the capital market in the yester years but are totally out of tune with fast market and the desired tempo of work at present. Unless the secondary market is reoriented so as to take charge of the new responsibilities cast on it by the recent developments, this will act as a drag on the future preface serious problems while trying to buy or sell scripts.

(e) **Inadequacy of investor service:** It is commonly felt that exchanges, particularly the smaller ones, have been unable to service their investors adequately; and have been able to make only a limited contribution to the spread of the equity cult in their region. The upgradation of existing stock exchanges thus has to be viewed as an integral component of increasing globalization of the Indian economy.

(f) **Poor Liquidity:** The Indian stock market suffers from poor liquidity. Barring a small proportion of some large established companies/institutions that are actively traded and highly liquid, most are traded infrequently and, hence, lack liquidity.

(g) **Scarcity of Floating Stocks:** There is a scarcity of floating stocks in India in general. This seems to be caused by:

(i) Joint stock companies, financial institutions, and large individual investors, who collectively own nearly three-quarters of the equity capital in the private sector, generally do not offer their holdings for trading.

(ii) Indian investors traditionally have sticky portfolio habits. Due to the scarcity of floating stocks, the market tends to be highly volatile and more easily amenable to manipulation.

(h) **Inadequate Professionalism:** While there are brokers who are highly competent and professional in their dealings, the majority seem to lack high professional standards.

Directions to Reform the Functioning of Stock Exchanges

The efforts to reform the functioning of stock exchanges in India have been as old as the stock exchanges themselves. It is interesting to discuss briefly the main recommendations of an expert study of trading in shares in Indian stock exchanges, which was commissioned in 1991 by the Department of Economic Affairs, Foreign Ministry, and Government of India with the following terms of reference:

(a) To examine the trading systems prevalent in the Indian stock exchanges with special reference to stock exchanges such as Mumbai, Kolkata, Delhi and Ahmedabad, covering both specified and non-specified shares, keeping in view the need to avoid unwarranted fluctuations in prices and crisis in stock exchanges, also the need for ensuring the market's liquidity and investor's confidence.

(b) To review the effectiveness of the system of regulation and market surveillance by stock exchanges trading operations.

(c) To look into the working of the *badla* system in the shares and its effects on trading.

(d) To examine any other manner that is relevant to the smooth and orderly operation of trading in shares.

(e) To make recommendations for improvements in the system of trading in shares and in maintaining the confidence in the stock market.

Main recommendations made by the expert study are as follows:

1. To introduce a uniform one-week settlement system in all stock exchanges and in all shares in order to unify the market on a national basis and, at the same time, to reduce the risk exposure of market participants to long settlement periods and also to counter the strong tendency towards excessive speculation and exempting the concentration of trading activity to a few shares only.
2. To replace the present margin system, because of its failure to prevent many defaults on several exchanges, by a system of "marking to the market" on a daily basis (i.e., debiting the losses and credit gains daily to the members having outstanding positions).
3. To do away with the carry forward system which is incompatible with the recommendation of the study and shorten the settlement period, for which the whole rationale would disappear with the adoption of the system "marking to the market" daily, as suggested above.

4. To insist that all the stock exchanges introduce formal mark-to-marking arrangements in the best manner in order to prevent exploitation of interests by market malpractices, and promote more orderly transactions of all securities.
5. To make the governing bodies of stock exchanges equally representative of the share brokers interest on one hand, and the public and the users of stock market services on the other and thus strengthen the exchange management.
6. To introduce in all stock exchanges a well-designed *management information system* (MIS), could be used by the authorities for restructuring and regulating then on proper lines.

The high-powered study group on Establishment of New Stock Exchanges, popularly known as *Phase Committee*, had in 1991 recommended the promotion of a new stock exchange at New Bombay to act as a 'National Stock Exchange'. The principal features of NSE would be to limit itself to listing only medium-sized companies, and focus on creating a market for debt instruments which had been wholly neglected until now by the Bombay Stock Exchange as well as other existing stock exchanges.

This exchange should be completely automated in terms of both trading and settlement procedures. The group further recommended that the concept of compulsory mark-to-market/jobbers should be introduced; having suggested many new features for NSE, over-the-counter exchange of India (OTCEI) had been established in 1992.

15.5 BENEFITS OF OTC EXCHANGE OFFERS

For Companies

It provides a method of raising funds through capital market instruments which are priced fairly. In OTC, the company will be able to negotiate the issue price with the sponsors who will market the issue.

It also helps in saving unnecessary issue expenses on raising funds from capital markets. The method of sponsor placing the scrip with members of OTC who will, in turn, offload the scrip to the public will obviate the need of a public issue. Therefore, almost all associated costs will be eliminated. It will help achieve a greater degree of management stability. The OTC exchange will list scrips over 20% of the capital made available for public trading. It will provide greater accessibility to a large pool of captive investor base, enhancing the fund's reign substantially. OTC exchange creates nationwide network, where investors are serviced (who are captive investor base for companies).

For Investor

Investment in stocks thus becomes easier. OTC exchange's wide networks bring the stock exchanges to every street and corner. It provides a greater confidence and fidelity of trade. Investors can look up the prices displayed at the OTC. He knows he is trading in scrips at the right market price as there is a transparency of price. It also enables transactions getting completed quickly. Investors can settle deals across the counter.

A money or scrip proceeds from the deal gets settled in a matter of days (if not earlier). It provides definite liquidity to investors. The market making systems in OTC has two-way prices and is quoted regularly providing sufficient opportunity for investors to exist. Investors get a greater sense of security because all scrips are being researched and members themselves invest in these scrips. In the case of public issue/offer for sale, the allotment will be done in 26 days and trading in 30 days. This immensely benefits investors naturally.

For Financial Environment

OTC exchange helps spreading the stock exchange operations geographically and integrates capital investments with a national forum. It encourages closely-held companies to go public and venture capital across the country to boost entrepreneurship.

Demutualisation of Stock Exchanges

Historically, stock exchanges were formed as 'mutual' organisations, which were considered beneficial in terms of tax benefits and matters of compliance. They are generally 'not-for-profit' and tax-exempted entities. The trading members who provide broking services, also own, control and manage such exchanges for their common benefit, but do not distribute the profits among themselves. The ownership rights and trading rights are clubbed together in a membership card which is not freely transferable and hence this card at times carries a premium.

In contrast, in a 'demutual' exchange, three sets of people own the exchange, manage it and use its services. The owners usually vest management to a board of directors which is assisted by a professional team. A completely different set of people use the trading platform of the exchange. These are generally 'for-profit' and taxpaying entities. The ownership rights are freely transferable. Trading rights are acquired/surrendered in terms of transparent rules. Membership cards do not exist. These two models of exchanges are generally referred to as '*club*' and '*institution*' respectively.

The most important development in the capital market is concerning the demutualisation of stock exchanges. *Demutualisation* of exchanges means segregating the ownership from management. This move was necessitated by the fact that brokers in the management of the stock exchange were misusing their position for personal gains. Demutualisation would bring in transparency and prevent conflict of interest in the functioning of the stock exchanges. The Minister of Finance in his own Union Budget speech of 2002-03, has made an important announcement that the process of demutualisation and corporatisation of stock exchanges is expected to be completed during the course of the year under reference.

There would be various benefits of demutualisation; a few are enumerated below:

- Stock exchanges owned by members tend to work towards the interest of members alone, which could on occasions be detrimental to the rights of other stakeholders. Division of ownership between members and outsiders can lead to a balanced approach, remove conflicts of interest, create greater management accountability, and take into consideration the interest of other players.

- To cope with competition, stock exchanges require funds. While member-owned stock exchanges have limitation in raising funds, publicly owned stock exchanges can tap capital markets.
- Publicly owned stock exchanges can be more professional as compared to member-owned organisations. Further, as a result of the role played by shareholders, strengthening of management and the organisation, there is greater transparency in dealings, accountability and market discipline.
- This would enhance management flexibility. A publicly held company is better equipped to respond to changes when compared to a closely held mutually-owned organisation. Further, a company can spin off its subsidiaries, get into mergers and acquisitions, raise funds, etc.

The concept of demutualised exchange most probably originated in India, where two exchanges (OTCEI in 1990 and NSE in 1992) adopted a pure demutualised structure from their birth. The Stockholm Stock Exchange was the first major stock exchange in the world to become demutualised. Since then, over 20 exchanges have been demutualised. Some of them like the Australian Stock Exchange, London Stock Exchange, and Singapore Stock Exchange have gone a step further by becoming a listed company. Many others, including commodity exchanges, are in the process of demutualisation.

15.6 FINANCIAL INSTRUMENTS

Equity and debt are the two basic instruments of raising capital from the primary markets. In the following table, some data are presented in terms of resources mobilized through debt and equity:

Table 15.2 Resource Mobilization through Debt and Equity (in %)

Year	Equity	Debt
1995-96	72.39	27.01
1996-97	55.99	44.01
1997-98	41.17	58.83
1998-99	15.34	84.66
1999-00	58.41	41.59
2000-01	52.79	47.21
2001-02	16.88	83.12
2002-03	18.00	82.00
2003-04	80.47	19.53
2004-05	83.96	16.04

2005-06	100.00	0.00
2006-07	100.00	0.00
2010-11	86.01	13.99
2011-12	92.83	7.17
2012-13	58.06	41.94
2013-14	54.65	45.35
Apr-Dec 2014	33.38	66.62
2015-16	45.89	54.11
2016-17	48.74	51.26

Source: NSE & SEBI Statistics, 2017

Corporates, in practice, offer a number of variations of equity and debt securities. They include:

(i) Ordinary shares: Ordinary (equity) shares represent the ownership position in a company. They have voting rights and receive dividends at the discretion of the board of directors.

(ii) Preference shares: The holders have a preference over the equity owners in the event of liquidation of the company. The preference dividend rate is fixed and known and is payable before paying dividend in the ordinary share capital. Companies in India now hardly issue preference shares.

(iii) Debentures: Debentures represent long-term debt given by holders of debentures to the company. Debentures may be secured (known as bonds) or unsecured, convertible or non-convertible, redeemable or non-redeemable. Debentures may be issued without an interest rate and are called zero-interest debentures (deep-discount bonds). They are issued at a price much lower than their face value.

(iv) Warrants: A company may issue equity shares or debentures attached with warrants. Warrants entitle an investor to buy equity shares after a specified time period at a given price.

(v) Derivative securities: Securities which derive value from the underlying security or an asset. Securities with options to buy or sell are called Options - derivative instruments.

(vi) Borrowing from financial institutions/banks: In India, besides issuing debentures, corporates raise debt capital through borrowings from financial institutions and banks. Banks are an important source of working capital requirement for corporates.

(vii) Private Placement: Instead of a public issue of securities, a company may offer to a few investors privately; that is less than 50 in number. This is referred to as *private placement* of securities. In recent times, private placement has become the most significant method of mobilizing funds by corporates. From about 30 per cent in 1990-91 it went to almost 100 per cent in 2006-07, as the route of private placement is preferred by corporates. A few reasons for this development are:

- Private placement of securities is subject to much less compliance than the public issues, and fund raising is fairly simple.
- Private placement is cost effective as compared to public issues.
- Private placement is time effective as deals can be easily and directly negotiated with a smaller number of investors.
- Private placement helps in tailoring the issue according to the needs of corporates.
- In case of a debenture issue, negotiated directly between the issuing company and the investors, there may be greater flexibility with respect to terms and conditions.

The investors in private placement may be financial institutions, commercial banks, other companies, shareholders of promoting companies, and friends and associates of the promoters.

The private placement market, however, has several limitations for the efficient functioning of the capital markets. There is little information available about this market and less transparency. The quantum of funds that can be raised may be rather limited.

(viii) Euro Issues: The increasing use of euro issues by the Indian corporate also indicates that Indian capital market is integrating with the international capital markets. Companies in India have also started raising funds via **euro issues** in the foreign capital markets. Euro issues include: foreign currency convertible bonds **(FCCBs)**, global depository receipts **(GDRs)** and American depository receipts **(ADRs)**. ADRs and GDRs are like shares and they are traded on the overseas stock exchanges. Indian corporate sector raised significant amount of funds by way of euro issues in the 1990s. Euro issues fetched Rs. 1,70,059 million in 2006-07 and Rs. 1,13,520 million in 2005-06 respectively.

15.7 MONEY MARKET

The money market is a mechanism which makes it possible for borrowers and lenders to come together. Essentially, it refers to a market for short-term funds. It meets the short-term requirements of the borrowers and provides liquidity of cash to the lenders.

Money market is the market in which short-term funds are borrowed and lent. The money market does not deal in cash or money but trades in bills, promissory notes and government papers, which are drawn for short periods. These short-term bills are known as *near money*.

Importance of Money Market

- Dealing in bills of exchange and commercial papers
- Acting as an outlet for the excess short-term funds of commercial banks
- Dealing in treasury bills and short dated government securities
- Guiding central banking policies
- Making central banking policies effective
- Reduction of disparities in interest rates
- Influencing the capital market

Features of a Developed Money Market

- Existence of an efficient and effective central bank
- Well organized commercial banking system
- Existence of specialised sectors
- Free flow of funds between the various sub-markets
- Adequate facilities for transfer of funds
- Uniformity in interest rates
- Availability of ample funds
- Availability of ample short-term credit instruments
- Sensitiveness to internal and external events
- Existence of specialized financial institutions

Weaknesses of the Indian Money Market

- Existence of unorganized money market
- Absence of integration
- Diversity in money rates of interests
- Seasonal stringency of money
- Highly volatile call money market
- Absence of the bill market
- Absence of well organized banking system
- Availability of credit investments

Money Market Instruments

Analysing specifically, the money market deals with the transactions of raising and supplying money in a short period not exceeding one year through various instruments. The following are important money market instruments:

- Treasury Bills (T-Bills)
- Central Government Securities (Gilt-edged securities)
- State Government and Public Sector Instruments
- Municipal Bonds
- Commercial Paper
- Certificates of Deposit
- Bills rediscounting
- Call/Notice Money Market
- Repurchase Agreements (Repos)
- Inter-bank participation
- Bank Deposits
- Term Money
- Corporate Debentures and Bonds
- Bankers Acceptance
- Commercial Bills
- Fringe Market

Reasons for Growth of Money Market in India

- Availability of new and more attractive instruments for investments such as short-term government papers and zero coupon bonds, besides other types of non-SLR instruments.
- Marketisation of government securities with adoption of auction system for all central government securities, and treasury bills of varying maturities.
- Increased professionalism in the banking industry with emergence of sophisticated instruments and technology changes, especially with the advent of more number of private sector participants.
- Emergence of risks of different nature in money markets on account of freeing of interest rates, removal of entry barriers and integration with the international financial markets. The total impact of interest rate deregulation has exposed the banks to greater vulnerability in trying to cope with money market related risks.
- Stimulation of the government securities market due to decision of the government to borrow at market related rates on the lines suggested by the Narasimham Committee. Taking into consideration the risk factor, there is no doubt that government securities including treasury bills offer a good return to the investor.

Capital Market vs Money Market

In this context, it is imperative that one should know the distinction between a capital market and a money market, which is briefly shown in the following table.

Table 15.3

Capital Market	Money Market
It is a market for long-term funds exceeding a period of one year.	It is a market for short-term loanable funds for a period of not exceeding one year.
This market supplies funds for financing the fixed capital requirements of trade and commerce as well as the long-term requirements of the government.	This market supplies funds for financing current business operations, working capital requirements of the corporate and short-term requirements of the government.
This market deals in instruments like shares, debentures, government bonds, etc.	The instruments that are dealt with in a money market are bills of exchange, treasury bills, commercial papers, certificate of deposit, etc.
Each single capital market instrument is of small amount. Each share's face value is Rs. 10. Each debenture value is either Rs. 100 or Rs. 1000	Each single money market instrument is of large amount. A treasury bill is for a minimum of Rs. 1 lakh. Each commercial deposit or commercial paper is for a minimum of Rs. 25 lakh.
Development banks, insurance companies, mutual funds, foreign institutional investors play a dominant role in the capital market.	The central bank and commercial banks are the major institutions in the money market.
Capital market instruments generally have secondary markets.	Money market instruments generally do not have secondary markets.
Transactions take place over a recognized stock exchange.	Transactions mostly take place over-the-phone and there is no formal place.
Transactions have to be conducted only through authorised intermediaries.	Transactions are conducted without the help of brokers.

Money Laundering

Money laundering poses a serious threat not only to the financial system of countries, but also to their integrity and sovereignty. The process of money laundering involves siphoning off money earned through illegal activities like extortion, drug trafficking, and gun running, etc. To prevent money laundering and associated activities, confiscation of proceeds of crime, an Act has been passed in the Parliament called 'The Prevention of Money Laundering Act, 2002'. Section 3 of the Act specifies certain acts which constitute money laundering. As per the section, a person is said to have committed an offence of money laundering if he:

(a) directly or indirectly attempts to indulge, or

(b) knowingly assists, or

(c) knowing is a party, or

(d) is actually in the process or activity with the proceeds of crime and projects it as untainted property, shall be guilty of an offence of money laundering.

Section 4 of the Act says that whosoever commits the offence of money laundering shall be punishable with rigorous imprisonment for a term which shall not be less than 3 years but which may extend to 7 years and shall also be liable to fine which may extend to Rs. 5,00,000. If the proceeds of crime involved in money laundering relate to any offence specified under paragraph 2 of part A of the Schedule to the Act, the individual shall be punishable with rigorous imprisonment for a term which shall not be less than 3 years but which may extend to 10 years and shall also be punishable with a fine which may extend to Rs. 5,00,000. Section 5 of the Act, confers the power to attach property involved in money laundering.

15.8 DEVELOPMENTS IN THE INDIAN STOCK MARKET

The globalization of financial markets and the consequential changes in the Indian segment have created a new thrust for desirable reforms.

Developed financial markets allocate capital through a supply and demand mechanism, establishing the cost of capital at the equilibrium of supply and demand for the securities. The financial services industry has assumed a key position by providing means for transfer of goods and services and payment thereof. In the process, they act as intermediaries between the countries with excess funds and those in need of funds, both for capital and trade purposes.

Financial reforms have brought about many changes. These reforms have removed the shackles of control and have promoted the free flow of investments, new instruments of investments and state-of-the-art technologies and procedures that are in operation in the other developed markets. With the larger availability of resources, industrial activity has received a boost. The active participation of foreign investors with resources and modern know-how has opened new vistas of growth and development in the Indian economy. Removal of restrictions and constraints, freedom to work within broad government guidelines and supportive policies that are investor-friendly, are the chief distinguishing features of the financial reforms.

The Foreign Exchange Control Act has been modified and rechristened as the Foreign Exchange Management Act (FEMA), symbolic of present times, which seek to promote development rather than control of inflow and outflow of investments.

The laws of securities in India were originally contained in the Capital Issues (Control) Act, 1947, the Securities Contract (Regulation) Act, 1956 and the Companies Act, 1956. The government, exercising the delegated powers under laws, prescribed detailed procedures in rules and regulations. With the promulgation of the Securities and Exchange Board of India Act (SEBI), 1992, the Capital Issues (Control) Act, 1947 and delegated legislation thereunder were repealed and SEBI was empowered to regulate all matters relating to capital issues in respect of listed companies.

These developments significantly changed the face of the Indian capital market. The market was thrown open to foreign investors with Indian companies being allowed to raise capital abroad and receive investments from foreign institutional investors (FIIs), in order to integrate Indian capital market with the global market; many evolutionary efforts have been taken. The changes in the capital market are not a one-shot affair and have to go through a learning curve.

The process of financial reforms is still under way and is likely to bring about even more drastic changes that may make the markets healthier and stronger. India's approach to financial sector reforms in general, and to the management of the external sector, in particular has served the country well, in terms of aiding growth, avoiding crisis, enhancing efficiency and imparting resilience to the system.

Impact of Liberalisation

It is needless to say that liberalisation has had a remarkable effect on both the economy in general and the capital market in particular. These measures for liberalisation initiated in 1991; by then government led to restoring of both domestic and international confidence in the Indian economy. The balance of payment position, which had reached alarming levels showed steady improvement, which was reflected in the growth of the foreign exchange reserves. The private sector has been given a place of pride in allocating resources for the government's five year plan.

Listed companies operate substantially under stock exchanges in India. The market capitalisation of listed companies has grown manifold and the market trends have been on the upswing as reflected on both BSE and NSE indices. The new policy of the government to privatise public sector enterprises (PSEs) by offloading part of the government holdings to mutual funds and financial institutions has opened up new opportunities for growth in the capital market. Public sector companies with a huge capital base have been listed with the stock exchanges following their partial disinvestment.

New Initiatives

Though the capital markets in India have evolved over a long period, they gathered considerable momentum only after various initiatives were undertaken by the government, SEBI beginning in early 1990s. The activity in the market picked up from 2003-04 significantly reflecting effectiveness of the measures initiated to develop the market and restore investor confidence. Various reforms initiated in the financial markets since the early 1990s have focussed on:

1. removing the restrictions on pricing of assets;
2. building of institutional and technological infrastructure;
3. strengthening the risk management practices;
4. fine-tuning of the market microstructure;
5. changes in the legal framework to remove structural rigidities; and
6. widening and deepening of the market with new participants and instruments.

The government has unveiled its policy permitting foreign institutional investors (FIIs) in both primary and secondary markets up to certain limits. FIIS from various countries have substantial resources. The government policy is expected to widen the capital base and take market activity to high levels.

Some noteworthy reforms that took place have been delineated hereunder:

During 2002-03

- Implementation of $T + 3$ rolling settlement for all listed securities across exchanges from April 2, 2002 to move $T + 2$ on April 1, 2003.
- Introduction of scientific model for risk management, based on Value-at-Risk (VaR).
- Introduction of Electronic Data Information Filing and Retrieval (EDIFAR) system to facilitate electronic filing of certain documents/statements by the listed companies and their immediate disclosure to the market participants.
- Launch of Securities Market Awareness Campaign.
- Introduction of rating corporate governance on the principles of wealth creation, wealth management and wealth sharing.
- Introduction of Straight through Processing (STP) for the securities transactions.
- Implementation of a comprehensive risk management system for Mutual Funds.
- Introduction of the dual fungibility of ADRs and GDRs.
- Establishment of the Central Listing Authority (CLA).
- Issuance of necessary guidelines/circulars for corporatisation and demutualisation of stock exchanges.
- Introduction of the trading of government securities on the stock exchanges.
- Posting all the orders passed by the Securities Appellate Tribunal (SAT) and the Board on SEBI website, to bring in regulatory transparency.
- Introducing the consultative process on policy formulation by putting all reports of committees and draft regulations on SEBI website for seeking comments, suggestions and opinions from various stakeholders and the public.
- Issuance of guidelines on delisting of securities from the stock exchanges.
- Establishment of inter-depository transfer through online connectivity between CDSL and NSDL.
- Review and amendment of the following regulations and guidelines – a measure of regulatory pro-activeness.
    - SEBI (Insider Trading) Regulations, 1992
    - SEBI (Underwriters) Regulations, 1993
    - SEBI (Debenture Trustees) Regulations, 1993
    - SEBI (Portfolio Managers) Regulations, 1993
    - SEBI (Foreign Institutional Investors) Regulations, 1995
    - SEBI (Mutual Funds) Regulations, 1996
    - SEBI (Substantial Acquisition of Shares and Takeovers) Regulations, 1997
    - SEBI (Depositories and Participants) (Amendments) Regulations, 2003
    - SEBI (Stock Brokers and Sub-Brokers) (Amendment) Regulations, 2003

    [**Source:** SEBI Annual Report, 2002-03]
- SEBI (Employee Stock Option Scheme & Employee Stock Purchase Scheme) Guidelines, 1999

- SEBI (Credit Rating Agencies) Regulations, 1999
- SEBI (Issue of Sweat Equity) Regulations, 2002
- SEBI (Procedure for Holding Enquiry by Enquiry Officer and Imposing Penalty) Regulations, 2002
- Announcement of accounting standards and disclosure practices of the Indian companies by ICAI in consultation with SEBI in accordance with international accounting standards.
- Expansion of the derivatives products basket.
- Introduction of benchmarking of all mutual funds schemes to facilitate the understanding of the investors about the performance of the funds.
- Introduction of nomination facility for the unit holders of mutual funds.
- Simplification of documentation procedure for FII registration and reduction of registration fee for FIIs.
- Memoranda of Understanding (MOU) for cooperation and information sharing were signed with international regulators like the Securities Commission of Mauritius and Securities and the Exchange Commission of Sri Lanka.

During 2003-04

With a view to making markets more competitive and compliant, SEBI has brought in the following new regulations:

- SEBI (Prohibition of Fraudulent and Unfair Trade Practices relating to Securities Market) Regulations, 2003
- SEBI (Ombudsman) Regulations, 2003
- SEBI (Central Database for Market Participants) Regulations, 2003
- SEBI (Self Regulatory Organizations) Regulations, 2004
- SEBI (Criteria for Fit and Proper Person) Regulations, 2004

Issue Norms: SEBI introduced an additional criteria of 'net tangible assets', 'minimum number of allottees in public issue' and 'profitability'.

Amendment to Book-Building Guidelines: In order to make price discovery process more realistic, companies were provided with some flexibility in the indication of price band either movable or fixed floor price in the Red Herring Prospectus. Qualified institutional buyers (QIBs) have been prohibited from withdrawing their bids after the closure of bidding.

Green Shoe Option: As a stabilization tool for the post-listing price of newly listed shares, SEBI has introduced the 'green shoe option' facility in IPOs.

Margin Trading: With a view to providing greater liquidity in the secondary securities market, SEBI has allowed corporate brokers with a net worth of at least three crores to extend margin trading facility to their clients in the cash segment of stock exchanges.

The brokers may use their own funds or borrow from scheduled commercial banks or NBFCs regulated by the RBI, but the total indebtedness for this purpose should not exceed five times the net worth.

Securities Lending and Borrowing: A clearing corporation/clearing house, after registration with SEBI, under the SEBI scheme for securities lending and borrowing, as an approved intermediary, may borrow securities for meeting shortfalls in settlement, on behalf of the members.

Secondary Market for Corporate Debt Securities: With a view to providing greater transparency and protecting the interests of investors in debt securities, SEBI has prescribed new guidelines for regulating private placement of debt securities issued by the corporate entities.

Full disclosure (initial and continuing) as per the Companies Act, 1956, SEBI (DIP) Guidelines 2000 and Listing Agreement are to be made by the companies. Credit rating of debt securities, appointment of debenture trustees, separate listing agreement, frequent furnishing of periodical reports to SEBI, etc. have been made mandatory to enhance the protection of investors in debt instruments.

Enhancing Market Safety and Reducing Credit Risk: Clearing and settlement cycle time has been further contracted to $T + 2$ with effect from April 1, 2003. This measure is expected to result in faster settlement, higher safety and lower settlement risk in the Indian capital market.

Foreign Institutional Investors (FIIs): FIIs have been allowed to participate in delisting offers to afford an exit opportunity. They have also been allowed to participate in sponsored ADR/GDR programmes. FIIs have also been permitted to participate in divestment by the government in listed companies.

Meaning of Depository

The term *depository* is defined as "a place where something is deposited for safekeeping, a bank in which funds or securities are deposited by others, usually under the terms of specific depository agreement."

Depository means "one who receives a deposit of money, securities, instruments, or other property, a person to whom something is entrusted, a trustee, a person or group entrusted with the preservation or safekeeping of something."

Before the introduction of depository system, the problems faced by the investors and corporates in handling large volume of paper were as follows:

(a) Bad deliveries
(b) Fake certificates
(c) Loss of certificates in transit
(d) Mutilation of certificates
(e) Delays in transfer
(f) Long settlement cycles

(g) Mismatch of signatures
(h) Delay in refund and remission of dividend, interest, etc.

The first depository in the world was set up way back in 1947 in Germany. The total number of depositories in the world then was only 32 and the number crossed 250 by the end of 2005. In India, the depository concept was introduced in 1996 with the enactment of Depositories Act, 1996. The operations of depositories are carried out in accordance with the regulations made by SEBI in this behalf, and the bylaws and business rules framed by the depository as per the powers given under the Depositories Act. The Central Government, in exercise of the power to make rules to carry out the provisions of the Act, framed the SEBI (Depositories and Participants) Regulations, 1996.

The major differences between physical and dematerialised share trading systems are:

Table 15.4

Physical	Dematerialised
1. Actual delivery of shares is to be exchanged	1. No actual delivery of shares is needed
2. Open delivery can be kept	2. No possibility of keeping delivery open
3. For sale transactions, no changes other than brokerage are levied	3. Sale transactions are also charged for
4. For buy transaction, delivery is to be sent to company for registration	4. No need to send the document to the company for registration
5. Stamp charges at 0.5% are levied for transfer	5. No stamp charges are required for transfer
6. Dematerialised processing time is too long	6. Dematerialised processing time is quite short

Benefits of the Depository System

- Growing and more liquid capital markets to provide financing and development stemming from more efficient post-trade systems with reduced transaction costs.
- Increase in competition in the international marketplace and attracting investors and fund managers by complying with stipulated international standards calling for an efficient and risk-free trading environment.
- Improved prospects for privatisation of public sector units by creating a conducive environment.
- Restoration of faith in the capital markets and the participants with systems to minimize settlement risk and fraud.
- Considerable reduction in the delay in registration, which currently impacts trading of the investing public.
- Reduction of risks associated with loss, mutilation, theft and forgery of physical scrip.
- Elimination of financial loss owing to loss of physical scrip.

- Greater liquidity from speedier settlements and reduction in delays in registration.
- Greater opportunities for investment offered by new instruments and services that can be provided only when the depository system is implemented and is operational and effective.
- Faster receipt of benefits and rights resulting from corporate action.
- Improved production of shareholder's rights resulting from more timely communications from the issuer.
- Reduced transaction costs through greater efficiency.

Facilities offered by Depository System

1. Opening of depository account
2. Dematerialisation
3. Rematerialisation
4. Settlement of trades in dematerialised securities
5. Account transfer
6. Transfer, transmission and transportation
7. Pledge and hypothecation
8. Redemption or repurchase
9. Stock lending and borrowing
10. Corporate action
11. Nomination
12. Account freezing
13. Demat of debt instruments
14. Dealing in government securities

Depositories in India

At present, two players are rendering depository services in India:

(i) National Securities Depository Limited (NSDL): The NSDL was registered by SEBI on June 7, 1996 as India's first depository to facilitate trading and settlement of securities in the dematerialisation form. The NSDL is promoted by IDBI, UTI and NSE to provide electronic depository facilities for securities traded in the equity and the debt markets in India. NSDL has been set up to cater to the demanding needs of the Indian capital markets. In the first phase of operations, NSDL has dematerialised scrip and replaced them with electronic entries.

(ii) Central Depository Services (India) Limited (CDSL): CDSL commenced its operations during February, 1999. CDSL was promoted by Stock Exchange, Mumbai in association with Bank of Baroda, Bank of India, and State Bank of India and HDFC Bank.

At present, the following stock exchanges are connected to the above depositories:

1. National Stock Exchange
2. The Bombay Stock Exchange, Mumbai
3. Calcutta Stock Exchange
4. Delhi Stock Exchange
5. Ludhiana Stock Exchange
6. Bangalore Stock Exchange
7. Over-the-Counter Exchange of India
8. Madras Stock Exchange
9. Inter Connected Stock Exchange
10. Ahmedabad Stock Exchange

Table 15.5 Progress of Dematerialization at NSDL and CDSL

Month		NSDL	CDSL
Apr-2004	Companies: Live	5,254	4,824
	DPs: Live	215	200
	DPs: Locations	1,729	977
	Demat Value (Cr.)	12,91,400	98,739
	Demat Quantity (Cr. Securities)	8,463	1,401
Dec-2013	Companies: Live	11,762	8,446
	DPs: Live	280	580
	DPs: Locations	14,349	11,491
	Demat Value (Cr.)	84,70,300	10,11,941
	Demat Quantity (Cr. Securities)	74,445	16,543
Apr-Dec 2014	Companies: Live	13,470	9,204
	DPs: Live	272	575
	DPs: Locations	15,864	11,428
	Demat Value (Cr.)	112,20,526	14,22,428
	Demat Quantity (Cr. Securities)	89,073	19,796
Apr-Dec 2015	Companies: Live	15,115	9,813
	DPs: Live	272	578
	DPs: Locations	25,793	16,359
	Demat Value (Cr.)	119,29,978	13,90,410
	Demat Quantity (Cr. Securities)	1,03,690	22,282

Source: NSDL and CDSL, 2013-14 & SEBI Handbook Statistics, 2015

The above table reveals that growth in dematerialization at NSDL and CDSL was phenomenal during Apr-2004 to Dec-2013 period.

Custodial Services

The meaning of 'custody' is 'duty of caring for, guarding'. It means that the valuable documents and papers should be carefully guarded by keeping them in a proper place, under tight security. A *custodian* is a person who has the custody of something, caretaker of a public building and property. A custodian is a caretaker of the securities and documents and in return, he receives some benefit for his services called *custodial charges*.

Since the work of a custodian is risky, costly and cumbersome, only entities can do such work of custodian services, which involve a lot of money, space requirement, full safety measures, etc. Institutions can do it successfully. Custodians are intermediaries between companies and clients (security-holders) and institutions (FIIs and MFs). They are intermediaries who are a link between real owners and entities. There is an arrangement agreement between custodians and real owners to act as custodians of those who handover ownership. Custodial services are a capital-intensive and technology-driven business.

Operations of a Custodian

A custodian's job includes receiving the shares on behalf of its customers from the brokers. In this, one must keep in mind that the purchase/sale decisions are taken by the customer and the custodian is required to just receive the delivery of these shares and hold it. For this, whenever the customers make any purchases or sales, they are supposed to send the contract note to the custodians along with the DIP or DIS, i.e., the purchase and sale instructions respectively. While holding the shares, the custodian has to exercise all the corporate actions on the shares like receiving of dividends, bonus shares, etc., and on the customer's instructions, apply for rights shares or has to hand over the renouncement forms to brokers in case the customer sells the same.

Stock Holding Corporation of India Ltd. (SHCIL)

This is a company incorporated under the Companies Act with an authorised capital of Rs. 25 crore and a paid-up capital of Rs. 10.5 crore subscribed by all-India financial institutions, namely IDBI, IFCI, ICICI, UTI, GIC and IRBI. SHCIL's operations are computer-aided and have offices at New Delhi, Kolkata and Chennai with its headquarters at Mumbai. Its prime aim is to simplify and expedite transactions, eliminating most of the paper work and thus simplifying the job on the lines of Depository Trust Company (DTC) of the USA or the Canadian Depository for Securities Limited (CDSL), which holds stocks on behalf of investors in its name. The SHCIL was formed with the following aims:

- To make it easy for an investor to buy/sell securities.
- To keep active share and debenture certificates in safe custody.

- To computerise trading among active investors of such institutions, mutual funds, etc.
- To create regional SHCs enabling growth in volume.
- To credit dividend and other payments directly to investors through central collection, and to act as a bank/custodian for shares.

The SHCIL renders services like:

- Clearing and settlement services
- Registration and transfer processing
- Depository services
- Corporate actions and benefits collection
- Management information system considering the pivotal services rendered by the SHCIL, NSE has considered using its services for the benefit of investors who are spread throughout the country. Without its services, the functions of NSE will not be complete and perfect. SHCIL, thus, is complementary to its function as a depository.

Circuit Breaker System

Stock market volatility is generally a cause of concern for both policy makers as well as investors. To curb excessive volatility, SEBI has prescribed a market-wide *circuit breaker system*, which brings about a coordinated trading halt in all equity and equity derivatives markets nationwide, when the index moves either way by 10%, 15% and 20%. The movement of Nifty-50, or the S&P Sensex, whichever is breached earlier, triggers the breakers. As an additional measure of safety, individual scrip-wise price bands of 20% either way have been imposed for all securities. However, in respect of securities for which derivative products are available or those included in indices on which derivative products are available, a daily price limit of 10% is applicable.

Disclosure Practices to Prevent Insider Trading

Listed companies are required to prescribe a *code for disclosure practices* as per regulation 12 (2) of the SEBI Regulation. A model code has been prescribed in Schedule II of the regulations to ensure adequate and timely disclosure of price sensitive information. A code prescribed by the company in this regard should have the following norms, which needs to be followed in practice:

- To ensure dissemination of price-sensitive information to stock exchanges on a continuous and immediate basis.
- To improve public access to price-sensitive information by announcements in media.
- Designate a Compliance Officer to oversee corporate disclosures of price-sensitive information to stock exchanges, analysts, shareholders and the public.
- To lay down procedure for responding to queries or request for verification of market rumours by stock exchanges and to decide whether a public announcement is necessary for verifying or denying rumours.

- Only public information should be provided to analysts/research persons or large investors like institutions. Price-sensitive information given to analysts, etc., should be simultaneously made public.
- Discussions/meetings with analysts, brokers, institutional investors should be held in the presence of at least two company representatives and preferably be recorded. Unanticipated questions from them may be taken into consideration and responded to later.
- To make press releases or post relevant information on company's website after every meeting with analysts or institutional investors.
- The company should use its website for providing investors direct access to significant background information and responses to the questions of analysts and investors.
- The stock exchanges may disseminate the disclosure made by listed companies through website or exchange network.

15.9 FINANCIAL STABILITY

From a financial stability perspective, it is necessary to have a balanced financial system whereby both financial markets and financial institutions play an important role. Notwithstanding a long history, the capital market in India remained on the periphery of the financial system. However, a series of reforms introduced since the early 1990s have brought about transformation of the capital market.

Free pricing in the primary capital market has allowed corporates to price their issues based on their fundamentals and conditions in the market. In the secondary market, the move to an electronic trading system has resulted in transparency in trades, better price discovery and lower transaction costs. The efficiency of the market has improved through faster execution of trades. The operational efficiency of the stock market has also been strengthened through improvements in the clearing and settlement practices and the risk management process.

Almost the entire delivery of securities now takes place in demutualised form. During the last 10-12 years or so, there has been no instance of postponement or settlements at two major stock exchanges (BSE and NSE), despite defaults by brokers. The cases of bad deliveries have become almost nil. The setting of trade/settlement guarantee funds has considerably reduced the settlement risk. The integrity and transparency of the market has improved with the wider availability of information regarding the corporate performance at quarterly intervals, which has improved the price discovery process. The trading and settlement framework in the Indian stock exchanges now compares favourably with the international best frameworks.

The future of the capital market holds promise on account of the fact that India is expected to continue to grow at relatively better growth than most parts of the world for several years ahead. The strong macroeconomic fundamentals and higher growth trajectory embarked upon by the Indian economy have also contributed to the strong upturn in resource mobilization from the primary capital market. Further, the Indian growth story is domestically inclined (creation of various physical and social infrastructures, a huge potential of making rural development, public/consumer spending on retail, discretionary, none-discretionary items, etc.) and as such, the external factors are likely to have rather less impact on the overall growth prospects. Moreover, the corporate India is gaining global credibility with improved visibility, productivity and performance. However, the global crude oil prices and the level of interest rates can pose constraints for sustained future growth rate.

Table 15.6 Growth of Market Participants in Securities Market

Particulars	No. as on 31-Dec-15	No. as on 31-Dec-13	No. as on 31-Mar-05
Securities Appellate Tribunal	1	1	1
Regulators	4	4	4
Depositories	2	2	2
Depository Participants	853	866	477
Qualified Depository of NSDL & CDSL	–	62	–
Stock Exchanges (Cash Market)	5	19	23
Stock Exchanges (Derivatives Market)	3	3	2
Stock Exchanges (Currency Derivatives)	3	4	–
Listed Securities	–	–	9,413
Brokers (cash segment)	4,824	9,150	9,519
Sub-brokers	36,683	54,846	13,291
Corporate Brokers (Cash Segment)	3,405	4,925	3,764
Brokers (Equity Derivatives)	2,762	3,072	1,003
Brokers (Currency Derivatives)	2,408	2,382	-
Mutual Funds	47	50	38
Investment Advisors	373	70	-
FIIs	Na	1,739	502
Sub-accounts	Na	6,394	-
Portfolio Managers	201	221	54
Custodians	19	19	11
Share Transfer Agents & Registrar to Issue	73	72	143
Merchants Bankers	191	198	124

Contd.

Bankers to an Issue	62	56	67
Debenture Trustees	31	32	35
Underwriters	2	32	43
Venture Capital Funds	200	210	43
Credit Rating Agencies	7	6	4
KYC Registration Agencies (KRA)	5	5	-
Foreign Venture Capital Investors	213	193	14
Alternate Investment Funds	189	90	-
Collective Investment Management Company	1	1	0
Approved Intermediaries (Stock Lending Schemes)	2	2	3
STP (Centralised Hub)	1	1	0
STP Service Providers	2	2	0
Sub-brokers	36,683	54,846	13,291
Corporate Brokers (Cash Segment)	3,405	4,925	3,764
Brokers (Equity Derivatives)	2,762	3,072	1,003
Brokers (Currency Derivatives)	2,408	2,382	-
Mutual Funds	47	50	38
Investment Advisors	373	70	-
FIIs	NA	1,739	502
Sub-accounts	NA	6,394	-
Portfolio Managers	201	221	54
Custodians	19	19	11
Share Transfer Agents & Registrar to Issue	73	72	143
Merchants Bankers	191	198	124
Bankers to an Issue	62	56	67
Debenture Trustees	31	32	35
Underwriters	2	32	43

Venture Capital Funds	200	210	43
Credit Rating Agencies	7	6	4
KYC Registration Agencies (KRA)	5	5	-
Foreign Venture Capital Investors	213	193	14
Alternate Investment Funds	189	90	-
Collective Investment Management Company	1	1	0
Approved Intermediaries (Stock Lending Schemes)	2	2	3
STP (Centralised Hub)	1	1	0
STP (Service Providers)	2	2	0

(**Source:** RBI, SEBI, DCA & DEA, 2014-15) – NA: Not available

Table: 15.7 Securities Turnover (Growth) on Stock Exchanges (Rs.in Million)

Stock Exchanges	1994-95	2004-05	Apr-13 to Dec-13	2015-16
NSE BSE	85,090 677,480	11,400,720 5,187,170	20,873,670 03,750,150	42,369,830 7,400,890
Kolkata	528,720	27,150	1,590	
Delhi	90,827	0	0	
Ahmedabad	56,508	0	0	
Uttar Pradesh	78,230	53,430	–	
Hyderabad	13,752	0	0	
MCX-SX	–	0	102,520	
OCTE	13,650	0	0	
Chennai	30,327	270	0	
Madhya Pradesh	7,968	0	0	
Vadodara	16,210	0	0	
Guwahati	2,853	0	0	
Others	1,07,819	–	–	
Total:	**1,709,434**	**16,668,740**	**24,727,930**	49,770,720

(**Source:** SEBI, NSE and Stock Exchanges)

16 Valuation of Equity Shares (and Capital Market Theory)

CHAPTER

Ordinary shares, preference shares and debentures are three important securities used by corporate sector to raise funds to finance their business activities. Ordinary shares provide ownership rights to ordinary shareholders. They are the legal owners of the company. As a result, they have residual claims on income and assets of the company. The preemptive right of the ordinary shareholders is maintained by raising new equity funds, through rights offerings. Rights issue does not affect the wealth of a shareholder.

Preference share is a hybrid security as it includes some features of both an ordinary share and a debenture. With regard to claims on income and assets, it stands before an ordinary share but after a debenture. Most preference shares in India have a cumulative feature, requiring that all past outstanding preference dividends are to be paid before any dividend to ordinary shareholders is announced. Preference shares could be redeemable, or irredeemable, i.e., perpetual, also it could be convertible or non-convertible.

16.1 CONCEPTS OF VALUE

How shares are valued? What is the role of earnings per share (EPS) and price-earnings ratios (P/E) in the valuation of shares? Do EPS and P/E really have significance in the valuation of shares? As we mentioned earlier in bond valuation, the *present value* is the most valid and true concept of value. Some other concepts of value are:

(i) Book Value: Book value is an accounting concept that reflects historical cost, rather than value. Book value per share is determined as net worth (difference between the book values of assets and liabilities) divided by the number of shares outstanding.

(ii) Replacement Value: This is the amount that a company would be required to spend if it were to replace its existing assets in the current condition, while ignoring the benefits of intangibles and the utility of existing assets.

(iii) Liquidation Value: It is the amount that a company could realize if it sold its assets, after having decided to terminate its business, generally a minimum value which a company might accept.

(iv) Going Concern Value: This is the amount that a company could realize if it sold its operating/running business. Going concern value would always be higher than the liquidation value, since it reflects the future value of assets and value of intangibles.

(v) Market Value: Market value of an asset or security is the current price at which the asset or the security is being sold or bought in the market. A number of factors influence the market value per share; therefore, it shows wide fluctuations. What is important is the long-term trend in the market value per share. In an ideal situation, where the capital markets are efficient and in equilibrium, market value should be equal to present (or intrinsic) value of a share.

The *present value* of a share is equal to the discounted value of stream of cash flows – the discount rate being the rate of return that investors expect from securities of comparable risk. Cash flows of an ordinary equity share consist of the stream of dividends and terminal price of the share. Unlike bond, cash flows of a share are not known. Thus, the risk of holding a share is relatively higher than the bond. Consequently, equity capitalization rate will be higher than that of a bond.

Present Value of Expected Stream of Benefits from Equity Shares

Fundamental analysis is centred on present value, which is computed as the discounted value of future of earnings. This poses two problems. One, it is neither specified (as in the case of preference shares) nor stated and their timings have to be estimated in a probabilistic manner, viz., dividends, cash flows and earnings.

The solution to the first problem is offered by past data, which is appropriately modified for future projections. A major modification to past data will be premised on materialised growth rates of return on equities. The second problem can also be viewed as a case of three alternatives not really conflicting with each other. And the question is: which cash flows are appropriate in the valuation of equity shares?

Now, if one buys equity and places it in all in a trust fund for oneself and his heir's perpetual benefit, what cash flows will be received to fund? The answer is '*dividends*' because this is the only cash distribution, which a company makes. Since a price is the present value of future dividends, investors' cash flows from equity shares as a combination of dividends and a future price at which the shares can be equivalent to the stream of all dividends to be received on the shares.

Finally, should one regard earnings as important and use them as a measure of future benefits? Obviously, the answer is 'yes'. All dividends are paid out of earnings. Moreover, a popular approach to valuation of equity known as P/E ratio uses earnings as its basis. Hence, earnings are important.

16.2 VALUATION OF ORDINARY EQUITY SHARES

The valuation of ordinary or equity shares is relatively more difficult. First, the estimates of the amount and timing of the cash flows expected by equity shareholders are uncertain. Second, the earnings and dividends on equity shares are generally expected to grow, hence this feature of variable dividend on equity shares makes the calculation difficult. The factors of growth and risk create greater complexity in the case of equity shares. We will discuss now the key determinants of intrinsic value and examine a framework helpful in estimating them.

Key Determinants of Intrinsic Value

As an equity shareholder, an investor expects to receive a stream of dividends from it which extends indefinitely into the future. So the intrinsic value of an equity share may be represented as follows:

$$\text{Value} = \frac{D_1}{(1+k)} + \frac{D_2}{(1+k)^{\wedge}2} + \ldots + \frac{D_n}{(1+k)^{\wedge}n}$$

where D_1, D_2 ... are dividends receivable at the end of year 1, year 2, and so on and k is the discount rate (required rate of return) applicable to the equity share being analysed.

If we assume that the dividend per share grows at a constant rate, denoted by the symbol g (growth rate), the intrinsic value may be represented as:

$$\text{Value} = \frac{D_1}{k-g}$$

To illustrate, consider the equity stock of M Limited:

E_1 (earning per share) = Rs. 3
b(dividend payout ratio) = 0.6
k(discount rate) = 0.15
g(growth rate) = 0.06

The intrinsic value per share of M Limited equity is:

$$\text{Value} = \frac{3.00\,(0.6)}{0.15-0.06} = \text{Rs. } 20.00$$

Examining the above formula and calculation, one finds that the key determinants of intrinsic value are:

- Earning per share
- Payout ratio
- Discount rate
- Growth rate

Valuation Rules

The influence of these determinants of intrinsic value may be expressed in terms of the following rules:

Rule 1: The higher the earnings per share, other things being equal, higher would be the intrinsic value.

Rule 2: The higher the payout ratio, other things being equal, higher would be the intrinsic value.

Rule 3: The higher the discount rate, other things being equal, lower would be the intrinsic value.

Rule 4: The higher the growth rate, other things being equal, higher would be the intrinsic value.

Further Analysis

It is helpful to analyse further the following key determinants: earning per share, discount rate, and growth rate.

Earning per share is equal to: (book value per share) (return on equity). So we get two sub-rules for valuation:

Rule 1(a): The higher the book value per share, other things being equal, higher would be the intrinsic value.

Rule 1(b): The higher the rate on equity, other things being equal, higher would be the intrinsic value.

The discount rate may be established as follows:

Risk-free rate of return + Risk premium
Since the discount rate is determined mainly by the risk-free rate of return and the risk level, we get the following sub-rules for valuation:

Rule 2(a): The higher the risk-free rate of return, other things being equal, lower would be the intrinsic value.

Rule 2(b): The greater the risk exposure, other things being equal, lower would be the intrinsic value.

Growth Rate, the most intractable element of the valuation exercise, truly tests the judgement of the analyst and/or the investor. The sustainable growth rate is equal to: (retention ratio)* (return on equity).

So we get the following sub-rules on valuation:

Rule 3(a): The higher the retention ratio, other things being equal, higher would be the intrinsic value.

Rule 3(b): The higher the rate on equity, other things being equal, higher would be the intrinsic value.

Estimation of Intrinsic Value

The procedure commonly employed by investment analysts to estimate the intrinsic value of a share consists of the following steps:

1. estimate the earnings per share for the current year,
2. forecast the growth rate in earnings per share,

3. assess the risk exposure,
4. establish a price-earnings multiple, and
5. develop a value anchor and a value range.

Impact of Growth and Discount Rates on P/E Multiple

Investment analysts pay a great deal of attention to the price-earning (P/E) multiple. How is this P/E multiple related to growth and discount rates? To answer this question, we divide one of the above referred equations by E, the earnings per share. Doing so, we get:

$$P/E = \frac{D/E}{k - g}$$

Given the above relationship, we can study the sensitivity of the P/E multiple to variations in k and g.

Dividend Capitalization

The value of a share depends on cash inflows (in the form of dividends) expected by investors and the risk associated with those cash inflows. So for shareholders in general, the expected cash inflows consist only of future dividends and, therefore, the value of an ordinary share is determined by the future dividend stream at the opportunity cost of capital. Hence, the value of a share is the present value of its future stream of dividends.

Growth in Dividends

Dividends do not remain constant. Earnings and dividends of most companies grow over time, at least, because of their retention policies. This policy would increase the ordinary shareholder's equity as well as the firm's future earnings.

Earnings Capitalization The dividend capitalization is basic share valuation model. However, under the following two different cases, the value of the share can be determined by capitalizing the expected earnings.

- When the firm pays out 100 per cent dividends, and does not retain any earnings.
- When the firm's return on equity (ROE) is equal to its opportunity cost of capital.

Thus, true growth, as opposed to mere expansion, is dependent on the existence of growth opportunities, to reinvest retained earnings at a rate higher than the capitalization rate, thereby creating net present value over and above the investment outlays required. The price of a 'growth stock' is not merely the capitalized value of earnings but it also includes the present value of growth opportunities. The earnings-price ratio will equal the capitalization rate only when growth opportunities are zero, otherwise it will either overestimate or underestimate the capitalization rate.

Caution in Using Constant Growth Formula

The constant growth formula is a useful rule of the thumb for calculating the present value of a share and the opportunity cost of capital. However, a blind faith in the formula can be misleading. One should be cautious in using the formula for the following:

- Estimation errors
- Unsustainable high current growth
- Errors in forecasting dividends

Equity Capitalization Rate

The required rate of return is equal to the risk-free rate of interest plus the risk premium to account for the equity share's risk which the owner has assumed. The risk premium would be different for different shares.

In a well functioning capital market, the *market price is the fair price of a share*. Therefore, the shareholders expect the share to earn a minimum return that keeps the current share price intact.

Linkages between Share Price, Earnings and Dividends

Why do investors buy shares? Do they buy them for dividends or for capital gain? Investors may choose between growth shares or income shares. *Growth share* offer greater opportunities for capital gains. Dividend yield (i.e., dividend per share as a percentage of the market price of the share) on such shares would generally be low since companies would follow a high retention policy in order to have a high growth rate.

Income shares, on the other hand, pay higher dividends, and offer low prospects for capital appreciation. Because of the high payout policy followed by the companies, their share prices tend to grow at a lower rate. Dividend yield on income shares would generally be high. Those investors who want regular income would prefer to buy income shares, which pay high dividends regularly. On the other hand, investors who desire to earn higher return (capital gain) would prefer to buy growth shares.

Active Equity Investment Styles

The primary styles of active equity management are top-down and bottom-up. A manager who uses a *top-down* equity management style begins with an assessment of the overall economic environment and a forecast of its near-term outlook and makes a general asset allocation decision regarding the relative attractiveness of the various sectors of the financial markets (e.g., equity, bond, real estate, and bullion and cash equivalents).

The top-down manager then analyses the stock market to identify economic sectors and industries that stand to gain or lose from the manager's economic forecast. After identifying attractive and unattractive sectors and industries, the top-down manager finally selects a portfolio of individual stocks.

EQUITY MANGEMENT

Active	Passive
Subjective	Objective
Complex rules	Simple rules
Few names	Many names
Appropriate weightings	Precise weightings

TRADING

Active	Passive
Worked transactions	Programme transactions
Few names	Many names
Cash reserves	Fully vested

MONITORING

Active	Passive
Infrequent	Constant
Approximate	Detailed

Share Valuation

Share valuation is the process of assigning a rupee value to a specific share. An ideal share of valuation technique would assign an accurate value to all shares. Share valuation is a complex topic and no single valuation model can truly predict the intrinsic value of a share. Valuation models can provide a basis to compare the relative merits of two different shares.

Equity valuations could be classified into the following categories:

1. Earnings valuation
2. Revenues valuation
3. Cash flow valuation
4. Asset valuation
5. Yield valuation
6. Member valuation

Rights Issues of Equity Shares

A rights issue involves selling of ordinary shares to the existing shareholders of the company. The law in India requires that the new ordinary shares must be first issued to the existing shareholders on a *pro rata* basis. Shareholders through a special resolution can forfeit this preemptive right. Obviously, this will dilute their ownership.

Value of a Right

Let us consider a company ABC has 9,00,000 shares outstanding, at current market price of Rs. 130 per share. The company needs Rs. 22.50 million (Rs. 2.25 crore) to finance its proposed modernization-cum-expansion project. The board of the company have decided to issue rights for raising the required money. The subscription/issue price (Ps) has been fixed at Rs. 75 per share. The subscription price has been set below the market price to ensure that the rights issue is fully subscribed.

We can determine the number of new shares to be issued to raise Rs. 22.50 million at Rs. 75 per share.

$$\text{No. of new shares} = \frac{\text{Desired funds}}{\text{Subscription price (Ps)}} = \frac{22,500,000}{75}$$

$$= 3,00,000 \text{ shares}$$

$$\text{In our example, the number of rights required are} = \frac{9,00,000}{3,00,000} = 3 \text{ rights}$$

This implies that to purchase a new share, an existing shareholder should have 3 rights and Rs. 75. What is the price of one share after rights offering? The price of the share after the rights issue is called *ex-rights* price (P_x). It is equal to the value of 3 rights plus Rs. 75. The formula for ex-rights issue (P_x) can be written as:

$$P_x = N * R + P_s$$

where N is the number of rights needed to buy one share

R is the value of a right

P_s is the subscription price.

This price can be found by using formula:

$$P_x = \frac{So * Po + s * P_s}{So + s} = \frac{So\,Po + sPs}{S}$$

where $S = So + s$. In our example, the price is:

$$= \frac{9,00,000 * 130 + 3,00,000 * 75}{9,00,000 + 3,00,000} = \frac{1,170,000 + 22,500,000}{12,00,000}$$

$$= \text{Rs.}116.25$$

In our example in company ABC rights issue, we know that a shareholder can buy one new share for Rs. 75 plus 3 rights. The company's share price after the ex-rights date is theoretically worth Rs. 116.25. Therefore, the total value of 3 rights together is Rs. 41.25 (Rs. 116.25 – Rs. 75), and the value of each right is Rs. 13.75 (Rs. 41.25/3).Thus the share price on the ex-rights date drops by Rs. 13.75 from the cum-rights (rights-on) price of Rs. 130 to the ex-rights price of Rs. 116.25 (Rs. 130 – Rs. 13.75). This drop is the value of one right.

16.3 EQUITY VALUATION MODELS

The purpose of equity valuation models is to identify whether a stock is mispriced. Underpriced stocks need to be purchased; overpriced stocks should be shorted. As most modern equity valuation models are based upon the present value theory, set forth in detail by John B. Williams in ***Theory of Investments Value***, the investment analyst must first turn to the present value estimation to know the intrinsic value of the equity shares.

Dividend Valuation Model

A difficult problem in using the dividend valuation model is the timing of cash flows from dividends. Since equity shares have no finite measure, the investor must forecast all future dividends. This might imply a forecast of intently long stream of dividends. Clearly, this would almost be impossible. And therefore, in order to manage the problem, assumptions are made with regard to the future growth of the dividend of the immediately previous period available at the time the investor wants to determine the intrinsic value of his/her equity shares. The assumptions can be:

(a) Dividends do not grow in future, i.e., the constant or *zero growth* assumption.
(b) Dividends grow at a constant rate in future, *i.e.*, the *constant* assumption.
(c) Dividends grow at varying rates in the future time period *i.e., multiple* growth assumption.

The following are a few dividend valuation models - with these assumptions:

(i) Zero growth case
(ii) Constant growth case
(iii) Multiple growth case

Financial Ratio Analysis

It is essential to obtain analytical insights using the data available in a balance sheet and a profit and loss account of any company. There are some widely popular tools of financial analysis which can be used to interpret the financial status and performance of a company. The tool kit of financial ratio analysis includes:

(i) Comparative balance sheet and P & L account: This exercise is done by comparing the financial statements for two or more years and studying the changes in assets, liabilities, income and expenditure.

(ii) Common size balance sheets and P & L accounts: This is a modified version of the first exercise. Figures in the financial statements are converted into percentages and studied. Since it is easier to analyse percentages than the absolute numbers.

These two method of using financial ratios is quite popular among the financial analysts. Several ratios are worked out using the financial data drawn from the balance sheet and the P & L account. These are then studied each by itself and also in conjunction with other ratios, in order to gain critical insights.

Financial ratios are helpful

- To bankers for appraising creditworthiness.
- To financial institutions for project appraisal.
- To investors for taking investment and disinvestment decisions.
- To financial analysts for making comparisons and recommending to the investing public.
- To credit rating agencies (like CRISIL, Moody's, etc.).
- To government agencies for reviewing and monitoring its fiscal packages and taxation policy.
- To company management for making intra-firm and inter-firm comparisons.

The Du Pont System of Ratio Analysis

The Du Pont Company developed a simple system of ratio analysis for analysing the financial statements. The significance of the Du Pont system lies in its sharp focus on the ultimate corporate objective, return on investment (ROI):

Productivity of Capital Profitability of Sales

= (Sales)/(Capital employed) * 100

= (Profit)/(Sales) * 100

Table 16.1 Framework for Ratio Analysis

Macro Level

Focus	Ratios	Reference group
Overall performance	ROI ratios	Top management, financial institutes, banks, investors
Equity returns	Equity ratios	–
Capital structure	Leverage ratios	–
Safety aspects	Coverage ratios	–

Micro Level

Working capital management	Activity ratios	Operations management, bankers, creditors, suppliers
Cash flows	Liquidity ratios	–
Overall profits	Profitability ratios	Senior management, lenders and investors

Type of Ratios:

Activity Ratios would include inventory turnover ratios, average collection period (debtors turnover), capital employed turnover, fixed assets turnover.

Liquidity Ratios would include current ratio, quick ratio or acid test ratio.

Profitability Ratios would include gross profit margin, net profit margin, operating (expenses) ratios.

Leverage Ratios would include debt-equity ratio, total debt to total capital employed ratio.

Coverage Ratios would include interest coverage, dividend cover, and debt service coverage ratio.

ROI Ratios would include return on assets; return on total capital employed, return on shareholder's net worth.

Equity Investor's Ratios would include earnings per share (eps), dividend per share, dividend pay-out ratio, dividend yield, earnings yield, price/earnings ratio (p/e ratio), book value per share, market price to book value.

Limitations of Ratio Analysis

Financial ratios have certain limitations. essentially, they are mere tools. What is important is how they are used, keeping in mind the following limitations:

1. Varying situations
2. No uniformity in definitions
3. No norms
4. No published accounts.

Integrated Study of Ratios: In view of these limitations of the various ratios, they should be studied together to yield a more meaningful picture.

Models Based on Price Ratio Analysis

Price ratios are widely used by financial analysts, more so even than dividend discount models. Of course, all valuation methods try to accomplish the same thing, which is to appraise the economic value of a company's stock.

P/E Approach to Equity Valuation

The first step consists of estimating future earnings per share. Next, the normal price-earnings ratio will be estimated. Product of these two estimates will give the expected price. For a single year holding period, with D_1 as the referred dividends in the coming year, the expected return of an investor can be found as under:

$$\text{Expected Return} = \frac{D_1(P_1 - P_0)}{P_0}$$

Reasons for Companies to have Negative Earnings

There are a number of reasons for a company to have negative earnings. Some of the reasons for negative earnings can be summarised as under:

- Cyclical nature of industry
- Unforeseeable circumstances
- Poor management
- Persistent negative earnings
- Early growth stage
- High leverage cost

Price-Book (P/B) Ratio

A very basic price ratio for a company is its price-book (P/B) ratio, sometimes called the *market-book ratio*. A price-book ratio is measured as the value of a company's equity issued divided by its book value of equity. Price-book ratios are appealing because book value represents, in principle, historical costs. The stock price is an indicator of current value, so a price-book ratio simply measures what the equity is worth today, relative to its cost. A ratio that is bigger than 1.0 indicates that the firm successfully created value for its shareholders. A ratio which is smaller than 1.0 indicates that the company is worthless for its value than the cost.

Price-Sales (P/S) Ratio

A price-sales (P/S) ratio is calculated as the current price of a company's stock divided by its current annual sales revenue per share. A high P/S ratio would suggest high sales growth, while a low P/S ratio might indicate sluggish sales growth.

Considerations in developing and selecting quantitative strategies

Many models can be used in combination with each other and especially in combination with sound judgement. The quantitative strategy in valuation models may be defined as *engineered investment strategies*. In developing these strategies, consideration must be given at least to three characteristics.

First, the strategy should be based on a sound theory. That is, there should be not only a reason why the strategy worked in the past, but, more importantly, a reason why it should be expected to work in the future. Second, the strategy should be put in quantified terms. Finally, a determination should be made of how the strategy would have performed in the past. This last characteristic is critical and is the reason why investment strategies are back-tested. An equity manager encounters many potential problems in the design, testing and implementation of engineered investment strategies. One such model is:

Random Valuation Model

The random valuation model begins with the promise that the next three years' growth of earnings, dividends, and price will be similar to those of the past ten years. This is similar to the *trend valuation equation* for estimating the rate of return, *r*.

In this model, the ten-year growth rate of earnings and dividends is used, along with the P/E ratio.

16.4 STOCK MARKET ANOMALIES AND FUNDAMENTAL INSIGHT OF CAPITAL ASSET PRICING MODEL

Despite these extraordinary changes, an annually rebalanced, passive approach to investing in equities, if it had been available could have performed very well. However, the belief that it should be possible to do "better" than to reflect the pattern of the stock market as a whole is supported by a wide body of research. This has focused on extensive analysis of stock market "anomalies", which are well-established patterns of stock market performance that do not conform with the predictions of the original simplified theory called the *capital asset pricing model* (CAPM).

In the original form, the CAPM said that the performance of any stock should be expected to reflect two things: the extent to which the stock is geared or a diluted "play" on the market as a whole; and as a considerable amount of company specific volatility. There have been numerous refinements to the CAPM to reflect research indicating that there are a number of sources of risk for a particular share price in the stock market which can help to explain share price performance. These include interest rate and foreign exchange exposure, corporate balance-sheet data, income and dividend information, as well as company capitalization, industry and geographical location. An understanding of these sources of risk can help in construction of equity portfolios, particularly if an investor has a view that a particular source of risk taking is likely to produce good results in the period ahead.

The CAPM provides a framework to determine the required rate of return on an asset and indicates the relationship between return and risk of an asset. The required rate of return specified by CAPM helps in valuing an asset. One can also compare the expected (estimated) rate of return on an asset with its required rate of return and determine whether the asset is fairly valued.

However, the fundamental insight of CAPM – the division of portfolio risk into undiversifiable, systematic market risk and diversifiable, idiosyncratic risk – has stood the test of time. It provides an invaluable framework for understanding how the activities of portfolio managers alter a portfolio's systematic and idiosyncratic risk exposures and so affect the performance and risk of that portfolio. An understanding of this insight, as well as its strengths and weaknesses, is an important aspect of the interface between finance theory and practical investment.

Among the weaknesses of CAPM is that it is now accepted that the original simplified theory does not fully explain the pattern of performance between different stocks. Low Beta stocks, with supposedly diluted exposure to the market, do not systematically underperform the stock market as the original theory suggested that they should. Furthermore, stocks with smaller market capitalization and certain measures of "value" stocks have shown an apparent persistence of superior performance that is inconsistent with the simplest versions of the theory.

Assumptions of CAPM

The CAPM envisages the relationship between risk and the expected rate of return on a risky security. Some of its important assumptions are given below:

- ***Market Efficiency***: The capital market efficiency implies that share prices reflect all available information. Also, individual investors are not able to affect the prices of securities. This means that there are large number of investors holding a small amount of wealth.
- ***Risk Aversion and Mean-Variance Optimization***: Investors are risk-averse and evaluate a security's return and risk, in terms of expected return and variance or standard deviation respectively. Investors prefer the highest expected returns for a given level of risk. This implies that investors are *mean-variance optimizers* and they form efficient portfolios.
- ***Homogeneous Expectations***: All investors have the same expectations about the expected returns and risks of securities.
- ***Single Time Period***: All investors' decisions are based on a single time period.
- ***Risk-Free Rate***: All investors can lend and borrow at a risk-free rate of interest. They form portfolios from publicly traded securities like shares and bonds.

Given these assumptions, CAPM provides a logical basis for measuring risk and linking risk and return. As such CAPM has the following implications:

- Investors will always combine a risk-free asset with a market portfolio of risky assets. They will invest in risky assets in proportion to their market value.
- Investors will be compensated only for that risk which they cannot diversify. This is the market related (systematic) risk.
- Investors can expect returns from their investment according to the risk. This implies a linear relationship between the asset's expected return and its Beta.

  However, in spite of its intuitive appeal and simplicity, CAPM suffers from practical problems and some of them are as follows:

  - It is based on unrealistic assumptions.
  - It is difficult to test the validity of CAPM.
  - Betas do not remain stable over time.

Value and Growth Managers

Value managers commonly have an investment process that starts with statistical screening of stock market databases for companies whose share price, earnings, dividend and balance-sheet data meet certain characteristics. A value stock will be one that has some combination of:

- higher than average dividend yield;
- lower than average ratio of the stock price to earnings per share or of the stock price to the book value of the company's assets per share; and
- lower than average ratio of the company's valuation to sales of or of valuation to cash flow.

There are some ratios that are used in constructing "value" indices of stock market performance. Individual managers use different combinations of these and other indicators to screen for value in the stock market. Apart from purely quantitative managers, the screening process is best seen as a step towards reducing the potential universe of investable companies to a manageable number, which the investment manager can then research qualitatively in depth. This stage, involving management, product and industry research and ad hoc analysis, is often be the most important part of the investment process.

But the screens are also important ingredients in describing a manager's investment style, and they define the universe of stocks that the manager may then research further. As stock prices evolve, managers should be able to relate their actual portfolios back to those screens to demonstrate that the portfolios remain true to the manager's descriptions of their investment style.

Value managers are divided into two camps:

1. "Deep" value managers invest in stocks that meet their qualitative and quantitative criteria irrespective of how unrepresentative the resulting portfolio may be of the market as a whole. In particular, they are happy to have a zero weighting in parts of the stock market where the value screens suggest that all stocks offer poor value.
2. "Relative" value managers manage the risks of their portfolios relative to the market as a whole, and so have discipline that forces the portfolio to hold some less expensive stocks in sectors that the screens suggest are absolutely expensive.

Growth managers are to exploit and profit from the relationship between growth of earnings and stock price performance. Companies generally do not post unusually strong earnings growth results year after year. But as the market discounts the strong earnings of those companies that are growing rapidly, their stock prices can rise very strongly.

This puts a premium on primary research into companies that may demonstrate unexpectedly rapid earnings growth in the future. Many growth managers also use statistical screening of databases, but this is generally a less powerful tool than successful qualitative industry or thematic research. Such research is notoriously difficult to undertake successfully and consistently. The statistical screens used by the index compliers to define "growth" stocks are earnings per share growth, sales growth and the ratio of retained earnings to equity capital (the internal rate of growth).

Table 16.2 Indian Equities: A Great Compounding Machine – (% return)

No.	Year ending March	BSE Sensex on 31/03/XXXX	Rolling 1 year returns	Rolling 5 year returns	Rolling 10 year returns	Rolling 15 year returns
0	Mar-79	100				
1	Mar-80	129	29			
2	Mar-81	173	35			
3	Mar-82	218	26			
4	Mar-83	212	-3			
5	Mar-84	245	16	20		
6	Mar-85	354	44	22		
7	Mar-86	574	62	27		
8	Mar-87	510	-11	19		
9	Mar-88	398	-22	13		
10	Mar-89	714	79	24	22	
11	Mar-90	781	9	17	20	
12	Mar-91	1168	50	15	21	
13	Mar-92	4285	267	53	35	
14	Mar-93	2281	-47	42	27	
15	Mar-94	3779	66	40	31	27
16	Mar-95	3261	-14	33	25	24
17	Mar-96	3367	3	24	19	22
18	Mar-97	3361	0	-5	21	20
19	Mar-98	3893	16	11	26	21
20	Mar-99	3740	-4	0	18	20
21	Mar-00	5001	34	9	20	19
22	Mar-01	3604	-28	1	12	13
23	Mar-02	3469	-4	1	-2	14
24	Mar-03	3049	-12	-5	3	15
25	Mar-04	5591	83	8	4	15
26	Mar-05	6493	16	5	7	15

Contd.

27	Mar-06	11280	74	26	13	16
28	Mar-07	13072	16	30	15	8
29	Mar-08	15644	20	39	15	14
30	Mar-09	9709	-38	12	10	6
31	Mar-10	17528	81	22	13	12
32	Mar-11	19445	11	12	18	12
33	Mar-12	17404	-10	6	18	12
34	Mar-13	18836	8	4	20	11
35	Mar-14	22386	19	18	15	13
36	Mar-15	27957	25			
37	Mar-16	25342	-9			
38	Mar-17	29621	17			

Source: BSE and SENSEX calculation methodology

Returns for a period of more than 1 year are shown on compounded annualised basis.

1. Sensex/equities are a great compounding machine
   Rs. 100 = Rs. 22,386 over a period of 34 years
2. Short-term returns in equity are volatile; hence equity investments should be made with a long-term horizon.
3. Long-term returns are less volatile; risk in equity reduces as holding period increases.
4. As holding period increases, chances of loss reduces.

Historical Capital Market Returns

What rates of returns on shares and other financial instruments have investors in India earned? We have used BSE-SENSEX (Bombay Stock Exchange Sensitivity Index) along with rates of return for the following financial instruments for the period 1981 to 2008.

1. **Ordinary shares:** SENSEX price data is used for calculating market return.
2. **Long-term GOI bonds:** This is a portfolio of GOI bonds with maturity over 15 years.
3. **Call Money Market:** This is a portfolio of inter-bank transactions.
4. **91-days Treasury Bills:** This is a portfolio of treasury bills of three-month maturity. The interest rate structure in India was controlled by the Government until the beginning of 1990s. The return on 91-day treasury bills remained fixed (arbitrarily) at 4.60% until 1993.

Table: 16.3 Year-by-Year Return (%) in different Asset Class: 1991-2012

Year	Sensex return	Call Money Market rates	Long-term Govt. bonds yield	91-day T-Bills rates	Inflation rate - CII (Income-tax)
1980-81	35.00	7.10	7.00	4.60	11.40
1981-82	26.00	9.00	7.20	4.60	12.50
1982-83	-3.00	8.80	7.70	4.60	7.80
1983-84	16.00	8.60	8.20	4.60	12.60
1984-85	44.00	10.00	9.20	4.60	6.30
1985-86	62.00	10.00	9.90	4.60	6.80
1986-87	-11.00	10.00	10.20	4.60	8.70
1987-88	-22.00	9.90	10.30	4.60	8.80
1988-89	79.00	9.80	10.60	4.60	9.40
1989-90	9.00	11.50	10.90	4.60	6.10
1990-91	50.00	15.90	11.50	4.60	11.60
1991-92	267.00	19.60	11.20	4.60	13.50
1992-93	-47.00	14.40	10.70	4.60	9.60
1993-94	66.00	7.00	13.10	8.90	7.50
1994-95	-14.00	9.40	12.60	9.10	10.10
1995-96	3.00	17.70	12.40	12.70	10.20
1996-97	0.00	7.80	11.60	9.70	9.40
1997-98	16.00	8.70	11.10	6.80	6.80
1998-99	-4.00	7.80	11.70	8.90	3.80
1999-2000	34.00	8.90	11.50	9.20	3.50
2000-01	-28.0	9.20	11.20	6.80	3.80
2001-02	-4.00	7.20	9.10	5.70	4.30
2002-03	-12.00	5.90	9.40	4.50	4.00
2003-04	83.00	4.60	6.60	4.80	3.90
2004-05	16.00	4.70	6.60	5.70	3.80
2005-06	74.00	5.60	7.50	6.50	4.40
2006-07	16.00	7.20	8.70	6.90	6.70

Contd.

2007-08	20.00	7.60	7.90	7.40	7.80
2008-09	-38.00				8.46
2009-10	81.00				3.93
2010-11	11.00				9.58
2011-12	-10.00				8.97
2012-13	8.00				7.36
2013-14	19.00				5.39
2014-15	25.00				2.06
2015-16	-9.00				
2016-17	17.00				

Source: NSE, SEBI & RBI

Table 16.4

Last 35 years Inflation Gold, FD, Sensex, PPF and LIC Bonus							
	Year	Inflation	Gold	FD	Sensex	PPF	LIC Bonus Rate
1	1979–80	17.12%	46%	7.00%	29.00%	8.25%	2.40%
2	1980–81	18.24%	31%	7.50%	34.00%	8.25%	2.80%
3	1981–82	9.33%	13%	8.00%	26.00%	8.50%	2.80%
4	1982–83	4.90%	0%	8.00%	–3.00%	8.75%	3.40%
5	1983–84	7.53%	8%	8.00%	16.00%	9.15%	3.40%
6	1984–85	6.47%	7%	8.00%	44.00%	9.50%	4.40%
7	1985–86	4.41%	7%	8.50%	62.00%	10.15%	5.20%
8	1986–87	5.82%	9%	8.50%	–11.00%	11.00%	5.80%
9	1987–88	8.14%	33%	9.00%	–22.00%	11.50%	6.20%
10	1988–89	7.46%	3%	9.00%	79.00%	11.80%	6.40%
11	1989–90	7.46%	2%	9.00%	9.00%	12.00%	6.60%
12	1990–91	10.26%	7%	9.00%	50.00%	12.00%	6.70%
13	1991–92	13.74%	25%	12.00%	267.00%	12.00%	6.70%
14	1992–93	10.06%	–5%	11.00%	–47.00%	12.00%	6.70%
15	1993–94	8.35%	10%	10.00%	66.00%	12.00%	6.70%
16	1994–95	12.60%	3%	11.00%	–14.00%	12.00%	6.70%

17	1995–96	7.99%	6%	12.00%	3.00%	12.00%	6.70%
18	1996–97	4.61%	2%	11.00%	0.00%	12.00%	7.10%
19	1997–98	4.40%	–14%	10.50%	16.00%	12.00%	7.10%
20	1998–99	5.95%	–2%	9.00%	–4.00%	12.00%	7.10%
21	1990–00	3.27%	3%	8.50%	34.00%	12.00%	7.10%
22	2000–01	7.16 %	2%	8.50%	–28.00%	12.00%	7.10%
23	2001–02	3.60%	2%	7.50%	–4.00%	9.50%	6.50%
24	2002–03	3.41%	16%	4.25%	–12.00%	9.50%	5.80%
25	2003–04	5.46%	7%	4.00%	83.00%	9.50%	5.10%
26	2004–05	6.48%	7%	5.25%	16.00%	9.50%	4.50%
27	2005–06	4.50%	12%	6.00%	74.00%	8.50%	4.00%
28	2006–07	6.60%	34%	7.50%	16.00%	8.50%	4.20%
29	2007–08	4.67%	8%	8.25%	20.00%	8.50%	4.20%
30	2008–09	8.06%	29%	8.00%	–38.00%	8.50%	4.20%
31	2009–10	3.81%	22%	6.00%	81.00%	8.50%	4.20%
32	2010–11	9.56%	22%	8.25%	11.00%	9.50%	4.20%
33	2011–12	8.93%	34%	9.00%	–11.00%	8.60%	4.20%
34	2012–13	7.00%	14%	9.00%	8.00%	8.80%	4.20%
35	2013–14	5.70%	–2%	9.00%	19.00%	8.70%	4.20%
Pre inflation Average		7.52%	11.46%	8.43%	24.00%	10.21%	5.27%
Post Inflation Average		7.52%	3.94%	0.91%	17.31%	2.69%	–2.24%

Source: Websites of RBI, Finance Ministry, Post-office, LIC & MCX

17 Commodity Market

CHAPTER

Ever since the dawn of civilization, commodity trading occupied an integral place in the lives of mankind. The very reason for this lies in the fact that commodities represent the fundamental elements of utility for human beings. The term, *commodity*, refers to any material, which can be bought and sold. Commodities in a market's context refer to any movable property other than actionable claims, money and securities. Over the years, commodity markets have been experiencing tremendous progress, which is evident from the fact that the trade in this segment is a boon for the global economy today. The promising nature of these markets has made them an attractive avenue for investment.

In the early days, people followed a mechanism for trading called barter system, which involved exchange of goods for goods. This was the first form of trade between individuals. The absence of a commonly accepted medium of exchange had initiated the need for the barter system. People used to buy those commodities, which they lacked and sell those commodities, which they had in excess.

The commodity trade is believed to have its genesis in ancient Sumeria. The early commodity contracts were carried out using clay tokens as medium of exchange. Animals are believed to have been the first commodities, which were traded, between individuals.

The internationalization of commodity trade can be better understood by observing the commodity market integration that occurred after the European voyages of discovery. The development of international commodity trade is characterized by the increase in volumes of trade across national boundaries and the convergence and price related to the identical commodities at different markets. The major thrust for the commodities trade was provided by the changes in demand patterns, scarcity and the supply potential, both within and across the nations.

Commodity markets are of great help not only for their participants but also for the economy as a whole. The twenty-four year bear market for commodities drastically reduced the prices of many commodities to their lowest levels. The present shift in trend in commodity trading complemented by the global increase in demand certainly holds a promising future for the investments in this segment.

17.1 WHAT IS A COMMODITY?

Any goods that are unbranded and are commonly traded in the market come under the term "commodities" (other than money, security and actionable claims).

Commodity Trading

Commodity markets are quite like equity markets. The commodity market also has two constituents, i.e., the spot market and derivative market. In case of a spot market, the commodities are bought and sold for immediate delivery. In case of a commodities derivative market, various financial instruments having commodities as underlying security are traded on the exchanges. It has been seen that traditionally in India, people have hedged their risks with gold and silver.

The Indian Connection

It is to be rightly said that India is a commodity based economy since more than 70% of the total population is engaged in primary sector directly or indirectly. Major industries of the economy like sugar, textile, metal, energy, etc., are based on various commodities. Commodity derivatives in India have had a chequered history. Commodity derivative markets started in India in cotton in 1875 and in oilseeds in 1900 in Bombay. Forward trading in raw jute and jute goods started at Calcutta in 1912. Forward markets in wheat had been functioning at Hapur in 1913 and in bullion in Bombay since 1920s. In 1919, the then Government of Bombay passed the Bombay Contract Control (War Provision) Act and set up the Cotton Contracts Board.

With a view to restricting speculative activity in cotton market, the Government of Bombay issued an ordinance in September 1939 prohibiting option business. The Bombay Options in Cotton Prohibition Act, 1939, later replaced the ordinance. In 1943, the Defense of India Act was utilized on a large scale for the purpose of prohibiting forward trading in some commodities and regulating such trading in others on an all-India basis.

In the same year, oilseeds forward contracts prohibition order was issued and forward contracts in oilseeds were banned. Similarly, orders were issued banning forward trading in food-grains, spices, vegetable oils, sugar and cloth. These orders were retained with necessary modifications in the Essential Supplies Temporary Powers Act 1946, after the Defence of India Act had lapsed. With a view to evolving unified systems, the Government of Bombay enacted the Bombay Forward Contracts Control Act, 1947.

17.2 LEGAL FRAMEWORK

After independence, the Constitution of India adopted by the Parliament on 26th January, 1950 placed the subject of "Stock Exchanges and Futures Market" in the Union list and therefore the responsibility for regulation of forward contacts devolved on the Government of India. The Parliament passed the Forward Contracts (Regulation) Act, 1952 which presently regulates forward contracts in commodities all over India. The

Act applies to goods, which are defined as any movable property other than security, currency, and actionable claims.

After independence, the Parliament passed Forward Contracts (Regulation) Act, 1952 which regulated forward contracts in commodities all over India. The Act applies to goods, which are defined as any movable property other than security, currency and actionable claims. The Act prohibited options trading in goods along with cash settlements of forward trades, rendering a crushing blow to the commodity derivatives market. Under the Act, only those associations/exchanges, which are granted recognition by the Government, are allowed to organize forward trading in regulated commodities.

The Act envisages three-tier regulation: (i) The *Exchange* which organizes forward trading in commodities can regulate trading on a day-to-day basis; (ii) the *Forward Markets Commission* provides regulatory oversight under the powers delegated to it by the Central Government, and (iii) the *Central Government* - Department of Consumer Affairs, Ministry of Consumer Affairs, Food and Public Distribution - is the ultimate regulatory authority.

The already shaken commodity derivatives market got a crushing blow when in 1960s, following several years of severe draughts that forced many farmers to default on forward contracts (and even caused some suicides); forward trading was banned in many primary or essential commodities. As a result, commodities derivative markets dismantled and went underground where to some extent they continued as OTC contracts at negligible volumes. Much later, in 1970s and 1980s the government relaxed forward trading rules for some commodities, but the market could never regain the lost volumes.

India is one of the top producers of a large number of commodities, and also has a long history of trading in commodities and related derivatives. The market has made enormous progress in terms of technology, transparency and the trading activity. Interestingly, this has happened only after government protection was removed from a number of commodities, and market forces were allowed to play their role. This should act as a major lesson for the policy makers in developing countries, that pricing and price risk management should be left to the market forces rather than trying to achieve these through administered price mechanisms. The management of price risk is going to assume even greater importance in future with the promotion of free trade and removal of trade barriers in the world. All this augurs well for the commodity derivatives markets.

Though the derivative markets survived the prohibition imposed from time to time, thanks largely to the grey markets; the participants have not been able to shrug off the scare of the markets being banned any time. It is not surprising that these markets have not developed as much as the markets in developed countries or even the securities market in our own country. The exchanges emerging from an earlier suffocating environment need a free and liberal regulatory and policy environment.

Despite a long history of commodity markets in India, they are still in their initial stages of development. The essential contribution of this scenario includes stringent regulatory restrictions and intermediate ban on commodity trading and policy interventions by the government. Commodity markets have a huge potential in the Indian context, particularly because of its agricultural based economy.

After gaining considerable popularity, major commodity exchanges in India had started the future contracts in various commodities years back, which can serve preferably to manage the risk that can arise due to adversity of expected prices of commodities besides the price discovery tool. The future contracts dealing in major commodity exchanges are standardized in nature.

With the government's initiative for agricultural liberalization, commodities' trading in India has gained increased momentum. To increase the efficiency of the markets the Forward Markets Commission (FMC), the governing body of commodity trading in India has taken several initiatives for the establishment of national level multi-commodity exchanges in India. These exchanges serve as platforms for facilitating transparent trading, trading in multiple commodities, electronic delivery systems and efficient regulatory mechanisms, creating world-class environment for Indian traders. In order to sustain the increasing volumes in commodities trade, the need for proper clearing and settlement systems, warehousing facilities and efficient pricing mechanisms have been identified. With the recent boom in commodities markets, Indian participants are gearing up for exploiting the potential opportunities in the future.

After 10 years of impressive growth, India is now the seventh largest economy in the world. Yet, to date, India's impact on global commodity markets has been muted. It is observed that India's industrial policies have altered the expansion path of its economy, putting the service sector to the forefront and likely reducing India's demand for metals. Sector-specific policies, such as those promoting self-sufficiency in agriculture, have altered India's demand for food commodities and its supplies of those commodities to international markets. Recent policy reforms in manufacturing have boosted output, which coincides well with an increase in India's demand for metals over the past 4–5 years. Continued policy reforms are likely to diminish the distorting influence of India's domestic and trade policies. India's demand for energy and metals should rise as some rebalancing occurs in its economic structure.

The growth of commodity market was remarkable during the last decade. Prices of all commodities are heading northwards due to rapid increase in demand for commodities. Developing countries like China are voraciously consuming commodities. That's why globally, commodity market is bigger than the stock market. It is the market where a wide range of products, viz., precious metals, base metals, crude oil, energy and soft commodities like palm oil, coffee, etc., are being traded. It is important to develop a vibrant, active and liquid commodity market. This would help investors hedge their commodity risk, take speculative positions in commodities and exploit arbitrage opportunities in the market. Value of contracts traded in commodity market represents the demand for trading and peoples' awareness regarding market. The inverse relation of commodity market with stock market shows the alterative ahead to investors whenever they feel bearish trend in the same.

The size of the commodities markets in India is quite significant. Of the country's GDP of Rs. 13,20,730 crore (Rs. 13,207.30 billion), commodities related (and dependant) industries constitute about 58%. Currently, the various commodities across the country clock an annual turnover of Rs. 1,40,000 crore (Rs. 1400 billion). With the introduction of futures trading, the size of the commodities market is likely to grow manifold from here on.

17.3 COMMODITIES FUTURE

Commodity future is a derivative instrument for the future delivery of a commodity on an agreed future date at a particular price. The underlying security in this case is a particular commodity.

If an investor purchases an oil future, he is entering into a contract to buy a fixed quantity of oil at a future date. The future date is called the *contract expiry date*. The fixed quantity is called the *contract size*. These futures can be bought and sold on the commodity exchanges.

The commodities include agricultural commodities like wheat, rice, tea, jute, spices, soya, groundnut, coffee, rubber, cotton, etc. Precious metals include gold, silver, platinum, etc. Base metals include iron ore, lead, aluminium, nickel, zinc, etc. Energy commodities include crude oil, coal, etc.

The number of retail investors participating in the market is increasing gradually after the introduction of commodities futures. The expected growth rate of commodity market is 40% annually over the next 5-7 years.

In commodity derivatives, the crux of future contracts is to lock up the future price of your commodity on the day of contract and cover the risk against price if it goes down in case of short and rise in case of long. This is basically used to transfer the risk. For example, if you are a producer of a commodity and expect a fall in future in selling price say at the time of harvesting, can short the commodity future in future market for specified quantity and get the agreed price, no matter where the price of such commodity goes.

Likewise if an industrialist knows the need of any commodity like cotton for textile over the year, he can make efforts to cover the demand-supply gap which can lead to hike in prices later on. While entering into future contracts of agricultural products, one should keep in mind the time of sowing and harvesting besides monsoon related factors, which lead to direct impact on the supply of that product.

Pricing of future contracts are directly related to the spot price and expected future price of an underlying asset, which here means a commodity. Simply stated, the change in spot price will lead to change in gain or loss of future contracts in the same direction. The gain or loss in future contracts will always be linear. The emergence of commodity derivatives has reduced transaction cost as well as enabled risk-free trading for producers, investors, and commodity traders and benefited both market participants and non-participants.

Benefits of Commodities Futures

1. **To Producers:** A producer of a commodity can sell the futures of the commodity, thereby ensuring that he can sell a particular quantity of his commodity at a particular price at a particular date.
2. **To Investors:** An investor has an alternative investment instrument where he can take a position as to future price and the spot price at a particular date in future and buy- and sell-options. He is not interested in taking deliveries of the commodities.
3. **To Commodity Traders:** A commodity trader can use these to ensure that he is protected against any adverse changes in the prices. He can enter into a futures contract for purchase or sale of a certain quantity of the underlying commodity at a particular price on a particular date, and be assured of the margins because both, purchase price as well as the sale price, are fixed. Traders do a good arbitrage in gold and silver. Whenever they find gold moving up, they short silver and similarly whenever they find silver moving up and gold likely to move down, they hedge their position.
4. **To Exporters:** Futures trading is very useful to the exporters as it provides an indication of the price likely to prevail, help the exporter in quoting a realistic price and thereby secure export contract in a competitive market. Having entered into an export contract, it enables exporters to hedge their risks by operating in futures market.

Policy Liberalization

In his budget speech of 28th February, 2002, the then Finance Minister announced expansion of futures and forward trading to cover all agricultural commodities. The economic survey for the year 2000-01 indicated the government's intention to allow futures trading in bullion. The policy statements of the government indicate its resolve to introduce reforms in commodity sector. A number of initiatives were also taken to decontrol the spot markets in commodities. The number of commodities listed as essential commodities has been pruned down to 17.

Accordingly, the FMC imposed some regulatory measures for the developed markets like:

- daily mark-to-market margining;
- time stamping of trades;
- notation of contracts and creation of trade guarantee fund;
- back-office computerization for the existing single commodity exchange and online trading for the new exchanges;
- demutualization for new exchanges; and
- one-third representation of independent directors on the boards of existing exchanges.

Commodity Export Scenario

India masters the global castor oil trade with its castor seeds and oil products. The yearly export of commercial castor oil from India turns out to be 2-2.4 lakh tonnes. India is known to be the fifth largest producer of aluminium in the world. Indian aluminium has a huge potential as its production far exceeds its domestic demand.

The export market for Indian organic agricultural products is expanding rapidly. Tea, coffee, spices, rice, wheat, pulses, oilseeds, fruits and vegetables, cashew nut, cotton, herbal products are the major organic products being exported from India.

Thus, the commodity market in India is growing rapidly with huge export potential. Though it is temporarily lagging behind the service sector in the matter of exports, it is sure to catch up within a few years.

Current Development in Commodity Market

The government has now allowed national commodity exchanges, similar to the BSE and NSE, to come up and let them deal in commodity derivatives in an electronic trading environment. These exchanges are expected to offer a nationwide anonymous, order-driven, screen-based trading system for trading. The FMC will regulate these exchanges.

Consequently, four commodity exchanges have been approved to commence business in this regard. They are:

(a) Multi-Commodity Exchange of India Ltd. (MCX) located at Mumbai
(b) National Commodity and Derivatives Exchange Ltd. (NCDEX) located at Mumbai
(c) National Board of Trade (NBOT) located at Indore
(d) National Multi-Commodity Exchange (NMCE) located at Ahmedabad
(e) Indian Commodity Exchange (ICEX) and ACE Commodity and Derivative Exchanges were also granted recognition as another two national multi-commodity exchanges in 2009 and 2010, respectively.

With the establishment of these exchanges, the commodity futures market has witnessed massive growth in India. For example, the total value of commodities traded has steadily increased, and after reaching Rs. 52.40 trillion in 2008-09, it has outperformed the domestic stock market. Certainly, the commodity market has grown to be among the major financial markets in India.

17.4 NEED FOR AN EXCHANGE-TRADED COMMODITY DERIVATIVES MARKET

The biggest advantage of having an exchange-based platform is the reach. A wider reach ensures greater participation, which results into a more efficient price discovery mechanism. In fact, it comes to a stage where the derivative market guides the spot market in terms of pricing.

Opportunities the Commodity Derivatives Provide to Investors

Futures contract in the commodities market, similar to equity derivatives segment, will facilitate the activities of speculation, hedging and arbitrage to all class of investors.

1. **Speculation:** It facilitates speculation by providing an opportunity to investors/ people, although not involved with the commodity, to trade on the views in the movement of commodity prices. The speculative position is taken with a small margin amount that is paid to the exchange, and the contract can be squared off any time during the trading hours.

2. **Hedging:** For the people associated with the commodities, the futures market can provide an effective hedging mechanism against price movements.

   For example, an oil-seed farmer may go short in oil-seed futures, thus 'locking' his sale price and in the process hedging against any adverse price movements. On the other hand, a processor of oilseeds may buy oilseed futures and thus assure him a supply of oilseeds at a predetermined price. Similarly, the oilseed processor may go short in oil futures, which may be bought by a wholesaler of oil.

   Also there is a saying that "gold shines when everything fails." Thus, gold can be used as a hedging tool against other investments.

3. **Arbitrage:** Traders may exploit arbitrage opportunities that arise on account of different prices between the two exchanges or between different maturities in the same underlying asset.

In India, whenever the futures price of a commodity increases sharply, it is usually regarded as the result of speculative activity, and the authorities tend to impose several kinds of regulations. However, the commodity market has significantly improved its efficiency with the increase of trade value during the recent period, suggesting that the futures market performs the function of price risk management and price discovery. Accordingly, in order to utilize the futures market, the Indian government will be required to further enhance its institutional infrastructure for smooth commodity transactions in line with market development, rather than to strengthen the restrictions on commodity transactions.

As a rapidly growing, large but poor economy, India's impact on global commodity markets is being shaped by some broad-based economic forces: India's population growth is increasing its demand for agricultural commodities, particularly for wheat and rice, but its per capita income growth is leading to a diversification of diet away from cereals and to fruit, vegetables, and dairy. Furthermore, its rapid GDP growth is naturally leading India to consume more energy commodities and metals, albeit to a lesser extent, than before.

But economic policies at work have distorted market outcomes: for example, the manufacturing sector has been held back in the past due to small-scale reservation, which has limited India's demand for metals, and price distortions in agriculture have shifted production towards cereals, rather than being reflective of average diets. Continued policy reforms are likely to diminish the distorting influence of India's domestic trade policies. Recent evidence of some dereservation in manufacturing appears to coincide well with a pickup in metal demand, as the growth in manufacturing output has risen. India's demand for energy and metals should rise as some rebalancing occurs in its economic structure. However, the outlook for India's demand for food commodities is less clear; it depends on the ongoing diversification of diet in India, and whether policies, including subsidies and price controls, continue to exert an influence on domestic production.

Department of Consumer Affairs, Government of India Forward Market Commission

Before participating in the commodity futures market please seek answers to the following questions:

1. Why am I participating in the commodity futures market? (as a hedger, trader or arbitrageur)
2. What should be my extent of participation?
3. Would it make any difference if I do not participate?
4. What is my risk bearing capacity?
5. How long should I hold my positions?
6. Have I read the commodity contract fully and understood its implication on my position?
7. How liquid is the contract I wish to participate in?
8. What would be my exit cost? Can I close out my position whenever I want? (*i.e.*, is the contract liquid enough to permit easy exit?)
9. Do I have adequate access to information about the fundamentals of the commodity that I wish to trade?
10. Does the product on the exchange serve any purpose of trading in the market?

Don'ts for dealing in the Commodity Futures

1. Do not fall prey to market rumours or tips.
2. Do not act based on bull/bear run of market sentiment.
3. Do not go by any explicit/implicit promise made by analysts/advisors/experts/ market intermediary until convinced.
4. Do not go by the reports/publications made in various print and electronic media without verification.
5. Do not trade in any commodity without knowing the risks and rewards associated with it.

Don'ts for dealing with Member (Commodity Broker) of the Commodity Exchanges

1. Do not undertake off-market transactions in commodities. It is both risky and illegal.
2. Do not deal with unregistered intermediaries. Ask for/know about their regulatory approval reference (FMC) before trading through the intermediary. The list of members is available on the website of the respective exchanges.
3. Do not deal with any intermediary not registered with the exchange on which you wish to trade.
4. Do not neglect to confirm in writing, orders for higher value given over phone.
5. Do not give authority to the Member of the Exchange to make 'sale' and 'purchase' decisions on your behalf and also do not surrender the right of receiving contract notes on a daily basis. Portfolio Management Schemes (PMSs) are not allowed in commodity market.

Rights of the Client

- In case of any dispute with a member regarding the trades done on a Commodity Exchange, the client can contact the Exchange for suitable redressal as per the byelaws of the Exchange including use of arbitration mechanism of the Exchange.
- All rights are available to a client for all exchange-traded transactions for which the client must have a duly authorized contract note of the broker.
- Approach the exchange management or the FMC for redressal of grievances.

Beware of the following

- No scheme for assured returns are allowed in commodity markets.
- Dabba (bucker shops) trading (trading outside the exchange platform) is illegal, punishable under the law and is highly risky.
- SMS's/emails/rumours and trading tips. Please do not be lured by such sources of information promising quick gains and unrealistic high returns.
- Advice through unconfirmed information such as websites/blogs/astrology predictions/or newspaper exposes one to undue risk.

Commodities (Gold, Silver, Precious Metals, and the like)

Table 17.1 shows the history of how gold prices have changed over a period of 90 years. Table 17.2 shows contracts traded in various segments of MCX from 2003. Table 17.3 displays the value and share of commodities traded at MCX, Mumbai during 2012-13.

Table 17.1 10 gm Gold Price History of 90 Years

Year	Price (Rs.)	Year	Price (Rs.)	Year	Price (Rs.)	Year	Price (Rs.)
1925	18.75	1948	95.87	1970	184.50	1992	4,334.00
1926	18.43	1949	94.17	1971	193.00	1993	4,140.00
1927	18.37	1950	99.18	1972	202.00	1994	4,598.00
1928	18.37	1951	98.05	1973	278.50	1995	4,680.00
1929	18.43	1952	76.81	1974	506.00	1996	5,160.00
1930	18.05	1953	73.06	1975	540.00	1997	4,725.00
1931	18.18	1954	77.75	1976	432.00	1998	4,045.00
1932	23.06	1955	79.18	1977	486.00	1999	4,234.00
1933	24.05	1956	90.81	1978	685.00	2000	4,400.00
1934	28.81	1957	90.62	1979	937.00	2001	4,300.00
1935	30.81	1958	95.38	1980	1330.00	2002	4,990.00
1936	29.81	1959	102.56	1981	1800.00	2003	5,600.00
1937	30.18	1960	111.87	1982	1645.00	2004	5,850.00
1938	29.93	1961	119.35	1983	1800.00	2005	7,000.00
1939	31.74	1962	119.75	1984	1970.00	2006	8,400.00
1940	36.04	1963	97.00	1985	2130.00	2007	10,800.00
1941	37.43	1964	63.25	1986	2140.00	2008	12,500.00
1942	44.05	1965	71.75	1987	2570.00	2009	14,500.00
1943	51.05	1966	83.75	1988	3130.00	2010	18,500.00
1944	52.93	1967	102.50	1989	3140.00	2011	26,400.00
1945	62.00	1968	162.00	1990	3200.00	2012	28,010.00
1946	83.87	1969	176.00	1991	3,466.00	2013	29,411.00
1947	88.62					2014	28,511.00
						2015	26,220.00
						2016	26,534.00

Source: Bullion Exchange, Mumbai

Table 17.2 Contracts Traded in Various Segments of MCX from 2003

Year	Contracts Traded (All)	Gold	Silver	Copper	Crude Oil	Cotton	Mustard Seed
2003	5176	3802	122	Nil	Nil	Nil	Nil
2004	2621019	724236	1583732	4151	Nil	422	678
2005	20349975	2773381	6481449	186921	5157811	5489	3826
2006	45635534	11988919	12496828	5293964	4466538	5136	17073
2007	68945925	10366705	15441649	15375506	13938813	2722	Nil
2008	94310537	26001228	23886120	14277796	20507001	Nil	Nil
2009	161173737	30423657	28510224	29602264	4109281	10118	Nil
2010	197206801	31581365	37766114	31341022	41537053	Nil	Nil

Source: Website of MCX

Table 17.3 Value and Share of Commodities Traded at MCX, Mumbai during 2012-13

Commodity	Volume	Value	Share in
	TRADED (Tonnes)	OF TRADE (Rs. in crore)	TRADE (%)
Silver	7.11	4086933.38	27.46
Gold	0.12	3720129.35	25.00
Crude Oil	8143.81	2981891.98	20.04
Copper	336.15	1443348.37	9.70
Natural Gas	39190500000	672892.89	4.52
Lead	523.42	616192.21	4.14
Nickel	46.66	432047.18	2.90
Zinc	389.25	416834.42	2.80
Aluminium	211.71	229582.03	1.54
CPO	213.31	106409.66	0.72
Others	142.70	174795.64	1.17
Total	10014.23	14881057.12	100

Source: Annual Report, Forwards Market Commission, GoI, 2012-13

18 Real Estate Market

CHAPTER

18.1 REAL ESTATE INVESTMENTS: CHARACTERISTICS

(a) **Higher capital requirement:** It is possible for an investor to participate in debt or equity through small investments say Rs. 5000 whereas in case of real estate, the amount required will be much higher.

(b) **Illiquidity:** Real estate is difficult to acquire and more difficult to sell because of absence of organized markets as in the case of bonds and equities. That makes it tough for the investor to search for real estate worth investing; time and money are spent in finding investment options. Thus, liquidity is a big problem indeed.

(c) **Title and legal problems:** The property laws are not investor friendly. Buying property involves a good marketable title. Numerous cases have come up where titles have been challenged many decades after transactions thereof have been entered into.

(d) **Government controls; policies, etc.:** Real estate holding involves a lot of legislation on who can own, e.g. documentation involving payment of stamp duties at arbitrary rates, mandatory registration, etc. Physical presence of both buyers and sellers needed for executing the transfer documents is also important. All these make real estate investments less attractive.

(e) **Legal complexities:** The legal contracts between property owners, financiers and tenants are quite complex and require legal interpretation and construction. This aspect of real estate brings in not only additional costs but the choice of right legal consultants.

(f) **Inefficient market:** Real estate doesn't have a marketplace as equities or bonds have. The market is highly localized where local factors play a vital role. There is a need for national and state markets to emerge in order to attract large scale investments.

Advantages of Real Estate

1. **Scope for capital appreciation:** The longer one holds on to properties, it has been observed, higher the capital appreciation. Demand for houses has been on the rise, thanks to increasing income levels and availability of easier housing loan facilities on both fixed and variable interest rates.
2. **Income stream:** Property rentals have been going up because of large scale employment generation in urban centres and where people from small places move to rental accommodation as ownership is beyond their reach at least in the initial years of employment.
3. **Sense of security:** Properties are considered less volatile; falling prices are rare compared to financial products like shares and bonds. Obviously these are perceptions and may not be right.
4. **Sense of pride:** It gives a sense of pride to the owner of a property that he stays in a house (even at times particular locality) and this cannot be measured in monetary terms.
5. **Self occupation:** House properties are bought more for self-occupation than for reasons of investment alone. However, sometimes retired people may shift from smaller homes to bigger ones or from one locality to another when their older homes fetch them handsome prices compared to purchase costs, thus proving to be a good investment.
6. **Tax shelter:** The income earned on rented properties is subject to some deduction; the tax on capital gains made on real estate can be saved through planning; a housing loan gives the investor tax concessions. These tax advantages make real estate an attractive proposition for high net worth individuals (HNIs), corporates, etc. Numerous tax advantages exist in the case of agricultural land; while capital gains on sale of agricultural land is fully exempt.

If an investor is able to analyze carefully, take professional advice and legal help and invests for long term, the appreciation could be high and this vehicle can yield handsome returns not only in percentage terms but in quantitative terms as well.

Disadvantages of Real Estate

1. Legal issues.
2. High cost of maintenance.
3. Municipal and other levies.
4. Inefficient market and illiquidity.

18.2 REAL ESTATE INVESTING

It is common to divide segments of a broadly defined real estate market into retail, office, industrial and residential. (Other categories include hotels and resorts and mixed category properties.)

In a number of international markets, private equity funds have become important participants in the real estate market. Private equity funds have a shorter time horizon than traditional institutional investors, commingled funds, or REITs (Real Estate Investment Trust), and they also bring a more aggressive attitude to leverage, with the introduction of high-risk, potentially high-return "mezzanine" debt into real estate transactions. These developments mean that investors now have more ways of gaining access to real estate returns than was previously the case. The REIT market provides access to each segment of the market.

Three things condition the experience of investors in real estate investing: the *performance* of the market; the *skill* of their advisors; and the degree of *leverage* involved in whichever vehicle used to access the market. This, in turn, depends upon the level of interest rates and the ease with which income yielding properties can support debt interest payments. As with all other markets, it is a routine weakness in appraising investment managers to fail to account properly for the impact of leverage on performance and risk.

Attractions of Investing in Real Estate

The traditional reasons for making investments in real estate equity include portfolio diversification; accessing premium and generally secure income yields; and the potential for attractive total returns that should be protected from inflation.

(i) Diversification: Appraisal valuation of properties complicate an assessment of the diversification qualities of real estate. Smoothing of performance results often gives short-term comfort to trustees and especially private investors who do not need to be confronted with the reality of market prices except when they transact. This paucity of reliable price information does not provide a substantive reason for favouring real estate investment. The market for REITs and similar vehicles in other countries gives both a *dependable market valuation* (although it may represent a premium or discount to property valuations) and a *time series of transaction prices,* which permits a market-based assessment of the contribution of real estate in an investment portfolio.

The conventional view is that the intrinsic volatility of well-diversified direct investments in real estate probably lies somewhere between that of bonds and that of equity. Since REITs are normally leveraged, the underlying volatility of the property portfolios within REITs will be lower. This provides evidence to support the conventional view of the volatility of the direct real estate market being between that of equities and bonds.

(ii) Income Yield: A recurring argument in favour of real estate investing is the provision of a dependable income that can be expected to increase in line with inflation. The ability to gain access to seemingly reliable income becomes particularly attractive to investors at times of low normal interest rates.

Over the period, the income for return for REITs have been somewhat lower than that on investment grade bonds, which have been subject to much less price risk. The income stream from REITs may appear stable, on average, but the price volatility has been comparable to equities. This means REITs cannot be regarded as "low risk" substitutes for a safe-heaven high-quality bond portfolio.

(iii) Inflation Hedge: Real estate investments always have one clear advantage over investments in conventional bonds: whereas bonds are eroded by any unexpected inflation, rents from real estate should always be expected to respond to inflation over time. This does not mean that rents will always move up with time. A market with excess or obsolete capacity should expect to see rents fall, and if monetary policy is tightened to restrain inflation, there is likely to be an adverse impact on rents.

Nevertheless, it is reasonable to assume that rents will increase faster than the rate of inflation which is higher. This, in turn, will be reflected in the value put on buildings, which should also respond to inflation. In this way, long-term investments in real estate provide an element of insurance against the biggest danger facing long-term investors in conventional bonds owing to erosion of wealth by inflation.

Worth of property and Expected Return

One of the attractions of real estate investing is that it is often easy to analyze individual investments in direct property quantitatively. Although this is no guarantee of investments succeeding, it helps to identify the opportunities that rely on unusually strong assumptions.

The financial appraisal of real estate requires assessment of a number of variables:

- Today's government bond yield.
- Market supply and demand forecasts as influences on prospects for rental incomes.
- Tenant creditworthiness.
- Property depreciation or obsolescence.

Rental Income

The return to be expected from a property is the discounted value of the expected rental income, net of expenses, plus the proceeds from selling the property at in the future.

The key variables in this evaluation are the future rate of change in rents (which is almost always assumed to be an increase) and the appropriate rate at which to discount that rental stream back to a present value or fair price for the property.

This focus on rental income is important to avoid two common mistakes. First, the value of a property has little to do with the cost of rebuilding it. It is the value of future rent that determines its value. Given the value of property, this can be broken down into the cost of rebuilding, proxies by the insurance value put on the property, and a residual, which is the value of the land underneath the building. Second, a property is never expensive because the land underneath it is expensive. It is always the other way round. Land is expensive because rents are high, and because rents are high, property is expensive. A third important feature for real estate investing follows from this: the price of land, the residual in property valuation, can be quite volatile.

It follows that investors rely on rental income, rather than capital appreciation, as the principal source of investment performance in real estate investing. This also explains why the income return from real estate investment is normally much higher than the income returns from mainstream equity investing. Nevertheless, investors should invest in real estate only if they expect to be rewarded for the incremental risk that they would be assuming, within the context of a balanced investment strategy.

It is not clear how much premium return over government bonds should be expected by financial investors in real estate in the long term. This required premium is reduced by the diversification benefits that real estate brings to a balanced investment strategy. It can be influenced by the degree of confidence that investors have in the quality of the investment process that they are able to deploy in investing in real estate markets.

Most importantly, as with private equity, direct investors in real estate should not assume that the market return will be accessible, unless a demonstrably skilful investment process is put in place. However, the more skill that is assumed, the easier it will be to justify a large allocation of an investment strategy to real estate. In this case, great caution needs to be exercised in interpreting past performance, in isolating the effects on performance of leverage during a rising market and in differentiating between skill and luck.

The Indian real estate sector has been a major beneficiary of the strong economic growth witnessed in India since the year 2000. The growth in the sector, supported by a series of reforms, has not only resulted in significant residential and commercial real estate, but also complemented the development of physical and social infrastructure of the country.

18.3 PRIVATE EQUITY FUNDING IN INDIAN REAL ESTATE

Post-global financial crises, private equity funds are increasingly considering only project-level funding in order to protect their investments in case of any defaults/failures by the equity. For project-level funding, it is relatively easy for private equity funds to assess the risks, vs returns and take apt investment decisions. Initially, real estate fund infused equity in various projects with an aim to get higher returns. However, private equity funds faced many issues in projects that had an equity exposure, such as:

- Losses due to project delays/terminations leading to developer's inability to garner sales and manage cash flows amidst decreasing capital values and subdued demand.

- In case of projects that had to be terminated, equity contributors were given the last preference and as a result, lot of capital was eroded, as the developer had to prioritize debtors.
- Exit opportunities for invested funds were also limited as the available pool of private equity diminished significantly, hedge funds largely exited and public markets dried up.

This led to private equity shying away from entering into pure equity deals in the Indian real estate sector. As a result, many deals executed post-2010 came in as structured deals, which were primarily debt transactions arranged in a manner that provided assured returns to the investor along with a possible upside as per the deal structure.

Structured debt transactions offer a very attractive investment option, giving the investors fully secured and full recourse high guaranteed returns in local currency. Encouraged by this structure, many new funds raised since 2010 have focused mainly on the structured deal strategy for investment in residential projects. The fund raising activity was slow in 2010 and 2011, but as the economy showed some signs of improvement and to be better equipped for the future, massive fund raising was witnessed between 2012 and 2014 (around USD 5.2 billion).

The value and number of structured debt real estate private equity deals have risen significantly from 2010. In terms of city-wise contribution, Mumbai leads with 33% share in total value and 32% share in total number in deals in 2014. In terms of asset-wise contribution, residential sector had a major share in structured debt deals. Around 80% (in value terms) and 94% (in number of deals) pertained to residential deals.

Structured debt office transactions were around 18% in value terms and 3% in terms of number of deals, while the rest came from retail and mixed-use assets. Domestic funds were very active in the structured debt transactions and accounted for 66% of total value of structured deals and 84% of total number of structured deals concluded between 2010 and 2014. (**Source:** Real Capital Analytics (RCA), Cushman & Wakefield Research)

18.4 KEY CHALLENGES IN STRUCTURED DEBT DEALS

Selecting the apt partner, in-depth analysis of the project (technical and financial viability) and collateral package assessment are key criterion in any lending decisions. This evaluation is crucial as real estate private equity structured debt investments are not covered under the Securitization and Reconstruction of Financial Assets and Enforcement of Security Interest (SARFAESI) Act, 2002 which is available to the banks and public financial institutions (PFIs) in India. Thus, a comprehensive due diligence on the commercials, partner and legal aspects for a debt transaction is extremely important.

However, existing formats of structured debt transactions will be under pressure or may become unsuitable in future, due to the following key reasons:

(a) **Changing market dynamics:** This product is primarily for residential projects where approvals are in place and sales have started. Post-global financial crisis, residential real estate sector in India has been battered and sales have slowed down significantly. New project launches across cities have also declined by around between 11% between 2012 and 2014. Hence, there is a drop in eligible projects/products due to both low sales velocity in existing projects and decline in new project launches.

(b) **End use constraint:** Developing residential projects on a continuous basis currently depends on land bank that developers have created over a period. However, many developers do not have a significant land bank and there is an increasing need to acquire new land parcels for launching projects. Massive investments are required for such land acquisitions. However, existing structured debt funds are prohibited from investing in these formats as per their internal rules.

(c) **Cash-flow mismatch:** In residential projects, cash-flows are lumpy, based on sales velocity, stage of construction and sales schemes adopted. In the initial period, there are high inflows and then free cash-flow becomes lumpy as payments are linked to construction schedules. Further, in lean markets, many sales have back-ended payments and there comes a stage when free cash-flows virtually become nil in the intervening project lifecycle. Monthly or quarterly coupon and principal servicing as opposed to sweep of free cash on IRR format is difficult. This is being increasingly faced by projects, which were launched and invested during 2010-2012.

(d) **Unsustainable cost of funding:** In residential projects that continue to garner good sales, developers consider refinancing the high cost debt at lower financing, which is available in Brownfield residential projects, thus shortening the effective YTM to 18-24 months as opposed to signed term of 36-48 months. In effect, this is bridge funding as opposed to a longer term high yield investment due to cost of funding. Further, the senior secured position does not allow any construction finance, which is much cheaper and costlier funds are used for working capital, making the project unviable. In some cases, banks also compete with the structured debt deals by providing funds at a cheaper cost.

(e) **Competition from other funding options:** Fund of fund managers and fund managers are also expected to increase their allocation in joint ventures and club deals over the next few years, emphasizing investors' desire for greater control over their investment. Some recent examples are APG's investment in Godrej Properties in 2012 and GIC's investment in Brigade Enterprises in 2014.

Possible Modifications in Structured Debt Deals

Structured debt deals are currently being commoditized and with increasing capital pools, it is leading to rate competition between the top funds. Hence, for structured debt to be sustainable, slightly different product structures would be more encouraging. A few innovations/charges that can be considered include: (i) end use; (ii) mezzanine structures; (iii) pricing and repayment; and (iv) asset diversification.

With these adapted features, structured funding would become a regular product as opposed to the current opportunistic product and may lead to massive incremental investments in the burgeoning Indian real estate sector.

Investments are real estate equity divide between ownership of properties directly by an individual investor (the direct or private market), through a commingled fund, or through stock exchange listed vehicles, most commonly REITS, a US innovation dating from the early 1970s. These vehicles represent the public or quoted market. REITS have grown substantially in the United States; similar entities have been introduced in range of jurisdictions including Australia, Brazil, Canada, France, Japan, Netherlands, and Singapore. In the United States, individual REITS specialize by sector of the market, with a minority investing primarily in commercial and residential mortgages.

18.5 INDIA REIT REGULATIONS – A HOLISTIC PERSPECTIVE

The Real Estate Investment Trust (REIT) – an investment vehicle that invests in rent-yielding completed real estate properties has the potential to transform the Indian real estate sector. Currently, developers incur huge capital expenditure especially in Commercial Real Estate (CRE), on land, construction, interior fit-outs, etc., which remains locked for years until the asset generates returns to break-even. REIT will help in attracting long-term financing from domestic as well as foreign sources. This could improve fund availability to real estate developers and reduce some burden on completed assets by allowing owners of such assets to raise capital from investors against issue of units. Further, for the investors, REIT can provide a new investment vehicle with ongoing returns, elevated transparency and governance standards.

Mandatory listing of the REITs on recognised stock exchanges will offer an easy entry and exit mechanism for investors. With respect to providing liquidity to the investors, REIT may be at par with equity shares trading on the exchange.

A REIT could help in bringing the much required professionalism and transparency in the real estate sector in India. It shall be governed by the SEBI guidelines, which would help ensure *transparency* and *accountability* of REITs. A REIT would have to appoint an independent trustee, managers, auditor and valuer to help ensure that the functioning of a REIT is transparent. Moreover, experiences in different facets of the real estate business are a prerequisite for the appointment of a manager in a REIT, thereby ensuring professionalism in real estate investments.

A REIT could provide developers and large investors of commercial real estate to tap into the REIT market for investment in the real estate assets. It could provide a long awaited exit opportunity to developers and private equity (PE) investors, with an option to retain a large share and diversify a smaller portion to unlock the potential of the assets. The liquidity generated could help developers with much needed capital to invest in future projects or complete existing projects. Moreover, a REIT as an investment vehicle has a huge opportunity in India. As on October 2014, India has a rent yielding office inventory to the tune of 425 million sq ft valued in excess of USD 52 billion. Apart from this, there are other properties like warehousing, retail malls, shopping centres, school buildings, etc., which could be considered for REIT.

Conducive Investment Environment

1. ***Growing economy:*** The thriving economy could be a key driver for growth of the REIT regime in the Indian market. The business confidence index has strengthened and the economy is looking forward to another phase of decent growth, with political stability and a government focusing on growth.

2. ***Increasing working age population:*** UN World Population prospects, projects Indian median population from 26.4 in 2013 to 36.7 in 2050; this signifies a large pool of young population in India. This employable young workforce demands employment and could attract global corporates especially in IT-ITES and promote the development of commercial real estate.

3. ***Housing and urban infrastructure requirement:*** To support the increasing population, huge investments are required to meet India's housing needs, and additional investments would be required for commercial and urban infrastructure to support the housing growth. India needs to develop almost 45 to 50 million housing units by 2028.

4. ***Disposable income and retirement savings:*** Increase in income of working age population, would result an increase in disposable income. This disposable income gives individuals flexibility to invest in long-term investment options for future savings.

5. ***Worldwide, an affordable office space:*** India is one of the countries globally offering affordable prime spaces, with high growth potential. The availability of such assets is expected to find takers for REITs in India.

Guidelines applicable to REITs: Fund raising conditions

Aspect	Guidelines
Initial offering of Units to third parties	• Only through public issue
Investment by Foreigners	• Allowed under REIT Regulations. However, subject to permission in keeping with the Department of Industrial Policy and Promotion (DIPP). It is also subject to the RBI guidelines and the government, as specified from time to time. • FDI is permitted in construction-development: townships, housing, etc. with an exit option to investors on completion of project or after development of trunk infrastructure. • Currently, the guidelines for foreign investment in REITs are awaited.
Listing	• Mandatory
Manager	• Can be a body corporate, company or LLP incorporated in India • An entity separate from the Sponsor • Minimum five years' experience in fund management or advisory services or property management in real estate industry or in development of real estate (at the manager or associate level). • Minimum two key personnel having minimum five years' experience in fund management or advisory or property management in real estate industry or in development of real estate. • Minimum 50% of the directors/members of the governing board have to be independent.
Minimum Net Worth of the REIT manager	• For a body corporate or a company: ₹ 100 million; • LLP: Net tangible assets of value ₹ 100 million
Offer size (assets under REIT)	• REIT assets of ₹ 5 billion at the time of public offering, minimum offer size: 2.5 billion; minimum float: 25%
Sponsor	• Sponsor may be any person(s) who set(s) up a REIT • Multiple (maximum: 3) • Minimum experience requirement: 5 years in development of real estate or fund management in the real estate industry (at the sponsor or associate level) wherein the sponsor is a developer; at least two projects of the sponsor should have been completed.
Net worth of the REIT sponsor	• ₹ 200 million (minimum) on an individual basis and ₹ 1000 million (minimum) on a collective basis. • Sponsors can collectively hold a minimum of 25% for the initial three years, investment followed by 15% thereafter. • A sponsor can redesignate another sponsor as long as the redesignated sponsor satisfies the qualifying requirements and holds the minimum percentage of units.
Ticket size for investors in REIT	• 2,00,000 for public (initial as well as follow-on) offer and 1,00,000 post listing. • Minimum 200 public unit holders at all times

Trustee	• Registered with the SEBI as a Debenture Trustee • Independent from the Sponsor/Manager
Acquisition and Disposition of assets	• For related party transactions, purchase or sale should be in accordance with two independent valuations and must be at a price not greater than (in case of purchases)/no lesser than (in case of sales), the average of the two independent valuations. • For non-related party transactions, purchase or sale should be in accordance with the valuation undertaken by the valuer of the REIT and shall be subject to prior approval of the unit holders, only if the purchase is at a value greater than 110% or the sale is at a value lesser than 90% of the value of the property as assessed by the valuer.
Asset class	• Rent-yielding assets (office, retail, hospitality, warehouses, conference centres, etc.).
Assets disposition	• Post the holding period of 3 years, asset churning is allowed, subject to prior permission of the unit holder, wherein the value of the transaction exceeds 10% of the value of the REIT assets in a financial year.
Asset location	• India
Asset restrictions	• At least 80% in completed and rent-generating real estate. • Completed and rent-generating properties from the date of purchase by REIT or SPV and under construction properties from the date of completion are to be held by the REIT for a minimum of 3 years. • A maximum of 20% of the total REIT assets may be invested in the following: - Debt of companies/body corporates in the real estate sector, - Mortgage Backed Securities (MBS), government securities, - Money market instruments/cash equivalents, - Listed equity of companies having 75% or more operating revenue from real estate activity, - Unutilised Floor Space Index (FSI) and Transferable Development Rights (TDR) for utilisation in investee projects. - Under-construction/completed properties but not rent-generating properties, subject to a cap of 10% of the value of the REIT assets • Investment in other REITs is not allowed.
Income distribution	• 90% of the net distributable cash flow is to be distributed among the unit holders not less than once every six months.
Income restrictions	• A minimum of 75% of the revenue of the REIT and the SPV, except gains arising from the disposal of properties, should come from rental, leasing and letting or any other income incidental to the leasing of assets.

Making REITs Successful in India

1. **Tax Related:** The REIT is being made a complete pass-through vehicle now (as against the old provisions) which allow pass-through only with respect to interest income from Special Purpose Vehicle (SPV) and rental income which is

taxed in the hands of the investors directly while capital gains and other income is taxed at a REIT level and exempt in the hands of the investors.

2. **Exchange Control Related:** Foreign portfolio investors and non-resident Indians should be permitted to invest in units of REIT without any cap or restriction on the units that can be acquired. Foreign sponsors should be allowed to acquire units of REITs under automatic route. It should be clarified that a REIT with majority foreign ownership would not be subject to downstream conditionality related to FDI.
3. **Stamp Duty Related:** In this regard, the government ought to consider making the stamp duty uniform across the states or consider waiving off the stamp duty where a REIT holds property over a specified period of years, in line with Singapore REITs or alternatively, the state governments could consider a one-time waiver of stamp duty on transfer of assets to REITs or SPVs owned by REITs.

In the near future, it is expected that the REIT vehicle will increase the depth of the Indian property market through enhanced transparency and governance standards along with monitoring of the REIT's performance on a regular basis by the financial media. The REIT Regulations fix the roles and responsibilities of stakeholders with respect to the underlying property in terms of valuation, structural audit, safety audit and insurance of the property at regular time periods. Besides adequate and timely disclosure on important developments relating to the REIT, it also prescribes the quantum and timelines for income distribution. In case of violations on aspects ranging from delay in allotment of units to distribution of income among unit holders, it has listed the consequences as well.

18.6 CHALLENGES AND REFORMS FOR REAL ESTATE SECTOR

The challenges in the Indian real estate sector can be broadly classified under five categories which are lack of suitable developable land, delays in obtaining approvals, issues in land title and insurance, inadequate funding challenges and shortage of manpower.

1. While there is a significant shortage of housing in urban regions, it is estimated that the top eight cities in India have approximately 6.5 lakh units of unsold housing stock. At the current rate of absorption, it may take over five years to clear the housing stock in regions, such as Delhi–NCR, which has the highest unsold inventory.
2. There is a scarcity of developable land in urban areas, and peripheral regions of cities lack appropriate urban infrastructure, which escalates the final project cost. This has resulted in significant surge in land prices in the urban areas. To address the issue of unavailability of land and promote stock of housing, several state governments have introduced land pooling policy. Land pooling, which has been successful globally, is increasingly being adopted by policy makers in

the states of Gujarat, Maharashtra, Delhi, Chhatisgarh, Tamilnadu, Punjab and Kerala.

3. One of the major issues that the real estate sector is facing is lack of clear land titles and land title insurance, which leads to litigations and causes project delays. Lack of clear land title and title issuance in India often makes it difficult for developers to acquire suitable land parcels. Absence of clear land titles sometimes results in long-drawn and expensive litigation for developers. Further, there is no single land policy in India and each state has its own policy which adds to the complexities. The property taxes, stamp duty, registration charges, FAR/FSI vary across states in India.

   The Indian Government has taken the initiative of digitising land records to address the issue of land titles. The full digitisation is expected to be completed by 2018. Further, the government enacted a new land acquisition policy in 2013 termed as Land Acquisition Resettlement and Rehabilitation (LARR) Act, 2013 in its bid to improve transparency and fairness in land transactions.

4. Despite the real estate sector contributing the third highest share to the Indian economy, the share in outstanding loans from banks to the sector is extremely low at 3 per cent. This results in limited access to long-term and low-cost funding channels, especially through the route of banks and external commercial borrowings (ECB). Arranging the initial funding can be a grave challenge affecting the housing supply to a large extent. The Reserve Bank of India (RBI) has the threshold for total maximum exposure to real estate, including individual housing loans and lending to developers for construction finance, for banks at 15 per cent, which is quite low and is curtailing the growth of the sector.

   Absence of long-term funding from banks is forcing developers to look at alternative sources of funds, most of which do not offer affordable interest rates and hence, the supply is being stifled. In the case of individual buyers, the persistently high inflation rates have made them suffer in multiple ways affecting their buying ability. Besides having lesser disposable incomes and savings, they are faced with increasing housing prices, further compounded by the higher interest rates on mortgages.

5. To improve the funding situation in India, the government is planning to relax the FDI norms in the real estate sector in addition to allowing FDI in farm lands. The reforms are expected to be cleared shortly and are expected to significantly ease funding crunch in India. The government has also allowed external commercial borrowing for development of affordable housing stock in the country.

6. Further, the government is in process of allowing Real Estate Investment Trusts (REITs) in India. Development of a healthy REIT market could help open up new funding avenues in the real estate sector.

7. Strict and prolonged regulatory process leading to delays:

   The process of obtaining construction permit has become difficult over the last several years and is among the major reasons contributing to the delays in real estate development. According to the report of Committee on Streamlining

Approval Procedures for Real Estate Projects (SAPREP) set up by the Ministry of Housing and Urban Poverty Alleviation, a developer has to follow at least 34 regulatory processes for obtaining construction permits and it takes an average of 227 days. According to the industry associations, the delay in obtaining approvals adhering to regulatory processes can raise the project cost by 40 per cent of the sales value.

To address the issues granting construction permit, the government is evaluating the single-window clearance mechanism. This has also been recommended by SAPREP committee which has given several recommendations to streamline the approval mechanism. Several cities in India such as Ahmedabad, Chennai, Cochin, Madurai, Ghaziabad, Pune, Trivandrum, Delhi and Kozhikode have already implemented the automated system for approving building plans.

8. Shortage of manpower and technology:

   Despite being the second largest employer in the country, the construction sector as a whole faces manpower shortage. Further, the sector is heavily dependent on manual labour, faces longer time lines for construction completions, which results in supply getting deferred. Hence, technologically faster and alternative methods of construction need to be adopted on a large scale, giving rise to training and skill development of manpower.

Urbanization is a trend which probably cannot be reversed or avoided in India. Having realized the potential and need for an adequate urban development strategy, the Government has taken significant steps by allocating significant amount of funds towards urban infrastructure, the fruits of which are now visible.

The constant focus of development is expected to support a strong growth for the real estate sector. As a growth enabler, it is essential to develop the real estate sector to support the growth of 300 other sectors and employment. However, a key challenge is the lack of technology and funding, where a massive gap exists. Realising the challenge at hand, several key reforms have been introduced recently and many more are lined up to improve global inflow of funds and promote growth of the sector.

The government has made an attempt to address some of these challenges to a certain extent, through the proposals announced in the Union Budget 2017-18, with focus on providing thrust to affordable housing and infrastructure. Some of the key announcements made for real estate and construction include:

- granting an infrastructure status to affordable housing projects, which has been a long standing demand of the supply side stakeholders;
- highest ever allocation to the infrastructure development (INR 3.96 lakh crore);
- relaxation in area requirements and time period for the completion of a project; and
- reduction in holding period to 24 months from 36 months for long-term capital gains tax on immovable properties.

> **"Truth is like a vast tree which yields more and more fruit, the more you nurture it." – Mahatma Gandhi**

19 Foreign Exchange Market

CHAPTER

The term *foreign exchange* refers to holdings of foreign currencies and also the act of trading one currency for another. The foreign exchange market is one of the important components of the international financial system. Especially, for the developing economy, the foreign exchange market is necessary for the conversion of currencies for short-term capital flows or long-term investments in the financial or physical assets of another country. The services of the foreign exchange markets are necessary not only for trade transactions but also for other financial receipts or payments between countries involving a foreign exchange transaction.

Globally, operations in the foreign exchange market started in major economies "way after the breakdown of the Bretton Woods system in 1971," which marked the beginning of floating exchange rate regimes in several countries. This resulted in foreign exchange markets becoming more volatile and more risky for the market players. Slowly these markets became less regulated. By the late 1980s, and the early 1990s foreign exchange flows shifted from being trade-related (flows connected with import and export seen in 1970s) to capital related (flows connected with raising money). Over the years, the foreign exchange market has emerged as the largest market in the world.

The decades of 1990s witnessed a perceptible policy shift in many emerging markets towards reorientation of their financial markets in terms of new products and instruments, development of institutional and market infrastructure and realignment of regulatory structure consistent with the liberalised operational framework. The changing contours were mirrored in a rapid expansion of foreign exchange market in terms of participants, transaction volumes, decline in transaction costs and more efficient mechanism of risk transfer. The foundation of European Monetary Union (EMU) and the year 2000 represented major landmarks.

Policies in respect of management of the exchange rate, foreign exchange reserve and external debt have received increasing emphasis in emerging market economies. The scope for exchange rate flexibility has generated considerable debate, particularly in view of recent build-up of reserves and movement in rupee currency. Furthermore, the need for careful assessment of the external debt situation has assumed an added significance on a day-to-day basis. It is the capital flows that influence the exchange rate and interest rate arithmetic of the financial markets, rather than real factors underlying trade competitiveness. Against this background, we will discuss some important areas, viz., structure, foreign exchange reserve and exchange rate.

The basic objectives of investment and financial management in international (or multinational) for corporates remains the same as in domestic scenario, i.e., the goal to maximize the shareholder value on a global basis. Multinational corporates, however, operate in more than one country and their operations involve multiple foreign currencies. Their operations are influenced by politics, geopolitical situation, laws of the countries where they operate and so on. Thus, they face a higher degree of risk as compared to domestic corporate entities. A matter of great concern for the multinational corporates is to analyse the implications of the changes in interest rates, inflation rates and exchange rates on their decisions and minimize the 'foreign exchange risk'. Exchange rates between and among currencies keep fluctuating on daily and even hourly basis. In the long run, the exchange rate between two currencies is determined by their relative demand and supply positions.

19.1 FOREIGN EXCHANGE MARKET

The foreign exchange market is the market where the currency of one country is exchanged for the currency of another country. According to Dr. Paul Elinzing, ["A Textbook on Foreign Exchange" (1966)] "Foreign exchange is the system or process of converting one national currency into another, and transferring money from one country to another;" most currency transactions are channelled through the worldwide interbank exchange market.

According to experts, foreign exchange rates between two (or more) currencies are determined by a wide range of factors, which include the following:

A change in the: 1. Home currency's money supply; 2. foreign currency's money supply; 3. home country's real income; 4. foreign country's real income; 5. home country's interest rate; 6. foreign country's interest rate; 7. home country's expected rate of inflation; 8. foreign country's expected rate of inflation; 9. home country's trade balance; and 10. foreign country's trade balance.

2. Speculation: There is a school of thought that believes that the thrust of movement of rates comes more from speculators than from international trade.
3. Intervention by the Central Bank: The Central Banks of different countries may step in to mop up currency in case it is appreciating or depreciating faster than desired.
4. Economic fundamentals: On account of advantageous fundamentals, the currency of the the country which is blessed with 'rich natural resources' is more likely to be strong.
5. Political stability: An uncertain political stability or an uncertain economic future is likely to lead to a weakening of the currency since international investors would not like to invest in these countries.

The foreign exchange market does not refer to a marketplace in the physical sense of the term. In fact, it consists of a number of dealers, banks and brokers engaged in the business of buying and selling foreign exchange. It also includes the central bank of each country and the treasury authorities who entered into this market as controlling authorities. Those engaged in the foreign exchange business are controlled by the Foreign Exchange Management Act (FEMA).

Evolution of the Foreign Exchange Markets in India

The origin of the foreign exchange market in India could be traced to the year 1978 when banks in India were permitted to undertake intra-day trade in foreign exchange. However, it was in the 1990s, that the Indian foreign exchange market witnessed far reaching changes along with the shifts in the currency regime in India. The exchange rate of rupee that was pegged earlier was floated partially in March 1992 and fully in March 1993, following the recommendations of the Report of the High Level Committee on Balance of Payments (Chairman: Dr. C. Rangarajan). The unification of the exchange rate was instrumental in developing a market-determined exchange rate of the rupee and an important step in the progress towards current account convertibility, which was achieved in August 1994.

Following the expert group headed by O.P. Sodhan recommendations report (June 1995), and beginning from January 1996, wide-ranging reforms have been undertaken for deepening and widening of the Indian foreign exchange market. Another internal technical group on the Foreign Exchange Market (2005) was constituted to undertake a comprehensive review of the measures initiated by the Reserve Bank of India and identify areas for further liberalisation or relaxation of restrictions in a medium-term framework.

India's shift from a protected economy to a market economy in 1991 opened up the floodgates. Developments in India during 1994-2009, have been both 'significant and meaningful'. Massive increase in foreign exchange reserves, growth in foreign trade, liberalization of foreign investment abroad, rationalization of import duty tariffs, current account convertibility, increased access to external commercial borrowings for companies, participation of FIIs in Indian capital markets, introduction of FEMA 1999, introduction of "rupee options" as a hedging mechanism (June, 2003), RBI allowing banks to establish offshore banking units and the introduction of Real Time Gross Settlement (RTGS) system; all mean that India has finally arrived in the global market place.

The conditions in the foreign exchange market have also generally remained orderly. While it is not possible for any country to remain completely unaffected by developments in international markets, India was also able to keep the spill-over effect of the Asian crisis to a minimum through constant monitoring and timely action, including recourse to strong monetary measures, when necessary, to prevent emergence of self-fulfilling speculative activities.

Broad Functions of Foreign Exchange Market

- To make necessary arrangements to transfer purchasing power from one country to another.
- To provide adequate credit facilities for the promotion of foreign trade.
- To cover foreign exchange risks by providing hedging facilities.

In India, the foreign exchange business has a three-tiered structure consisting of:

1. trading between banks and their commercial customers;
2. trading between banks through authorised dealers; and
3. trading with banks abroad.

Structure of the Foreign Exchange Market

The foreign exchange market in India comprises of

(a) the Reserve Bank of India at the apex;
(b) authorised dealers (ADs) licensed by the RBI; and
(c) customers such as exporters and importers, corporate and other foreign exchange earners.

Apart from these main market players, there are foreign exchange money changers who bring buyers and sellers together but are not permitted to deal in foreign exchange on their own account. The ADs are governed by the guidelines framed by the Foreign Exchange Dealers Association of India (FEDAI). Dealings in the foreign exchange market include transactions between ADs and the exporters, importers and other customers, transactions among ADs themselves, transactions with overseas banks and transactions between ADs and the RBI.

The market trades freely in spot and forward exchange contracts, and to a limited extent in derivatives. The efficiency/liquidity of the market is often gauged in terms of bid/offer spreads. Wider spreads are an indication of an illiquid or a one-way market. In India, the normal spot market quote has a spread of 0.25 to 0.50 paise (the difference), while the swap quotes are available at 1 to 2 paise a spread. The total turnover in the foreign exchange market has been showing an increasing trend over the years.

Foreign Exchange Market Components

There are three major components in the foreign exchange market depending upon the transactions between the:

1. public and banks at the base level;
2. banks dealing with foreign exchange involving conversion of currencies; and
3. banks and the RBI involving purchase and sale of foreign currencies.

Role of the Reserve Bank of India

The Reserve Bank of India as the central banking authority also controls the foreign currency operations. It fixes the buying and selling exchange rates from time to time based on the parity of unspecified currencies – *basket of currencies*. While the RBI does not enter the foreign exchange market to support the Indian rupee like the Bank of England, it buys spot and forward sterling up to 9 months forward and sells only spot sterling. Thus, RBI continues to maintain the external value of the Indian rupee. Also the RBI buys major currencies like US dollars, Deutsche Mark and Japanese yen, both spot and forward up to 6 months at exchange rates based on the previous day's closing rate in the London Exchange Market for the respective currencies.

The RBI's role in the Indian foreign exchange market has been more towards guiding the banks in their exchange operations and developing the exchange markets by giving appropriate directives from time to time. The RBI has so far not found it necessary to operate directly in the foreign exchange market with a view to stabilising the external value of the Indian rupee.

India's Foreign Exchange Reserves

Since the inception of economic reforms there has been a steady increase in the Indian forex reserves. The following table presents the growth of foreign exchange reserves over a period of time.

Table 19.1 Trends in India's Foreign Exchange Reserves

End of March	SDR	Gold	Foreign Currency Assets	Total Reserves Rs. in Crore
1950-51	-	118	911	1,029
1960-61	-	118	186	304
1970-71	112	183	438	733
1980-81	497	226	4,822	5,544
1990-91	200	6,822	4,388	11,416
2000-01	11	1,271.1	18,448.2	20,007.7
2010-11	456.9	2,297.2	27,433	30,481.8
2011-12	446.9	2,702.3	26,006.9	29,439.8
2012-13	432.7	2,569.2	25,972.6	29,204.6
2013-14	447	2,063	28,932	31,613
2014-15	402	1,908	32,893	35,330
2015-16	150	2,060	33,740	36,190
30-Dec-2016	143.24	1,998.29	33,658.25	36,029.68

Source: Economic Survey and RBI website

From March 1993 to April 2008, Indian economy has added as much as Rs. 12,16,856 crore to its foreign exchange reserves. The build-up of reserves is a result of conscious policy, which takes into account the composition of balance of payments and 'liquidity risks', associated with different types of flows and requirements. The RBI stated that the increase in reserves in the recent period has been on account of capital and other inflows. The major sources of this increase are:

- Foreign investment
- Banking capital
- Increase in other types of capital flows (e.g., foreign institutional investments)
- Short-term credit
- Remittances by Indian nationals working in foreign countries
- Valuation changes in reserves

19.2 EXCHANGE RATE MANAGEMENT: THE INDIAN EXPERIENCE

Against the backdrop of international experience, it would be useful to review the management of the exchange rate in India in a historical perspective. India's exchange rate policy has evolved in tandem with international and domestic developments. The period after independence in 1947 was followed by a fixed exchange rate regime where the Indian rupee was pegged to the pound sterling on account of historic links with Britain and this was in line with the Bretton Woods System prevailing at that time.

A major event was the devaluation of the Indian rupee by 36.5 per cent on June 6, 1966. With the breakdown of the Bretton Woods System in the early 1970s and the consequent switch towards a system of managed exchange rates, and with the declining share of the UK in India's trade, the Indian rupee, effective from September 1975, was delinked from the pound sterling in order to overcome the weaknesses of pegging to a single currency. Even after the rupee was delinked from the pound sterling, the role of exchange rate remained muted for quite some time; given the widespread rationing of foreign exchange through the elaborate system of licensing, there were other quantitative restrictions and exchange control. During the period of 1975 to 1992, the exchange rate of rupee was officially determined by the RBI within a nominal band of +/−5 per cent of the weighted basket of currencies of India's major trading partners.

Over the years, the Indian rupee depreciated sharply against pound sterling, American dollar and other hard currencies for the following reasons:

(a) India imports more than its exports. Hence, the demand for hard currencies is more than their supply.

(b) The foreign debt of India is mounting, assuming alarming proportions. The credit rating for India was downgraded by Moody's in 1990.

(c) The domestic inflation rate in India has been around 8 per cent to 10 per cent.

(d) As a major importer of oil, India is vulnerable to situations like the Gulf crisis of 1990.

The RBI performed a market-clearing role on day-to-day basis which introduced high variability in the size of reserves. The periodic adjustments in the exchange rate were, however, not enough to maintain external competitiveness as competitor countries had undertaken significant adjustments in their exchange rates despite their lower inflation. The exchange rate regime of this period can be best characterized as an adjustable nominal peg with a band, with the nominal exchange rate being the operating variable to achieve the intermediate target of a medium-term equilibrium path of the real effective exchange rate (REER).

The important message that comes out of the analysis of various episodes of volatility and policy response is that flexibility and pragmatism are needed in the exchange rate policy in the developing countries, rather than adherence to strict theoretical rules. There is a need for central banks to keep policies/instruments in hand for use in difficult situations.

Table 19.2 Exchange Rate of Indian Rupee (Rupees per unit of foreign currency)

Annual average	US $	Pound Sterling	German Mark	Japanese Yen	SDR
1984-85	11.89	14.87	3.990	0.049	11.93
1985-86	12.24	16.85	4.560	0.056	12.92
1987-88	12.97	22.09	7.400	0.094	17.12
1988-89	14.48	22.60	8.050	0.113	19.26
1989-90	16.65	26.92	0.090	0.117	21.37
1990-91	17.94	33.19	11.440	0.128	24.85
1991-92	24.47	42.93	14.750	0.186	33.89
1992-93	28.86	48.83	18.410	0.233	37.14
1993-94	31.37	47.20	18.740	0.291	43.96
1994-95	31.40	48.82	20.20	0.316	45.79
1995-96	33.45	52.35	23.40	0.348	50.48
1996-97	35.50	56.36	22.92	0.316	50.89
1997-98	37.16	61.02	20.96	0.303	50.67
1998-99	42.07	69.55	24.18	0.331	57.51
1999-2000	43.33	69.85	44.79	0.391	58.93
2000-01	45.68	67.55	41.48	0.414	59.55
2001-02	47.69	68.32	42.18	0.382	60.21
2002-03	48.40	74.82	48.09	0.397	64.13
2003-04	45.95	77.74	53.99	0.407	65.69
2004-05	44.93	82.86	56.55	0.418	66.93

2005-06	44.27	79.05	53.91	0.391	64.49
2006-07	45.25	85.64	58.05	0.387	67.25
2007-08	40.26	80.84	57.06	0.353	62.65
2008-09	45.99	78.32	65.06	0.462	71.28
2009-10	47.44	75.78	67.05	0.511	73.73
2010-11	45.56	70.88	60.23	0.533	69.72
2011-12	47.92	76.39	65.89	0.607	75.31
2012-13	54.41	85.97	70.07	0.659	83.03
2013-14	60.50	96.30	81.17	0.604	92.26
2014-15	61.14	98.57	77.52	0.558	90.80
2015-16	65.47	98.73	72.29	0.546	91.35

Source: Economic Survey (RBI controlled the exchange rate till 1993-94) and RBI handbook

Foreign Exchange Management Act (FEMA), 1999

The Foreign Exchange Regulations Act (FERA), 1973 was repealed and was replaced by a new legislation – Foreign Exchange Management Act (FEMA), 1999 – with effect from June 2000. The objective of the new legislation as stated in the Preamble to the Act was to facilitate external trade and payments and promote the orderly development and maintenance of the foreign exchange market in India – a shift in the approach from "conservation of foreign exchange resources of the country and proper utilisation thereof" under the old Act. The shift in the policy approach entailed significant implications for the operations of the RBI.

The Government of India, in one of the notifications, has designated RBI as the compounding authority for all contravention(s) under the FEMA, except for those involving *hawala* transactions for which the Directorate of Enforcement would be the compounding authority. The new procedure would provide quick and hassle-free disposal of the cases involving contravention(s) of FEMA.

Under the new system, all current account payments except those notified by the government are eligible for appropriate foreign currency in respect of genuine transactions from the authorised dealers without any restrictions. The surrender requirements in respect of exports of goods and services continue to operate. The RBI would, however, have the necessary regulatory jurisdiction over capital account transactions.

The RBI has delegated considerable powers to the authorised dealers to release foreign exchange for a variety of purposes and has been focusing on the development of the foreign exchange market. In order to deepen the foreign exchange market, a large number of products have been introduced and the entry of newer players has been allowed. Additional hedging instruments, such as foreign currency-rupee options have been introduced and authorised dealers have been permitted to use innovative products like cross-currency options, interest rate and currency swaps, caps/collars and forward rate agreements (FRAs) in the international markets.

Asian Clearing Union

For many years now, regional cooperation for benefiting trade and payments has been a subject of serious consideration all over the world. In the Asian region, the initiative on these matters was taken by ECAFE (since renamed as Economic and Social Council for Asia and Pacific) and as a first step for securing regional cooperation amongst its members, the Asian Clearing Union (ACU) was established on 9th December 1974. There are six member countries, *viz*. Bangladesh, India, Iran, Nepal, Pakistan and Sri Lanka.

The central banks of these countries are the participating members of the ACU. Asian Monetary Unit (AMU) is the common unit of account of ACU. The Reserve Bank of India is one of the founder members of ACU. The headquarters of ACU is located in Tehran (Iran). The clearing operations under the arrangement commenced on 1st November 1975. ACU was set up with the objective of:

1. facilitating payments for current international transactions within the ECAFE region on a multilateral basis;
2. reducing the use of extra-regional reserve currencies to settle such transactions by promoting the use of participant's currencies or AMU;
3. effecting thereby economies in the use of foreign exchange and a reduction in the cost of making payments for such transactions; and
4. continuing with the expansion of trade and promotion of monetary cooperation among various countries.

Asian Currency Unit

The term 'Asian Currency Unit' refers to the deposits placed with banks in Singapore, which are specially licensed by the Monetary Authority of Singapore to operate in the Asian Dollar market. The deposits are usually non-resident US dollar deposits but deposits in Deutsche mark, dutch guilders, Swiss francs and Japanese yen are also transacted.

The market for ACU has grown fast, making Singapore a prominent world financial centre. Singapore's geographical location (which gives it access to both Asian and European markets on the same day), a liberal monetary policy and a wide range of international banking facilities have helped the centre to gain this position. The Monetary Authority of Singapore has recently commenced issuing licences to foreign banks to exclusively operate as off-shore units dealing in the inter-bank Asian Dollar market. This step is likely to induce further development of the Asian Dollar market.

19.3 OPERATIONS OF THE CURRENCY EXCHANGE MARKETS

Settlement of international trade transactions usually takes place in denominated currencies which are well accepted by the international trading community. This necessitates the existence of foreign exchange markets which will reflect the interactions between suppliers and the demand for currencies. Currency exchange markets function through sophisticated network of communications, usually computer terminals. With such markets located in major centres like New York, London, Tokyo, etc., they operate 24 hours of the day and the daily turnover is in billions of dollars. Thus, these markets are a critical element of the world's financial system.

The market participants are usually dealers who buy and sell currencies. The official monetary authorities are also important participants in that they intervene to smoothen the fluctuations. Transactions in the markets are done in spot and forward basis. Long-term exchange rates are determined on the basis of the relative economic fundamentals (including inflation, interest rates, current account position in the balance of payments, real income levels, etc.) and a broad set of political and social environments. Short-term movements occur based on short-run changes in these variables. For instance, strikes, general elections, health of leaders, weather, climatic conditions, geo-political situation, etc.

If the determination of exchange rates is left purely to the market mechanism, it is said to be a clean floating exchange rate regime, while allowing market forces to determine the long-term rates and keeping central bank intervention discretionary in the short term is known as *managed floating exchange rate regime*. When the monetary authorities seek to maintain the exchange rate within a narrow margin of pre-determined value in terms of another currency, it may be said to be a fixed exchange rate regime. In fact, the Exchange Rate Margin (ERM) is a somewhat refined example of this system.

Interbank market is the wholesale market in which major banks trade with each other. Forex market is a worldwide market of an informal network of telephone, telex, satellite, facsimile and computer/internet communications between the forex market participants, which include banks, foreign exchange dealers, arbitrageurs and speculators. The foreign exchange market operators are guided by different motives when they deal in the market. Following are the roles played by various participants in the foreign exchange market:

- **Arbitrageurs:** They seek to earn risk-free profits by taking advantage of differences in exchange rates among countries.
- **Traders:** They engage in export or import of goods to a number of countries. They operate in the foreign exchange market because exporters receive foreign currencies which they have to convert into local currencies, and importers make payments in foreign currencies which they purchase by exchanging local currency. They also operate in the foreign exchange market to hedge their risk of fluctuation in currencies.
- **Hedgers:** Multinational corporates have their operations in a number of countries and their assets and liabilities are designated in foreign currencies. The foreign exchange rates fluctuations can cause diminution in the home currency value of their assets and liabilities. They operate in the foreign exchange market as *hedgers* to protect themselves against the risk of fluctuations in the foreign exchange rates.

- **Speculators:** They are guided purely by the profit motive. They trade in foreign currencies to benefit from the exchange rate differences/fluctuations. They take risks in the hope of making profits.

Authorised Banks

To deal in foreign exchange in the United Kingdom, banks must be duly authorised by the Treasury on the recommendation of the Bank of England. Currently, there are some 244 authorised banks, although with the opening of branches and subsidiaries of foreign banks in London and various consortium banks, this number is constantly increasing. These banks generally deal with other banks in London through the medium of brokers. For a brokerage firm to operate in the London foreign exchange market, membership of the Foreign Exchange and Currency Brokers' Association (FECDBA) is obligatory, and moreover the firm must be specifically authorised by its association to provide brokerage services in foreign exchange.

At present, there are 16 firms in the FECDBA of which 11 are authorised to provide this service. Banks are free to deal directly with other overseas banks, and do so by means of telephone, telex, email while dealings through banks within Britain are generally conducted by direct telephone lines. Authorised banks participating in the market normally have a separate dealing room, where telephone lines are arranged on individual switchboards, enabling all dealers to listen in, thus keeping themselves informed on exchange rate movements. The dealers have direct lines to brokers and to other banks and important customers. A deal conducted by telephone is confirmed in writing.

Currency Dealing

The US dollars and some of the leading European currencies, received on deposit by authorised banks can be lent either in the same currency or converted by the bank into another currency. Members of the FECDBA usually act as *intermediaries* between authorised banks in currency deposit business, although banks are free to deal directly by with other banks in other countries, if they so desire. United Kingdom residents other than banks are normally given exchange control permission for foreign currency borrowing to finance domestic expenditure, only when the borrowing is for a period of at least two years. The financing of overseas as distinct from domestic investment by residents through foreign currency borrowings is not affected by this restriction and is normally allowed by the Bank of England.

The term 'foreign exchange' covers in its broadest sense, all payments and receipts denominated in foreign currency. There are, however, other separate markets, for example, in investment currency and in foreign bank notes. Because of the specialised nature of these markets, transactions are normally handled within the banks by specific departments or officials.

Domestic Currency and Foreign Currency

The term "domestic currency" means the currency in which the CFO reports his company's performance to the stakeholders. Often, this term is also referred to as *home currency*.

The term "foreign currency" means any currency other than the domestic currency. For an Indian company, USD is a foreign currency. For a Hong Kong based company GBP is a foreign currency. The foreign currency is not only a medium of exchange but is also a store of value (an asset). As an asset, foreign currency has purchasing power, at times greater and at times less than the domestic (home) currency. Hence, it becomes necessary to know about its price, also known as *exchange rate.*

19.4 FOREIGN EXCHANGE RATES

Foreign exchange is the rate at which one currency is exchanged, i.e., bought and sold, for another currency. For any currency, there is an exchange rate for every other traded currency in the forex markets. A foreign exchange rate is the price of one currency quoted in terms of another currency at a given point of time. When the rate is quoted per unit of the domestic currency, it is referred to as **direct quote**. Thus, the US $ and INR exchange rate would be written as US $ 0.02538/INR. When the rate is quoted as units of domestic currency per unit of the foreign currency, it is referred to as **indirect quote**. If we say that the price of one US $ in INR is 39.40, that is INR 39.40/US $.

Direct Quote

Direct quotes express the exchange rate in terms of "home currency per unit of the foreign currency." In other words, it is the number of home currency units required to buy or sell one unit of foreign currency. For example, Rs. 62 per USD is a direct quote for USD in India. In a direct quote, the **foreign currency** is the commodity which is being bought and sold. Internationally, people prefer direct quotes. In essence, one (in India) would say "I want to buy or sell US $."

Indirect Quote

An indirect quote expresses the exchange rate in terms of "foreign currency per unit of home currency." In other words, it is the number of units of foreign currency required to buy or sell one unit of home currency. For example, Re 1 = 0.02 USD is an indirect quote for the rupee. In an indirect quote, the commodity being bought and sold is the **home currency**. In indirect quote, people (in India) would say "I want to buy or sell rupees."

Link between Direct and Indirect Quotes

What is direct quote for a given currency in one country (i.e., for $ in India) is an indirect quote for that currency in the other country (for $ in USA). Thus,

Rs. 62 per dollar is a direct quote for USD in India and an indirect quote for USD in US. Arithmetic tells us that Rs. 62 per dollar can also written as 1 INR = 1/62th portion of $ or 0.02 per dollar. This is a direct quote for the INR in USA and an indirect quote for INR in India. Thus, the rule reads: "an indirect quote is the reciprocal of the direct quote and vice versa."

Concept Problem

A Mumbai banker has given the following quotes. Identify whether they are direct or indirect. For each direct quote, give the corresponding indirect quote and vice versa.

Currency	Rate	Quote
SEK	6.16	Rs. per Kroner
Euro	0.0148	€ per Re
SGD	0.0299	SGD per Re
AED	13.85	Rs. per UAE Dirham

Solution:

Quote	Rate	Nature of Quote	Other Quote	Rate	Nature of Quote
Rs. Per Kroner	6.16	Direct	SEK per Re	0.1623	Indirect
€ per Re	0.0148	Indirect	Re per €	67.5676	Direct
SGD per Re	0.0299	Indirect	Re per SGD	33.4448	Direct
Rs. Per UAE Dirham	13.85	Direct	AED per re	0.0722	Indirect

The home currency is rupee (since it is a Mumbai based banker).

American Term and European Term

Exchange rates for most currencies are priced based on demand and supply. With over 100 currencies in the global market, it would be an extremely cumbersome job to fix the price of every currency in relation to every other currency.

To obviate this, internationally all currencies are marked against only a single currency namely the dollar. Thus, the rupee is expressed against the dollar; the yen is expressed against the dollar, etc. These quotes are expressed in the direct mode for the respective currency, i.e., respective currency per USD. This is where the concept of American term and European term steps in.

The rule says, "A quote which is a direct quote for the American is said to be in American terms. A quote which is an indirect quote for the American is said to be in European terms."

To be either in American or in European terms, one of the currencies involved should be the USD. International quotes except for £, €, SA Rand, AU$ and NZ$ are all expressed in European terms.

Cross-rates

Traditionally, a "cross-rate denotes an exchange rate that does not involve the home currency." A *cross-rate* is exchange rate between two countries that are not quoted against each other, but are quoted against one common currency. Currencies of many countries are not freely traded in the forex market. Therefore, all currencies are not quoted against each other. Most currencies are, however, quoted against the US dollar. The cross-rates of currencies that are not quoted against each other can be quoted in terms of the US dollar.

Given the exchange rates of two currencies, we can find the exchange rate for the third currency. For example, the US $-Thai baht exchange rate is: US $ 0.02339/Baht, and the US $/INR exchange rate is US $ 0.02538/INR. What is the Baht/INR exchange rate?

$$\frac{\text{US\$ }0.02538}{\text{INR}} \Big/ \frac{\text{US\$ }0.0339}{\text{Baht}} = \frac{\text{US\$ }0.02538}{\text{US\$ }0.02339} * \frac{\text{Baht}}{\text{INR}} \frac{\text{Baht }1.085}{\text{INR}}$$

Thus, one Indian rupee should cost: 0.02538/0.02339 = baht 1.085.

Cross Multiplication is different from cross-rate. "Cross multiplication is a mechanism used to derive the exchange rate for a set of currencies, when the exchange rates for two other sets of currencies are available."

Thus, for example, cross multiplication is used to find the exchange rate between INR and USD when the exchange rate between rupee and pound and that between pound and USD are available. The following rules are employed:

Math Rule 1: Bid (A/B) = Bid (A/C) = Bid (C/B) This means that the purchase price of B in relation to A is the product of the purchase price of C in relation to A and the purchase price of B in relation to C.

Math Rule 2: Ask (A/B) = Ask (A/C) = Ask (C/B) This means that the selling price of B in relation to A is the product of the selling price of C in relation to A and the selling price of B in relation to C.

Math Rule 3: The relationship between bid and ask is:

$$\text{Bid }(A/B) = 1/\text{Ask }(B/A)$$
$$\text{Ask }(A/B) = 1/\text{Bid }(B/A)$$

This is to be used when A/B needs to be computed but B/A is available.

Bid-ask Spread

The foreign exchange dealers are always ready to buy or sell foreign currencies. The quotations are given as bid-ask price. The difference between the buying (bid) and selling (ask) rates is the operator's (bank's) spread. *Bid-ask spread* is the difference between the bids and ask rates of a currency. It is based on the breadth and depth of the market for that currency and its volatility. This spread is cost of transacting in the foreign exchange market. It is computed as:

$$\text{Spread} = \frac{\text{Ask price} - \text{Bid price}}{\text{Ask price}}$$

The following two factors determine the size of spread:

1. **Stability of Exchange Rate:** If the exchange rate is expected to be stable, the spread will be narrow. If the exchange rate is volatile, the spread will be wider.
2. **Depth of the Market:** "Depth" refers to the volume of transactions in the market. A 'deep' market has a high volume of transactions with several dealers simultaneously engaged in transacting business. In this case, the spread will be narrower than for a "thin" market where there is low volume of transactions and a few dealers.

Two-Way Quote

A banker gives a two-way quote. That is, "bid quote" and an "ask quote". When a banker is asked about the foreign currency rates, he does not enquire whether you want to buy or sell. He simply indicates both quotes. By convention, in the direct quote, the bid quote precedes the ask quote. For example, a two-way quote in INR for USD will read: Re/$ – 50.25 – 50.75.

This quote can be interpreted as follows

(a) Here, the first figure Rs. 50.25 denotes the rate at which bank "bids" or "buys" the second currency, in the pair of currencies, namely, US dollar (it is the bank's rate for buying USD by tendering rupees).

(b) The second figure Rs. 50.75 denotes the rate at which the banks "sells" the second currency in the pair of currencies, namely, US dollar (it is the bank's rate for selling $ in order to get Rupees).

(c) In short, the bank buys $ at Rs. 50.25 and sells at Rs. 50.75.

Applicable Rate?

If one were to buy $ from the bank, the relevant rate is the rate at which bank will sell $. That is, the 'ask rate' of Rs. 50.75. This is because when you buy $, the bank sells $. Similarly, if one were to sell $ to the bank, the relevant rate is the "bid rate" of Rs. 50.25. This is because when you sell $, the bank buys $.

In short, the bank buys at Rs. 50.25 and sells at Rs. 50.75 which means that you sell $ at Rs. 50.25 and buy $ at Rs. 50.75. Actually, in a two-way quote, it is easy to identify the rate you need. However, the rule is: "**The bank always wins.**"

Spot Exchange Rates

It is the rate at which a currency can be bought or sold for immediate delivery which is within two business days after the day of trade. Financial newspapers generally provide information on exchange rates. For example, if an investor wants to buy pound sterling, a bank will sell one £ for INR 79.084. These rates are *wholesale rates* for trades among dealers in the interbank market. Financial dailies also quote cross-rates.

For example, if a spot transaction is concluded on a Friday, the settlement will be on the following Tuesday with Saturday and Sunday being holidays (Monday being the first working day and the second working day happens to be Tuesday). In some countries, *e.g.* Bahrain, the weekly closing day is a Friday and, Sunday a working day. The two-day time differential is a reasonable cushion for actual movement of funds through approved banking channels, necessitated by different time zones.

19.5 FORWARD EXCHANGE RATES

It is the rate that is currently paid for the delivery of a currency at some future date. In the forward market, currencies are traded for future delivery. Once the rate is contracted, both parties, namely, the customer and the dealer-banker are obliged to perform on specified future date irrespective of the exchange rate prevailing on that date. In terms of the volume of currency transactions, the spot exchange market is much larger than the forward exchange market.

Forward rates (for example, 30-day, 90-day, or 180-day forward rates) for a few currencies are quoted in the forex market. Most banks will, however, quote currency forward rates to the traders. Forward exchange cover is made available to traders as a form of insurance that protects them against exchange risks arising from a move in foreign exchange rates between the time when their underlying contracts are arranged and the time when the currency is to be received or paid.

Forward Premium/Appreciation or Discount/Depreciation

Relative to "spot rates", forward rates can either be favourable or adverse. This is referred to as "premium or discount", attributed respectively to appreciation or depreciation in value of one currency against another. An exchange rate quoted for a forward date thus usually involves a *premium* or *discount* as compared to spot rate, depending on interest rate differentials between various international centres and general expectations about relative movements between currencies.

Rule 1: In a direct quote, since the foreign currency is the commodity, if the forward rate is greater than the spot rate, the foreign currency is appreciating and the home currency is depreciating.

Rule 2: In a direct quote, if the forward rate is less than the spot rate, the foreign currency is depreciating and the home currency is appreciating.

Relationship	Foreign Currency	Home Currency
$F > S$	Appreciating	Depreciating
$F < S$	Depreciating	Appreciating

Concept Problem

In the following cases, identify as to which currency is appreciating and which is depreciating. Spot 140 Yen per $ 1; Forward 142 Yen per $1. Spot 1£ = Rs. 70; Forward 1£ = Rs. 68.

Solution:

		Status			
Currency	**Country**	**Given**	**Hence**	**Relationship**	**Hence**
Yen	Japan	Home/Forex ¥/$	Direct	F > S	USD is appreciating
Pound	England	Forex/Home Rs./£	Indirect	F < S	INR is appreciating

The same can be cracked differently by viewing every quote as a Direct Quote.

		Status		
Currency	**Product**	**Relationship**	**Appreciating**	**Depreciating**
¥/$	Dollar	F > S	Dollar	Yen
Rs./£	Pound	F < S	INR	Pound

Forward rate premium or discount may be shown as an annualised percentage deviation from the spot rate. Suppose that US $-INR spot exchange rate is US $0.025063/INR. An investor can purchase US dollar at this exchange rate for immediate delivery (within two business days).

Instead of buying US dollars immediately, an investor can enter into an agreement with a bank to deliver him/her US dollars after six months. The bank has quoted a six-month forward rate of US $ 0.024390/INR. Is the six-month forward rate of US dollar at a premium or at a discount?

An investor may observe that the forward rate of dollar is lower than the spot rate. If investor purchases US dollars for a six-month delivery, he/she will get fewer dollars for rupees than in a spot purchase. Since forward dollars are more expensive than spot dollars, the dollar is said to be trading at a premium relative to the Indian rupee. For a direct quote, the annualized forward discount or premium can be calculated as follows:

Forward premium or discount = Spot rate – Forward rate/Spot rate * 360/days

For a six-month forward, the annualized premium is as follows:

6-month forward discount or premium

= 0.025063 – 0.02439/0.02439 * 360/180 = 5.5%

We can also say that the forward rupee is selling at a discount of 5.5 per cent relative to the dollar. In terms of indirect quote, the INR/$ spot exchange rate is INR 39.90/$ and forward rate is INR 41.00/$. For an indirect quote, the forward premium or discount for six months can be calculated as follows:

Forward premium or discount = Forward rate – Spot rate/Spot rate * 360/180

= 41.00 – 39.90/39.90 *2 = 5.5%

Forward contracts are tailor-made according to the corporate needs. The parties to a forward contract can negotiate the terms in accordance with the currency, amount, premium/discount or any other issue.

Swap Points: Forward exchange rates can be quoted either as outright forward exchange rate, or as an adjustment to spot rates (ask the swap points).

Outright forward means expressing the forward rate in the same manner as the spot. Thus, a three-month forward rate of Rs. 70 per € is an outright forward rate. The difference between the outright forward rate and spot rate is called the *swap differential of swap points*.

Remember that swap points are not the same as spread. While spread is the difference between bid and ask, swap is the difference between forward and spot.

Term	Bid	Ask	Spread
Spot	A	B	B – A
Forward	C	D	D – C
Swap	C – A	D - B	

Forward Rate, Premium and Discount

The swap point can represent either a premium or a discount. We know that in direct quote if F > S, the foreign currency is appreciating and the home currency is depreciating. In a direct quote, if the commodity (foreign currency) is appreciating, add the swap points to arrive at the forward rate. If it is depreciating, deduct the swap points from the spot rate to arrive at the forward rate.

If the quote is indirect, naturally opposite effect will have to be given. If the commodity (home currency) is appreciating, deduct the swap points. If the commodity is depreciating, add the swap point.

Concept Problem: Consider the following rates and suggest which currency is quoting at premium and which at a discount.

Quote	Spot	Forward	Period
Rs./HKD	6.56	6.58	1 month
Rs./SGD	33.50	33.25	3 months

Solution:

Price	Product	Spot	Forward	Relationship	Price	Product
Rs	HKD	6.56	6.58	F > S	Depreciating	Appreciating
Rs	SGD	33.50	33.25	F < S	Appreciating	Depreciating

Financial Swaps

Financial swap means an exchange of a specific stream of payments over an agreed period of time between two parties. Financial swaps enable two parties with advantages in different segments of the market to exchange their obligations. Banks arrange these transactions for a fee.

Interest Rate Swap

An *interest rate swap* is a legal agreement between two or more parties to exchange only their interest obligations in the same currency. This, obviously, does not entail the exchange of the principal sums. By swapping his interest obligations for another, a borrower can raise funds at a fixed rate, when interest rates are rising and then, switch to a floating rate in case interest rates fall and vice versa. An example of mechanism of interest rate swap between two companies is given in the table below.

Net Costs	Company X	Company Y
Fixed rate outflow	11.50%	12.75%
Fixed rate inflow	12.75%	-
Floating rate outflow	Libor* + 1.50%	Libor + 1.50%
Floating rate inflow	Libor + 1.50%	-
Net	Libor + 0.25%	12.75%
Alternative cost	Libor + 0.75%	13.00
Savings	0.50%	0.25

* London interbank offered rate

Any borrower of foreign currency exposes himself to two types of risk: exchange risk and interest rate risk. Raising a long-term currency loan at a fixed rate of interest in a rising interest rate environment is alright. But if interest rates stop rising, and on the contrary, fall sharply in a short period of time, the decision to borrow at a fixed rate may prove to be wrong.

Currency Swap

It is an exchange of cash flows, in different currencies, between the two parties. In a currency swap, two parties exchange specified amounts of two currencies today and agree to reverse the transaction at a future date. The interim interest amounts are also exchanged during the currency of the loans.

19.6 INTERNATIONAL PARITY RELATIONSHIPS

The forex markets are considered efficient when exchange rates impound all available information and adapt expeditiously to new information. It is not possible for investors to earn abnormal profits in an efficient forex markets.

Speculators or arbitrageurs will have opportunities to consistently earn large profits without any increase in risk only when the forex markets are inefficient. In an efficient forex market comprising large number of traders, have access to information without much cost, the arbitrage activity will ensure that the disparities in the exchange rates are eliminated. It will also ensure that the exchange-adjusted prices of similar goods and financial assets will be equal in all the countries. This economic behaviour is referred to as the **law of one price**.

In a highly competitive forex market, free from government intervention, both spot and the forward exchange rates should be affected significantly by the current expectation of future events. They should change in expectation of a change in interest rates. In an efficient market, the change in interest differential will get reflected quickly in both spot and forward exchanges rates.

Interest rates are influenced by inflation rates. If we assume that the forex markets are efficient, then interest rates, inflation rates and exchange rates will have equilibrium relationships. Following are four international parity relationships:

1. Interest rate parity (IRP)
2. Purchasing power parity (PPP)
3. Forward rates and future spot rates parity
4. International Fisher effect (IFE)

Interest Rate Parity (IRP)

The interest rate parity characterizes the relationship between interest rates and exchange rates of two countries. It states that the exchange rates of two countries will be affected by their interest rate differential. In other words, the currency of a high interest rate country will be at a forward discount relative to the currency of a low interest rate country and vice versa. This implies that the exchange rate (forward and spot) differential will be equal to the interest rate differential between two countries. i.e.,

Interest differential = Exchange rate (forward and spot) differential

Interest rate parity states that the high interest rate on a currency is offset by the forward discount and that low interest rate is offset by the forward premium. Arbitrage will ensure that this happens.

Working of IRPT

Step 1: Maturity value in the currency of first country:

(i) Invest the money available in the country of the currency at the given interest rate.

(ii) Compute maturity value at the end of the year.

Step 2: Maturity value in the currency of second country:

(i) Buy the currency of the second country, by applying the spot rate.

(ii) Invest the proceeds of step 2(i) at the given interest rate.

(iii) Compute the maturity value at the end of the year.

Step 3: Convert the maturity value of step 2(iii) into the currency of the first country by using the one year forward rate. This value is the same as in step 1(ii).

Interest rate parity works fairly well in the international capital markets where no restrictions exist for the flow of funds from one country to another and no tax asymmetries exist.

What if the Interest Rate Parity Theory does not hold good?

(i) Enter Arbitrage

As mentioned the forward rate would reflect IRPT. If the forward rate did not reflect IRPT, arbitrage opportunities would open up and an intelligent investor can rake in mullah.

Arbitrage means "one commodity/security commands two different prices in two different markets such that it is advisable to buy the commodity/security from the market where it is cheaper and simultaneously sell it in the market where it is dearer. This will lead to risk-free profits."

(ii) Identifying Arbitrage Opportunities

An investor can identify arbitrage opportunity in one of the two ways. One, compute what should be the forward price (*theoretical price*) and compare it with what is the forward price (*actual forward rate*). If two are not equal, there exists an arbitrage opportunity. Two, compute what should be the home country interest rate (theoretical interest rate) for the given forward rate and compare it with what is the actual home country rate (actual interest rate). If the two are not equal, there exists an arbitrage opportunity.

Note: When the actual home country interest rate is less than the theoretical home country interest rate, it means that the home country is offering a rate which is less than what investors want. Hence, money will flow out of home country. Similarly, when actual home country interest rate is higher than the theoretical home country interest rate, it means that the home country is offering a rate which is higher than what investors want. Hence, money will flow into home country from foreign countries.

(iii) Confirmation of Existence of Arbitrage Opportunity

Step 1: Borrow money from the country where money would flow out.

Step 2: Convert the borrowed money at spot rate.

Step 3: Invest the proceeds in another country where money is flowing in.

Step 4: Take **forward cover** to eliminate risk.

Step 5: Realise proceeds from the investment

Step 6: Reconvert at the **forward rate** to the currency of borrowing.

Step 7: Repay principal and pay interest on borrowed money.

Step 8: Count **arbitrage gain** (with the use of step 6 and 7).

Eurocurrency markets are such international capital markets where there are minimum restrictions and controls, and the market forces determine interest rates.

Purchasing Power Parity

In absolute terms, *purchasing power parity* states that the exchange rate between the currencies of two countries equals the ratio between the prices of goods in these countries. Further, the exchange rate must change to adjust to the change in the prices of goods in the two countries. In relevant terms, purchasing power parity states that the exchange rate between the currencies of two countries will adjust to reflect changes in the inflation rates of two countries. In formal terms, it implies that the expected inflation differential equals the current spot rate and the expected spot rate differential. Thus,

Inflation rate differential = Current spot and expected spot rate differential

Expectation Theory of Forward Rates

What would be the relationship between the forward rates and the expected spot rates in the future? Suppose an exporter who is expecting to receive US dollars in the future. He/she has two choices. He/she can wait until dollar payment is received and then convert it into rupees. Here the exporter is exposed to the risk of drop in the value of the dollar in the future. The second alternative is that he/she fixes the price of dollar today and sells US dollar forward. The exporter is thus able to avoid risk of a possible fall in the value of dollar.

On the other hand, suppose an importer who is required to make payment in US dollars in future. Here importer will do the opposite. He/she will buy dollars forward to avoid the risk of possible appreciation in the value of dollar in future. If both exporters and importers are in large numbers, the forward rate of US dollar relative to Indian rupee will be very close to the expected future spot rate. This is the **expectation theory of forward exchange rates**. The expected future spot rate depends on the expectations of forex market participants. If they prefer to hedge their forex risk or if they are risk neutral, then the forward rate must be equal to the expected future spot rate.

In general, when forward rate for any currency is higher than the market participants' prediction of the expected future spot rate, they will tend to sell the foreign currency forward. This should cause a fall in the forward rate until it equals the expected future spot rate. Similarly, when the forward rate is lower than the expected future spot rate, market participants will purchase the foreign currency forward.

As a consequence, the forward rate will rise until it reaches the expected future spot rate. The expectation theory of forward exchange rates states that the forward rates provide the best and unbiased forecast of the expected future spot rate. In formal terms, it means that the forward and current spot rate differential must be equal to the expected spot rate and current spot rate differential. Thus,

Forward and current spot rate differential = Expected and current spot rate differential

In simple terms, the forward rate must be equal to the expected future spot rate. Thus,

Forward rate = Expected future spot rate

The expectation theory works on an average. The actual future spot rates have been found to differ from the earlier forward rates. It is very difficult to predict accurately the exchange rates. However, the forward rate is the best possible forecaster of the expected future spot rate.

Pure Expectation Theory

Market expectations as to the foreign exchange rates determine the foreign exchange rate! This merely indicates that we would first make an estimate of future interest rate and compare it with our own judgement of interest rates.

1. Judgement of a Future Interest Rate

Suppose an investor has Rs. 1,00,000 for investment. He/she wishes to invest in a bank. The banker informs the investor that the interest rate for 1 year deposit is 6%, and for a 2-year deposit is 8%. This might indicate to the investor about the likely interest rate scenario one year hence.

The current interest rate structure of 6% and 8% respectively, for 1 and 2 years deposits implies that the market expects the interest rates to rise in a year to 10.038%.

Where reliable data is available, the logic of predicting future interest rates can be extended to further periods into the future also. These interest rates are also referred to as **forward interest rates**.

2. How is This Helpful?

Armed with a prediction of future spot interest rate, the investor would now obtain the actual future interest rate. If the two are not equal, and investor tends to gain (interest-arbitrage profits) from such a situation, until such time that demand-supply forces interact in a manner which would bring about equilibrium.

3. Link between Forward Rate and Spot Rate

Now, for most major currencies, on any give date, there is a spot rate and a forward rate, say for a year. The percentage difference today between the forward rate and the spot rate is the change expected in the spot rate. Investors have their own estimates of "future spot exchange rates" (what they expect the spot rate to be in future). Armed with this, they proceed to buy and sell currencies.

Weak currencies strengthen, while stronger ones dwindle. Ultimately, it is the type of investor which is the predominant player in the market (speculators, hedgers, or the 'safety-first' category!) that would decide whether forward rate is less than or equal to "future spot rate."

This means apart from interest rates or inflation rates, there are two other variables, namely: (a) expectation of the market itself, and (b) speculators and hedgers in the market, that determine the exchange rate movements.

International Fisher Effect

We know that the normal interest rate comprises a real interest rate and an expected rate of inflation. The nominal rate of interest adjusts when the inflation rate is expected to change. The nominal interest rate will be higher when a higher inflation rate is expected and it will be lower when a lower inflation rate is expected. This is referred to as the **Fisher effect**.

Irving Fisher argued that, over time, money-interest rates change to reflect changes in anticipated inflation rates. It is formally expressed as:

1 + Nominal interest rates = (1 + real interest rate)/(1 + inflation rate)

(The nominal rate of interest also includes cross-product term, in practice however, this term is ignored.)

If the international capital markets are perfect, then the equivalent risk investments in two countries should offer the same expected real rate of return. This is ensured by arbitrage. If the **expected real rate of return** is higher in one country than in another, capital would flow from the second to the first country, and investors will have opportunities to make risk-free arbitrage profit.

The arbitrage activity will persist until equilibrium is established in the expected real returns in two countries. If real rates of return are the same in two countries, then, as per Fisher effect, the nominal rates on interest in two countries will adjust exactly for the change in the inflation rates. In formal terms, the **international Fisher effect** states that the nominal interest rate differential must be equal to the expected inflation rate differential in two countries.

Thus, Nominal interest rate differential = Expected inflation rate differential

In effect, the international fisher effect implies that the expected future spot rate of a currency with a higher interest rate will tend to fall in value in the long run and the expected future spot rate of a currency with a lower interest rate will tend to rise in value in the long run. Thus, the interest rate differential between two countries should provide an unbiased forecast of future change in the spot rate.

International Fisher effect suggests the following:

- Changes in interest rates reflect the changes in anticipated inflation rates, and interest rate differentials provide an unbiased predictor of future changes in spot exchange rates.
- Currency of countries with relatively high interest rates is expected to depreciate, because higher interest rates are considered necessary to adjustments to spot exchange rates.
- Given the free movement of capital internationally, the real rate of return in different countries will equalise as a result of adjustments to spot exchanges rates.

The international Fisher effect reinforces the interest-rate parity and purchasing power parity theories, by highlighting the "inflation" element in nominal interest rates.

Since the forward rate is an unbiased predictor of the spot rate, the international Fisher effect follows from interest rate parity, purchasing power parity and the expectation theory of forward exchange rate.

According to international Fisher fffect, the interest rate differential must be equal to the inflation rate differential, and the interest rate differential provides a forecast of the expected future spot rate. If the expectation theory of exchange rate holds, then the forward rate should be equal to the expected future spot rate.

Before we move further, let us understand few basic elements in risk.

1. **Risk** is the possibility that the actual result from an action will deviate from the expected level of result. The greater the "magnitude" of deviation, and greater the probability of its occurrence, the greater is the risk!
2. **Exposure** as understood in risk management indicates a situation of being open or being vulnerable to risks.

Risk Management

Any business takes various steps for reducing the risk by adopting appropriate techniques or policies. Risk management focuses on identifying and implementing such techniques or policies, lest the business should be left exposed to uncertain outcomes. Therefore, a business entity is generally keen on avoiding particular kind of risks, rather wishes to "reduce" risks to acceptable levels.

For risk reduction, a business entity has one or two options:

- **Pooling:** When certain types of risk which are unacceptable to business entities that face risk, are pooled, taken over and assumed by a third party ("insurer"), thus risk is shifted/transferred for a price called "risk premium."
- **Hedging:** Hedging is a technique that enables an investor to minimise the effect of adverse outcomes in a particular or given situation. Parties come together under an agreement in terms of which risk of one party gets cancelled by the risk of another.

Risk minimization is not the only strategy. A business entity may still choose to remain "exposed", in anticipation of reaping profits from its risk-taking policies!

19.7 FOREIGN EXCHANGE RISK

An international firm deals in foreign currency. It is expected to receive or make payment in foreign currency. The exchange rate between the firm's domestic currency and the foreign currency may rise or fall by the time the firm receives or pays the cash flows in the foreign currency. This exposes the firm to what is called the *foreign exchange risk*. Foreign exchange risk is the risk that the currency value of cash flows, denominated in foreign currency, may change because of the variation in the foreign exchange rate. There would not be any foreign exchange risk if the exchange rates were fixed. We can distinguish between three types of foreign exchange exposures:

1. Transaction exposure
2. Economic exposure
3. Translation exposure

Transaction Exposure: Transaction exposure involves the possible exchange loss or gain on the existing foreign currency denominated transactions. For example, an importer of goods and/or services is required to make payment after three months or six months as per the terms of purchasing contract, after receiving delivery of goods/services. The usual problem arising is that an importer cannot predict what the exchange rate would be after three or six months. There is uncertainty whether his/her domestic currency will appreciate or depreciate in relative terms with the foreign currency. Therefore, the importer is exposed to transaction risk.

Economic Exposure: It refers to the change in the corporate value of corporate caused by the unexpected changes in the exchange rate. It is also referred to as **operating exposure** or the long-term cash flow exposure. Thus, the exchange risk may be defined as the variability of the corporate value resulting from the unanticipated exchange rate changes. The changes in the foreign exchange rate affect cash flows from operations. The corporate value is affected by the unexpected changes in the expected cash flows.

The expected cash flows can change due to various factors. The input costs, prices of goods or investments can cause the cash flows to change. The cash flows are also affected by changes in the pricing policy. A shift in the exchange rate could affect the immediate cash flows as well as the cash flows in the future. The future cash flows are affected because a change in exchange rate could also affect the price, volume, market share and competitiveness of corporates.

Economic exposure has two components: *transaction exposure* and *real operating exposure*. Transaction exposure involves the possible exchange rate loss or gain on existing foreign currency denominated transactions. The real operating exposure takes into account the impact of both the exchange rate changes and the inflation rate changes. The exchange rate and inflation rate changes together could have serious effects on the magnitude of cash flows.

A corporate economic exposure depends on the structure of the input and the output markets. The corporate can manage the effects of exchange rate changes on its competitiveness by adjusting markets, product mix and input sourcing. Since, ultimately it is corporate competitive position that gets affected; (these economic risks affect the "potential", rather than the "performance" per se) the exchange rate exposure should be dealt with strategically by buying suitable insurance cover against such risks. The objective should be to smoothen the flows of cash under the variable exchange rate situations.

Translation Exposure: It refers to the exchange gain or loss occurring from the difference in the exchange rates at the beginning and end of the accounting period. It is the effect of a change in exchange rate on the reported profits and financial position.

This accounting gain or loss need not be economic gain or loss. A corporate is exposed to translation loss if it uses current exchange rate to translate its assets and liabilities. There are four methods that are in use in translating assets and liabilities.

- ***Current/Non-Current Method***: Under this method, current assets and current liabilities are translated at the current rate and non-current assets and non-current liabilities at the historic rate. Profit and loss statement items are translated at the average exchange rate of the period. However, revenues and expenses related to non-current assets and non-current liabilities are translated at historic rate.
- ***Monetary/Non-Monetary Method***: Under this method, monetary balance sheet accounts such as cash, account receivables, payables and long-term debt are translated at the current rate. Non-monetary accounts such as inventory, fixed assets and long-term investments are translated at the historic rate. The profit and loss statement items are translated at the average exchange rate during the period. However, revenue and expense accounts related to non-monetary balance sheet accounts are translated at the historic rates.
- ***Temporal Method***: This method is similar to the monetary/non-monetary method with the only difference that inventory may be translated at the current rate when it is shown at market rate.
- ***Current Rate Method***: Under this method, all balance sheet and income statement items are translated at the current rate.

Political Risk refers to the consequences that political activities in a country may have on the value of a corporate overseas operations. While political risks can cause either a negative or a positive effect on the value of a corporate, we will limit our discussion to adverse effects only.

- Discrimination against foreign businesses
- Compulsory acquisition of properties by government
- Boycott of products (mostly during war time)
- Rules specifying use of labour and materials (companies' cost control measures) or price setting constraints
- Exchange controls. Limitations on the extent to which a country's currency can be used to transfer funds or restrictions on the conversion of a currency into other currencies (e.g., regulations prevailing in Nigeria)
- Tax regulations biased against foreign investments, or foreign operations (e.g., GAAR in India)

19.8 HEDGING FOREIGN EXCHANGE RISK

Some companies have a policy of partially covering their exposure. This policy suffers from subjectivism as there is no sound method of deciding how much to cover and how much to keep uncovered. The corporate risk remains unlimited in the partially covered exposure. In fact, keeping the foreign exchange exposure totally or partially uncovered tantamount to speculation.

There are three alternatives available to companies to hedge against the foreign exchange exposure:

- Forward contracts
- Foreign currency option
- Money market operations
- Currency futures (a derivative instrument)
- Option contracts (a derivative instrument)

The hedging techniques of foreign currency option and money operations may not be available to corporates in many countries, particularly developing countries. However, a large majority of corporates can cover their foreign exchange exposure through forward contracts.

Forward Contract

It involves the contract between two parties (obliged to perform) for either purchase or sale of specified quantity of specified currency, for the price which is agreed today, while the performance of the contract would be carried out at a specified future date.

A corporate can take a full forward cover against its foreign exchange exposure and entirely hedge its risk. The advantage of this approach is that corporate management can concentrate on its operations rather than worrying about the foreign exchange (loss) or gain. Most international companies have the policy of covering hundred per cent of their foreign exchange risk. In forward contract the cost remains the same, irrespective of the spot rate.

- ***Cost of forward contract*** is the difference between the forward rate and the expected spot rate (not the current spot rate) at the time cash flows are paid or received.
- ***The length of time (depth)*** up to which one can stretch forward depends upon demand levels. The longer is the time period, the wider is bid-ask spread. The size for spread for a given currency increases with maturity.

Closure of Forward Contracts

As an entity one enters into forward contract either as a *buyer* of foreign currency (importer) or *seller* of foreign currency (exporter). The forward contact can be closed either on: (a) due date of settlement, or (b) on any date prior to the date of settlement of the forward contract. Closing of contract can be done either by:

- Honouring the contract
- Rollover of the contract (i.e., extending the contract)
- Cancelling the contract

Foreign Currency Option

The foreign currency option is the right (not an obligation) to buy or sell a currency at an agreed exchange rate (exercise price) on or before an agreed maturity period. The right to buy is called a **call option** and right to sell, a **put option**. A foreign currency option holder will exercise his right only if it is advantageous to do so. Except for the cost of option premium, the foreign currency option provides a unique hedging alternative; an investor can avoid the loss by exercising his/her option and gain from the favourable changes in exchange rate by not exercising the option.

Money Market Operations

Another hedging technique is the money market operations. If interest rate parity holds, the difference in the forward rate and the spot rate is the reflection of the differences in the interest rates in two countries. A money market is a market for short-term instruments. In this market, a business entity lends or borrows for a short period of time. The salient features are:

1. **Time Period:** The time can range from an "overnight" time period (a day comprising 24 hours from the close of business hours on day-1 till close of business hours on day-2) to generally six to twelve months.
2. **Interest Rate:** Each time, a period will have its own interest rates; lowest for overnight periods, and increasing gradually with the tenure of borrowing/lending.
3. **Nominal Annual Rates:** Money market rates are always given in nominal annual rates. If a rate of 8% is quoted, it means 8% per annum and will have to be adjusted for the relevant time period. A three-month tenure would thus carry interest at 2% (8 *3/12).
4. **Different Rates:** Interest of deposit rates differ from country to country, and hence currency to currency.

Decision Process in Money Market Hedging

Decision process for covering a transaction-risk exposure, through money market hedging is based on: (a) interest rate structure in two countries; (b) which of the two currencies is appreciating against the other; and (c) whether an entity is an exporter or importer. The table below describes the possibilities in money market hedging for both the importer as well as the exporter.

Money Market Hedge for	Possibility Exists, if in Absolute Terms
Importer	Borrowing and lending rates are lower in foreign currency than in domestic currency and there are signs of domestic currency depreciating.
Exporter	Borrowing and lending rates are higher in foreign currency than in domestic currency and there are signs of foreign currency depreciating.

The problem with the money market alternative is that all markets are not open and all currencies are not fully convertible. For example, the Indian rupee is not fully convertible and there are restrictions on the free flow of funds outside the country.

Comparison of Forward Cover with Money Market Hedge

There are two ways of computing: (i) compare the cash flows under the two alternatives and; (ii) compare the rates under the two alternatives.

Method	Exporter	Importer
Cash flow	Whichever gives higher domestic currency inflow	Whichever gives lower domestic currency outflow
Effective rate	Whichever gives higher effective rate	Whichever gives lower effective rate

Covered Interest Arbitrage: In the financial market, one knows with certainty: 1) spot rate, and 2) fixed interest rates for a specified period. In addition, one can have a forward exchange rate, which is merely the "predicted" rate. There can be situations where the "predicted" forward rate is out of alignment with money market rate. When and if, it happens, it will be possible for speculators to make risk-free money.

Concept Problem: You are approached for an advice by a US based businessman enjoying a surplus cash of US $ 500,000 and looking for short-term investment opportunities. Money market rate in USA is 4% while in London, it is 7.2%. You notice spot exchange rate is $1.5865–1.5887 per GBP. Three-month forward rate is $1.5795 –1.5807. What will be your advice?

Solution:

Investment in USA	Calculation	Result
(a) Money available		500,000 dollars
(b) Interest rate		4% p.a. or 1% quarter
(c) Maturity	(a) * 1.01	505,000

Investment in London		
(d) Money available		500,000 dollars
(e) Buy P Spot Ask rate	(d) / 1.5887	314,723 P
(f) Interest rate		7.20% p.a. or 1.80% quarter
(g) Maturity	(e) * 1.018	320,388 P
(h) Reconvert Forward Bid	(g) * 1.5795	506.053

It is advisable to convert money first and then invest in London. Hence, arbitrage opportunity exists.

19.9 INTERNATIONAL CAPITAL INVESTMENT ANALYSIS

The basic principle applicable to an international investment decision is similar to a domestic investment decision. The incremental cash flow of the investment should be discounted at an opportunity cost of capital appropriate to risk of the investment. The investment should be accepted if the net present value is positive. One factor that distinguishes the international investment decision from the domestic one is that cash flows are earned in foreign currency. The fact should be considered while estimating the incremental cash flows.

Let us consider an example to illustrate the evaluation of an international investment decision for a project. Suppose a Taiwanese toy manufacturing corporate is thinking of an investment for making toys in Thailand. It is estimated that the initial project cost will be 12.5 million in Thai baht. The project will have a target debt ratio of 40 per cent. It is expected to generate the following free cash flows (net cash flows after tax) in baht for the next eight years.

Year	1	2	3	4	5	6	7	8
National Cash Flows (Baht in millions)	2.50	2.73	2.97	3.24	3.53	3.85	4.19	4.57

The following are the key assumptions about the project in Thailand.

	Taiwan (T$)	Thailand (Baht)
Inflation rate	12.9%	6.1%
Government bond yield	12.3%	9.4%
Risk premium	11.0%	8.0%
Interest rate	15.5%	12.4%
Tax rate	35.0%	30.0%
Spot exchange rate		
1 Baht = 0.8160 Taiwanese dollar (T$)		

- How should the project be evaluated?
- Should it be undertaken?

As stated earlier, we can discount the free cash flows of the project by its Weighted Average Cost of Capital (WACC) to determine its NPV. We should accept the project if NPV is positive. There are alternative ways to state the free cash flows and the discount rate. We can either use the Taiwanese dollar cost of capital to discount free cash flows in Taiwanese dollars or the Thai baht cost of capital to discount free cash flows in Thai baht.

Table 19.3 NPV Calculation of the Project (Taiwanese dollar)

Year	Net Cash Flows (Baht)	Estimated Exchange Rate	Net Cash Flows (T$)	PV Factor at 19%	Present Value
0	-12.50	0.8160	-10.20	1.0000	-10.20
1	2.50	0.8383	2.10	0.8403	1.76
2	2.73	0.8612	2.35	0.7062	1.66
3	2.97	0.8848	2.63	0.5934	1.56
4	3.24	0.9089	2.94	0.4987	1.47
5	3.53	0.9338	3.30	0.4190	1.38
6	3.85	0.9593	3.69	0.3521	1.30
7	4.19	0.9855	4.13	0.2959	1.22
8	4.57	1.0125	4.63	0.2487	1.15
Net Present Value (T$, in millions)					**1.30**

NPV in Taiwanese dollars = 1.61 * 0.816 = 1.30

The above table shows the NPV calculation of the project in terms of Taiwanese dollars. The project has a positive NPV of T$ 1.30 million. The firm should accept it.

Table 19.4 NPV Calculation of the Project (in Thai Baht)

Year	Net Cash Flows (Baht)	PV Factor at 15.8%	Present Value
0	-10.00	1.000	-12.50
1	2.50	0.864	2.16
2	2.73	0.746	2.04
3	2.97	0.644	1.91
4	3.24	0.556	1.80
5	3.53	0.480	1.70
6	3.85	0.415	1.60
7	4.19	0.358	1.50
8	4.57	0.309	1.41
Net Present Value (Baht, in million)			**1.61**

Estimating Beta: Beta of a foreign investment can be calculated by regressing the project investment return to a benchmark market index. An appropriate benchmark market index depends on whether the international financial markets are integrated or segmented. In fully integrated international markets, both corporate and individual investors are free to invest anywhere in the world.

In the above Thailand project case, the project's cost of capital does not depend on any country. Investors could diversify internationally and obtain international diversification benefits themselves. In Thailand project case, Beta is calculated relative to the world market index.

In practice, international markets may be segmented. In a number of countries, particularly in emerging markets, only corporates are allowed to invest internationally, and not individual investors. Further, investors typically invest in their home markets even if they are allowed to invest in foreign markets. Hence, they would expect to earn the risk-free rate of home markets plus risk premium in home markets multiplied by the foreign investment's Beta relative to the home market index.

In the Thailand project example, we assume that the Taiwanese investors mostly invest in the home market. Therefore, the Beta of the project in Thailand should reflect the Taiwanese corporate risk of investing in a project in Thailand. We can take an indirect approach to estimate the Beta of the toys manufacturing project in Thailand. We can first estimate the Betas for a sample of Thai toys firms relative to the Taiwanese market index. Then we can find the average (simple or weighted) of these Betas and use the average Beta as a proxy for the Beta of investment in Thailand.

Investment Evaluation: Parent Vs Project

Foreign investment should be evaluated from the parent's point of view. Generally, the parent will have control over cash flows of the foreign project that are the basis for remittance of dividends, reinvestment of cash flows anywhere or repayment of debt by the parent. In this case, the parent's cash flows are also project's cash flows, and there is no need for separate valuation of the investment project.

In many situations, there may be significant difference in the parent's and project's cash flows. These differences may arise because of the host country's current and future policy of exchange controls and taxes on foreign profits of the parent company.

Restrictions on Remittances: The parent may not be allowed by the host country to appropriate the project's cash flows; there may be restrictions on the dividend repatriation; the reinvestment of cash flows may be restricted; the project's cash flows may not be allowed to service the firm's debt taken outside the host country.

Differences in Taxes: There may be difference in the tax rates in the parent country and the country where the subsidiary operates. The earnings may be taxed in the host country, but not in parent's country. Alternatively, if the tax rate in the parent's country is higher on the remitted earnings, the parent may have to pay differential tax. In some cases, there is no tax treaty between two countries and earnings of the subsidiaries are taxed twice – once by the host government and then by the parent government if remitted.

Cash Flows to Parent: There are many ways by which a parent company could obtain cash flows from its foreign project. There may be restrictions on the dividend repatriation, but the host government may allow payment of royalty or licence and management fees to parent. The parent may supply material or components to the project at a profit to 'recover' cash flows when there are restrictions on transfer of cash flows.

When the cash flows of a project are different from the parent's cash flows, the parent will be interested in evaluation of the project from both parent's and project's viewpoints. An investor should follow the principle of relevant cash flows to the project and parent in performing the investment analysis.

Political Risk of Foreign Investments

Investment in a foreign country is not only exposed to exchange rate, but also to political risk. A corporate which is deciding to make investment in another country, must vouch for the political risk in the host country. A corporate exposure to political risk depends on the host country's political system, its economic conditions and the government's policies and actions towards foreign direct investment (FDI) that affect the corporate investments and cash flows.

A country with large deficit relative to the gross domestic product (GDP), high growth of money expansion, fully or partially controlled exchange rates, enormous public sector enterprises, huge low-yielding government expenditures, controlled prices and interest rates and trade restrictions would have potentially high political risk. A country with poor economic performance, low degree of economic integration with the world system and controlled political regime poses a high degree of political risk.

The most important, but now less frequent political risk is the **risk of appropriation**. The most frequent political risks arise on account of the host government's regulations that constrain the efficient operations of the foreign corporate. There are conflicts of goals between the host government and the foreign corporates that lead to regulatory constraints on the foreign corporate activities. The host government may restrict regulation of dividends, may impose additional taxes on the income of foreign corporate or may control prices of its output after the corporate has made investment in the host country.

Total avoidance of political risk is not possible as all countries do have some degree of political risk. A corporate should have a strategy of managing political risk. It can insure its foreign investment with international insurance companies. But the insurance against political risk is not a guarantee against the economic value as it only guarantees the initial investment. The most appropriate strategy for the corporate is to increase its bargaining power. If expropriation is a threat, the corporate can increase the cost of expropriation and benefits of not expropriating to the host country. It can enter into contracts, which interlocks the interests of host government, customers and major international suppliers of funds and host country's financial institutions.

Foreign Political Risks and Investment Evaluation

There are two ways in which a corporate can handle political risks in investment evaluation. The corporate may *increase the cost of capital* (discount rate) to allow for political risks. In practice, it is very difficult to adjust the cost of capital for political risks. Hence, an alternative available to the corporate is to *adjust the investment's cash flows* to account for political risk. It is relatively easy to adjust cash flows by making conservative forecasts of cash flows when political risks are high.

The Way Forward

The Indian foreign exchange market has undergone transformation from a closed and heavily controlled setting of the 1970s and the 1980s to a more open and market oriented regime since the mid-1990s. The foreign exchange market, which witnessed deregulation in conjunction with current account convertibility and liberalization of capital controls in many areas, lent considerable support to the external sector reform process. The criticality of a well-functioning market with its ability to trade and settle transactions in new products and adapt itself quickly to the changing regulatory and competitive environment has been demonstrated well in the Indian context. The bid-ask spread of rupee/US dollar rate has been almost converged with that of other major currencies in the international market.

Moving forward, further initiatives for developing the Indian foreign exchange market need to be aligned with the external sector reforms, particularly the move towards:

(a) further liberalization of the existing capital control, for which a fresh roadmap has been provided by the Committee on FCAC;

(b) reform in other segments of the financial market; and

(c) greater integration of the Indian economy with the outside world.

These among other things, would imply that:

(i) an increasing number of Indian corporates will become global players; and

(ii) more and more non-resident entities operating in India will be exposed to risks related to changes in exchange as well as interest rates.

With steady integration of the Indian economy globally, the foreign exchange market will be required to deal with large capital inflows. To meet the needs of corporate, the foreign exchange market needs to introduce more instruments, invite and engage with more participants and improvise market infrastructure in respect of trading and settlement. Other factors would include:

- introduction of more derivative products;
- diversification of custom base with heterogeneous expectations;
- entrenchment of modern risk management systems, procedures and governance in banks and other corporate clients; and
- adoption of accounting and disclosure norms in respect of derivatives by banks.

CHAPTER 20

Financial Derivatives Market

The economy is driven towards the free market economy. Further, with the integration of the financial markets and free mobility of capital, risks also multiply and risk management becomes quite significant. The world of high finance is all about risk. You would have your job on the line if you do not protect your company against risk. Price risk is amongst the most crucial risks that a business faces.

In this context, derivatives occupy an important place as a risk reducing tool. Investors, including corporate, are risk averse. They aim at reducing risks by hedging through derivatives. Derivatives include options, forward contracts, futures contracts and swaps. Derivative products provide certain important economic benefits such as risk management or redistribution of risks away from risk averse investors, towards those willing and able to bear risk. Derivatives also help in price discovery and efficient allocation of capital in the economy.

The emergence of the market for derivative products, most probably forwards, futures and options, can be traced back to the willingness of risk-averse economic agents to guard themselves against uncertainties arising out of fluctuations in asset prices. In a dynamic market environment, various stakeholders including corporates, a portfolio manager, an investor faces several kinds of risk. Corporate firm's profitability fluctuates due to unanticipated changes in demand, selling price, costs, taxes, interest rates, technology, exchange rate and host of other factors. Managers may not be able to fully control these risks, but, to some degree, they can decide the risks that the firm should undertake. From several options, they create operating flexibility that might bail them out in difficulties. Managers reduce their risk exposure by entering into *financial contracts*.

By their very nature, the *financial markets* are marked by a very high degree of volatility. Through the use of derivative products, it is possible to partially or fully transfer price risks by locking-in asset prices. As instruments of risk management, these generally do not influence the fluctuations in the underlying asset prices. However, by locking-in asset prices, derivative products minimize the impact of fluctuations in asset prices on the profitability and cash flow situation of risk-averse investors.

Derivatives history goes back to the Middle Ages when farmers and merchants used to seal the prices of harvest in advance through forward trading. This method helped them to protect against any undesirable price structure. The Chicago Board of Trade (CBOT), USA, formalized this process in 1848 by introducing fluctuations exchanged traded futures. Initially, its main task was to act as a market provider and guarantor of trades. Slowly this market picked up and spread across various regions, and subsequently a proper derivatives market developed with many variants like options and swaps on various underlying assets in commodities and financial instruments.

Derivative products initially emerged, as hedging devices against fluctuations in commodity prices and commodity-linked derivatives remained the sole form of such products for almost three hundred years. The financial derivatives came into spotlight in post-1970 period due to growing instability in the financial markets and are fairly a recent feature even in developed countries. Currency futures first emerged in the USA in 1972, followed by interest rate futures. Stock index futures and options emerged only in 1982.

A new dimension was added to the derivatives market in 1982, when Kansas City Board of Trade (USA) introduced trading in index futures. In this case, the underlying section was not any visible commodity but a quantitative index of the stock market. Soon the market volumes multiplied manifold and derivatives became a popular tool for risk management against uncertainties in today's business environment. Since their emergence, these products became very popular and by 1990s, spread rapidly to other developed countries, accounting for about two-thirds of total transactions in derivative products.

Derivatives have come to be recognized as the most cost efficient way of hedging risks in certain types of commercial and financial transactions and therefore, countries not providing such globally accepted risk-hedging facilities are disadvantaged in today's rapidly integrating global economy. In recent years, the market for financial derivatives has grown tremendously both in terms of variety of instruments available, their complexity and also turnover. In the class of equity derivatives, futures and options on stock indices have gained more popularity than on individual stocks, especially among institutional investors, who are major users of index-linked derivatives.

Even small investors find them useful due to high correlation of the popular indices with various portfolios and ease of use. The lower costs associated with index derivatives vis-*á*-vis derivative products based on individual securities are another reason for their growing use.

20.1 DERIVATIVE

Derivative is a product, a financial instrument whose value (pay-off) is derived from the value of one or more basic variables, called bases (underlying asset, such as stocks, bonds, currencies, commodities, precious metals, market index, or reference rate, i.e., interest rate and foreign exchange rate), in a contractual manner. These instruments are so called because they derive their value from the underlying instruments and have no intrinsic value of their own. Derivatives are tools used by a firm/portfolio manager, or an investor to reduce risk exposure. Forwards, futures, options, swaps, caps floor collar, etc., are commonly used derivatives. The world over, derivatives are a key part, an integral part of the modern financial system.

Derivatives are structured products and are increasingly used to manage risk. Derivatives are off-balance sheet transactions and they cannot be put on balance sheet unless the underlying assets are bought and paid for.

Characteristics of Derivatives

- Derivatives possess a combination of novel characteristics not found in any form of assets.
- It is comfortable to take a short position in derivatives than in other assets. An investor is said to have a short position in a derivatives product if he is obliged to deliver the underlying asset in specified future date.
- Derivatives traded on exchange are liquid and involve the lowest possible transaction costs.
- Derivatives can be closed/matched with specific portfolio requirements.
- The margin requirements for exchange-traded derivatives are relatively low, reflecting the relatively low level of credit-risk associated with derivatives.
- Derivatives are traded globally having strong popularity in financial markets.
- Derivatives maintain a close relationship between their values and values of underlying assets; the changes in values of underlying assets will have effect on value of derivatives based on them.
- In a Treasury bond futures contract, the derivatives are straightforward.

20.2 DEVELOPMENT OF DERIVATIVE MARKETS IN INDIA

Derivative markets have been in existence in India in some form or other for a long time. In the area of commodities, the Bombay Cotton Trade Association started futures trading in 1875 and, by the early 1900s India had one of the world's largest futures industries. In 1952, the government banned cash settlement and options trading and derivative trading shifted to informal forward markets. In recent years, government policy has changed, allowing for an increased role for market-based pricing and less suspicion of derivatives trading. The ban on futures trading of many commodities was lifted starting in the early 2000s, and national electronic commodity exchanges were created.

In the equity markets, a system of trading called *badla* involving some elements of forward trading had been in existence for decades. However, the system led to a number of undesirable practices and it was prohibited.

The economic liberalization of the early 1990s facilitated the introduction of derivatives based on interest rates and foreign exchange. A system of market-determined exchange rate was adopted by India in March, 1993. In August 1994, the rupee was made fully convertible on current account. These reforms allowed increased integration between domestic and international markets, and created a need to manage currency risk. In India, many market participants, especially FIIs and Mutual Funds, pressed for effective hedging tools through derivatives. Therefore, NSE and BSE followed the recommendations of Prof. L. C. Gupta committee and introduced Index Futures on Nifty and Sensex respectively from June 12, 2000.

Development and Regulation of Derivative Markets in India

The SEBI Board in its meeting on June 24, 2002 considered some important issues relating to the derivative markets, including:

- Physical settlement of stock options and stock futures contracts.
- Review of the eligibility criteria of stocks on which derivative products are permitted.
- Use of sub-brokers in the derivative markets.
- Norms for use of derivatives by mutual funds.

The recommendations of the Advisory Committee on Derivatives on some of these issues were also placed before SEBI Board. The Board desired that these issues be reconsidered by the Advisory Committee on Derivatives (ACD) and requested a detailed report on the aforesaid issues for the consideration of the Board.

20.3 DERIVATIVES CONTRACT TRADING

The most notable development concerning the secondary segment of the Indian capital market is the introduction of derivatives trading in June 2000. The Securities and Exchange Board of India (SEBI) approved derivatives trading based on futures contracts at both BSE and NSE in accordance with the rules/bylaws and regulations of the stock exchanges. Both BSE and NSE made a beginning with equity derivatives with the introduction of stock index futures.

To make Indian capital market more efficient and world-class, derivatives as new products have been permitted. Interest rate futures contracts were introduced in June 2003 and futures and options contracts on sectoral indices were introduced in August, 2003.

Regulatory Objectives

It is inclined towards positive regulation designed to encourage healthy activity and behaviour. It has been guided by the following objectives:

(a) Investor Protection: Attention needs to be given to the following four aspects:

(i) *Fairness and Transparency*: The trading rules should ensure that trading is conducted in a fair and transparent manner. Experience in other countries shows that in many cases, derivatives brokers/dealers failed to disclose potential risk to the clients. In this context, sales practices adopted by dealers for derivatives would require specific regulation. In some of the most widely reported mishaps in the derivatives market elsewhere, the underlying reason was inadequate internal control system at the user-firm itself, so that overall exposure was not controlled and the use of derivatives was for speculation rather than for risk hedging. These experiences provided useful lessons for US designing its regulations.

(ii) *Safeguard for Clients' Money*: Money and securities deposited by clients with the trading members should not only be kept in a separate clients' account but should also not be attachable for meeting the broker's own debts. It should be ensured that trading by dealers on own account is totally safeguarded from that of the clients.

(iii) *Competent and Honest Service*: The eligibility criteria for trading members should be designed to encourage competent and qualified personnel so that investors/clients are served well. This makes it necessary to prescribe qualification for derivatives brokers/dealers and the sales persons appointed by them in terms of knowledge base.

(iv) *Market integrity*: The trading system should ensure that the markets' integrity is safeguarded by minimizing the possibility of defaults. This requires framing appropriate rules about capital adequacy, margins, clearing corporation, etc.

(b) **Quality of Markets:** The concept of "quality of markets" goes well beyond market integrity and aims at enhancing important market qualities, such as cost-efficiency, price-continuity, and price-discovery. This is a much broader objective than market integrity.

(c) **Innovation:** While curbing any undesirable tendencies, the regulatory framework should not stifle innovation which is the source of all economic progress, more so because financial derivatives represent a new rapidly developing area, aided by advancement in information technology.

Legality of Derivatives

Derivatives are governed by the following laws in India:

1. The Indian Contract Act, 1972
2. The Foreign Exchange Management Act (FEMA), 1999
3. The Securities Contracts (Regulation) Act (SCRA), 1956
    - This Act was amended in 1999 for the purpose of providing for trading in derivatives.
4. The Reserve Bank of India Act, 1934
    - Amended in 2006 (brought into force in January 2007). The amended Act empowers the RBI to undertake the business of dealing in derivatives.

Making the derivatives accounting more transparent, RBI on 13 October, 2008 asked the banks to treat the amounts remained unpaid under the contract for over 90 days as non-performing assets (NPA). "The overdue receivables representing positive mark-to-market value of a derivative contract will be treated as a non-performing asset, if remain unpaid for 90 days or more," the RBI said in a notification.

In case the receivables remain unpaid for over three months, the central bank said, the other fund-based facilities granted to the clients should be classified as *non-performing assets* in accordance with the asset classification norms. RBI has also said that the unrealized amount from derivatives trade already shown in the P&L (profit and loss) account be mentioned in the "suspense account."

Use of Derivatives

The opportunities to use derivatives to hedge risks are not available to all companies. In many countries, particularly the developing countries, no derivatives or a very few types of derivatives are available. Even in developed economies where derivative markets are well developed, all companies do not make full use of the derivatives. Most surveys on the use of derivatives reveal that derivatives are popular among the large listed companies in US. About half of the publicly traded firms use one or the other form of derivatives. Among the companies using derivatives, the most widely used derivatives are interest rate derivatives and the foreign exchange rate derivatives.

Should corporates continue using derivatives? Of course, corporates must use derivatives to hedge risk, but with great care and caution. They must use derivatives only for reducing risk and not for speculation.

The following factors have been driving the growth of financial derivatives:

1. Increased volatility in asset prices in financial markets.
2. Increased integration of national financial markets with the international markets.
3. Marked improvement in communication facilities and sharp decline in their costs.
4. Development of more sophisticated risk management tools, providing economic agents a wider choice of risk management strategies.
5. Innovations in the derivative markets, which optimally combine the risks and returns over a large number of financial assets, leading to higher returns, reduced risk as well as transaction costs as compared to individual financial assets.

Derivatives have emerged as tools for integration because they allow the users to unbundle risks and repackage them to create whatever kind of solution they need.

Derivative tools need to tackle old problems in different ways. It has been argued that derivatives do not result in managing risk. Rather, they facilitate the transfer of risk from those who are risk averse to those who are willing to assume risk.

This is an important economic function being performed by them because there are certain players like insurance companies, pension funds, etc., which are ready to bear risk on account of their larger capital base and diversified portfolio. The uses of derivative instruments are generally attributed to:

- ***Risk Sharing***: The major economic function of derivatives is typically seen as risk sharing; derivatives provide a more efficient allocation of economic risks.
- ***Implementation of Asset Allocation Decisions***: Derivatives are useful in implementing asset allocation strategies on account of their property of low cost of diversification and leverage.
- ***Information Gathering***: If risk allocation is the major function of derivative instruments and because risk is also related to information, derivative markets also affect the information structure of the financial system, which itself is a major determinant of the dynamics and the stability of the economic system.

20.4 CLASSIFICATION OF DERIVATIVES

Derivatives are broadly classified as financial and non-financial. Non-financial derivatives cover vast segment of commodities, metal, weather, etc. Financial derivatives are: forwards, futures, options, credit and swaps.

Financial Derivatives: Financial derivatives find their utility in risk control and management as well as in hedging. Banks, Mutual Funds, and insurance companies find derivatives very useful in managing their portfolio effectively. There are three types namely:

- *Currency futures* where the position involves foreign currencies.
- *Interest rate futures* where the position involves fixed income securities.
- *Equity futures* where the position involves equities.

Weather Derivatives: Weather is an important aspect that affects volume of production and sales as also the price of the products. Weather derivatives are the new invention of financial markets. The price volatility of such products tends to be high. To that extent, revenues of the companies are adversely affected by weather conditions. The potential profits of a company may be turned into losses due to high price volatility and less production. Agriculture product processing, power generation, oil exploration, tourism, insurance are all affected by weather. Hedging through weather derivatives minimises the risk exposure of these companies. Weather derivatives are traded both in over-the-counter (OTC) and other exchanges.

Weather derivatives enable businesses to hedge against unanticipated temperature swings, thus enabling them to cover the loss of revenue. This sector of hedging and risk management products represents a fast growing derivative market. Trading in weather derivatives provides both buyers and sellers to establish a platform to manage risk in the case of hedgers and profit from risk in the case of sellers more effectively. The most actively traded products among the weather derivatives are based on temperature measures. The individual contracts are calendar month futures contracts on Heating Degree Days (HDD) and Cooling Degree Days (CDD) as well as options on futures. These are based on HDD and CDD.

Credit Derivatives: In recent years, credit derivatives have evolved as major risk management tools. The new international rules of the Basle Accord, 1988 brought credit derivatives into existence.

Broadly speaking, a credit derivative is an instrument which allows credit risk to be priced and traded independently of market risk like interest rate and currency risk. Credit derivatives offer a way to mitigate credit risks associated with loans and emerging market government bonds by splitting debt investments into several risk components like credit, interest rates, currency, etc., valuing them separately, and then assuming acceptable risks on some components while hedging unacceptable or inadequately compensated risks in others. Thus, credit derivatives would change the way in which credit risk is managed by facilitating distribution of risk outside the banking system to MFs, insurance companies and the corporate sector.

A *credit derivative* is a financial instrument used to mitigate or assume specific forms of credit risk by hedgers and speculators. Though the credit derivative has been invented to hedge the risk of banks, it has also become popular in insurance companies, asset management companies, mutual funds, hedge funds, pension funds, corporate treasurers, etc.

In any financial transaction, the two primary types of risks faced by firms are *market risk* and *credit risk*. When the changes of interest rates, exchange rates, stock prices or commodity prices affect the firm's value, it is market risk. However, when the firm fails to meet obligated payments of counter parties on time it is termed as credit risk or default risk.

Credit derivatives allow users to isolate; price and trade firm-specific credit risk by unbundling a debt instrument or a basket of instruments into its component parts and transferring each risk to those best suited or most interested in managing it.

Credit derivatives market is yet to take off in India. One of the reasons attributed is *lack of liquidity* in the domestic corporate bond market where the average daily trading volume is low. For credit derivatives, market needs to have more depth in liquidity. It is the multitude of issuers with varied credit ratings and participants with different risk appetite, that will contribute to the liquidity and create a robust market. A deep and liquid corporate bond market will help in effective pricing of credit. The regulators – RBI, SEBI, IRDA need to explore possibilities and create a level-playing field for all the participants in this market. However, all these would need to be preceded by a policy framework and a thorough understanding of the associated risks of trading in derivative products by market participants.

Commodity Derivatives: Though India is considered a pioneer in some form of derivatives in commodities, the history of formal commodity derivatives is rather chequered. The derivatives market for Cotton futures was set up in Mumbai, followed by the establishment of futures market in edible oilseeds complex, raw jute goods and bullion. Organised futures markets in India dates back to the setting of Bombay Cotton Trade Association Ltd., in 1875. Organised futures trading in oilseeds were started in India with the setting of Gujarati Vyapari Mandali back in 1900.

The basic difference between the commodity exchange and the stock exchange is that in a commodity exchange, actual physical products that are non-financial in nature are traded. These include agricultural products such as wheat, castor, groundnut or sesame and industrial products, such as zinc, nickel and also precious metals, like gold and silver. In the case of commodities, a contract can vary widely on the basis of the quality of the underlying asset. Further, unlike equity futures, which have a life cycle of three months, in the case of commodity futures, the contract duration can vary and in some cases extend up to six months.

India Commodity Futures: In India, a number of commodities in various categories can be traded on commodity exchanges. These include bullion (gold and silver), oil and oilseeds (castor, soya, rapeseed/mustard oil, crude palm oil, RBD palmolein), grains and pulses (wheat and rice), soft commodities (cotton, sugar, coffee) and spices and plantations (pepper and rubber), etc.

The main national level multi-commodity exchanges are:

1. National Commodity and Derivative Exchange, Mumbai (NCDEX)
2. Multi Commodity Exchange of India Ltd., Mumbai (MCX)
3. National Multi Commodity Exchange of India Ltd., Ahmedabad (NMCE)
4. National Board of Trade, Indore (NBOT)

Currency Derivatives: A currency futures contract is a derivative financial instrument that acts as a conduit to transfer risks attributable to volatility in prices of currencies. It is a contractual agreement between a buyer and a seller for the purchase of sale of a particular currency at a specified future date, at a predetermined price. The fundamental advantage is hedging risks. In a currency futures contract, one of the "pair" of currencies is invariably the US$. That is, an investor can buy or sell a futures contract only with reference to the USD.

For the first time in India, individuals are allowed to punt in foreign currency, just as they bet on stock and commodity futures. Till now, only banks could do that, but only up to a limit. All others had to have an actual underlying exports or imports, or at least a proof of it. Now traders and punters, snooping around for a new market, may try their hand in currency futures.

Fixed Income Derivatives: Introduction of fixed income derivatives on the stock exchanges ushers in a new era in the Indian debt market. Globally, fixed-income derivatives form a large portion of the financial derivatives market on the exchanges. In India with over-the-counter (OTC) products introduced in 1999, these derivatives have seen exponential growth in terms of volume.

Deregulation of interest rates in the economy has exposed market participants to a variety of risks. It was to manage and control risks and to deepen the money market that fixed-income derivatives were permitted in the OTC market.

Recently, a SEBI group on Secondary Market Risk Management issued a consultative document. This sets a timeframe for introduction of a few exchange-traded interest rates derivatives, which can provide as an effective hedging mechanism for interest rate risk and even for the OTC derivatives market. Existing participants in the OTC market are banks, primary dealers and certain large corporate houses. According to market sources, daily volumes in the OTC market range anywhere between Rs. 500-800 crore. Interest rate derivatives have been a resounding success in India. The outstanding amount has risen to over Rs. 1,50,000 crore.

20.5 MARKET PLAYERS/OPERATORS IN THE DERIVATIVES MARKET

Hedgers: Players (and operators) who want to reduce and transfer a risk component to safeguard their existing portfolio holding. They are not in a derivatives market to make profit. Apart from equity markets, hedging is common in the foreign exchange markets where fluctuations in the exchange rate have to be taken care of in the foreign currency transactions or could be in the commodities market where spiralling oil prices have to be tamed using the derivative instruments.

Speculators: Players who intentionally take the risk from hedgers in pursuit of profit (in a short span). They are willing to take risks and they depend on whether the markets would go up or come down.

Arbitrageurs: Players who operate in different markets simultaneously, in pursuit of arbitrage gain wanting to gain price mismatch with almost 'no risk'. They buy in one market and sell in another. They could be making money even without putting their own money in and such opportunities often come up in the market but last for very short timeframe. This is because as soon as the situation emerges arbitrageurs take advantage and demand-supply forces drive the market back to normal.

20.6 HEDGING

The term 'hedging' is fairly clear. It covers derivatives market positions that are designed to offset the potential losses from the existing cash market positions. *Hedging* is used for reducing risk by using derivatives. It helps to:

(a) reduce costs of financial distress;
(b) isolate the effects of changes in external factors like interest rates and foreign exchange rates on profitability; and
(c) allow corporate managers to focus on improving operating efficiency.

Some examples will offer more clarity:

- An income fund has a large portfolio of bonds. This portfolio stands to make losses when interest rates go up. Hence, the fund may choose to go short on interest rate futures in order to offset this loss.
- An income fund has a large portfolio of corporate bonds. This portfolio stands to make losses when credit spreads of these bonds degrade or when default takes place. Hence, the fund may choose to buy credit derivatives, which pay when these events happen.

- Every equity portfolio has exposure to the market index. Hence, the fund may choose to sell index futures, or buy index put options, in order to reduce the losses that would take place in the event that the market index drops.

The regulatory concerns are about (a) the effectiveness of hedge and (b) its size.

Objectives of Hedging

Hedging is a financial instrument whose sensitivity to a particular financial price offsets the sensitivity of the firm's core business to that price. There are three issues that define the objectives of hedging.

(i) *Hedging objective of the form:* Some hedging programmes in the corporate world will choose reduction in the variability of corporate income as an appropriate target, i.e., an investor purchases the stock of those companies in order to take advantage of its core business expertise.

(ii) *Firm's exposure to financial price-risk:* It is important to measure and to have some notion of the firm's potential liability from financial price risk on a daily basis. It is no less critical for a company with billions of dollars of internationally driven revenue to do so.

There are three types of risk for every particular financial price to which the firm is exposed.

Transactional risks reflect the pejorative impact of fluctuations in financial prices on the cash flows that come from purchases or sales.

Translation risks describe the changes in the value of a foreign asset due to changes in financial prices, such as the foreign exchange rate.

Economic exposure refers to the impact of fluctuations in financial prices on the core business of the firm.

(iii) The various hedging instruments available to the Corporate Treasurer and how do they behave in different pricing environment: The difference between a mediocre corporate treasurer and an excellent one is their ability to operate within the context of their shareholder-delineated limits and choose the hedging structure for a particular exposure and economic environment.

Besides the above objectives, there are some advantages of better risk management through hedging:

(a) **Debt Capacity Enhancement:** Financial risk management helps to understand and manage investment and financing risk. It reduces a firm's costs of financial distress. Hence, the firm can increase debt capacity and interest tax shield.

(b) **Increased Focus on Operations:** Financial risk management requires managers to hedge against possible movements in interest rates and exchange rates. These factors are not under the control of managers nor can they predict their behaviour. Hedging against such risks encourages managers to concentrate their efforts on improving operations.

(c) **Isolating Management Performance:** Hedging helps to separate out the effects of fluctuating external factors (interest or exchange rate) and good or bad management on the firm's profitability.

Hedging with Futures Contracts

There are six steps involved in the technique of hedging through futures. These are:

1. Estimating target outcome (with reference to the spot rate available on a given date).
2. Deciding on whether futures contract should be bought or sold.
3. Determining number of contracts (this is necessary, since contract size is standardized).
4. Identifying profit or loss on target outcome.
5. Closing on futures position.
6. Evaluating profit or loss in futures.

The derivative market also known as *credit market* (of which futures market is a segment) is one where the price is agreed on one day and delivery and settlement is made on a specified future date. The primary objective of hedging is to reduce "price risk" of a position taken in the cash market. An investor can hedge with a futures contract by taking a position that is the opposite of one in cash market. Position can be "long" or "short." The term long means *bought position* and the term short means *sold position*.

Rule 1: An investor should sell futures if he/she has long position on the asset in cash market (*short hedge*).

Rule 2: An investor would buy futures if he/she has a short position on asset in cash market (*long hedge*).

Table 20.1

Spot position	Futures	Price	Spot	Futures
Buy (Go Long)	Sell	Goes up	Gain	Loss
	(Go Short)	Falls	Loss	Gain
Sell (Go Short)	Buy	Goes up	Loss	Gain
	(Go Long)	Falls	Gain	Loss

Essentially, gains in the spot market are offset by loss in the futures market and loss in the spot market is offset by gains in the futures market. This does not necessarily give a return but helps eliminate price risk.

Hedging strategy is a strategy where an investor plans to limit his/her loss in one position by simultaneously taking an opposite position in the same or another market.

This opposite position could be in the same asset or in some other asset. An investor could use options to hedge position in stocks. Let us consider the following four situations:

No. 1: Hedging a long position in a stock (Long stock, long put): Buy a put (right to sell)
No. 2: Hedging a short position in a stock (Short stock, long call): Buy a call (right to buy)
No. 3: Hedging a long position in a stock (Long stock, short call): Write calls
No. 4: Hedging a short position in a stock (Short stock, short put): Write puts.

Table 20.2 Working of the Heading Strategy

Current Position	Objective	Suggested Action
Long stock	Minimize loss	Buy put
Short stock	Minimize loss	Buy call
Long stock	Enhance gain	Write a call
Short stock	Enhance gain	Write a put

Hedging an investment in a stock with a short position in another stocks' futures is not an acceptable hedge because of effectiveness concerns. This would be true even for merger arbitrage where long and short positions in two merging companies are combined to benefit from deviations of market prices from the swap ratio.

Hedging with options would be regarded as *over-hedging* if the notional value of the hedge exceeds the underlying position of the fund even if the option delta is less than the underlying position.

Covered call writing is hedging if the effectiveness and size conditions are met. Again the size of the hedge in terms of notional value and not option delta must not exceed the underlying portfolio.

The position is more complicated if the option position includes long calls or short puts. The worst-case short exposure considering all possible expiration prices should meet with the size condition.

Transactions not Involving US $: Futures Contracts

If an entity were to buy or sell currency with another currency neither of which is US$. It needs to deal in more than one type of contract. (Recall the process of deriving cross rates.) The hedging process thus gets a little more complex than the use of forward markets and therefore, contributes to their relative lack of popularity.

20.7 SWAPS

A *swap* can be defined as "the exchange of one stream of future cash flows with another stream of cash flows with different characteristics." A swap is an agreement between two or more people/parties to exchange sets of cash flows over a period in future. Thus, swaps are similar to futures and forwards contract in providing hedge against financial risk. The development of the swaps in 1980 is a significant development.

In finance, a swap is a derivative in which two counterparties agree to exchange one stream of cash flows against another stream. These streams are called the *legs* of the swaps. The cash flows are calculated over a notional principal amount, which is usually not exchanged between counterparties. Consequently, swaps can be used to create unfunded exposures to an underlying asset, since counterparties can earn the profit or loss from movements in price without having to post the notional amount in cash or collateral.

Swaps can be used to hedge certain risks such as interest rate risks, or to speculate on changes in the underlying. Most swaps are traded over-the-counter (OTC), *tailor made* for the counterparties. Some types of swaps are also exchanged on futures markets, for instance Chicago Mercantile Exchange Holding Inc., the largest US futures market, the Chicago Board Options Exchange and Frankfurt-based Eurex AG.

The following are generic types of swaps, in order of their quantitative importance:

1. **Interest Rates Swaps:** It is an agreement whereby one party exchanges one set of interest rate payments for another. The most common arrangement is an exchange of fixed interest rate payment for another rate over a time period. The interest rates are calculated on notional values of principals. It can be used by hedgers to manage their fixed or floating assets and liabilities. They can also be used by speculators to replicate unfunded bond exposures to profit from changes in interest rates. As such, these are very popular and highly liquid instruments.

   Interest rate swaps can be *fixed-for-fixed*, *fixed-for-floating* or *floating-for-floating*. The legs of the swap can be of the same currency or different currencies.

   - Fixed-for-floating rate swap – same currency
   - Fixed-for-floating rate swap – different currencies
   - Floating-for-floating rate swap – same currency, different Index
   - Floating-for-floating rate swap – different currencies

2. **Asset Swaps:** An asset swap is a derivative security that can be viewed, in its simplest version, as a portfolio consisting of a fixed-rate note and an interest-rate swap that pays fixed and receives floating, to the stated maturity of the underlying fixed-rate note. The fixed rate on the interest-rate swap is conventionally chosen so that the asset swap is valued at par when traded. Because of the mismatch in termination with default between interest-rate swap embedded in the asset swap and the underlying fixed-rate note, the asset-swap spread does not on its own provide precise information for default-swap pricing.

3. **Currency Swaps:** These are agreements whereby currencies are exchanged at specified exchange rates and at specified intervals. It involves an exchange of cash payments in one currency for cash payments in another currency. Most

international companies require foreign currency for making investments abroad. These firms find difficulties in entering into new markets and raising capital at convenient terms. Currency swap is an easy alternative for these companies to overcome this problem. The basic purpose is to lock in the rate.

4. **Credit Swaps:** Credit swaps is a form of derivative security that can be viewed as default insurance on loans or bonds. Credit swaps pay the buyer of protection a given contingent amount at the time of a given credit event, such as default. The contingent amount is often the difference between the face value of a bond and its market value, paid at the default time of the underlying bond. This special case defines a "default swap." In return, the buyer of protection pays an annuity premium until the time of the credit event, or the maturity date of the credit swap, whichever is first.

   Credit swaps are perhaps the most popular, credit derivatives. As opposed to many other forms of credit derivatives, payment to the buyer of protection in a credit swap is triggered by a contractually defined event, which must be documented.

5. **Commodity Swaps:** A commodity swap is an agreement involving the exchange of a series of commodity price payments (fixed amount) against variable commodity price payments (market price) resulting exclusively in a cash settlement (settlement amount).

   The buyer of a commodity swap acquires the right to be paid a settlement amount (*compensation*) if the market price rises above the fixed amount. In a contract, the buyer of the commodity swap is obliged to pay the settlement if the market price falls below the fixed amount.

   Both streams of payment (fixed/variable) are in the same currency and based on the same nominal amount. While the fixed side of the swap is of the benchmark nature (it is constant), the variable side is related to the trading price of the relevant commodities quoted on a stock exchange or otherwise published on the commodities futures market on the relevant fixing date or to a commodity price index.

6. **Equity Swaps:** An equity swap is a special type of total return swap, where the underlying asset is a stock, a basket of stocks, or a stock index. Compared to actually owning the stock, in this case you do not have to pay anything up front, but you do not have any voting or other rights that stock holders have.

Risk of Commodity Swaps and Commodity Options with Cash Settlement

If the trend does not live up to your expectations, you will have to pay the difference between the underlying price when you signed the agreement and the current market price when the transaction reaches maturity. That difference constitutes the loss. Though the maximum amount of loss cannot be determined in advance, it may possibly exceed the security posted.

The interest rate and currency swap markets enable firms to arbitrage the differences between capital markets. They make use of their comparative advantage of borrowing in their domestic market and arranging swaps for interest rates or currencies that they cannot easily access.

20.8 SWAPTION

A *swaption* is an option granting its owner the right but not the obligation to enter into an underlying swap. While options can be traded on a variety of swaps, the term "swaption" typically refers to options on interest rate swaps. There are two types of swaption contracts:

(a) A payer swaption gives the owner of the swaption the right to enter into a swap where they pay the fixed leg and receive the floating leg.

(b) A receiver swaption gives the owner of the swaption the right to enter into a swap where they will receive the fixed leg, and pay the floating leg.

The buyer and seller of the swaption agree on:

- The premium (price) of the swaption
- The strike rate (equal to the fixed rate of the underlying swap)
- Length of the option period (which usually ends two business days prior to the start date of the underlying swap)
- The term of the underlying swap
- Notional amount
- Amortization, if any
- Frequency of settlement of payments on the underlying swap

Properties of Swaption

Unlike ordinary swaps, a swaption not only hedges the buyer against downside risk, but also lets the buyer take advantage of any upside benefits. Like any other option, if the swaption is not exercised by maturity, it expires.

If the strike rate of the swap is more favourable than the prevailing market swap rate, then the swaption will be exercised as detailed in the swaption agreement.

It is designed to give the holder the benefit of the agreed upon strike rate if the market rates are higher, with the flexibility to enter into the current market swap rate if they are lower.

The converse is true if the holder of the swaption receives the fixed rate under the swap agreement. Investors can also use swaptions to trade the volatility of the underlying swap rate.

Swaption Styles

There are three styles of swaption. Each style reflects a different timeframe in which the option can be exercised.

- *American swaption,* in which the owner is allowed to enter into the swap on any day that falls within the range of two dates.
- *European swaption,* in which the owner is allowed to enter into the swap only on maturity date.
- *Bermudan swaption,* in which the owner is allowed to enter the swap only on certain dates that fall within a range of the start (roll) date and end date.

20.9 DERIVATIVE PRODUCTS

Derivative is a product/contact that does not have any value of its own. It derives value from some underlying.

1. Forward Contracts

- It is a *one-to-one bipartite* contract, to be performed in the future, at the terms decided today.
- It offers *tremendous flexibility* to the parties to design the contract in terms of price, quantity, quality (in case of a commodity), delivery time and place.
- Both parties are *assured of price* at which deal will go through.
- *No money is involved* at the time of the deal is signed, i.e., no deposit or premium is required to be paid, normally, since both the parties have equal rights and equal obligations.
- These are not traded on the exchange; they are said to be *traded* over-the-counter (OTC).
- Forward contracts however suffer from *poor liquidity and default risk,* as no secondary market exists.

  Forward contracts are tailor-made to suit the needs of buyers and sellers. Both parties (buyer and seller) can enter into a forward contract for any goods, commodities, or assets and can choose delivery date for any quantity of goods or commodities. There should always be *willingness* of buyers and sellers for entering into a forward contract. Though forward contracts are entered into for different goods, commodities or assets, etc., the foreign currencies forwards have the largest trading.

2. Future Contracts

- These are *organised/standardised* contracts, which are traded on the exchanges, subject to rules and regulations, that facilitate the secondary market trading and thus, are very liquid in nature.

- In future contract, clearing corporation/clearing house provides the *settlement guarantee* for each and every trade/(s) to buy or sell a commodity, security or currency at a predetermined future date at a price agreed upon today.
- These are standard contracts for quality, quantity, delivery date, time and place.
- The minimum, and sometimes the maximum amount by which the price would change, is specified.
- The *terms* of the futures contracts are not negotiable.
- The buyers and sellers of the futures contracts are required to deposit some cash or securities as 'margin' and maintain it. The *margin amount* changes with changes in daily prices. This is done to ensure that the buyers and sellers honour the deal.
- In case of future contracts, there is daily *closing* and *reopening* of the position which is called **marked to market**. Marked to market means that profit and loss on a future contract is calculated each day, and if there is a profit, one receives it from exchange, but if there is a loss, one needs to pay to the exchange.

One wonders whether future contracts are like forward contracts as both serve the same purpose and operate through a contract between counterparties. The difference is in terms of standardization and method of operation. Future contracts have standardized contract size and they trade only on the organised exchanges. Thus, future contracts are forward contracts traded on organised exchange in standardized contract size.

In futures contracts, like in the forward contracts, one party would lose and another will gain. The profit and loss will depend on the agreed future price and the actual spot at the time of contract maturity. One could use futures contracts to hedge risk. But in forward contracts, on the due date the seller has to deliver to the buyer and the buyer will pay seller the agreed price.

Set of Assumptions

- No seasonal demand and supply in the underlying asset.
- Storability of the underlying asset is not a problem.
- The underlying asset can be sold or stored.
- No transaction costs; no taxes.
- No margin requirements. So the analysts relate this to a forward contract (rather than futures contract).

Rules for Valuation are based on the concepts of 'continuous compounding' and 'short selling'.

1. **Continuous compounding:** All of us are familiar with compounding. There are three links to compounding, namely, continuous compounding, continuous discounting and equivalent rates.
   (i) **Continuous compounding** refers to the frequency with which interest is payable. The most popular example of compounding is annual compounding.

In general, $A = P * (1 + r/m)^{m*n}$, where m is the number of compounding in a year. For annual compounding m = 1, for half yearly compounding m = 2, for daily compounding m = 365, etc. We can even compound on a continuous basis! In this case, the formula drips down to **$A = P * e^{r*t}$** where "e" is the exponential value, "r" is the rate per annum and "t" is the time in years, A is compounded value and P is amount to be compounded. To summarise, as the number of compounding periods increase, the EAR (*Effective Annual Rate*) also increases.

Concept Problem: Mr. B lent Rs. 1,00,000 to Mr. Y at 12% per annum continuous compounding for 3 months. What is the maturity value?

Solution: Applying the formula $A = P * e^{r*t}$

$$= 100000 * e^{0.12 * (3/12)} = 100000 * 1.03045$$
$$= 1{,}03{,}045$$

(ii) Continuous Discounting is the process by which we find today's value (also known as *present value*) of tomorrow's money. The compound value formula can be turned around to find the present value formula. Where continuous compounding is involved, the present value factor is e^{-r*t}. Like present value tables, we have the e^{-x} table which gives the value of continuous discounting. Here the formula is:

$$\mathbf{A = P * e^{-r*t}}$$

Concept Problem: Mr. H is going to receive Rs. 8000 as dividend from a stock 3 months from now. What is the present value of the dividend if the risk-free continuous compounding is 16% p.a.?

Solution: Applying the formula $A = P * e^{-r*t}$

$$P = 8000 * e^{-0.16 * (3/12)}$$
$$P = 8000 * e^{-0.04} = 8000 * 0.96079$$
$$= 7{,}686.32$$

(iii) Equivalent Rates: Derivative pricing is done using continuous compounding. In real life, however, people use annual or semi-annual compounding. Hence, it is necessary to find equivalent rates. For example, if a certain rate of interest with half-yearly compounding is given, we should find the interest rate which will yield the same amount if continuous compounding is done. The formula is:

Normal to continuous: $r2 = m(e^{r1/m} - 1)$

Continuous to normal: $r2 = m(e^{r1/m} - 1)$

Where r1 = normal rate; r2 = continuous compounding rate.

Concept Problem: An interest rate is quoted at 18% per annum with half-yearly compounding. What is the equivalent continuous compounding rate?

Solution: r1 = 18%; m = 2; r2 = ?

We know r2 = m(e^ r1/m – 1)

= 2 (e^ 01.18/2 – 1)

= 2 (1,09417 – 1) = 18.84%

Concept Problem: Mr. D gives a loan on which he quotes 24% per annum continuous compounding. Calculate the equivalent rate if compounding was done quarterly.

Solution: Given r1 = 24% (0.24); m = 4

Applying the formula r2 = m(e^ r1/m – 1)

r2 = 4[Log(0.24/4 + 1)]

= 4 log 1.06

= 4 * 0.5827 = 24.73%

Actual Pricing Futures (AFP)

One of the models for Cost and Carry Future Pricing:

Fair price (FFP) = Spot price + Cost of carry – Inflows

Cost of carry = financing storage and insurance cost

If futures price > fair price, buy in the cash market and simultaneously sell in futures market.

If futures price < fair price, sell in the cash market and simultaneously buy in futures market.

The arbitrage between cash and futures market will remain till prices in the cash and futures market gets aligned.

Actual FP vs FFP	Valuation	Spot	Borrow/Invest	Forward
AFP < FFP	Under	Sell	Invest	Buy
AFP > FFP	Over	Buy	Borrow	Sell
AFP = FFP	No change	No action	No Arbitrage	No action

Situation 1: Securities Providing No Income

The security in which a forward position is taken, does not generate any income during the period of the forward contract. Some examples are non-dividend paying shares and deep discount bonds.

Formula: If there is no arbitrage gain the forward price should be: F = So * e^ rt, where F = Theoretical forward price; So = Current spot price; r = Rate of interest (risk-free) with continuous compounding and t = no. of years

Concept Problem: X Ltd. a company that historically has not paid any dividend and has no plans to do so in the future, is currently quoting on the exchange at Rs. 60. An investor wishes to enter into a futures contract on this stock maturing in 3 months time.

(a) If the risk-free rate of return is 8% per annum continuously compounded, what he/she can expect the futures price to be?

(b) If the futures contract was priced at Rs. 64, what action would investor take? In case it is priced at Rs. 61, will investor's decision change?

Solution: Step 1: Compute Fair Future Price **(FFP)**

So = Rs. 60, r = 8%, t = 3 months (0.08 * 0.25)

FFP = So * e^ rt = 60 * e^ 0.02

= 60 * 1.0202 = 61.21

Decision:

Actual FP vs FFP	Valuation	Spot	Borrow/Invest	Forward
64 > 61.21	Over	Buy	Borrow	Sell
61 < 61.21	Under	Sell	Invest	Buy

Situation 2: Securities providing a known Cash Income

The security in which a forward position is taken, generates a cash income during the currency of the position. Some examples are dividend paying shares, preference shares or bonds due for interest payment.

Formula: If the income is designated as Y to be received one month from today. The present value of the income is designated as I, where I = Y * e^ rt. The initial outlay can then be considered as S – I. If there is no arbitrage gain, the forward price should be:

F = (So – I) * e^ rt

Steps involved:

1: Compute present value of cash income as I = Y * e^ rt

2: Compute adjusted So as S – Step 1

3: Compute theoretical forward price using the same formula as in step except that it will now be used with reference to So as computed in step 2

FFP = A So * e^ rt

Concept Problem: A Ltd. is quoting at Rs. 40 in the market. A six-months futures contract on 100 shares of A Ltd. can be bought. The risk-free rate of return is 12% per annum continuously compounded. A Ltd. is certain to pay a dividend of Rs. 2.50 per share 3 months from now. What should be the value of futures contract? If the futures contract is priced at Rs. 4100 what action would follow? If it is priced at Rs. 3800 what would investor do?

Solution: Step 1: Compute Fair Future Price

Present value of dividend income = 2.50 * 0.97 = 2.43 = Rs. 242.61 on 100 shares

Adjusted So = 4000 – 242.61 = Rs. 3757.39

FFP = A So * e^ rt = 3757.39 * e^ 0.12*5

= 3757.39 * 1.06 = Rs. 3990

Step 2: Decision

AFP	FFP	Valuation	Future	Spot
4100	3990	Over	Sell	Buy
3800	3990	Under	Buy	Sell

Situation 3: Securities Providing a Known Yield

The share is expected to give a dividend over a time period. This is similar to situation 2 except that the income is expressed as a percentage of spot price.

Formula: Theoretically, the yield is assumed to be paid continuously at r rate of return. This can be considered *negative cost*. Hence, deduct the yield from rate. Consequently, at no arbitrage, the formula would be: F = So * e^ (r-y) * t

Concept Problem: If P Ltd. provided a dividend yield of 4% per annum, the current value of P is Rs. 500, the continuously compounded risk-free rate of interest is 8% per annum, what would be the value of a 3-month futures contract? If the futures price is Rs. 510 what action would follow? Will the position change if the price is Rs. 490?

Solution: Step 1: Compute FFP

FFP = So * e^ (r-y) * t = 500 * e^ 0.01

= 500 * 1.01005 = Rs. 505

Step 2: Decision

AFP	FFP	Valuation	Future	Spot
510	505	Over	Sell	Buy
490	505	Under	Buy	Sell

Simple Strategies in Futures Market

The following simple strategies are popular in the futures market:

(i) *Commodities Futures Market*

- Buy a future to agree to take delivery of a commodity to protect against a rise in price in the spot market as it produces a gain if spot market prices rise. Buying a future is said to be going long.
- Sell a future to agree to make delivery of a commodity to protect against a fall in price in the spot market as it produces a gain if spot prices fall. Selling a future is said to be going short.

Type of Commodities: Carry type commodities are commodities that are held for purposes of investment rather than for purposes of consumption. Gold is a typical example. Let's look at the following points:

- If the storage cost is NIL, this translates into securities providing no income. The same formula can be adopted.
- If storage cost is involved, the storage cost can be considered negative cash income. The steps adopted in securities providing known income can be followed.
- If storage cost is considered being proportional to the price of commodity, it can be considered negative yield. The procedure of securities providing known yield can be adopted.

Concept Problem: Consider a six-month gold futures contract of 100 gm. If the spot price is Rs. 600 per gm and it costs Rs. 3 per gm for the six-monthly period to store gold and the cost is incurred at the end of 2 months. If the risk-free rate of interest is 12% per annum continuously compounded, compute the futures price. If the futures were available at Rs. 620, what action would follow? Would the position change if the futures were available at Rs. 660?

Solution: Step 1: PV of storage cost, i.e., Rs. 3 * 100 gm = Rs. 300

PV = 300 * e^ rt = e^ -0.12*0.167 = 300 * e^ -.02
= 300 * 0.98020 = Rs. 294

Adjusted So = 60000 + 294 = Rs. 60,294
Compute Fair Future Price, *i.e.* Adjusted So * e^ rt

= 60294 * e^ 0.12*.05
= 60294 * e^ 0.06
= 60294 * 1.06184 = Rs. 64,022 or 640 per gm

Step 2: Decision

AFP	FFP	Valuation	Buy	Sell
640	620	Under	Futures	Spot
640	660	Over	Spot	Futures

Non-carry type commodities are commodities that are held for purposes of consumption and not for investment. Example: rice, wheat, etc. Let's look at the following points:

- The cost of carry model cannot apply since the commodity is not held for investment.
- The cost of carry model provides only an upper band. In other words, the fair price will not exceed the sum of the spot price and the carrying costs less carry return.
- The arbitrage argument does not work. Investors who stock price keep it for consumption and not for investment. If the futures price is undervalued, they will not sell rice in the spot market and buy in the futures market, because they cannot consume the futures contract!

Consequently, in valuing of non-carry commodity futures we need to introduce a concept called *convenience yield*. This is the return that an investor realizes for carrying inventory over his/her immediate need. It is considered as negative cost. The formula will be:

$$F = (So + S) * e \{(r\text{-}c)\ t\}$$

Concept Problem: The spot price of steel scrap is Rs. 5000 per tonne. The 1-year futures price is Rs. 5802. The interest rate is 15%. The present value of storage cost is Rs. 250 per tonne. Compute the convenience yield assuming that the futures are fairly priced.

Solution: Applying the formula F = (So + S) * e {(r-c) t}, we get

$$5802 = (5000 + 250) * e\text{^}\ (0.15\text{-}c)t$$
$$= 5250 * e\text{^}\ (0.15\text{-}c)$$
$$1.1052 = e\text{^}\ (0.15\text{-}c)$$

This corresponds to e^ 0.10. Hence c = 5%

(ii) *Interest Rate Future*

- Selling short on interest rate futures contract protects against a rise in interest rates.
- Purchasing long an interest rate futures contract protects against a fall in interest rates.

(iii) *Future Rate Agreements (FRAs)*

- Selling short on FRA protects against a fall in interest rates.
- Purchasing long on FRA protects against a rise in interest rates.

(iv) *Currency Futures*

- Buying long currency futures protects against a rise in currency value.
- Selling short currency futures protects against a fall in currency value.

  Both Interest Rate Futures and Currency Futures are called **Financial Futures** and firms can hedge their exposure through financial futures. Financial futures, like commodity futures, are contracts to buy or sell financial assets at a future date at a specified price. Introduced in 1972 in USA, the trading in financial futures far exceeds trading in commodity futures.

(v) *MIBOR Futures*

It is a futures contract where the Mumbai interbank offered rate – an average of interbank rates quoted by a money market participants – is the underlying benchmark. A participant could sell MIBOR futures if he sees interest rates rising and buy them if he feels rates would fall. The futures contract would be available up to 12 months for each month.

(vi) *Index Futures*

The stock index tracks the changes in a basket of stocks. The value of a index futures contract can be ascertained using the cost of carry model.

Here, the spot price is the "Spot Index points", the carry cost is the interest on the value of stock underlying the index, while "Carry return" is the value of dividends receivable between day of valuation and delivery date. The situation using *Known Income* or *Known Yield*, as the case may be, can be applied.

Concept Problem: A 3-month futures contract on NIFTY is available at a time when the NIFTY is quoting 1800 points. Continuously compounded risk-free rate is 10%. Continuously compounded yield on the Nifty stocks is 2% per annum. One future contract equals 200 Nifty. How much investor would pay for Nifty futures? If the Nifty forward trades at 1825 what action would follow?

Solution: This falls under Known Yield.

Step 1: Compute FFP using formula So * e^ (r-y)t

= 1800 * e^ (0.10 – 0.02)*0.25

= 1800 * e^ 0.02 = 1800 * 1.02020 = 1836

Step 2: Decision

Since actual forward price (1825) is less than fair forward price (1836), the investor would buy Nifty futures.

It may refer to a choice or alternative or privilege or opportunity or preference or right. To have options is normally regarded good. Options are valuable since they provide protection against unwanted occurrences. They provide alternatives to bail out from a difficult situation. Options can be exercised on the occurrence of certain events. Options may be explicit or implicit. The underlying asset could be a share or any other asset.

Options have assumed considerable significance in finance. They can be written on any asset, including shares, bonds, portfolios, stock indices, currencies, etc. They are quite useful in risk management. Options are instruments whereby the right is given by the option seller to the option buyer to buy or sell a specific asset at specific price on or before a specific date. Some important features of options are:

- *Option Seller:* One who writes/gives the option. He has an obligation to perform, in case option buyer desires to exercise the option and has high degree of risk.
- *Option Buyer:* One who buys the option. He has the right (but no obligation) to buy and exercise the option. He has limited liability.
- Options provide flexibility to investors' needs.
- *American Option:* An option that can be exercised any time on or before the expiry date.
- *European Option:* An option that can be exercised only on expiry date.
- *Strike Price/Exercise Price:* Price at which the option can be exercised.
- *Expiration Date:* Date on which the option expires.
- *Exercise Date:* Date on which the option gets exercised.

- *Option Premium:* The price paid by the option buyer to the option writer/seller for granting the option. The premium usually is paid in advance, whether or not the holder exercises his option.

3. Options

- An investor who writes a call option against stock held in his portfolio is said to be selling *covered options*.
- Options sold without the stock to back them up are called *naked options*.
- The clearing house guarantees performance. Consequently, there is no risk of default.
- *Mark to market margin*: Since the clearing house acts as a guarantor, it would require parties to make and maintain deposit (margin) with it.

Types of Options

- **Call Option:** *Option to buy*. It gives the holder a 'right to buy' an underlying asset by a certain date for a certain price. The seller is under the obligation to fulfil the contract and is paid a price for this, called "call option premium." The call option holder's opportunity to make profits is unlimited. It depends on what the actual market price of the underlying share/asset is when the call option is exercised. The greater the market values of the underlying asset, the larger the value of the option. A call option's value will increase with increase in the share price, the rate of interest, volatility and time to expiration. It will decline with increase in the exercise price. The value of call decreases in the case of dividend paying shares. At expiration, the maximum value of a call option is: Max [(St – E), 0].

- **Put Option:** *Option to sell*. It gives the holder a 'right to sell' an underlying asset by a certain date for a certain price. The buyer is under the obligation to fill the contract and is paid a price, called "put option premium." A put buyer gains when the share/asset price falls below the exercise price. The potential profit of the put buyer is limited, since share/asset price cannot fall below zero. The potential loss of the put option seller is limited to the exercise price. A put option's value will increase with increase in the exercise price, volatility and time to expiration. It will decrease with increase in the share price, and the rate of interest. The value of put increases in the case of dividend paying shares. The value of put option at expiration is: Max [(E – St), 0].

- **Index Options:** Index options are call or put options on the stock market indices. In India, the SENSEX options are European-type options and expire on every last Thursday of the contract month. The put and call index option contracts with 1-month, 2-month and 3-month maturity are available. The settlement is done in cash on a T + 1 basis and the prices are based on expiration price as may be decided by the exchange. Option contracts will have a multiplier of 100.

- **Currency Options:** Currency options are similar to stock market options.

Following are the three features of options:

Premium: Option contracts carry a premium which is not refundable. The premium depends on volatility in exchange rates, exercise price, time to expiry, interest and inflation rate differentials.

Exercise Price: In exchange trade, options are generally indicated as three-tier exchange rate.

Standardization: In exchange traded options, the contact size as also the time to maturity (tenure) are standardised.

Types of Currency Options

Over-the-Counter Options (OTC-C): Such options contracts are generally written by banks to incorporate tailor-made conditions to suit the needs of customers. Major users are medium enterprises, who may not have adequate expertise to evaluate the price for an option. OTC-C also includes average rate options, a popular variety of OTC-Os.

Exchange Traded Options: These options are standardised both as to delivery dates and contract size. However, an element of negotiability is built in, in the area of option premium and the price at which option will be exercised.

The distinction between OTC options and exchanged traded OTC-O are summarised hereunder.

Table 20.3

OTC Options	Exchange Traded Option
Available in a wide range of currencies	Available for select major currencies
Available for cross-currencies, e.g., €/¥	Available only against the US $
Time towards maturity is kept flexible, and is available even for periods longer than 1 year	Available for standardised periods only
Pricing or premium is decided by the writing bank, hence negotiable	Pricing or premium is market driven, and hence non negotiable
Relatively illiquid securities, and are not transferable	Securities are available and hence liquid

Mechanics of Hedging through Options is a simple four-step process:

1. Decide on Call or Put options (i.e., whether to buy or sell a currency).
2. Determine the number of contracts.
3. Select an acceptable exercise price; pay the premium and conclude the contract.
4. On maturity, (i) if market rate is less favourable, exercise your option under the contract; and (ii) if market rate is more favourable, ignore the contract and buy or sell in the market.

Some Strategies in Options

After having understood about the options, an investor needs to formulate strategies that would help him/her make profits. For the same, following are to be understood:

- What are the ramifications of changes in stock options on the various parties to the derivative contract?
- What are in-the-money, at-the-money and out-of-the money options?
- What are intrinsic value and time value?
- What are pay-off graphs and how are they drawn?
- What happens on the expiry date?
- What is the value of an option on the expiry date?
- What is break-even price?
- What would happen if the market price is not in line with the theoretical value of the option?

1. Stock Price Movements and Value

A call option gives its owner the right to buy a stock at a specified price on or before the expiry date. A put buyer buys the right to sell shares. The following table(s) summarize the position.

Rule 1:

Party	Increase in Price	Decrease in Price
Call holder	Favourable	Adverse
Call writer	Adverse	Favourable
Put holder	Adverse	Favourable
Put writer	Favourable	Adverse

Rule 2:

Option	Right to	EP < MP	EP > MP
Call	Buy	Exercise	Lapse
Put	Sell	Lapse	Exercise

EP = the buying price and MP = the selling price

Concept Problem: The strike price and the expected price on expiry are as given in Columns 1 and 2 respectively. The option expires 3 months down the road. What position would you take? The actual price on the expiry date is given in Column 3.

Exercise Price (EP)		Expected Market Price on Expiry (EMP)	Actual Market Price on Expiry
(i)	180	160	180
(ii)	125	125	130
(iii)	160	175	155
(iv)	170	155	160
(v)	150	160	150
(vi)	110	110	100
(vii)	150	155	165
(viii)	170	160	180
(ix)	95	95	95

Solution:

Exercise Price (EP)		Expected Market Price on expiry	Relationship	Option Chosen (*)
(i)	180	160	EP > EMP	Put
(ii)	125	125	EP = EMP	No action
(iii)	160	175	EP < EMP	Call
(iv)	170	155	EP > EMP	Put
(v)	150	160	EP < EMP	Call
(vi)	110	110	EP = EMP	No action
(vii)	150	155	EP < EMP	Call
(viii)	170	160	EP > EMP	Put
(ix)	95	95	EP = EMP	No action

* As per the Expected Price (EP).

It is the purchase price in case of a Call and sale price in case of a Put. We want to buy low, sell high. Hence, if the EP is less than the Expected Market Price, we should buy the right to buy at EP. That is, we should buy a Call. If the EP is greater than the Expected Market Price, we should buy the right to sell at EP. That is, we should buy a Put.

2. Classification of Options

- In-the-money – These result in positive cash flow for the investor (gain).
- At-the-money – These result in zero cash flow to the investor, neither a gain nor a loss.
- Out-of-the-money – These result in a negative cash flow for the investor (loss).

The exercise price or strike price is fixed by the exchange. The exchange announces the above three prices. In this context, the option premium paid to buy these options is to be ignored since it represents a sunk cost.

Rule 1:

Relationship	Call Buyer	Put Buyer
EP > MP	Out-of-the-money	In-the-money
EP = MP	At-the-money	At-the-money
EP < MP	In-the-money	Out-of-the-money

Rule 2:

For Buyer	For Writer
OTM : Bad	Good
ATM : Bad	Good
ITM : Good	Bad

Concept Problem: State whether each one of the following is ITM; ATM or OTM.

Option	Exercise Price (EP)	Stock Price (SP)
Call	60	55
Call	50	50
Call	110	105
Call	30	35
Put	110	100
Put	105	105
Put	12	15
Put	25	20

Solution:

Option	EP	SP	Action	Action
Call	60	55	OTM	Lapse
Call	50	50	ATM	Indifferent
Call	110	105	OTM	Lapse
Call	30	35	ITM	Exercise
Put	110	100	ITM	Exercise
Put	105	105	ATM	Indifferent
Put	12	15	OTM	Lapse
Put	25	20	ITM	Exercise

3. Intrinsic Value and Time Value

An option's premium consists of two parts: (a) *intrinsic value* and (b) *time value.*

Intrinsic value is that part of the option premium which represents the extent to which the option is in the money. This means that in respect of options that are at-the-money or out-of-the-money, there is no intrinsic value, i.e., intrinsic value cannot be negative.

Time value is the difference between Option Premium and Intrinsic Value and is the premium paid for the time value of money. Time value falls with time and falls to zero on the expiry date. It cannot be negative.

Concept Problem: A stock with a current market price of Rs. 50 has the following exercise price and call option premium. Compute intrinsic value and time value.

Exercise Price	45	55	50	52	48
Premium	5	7	4	5	6

Solution:

Exercise Price	Option Premium	Nature	Intrinsic Value	Time Value
45	5	ITM	5	0
55	7	OTM	0	7
50	4	ATM	0	4
52	5	OTM	0	5
48	6	ITM	2	4

Effect of Increase in the Relevant Parameters on Option Prices

***Spot Prices*:** In case of a call option the pay-off for the buyer is max (S – Xt, 0) therefore, more the Spot Price, more is the pay-off and it is favourable for the buyer. It is the other way round for the seller, more the Spot Price higher are chances of his going into a loss.

In case of a put option, the pay-off for the buyer is (Xt – S, 0) therefore, more the Spot Price more are chances of going into a loss. It is the reverse for Put Writing.

***Strike Price*:** In case of a call option the pay-off for the buyer which is linked to the relationship of a higher strike price and that would reduce the profits for the holder of the call option.

Time to Expiration: More the time to expiration, more favourable is the option. This can only exist in case of European Option. The option contracts mature only on the date of maturity.

Volatility: More the volatility, higher is the probability of the option generating higher returns to the buyer. The downside in both the cases of call and put is fixed, but the gains can be unlimited. If the price falls heavily in case of a call buyer then the maximum he loses is the premium paid and nothing more than that. More so, he/she can buy the same shares from the spot market at a lower price. Similar is the case of the put option buyer.

Risk-free Rate of Interest: In reality, the rate of interest and the stock market is inversely related. But theoretically speaking, when all other variables are fixed and interest rate increases, this leads to a double effect: increase in expected growth rate of stock prices, discounting factor increases making the price fall.

In case of the put option, both these factors increase and lead to a decline in the put value. A higher expected growth leads to a higher price taking the buyer to the position of loss. The discounting factor increases and the future value becomes lesser.

In case of call option, these effects work in the opposite direction. The first effect is positive as at a higher value in the future, the call option would be exercised and would give a profit. The second effect is negative as is that of discounting. The first effect is far more dominant than the second one, and the overall effect is favourable on the call option.

Dividends: When dividends are announced, then the stock prices ex-dividend are reduced. This is favourable for the put option and unfavourable for the call option.

Risk Hedging with Options

We have understood that option is a right and does not constitute any obligation on the part of the buyer or seller of the option to buy or sell the underlying asset.

A foreign currency option is a handy method of reducing foreign exchange risk. Similarly, options on interest rates and commodities are quite popular with corporate managers to reduce risk, i.e., buying an option shields a company from increase in price of a commodity while the company can continue benefiting from the decrease in price. Thus, option creates an opportunity to guard against risk and benefit from changes in the prices. The cost of this opportunity is *option premium*. Many options trade on option exchanges. However, in practice, banks and companies strike private option deals.

There is a hidden option in the case of an ordinary share that arises because of the limited liability of the shareholders. Shareholders have a call option on the firm which has an exercise price equal to the required payment for debt. Shareholders will exercise their option to keep the firm (by making required payment to debt-holders) if the value of the firm is higher than the debt payment.

20.10 DERIVATIVES: A NEW WAY TO TRADE

SEBI approved derivatives trading in June 2000. The first instruments to be traded were index futures based on NSE's NIFTY and BSE's SENSEX. This was followed by trading on the two indices in June 2001 and options in 30 individual securities in July 2001. A future trading in individual stock was permitted in November 2001. The National Stock Exchange (NSE) has achieved a record of sorts.

During 2007, the NSE and BSE turnover added up to Rs. 1,21,60,701 crore, showing a quantum growth over 2006. During 2007, as a proportion of market capitalization of Nifty, the turnover in NSE spot and derivatives markets was 87.8 per cent and 339 per cent respectively.

Table 20.4 Growth and Turnover in Derivatives (Rs. Crore)

Year	BSE Average Trade	No. of NSDL	NSE Size	BSE Accounts (Nos.)
2001	2,58,983	36,58,098	39,848	2,076
2002	3,00,334	38,13,336	3,45,443	928
2003	4,25,077	46,12,884	14,31,142	9,103
2004	4,88,790	59,69,095	25,86,736	-
2005	5,01,946	N.A.	39,26,843	1,965
2006	6,35,241	N.A.	70,46,665	18,971
2007	7,82,521	N.A.	1,19,40,877	2,19,824

Table 20.5 Trends in Equity Derivatives Market NSE BSE

Particulars	Jan-17	Feb-17	Percentage changeover month	Jan-17	Feb-17	Percentage changeover month
1	2	3	4	5	6	7
A. Turnover (Rs. Crore)						
(i) Index Futures	3,24,469	3,51,773	8.4	0	0	NA
(ii) Options on Index						
Put	31,37,877	34,34,199	9.4	0	0	NA
Call	33,37,204	38,51,292	15.4	0	0	NA
(iii) Stock Futures	9,63,574	10,88,456	13.0	7	8	12.2
(iv) Options on Stock						
Put	1,77,441	1,89,337	6.7	0	0	NA
Call	3,64,053	4,33,282	19.0	0	0	NA
Total	**83,04,618**	**93,48,339**	**12.6**	**7**	**8**	**12.2**

B. No. of Contracts						
(i) Index Futures	47,92,429	48,81,690	1.9	0	0	NA
(ii) Options on Index						
Put	4,59,51,150	4,69,60,409	2.2	0	0	NA
Call	4,68,99,629	5,06,98,955	8.1	0	0	NA
(iii) Stock Futures	1,45,12,081	1,54,36,866	6.4	97	99	2.1
(iv) Options on Stock						
Put	26,89,907	27,07,278	0.6	0	0	NA
Call	33,15,699	58,32,798	75.9	0	0	NA
Total	**11,81,60,895**	**12,65,17,996**	**7.1**	**97**	**99**	**2.1**
C. Open Interest in terms of Value (Rs. Crore)						
(i) Index Futures	21,837	25,778	18.0	0	0	NA
(ii) Options on Index						
Put	65,074	60,369	-7.2	0	0	NA
Call	68,369	65,010	-4.9	0	0	NA
(iii) Stock Futures	77,930	85,679	9.9	1	1	45.5
(iv) Options on Stock						
Put	6,424	6,166	-4.0	0	0	NA
Call	11,630	11,227	-3.5	0	0	NA
Total	**2,51,264**	**2,54,229**	**1.2**	**1**	**1**	**45.5**
D. Open Interest in terms of No. of Contracts						
(i) Index Futures	3,29,432	3,71,379	12.7	0	0	NA
(ii) Options on Index						
Put	9,82,705	8,73,614	-11.1	0	0	NA
Call	10,27,463	9,31,685	-9.3	0	0	NA
(iii) Stock Futures	12,05,320	12,51,267	3.8	10	14	40.0
(iv) Options on Stock						
Put	95,805	87,750	-8.4	0	0	NA
Call	1,74,555	1,61,217	-7.6	0	0	NA
Total	**38,15,280**	**36,76,912**	**-4**	**10**	**14**	**40.0**

Source: SEBI Bulletin

Derivative Security

A *derivative security* is a security whose value depends upon the values of other basic variables backing the security. In most cases, these variables are nothing but the prices of traded securities. A derivative security is basically used as risk management tool and it is resorted to cover the risks due to price fluctuations.

Just like forward contract which is a derivative of a spot contract, a derivative security is derived from other trading securities backing it. Naturally, the value of a derivative security depends upon the values of the backing securities. Derivative helps to break the risks into various components such as *credit risk, interest rates risk, exchange rates risk* and so on. It enables the various risk components to be identified precisely and priced them and even traded them if necessary. Financial intermediaries can go for derivatives since they will have greater importance in the near future. In India, some forms of derivatives are in operation, for example, forwards in forex market.

20.11 FOREIGN EXCHANGE DERIVATIVES

Foreign exchange derivatives, also called *forex derivatives,* are instruments that are held by an Indian equity because of their foreign exchange exposure. These are meant to take care of the risk arising out of the movement of foreign currencies against expectations. Derivatives play a crucial role in developing in foreign exchange market as they enable market players to hedge against underlying exposures and shape the overall risk profile of participants in the market.

In India, various informal forms of derivatives contracts have existed for a long time though the formal introduction of a variety of instruments in the foreign exchange derivatives market started only in the post-reform period, cross-currency derivatives with the rupee as one leg were introduced with some restrictions in April 1997. Rupee foreign exchange options were allowed in July 2003. The most widely used derivative instruments are the forwards and foreign exchange swaps (rupee-dollar). Options are also in use in the market.

Foreign Exchange Derivative Instruments in India

1. Foreign Exchange Forwards

Authorised dealers (ADs) (Category-I) are permitted to issue forward contracts to persons residing in India with crystallized interest rate exposure and based on past performance/actual import-export turnover, as permitted by the RBI and to persons outside India with genuine currency exposure to the rupee, as permitted by the RBI. The residents in India generally hedge crystallized foreign currency/foreign interest rate exposure or transform exposure from one currency to another permitted currency. Resident, outside India enters into such contracts to hedge or transform permitted foreign currency exposure to the rupee, as permitted by the RBI.

2. Foreign Currency Rupee Swap

A resident of India who has long-term foreign currency or rupee liability is permitted to enter into such a swap transaction with ADs (Category-I) to hedge or transform exposure in foreign currency/foreign interest rate to rupee/rupee interest rate.

3. Foreign Currency Rupee Options

ADs (Category-I) approved by the RBI and ADs (Category-I) who are not market makers are allowed to sell foreign currency rupee options to their customers on a back-to-back basis, provided they have a capital to weighted assets ratio (CRAR) of 9 per cent and above. These options are used by customers who have genuine foreign currency exposures, as permitted by the RBI and ADs (Category-I) for the purpose of hedging trading books and balance sheet exposures.

4. Cross-Currency Options

ADs (Category-I) are permitted to issue cross-currency options to a person residing in India with crystallized foreign currency exposure, as permitted by the RBI. The clients use this instrument to hedge or transform foreign currency exposure arising out of current account transactions. ADs use this instrument to cover the risk arising out of market-making in foreign currency rupee options as well as cross-currency options, as permitted by the RBI.

5. Cross-Currency Swaps

Entities with borrowings in foreign currency under External Commercial Borrowings (ECB) are permitted to use cross-currency swaps for transformation of and/or hedging foreign currency and interest rate risks. Use of this product in a structured product not conforming to the specific purposes is not permitted.

Off-shore Derivatives

In the context of the Indian market, *off-shore derivatives instruments* (ODIs) are investment vehicles used by overseas investors for an exposure in Indian equities or equity derivatives. These investors are not registered with SEBI, either because they do not want or due to regulatory restrictions. These investors approach a *foreign institutional investor* (FII), who is already registered with SEBI. The FII makes purchases on behalf of these investors and the FII's affiliate issues them ODIs. The underlying asset for the ODI could be either stocks or equity derivatives like Nifty futures.

Instruments present in the form of derivatives are meant as *hedging products*. These ensure that the risk is contained and it helps them to create a position that will take care of unforeseen happenings in the foreign exchange market due to volatile movement in the currencies across the world.

Investors have to keep an eye on the impact on these instruments because companies that use them can be impacted by their improper use. There can be some sudden unaccounted hit for the company leading to a loss in value for the investor and their holdings. This makes understanding of the terms also very important.

Foreign Institutional Investors (FIIs): To strengthen the "know your client" regime and in the interest of greater efficiency of the market, it has been made mandatory for the FIIs, to report issuance/renewal/cancellation/redemption of offshore derivatives instruments against underlying Indian securities. Issuance of such derivatives has been limited only to regulated entities.

Participatory Notes (P-Notes)

P-Notes or PNs are instruments issued by registered foreign institutional investors to overseas investors, who wish to invest in the Indian stock markets without registering themselves with the market regulator, the SEBI.

PNs are one of the categories of the ODIs. At a basic level, the underlying asset class could be stocks and returns would be directly related to the appreciation in prices of those stocks. In some complex forms, returns could be linked to the appreciation in Nifty over a given time frame and could be even linked to combination of change in Nifty and a basket of stocks. For instance, the holder of a P-Note may be promised a return of 10% if Nifty rises by 5% within a month. Other categories of ODIs include equity-linked notes, capped return notes, participating return notes, etc.

International access to the Indian capital market is limited to foreign institutional investors (FIIs). The market has found a way to circumvent this by creating P-Notes, which are said to account for half the $ 80 billion that stands to the credit of FIIs. Investing through P-Notes is very simple and hence very popular. It keeps the investor's name anonymous. Some investors use it to save on costs, record keeping overheads and regulatory compliance overseas.

P-Notes are issued to the real investors on the basis of stocks purchased by the FII. The registered FII looks after all the transactions, which appear as proprietary trades in its books. It is not obligatory for the FIIs to disclose their client details to the SEBI unless asked specifically. PNs are banned by SEBI in October 2007.

Myths and Realities about Derivatives

The myth is that: "derivatives increase speculation and do not serve any economic purpose."

Reality

Numerous studies of derivative activities have led to a broad consensus, both in the private and public sectors that derivatives provide numerous and substantial benefits to the various/different users. Derivatives are a low cost, effective method for users to hedge and manage their exposure to interest rates, commodity prices, security prices, exchange rates, and so on.

The need for derivatives as a hedging tool was felt first in the commodities market. Agricultural futures and options helped farmers and processors hedge against the risk of commodity price fluctuations. After the fallout of Breton Woods Agreement, the financial markets in the world started undergoing radical changes. The period was marked by some remarkable innovations in the financial markets such as:

- introduction of floating rates for currencies;
- increased trading in variety of derivative instruments; and
- on-line trading in the capital markets.

As the complexity of instruments increased manifold, the accompanying risk factors grew in gigantic proportion. This situation thus led to more development in derivatives as risk management tools for various market participants.

Looking at the equity market, derivatives allow corporations and institutional investors to effectively manage their portfolios of assets and liabilities through instruments like stock index futures and options. An equity fund for example, can reduce its exposure to the stock market quickly and at relatively low cost without selling off part of its equity holding by using stock index futures or index options.

By providing investors and issuers with the wider array of tools for managing risk and raising capital, derivatives improve the allocation of credit and the sharing of risk in the global economy, lowering the cost of capital formation and stimulating economic growth. Now that the global markets for trade and finance have become more integrated, derivatives have strengthened these important linkages between global markets, increasing the liquidity and efficiency, thus facilitating the flow of trade and finance.

UNIT-IV

21 Portfolio Management

CHAPTER

It is the art and science of making decisions about investment mix and policy, matching investments to objectives, asset allocation for individuals and institutions, and balancing risk vs performance. *Portfolio management* refers to the management of a portfolio of investments to achieve the investment objectives like safety, profitability, liquidity and capital appreciation. Portfolio management is all about strengths, weaknesses, opportunities and threats in the choice of debt vs equity, domestic vs international, growth vs safety, and numerous other tradeoffs encountered in the attempt to maximize return at a given appetite for risk.

21.1 IMPORTANT STEPS IN PORTFOLIO MANAGEMENT PROCESS

1. Defining investors, goals and constraints
2. Developing Investment strategy (asset allocation mix)
3. Implementing the investment strategy
4. Monitoring, reviewing and updating

Portfolio management begins with identifying the securities for investment and determining the proportion of the investor's wealth to be invested in each. Thus, portfolio construction would address itself to three major issues, i.e., **selecting**, **timing**, and **diversification**. Portfolio revision would include examining the performance for average return, and risk against certain yardsticks or norms. Some investments are retained and some are disinvested to achieve the target rates of return.

Portfolio Construction is the process of blending together broad asset classes so as to obtain optimum return with minimal risk. The strategy of successful portfolio management is not to put all the eggs into one basket. If the investors hold a well-diversified portfolio of assets, then their concern should be the *expected rate of return* and *risk of the portfolio* rather than individual assets and the contribution of individual asset to the portfolio risk.

21.2 FACTORS FOR PORTFOLIO CONSTRUCTION

- Investment philosophy
- Approach
- Investment horizon
- Risk control
- Consistency/volatility
- Size of fund

Securities included in a portfolio are associated with each other. Therefore, **portfolio risk** also accounts for the covariance between the returns of securities. The magnitude of portfolio risk will depend on the correlation between securities. As the number of different securities in the portfolio increases, **diversification** helps in reducing the risk.

The investment or portfolio opportunity represents all possible combinations of risk and return, resulting from portfolios, formed by varying proportions of individual assets, securities. It presents the investor with the risk-return tradeoff. An **efficient portfolio** is one that has the highest expected returns for a given level of risk.

Building a successful investment plan for the twenty-first century may require a fundamental change in the way we think about investing. For instance, while taking less risk, a portfolio comprising only 60% equities that outperforms the Nifty 500 by a wide margin should certainly be considered a superior portfolio. Furthermore, new advances in investment and finance offer us solutions both simpler and more elegant (and different) than what we grew up with.

Turning One's Goals into a Strategy

Every strategy has certain performance implications. The word *strategy* implies a conscious effort to achieve stated goals. Their concern is to at least meet their minimum acceptable return levels without taking excessive risk. They desire a comfortable and stress-free retirement.

The asset allocation design will determine results in both short-term and long-term. Both risk and returns will be driven more by asset allocation than stock selection or market timing.

Specification of Investment Objectives: The commonly stated investment goals are capital preservation, current income, growth (capital appreciation), total return and stability. Since income and growth represent two ways by which return is generated and stability implies containment of risk, investment objectives may be expressed more clearly in terms of return and risk.

Risk-Reward Concept

This is a general concept underlying anything by which a return can be expected. In theory, the higher the risk, the more one should receive for holding the investment, and lower the risk, the less one would receive.

Determining One's Risk Preference

With so many different types of investments to choose from, how does an investor determine how much risk he or she can handle? Every individual/investor is different, and it is hard to create a steadfast portfolio model applicable to everyone all the time.

Portfolio Strategies

(i) Passive: These strategies do not seek to outperform the market but simply to do as well as the market. The emphasis on minimizing transaction costs and time spent in managing the portfolio because any expected benefits from active trading or analysis are likely to be less than the costs. Passive investors act as if the market is efficient and accept the consensus estimates of return and risk, accepting current market price as the best estimate of a security's value. *Index funds* are a typical example of passive portfolio management.

(ii) Active: These are investors who pursue active investment strategies believing that they can identify undervalued securities. These investors generate more search costs (both in time and money) and more transaction costs, but they believe that the marginal benefit outweighs the marginal cost incurred. One of the most traditional and popular form of active stock strategies is the selection of an individual stock identified as offering superior return-risk characteristics.

Pursuit of an active strategy assumes that investor possesses some advantage relative to other market participants. Such advantage could include superior analytical skills, superior information, or the ability or willingness to do what other investors, particularly institutions, are unable to do. The reason for this active approach is obvious – the potential rewards are very large, and many investors feel confident that they can achieve such rewards even if other investors cannot.

Security research is an essence in active fund management and is carried out through analysis such as: fundamental, technical and quantitative (including mathematical models, and computer based models).

21.3 APPROACHES USED AND INVESTMENT STYLES IN ACTIVE PORTFOLIO MANAGEMENT

There are a range of different styles of portfolio management that any institution can adopt. For example, growth, value, growth at a reasonable price (GARP), market neutral, small capitalisation, indexed, etc. Each of these approaches has its distinctive features, adherents and, in any particular financial environment, possess distinctive risk characteristics.

Value Investing

This value investing style is also called *conservative investing*. In the case of value investing, bargains are often measured in terms of market prices that are below the estimated current economic value of tangible and intangible assets. Value investors pick up shares at attractive low prices. They are characterised by maintaining a portfolio of market under performers, equipment, or other financial holdings in subsidiaries or other companies, and real estate.

Value investors, who select only cheap shares that are very infrequently traded, are called *deep-value investors*. Some value investors focus on companies at the brink of bankruptcy or in the midst of bankruptcy proceedings. The value investors' portfolio will have shares that have been undervalued by the market. Such value investing is suitable in a market economy that is facing depression.

Most value investors focus on tangible assets such as plant. Cyclical shares also become a favourite with value investors when recession hits and economically sensitive shares get less importance due to short-term investors focusing on temporarily adverse sales and earnings information. Underlying earnings or dividends must sustain, and value of those assets must be realizable.

Growth Investing

The strategy of growth investors is to identify the shares whose future returns are expected to grow at a fast rate while outperforming the markets on a consistent basis. Growth investment style identifies shares based on the growth potential of companies. These types of investors look into the future potential returns from the company. Historical returns need not exhibit a close relationship with growth rate or historical earnings per share.

Growth investors consider several factors to identify superior performing securities for purchase. Some of the factors that are looked into are short run and long run high growth rates from sales and EPS, high profit margin and notable increase in projected earnings for both three and five years. Growth companies are also identified through comparison with industry averages. If the company has superior expected growth rates compared with the industry averages, such companies are considered growth companies. Focus is more on how much a company is growing.

Growth shares also show distinctive cost advantage over other companies and are marked by high pay scales to attract talented employees. It is not always possible to identify the growth shares in all capital market situations. Many investors might arise, which would make the identification of the growth shares very difficult. Also, the identified growth shares might change their characteristics and might often result in unexpected losses for the investor.

21.4 DIVERSIFICATION

Diversification is a risk-management technique that involves a wide variety of investments like shares, bonds, bullion, real estate, etc., within a portfolio in order to minimize the impact that any one security will have on the overall performance of the portfolio. Shares of companies engaged in different industries are included in the portfolio. Diversification lowers the risk of one's portfolio yet provides better return per unit of risk.

Against the background of asset allocation, portfolio managers consider the degree of diversification that makes sense for a client (given its risk preferences) and construct a list of planned holdings accordingly. The list will indicate what percentage of the fund should be invested in each particular stock or bond. Effective diversification requires management of the correlation between the asset returns and the liability returns, issues internal to the portfolio (individual holdings volatility), and correlations between the returns. In a market meltdown, correlation between securities increases and decreases benefit of diversification.

Following are the three main practices that ensure better diversification:

1. Spread the portfolio among multiple investment vehicles such as cash, stocks, bonds, mutual funds and perhaps even some real estate.
2. Vary the risk among securities. There need not be any restrictions in choosing only blue chip stocks. Rather, it would be wise to pick investments with varied risk levels; this will ensure some losses are offset by other areas.
3. Vary securities by industry. Vary investments by time maturity, across asset class, across entities. This will minimize the impact of risks.

"**Do not put all the eggs in one basket**" is an old saying about diversification. The purpose of diversification is to reduce or eliminate unsystematic risk by distributing investments to various asset classes or within the same asset class to various securities. Diversification is best achieved when returns from securities are negatively correlated.

Diversification is the most important component that can help investor achieve his/her long-term financial goals while minimizing risk. However, one needs to remember that diversification is not the guarantee against loss. No matter how much diversification one employs, investing does involve taking on some risk.

A normal investor often frequently asks the question: how many stocks should be bought in order to reach optimal diversification? According to portfolio theorists, adding about 20 securities to one's portfolio reduces almost many of the individual security's risk. This assumes that one may buy stocks of different sizes from various industries.

It is sensible to hold a certain number of securities and monitor the same periodically, rather than holding too many securities in a portfolio. The following would be important while making diversification across the board in the securities portfolio:

(a) The number of securities should be limited to say 14 to 16.

(b) The securities should ideally belong to different industrial sectors, indeed even different geographical regions.

(c) The correlation of market movements may be built into the process of selecting stocks.

Common Portfolio Approaches Include

Top-Down Approach: Economic, Industry and Company (E-I-C) approach is followed. Belief and assumption made here is that every company depends on its industry, and every industry on the economy. There is risk while comparing with fully-invested portfolio. E-I-C can lead to underperforming thus less return to investors when markets run up.

Bottom-Up Approach: Focus is on individual merits and inherent strength of companies. Industry prospects and sensitivity to economy are a part of company evaluation, not elimination criteria. It improves focus in the process while evaluating companies rather than spending time on predicting market movements and economy prospects. The belief is: over a longer term, inherent strengths make or break a company – a merit that will be rewarded by the market. Following this approach can identify opportunities that may go unnoticed in a top-down approach.

21.5 OPTIMAL PORTFOLIO: SELECTION AND DIFFICULTIES

The optimal portfolio concept falls under the '*modern portfolio*' theory. The theory assumes (among other thing) that investors financially try to minimize risk while striving for the highest possible return. The theory states that investors will act rationally, always making decisions aimed at maximizing their return with acceptable level of risk.

Harry Markowitz ("The Legacy of Modern Portfolio Theory") used the optimal portfolio in 1952, and it shows us that it is possible for different portfolios to have varying levels of risk and return. Each investor must decide how much risk they can handle and then allocate (or diversify) their portfolio according to this decision.

The optimal-risk portfolio is usually determined to be somewhere in the middle of high and low (risk-return) level. If one goes higher up on the level, he/she takes proportionately more risk for a comparatively lower return. On the other hand, low risk/low return portfolios are pointless because one can achieve similar return by investing in risk-free government securities. Optimizing the portfolio is not something one can calculate easily. There are computer programs that are dedicated to determining optimal portfolios by estimating hundreds (and sometimes thousands) of different expected returns for each given amount of risk.

Notion of Portfolio

The term *portfolio* means a basket or a combination of securities. Thus, if one invests in soft drink business and coffee business, he/she is creating a portfolio of businesses. Similarly, if one invests in ACC and Hero Motor Corp he/she is building a portfolio of stocks. Let us now discuss how one can compute the return and risk of a portfolio.

Principle 1: Return of Portfolio

The *return of a portfolio* is the weighted average return of the securities constituting the portfolio with the market value of investment being the assigned weight. There are two different ways of computing this. One being, "first principles" and the second, "formula based" method. These are discussed briefly here.

Method 1: First Principle: Under this method, an investor could compute the return of the portfolio for each possible outcome by using the formula $\Sigma Rp = (W * R)$, where W is the weight of the security in the portfolio and R is the expected return. The portfolio would now resemble a 'single security'. One can then proceed to compute the return of this 'single security' using the formula $\Sigma Rp = (W * R)$ and this would be the return of portfolio, where P is the probability of return. The steps involved are:

Step 1: Convert the securities into a portfolio (and then regard it as a single stock) with the help of the investment weight and arrive at the return for each observation with the formula $\Sigma Rp = (W * R)$.

Step 2: Now that portfolio resembles a single stock, compute its return using the formula $\Sigma Rp = (W * R)$.

Method 2: Formula Based

Under this method, an investor could compute the return of a portfolio of securities as the weighted average of return of the securities constituting the portfolio.

Step 1: Compute the expected return of each stock taking into account the various observations and the probabilities of occurrence. Use the formula $\Sigma(P * R)$.

Step 2: Compute the return of the portfolio using the formula $\Sigma Rp = (W * R)$ where W would be the weight of each security in the portfolio.

Portfolio Return: Two-Asset Class

The return of a portfolio is equal to the weighted average of the returns of individual assets (or securities) in the portfolio with weights being equal to the proportion of investment value in each asset.

For example, an investor has an opportunity of investing his/her wealth in either asset X or asset Y. The possible outcomes of two assets in different states of economy are given in following table.

Table 21.1 Possible Outcomes of Two Assets, X and Y (Return in %)

State of Economy	Probability	Asset X	Asset Y
A	0.10	-8	14
B	0.20	10	-4
C	0.40	8	6
D	0.20	5	15
E	0.10	-4	20

The expected rate of return of X is the sum of the product of outcomes and their respective probability, i.e.,

$E(Rx) = (-8 * .1) + (10 * .2) + (8 * .4) + (5 * .2) + (-4 * .1)$
$= 5\%$

Similarly, the expected rate of return of Y is:

$E(Ry) = (14 * .1) + (-4 * .2) + (6 * .4) + (15 * .2) + (20 * .1)$
$= 8\%$

Suppose the same investor decides to invest 50 per cent each in both the assets (X and Y). What is the expected rate of return of a portfolio now?

This can be done in two steps. First, calculate the combined outcome under each state of economic condition. Second, multiply each combined outcome by its probability. The calculation is shown in the following table.

Table 21.2 Performance of 3 Different Asset Classes for 1995-2012 (in %)

State of Economy	Probability	Combined Return (%) X (50%) & Y (50%)	Expected Return (%) Column (2) * (3)
A	0.10	(-8 * 0.5) + (14 * 0.5) = 3.0	0.10 * 3.0 = 0.30
B	0.20	(10 * 0.5) + (-4 * 0.5) = 3.0	0.20 * 3.0 = 0.60
C	0.40	(8 * 0.5) + (6 * 0.5) = 7.0	0.40 * 7.0 = 2.80
D	0.20	(5 * 0.5) + (15 * 0.5) = 10.0	0.20 * 10.0 = 2.00
E	0.10	(-4 * 0.5) + (20 * 0.5) = 8.0	0.10 * 8.0 = 0.80
			6.50

There is a direct and simple method of calculating the expected rate of return on a portfolio in which the expected rates of return on individual assets and their weights are known. The expected rate of return on a portfolio is the weighted average of the expected rates of return on assets in the portfolio. In the above example, the expected rate of return is as follows:

$$E(Rp) = (0.5 * 5) + (0.5 * 8) = 6.5\%$$

21.6 PORTFOLIO RISK

Calculation of portfolio risk is not similar to weighted average of individual assets' total risk. Portfolios' risk is sometimes substantially different from individual asset's risk. It is quite possible that the individual assets may be substantially risky with sizeable standard deviations and when combined, may result in a portfolio which is at a very low risk.

Principle 2: Computation of Risk of a Portfolio

The risk of a portfolio is NOT the weighted average risk of the securities constituting the portfolio. The risk of a portfolio is dependent on a few statistical measures such as standard deviation, covariance and correlation.

Covariance: The link between the variability of returns in two independent securities is called *covariance*. We may use the statistical jargon: "Covariance is a measurement of the co-movement between two variables." The covariance (Cov) between two securities may be positive, negative or zero.

When we consider two assets, we are concerned with the co-movement of assets. Covariance of returns on two assets measures their co-movement. Three steps are involved in the calculation of covariance between two assets:

- Determining the expected returns on assets
- Determining the deviation of possible returns from the expected return for each asset
- Determining the sum of the product of each deviation of returns of two assets and respective probability.

Let us consider the data of security *X* and *Y* given in the following table:

Investments in Securities *A* and *B* (returns in %)

Economic Condition	Probability	Security *X*	Security *Y*
Good	0.5	40	0
Bad	0.5	0	40

Table 21.3 Covariance of Returns of Securities *X* and *Y* is Calculated (returns in %):

State of Economy	Probability	Returns		Deviation from Expected Returns		Product of deviation and Probability (Covariance)
		X	Y	X	Y	
A	0.1	-8	14	-13	6	-7.8
B	0.2	10	-4	5	-12	-12.0
C	0.4	8	6	3	-2	-2.4
D	0.2	5	15	0	7	0.0
E	0.1	-4	20	-9	12	-10.8
		E(Rx) = 5	E(Ry) = 8			Covar = –33.0

Table 21.3 shows the calculation of variations from the expected return and covariance, which is the product of deviations of returns of securities *X* and *Y* and their associated probabilities.

1. **Positive Covariance:** Returns of *X* and *Y* could be above or below their average returns at the same time. In either situation, this implies positive relationship between two returns. A positive value for covariance indicates that the returns of the two assets tend to go together.

2. **Negative Covariance:** Return of *X* could be above its average return while return of *Y* could be below its average return and vice versa. This denotes a negative relationship between returns of *X* and *Y*. The covariance would be negative. A negative value for covariance indicates that the returns on two assets bear a tendency to offset each other.

3. **Zero Covariance:** Returns on X and *Y* could show no pattern; that is, there is no relationship. In this situation, covariance would be zero. In reality, covariance may hardly be zero due to randomness and the negative and positive terms may not cancel out each other. A zero value for covariance would imply that there is no distinct relationship between the movements in returns in respect of the two securities.

***Correlation*:** How can one find relationship between two variables? Correlation is a measure of linear relationship between two variables (say, returns of two securities, *X* and *Y* as discussed above). As we noted, covariance of returns of securities *X* and *Y* is a measure of both variability of returns of securities and their association. Thus, the formula for covariance of returns on *X* and *Y* can also be expressed as follows:

$$\text{Covariance } XY = \text{Standard deviation } X * \text{Standard deviation } y * \text{Correlation } XY$$

$$= \sigma x \, \sigma y \text{ Cor } xy$$

The value of correlation, called the **correlation coefficient**, could be positive, negative or zero. It depends on the sign of covariance since standard deviations are always positive numbers. The correlation coefficient always ranges between −1.0 and +1.0. A correlation coefficient of +1.0 implies a **'perfectly positive correlation'** while a correlation coefficient -1.0 indicates a **'perfectly negative correlation'.** The correlation between the two variables will be zero (or not different from zero) if they are not at all related to each other. Many a times and in a number of situations, returns of any two securities may be weakly correlated (positively or negatively).

Correlation (rho) supplements and upgrades the covariance values in order to help comparison with corresponding values for other pairs of securities constituting the portfolio.

Measuring Correlation: Correlation coefficient for the two securities is derived by the formula:

$$\frac{\text{Covariance } xy}{(\sigma x) * (\sigma y)}$$

Portfolio risk will be maximum when two components of a portfolio stand perfectly positively correlated; and will be minimum when the same are perfectly negatively correlated.

Let us calculate correlation by using the above data given in table. The covariance is –33.0. We can calculate the standard deviation of securities *X* and *Y* which are 5.80 for *X* and 7.63 for *Y*. The correlation of these securities *X* and *Y* are as follows:

$$\text{Cor xy} = \frac{-33.0}{5.80 * 7.63} = \frac{-33.0}{44.25} = -0.746$$

Securities X and Y are negatively correlated as their relationship is indicated by −0.746. An investor can reduce his/her risks by investing in both the securities instead of one.

Minimum Variance Portfolio

The minimum variance portfolio is also called the optimum portfolio. However, investors do not necessarily strive for the minimum variance portfolio. A risk-averse investor will have a tradeoff between risk and return. His/her choice of a particular portfolio depends on his/her risk preference.

We can use the above stated general formula for estimating optimum weights of two securities X and Y so that the portfolio variance is minimum.

Measuring Portfolio Risk for Two Assets

Like in the case of individual assets, the risk of a portfolio could be measured in terms of its variance or standard deviation. As stated earlier, the portfolio return is weighted average of returns on individual assets. The portfolio variance or standard deviation depends on the co-movement of return on two assets. There are two different ways of computing this. The first is called "first principle." The second is called "Formula based method."

Method 1: First Principles

This is a derivation-based method. Under this method, we simply convert the portfolio into a proxy single security. We compute the return of a portfolio for each possible outcome by using the formula $\Sigma(W*R)$, where W is the weight of the security in the portfolio and R is the expected return. The portfolio would now resemble a "single security." For computation, the steps involved are:

Step 1: Convert the securities into a portfolio (and then regard it as a single stock) with the help of the investment weight and arrive at the return for each observation.

Step 2: Treat the portfolio arrived at in Step 1 as a single security. Compute its standard deviation in the same way as the standard deviation of a single security.
This standard deviation would be the risk of the portfolio.

Method 2: Formula Method

The three essential elements that go to make up portfolio risk are:

1: Standard deviation of each security

2: Proportion (or weight) of investment in each security

3: Covariance of the pair of securities.

Armed with these figures, one just needs to do multiplication and addition! Here's how:

Step 1: Compute covariance between the two stocks

Step 2: Compute correlation

$$\sqrt{[(\sigma x)^\wedge 2\ (wx)^\wedge 2] + [(\sigma y)^\wedge 2\ (wy)^\wedge 2] + [2 * (\sigma x)*(wx)*(\sigma y)*(wy) * (\text{Cov } xy)]}$$

where
$(\sigma x)^\wedge 2$ = Variance of security X
$(\sigma y)^\wedge 2$ = Variance of security Y
(wx) & (Wy) = Proportion of investment in securities X and Y
(Cor xy) = Correlation coefficient of securities X and Y

Step 3: Apply the formula

Relationship between Correlation and Risk Reduction

In general, the correlation between the two securities can be +1, –1 or range between –1 and +1. Their meaning and impact on risk reduction is explained.

Table 21.4

Value of Correlation	Nature of Correlation	Movement of Return	Risk Reduction
+1	Perfect positive	Same direction	Not possible
-1	Perfect negative	Opposite direction	Can be reduced to near zero
0 to 1	Positive	Same direction but not in same proportion	Possible but not near to zero
0 to –1	Negative	Opposite direction but not in same proportion	Possible but not near to zero

Portfolio Risk-Return Analysis: Two-Asset Scenario

Let us recapitulate that the portfolio return depends on the proportion of wealth invested in two assets, and is in no way affected by correlation between asset returns. In contrast, the portfolio risk depends on both correlation and proportions (weights) of the assets forming the portfolio.

Let us consider an example to understand the implications of asset correlation and weights for the portfolio risk-return relationship. Suppose two securities, *A* and *B* have the following characteristics:

	A	B
Expected return (%)	12.00	18.00
Variance	256.00	576.00
Standard deviation	16.00	24.00

Further, assume five possible correlations between the returns of these securities:

(i) Perfectly positive correlation +1
(ii) Perfectly negative correlation –1
(iii) No correlation 0.0
(iv) Positive correlation 0.5
(v) Negative correlation –0.25.

The first three relationships are special situations. They are not rare, but they may not be very common either in practice. In the real world, returns of securities have a tendency to move together in the same direction. Sometimes they move in opposite direction too. Thus, a positive or negative correlation is more likely between two risky securities.

Given the characteristics of A and B and their correlation, what are the interactions between risk and return of portfolios that could be formed by combining them?

Table 21.5

			Portfolio Risk, σp (%)				
			Correlation				
Weight		**Portfolio Returns**	**+1.00**	**–1.00**	**0.00**	**0.50**	**–0.25**
A	B	Rp	Σp	Σp	Σp	Σp	Σp
1.00	0.00	12.00	16.00	16.00	16.00	16.00	16.00
0.90	0.10	12.60	16.80	12.00	14.60	15.74	13.99
0.80	0.20	13.20	17.60	8.00	13.67	15.76	12.50
0.70	0.30	13.80	18.40	4.00	13.31	16.06	11.70
0.60	0.40	14.40	19.20	0.00	13.58	16.63	11.76
0.50	0.50	15.00	20.00	4.00	14.42	17.44	12.65
0.40	0.60	15.60	20.80	8.00	15.76	18.45	14.22
0.30	0.70	16.20	21.60	12.00	17.47	19.64	16.28
0.20	0.80	16.80	22.40	16.00	19.46	20.98	18.66
0.10	0.90	17.40	23.20	20.00	21.66	22.44	21.26
0.00	1.00	18.00	24.00	24.00	24.00	24.00	24.00
			Minimum Variance Portfolio				
Weight A			1.00	0.60	0.692	0.857	0.656
Weight B			0.00	0.40	0.308	0.143	0.344
Σ			256.00	0.00	177.23	246.86	135.00
Σ (%)			16.00	0.00	13.31	15.71	11.62

A is a low return and low risk security as compared to *B*, which has high return and high risk. If one holds 100 per cent investment in *A*, his/her expected return is 12 per cent and standard deviation is 16 per cent. On the contrary, if one invests entire wealth in *B* he/she may expect to earn a higher return of 18 per cent, but the standard deviation, 24 per cent, is also higher.

How would the expected return and risk change if portfolio *A* and *B* are combined in different proportions? In the above table, we show the calculation of the portfolio return and risk for different combinations (weights) of *A* and *B* under different assumptions regarding the correlation between them.

21.7 PERFORMANCE MEASUREMENT

Performance is often the acid test of portfolio management, and in the institutional context, accurate measurement is a necessity. The leading performance measurement firms compile aggregate industry data, e.g., showing how portfolio in general performed against given indices as well as peer groups over various time periods.

Benchmark Portfolios for Performance Evaluation

Benchmark portfolio is a tool for the meaningful evaluation of the performance of a portfolio manager. The more the benchmark reflects the manager's stated style, the more accurately the performance due to a manager's skills can be assessed. Specialized benchmarks are called "normal portfolios". They are specially constructed by mutual consent of the client and the manager to reflect the client's need and the manager's style.

Some management firms develop a normal portfolio, which they can use for all clients, and some develop it separately for each type of client. When benchmarks are designed in advance, the portfolio manager knows what the specific objectives are and tailors the portfolio accordingly. The benchmark should reflect the appropriate investment environment in which the manager works. Without a yardstick for proper comparison, it becomes difficult to distinguish between active management skills and random results.

Rather than using a market index like the Bombay Stock Exchange's Sensitive Index (SENSEX) to the Economic Times (ET) Index, a benchmark portfolio would use a portfolio with predominantly value-oriented shares for a value manager, growth-oriented shares for a growth manager and small capitalization shares for a small cap (size) manager. It is quite natural for an investment manager to perform better than the benchmark, though the benchmark may itself underperform in relation to a market index. The process of constructing a benchmark portfolio involves:

(a) defining the universe of stock to be used for the benchmark portfolio; and

(b) defining the weightage of the stocks in the universe.

Performance attribution analysis, as mentioned earlier, is a means of evaluating an investment manager's performance, the return and the sources of return relative to a benchmark portfolio. This analysis looks at an investment manager's total 'excess' return, or 'active management return' (AMR) relative to its benchmark over a given period.

Determinants of Portfolio Performance

Performance of the portfolio depends on certain critical decisions taken by a portfolio manager. An evaluation of these decisions helps one to determine the activities that need efficiency for better portfolio performance. The popular activities associated are:

1. Investment policy
2. Stock selection
3. Market timing

The risk-adjusted performance measures discussed earlier primarily provide an analysis on the overall performance of a portfolio without breaking it up into sources or components. Eugene Fama has given a framework towards this purpose.

21.8 MODERN PORTFOLIO THEORY

It established the quantitative link existing between portfolio risk and return. The Capital Asset Pricing Model (CAPM) developed by Sharpe ("Mutual Fund Performance", Jan, 1966) highlighted the notion of rewarding risk and produced first performance indicators, be they risk-adjusted ratios (Sharpe ratio, information ratio) or differential returns compared to benchmarks.

So far we have seen that for ascertaining returns for a given level of risk:

- The stock market is not concerned with diversifiable risk.
- The stock market is not concerned with whether an investor holds a diversified portfolio.
- The compensation that stock market pays to an investor will be limited to only non-diversifiable risk.

So we have on one side a non-diversifiable portion of the "risk", and on the other side "returns" that an investor seeks. A link needs to be established between the two. We will discuss four principles for the purpose.

Principle 1: The required return is mandated by CAPM

We can establish a link by laying down what is the return that one should look forward to get for an assumed level of risk. It is easy for anyone to earn risk-free (Rf) rate of return, say 6%.

Whereas the stock market earns certain rate of return (Rm). Let us assume that it is 15%. So an investor who has potential to earn this excess return over and above the risk-free return is called the *risk premium* (Rm – Rf). It is the reward for undertaking risk by investing in stock market. The risk premium here is 15% – 6% = 9%.

If an investment is as risky as the stock market, the risk premium to be earned is 9%. Suppose an investment is 30% riskier than the stock market, it naturally carried a risk premium more than the risk premium of market, i.e., 9% + 30% of 9% = 11.7%.

How much more risky is an investment with reference to the market, is identified by Beta. Hence, the risk premium that a stock should earn is Beta times the risk premium from market [$\beta * (R_m - R_f)$].

So far we have talked and explained only the risk premium. The total return from an investment is the risk-free rate of return plus the risk premium. Therefore, the required rate of return from a stock would be: $R_j = R_f + [\beta * (R_m - R_f)]$.

Substituting the data in our example, it would be: 6% + [1.17 * (15% - 6%)] = 16.53%

Principle 2: Security Market Line (SML)

A graphical representation of CAPM is called the *security market line* (SML). This line indicates what rate of return is required to compensate for a given level of risk.

The line (in a graph) points to $R_m - R_f$, i.e., the risk premium element, and the fact that higher is the Beta value for a security, higher would be its risk premium relative to the market. Thus, upward sloping line is called the "security market line". It measures the relationship between risk and premium.

Concept Problem

T-Bills give a return of 5%. Market return is 13%. (i) What is the market risk premium? (ii) Compute Beta value and required returns for the following combination of investments.

T Bill	100	70	30	0
Market	0	30	70	100

Solution:

Part (i): Risk premium = $R_m - R_f$ = 13% – 5% = 8%

Part (ii): Beta value and required rate of return:

Beta is weighted average β investing in portfolio consisting of market (β = 1) and treasury bills (β = 0).

Table 21.6

Portfolio	T Bills : Market	β	$R_j = R_f + \beta * (R_m - R_f)$
1	100 : 0	0	5% + 0 * (13-5) = 5%
2	70 : 30	0.7(0)+0.3(1) = 0.3	5% + 0.3 * (13-5) = 7.40%
3	30 : 70	0.3(0)+0.7(1) = 0.7	5% + 0.7 * (13-5) = 10.60%
4	0 : 100	1.0	5% + 1.0 * (13-5) = 13.00%

As we know that Security Market Line (SML) is likely to provide a relationship between the systematic risk (β) and return on an asset. Fama used this framework to break the actual realized return into two parts. A part of the return may be due to the size of risk that the asset carries and the remaining due to the superior selectivity skills of the portfolio manager. The excess return-form of SML can be used to estimate the expected returns. If actual return is more or less than such expected returns, it can be attributed to superior or inferior stock selection. Then, total excess return on a portfolio (say A) = Selectivity + Risk.

Principle 3: Risk-free Rate of Return

One of the underlying assumptions of the CAPM is that there is only one risk-free rate. It also presupposes that the return on a security includes both dividend payments and capital appreciation. These have to be factored in making a judgement of Beta and computing the required rate of return.

Concept Problem

Blueline Ltd. expects that considering the current market prices, the equity share holders should get a return of at least 15.50% while the current return on the market is 12%. RBI has closed the latest auction for Rs. 4000 crore of 182-day bills for the lowest bid of 4.30%, although there were bidders at a higher rate of 4.60% also for less than Rs. 10 crore. What is Blueline Ltd.'s Beta?

Solution:

Step 1: Determining the risk-free rate

Here two risk free rates are given. The aggressive approach would be to consider 4.60% while a conservative approach would have it at 4.30%. If we want to moderate; the simple average would be fine. So the average of 4.30 and 4.60 are taken.

Step 2: Apply CAPM

$$15.5 = 4.45 + \sigma * (12 - 4.45) \quad : \beta * (12 - 4.45) = 15.5 - 4.45$$

$$\beta * (7.55) = 11.05 \quad : \beta = 11.05/7.55 = 1.464$$

Principle 4: Undervalued and Overvalued Stocks

The CAPM is not an academic model. It can be put to use to help the investor decide whether he/she should buy, sell or hold stocks.

Remember that the CAPM provides the required rate of return on a stock after taking into account the risk involved in the investment. Based on current market price or based on any other judgemental factor, it is possible to identify as to what would be the expected return across a period of time. By comparing the required return with the expected return, we can make investment decisions.

Rule 1: CAPM < Expected return: Buy

If the required return (as computed by CAPM) is less than the expected return (calculated using any other factor), it would mean that the stock is undervalued. This is because the stock gives more return than what it should give. Hence, such stocks should be bought.

Rule 2: CAPM > Expected return: Sell

Similarly, if the required return is higher than the expected return it would mean that the stock is overvalued. This is because the stock gives less return than what it should give. Hence, such stocks should be sold.

Rule 3: CAPM = Expected rate of return: Hold

Finally, if the required return equals the expected return the stock is rightly valued. Hence, such stocks should be held.

An alternative: Another way of looking at this situation is to figure out what should be the current market price (also known as *Fair Market Price*–FMP). Based on CAPM, we can compute that by using the Gordon's model for share valuation with the cost of equity being CAPM's required rate of return.

$$\text{Hence, FMP} = \frac{D_1}{(Ke - g)}$$

If the actual market price (AMP) is less than the FMP, the stock is undervalued and should be bought. If AMP is greater than FMP, the stock is overvalued and should be sold. If the two are equal, then it is correctly valued, and hence stocks should be held.

Table 21.7

Price Relationship	Return Relationship	Valuation	Action
AMP < FMP	Required return < Expected return	Under	Buy
AMP > FMP	Required return > Expected return	Over	Sell
AMP = FMP	Required return = Expected return	Correct	Hold

Sharpe's Single Index Market Model

Sharpe assumed that, for the sake of simplicity, the return on a security could be regarded as being linearly related to a single index like the market index. Theoretically, the market index should consist of all the securities trading in the market. However, a popular average can be treated as a surrogate for the market index. The acceptance of the idea of a market between individual securities is because any movement in securities could be attributed to movements in the single underlying factor being measured by the market index. The simplification of the Markowitz model has come to be known as the *Market Model* or *Single Index Model* (SIM).

In an attempt to capture the relative contribution of each stock towards portfolio risk, William Sharpe has developed a simple but elegant model called the "Market Model." His argument is like this: We appreciate that the portfolio risk declines as the number of stocks increases but to an extent. The part of the risk which cannot be further reduced even when we add a few more stocks into a portfolio is called *systematic risk.*

That undiversifiable risk is attributed to the influence of systematic factors principally operated in a given market. If one includes all traded securities in a market in his portfolio, that portfolio reduces the risk of the extent of market influences. In such a case, one can easily capture every individual stock's contribution to portfolio risk by simply relating its returns with that of the market index. Such a relationship is expected to give us the market sensitivity of the given scrip.

This is exactly the relationship that William Sharpe has estimated with a simple regression equation considering the returns or Market Index, such as S&P SENSEX, ET Index, NSE Index or RBI Index as independent variable and returns on individual stocks as dependant.

$$R_{it} + \alpha_i + \beta_{mt} - C_{it}$$

where R_{it} = Return on ith security during t(th) holding period
R_{mt} = Return on a Market Index during t(th) holding period
α = Constant term
β_{mt} = Market Beta or Market Sensitivity of a given stock

Since the regression coefficient (Beta) indicates the manner in which a security's return changes systematically with the changes in market, this linear line is also called *Characteristic Line*. The slope of the line is called *Beta*. It gained popularity in security analysis as a relative market risk. Beta is 'one' for such a stock, which is said to have the risk exactly equal to that of the market.

21.9 BETA COEFFICIENT

The market related risk, which is also called 'systematic risk', is unavoidable even by diversification of the portfolio. The market will not reward an investor for holding diversifiable risk. The logic is simple: the investor is expected to diversify such risk. By not diversifying, he/she isn't being efficient. One can't get rewarded for inefficiency! The market therefore rewards an investor only for the non-diversifiable risk. Hence, the only relevant risk is the *non-diversifiable risk* and so the investor must know how much non-diversifiable risk he/she is taking.

Beta is a measure of non-diversifiable risk. *Beta coefficient* is a relative measure of the volatility of stock price in relation to movement in stock index of the market; therefore, Beta is the index of systematic risk. In other words, Beta of a stock measures the sensitivity of the stock with reference to a broad based market index. The broad based index, for instance, in India, could be the Sensex or the Nifty.

A Beta of 1.0 indicates average level of risk, while the security's return fluctuates more or less than that of market portfolio. A zero Beta means no risk. The degree of volatility is expressed as follows:

- If the Beta is less than 1.0, it is less sensitive to market risk, the security is *conservative*. Here, securities move slower than the movement in the stock market.
- If the Beta is more than 1.0, it is more sensitive to market risk, the security is *aggressive*. Here, securities move faster than the movement in the stock market.

- If the Beta is 1.0, it is called *unity stocks*. Such stocks mimic the market. They move in tandem with the market. This has two simple implications.

  Implication 1: An investor gets extra reward for taking risk. This is called *risk premium*. If the stock market as a class (measured by the Index) gives a risk premium of say 10% and the Beta of a stock is 1.2, the risk premium from this stock ought to be 1.2 times, i.e., 12%.

  Implication 2: Put another way, this would mean that the Beta of a stock indicates the sensitivity of a stock to changes in the returns from the stock market. If the stock market as a class (measured by the Index) changes by 5%, a stock with Beta of 1.2 should change by 5 * 1.2 = 6%.

Table 21.8

Beta	Nature	Investor	Risk	Speed	Preference
>1	High	Aggressive	Higher	Faster	Rising market
1	Unity	Copycat	Same	Same pace	Sideways market
<1	Low	Conservative	Lower	Slower	Falling market

Calculation of Beta

In statistical terms, the risk of a stock is measured by its standard deviation. In relation to a market, it is its covariance with the market. If this covariance is standardized for the covariance of the market, we get the Beta value. Beta is a standardized measure of covariance of return of an asset and that of the market. Alternative ways of computing Beta are given in Table 21.9.

Table 21.9

Formula 1 (for Beta)	Formula 2 (for Beta)	Formula 3 (for Beta)
$\beta = \dfrac{\Sigma XY - nXY}{\Sigma Y \wedge 2 - nY \wedge 2}$	$\beta = \dfrac{\text{Covariance jm}}{(\sigma m) \wedge 2}$	$\dfrac{\beta = \sigma j}{\sigma m * \text{Corr jm}}$
where,	where,	where,
X = Return (%) from stock	Covariance jm = Covariance between stock and market	σj = Standard deviation of stock
Y = Return (%) from the stock market as a class		σm = Standard deviation of market returns
n = number of observations	Variance m$(\sigma = m)\wedge 2$ = Variance of the market	σj corr jm = Correlation between returns from stock and stock market
X = Arithmetic mean of rate of returns from the stock		
Y = Arithmetic mean of rate of returns from the market		

Prediction of Beta

Beta, as commonly defined, represents how sensitive the return of an equity portfolio (or security) is to the return of the overall market. It can be measured by regressing the historical returns of a portfolio (or security) against the historical returns of an index; the resulting slope of this regression line would be the historical beta. This can be useful for attributing relative performance to various sources or for explaining active risk over a certain period of time.

Portfolio managers are quite interested in what the Beta of a portfolio (or security) will be in the future, or what the realized Beta will be. As one might expect, predicting the value of Beta can be a complicated process.

In the past, when returns were typically available no more frequently than monthly, historical Betas were not very reliable predictors of realized Betas; achieving statistical significance usually meant using returns from past periods that were no longer relevant. In the 1970s, Barra ("Style Timing: Value versus Growth") pioneered the use of multi-factor equity models to calculate, among other things, predicted Betas that were based on statistically significant historical relationships between equity returns and a number of risk factors, with the belief that predicted Betas calculated in this manner would be better predictors of realized Betas than historical betas.

21.10 ALPHA

We used Beta to estimate the "required return" of a single security (or a portfolio), relative to the market return. There can be many securities providing returns either above or below the estimates of return shown by CAPM. *Alpha* is an indicator of the extent to which the actual return of a stock deviates from those predicted by its Beta value. It is denoted by the symbol α and is given by the following formula:

Alpha = Return mandated by CAPM – Actual return earned

A share's Alpha value is a measure of its abnormal return, and represents the per cent by which the share's returns are currently above or below the required return, given by the systematic risk.

Computation of Alpha

The Alpha value can be arrived at by taking the simple average of returns in excess of Beta value. The steps involved are:

Step 1: Compute the required return mandated by CAPM

Step 2: Compute the actual return for a set of observations

Step 3: The difference between the two is computed

Step 4: Final Alpha is the simple average of step 3 for various observations.

Interpretation of Alpha

Alpha values assume significance in the investment market. They help an investor decide whether stocks are undervalued, overvalued or rightly valued. The following rules would help make the choice.

Rule 1: A positive Alpha value indicates that the expected return from this stock could be higher than that mandated by CAPM to the extent of Alpha value. Hence stocks with positive Alpha value should be considered undervalued stocks. Such stocks should be bought.

Rule 2: A negative Alpha value indicates that the expected return from this stock will be less than that mandated by CAPM to the extent of the Alpha value. Hence stocks with negative Alpha value should be considered overvalued stocks. Such stocks should be sold.

Table 21.10

Alpha	Valuation	Action
Positive	Under	Buy
Zero	Correct	Hold
Negative	Over	Sell

Sale of overvalued stocks and purchase of undervalued stocks would mean that over time, the value of the stocks will touch the values suggested by CAPM and hence the Alpha value will over time become zero.

A Note of Caution

Overvalued and undervalued stocks are to be spotted only with the help of Alpha values that are reasonable. We should keep in mind that Alpha value has limited utility and it has no predictive value. Alpha value should not be taken as a basis for a logical decision to invest or not to invest in a stock/share/scrip.

Example: If Beta is 1.40; R is 5.25%, and Rm is 11% what should be the return on the share? If the Alpha value is: (i) +1.5, (ii) 1, (iii) 0 and (iv) –2.35, what would the current expected return from the stock? What investment action could be suggested?

Solution:

Step 1: Compute the required return under CAPM

$$R_j = 5.25 + \beta * (11.00 - 5.25) = 5.25 + 1.40 * (5.75) = 13.30\%$$

Step 2: Compute current return

Current return = Expected CAPM return + Alpha Value

Table 21.11

	1	2	3	4
Required return (%)	13.30	13.30	13.30	13.30
Alpha value (%)	1.50	1.00	0.00	-2.35
Current return	14.80	14.30	13.30	10.95
Action	**Buy**	**Buy**	**Hold**	**Sell**

Multi-factor Models

These models were developed as an alternative to the CAPM, allowing a better description of portfolio risks and a more accurate evaluation of a portfolio's performance.

For example, Fama and French "Common Risk Factors in the Returns on Stock and Bonds" (1993) have highlighted two important factors that characterize a **company's risk** in addition to **market risk**. These factors are the book-to-market ratio and the company's size as measured by its market capitalization. Also of interest for performance measurement is Sharpe's (1992) *style analysis model,* in which factors are style indices. This model allows a custom benchmark for each portfolio to be developed, using the linear combination of style indices that best replicate portfolio style allocation, and leads to an accurate evaluation of portfolio alpha.

Markowitz Model: The Mean-Variance Criterion

Dr. Harry Markowitz is credited for developing the first modern portfolio analysis model since the basic elements of modern portfolio theory emanate from a series of propositions concerning rational investor behaviour set forth by Markowitz, then of the Rand Corporation, in 1952, and later in a more complete monograph sponsored by the Cowles Foundation. It was this work that has attracted everyone's perspective regarding portfolio management.

Markowitz used *mathematical programming* and *statistical analysis* to arrange for the optimum allocation of assets within a portfolio. To reach this objective, Markowitz generated a portfolio within a reward-risk context. In other words, he considered the variance in the expected returns from investments and their relationship to each other in constructing portfolios. In doing so by directing the focus, Markowitz, and others following the same reasoning, recognized the function of portfolio management as one of composition, and not individual security selection – as it is more commonly believed.

Decisions as to individual security additions to and deletions from an existing portfolio are then predicted on the effect such as manoeuvre has on the delicate diversification balance. In essence, Markowitz's model is a theoretical framework for the analysis of risk return choices. The model requires expected return and standard deviation estimates for each security to be considered for inclusion in the portfolio.

Decisions are based on the concept of *efficient portfolio*. A portfolio is efficient when it is expected to yield the highest return for the level of risk accepted or, alternatively, the smallest portfolio risk for a specified level of expected return. To build an efficient portfolio an expected return level is chosen, and assets are substituted until the portfolio combination with the smallest variance at return level is found. As this process is repeated for other expected returns, a set of efficient portfolio is generated.

Assumptions

The Markowitz model is based on several assumptions regarding investor behaviour.

(i) Investors consider each investment alternative as being represented by a probability distribution of expected returns over some holding period.

(ii) Investors maximize one period's expected utility and progress along the utility curve, this demonstrates diminishing marginal utility of wealth.

(iii) Individuals estimate risk on the basis of the variability of expected returns.

(iv) Investors base their decisions solely on expected returns and variance (or standard deviation) of returns only.

(v) For a given risk level, investors prefer high returns to lower returns. Similarly, for a given level of expected return, investor prefers less risk to more risk.

Factor Model

The CAPM is also known as the Arbitrage Pricing Theory Model. It provides a link between expected returns on a share and the expected returns on market index. The essence of CAPM is that investors will be rewarded for only non-diversifiable risks. These non-diversifiable risks can be traced to macroeconomic factors. Some examples are: interest rates, inflation, GDP, balance of payments, foreign exchange reserves, etc.

Now will these macroeconomic factors affect all the businesses operating in the market in the same manner? That's unlikely. Because macroeconomic factors like foreign exchange implications, inflation, GNP and the like have varying degrees of impact on the returns of business entities that comprise the market.

One can therefore, argue that:

- The responsiveness of a business entity to each of these factors will be different.
- Hence, a business entity can have a Beta for a change in foreign exchange reserves, another Beta for a change in GNP, and third Beta for a change in inflation rates, etc.
- Using the sensitivity of the firm to two or more such factors that are relevant, the expected return on a given stock can be estimated.

The steps involved are:

Step 1: Identifying the macroeconomic factors.

Step 2: Assessing the risk premium for taking on factor risk. Towards this have R_m for each variable. Thus, one has R_m Interest, R_m GNP, etc. From this, deduct R_f to arrive at risk premium.

Step 3: Readjust the risk premium, to fall in line with sensitivity of the selected firm/stock to each of these factors.

Criticism against Factor Model

Macroeconomic factors that affect the performance and results of entities are many. There is no unanimity about which macroeconomic factor should be taken in, and which ones to be ignored. Further, it is extremely difficult to measure in terms of Beta value, the sensitivity of an investment to the changes in these macroeconomic factors.

21.11 OTHER PORTFOLIO SELECTION MODELS

Some other portfolio selection models that seem to hold great promise to practical application are briefly discussed here. One such model is *multi-index model.* There are different variants of this model and each of them is developed to capture some of the non-market influence that causes shares to move together (recall that single-index model accounts for only market-related influence).

The non-market influences, in essence, include a set of economic factors or industry (or group) characteristics that account for common movement in share prices. While it is easy to find a set of indices that are associated with non-market effects over any period of time, it is quite another matter to find a set that is successful in predicting covariances that are not market related. There is still a great deal of work to be done before multi-index models consistently outperform the simpler one.

Another model that takes into account a wide spectrum of practical consideration in portfolio selection is the *goal-programming model*. In real life, an investor's goals and desires transcend the notion of a tradeoff between only risk and return. For example, an investor may prefer to invest some minimum amount in several different shares, but at the same time he or she may not like individual investments to exceed a specified limit. Additionally, he or she prefers dividend income to capital appreciation.

Expected Return on a Portfolio

The expected return on a portfolio is simply the weighted average – the expected returns of the individual securities in the given portfolio.

$$R_p = W_1 R_i + W_2 R_{ii} + ... + W_n R_n$$

where R_p = Expected rate of return in a portfolio

W_1 = Proportion of asset invested in total investment

R_i = Expected rate of return as ith security

n = Number of securities in a given portfolio

Illustration:

The following data relates to the annual rates of returns earned from two stocks, viz., M (an agro-based industry) and W (a construction industry) whose rates of return are perfectively negatively correlated.

Year	Stock M	Stock W
2006	40%	-10%
2007	-10%	40%
2008	35%	-5%
2009	-5%	35%
2010	15%	15%
Average Return	15%	15%
Standard Deviation	22.6	22.6

Solution:

Table 21.12 Portfolio rates of return and risk of M and W

Year	Return on M	Return on W	Portfolio MW Return
2006	40%	-10%	Rp = (0.5 * 0.4) + (0.5 * –0.1) = 0.15 or 15%
2007	-10%	40%	Rp = (0.5 * -0.1) + (0.5 * 0.4) = 0.15 or 15%
2008	35%	-5%	Rp = (0.5 * 0.35) + (0.5 * -0.05) = 0.15 or 15%
2009	-5%	35%	Rp = (0.5 * -0.05) + (0.5 * 0.35) = 0.15 or 15%
2010	15%	15%	Rp = (0.5 * 0.15) + (0.5 * 0.15) = 0.15 or 15%
Average	15%	15%	
S.D.	22.6%	22.6%	

Both the stocks are quite risky if they are held in isolation. But when they are combined to form a portfolio MW, their risk level is low. The rate of returns of these individual stocks move counter cyclically to one another. Statistically, such a relationship is called negatively correlated. Therefore, one conclusion is drawn that a portfolio with negatively correlated stocks reduces the risk significantly.

21.12 RISK-ADJUSTED PERFORMANCE MEASUREMENT

Performance measurement should not be reduced to the evaluation of portfolio returns alone, but must also integrate the measure of risk taken. Several other aspects are also part of performance measurement: *evaluation*, if portfolio managers have succeeded in reaching their objective, i.e., if their return was sufficiently high to reward the risks taken; how they *compare* with their peers; and finally whether the portfolio management *results* were due to luck or the manager's skill.

Portfolio Performance and Risk Adjusted Methods

Modern portfolio theory provides a variety of measures to measure the return on a portfolio as well as the risk. When a portfolio carries a degree of risk, the return from it should be evaluated in terms of risk. More specifically, it is better to evaluate the performance of a fund in terms of return per unit of risk. In case of a well-diversified portfolio the standard deviation could be used as a measure of risk, but in case of individual assets and not so well-diversified portfolio, the relevant measure of risk could be the systematic risk, which can be assessed using the Beta coefficient (β). Beta signifies the relationship between covariance (individual stock and market) and variance of market.

There are three popular measures to estimate the return per unit of risk from a portfolio.

1. Sharpe's Ratio
2. Treynor's Measure
3. Jensen's Differential Returns (Alpha)

Sharpe's Ratio: A ratio was developed by Nobel laureate William F. Sharpe to measure risk-adjusted performance. The Sharpe ratio is the simplest performance measure and is calculated by subtracting risk-free rate such as that of the 10-year Central Bank's bond or G-Sec. from the rate of return for a portfolio dividing the result by standard deviation of the portfolio returns. It measures the return, of a portfolio in excess of the risk-free rate, compared to the total risk of the portfolio. These excess returns, attributable as reward for investing in risky assets, are validated in terms of return per unit of risk. The ratio is calculated as follows:

$$S = \frac{E[R] - R_f}{\sigma}$$

where $E[R]$ = Expected rate of return

R_f = Risk-free rate

β = Portfolio standard deviation

The Sharpe ratio tells us whether the returns of a portfolio are due to smart investment decisions or a result of excess risk. This measurement is useful because although one portfolio or fund can reap higher returns than its peers, it is only a good investment if those higher returns do not come with too much additional risk. The greater a portfolio's Sharpe ratio, the better its risk-adjusted performance will be.

A variation of the Sharpe ratio is *Sortino ratio*, which removes the effects of upward price movements on standard deviation, instead measures only the return against downward price volatility.

Treynor Measure (Reward to Volatility Ratio): This measure was developed by Jack Treynor in 1965. Treynor (helped develop CAPM) argues that, using the characteristic line, one can determine the relationship between a security and the market. Deviations from the characteristic line (unique returns) should cancel out if one is holding a fully diversified portfolio.

Jack Treynor was interested in a performance measure that would apply to all investors regardless of their risk preferences. He argued that investors would prefer a *capital market line* (CML) with a higher slope (as it would place them on a higher utility curve). The slope of this portfolio possibility line is:

$$T_i = \frac{R_m - R_f}{\beta i}$$

where, R = market return; R_f = risk-free return; βi = SD

A larger T value indicates a larger slope and a better portfolio for all investors regardless of their risk preferences. The numerator represents the risk premium and the denominator represents the risk of the portfolio; thus the value, T, represents the portfolio's return per unit of systematic risk. All risk-averse investors would want to maximize this value. The Treynor measure only measures systematic risk – it automatically assumes an adequately diversified portfolio.

(iii) Jensen's Differential Returns (Alpha)

Jensen's measure is an absolute measure of performance, adjusted for risk. This measure assesses the portfolio manager's predictive ability. The objective is to calculate the return that should be expected for the fund given the risk level and comparing it with the actual return realized over a period.

Portfolio alpha (Jensen measure) is obtained by measuring the difference between the return of the portfolio and that of a benchmark portfolio. This measure appears to be the only reliable performance measure to evaluate active management. In fact, we have to distinguish between normal returns, provided by fair reward for portfolio exposure to different risks, and obtained through passive management, from abnormal performance (outperformance) due to the manager's skill (or luck), whether through market timing, stock picking, or good fortune. Performance measured by **alpha**, allows the evaluation of the manager's true performance (but then, only if you assume that any outperformance is due to skill and not luck).

Jensen Measure of Differential Returns with Risk Measured by Beta

The Jensen measure of differential returns for portfolios p(i) and p(ii) is

The model used is: $R_t + R_f + \alpha + \beta + (R_m - R_f) + e$

or

$$= Rp(\text{i}) - Rp(\text{ii}) = (R_m - R_f)\ [\beta p(\text{i}) - \beta p(\text{ii})]$$

where R_t = Average return on portfolio for period t

R_f = Risk-free rate of return for period t

α = Intercept that measures the forecasting ability of the portfolio manager

β = A measure of systematic risk

R_m = Average return on the market portfolio

e = Error term

The variables are expressed in terms of realized return and risk.

Applying the Jensen Measure

This requires that one will use a different risk-free rate for each time interval during the sample period. One must subtract the risk-free rate from the returns during each observation period rather than calculating the average returns and average risk-free rate as in the Sharpe and Treynor measures. Also, the Jensen measure does not evaluate the ability of the portfolio manager to diversify, as it calculates risk premium in terms of systematic risk (Beta). For evaluating diversified portfolios (such as most mutual funds), this is probably adequate. Jensen found that mutual returns are typically correlated with the market at rates above 0.90%.

21.13 PORTFOLIO REVISION

In the entire process of portfolio management, portfolio revision is as important as portfolio analysis, selection and execution. Keeping in mind the risk-return objectives, an investor selects a mix of securities from the given investment universe. In the dynamic world of investment, it is only natural that the portfolio may not perform as desired or opportunities might arise turning the desired into less than the desired outcome. In every such situation, a portfolio revision is warranted.

Portfolio revision involves changing the existing mix of securities/asset class. The objective of portfolio revision is similar to the objectives of portfolio selection, i.e., maximizing the return for a given level of risk or minimising the risk for a given level of return. The process of portfolio revision may also be similar to the process of portfolio selection. This is particularly true where active portfolio revision strategy is followed. Where passive portfolio revision strategy is followed, mechanical formula plans may be used.

Need for Portfolio Revision

No plan can be perfect to the extent that it would not need revision sooner or later. Investment plans are certainly not. In the context of portfolio management, the need for revision is even more because the financial markets are continually changing. Thus, the need for portfolio revision might simply arise because the market witnesses some significant changes since the creation of portfolio.

Further, the need for portfolio revision may arise because of some investor-related factors such as:

(i) availability of additional wealth;
(ii) changes in the risk attitude and the utility function of the investor;
(iii) change in the investment goals of the investor; and
(iv) the need to liquidate part of the portfolio arises from providing funds for some alternative uses.

The other valid reasons for portfolio revision such as short-term price fluctuations in the market also exist. There are, thus, numerous factors, which may be broadly called *market related, regulatory related*, and *investor-related*, which spell the need for portfolio revision.

Portfolio Revision Strategies

There are two broad aspects of portfolio management, namely, *effective investment planning* and *constant review* and *revision of investment*. Constant review and revision of investment requires:

(i) continuous monitoring of quality management of the companies in which investment has already been made;

(ii) continuous financial analysis and trend analysis of the companies' balance sheets, profit and loss account to choose sound companies and offload investment made in companies where the performance is slackening; and

(iii) continuous analysis of the securities market trends.

As there are numerous factors motivating revision of portfolio, so are there numerous strategies of portfolio revision. Broadly speaking, investors may, depending on their investment objectives, skill and resources, follow active or passive strategies for portfolio revision. *Active strategy* of portfolio revision involves a process similar to portfolio analysis, selection and execution which is based on an analysis of fundamental factors covering economy, industries, companies, market related as well as other technical factors. As against this, under *passive strategy* some kinds of formula plans are followed for revision.

Portfolio Revision Practices

In the US, both active and passive portfolio revision strategies have been prevalent. Studies about portfolio revision strategies followed by US investors show that efficient market hypothesis is slowly but continuously gaining believers and these converts revise their portfolio much less often than they were doing previously because of their rising faith in market efficiency. Institutional investors in the US, on the other hand, have shown a definite tendency in the recent past for active revision of their portfolios. This is reportedly motivated by their desire to achieve superior performance by frequent trading to take advantage of their supposedly superior investment skills and resources.

Some research studies undertaken in the US about the market timing and portfolio revision are suggested as follows:

(a) F. Black ("The Capital Asset Pricing Model: Some Empirical Tests") (1972) found that monthly and weekly revision could be a rewarding strategy. Though when transactions costs were considered, the results were less impressive, but of course, still significantly positive.

(b) H.A. Latane et al. ("Quarterly earnings reports and subsequent holding period returns") (1974) concluded that complete portfolio revision every six months would have been a rewarding strategy.

(c) Sharpe ("Mutual Fund Performances", Jan., 1966) wrote: "A manager who attempts to time the market must be right roughly three times out of four, in order to outperform the buy-and-hold portfolio. If the manager is right less often, the relative performance will be inferior because of transaction costs and the manager will often have funds in cash equivalents when they could be earning higher returns available from common stock."

Institutional investors who continue to be dominant in the Indian stock market seem to resort to active portfolio revision mainly for statutory reasons. Another feature of their portfolio revision is that they continue to emphasize individual securities rather than portfolio risk-return changes.

21.14 FORMULA PLANS – FORMULA INVESTING

Investment technique is based on a predetermined timing or asset allocation model that eliminates emotional decisions. One such type of formula investing, called *rupee cost averaging*, involves putting the same amount of money into a stock or mutual fund at regular intervals, so that more shares/units will be bought when the price is low and less when the price is high.

Another formula investing method calls for *shifting funds from stocks to bonds* or vice versa as the stock market reaches particular price levels. If stocks rise to a particular point, a certain amount of the stock portfolio is sold and put in bonds. On the other hand, if stocks fall to a particular low price, money is brought out of bonds and converted into stocks.

Somewhat similar to the constant-rupee plan is the *constant-ratio formula*. It is one of the oldest formulas in existence, having been used as long as 20 years ago. More important, it still stands up today, and is widely used, despite the drastic changes, which have taken place in the market.

Basic Assumptions and Ground Rules of Formula Plan

- The stock prices move up and down in cycle.
- Stock prices and the high-grade bond prices move in opposite directions.
- Investors cannot or are not inclined to forecast direction of the following fluctuations in stock prices, which may be due to lack of skill and resources or their belief in market efficiency or both.

Constant Rupee-Value Plan

It is an investment strategy designed to reduce volatility in which securities, typically mutual funds, are purchased in fixed rupee amounts at regular intervals, regardless of what direction the market is moving.

Rupee Cost Averaging

Periodic investment of a fixed rupee amount, as in a particular stock or fund or in the market as a whole, on the belief that the average value of the investment will rise over time and that it is not possible to foresee the intermediate highs and lows.

Law of average as popularly known; where the investor reduces the cost of acquiring the asset by purchasing at different prices. The systematic investment plans in mutual funds, consistent with periodic new purchases of shares, allows a lower cost per share owned over time.

You invest a fixed amount of money at regular intervals, regardless of whether the market is high or low. This approach reduces the effects of market fluctuation on the average price you pay for your shares.

Investopedia says: "Eventually, the average cost per share of security/per unit will become smaller and smaller. Rupee-cost averaging lessens the risk of investing a large amount in a single investment at the wrong time. In the UK, it is known as "pound-cost averaging" and in the US, it is known as "dollar-cost averaging".

Constant-Ratio Plan

This is an investment strategy in which the portfolio's composition by asset class is maintained at a certain level through periodic adjustments. When the balance is upset, it is periodically restored by moving money from over-performing assets to under-performing ones. This system prevents one asset class from dominating the portfolio. This is one way to maintain a desirable, more balanced portfolio of asset class.

The *constant-ratio plan* specifies that the value of the aggressive portfolio to the value of conservative portfolio will be held constant at the predetermined ratio. This plan automatically forces the investor to sell stocks as their prices rise, in order to keep the ratio of the value of their aggressive portfolio to the value of conservative portfolio constant. Likewise, the investor is forced to transfer funds from conservative portfolios to aggressive portfolios as the price of stocks fall.

Variable-Ratio Plan

Variable-ratio plan is a more flexible variation of constant ratio plan. Under the variable ratio plan, it is provided that if the value of aggressive portfolio changes by certain percentage or more, the initial ratio between the aggressive portfolio and conservative portfolio will be allowed to change as per the predetermined schedule. Some variations of this plan provide for the ratios to vary according to economic or market indices rather than the value of the aggressive portfolio. Still others use moving averages of indicators.

Constraints in Portfolio Revision

A look into the portfolio revision practices as discussed above highlights that there are a number of constraints in portfolio revision, in general and active portfolio revision, in particular. Let us indicate some common constraints in portfolio revision as follows:

(i) Transaction cost
(ii) Taxes
(iii) Statutory stipulation
(iv) No single formula

Limitations

Indeed, none of the formula plans are a royal road to riches. First, as an effort to provide mechanical rules for portfolio revision, they make *no provision* for what securities should be selected for investment. Second, formula plans by their nature are *inflexible*. This inflexibility makes it difficult to know if and when to adjust the plan to new conditions emerging in the investment environment. Finally, in the absence of much faith in the market efficiency, particularly in the developing stock markets, there may *not be many followers* of formula plans for portfolio revision.

Systems and Controls

For managing a portfolio, it is not only the creation, recreation and regrouping of various securities that are important for achieving the desired rate of return, but various kinds of systems and controls are also needed.

Asset allocation

The different asset class definitions are widely debated, but **four** common divisions are "stocks, bonds, real-estate and commodities." The purpose is to reduce the risk by diversifying the portfolio. Asset classes exhibit different market dynamics, and different interaction effects; thus, allocation of money among asset classes will have a significant effect on the performance of the portfolio.

Arguably, the skill of a successful manager resides in constructing the asset allocation, and separately the individual holdings, also the market timing so as to outperform certain benchmarks and stock indices.

Power of Asset Allocation

- Most experienced investors learn that the key to long-term success lies in a coherent strategy for allocation among broad categories of assets for achieving long term financial goals.
- By diversifying across asset classes, one can enhance return potential while minimizing risk.
- Stock selection (or mutual fund selection) and market timing are nearly impossible in the long term.

Importance of Asset Allocation

- Portfolio diversification
- Fund variability
- Reduction of risk
- Risk adjusted returns
- Liquidity

"Keep-it-simple" long term asset allocation models

"Diversify, diversify," asset allocators often say. In fact, in designing low-risk strategies, the starting point for asset allocation, should be to design the best hedge to neutralise risks of failing to meet objectives. Diversification becomes an issue as an investor moves from this "best hedge".

identification of Asset Classes

1. List all available assets
2. Measure returns and standard deviation of returns

3. Form groups from this package such that there is
   - Homogeneity within the group and
   - Heterogeneity across the group

Global Investing

- Investing in a wide range of countries allows investors to reduce the general impact of risks inherent in their respective home markets on their assets and net worth thereof.
- Certain markets have a negative or low corelation with other markets in the world, e.g., Canada and China.

In today's global financial village, it is imperative for a global private banker to help clients with their global financial assets.

21.15 PRIVATE EQUITY

It is useful to think of market in two distinct parts. The first is *start-up venture capital*. The second is market for *leveraged buy-outs of existing businesses*. The market is commonly divided further, with venture capital differentiated between the seed capital and early-stage venture capital, whereas the later stages of investing differentiate between buy-outs and expansion capital. Another important area for private equity fund is the *funding* or *co-financing of public-sector projects*.

Expansion capital may take the form of "mezzanine" financing, which is the riskiest form of debt obligations. It will often have options to convert into equity if the firm fails to meet the terms of its debt, which will be priced to deliver a high rate of return. Mezzanine finance is expensive for companies. Management buy-outs occur when an existing management team is supported with external private equity, for example, when a family business is sold, or a larger firm decides that an existing division is no longer a core business for the parent company.

The word "leverage", a *leveraged buy-out* (LBO), refers to the financing of the deal, when the new private equity owners will have leveraged their equity ownership. This may occur, for example, through the issue of asset-backed loans, the sale of high yield bonds or, where bond or loan covenants are weak, by restructuring the company's balance-sheet such that existing debt becomes devalued and so higher yielding. This focus on the use of leverage is the principal reason private equity should, in general, be regarded as more risky than the quoted equity.

The private companies often look similar to the quoted companies with which they compete. However, this does not mean that the risks for the investors are comparable with those of the stock market. The first difference is *illiquidity*, and the much greater difficulty of transferring a part ownership in a private company than one in a public company. The second is that there are *systematic biases* in the characteristics of private companies compared with the quoted companies (for example, private companies will have a bias towards small and medium sized companies). Nevertheless, it might be thought that the inherent risk or volatility of their aggregate value should be broadly comparable to that of the quoted companies.

After 1999, and early 2000, experience of many private equity investors, as a bias towards new companies in the volatile technology sectors became a feature of many private equity funds, especially venture capital funds. That this occurred is unsurprising, as a bias towards whatever is the latest "new, new thing" will always be a characteristic feature and risk of early-stage venture capital investing.

Individual venture investments will always be subject to considerable stock-specific risk and, diversifying this risk, venture portfolios tend to hold more positions (though they may focus on a particular sector or theme) than buy-out portfolios. The financing structure is critical to the risk of leveraged buy-out investments. Typically, these are, as their name suggests, highly leveraged, more so than otherwise similar quoted businesses. For this reason, the intrinsic volatility of the private equity market, however well diversified, is probably significantly higher than that of the quoted equity market. Investors should not be satisfied with an expected return that does not compensate them for this leverage. Moreover, it makes no sense to pay performance fees simply to leverage an investment portfolio. Any investor can achieve this at minimal cost by buying equity index futures contracts.

Private equity is about exploiting information advantages by identifying entrepreneurial skill. It is not about being financially conservative. It may form a component of an efficient diversified approach to investing, but within that it clearly forms part of an inspirational strategy to accumulate wealth.

This leads to several conclusions.

- Well diversified fund of fund arrangements are likely to diversify precious elements of information advantage.
- If high leverage persists across the funds, intrinsic volatility may still be surprisingly high even with a well-diversified fund of funds.
- It can be entirely appropriate to have a modest allocation to a small number of funds (even from just one team), so long as the combined allocation to private and quoted equity is reasonably balanced.
- A common danger in private equity investing is to fail a quoted diversified equity over time. Once a preferred arrangement has been selected, it makes sense to maintain a commitment to the market over time, most probably staying with the same team (or teams). Otherwise, risks that were particularly prevalent in the market at a particular point in time (for example, high leverage or exposure to particular themes in venture capital investing) will unduly characterize the investor's experience of investing in private equity.

Private Equity Returns

Private equity performance data suffer (as do those for private equity risk) from the absence of market indicators of the value of private businesses. The need to rely on appraisal estimates for interim valuations smoothens the reported performance included in published calendar year performance results. Appraisal valuations are still useful as they provide important management information for investors on what is "work in progress". However, the only private equity performance data that really matters is the **internal rate of return (IRR)** earned on investments. This combines the amount invested, the amount received back and the time interval in between. In substance, these are only financial magnitudes that the investor knows for certain when investing in private equity (or any private investment). The **IRR** is the standard rate of return reported for funds and individual investments, but it is important to note that unrealized investments will be included at an appraisal value in reports of fund **IRRs**.

In mutual fund investing, it is agreed that past performance in league tables is a poor predictor of future league table performance. But in private equity, there have long been suggestions that success is repeatable and there is now increasing evidence from academic research that this may be the case. One of the problems in comparing the performance of private equity managers is the impossibility of obtaining reliable values for private businesses and the difficulty of comparing the performance of a manager, or a private equity fund, with that of the stock market.

Some useful statistics are been given hereunder, for three asset classes Stock, Bond, and Gold. The period chosen is from 1995 to 2012.

Table 21.13 Performance of Three Different Asset Classes 1995 – 2016 (in %)

Year	Stock/Equity	Bond/Debt	Gold	Average Return
1995	–23	3	14	–2
1996	–1	13	–3	3
1997	20	24	–14	10
1998	18	8	8	0
1999	67	16	2	29
2000	–15	13	1	0
2001	–16	25	6	5
2002	3	23	24	17
2003	72	12	13	33
2004	11	–1	1	3
2005	36	6	22	22
2006	40	6	21	22
2007	55	7	17	26
2008	–52	27	31	2
2009	76	–6	19	30
2010	18	6	24	16
2011	–25	6	31	4
2012	28	12	9	16
2013	6	–18	2	–3
2014	32	2	18	17
2015	–4	–6	8	–1
2016	4	11	15	10

Source: Data is historical. Stocks: S & P CNX Nifty; Bonds: I-Sec Sovereign Bond Index Bloomberg and Axis Mutual Fund, India.

As can be seen, except for two years at least two assets delivered positive returns each year. An equally weighted portfolio delivered negative returns only thrice in 20 years. This has happened despite negative returns in various years in stocks, bonds and gold showing the power of true diversification.

Table 21.14 Indian Domestic Investors Portfolio Holding - Total Assets of US $ 6 Trillion (Figure in %), Mar. 2014

Property	Gold	Bank FDs	Insurance	PF & Pension	Equities	Cash
56.10	14.20	15.00	5.20	4.10	2.30	3.10

(Source: RBI, SEBI, CLSA – March, 2014**)**

The above table reveals that Indians' holding of assets is skewed and more tilted towards physical assets, viz., property and gold **(70.30%),** whereas only **26.60%** in financial assets (comprising bank FDs, insurance, PF and pension, and equities).

Table 21.15 Financial Savings of Indian Households - Break-up

Savings & Deposits	(%)	(Value in Rs. lakh crore)
Cur Depo	2.54	4.37
FD/Bond	21.40	36.81
Svg Depo	12.55	21.59
Cash	9.67	16.63
Small Svg	3.83	6.59
P.F.	6.69	11.51
	56.68	97.49
Dir Eq.	17.23	29.64
MF	3.63	6.24
	20.86	35.88
Insurance	14.81	25.47
Pension Fund	2.28	3.92
NRI Depo	4.81	8.27
Alternate Assets	0.45	0.77
International Asset	0.11	0.19
	100	**172.00**

Source: Karvy Private Wealth Report (Financial savings) Dec. 2016, Vol. 7

22 CHAPTER Mutual Fund

Historically, mutual fund investment traces its origin to the early pioneering investments of Scottish and English investors in the American West in the 1800s, and later of the early global portfolio investors in Japan in the 1960s. Globally, mutual funds have been a popular investment option.

Concept of Mutual Fund

Various authors have defined a mutual fund in different ways. According to Pierce ["Deposit Demand, 'Hot Money', and the Viability of Thrift Institutions" (1974)] James L, it is non-depository or non-banking financial intermediary which acts as an 'important vehicle for bringing wealth holders and deficit units together directly."

Fred et al. (1995) in their book *Essential of Managerial Finance* state that mutual funds are corporations that accept dollars from savers and then use these dollars to buy stock, long-term bonds, short-term debt instruments issued by business or government. These corporations pool funds and thus reduce risk by diversification.

The Securities and Exchange Board of India (SEBI) (Mutual Funds) Regulations, 1993 defines a *mutual fund* as a "fund established in the form of a trust by a sponsor to raise monies by the trustees through the sale of units to the public under one or more schemes, for investing in securities in accordance with these regulations."

A mutual fund is a trust that pools the savings of very large number of investors who share a common financial goal and invest in capital market instruments such as shares, debentures, and also in gold as per each scheme's objectives. It is one of the important routes for every investor towards: variety, diversification, capital appreciation, liquidity, less paperwork, convenience, professional management, regulatory oversight and low cost.

Mutual funds are financial intermediaries in the investment business. Funds they collect from investors, and manage on behalf of them "pass through entities" with losses and gains accruing to the investors only. Mutual fund investors receive *pro rata* (in the proportion of their individual investments) shares of earnings from the assets, minus management and other fees. Dividends and capital gains are automatically reinvested. As the portfolios are large, the risks are spread over a large number of investors.

Mutual fund units are investment vehicles that provide means of participation in the stock, bond, gold or property market for people who have neither the time, nor the expertise for analysing, buying, selling and constant monitoring of their personal portfolios, or to undertake direct investment in equities or other assets successfully. Mutual funds also provide a route into specialist market where direct investment often demands more time and updated knowledge than an investor or his financial advisor may possess.

22.1 HISTORY OF MUTUAL FUNDS INDUSTRY IN INDIA

The mutual fund industry originated in India with the introduction of the concept of mutual funds by UTI in the year 1963. As a government monopoly, the industry for 25 years had a stunted growth. Though the growth was slow, but it accelerated from the year 1987 when non-UTI players entered the industry.

The mutual fund industry can be broadly classified into four phases according to the development of the sector.

First Phase (1964-87)

The Unit Trust of India (UTI) was established in 1963 by an Act of Parliament. It was set up by the Reserve Bank of India and functioned under the regulatory and administrative control of Reserve Bank of India. In 1978, UTI was delinked from the RBI and the Industrial Development Bank of India (IDBI) took over the regulatory and administrative control in place of RBI. The first scheme launched by UTI was Unit Scheme 1964.

Second Phase (1987-93) (Entry of Public Sector Funds)

Entry on non-UTI mutual funds: SBI Mutual Fund was the first followed by Canbank Mutual Fund (Dec, 1987), Punjab National Bank Mutual Fund (Aug, 1989), Indian Bank Mutual Fund (Nov, 1989), Bank of India (June, 1990), Bank of Baroda Mutual Fund (Oct, 1992), LIC in 1989 and GIC in 1990.

Third Phase (1993-2003) (Entry of Private Sector Funds)

With the entry of private sector funds in 1993, a new era began in the Indian mutual fund industry, giving the Indian investors a wider choice of fund families. 1993 was also the year in which the first Mutual Fund Regulations came into being, under which all funds, except UTI were to be registered and governed. The erstwhile Kothari Pioneer (now merged with Franklin Templeton) was the first private sector mutual fund registered in July, 1993.

Fourth Phase (Since February, 2003)

This phase was a bitter experience for UTI. It was bifurcated into two separate entities. One is Specified Undertaking of the Unit Trust of India with Asset Under Management (AUM) of Rs. 29,835 crores (as on January, 2003). The Specified Undertaking of Unit Trust of India, functioning under an administrator and under the rules framed by Government of India and does not come under the purview of Mutual Fund Regulations.

The second is the UTI Mutual Fund Ltd., sponsored by SBI, PNB, BOB and LIC. It is registered with SEBI and functions under the Mutual Fund Regulations. With the bifurcation of the erstwhile UTI, which had in March, 2000 more than Rs. 76,000 crore of AUM and with the setting up of a UTI Mutual Fund, conforming to the SEBI Mutual Fund Regulations, and with recent mergers taking place among different private sector funds, the mutual fund industry has entered the current phase of consolidation and growth.

22.2 ORGANISATION OF MUTUAL FUNDS

A mutual fund can be constituted either as a corporate entity or as a trust. In India, UTI was set up as a corporation under an Act of Parliament in 1964. Indian banks when permitted to operate mutual funds were asked to create trusts to run these funds. The basic difference between corporation and a trust is that in the case of the former, the liability is limited whereas in case of latter, it is unlimited.

Also, a corporation enjoys the status of separate legal entity that can act on its own behalf. A trust established by one or more sponsors has to work on behalf of its trustees, akin to the promoter of a company, and hold its property for the benefit of the unit holders. Indian banks operating mutual funds had made a convincing plea before the government to allow their mutual funds to constitute them as 'Asset Management Companies'. The Department of Company Affairs, Ministry of Law, Justice and Company Affairs issued guidelines in respect of registration of Asset Management Companies (AMCs), in consultation with Securities and Exchange Board of India (SEBI), as follows:

(a) **Approval of AMC by SEBI:** As per guidelines, AMC shall be authorised for business by SEBI on the basis of certain criteria and the Memorandum and Articles of Association of the AMC would have to be approved by SEBI. Accordingly, no company can register an AMC under the Companies Act, 1956 without the Memorandum and Articles of Association being approved by SEBI.

(b) **Authorised Capital of AMC:** The primary objective of setting up of an AMC is to manage the assets of the mutual funds and other activities, which it can carry out, such as, financial services consultancy, which do not conflict with the fund management activity and are only secondary and incidental. That being so, it may not be practical to expect a company to be set up with a paid up capital of Rs. 10 crore to carry on only incidental activities, without any assurance of its receiving an approval from SEBI to act as an Asset Management Company for a Mutual Fund. There should, therefore, not be any objection in registering an AMC if the authorised capital of such a company is approved by SEBI.

Other major players who play a part in running a mutual fund are as follows:

a. Registrar and Transfer Agents

Their major responsibilities include:

1. Receiving and processing the application form of a mutual fund,

2. Issuing of unit/share certificates/account statement on behalf of mutual fund.
3. Maintain detailed records of unit holders transactions.
4. Purchasing, selling, transferring and redeeming the units/shares.
5. Issuing of income/dividend warrants, broker cheques/crediting brokerage directly into bank account, etc.
6. Creating security interest on units/shares for allowing loans against them.

b. Advertiser

Major responsibilities include:

1. Helping mutual fund organizers to prepare a media plan for marketing the fund/scheme.
2. Issuing/buying a space in newspapers and other electronic media for advertising the various features of a fund/scheme.
3. Arranging hoardings at public spaces.

c. Advisor/Manager

It is generally a corporate entity that does the following jobs:

1. Professional advice on the fund's/scheme's investments,
2. Advise on asset management services.

d. Trustees

They provide overall management services, and are responsible and accountable for performance and regulatory compliance of mutual fund affairs and charge management fee.

e. Custodian

A custodian is again a corporate entity carrying out the following jobs:

1. Holds securities.
2. Receives and delivers securities,
3. Collects income/interest/dividends on the securities,
4. Holds and processes cash.

Besides the above, there are other players also:

(a) Fund administrator
(b) Fund accounting services
(c) Legal advisors
(d) Fund officers
(e) Designated analysts
(f) Underwriters/distributors

Dynamics in the Mutual Funds

There are fundamental dynamics in the Indian mutual fund industry, such as: The trend towards open ended funds, and the awareness among individual investors about how mutual funds work and the value they add.

Table 22.1 The Nest-Eggs

Features	Mutual Fund	Pension Scheme	Provident Fund
Investor	Individual	Individual	Company
Objective	Variety of purposes	Retirement planning	Retirement planning
Time horizon	Variable	Long term	Long term
Participation	Voluntary	Voluntary	Mandatory
Contribution	Initial and/or regular	Regular	Regular
Pre-mature exit	At will	At will	Penalised
Tax concessions	ELSS and RGESS	At investment only	Yes (EEE)
Fund manager's discretion	Highest	Medium	Limited
Investment products	Equity, debt, gold, cash and alternate	Equity and debt	Debt
NAV publication	Daily	Daily for equity option	Not applicable

Advantages of Investing in Mutual Funds

By investing in various mutual fund schemes, small investors or middle-income investors seek the following advantages compared to other types of investments:

1. Investment variety and spread in different industries.
2. Capital appreciation without having to watch the upward or downward performance curves of different scrip.
3. No impulsive decision-making regarding purchase or sale of share/securities, since the funds are managed by professionals and expert, who have access to the latest detailed information regarding the stock market and individual scrips.
4. Liquidity through buyback arrangements of the mutual fund or listing on some stock exchanges after a certain lock-in period.
5. Even the smallest dividend or capital gain gets reinvested, thus enhancing the effective return.
6. Freedom from paperwork.
7. Tax benefits on invested amounts/returns or dividends/capital gains.

Apart from the above, other advantages of mutual funds are:

- Portfolio diversification
- Management of risk through widespread among asset class and different time horizon
- Liquidity
- Convenience, transparency and flexibility
- Professional management, and low cost
- Regulatory oversight
- The emergence of a class of educated/certified intermediaries who will advise and recommend mutual funds as financial planners/counsellors rather than mere Meaning of 'purveyors' is-supplier (in the context of only selling financial products)./agents/sellers of financial products
- Rating of various mutual fund schemes by independent agencies as investors look for an unbiased source of information on the performance.

The combined effect of all the above factors will result in more benefits to investors.

Drawbacks of Mutual Funds

- **No Guarantee:** No investment is risk-free. If the entire stock market declines in value, the value of mutual fund shares will go down as well, no matter how balanced the portfolio is.

  Investors encounter fewer risks when they invest in mutual funds than when they buy and sell stocks on their own. However, anyone who invests through a mutual fund runs the risk of losing money.
- **Fund management expenses:** All funds charge administrative fees to cover their day-to-day expenses. Some funds also charge sales and marketing 'load' to compensate distributors, brokers, financial planners.
- **Management Risk:** When one invests in a mutual fund, he/she depends on the fund's manager to make the right decisions regarding the fund's portfolio. If the manager does not perform as you had hoped, one might not make as much money on his/her investments as expected.

Of course, one can invest in index funds, and can forego management risk, because these funds do not employ active strategy and fund manager's role is limited to follow index stocks.

Investment (including mutual fund) is a money game with risks and returns. Investors need to play the game carefully and achieve a right tradeoff between the risks and returns. Otherwise, there are chances he/she will end up getting stuck between the bulls and bears.

22.3 CLASSIFICATION AND TYPES OF MUTUAL FUND SCHEMES

A wide variety of mutual fund schemes exists to cater to the needs such as financial position, risk tolerance and return expectations, etc. These can be classified in different types as explained below:

By Structure: Open-ended, close-ended and interval schemes

By Investment Objective: growth, income, balanced and money market schemes

Other Schemes: Tax saving and special schemes

Open-end Mutual Fund: Here, the fund is ready to sell new units and repurchase issued units. An investor can buy or redeem units from fund at a price based on the Net Asset Value (NAV) per unit. It does not have a fixed maturity date. Unit capital of fund is not fixed.

Close-end Mutual Fund: It makes a one-time sale of fixed number of units, offered in an NFO only. Units are redeemed upon maturity. Units have to be compulsorily listed on a stock exchange in order to provide liquidity. The size of a listed closed end fund is kept constant.

Medium-to Long-Term Funds

Equity growth funds: Invest in equities of growth stocks that exhibit and promise above average growth of earnings of over a period of time.

- **ELSS funds:** The investment into ELSS qualify for deduction under section 80-C of Income-tax Act and comes with a lock-in period of 3 years.
- **RGESS funds:** First time investors into market get additional benefit under section 80-CCG of Income-tax Act, which also comes with a lock-in period.
- **Income funds:** Invest in fixed income generating debt instruments, issued by government, public and private companies, banks, financial institutions and other entities.
- **Balanced and MIP funds:** It is a hybrid category, whereby allocation is made into equity (20% to 65% and Debt 35% to 80%) as per scheme's objectives.
- **PE Dynamic funds:** Here on a periodic basis, fund house adjusts scheme's asset allocation as per some defined criteria (e.g., PE ratio) whereby volatility is reduced.
- **Indexed funds:** It mimics the underlying index (e.g., S & P BSE or Nifty-50) and the fund manager's role is passive since it follows the index portfolio.
- **Exchange traded funds:** It offers the best features of open and closed mutual fund schemes. It can be purchased and sold at real time price rather than NAV.
- **Gold exchange traded funds:** Here the underlying asset is gold. The advantages are low cost, transparency in price, option to hold it in electronic form.

- **Thematic and sectoral funds:** It invests in a narrow segment and/or in a particular sector of the market (e.g., pharma, banking, infrastructure, PSU, etc.)
- **Fixed maturity plans:** These debt schemes have a defined maturity from 3 months to 3 years and money is compulsorily returned to investors at the closure of fund. Units are listed on a stock exchange for liquidity to the investors.
- **Overseas opportunities/international diverse equity funds:** Mostly these are feeder funds which invest the funds of local investors into a country/region specific equity scheme, thus providing diversification of various and different countries/locations/geography.
- **Off-shore funds:** It has non-residential investors and are regulated by the provisions of the countries where these are registered. Further, these funds are governed by the rules and their performance is approved and monitored by the Department of Economic Affairs, Ministry of Finance and the directives of RBI.

Short-Term Funds

In order to reduce interest risk, some mutual fund schemes are mandated to invest in debt securities with short maturity, say around 1 year or so.

Liquid funds: The investment is made into most liquid assets (e.g., 90 days Treasury Bills, Certificate of Deposit, Commercial Paper, etc. These can be encashed at short notice; they offer low return and the capital is mostly safe.

- ***Arbitrage funds:*** Arbitrage funds typically look for small, marginal difference in price between two platforms or between two markets and trade simultaneously to make 'Gain'.

22.4 RGESS

Rajiv Gandhi Equity Savings Scheme (RGESS), is a tax saving scheme announced in the Union Budget 2012-13 (Para 35) and further expanded vide Union Budget 2013-14 (Paras 61 & 144). The scheme is designed exclusively for first time individual investors in securities market, whose gross total income for the year is below a certain limit. In 2013-14, the income ceiling of the beneficiaries was raised to Rs. 12 lakh from Rs. 10 lakh specified in 2012-13. The investor would get under Section 80CCG of the Income Tax Act, a 50% deduction of the amount invested during the year, up to a maximum investment of Rs. 50,000 per financial year, from his/her taxable income for that year, for three consecutive assessment years.

Objective

As announced in the Union Budget 2012-13, the objective of the scheme is to encourage the flow of savings and to improve the depth of domestic capital markets. This would help in promoting an 'equity culture' in India. The scheme aims at widening the retail investor base in the Indian securities markets and also furthers the goal of financial stability and financial inclusion.

Legal Provision

A new section 80CCG in the Income Tax Act, 1961 on 'deduction in respect of investment under an equity savings scheme' was introduced vide Finance Act, 2012 and amended vide Finance Act, 2013, to give tax benefits to 'New Retail Investors' whose gross annual income is less than or equal to Rs. 12 lakh, for investments in 'eligible securities' up to Rs. 50,000 in a single financial year, for three consecutive assessment years.

The details of the RGESS were first notified on 23 November, 2012 (Section No. 2777(E); Notification No. 51) and vide subsequent corrigendum dated 5 December, 2012 (Section No. 2835(E); Notification No. 53) by Department of Revenue. The operational guidelines were issued by SEBI on 6 December, 2012. Subsequent to the Union Budget 2013-14, Section 80CCG was amended vide Finance Act, 2013, to expand the scope of the Scheme. The notification dated 23 November, 2012 was accordingly amended vide notification dated 18 December, 2013 (Section No. 3693 (E); Notification No. 94).

Linked Savings Scheme (ELSS) vs RGESS

ELSS and RGESS are entirely different schemes: They pertain to different asset classes with ELSS offering passive investment avenues. ELSS is meant for indirect participation in the stock market, whereas RGESS aims at encouraging direct participation in the stock market. The operational differences are given below.

Table 22.2

ELSS	RGESS
Investments are to be strictly in mutual funds	Investments are to be made directly in listed equity.
100% deduction (up to Rs. 1,00,000) is allowed under ELSS	Only 50% deduction of the investment made (up to max. of Rs. 25,000 in any one year) is allowed under RGESS.
ELSS benefits can be availed by an investor every year	RGESS benefits are limited to the new investors and can be availed for only 3 consecutive years.
The ELSS benefit is coming under Section 80C of the IT Act which has an aggregate limit of Rs. 1,00,000 for all such eligible instruments like LIC policy, PPF, etc.	RGESS deduction is available under Section 80CCG. This is a separate investment limit exclusively for RGESS, over and above the Section 80C limit of Rs. 1 lakh.
Lock-in period of 3 years	Lock-in period of 3 years. However, trading allowed after one year, subject to conditions.
Since investments are in mutual funds, it is perceived to be less risky.	Since investments are in equity, risk is perceived to be higher.

Who all will be covered under RGESS Scheme? Who is a new investor?

The scheme is open for all *new retail investors* who have gross total income less than or equal to Rs. 12 lakh. A new retail investor is one:

- who is a resident individual (the benefit cannot be availed by Hindu Undivided Family (HUF) corporate entities/trusts etc.);
- who has not opened a Demat account and has also not done any trading in the derivative segment till RGESS account opening date or the first day of the "initial year" in which he brings in the RGESS eligible investment into the account, whichever is later; and
- who has opened a Demat account and has not made any transactions in equity and/or in the derivative segment till designating such account as RGESS or the first day of the "initial year" in which he brings in the RGESS eligible investment into the account, whichever is later.

In case of joint accounts, only the first account holder will not be considered a new retail investor. In case of joint accounts, only the first account holder will not be considered a new retail investor. All or other joint holders or nominees of the existing account holders will be considered new retail investors for the purpose of opening of a fresh RGESS account, if otherwise eligible.

In case the Demat account is opened as a first holder, but there are no transactions in the equity or derivative segment, then the first account holder is eligible to be a new retail investor.

For taking the benefits under RGESS, the new retail investor will have to submit a declaration, as in Form 'A', to the depository participant (DP) at the time of account opening or designating his existing Demat account.

Eligible securities, which are brought thereafter into such an account, will be automatically subject to lock-in up to a value of Rs. 50,000, unless the investor specifies otherwise through Form 'B' specified in this regard.

22.5 IMPORTANT POINTS TO CONSIDER WHILE INVESTING INTO MUTUAL FUND SCHEMES

Mutual fund is one of the best investment tools for the retail investor as it offers the twin benefits of good returns and also the choice of equity, debt, gold or combination of two or more asset class in a single scheme. Following are important points to be kept in mind.

Past Performance: While past performance is not an indicator of future, it does throw light on investment philosophies of the fund, how it has performed in the past and kind of returns it is offering to the investor over a period of time in future. One also needs to check out 1, 2, 3, 5 years returns for consistency. How did fund perform in the bull and the bear markets in the immediate past? These are some aspects an investor must take into consideration at the time of investing.

Know Your Fund House and Fund Manager: The success of a fund to a great extent depends on the fund manager as well as on company's processes of selecting sector/stock and quantum of amount invested, with its research team.

Does it suit your risk profile?: One needs to have the knowledge of risk, risk appetite, time horizon and expectation of return, while selecting a particular mutual fund scheme.

Read the scheme prospective information document: The prospective says a lot about the fund. Reading of the fund's prospective/information document provides its investment strategy and the risk that it will expose you to.

What it costs you?: A fund with high costs must perform better than a low-cost fund to generate the same returns for you. Finally, avoid picking a fund simply because it has shown spurt in value in current rally. Ferret out information of a fund for at least three to five years.

Independent Ranking and Rating

- Several research agencies use the daily NAV information, and disclosures in the fact sheets, to rate and rank mutual funds.
- Various funds are categorised for such rankings, based on their objectives, so that comparisons can be made with the same peer group.
- Both quantitative and qualitative measures are used, and a final ranking depends on the overall score of a fund.
- More information on fund rankings can be found at: www.valueresearchonline.com

Net Asset Value (NAV)

The performance of a particular scheme of a mutual fund is denoted by Net Asset Value (NAV). NAV is the market value of securities held by each scheme. Since the market value of the securities/assets change every day, the NAV also varies on a day-to-day basis. The NAV per unit is the market value of securities/assets (minus liabilities accrued) of a scheme divided by the total number of units of the scheme on any particular day.

NAV is calculated as follows:

Fair market value of Scheme's Investments + Receivables + Accrued income + Others

$$\text{NAV} = \frac{\text{Assets} - \text{Accrued expenses} - \text{Payables} - \text{Other liabilities \& provisions}}{\text{Number of units outstanding}}$$

Mutual funds have become a major vehicle for mobilization of saving particularly from the household sectors for investment into various markets in many parts of the world. In view of its growing importance, it has become necessary to evolve a comprehensive set of prudential guidelines for the all-round development and regulation of mutual funds and for ensuring investor protection.

The mutual fund industry the world over has undergone a profound transformation since 1990s. The changed operating environment for the mutual fund sector, underpinned by globalization, deregulation, advances in information technology and awareness has resulted in intense competitive pressures. Mutual funds have responded to this challenge by diversifying through organic growth, innovative new products and building trust with the investors.

Mutual fund advisors/distributors market their schemes through Systematic Investment Plan' (SIP). The issue of wrong timing is supposed to be addressed by averaging purchases, which is known as 'SIP'. SIP works on the strategy of *rupee cost-averaging*. Study also compares public sector and private sector mutual funds on the basis of their performance using Sharpe and Treynor ratios.

Due diligence on MF-Asset Management Companies (AMCs):

- ☐ Focus on various qualitative parameters such as AMCs pedigree, assets under management, service capabilities, etc.
- ☐ Regular interaction with AMC marketing/product team/fund managers for appraising any change in investment process.
- ☐ Quarterly update on the fund in terms of the fund manager's view on the fund.

Selection parameters:

- ☐ Pure return/performance parameters considered: six months, 1, 3 and 5 years return
- ☐ Greater importance provided to consistency of outperformance. Other parameters are:

Equity		Debt	
Sector Allocation	Standard Deviation	Yield to Maturity	Exit load
Jenson's Alpha	Stock Selection	Modified Duration	Expense Ratio
	Average Maturity		Credit Rating of Papers

Recommendation/Suggestion: Mutual funds provide investors a mixture of **liquidity, return and safety** in accordance with scheme objectives *vis-a-vis* its performance. For many investors mutual funds is a preferred route as it serves a link to stock markets whereby savings thus mobilized, are invested in diversified portfolio of stocks.

With a view to strengthening the position, specifying accountability and protecting the interest of investors, SEBI has defined the roles of Chief Executive Officer and Fund Manager of mutual funds.

Regulatory practices should be fair to all concerned in the marketplace. In order to enhance fairness, a uniform cut-off time for calculating and applying NAVs, both for subscription and redemptions have been prescribed.

Skewed holdings in mutual fund schemes may lead to distortion. To avoid any distortion in the unit holding pattern and its impact, minimum number of investors in a scheme has been prescribed. Further, it has been specified that no single investor should hold more than 25% of the corpus of any scheme/plan.

Opportunities for investing have been widened for mutual funds by allowing them to invest in derivative securities. They have also been permitted to invest up to 10% of the net assets as on January 31st of each year in foreign securities with the limit of minimum US $ 5 million and maximum of US $ 50 million.

22.6 Return on Investment in Mutual Fund

The investor who invests in mutual fund units can receive returns in the following ways:

Capital Appreciation: Profit earned on sale of units at a higher NAV than the original cost.

Income Distribution: When a fund makes a profit on its investment, this profit will be (*dividend*) given to investor as a dividend which can be reinvested in the fund or retain it in the form of cash.

Return on Mutual Fund

$$r = \frac{(\text{NAV}t - \text{NAV}t - 1) + \text{I}t + \text{G}t}{\text{NAV}t - 1}$$

where r = Return on mutual fund

NAVt = Net asset value at the time period t

NAV$t - 1$ = Net asset value at the time period $t - 1$

It = Income at the time period t

Gt = Capital gain distribution at the time period t

Required Return on Mutual Fund Investment (as a percentage)

$$R_2 = \frac{1}{\text{1-Initial expenses (\%)} * R_1 + \text{Recurring expenses (\%)}}$$

where R_1 = Personal return of investor

R_2 = Mutual fund earnings

Effective Yield on Mutual Fund Investment

$$\frac{\text{Dividend} + \text{Capital Appreciation}}{\text{Initial Investment}} \times \frac{365}{\text{No. of Days}} \times 100$$

Illustration:

Mr. SBK has invested in three mutual fund schemes as per the information given below:

Table 22.3

Particulars	MF A	MF B	MF C
Date of investment	12/1/2009	1/1/2010	3/1/2010
Amount of investment	50,000	100,000	50,000
Net asset value (NAV) at entry date	10.50	50.50	120.30
Dividend received up to 31-03-2010	950.00	1600.00	Nil
Unit NAV as on 31-03-2010	10.40	51.50	119.50

Calculation of Effective Yield on per annum basis in respect of three mutual fund schemes to Mr. SBK up to 31-03-2010

Particulars	MF A	MF B	MF C
(a) Investment	50,000	100,000	50,000
(b) Number of units	4761.9048	1980.1980	415.6276
(c) Unit NAV as on 31-03-2010	10.40	51.50	119.50
(d) Value of investments on 31-03-2010	49523.81	101980.20	49667.50
(e) Increase/decrease in investments	-476.19	1,980.20	-332.50
(f) Dividend received	950.00	1600.00	0.00
(g) Total yield ($e + f$)	473.81	3580.20	-332.50
(h) Number of days of investment	122	91	31
(i) Effective yield p.a.	2.84%	14.36%	-7.83%

Table 22.4 An illustration showing how *XIRR* is used to obtain CAGR

Date	Transaction	Amount
15-Jan-10	Purchase - XYZ Income Fund	-10000
14-Feb-10	Purchase - PQR Equity Fund	-15000
22-Mar-10	Purchase - ABC FMP	-10000
15-Nov-11	Dividend - XYZ Income Fund	900
04-Jan-12	Dividend - PQR Equity Fund	1000
02-Apr-12	Redemption - ABC FMP	11000
14-Apr-12	Redemption - PQR Equity Fund	6000
31-Dec-12	Current value of XYZ Income Fund	12000
31-Dec-12	Current value of PQR Equity Fund	14000
	CAGR obtained using XIRR function	**10.29%**

Compounded Annual Growth Rate (CAGR) in Mutual Funds

- Mutual funds use CAGR to compute returns for the fund and benchmark for periods longer than one year. Can be used efficiently to show long-term returns to investors.
- Investors can use the CAGR to show returns for longer period, using XIRR
  (a) XIRR refers to rate of return an investor makes (when information are for different dates and multiple outflows & inflows has taken place) from his/her total mutual fund portfolio. It enables simple use of CAGR in practice.
  (b) Takes into account all transactions and different holding periods of investor.

22.7 ROLE OF MUTUAL FUNDS IN THE INDIAN STOCK MARKET

Mutual fund usually plays an important role in the development of the capital market since they are an ideal vehicle for investment by retail investors.

- MF pools the investment of small investors together, thereby increasing participation in the stock market.
- MFs being institutional investors can better analyse various economy/industry/company related situations and related factors generally not available or accessible to individual investors, thereby providing informed decisions to the small investors.
- MFs can diversify portfolio in a better way due to its expertise of managing relatively large amounts/bigger corpus.
- Growing interest of investors in the equity market over the years could also be gauged from the resources mobilised by mutual funds.

Mutual funds in India, because of their small size and slower growth in the recent past, have tended to play only a limited role in the stock market. The share of mutual funds in total turnover of the stock markets (BSE + NSE), which was 4.9 per cent in January 2000, increased to 12.5 per cent by January 2008. However, this constitutes less than 12.28 per cent of GDP which is very low in comparison with about 39 per cent in Brazil, 45 per cent in Korea and 82 per cent in USA.

One of the major reasons for this is that the penetration of mutual funds, especially in the rural areas remains small. According to the survey carried out by SEBI-NCAER (2000), mutual funds have been found to be popular mainly with the middle and high income groups and have not been found to be an attractive investment avenue for the low income groups.

Thus, if the mutual funds have to grow fast, they would need to devise appropriate schemes to attract the saving of low income groups, especially in rural areas. This would ensure participation of all categories of investors into the capital market, which is so crucial for its long-term development. Mutual funds with large funds at their disposal are also required to act as a counterweight to FIIs, which generally exerts a significant influence on the stock market.

Table 22.5 Status of Mutual Funds Industry in India for the Period Apr - Sept 2014

		No. of Schemes	No. of Folios	Funds Mobilized	Repurchase/ Redemption	Net Inflow (+ve)/ Outflow(–)	Net Assets as on September	Average Asset under Management
		Total	Total	Total	Total	Total	Total	
				Rs. Crore	Rs. Crore	Rs. Crore	Rs. Crore	
A	INCOME/DEBT ORIENTED SCHEMES							
i	Liquid/Money Market	53	318160	5105768	5075173	30595	184525	290694
ii	Gilt	47	50937	2020	2890	-869	5619	5570
iii	Debt (other than ass. re)	1252	6760955	224819	256686	-31867	454495	459189
iv	Debt (assured return)	0	0	0	0	0	0	0
v	Infrastructure Development	4	29	188	0	188	1120	1117
	Sub total	**1356**	**7130081**	**5332795**	**5334748**	**-1954**	**645759**	**756570**
B	GROWTH/EQUITY ORIENTED SCHEMES							
i	ELSS	52	6098912	2278	2898	-619	32813	33023
ii	Others	335	23586895	67280	33490	33790	247585	246533
	Sub total	**387**	**29685807**	**69559**	**36388**	**33171**	**280397**	**279556**
C	BALANCED SCHEMES							
i	Balanced schemes	26	1830761	3632	2110	1522	18277	18063
D	EXCHANGE TRADED FUND							
i	GOLD ETF	14	479142	46	1024	-978	7277	7397
ii	Other ETFs	29	216931	3295	4241	-946	4737	4952
	Sub total	**43**	**696073**	**3341**	**5265**	**-1924**	**12013**	**12349**
E	FUND OF FUNDS INVESTING OVERSEAS							
i	Fund of funds investing overseas	31	166285	465	763	-298	2968	3075
F	Fund of Funds Scheme (Domestic)	42	847514	1886	1691	195	5913	6028

Contd.

	GRAND TOTAL*	**1843**	**39509007**	**5409791**	**5379274**	**30517**	**959414**	**1069613**

No. of schemes also includes serial plans.

Note: Erstwhile UTI has been divided into UTI Mutual Fund (registered with SEBI) and the Specified Undertaking of UTI (not registered with SEBI). Above data contains information only of UTI Mutual Fund. *The grand total is not the aggregation of subtotal. Further, the sum of number of investors for each scheme type will not match the subtotal under each scheme type as investors may be common across different schemes of different mutual funds. In addition, the above table is collation of unique investors from individual fund houses.

Source: SEBI, October 2014

Table 22.6 Asset Under Management & Folios Category-wise Aggregate (On Sept. 30, 2014)

Types of Schemes	Investor Classification	AUM (Rs. Cr)	% to Total AUM (Rs. Cr)	No. of Folios	% to Total No. of Folios
Liquid/Money Market	Corporates	151982.01	82.36	25677	8.07
	Banks/FIs	13037.45	7.07	681	0.21
	FIIs	899.68	0.49	77	0.02
	High Net worth Individuals*	15682.12	8.5	50975	16.02
	Retail	2924.04	1.58	240750	75.67
	Total	**184525.3**	**100**	**318160**	**100**
	Grand Total	**184525.3**		**318160**	
Gilt	Corporates	3433.7	61.11	2687	5.28
	Banks/FIs	32.1	0.57	31	0.06
	FIIs	7.31	0.13	2	0
	High Net worth Individuals*	1769.83	31.5	4852	9.53
	Retail	375.75	6.69	43365	85.13
	Total	**5618.7**	**100**	**50937**	**100**
	Grand Total	**190144**		**369097**	
Debt Oriented	Corporates	253667.85	55.68	104179	1.54
	Banks/FIs	5241.04	1.15	1053	0.02
	FIIs	4433.39	0.97	36	0
	High Net worth Individuals*	158522.86	34.79	604893	8.95

	Retail	33749.98	7.41	6050823	89.5
	Total	**455615.11**	**100**	**6760984**	**100**
	Grand Total	**645759.11**		**7130081**	
Equity Oriented	Corporates	34260.56	12.22	147366	0.5
	Banks/FIs	888.88	0.32	842	0
	FIIs	4249.8	1.52	74	0
	High Net worth Individuals*	77862.89	27.77	494546	1.67
	Retail	**163135.26**	**58.18**	**29042978**	**97.83**
	Total	**280397.4**	**100**	**29685806**	**100**
	Grand Total	926156.51		36815887	
Balanced	Corporates	2249.11	12.31	11374	0.62
	Banks/FIs	50.83	0.28	59	0
	FIIs	0	0	0	0
	High Net worth Individuals*	6788.4	37.14	46234	2.53
	Retail	9188.18	50.27	1773094	96.85
	Total	**18276.53**	**100**	**1830761**	**100**
	Grand Total	**944433.04**		**38646648**	
Gold ETF	Corporates	3665.8	50.38	4010	0.84
	Banks/FIs	2.71	0.04	5	0
	FIIs	2.96	0.04	4	0
	High Net worth Individuals*	1087.18	14.94	7282	1.52
	Retail	2517.93	34.6	467841	97.64
	Total	**7276.58**	**100**	**479142**	**100**
	Grand Total	**951709.61**		**39125790**	
ETFs (other than Gold)	Corporates	752.66	15.89	5628	2.59
	Banks/FIs	2144.57	45.28	30	0.01
	FIIs	329.71	6.96	20	0.01
	High Net worth Individuals*	851.05	17.97	3737	1.72
	Retail	658.77	13.91	207516	95.66

Contd.

	Total	**4736.75**	**100**	**216931**	**100**
	Grand Total	**956446.37**		**39342721**	
Fund of Funds investing Overseas	Corporates	596.44	20.1	1392	0.84
	Banks/FIs	0.01	0	1	0
	FIIs	0	0	0	0
	High Net worth Individuals*	1662.78	56.03	11068	6.66
	Retail	708.56	23.87	153824	92.51
	Total	**2967.79**	**100**	**166285**	**100**
	Grand Total	**959414.16**		**39509006**	
* Defined as individuals investing Rs. 5 lakhs and above					

(Source: AMFI, September 2014)

The above table gives us interesting information about number of folios vs. AUM of three important classes of investors:

Table 22.7 Industry AUM & Folios Category-wise as on Mar. 31, 2017

Category	Number of folios	% to total folios	AUM (Rs. Cr)	% to total AUM
Retail	37980191	96.13	213258.47	22.23
HNIs	1223587	3.10	264227.11	27.54
Corporate	302313	0.77	450608.13	46.97

Table 22.8 Investor Category-wise MF AUM & Folios – A Summary

Types of Schemes	Investor Classification	AUM (Rs. Cr)	% to Total AUM	No. of Folios	% to Total Folios
Liquid/Money Market	Corporates	270599.6	86.15	34547	4.38
	Banks/FIs	11797.35	3.76	607	0.08
	FIIs	53.03	0.02	20	0
	High Net worth Individuals*	25836.6	8.23	87428	11.08
	Retail	5799.3	1.85	666258	84.46
	Total	**314085.89**	**100**	**788860**	**100**

Gilt	Corporates	9124.77	61.34	5073	5.89
	Banks/FIs	173.33	1.17	62	0.07
	FIIs	219.9	1.48	14	0.02
	High Net worth Individuals*	3831.29	25.76	10709	12.43
	Retail	1525.94	10.26	70324	81.6
	Total	**14875.23**	**100**	**86182**	**100**
Debt Oriented	Corporates	434466.92	58.26	134678	1.48
	Banks/FIs	10686.91	1.43	1750	0.02
	FIIs	8673.65	1.16	63	0
	High Net worth Individuals*	224630.57	30.12	917325	10.05
	Retail	67232.87	9.02	8070797	88.45
	Total	**745690.91**	**100**	**9124613**	**100**
Equity Oriented	Corporates	78564.33	14.45	331176	0.81
	Banks/FIs	896.19	0.16	740	0
	FIIs	3329.82	0.61	106	0
	High Net worth Individuals*	174322.45	32.07	1171529	2.87
	Retail	286428.43	52.7	39322660	96.32
	Total	**543541.22**	**100**	**40826211**	**100**
Balanced	Corporates	10163.12	11.99	50505	1.42
	Banks/FIs	98.75	0.12	89	0
	FIIs	64.62	0.08	6	0
	High Net worth Individuals*	44114.51	52.04	306595	8.64
	Retail	30321.99	35.77	3191717	89.94
	Total	**84762.99**	**100**	**3548912**	**100**
Gold ETF	Corporates	2503.04	45.68	2498	0.69
	Banks/FIs	13.03	0.24	6	0
	FIIs	0.79	0.01	1	0
	High Net worth Individuals*	1035.11	18.89	7243	1.99
	Retail	1927.84	35.18	354362	97.32
	Total	**5479.81**	**100**	**364110**	**100**

Contd.

ETFs (other than Gold)	Corporates	37113.02	83.52	10805	1.96
	Banks/FIs	2633.76	5.93	41	0.01
	FIIs	336.97	0.76	15	0
	High Net worth Individuals*	1652.61	3.72	6847	1.24
	Retail	2699.28	6.07	533309	96.79
	Total	**44435.64**	**100**	**551017**	**100**
Fund of Funds investing Overseas	Corporates	345.94	19.8	708	0.65
	Banks/FIs	0.01	0	1	0
	FIIs	0	0	0	0
	High Net worth Individuals*	792.61	45.36	4846	4.42
	Retail	608.73	34.84	104171	94.94
	Total	**1747.29**	**100**	**109726**	**100**
	Grand Total	**1754618.99**		**55399631**	

* Defined as individuals investing Rs. 5 lakh and above

Table 22.9 AUM in percentage as on March, 2017

Category	AUM (in %)
Individuals	54.1%
Institutions	45.9%

Source: AMFI website

The Way Forward

The future of mutual funds in India is inextricably linked to the growth of the Indian economy, savings and investment patterns, government policy towards private sector and the development of capital market. The government has provided the initial impetus for launching funds by providing tax concessions and tax exemptions. The creators of the funds are trusted banks with a good track record. The first step has, therefore, been taken very carefully, ensuring success and building up investor confidence in the new instrument.

Mutual funds in India have a significant and centrestage role to play in spreading equity cult. The wider range of products/services offered by funds will make the investor quality conscious. And, private sector has been in the forefront in mobilising savings, through mutual funds by offering tailor-made solutions for the variety of product baskets to the investor. Towards this, following measures need to be implemented to move forward.

Measures towards improvement

- Greater clarity to the role of trustees.
- Allow mutual funds to invest through specialized schemes in real estate, money market instruments, mortgage-backed securities, securitised debt and gilt-edged instruments.
- Unit holders to be given voting rights to be exercised specifically in matters such as change in investment policy and fee structure.
- Diversification of operations by AMCs. They should be allowed to undertake related activities such as portfolio management services and offshore funds.
- Fund managers of close ended schemes may be permitted, with some safeguards, to trade on their own account to bring down market price-NAV gaps (discounts).
- Mutual funds should be permitted to borrow in certain cases, subject to ceiling and cost related parameters.
- Voting rights for mutual funds in companies in which they have substantial holding.

Some of the key prerequisites for success in the Indian mutual fund space are: innovating marketing, brand building, distribution network, usage of state of the art technology, high quality of fund management and persistent good track record, skilled manpower, robust risk management, targeting different stakeholders (including low-income groups in rural areas), continuous research, and a well-oiled sales and management machinery.

23

Insurance Planning

CHAPTER

Insurance is a form of risk management used to primarily transfer risks. It means transferring risk from one entity to another.

"Pooling of fortuitous losses by transfer of such risks to insurers, who agree to indemnify insured for such losses, to provide other pecuniary benefits on their occurrence, or to render services connected with the risk may be termed *insurance planning*." (American Risk and Insurance Association)

23.1 MEANING OF RISK

Risk implies a condition where there is a possibility of *an adverse deviation* from a desired outcome.

Meaning of Risk Management

Identifying potential risks and making decisions so as to reduce the possibility and/or impact of the risks. It is a systematic approach to analyzing risk and evaluating methods that will reduce the impact in the event the risk turns into reality, e.g., loss of life, damage to an asset (house, car, etc.).

Objective

The objective of risk management is to avoid, minimize or control the impact of losses to an individual due to sudden accident/catastrophe that may be caused to him/her.

Methods of Risk Management

1. **Avoidance:** Trying to avoid the risk as far as possible through measures which are not hazardous.
2. **Reduction:** Steps taken for reduction in chances and severity of the losses.
3. **Retention:** Keeping or retaining the risk with oneself.

4. **Transfer:** Handing over one's risk to someone else. A commercial and most important form of 'transfer' of risk is through *insurance*.
5. **Sharing:** Having common purpose called *risk sharing pools* to which every member would contribute his/her share. It is a private arrangement.

Personal Risk Management: Risk Control and Risk Financing

'Risk control' measures intend to minimize the risk to which an entity is exposed to. This is accomplished by avoiding the action that gives risk to risk. Avoiding risk is an appropriate strategy for high severity risk. It includes restraining self from such conditions or action which might carry risk. An example would be not buying a property or doing business in order to not take on the liability that comes with it.

Another would be not flying in order not to take risk that the airplane might be hijacked. Avoidance may seem the answer to all risks, but avoiding risks also means losing out on the potential gain that accepting (retaining) the risk may have allowed. Not entering a business to avoid the risk of loss also avoids the possibility of earning profits.

Protecting your Wealth

While one cannot predict the outcome of a "financial decision", by careful analysis and preparation, the **risk** can be mitigated.

Normally, one is concerned with "**pure risks**" that can cause financial insecurity, the type of which are categorized as: Personal, Property and Liability Risks.

(i) Personal Risks: Risk of premature death, poor health, temporary or permanent disability, and insufficient income during retirement.

(iii) Property Risks: Personal property possesses the risk of getting damaged or destroyed or lost due to different causes. Two major losses it creates are: direct loss, and indirect or consequential loss.

(iii) Liability Risks: They arise from the possibility of being held legally liable for the loss to another reason. Further it is categorized into:

- Statutory liability, e.g., third party liability in Motor Vehicle Act; Workmen Compensation Act, etc.
- Under common law, e.g., libel and slander
- Under contract, i.e., contractual obligations.

These liabilities may arise in personal or professional capacity.

Concept of Risk Financing

Paying for the losses in case an eventuality occurs is called risk financing. The retention of risk can be voluntary or involuntary. There are two ways to finance risk: (a) Retain, and (b) Transfer.

23.2 INSURANCE

Insurance transfers the risk from an individual to a group. It provides an important means of ensuring risk from interfering with a client achieving his/her financial objectives.

Insurance is a contract between two parties – the *insurer* (the insurance company) and the *insured* (the person or an entity seeking the cover) wherein the insurer agrees to pay the insured for financial losses arising out of any unforeseen events in return for a regular payment of 'premium'.

Insurance can be used as a tool to shield an individual against potential risks like travel accidents, death, unemployment, theft, property destruction by natural calamities, fire mishaps, unintentional public liabilities, etc.

Characteristics of Insurance

- **Pooling of losses:** Spreading of losses incurred by a few over the entire group so that, in the process average loss is substituted and shared for actual loss. Grouping of large number of similar exposure units helps operation of law of large number of similar perils.
- **Law of Large Numbers:** "Greater the number of exposures, the more closely will the actual results approach the probable results that are expected from an infinite number of exposures." Advantage of law of large numbers is sharing of losses and prediction of future losses. Large group of similar units, need not be identical, are subject to the same peril or group of perils.
- **Fortuitous losses:** A fortuitous loss is unforeseen, unexpected and occurs as a result of chance. This could be accidental, unintentional and at random.
- It is essential that the person insuring must be the **one who will suffer should the loss occur.** It means a person can insure his own asset/property, but he/she cannot insure his/her friend's asset or property.
- **Determinable and measurable:** Loss should be definite as to *cause, time, place* and the *amount*. It must involve loss which can be measured in actual money rather than, for example, sentimental or emotional value.
- **Chance of loss must be calculable:** Insurer must be able to calculate loss with some accuracy, average frequency and average severity of future losses.
- **Premium must be economically feasible:** Premiums should not only be affordable but also less than the value of the policy.
- **Not to be catastrophic:** Large proportion of exposure units should not incur losses at the same time.
- **To be insurable**: It must not be against public policy to have that insurance protection. For example, in the public good, allowing for insurance protection against a fine imposed by the court. A fine is a penalty to be met by the offender

and it would contravene what society considers right and proper if a person could take out a policy of insurance to pay such fine.

- **Risk transfer:** Risk which involves the chances of loss or no loss but never a gain is referred to as *pure risk*. It is transferred from insured to insurer, who typically is in a stronger financial position to pay the loss than the insured himself/herself.
- **Indemnification:** Insured is restored to his or her approximate financial position prior to the occurrence of the loss. This characteristic of the insurable risk is that 'it does not involve any prospect of **gain** or **profit**'.

Insurance thus, is the means by which those unfortunate enough to be the victim of some financial loss can gain reasonable compensation.

Principles of Insurance

Utmost good faith is a positive duty voluntarily to disclose, accurately and fully, all facts or materials to the risk being proposed.

Insurable interest is the financial interest of the proposer by which he stands benefited by the safety or continuous existence of an asset, and the damage to that asset results in loss of a legal right or creation of legal liability for him.

The following are other principles of insurable interest towards various conditions:

Contract of Alienator	: Uncertain event
Contract of Unilateral	: only "insurer" makes a promise
Contract of Conditional	: Restrictions
Contract of Personal	: Freely assigned
Contract of Adhesion	: Must be accepted in "total" by the insured

Creation of Insurable Interest

(a) By Common Law, e.g., person owning a house
(b) By Contract – It arises by virtue of a contract entered into
(c) By Statue – An act of parliament may create an insurable interest by granting some benefit or imposing some duty.

Assignment: It refers to transfer of title of the policy from one insured to another.

Nomination: Nominee has the right to receive the policy proceeds payable to him, BUT does not have any right to sue the insurer.

Requirements of an Insurance Contract

Offer and acceptance, Consideration, Competent parties, Common intention, Legal purpose.

These are few important requirements for anyone to buy any insurance policy in India, and as governed by IRDA.

Advantages of Insurance

- **Indemnification of loss:** It restores individuals to their former financial condition. As a result, it reduces the amount of disruption that such losses would otherwise cause.
- **Reduction of anxiety:** It reduces stress and anxiety as individuals need not worry about financial insecurity in case of adverse events.
- **Sources of investment funds:** The premium collected by the insurance companies are accumulated and invested. This promotes capital investment and aid in economic growth.
- **Loss prevention:** Since insurance companies benefit if incidence of loss does not occur, they actively promote best practices for loss prevention amongst the insured.
- **Enhancement of credit:** Insurance makes a borrower to command credit risk because it acts as collateral to the lender. The lender knows that in case of any adverse event which causes financial losses or affects the income potential of the borrower, the insurer will restore the borrower to his formal financial position.

Disadvantages of Insurance

- **Costs of doing the business:** The costs for the administration, sales, marketing, etc., incurred by the insurers for the purpose of doing business are also recovered.
- **Fraudulent claims:** Many insured submit fraudulent claims to insurance companies by faking losses resulting in the increased cost of insurance affecting all others insured.
- **Inflated claims:** While the loss is actual and accidental, many policy holders inflate the severity of the loss so as to profit from insurance, and this would again lead to high premiums for all the insured.
- **Time and effort** in indemnifying right insurer, right amount of coverage and negotiation of premium.
- **Lax attitude** may creep in.

23.3 FUNCTIONS OF INSURANCE

1. Primary Functions

(i) *Provide protection* against future risks, accidents and uncertainties. Insurance cannot check the realization of risk, but can certainly provide for the losses of risk. Insurance is actually prevention against economic loss, by sharing the risk with others.

(ii) *Collective bearing of risk:* Insurance is a means by which a few losses are shared among larger number of people. All the insured contribute the premium towards a fund and is paid to the people who incur a loss due to the occurrence of an insured risk.

(iii) *Assessment of risk:* Insurance determines the probable volume of risk by evaluating various factors that give risk. Risk is the basis for determining the premium rate also.

2. Secondary Functions

(i) *Prevention of losses:* Insurance cautions individuals and businessmen to adopt suitable devices to prevent unfortunate consequences of risk by observing safety instructions; for example, installation of automatic sparker or alarm systems, etc. Prevention of loss causes lesser payment to the insured by the insurer and this will encourage for more savings by way of premium. Reduced rate of premiums stimulate for more business and better protection to the insured.

(ii) *Small capital to cover larger risks:* Insurance relieves the businessmen from security of investments, by paying small amount of premium against larger risks and uncertainties.

(iii) *Contribution towards the development of larger industries:* Insurance provides development opportunity to those larger industries having more risks in their set up. Even the financial institutions may be prepared to give credit to sick industrial units which have insured their assets including plant and machinery.

3. Other functions

(i) *Means of savings and investment:* Insurance serves as savings and investment; insurance is a compulsory way of savings and it restricts the unnecessary expenses by the insured. People also invest in insurance for the purpose of availing income-tax exemptions (benefits).

(ii) *Source of earning foreign exchange:* Insurance is an international business. The country can earn foreign exchange by way of issue of marine insurance policies and various other ways, like for example, permitting joint venture with foreign insurance company (as one of the business partners) who bring in capital in terms of FDI.

(iii) *Risk-free trade:* Insurance promotes exports, which makes the foreign trade risk free with the help of different types of policies under marine insurance cover.

23.4 TYPES OF LIFE INSURANCE / RISK COVERS

1. Term Cover

Term insurance is a *pure risk cover product*. It pays a death benefit only if the policy holder dies during the period for which one is insured. Term insurance generally offers the cheapest form of life insurance. Term life insurance provides for life insurance coverage for a specified term of years for a specified premium. The policy does not accumulate cash value.

The three factors to be considered in terms insurance are: a) sum assured (death benefit); b) premium to be paid (cost); and c) length of coverage (term). Various insurance companies sell term insurance with many different combinations of these three basic parameters. The term can be for one or more years. The premium can remain at a level or increase depending on each term insurance policy type and the contract.

2. Endowment

It is a *level premium plan* with a savings feature. At maturity, a lump sum is paid equal to the sum assured (plus bonus). If death occurs during the term of the policy, then the total amount of insurance and any bonus accrued are paid out.

Endowments are considered most expensive (in terms of annual premiums) than either whole life or universal life. In India, endowment insurance is a popular plan providing protection to self and the family. It serves as a source of financial needs during active life. It also acts as one of the tools for retirement planning.

There are a number of products in the market that offer flexibility in choosing the term of the policy; one can choose the term from 5 to 30 years. There are products in the market that offer non-participating (no profits) version, the premiums for which are cheaper.

3. Whole Life Insurance

It provides life insurance cover for the *entire life of the insured person* or up to a specified age (age varies from company to company). Generally, the premium payable remains the same throughout the tenure of policy period.

Whole life insurance is mainly devised to create an estate for the heirs of the policy holders. It is also suitable for people of all ages who wish to protect their families from financial crisis that may occur owing to the policy holder's sudden and untimely death. However, the primary disadvantages of whole life are *premium inflexibility* and the *internal rate of return (IRR) remaining lower* and may not be competitive with other saving alternatives. Riders (clause or a condition) can be availed to increase the death benefit by paying additional premium. Alternatively, death benefit can also be increased through the use of policy bonuses.

4. Unit Linked Insurance Plans (ULIP)

Unit-linked insurance plan or market-linked plan (ULIP) is a financial product that offers life insurance as well as investment in the financial markets. Unit-linked insurance plans invest in a basket of securities (including the listed shares of companies), which allows to choose between investment options predominantly in equity or debt or a mix of both.

One major advantage of ULIPs is that they leave *asset allocation decision* in the hands of investors themselves. Investors have *total control* of how to distribute investible funds among the investment products. ULIPs typically have charges like: premium allocation, fund management, policy administration, mortality, etc. Investors are advised to refer, read investment strategy to understand asset allocation under ULIP.

In the market, there are a few variants of ULIP available:

(a) Unit Linked Endowment Plans: Here one can conveniently choose flexible payment tenure (say, pay premium for first 10 years only) and can continue to avail life cover for another 10 years. Similarly, one has the freedom to choose asset allocation and then change it depending upon market conditions or owing to life stage, multiple times during policy period.

(b) Unit Linked Children's Plans: This is another variant of ULIP with some unique features that are offered in this kind of policy:

(i) option of double-death or triple-death benefit (double or triple the sum assured) if the particular rider is opted; and

(ii) options to make withdrawals once the child completes certain age or for his/her educational needs after some stage (for example: after 10th, 12th, graduation, etc.).

5. Pension Plans

Pension plans or *retirement plans* are those in which normally an investor invests till his/her retirement period. Thereafter, monthly pension (annuity) is paid from the funds so accumulated. However, one more option at the vesting age is: a person can withdraw 1/3rd of his/her corpus in lump sum (for various needs he/she may have) and the balance 2/3rd is paid compulsorily paid as pension according to the option chosen. The following are various annuity options:

(a) Annuity for life

(b) Joint life last survivor annuity

(c) Joint life last survivor with return of purchase price

(d) Annuity guaranteed for certain periods

(e) Life annuity with return of purchase price

(f) Increasing annuity

6. Keyman Insurance

Keyman insurance offers the employer protection in the event of the untimely death or disability of a key person – a CEO, a CFO, a CMO or owner of a business. Any person can be a key person who has specialized skills and whose loss can cause a financial strain on the company. Keyman insurance provides a financial cushion to the company for:

- loss of sales affected;
- cost of recruiting and training a suitable replacement;
- delay of business projects; and
- arrangement of timely funds at competitive/cheaper rates.

23.5 LIFE INSURANCE: NEED ANALYSIS

Human Life Approach/Human Life Value (HLV)

The *human life value* is the present value of the person's future earnings. Human life value of any person can be measured by capitalized value of that part of his income or income earning capacity devoted or meant for dependents arising out of economic forces incorporated within his being, like character, health, education, training, experience and ambition.

It is usually calculated by taking into account a number of factors including but not limited to the insured individual's age, gender, planned retirement age, occupation, annual income, employment benefits, as well as the personal and financial information of the spouse and/or dependent children. This method is typically used for families with working family members, and in its relation to spouse or dependent children.

While using this method, one needs to remember to include only the post-tax pay (net) and then make adjustments for personal expenses, add value for health insurance or other employee benefits (as applicable) to the income figure so arrived.

Information Required

- The number of years the individual is likely to earn (retirement age – present age).
- Average annual earnings during the 'earning years'.
- Amount of personal expenses, e.g., tax deductions in employment, life insurance premium, hobbies, etc.

Method of Calculation

Example: Shyam is earning Rs. 12 lakh p.a. and expects his income to increase by 5% every year. He also expects a growth of 10% p.a. on his investments. He has 18 years of working life left as he would like to retire at the age of 58. He has existing investments (assets) worth Rs. 40 lakh and a house worth Rs. 60 lakh. Calculate insurance as per human life approach.

Table 23.1

Income growth	**5%**
Expected return on savings	10%
No. of working years left	18
Current income	Rs. 12,00,000
Human Life Value	Rs. 13,611,561

Year	Income
1	1200000
2	1260000
3	1323000
4	1389150
5	1458608
6	1531538
7	1608115
8	1688521
9	1772947
10	1861594
11	1954674
12	2052407
13	2155028
14	2262779
15	2375918
16	2494714
17	2619450
18	2750422
NPV at 10%	Rs. 13,611,561

Life insurance still required is Rs. 1.36 crore as HLV considers only replacement of income. However, for practical purposes, the value of investments may be deducted from the insurance requirements to reduce the insurance value and consequently cost as well.

Need Based Approach

This is a method calculating how much life insurance is required by an individual/family to cover their needs (i.e., expenses). These include things like funeral expenses, legal fees, estate, gifts and taxes, probate fees, medical deductibles, emergency funds, mortgage expenses, rent, debt and loans, college, childcare, schooling and maintenance costs, etc. The need based approach uses two variables:

1. How much will be needed at death to meet obligations?
2. How much future income is needed to sustain the household?

While calculating expenses, one is advised to overestimate the needs a little (slightly more). Since if it is underestimated, person will not realize his/her mistake until it's too late. One also needs to be careful in overestimating, as compounding over long period would mean much higher outgo of premium.

Needs are divided into three types:

- *Cash Needs* – Funeral expenses, uninsured portion of medical bills, legal charges, etc.
- *Income Needs* – Income for the family
- *Special Needs* – Debt, children's education, marriage, contingencies, etc.

What is already available to meet these needs?

Investments and deposits; death benefit from employer; existing life insurance; and other assets.

Method of calculation:

Example: Mr. Ashwin Kumar, a businessman has given the following expenses. Calculate amount of insurance required on need based approach. He also has investments worth Rs. 25 lakh and a house worth Rs. 60 lakh

Table 23.2

Current expenses	**20000**
Less: Insurance premium paid	2500
Less: EMI	2500
Net Expenses	**15000**
Less: Proportion of personal expenses	10%
Personal expenses	1500
	13500
Age of dependent	26
Life expectancy of dependent	85
Annual expenses	162000
Expected inflation	7%
Expected return	9%
No. of years	59
Expense protection	8773197
Liability protection	800000
Total insurance required	**9573197**

Rs. 95.73 lakh – Rs. 25 lakh = Rs. 70.73 lakh needed as life cover to provide adequate protection to his dependent.

Few things to consider while choosing the right insurance company:

1. **Product price (premium and charges):** One needs to compare the prices and various charges involved in life insurance policy one intends to buy. Make sure

that the insurance company offers a pricing that complements your need and it must not overshoot your budget.

2. **History:** One needs to look at track record of any insurance company, *e.g.* how long the company has been in business, claim settlement ratio, and so on. One can also refer to the website of IRDA and insurer ratings that are available with the respective company.
3. **Service Quality:** Here one needs to evaluate approach and attitude of an insurance company and its officials with respect to answering any query, listening to customers, resolving issues (if any), and so on. If the company and its people remain engaged in sales pitch only without understanding the needs, then it is best to avoid them.
4. **Some financials:** It is worth to check out the crucial numbers like new premium mobilized, business growth, market share, total assets, the ability to settle claims, etc. It also makes sense to look out for the number of complaints or bad reviews a company may have.

23.6 NON-LIFE/GENERAL INSURANCE

General insurance business in India was nationalized w.e.f. 1st January, 1973 by the General Insurance Business (Nationalization) Act, 1972. More than 100 non-life insurance companies including branches of foreign companies operating within the country were amalgamated and grouped into four companies, *viz.* New India Assurance Company Ltd; National Insurance Company Ltd; United India Insurance Company Ltd; and Oriental Insurance Company Limited with their head offices in Mumbai, Kolkata, Chennai and New Delhi respectively.

General Insurance Corporation (GIC) which was the holding company of these four public sector general insurance companies has since been delinked from the latter and has been approved as the "Indian Reinsurer" (insurance company transferring all or part of the risk by some contract to another insurance company) since November 3, 2000. The share capital of GIC and that of four companies are held by the Government of India. All the five entities are government companies registered under the Companies Act.

Principle of indemnity: It is the mechanism by which the insurer provides financial compensation in an attempt to make good the loss suffered by the insured.

There are two corollaries to the principle of indemnity – subrogation and contribution.

Subrogation is the right of an insurer, having indemnified the insured, under a legal obligation to do so, to stand in the place of that (insured) and avail himself (insurer) of all the rights and remedies of that other, whether already enforced or not.

Contribution is the right of the insurer to call upon others similarly (but not necessarily equally) liable to the same insured to share the cost of an indemnity payment.

An insurance policy is designed to provide compensation only for losses that are caused by "insured perils".

- What is the root cause of the loss?
- Is the peril indemnified above, specifically covered under the insurance policy?

Proximate cause (direct, most dominant and effective) is the active efficient cause that sets in motion a train of events which bring about a result, without the intervention of any force started and working independently from a new source.

Suppose a fire breaks out in a building containing a library but is swiftly brought under control by firemen. However, the water used by the firemen to control the fire, damages the books.

CAUSE: It is "fire" only. This is so because the water would not have been sprayed on the books if the fire had not broken out.

23.7 SOME PRODUCTS IN NON-LIFE INSURANCE

Property Insurance: Property insurance provides protection against fire, theft, etc. Property insurance generally means insuring the structure and the contents of the building against natural and manmade disasters. Property insurance covers fire, burglary, theft, etc.

Following are excluded (and not covered) under property insurance:

- Wilful destruction of property
- Loss/damage due to wear and tear
- Art and antiques

Motor Insurance: Under motor insurance, the insurer indemnifies the insured in the event of accident caused by or arising out of the use of the motor vehicle anywhere in India against all sums including claimant's cost and expenses which the insured becomes legally liable to pay in respect of:

(i) death or bodily injury to any person;

(ii) damage to the property other than property belonging to the insured or held in trust or custody or control of the insured.

The insurance of motor vehicle against damage is not made compulsory but the insurance of the third party liability arising out of the use of the motor vehicle in public is made compulsory. No motor vehicle can ply in public place without motor insurance.

Health Insurance–Mediclaim Policy: Health insurance protects the policy holder and his/her family against any financial contingency arising due to a medical emergency. Earlier only group insurance was available but now a lot of innovations have been introduced. The claim is reimbursed to those patients (policy holders) who are admitted in a hospital for treatment that require at least 24-hour stay in a hospital. However, in some cases where patients (policy holders) cannot be admitted to the hospital, domiciliary treatment at home is considered with a lower amount of reimbursement. Medical expenses incurred 30 days prior and 60 days after hospitalization are covered under the policy.

Any one illness will be deemed to mean continuous period of illness and it includes relapse within 45-days from the day of discharge from the hospital. Thereafter, it is treated as fresh insurance. Normal exclusions include all diseases/injuries which are pre-existing at the time of taking the cover. However, some policies cover pre-existing diseases as well after a specified period of time.

Health Insurance – Critical Illness: This policy provides for a lump sum benefit to be paid if insured contracts certain specified diseases such as cancer, heart attack, stroke, kidney failure or multiple sclerosis (one is advised to refer to policy terms and conditions). However, there is no payment in case of death of a policy holder; thus, it differs from life insurance. The lump sum amount received under the policy can be used by the insured in a manner which he thinks fit and thus free to use it. Critical illness policies are available either with life insurance policies as rider or as standalone policies and as many as 30 critical illnesses (as specified) can be covered.

Personal Accident Insurance: This type of policy provides that if the insured shall sustain any bodily injury resulting solely and directly from accident caused by external violent and visible means, then the insurer shall pay to the insured or his legal/personal representative, as the case may be, the sum or sums set forth, in the policy. Below mentioned conditions are covered under personal accident insurance.

1. Permanent total disablement
2. Permanent partial disablement
3. Temporary total disablement

In the event of any of the above or combination of any such disablement that occurs, for which insured is not able to (not in a position to) resume his normal duty, the policy holder would get 1% of sum insured for maximum of 100 weeks, provided he/she obtains and submits the medical certificate from a qualified doctor.

Liability Insurance: The purpose of liability insurance is to provide indemnity in respect of damages payable under the law for personal injury to third party or damages to their property. This legal liability may arise under common law on the basis of negligence or under any statutory law on no fault basis, i.e., when there is no negligence.

"No occupation is at once idler and more fruitful than entertaining one's own thoughts." –Montaigne

24 Retirement Planning

CHAPTER

Retirement planning is an essential element of any financial/investment plan and is a comprehensive process for determining how much money you will need when you retire. It also helps you identify the best ways to save for retirement given your financial situation. The necessities and desires in life do not cease with retirement and there will have to be a form of substitution for his/her current income which may allow an individual to maintain similar standard of living. The planning which goes into substitution of this income constitutes the core of retirement planning.

A proper retirement planning requires longer period of time – from the day you start working until well beyond your actual retirement date. In fact, it's never too early to start planning for your retirement. Varied factors impact the planning such as, current age, retirement age, life expectancy, investment horizon, number of dependants, the dependency period, risk profile of the person, how much money will be required to cover his (and his family's) monthly expenses—areas of personal interest, medical costs, etc.

Each person's situation is unique with respect to life cycle stages, financial goals and risk profiles and so, retirement planning isn't a 'one-size-fits-all' plan. Retirement planning is an on-going process. The undernoted steps summarise essence of sound retirement planning:

- Analyse your current financial situation.
- Identify your future financial needs/goals/requirements.
- Compute the gap between your current financial position and future financial requirements.
- Fill the gap by creation of an asset allocation through one's savings and a basket of retirement products that would generate regular income and capital protection over a period of time. Shifts in asset allocation before and during retirement as part of overall retirement plan.
- Monitor the retirement plan at regular intervals.

A. Types of annuities, pension plans,

B. NPS

C. Reverse mortgage and features of available products

24.1 TWO APPROACHES IN RETIREMENT PLAN

A good retirement plan provides adequate corpus for the sunset years without compromising on the standard of living of the person. It also involves smart *selection of retirement products* not only to save for retirement but also to help save on taxes. The process of approximating one's retirement needs can be done in two ways:

(a) Expense method or 'expense protection' method
(b) Income replacement method

(i) Expense Protection Method

Under this method, monthly/annual expenses of the person (just before retirement) are estimated. The figure so arrived at is adjusted for inflation rate and the concluding amount indicates the corpus required by the person upon retirement which should be able to generate regular income equal to the expenses so arrived at.

In many cases, the monthly/annual expenses required by the person on retirement is taken as percentage of the monthly/annual expenses of that person just before retirement – the assumption being that one's post-retirement expenses will not include certain expenses (such as transport, home loan EMI, etc.) and so, it would be a lesser amount than his expenses just before retirement or it is assumed that he/she will take a lifestyle shift once retired.

Expense protection is a slightly cumbersome method due to detailed listing out of expenses as many people do not keep a tab/record of each and every expense incurred, the lack of which would make determination of retirement corpus inaccurate. The process involves preparing a list of pre- and post-retirement (current and future) expenses and arriving at the total expense list.

Following are the steps involved in calculating retirement needs through expense protection method:

Step 1: Find out 'current annual expenses' (including insurance premiums and loan EMIs)

Step 2: Determine present value of 'post-retirement expenses'

Step 3: Add step 1 and 2

Step 4: Deduct work related expenses from step 3

Step 5: The amount so arrived in step 4 is to be inflation adjusted corpus and must last as long as the 'dependency period' (post-retirement period).

Common 'Post Retirement' Expenses

1. Food and clothing
2. Housing
   (a) Rent

(b) Property tax, property maintenance and repairs
(c) Home insurance

3. Utilities
   (a) Gas
   (b) Electricity
   (c) Water
   (d) Telephone, mobile, internet
   (e) TV/Cable, DTH bills
4. Transport (local conveyance)
5. Insurance premium
   (a) Medical
   (b) Personal accident
   (c) Motor
6. Income tax
7. Liabilities
   (a) Personal loans
   (b) Vehicle loans
   (c) Credit card payment
8. Recreation
   (a) Travel
   (b) Dining out
   (c) Hobbies
9. Miscellaneous expenses (not part of the above expenses)

Income Replacement Method: This is another method of estimating one's retirement needs. Here, instead of estimating retirement needs on an individual's numerous and limitless expenses, his/her 'income just before retirement' is considered. It works on the premise that a certain percentage of the 'income just before retirement' will be sufficient for rest of the person's retired life.

Sources of 'Post-Retirement' Income

1. Savings and retirement proceeds from investments
2. Pension annuity from employer and/or insurer/mutual fund
3. Post-retirement job to supplement income, e.g., teaching, part-time consultancy, etc.
4. Reverse mortgage
5. Regular income from investments in form of dividend and interest
6. Other sources

Inflation-adjusted return and nominal return on investments

While calculating the retirement needs, one should necessarily factor inflation into the working of expenses. It is important to understand two terms at this stage:

(a) **Nominal rate of return**: Rate at which money invested grows.

(b) **Real rate of return**: Rate at which the purchasing power of an investment increases.

To protect your retirement savings against inflation, one needs to earn return more than the inflation. The portfolio must consist of instruments that give regular returns, as well as those that offer scope for capital appreciation.

Rate of return on an investment after adjusting for inflation effect:

$$\text{Inflation-Adjusted Return} = \frac{(1 + \text{Return})}{(1 + \text{Inflation rate}) - 1}$$

Gratuity

Gratuity is a part of salary that is received by an employee from his/her employer in gratitude for the services offered by the employee in the company. Gratuity is defined benefit plan and is one of the many retirement benefits offered by the employer to the employee upon leaving the job or completing his/her service contract period. An employee may leave his/her job for various reasons, such as retirement/superannuation, for a better job elsewhere, on being retrenched or by way of voluntary retirement.

How does Gratuity work?: An employer may offer gratuity out of his own funds or may approach a life insurer in order to purchase a group gratuity plan. In case the employer chooses a life insurer, he has to pay annual subscription as decided by the insurer. The employee is also free to make contributions to his/her gratuity fund. The gratuity will be paid by the insurer based upon the terms of the group gratuity scheme (contract).

Provident Fund

There are many investment vehicles in our country for the purpose of saving for one's retirement. But the most popular one among them has been 'provident fund'. For a long time, provident fund has been the primary investment vehicle for an individual's retirement nest until the entry of mutual funds and other new innovative products such as ULIP (unit linked insurance plan), and so on.

Provident fund is considered a debt instrument as majority (at least 90%) of the corpus is invested in debt. Let us understand now the working of the provident fund.

A fixed sum (%) is deducted from employee's salary as contribution to provident fund.	Employer also contributes his/her share to the provident fund.

The money so pooled is invested in various instruments, majority is debt.

(i) On maturity, an employee gets his contribution + Employer's contribution and interest accrued thereon and/or before maturity (due to premature withdrawal, death of the deposit holder, etc.)

(ii) In case of death of the deposit holder/employee, the sum so accumulated is paid to his/her legal heirs.

Types of Provident Fund

(a) Statutory Provident Fund

(b) Recognised Provident Fund

(c) Unrecognised Provident Fund

(d) Public Provident Fund

Let us understand the types and differences between them through the following table:

Table 24.1

	Statutory Provident Fund	Recognised Provident Fund	Unrecognised Provident Fund	Public Provident Fund (PPF)
What is it?	SPF was set up under the provisions of the Provident Act, 1925. It is maintained by the central, state governments and their establishments.	RPF is recognised by the Commissioner of Income Tax. The Employees' PF (EPF) and Miscellaneous Provisions Act, 1952 apply for RPF.	This type of PF is not recognised by the Commissioner of Income Tax.	This type of PF is covered under the PPF Act, 1968.
It covers whom?	All employees of central and state governments, and government establishments.	It automatically covers any establishment that employs 20 and more persons. Establishments with less than 20 are free, and encouraged to join RPF.	N.A.	All individuals (whether salaried, self-employed, employed or not) and minors (through individuals acting as their guardians).

24.2 TYPES OF RETIREMENT/PENSION PLANS

A pension plan is nothing but an annuity. Both terms are used interchangeably. Typically, annuities are bought to income during one's retired life, which is why they are called pension plans. Pension plans are *perfect investment instruments* for a person who after retiring from service has received a large sum as superannuation benefit. One can pay for a pension plan either through an annuity or through instalments that are annual in most cases.

The two most common types of pension plans are: (a) Defined Contribution (or the money purchase plan) and (b) Defined Benefit plan. Sometimes these two plans are combined and the combination is thus known as *hybrid plans* or *combination plans*.

Defined Benefit (DB) Plans: In these kinds of plans, the benefit to be paid to the employee is defined or fixed at the beginning of the plan, e.g., final year's salary multiplied by number of years of service. Here the employer funds the plan and the employee reaps the rewards upon retirement. The employer has to use actuarial assumptions like retirement age, mortality, expected life span, expected compensation increase and other demographic assumptions to estimate the pension liability and accordingly contribute to the pension plan.

From an employer's perspective, defined benefit plans are an on-going liability. Returns on the plans are assumed and estimated in such a way to get the desired pay-out to the employee. The investment risk is borne by the employer in the defined benefit plan.

Defined Contribution (DC) Plans: This is also known as *money purchase plan*. Under this plan, the contribution to the pension plan by the employee is fixed (say 12% of salary) and the same is matched by the employer. The money is placed in the investment instruments selected by the beneficiary in his/her investment account. After the person retires, these investments along with interest are used to buy pension or annuity.

However, under DC plan, one cannot be sure of the final pension amount at retirement. Ultimately, the pension benefit that a person is going to receive after the retirement will depend upon the performance of the investment made. Unlike a DB plan, where the employee knows exactly what his or her benefits will be upon retirement, there is no such certainty regarding investments in DC plan.

Apart from pension plans of employers, there are two broad categories of pension plans from life insurers in India: *Traditional endowment policies* and *unit-linked policies*. They differ primarily in the way the money of the policy holder is invested and grows during the accumulation phase.

Mutual funds have also stated offering pension plans, which are targeted towards saving for one's retirement. These are debt-oriented balanced funds that take equity exposure of up to 40 per cent and invest the balance in debt instruments. Though they are hybrid in nature, their equity exposure is much lower than balanced funds that invest up to 65 to 70 per cent in equity.

24.3 ANNUITY

An *annuity* is a contract between the insurer and an individual whereby the insurer agrees to pay a specified amount in future in exchange for money now paid by the individual. It is an investment that you make, either in a lump sum or through instalments over a specified period of time (called the 'accumulation period'), in return for which you receive a specific sum at regular intervals (either annually, semi-annually, quarterly or monthly), either for life or for a fixed number of years. This period when annuitant receives the payments is known as *distribution phase*. One important aspect is to make sure that the payments you receive will meet your income needs during retirement.

Annuities are also popularly known as 'pension plans'. This is because they are typically bought to generate regular income during one's retired life. Annuities can be viewed as a solution to one of the biggest financial insecurities of old age; outliving one's retirement corpus. One important aspect is to make sure that the payments you receive will meet your income needs during retirement.

Types of Annuities

There are two basic types of annuities: deferred and immediate.

(a) Deferred Annuity – Here, your money is invested for a specified period of time until you are ready to begin taking withdrawals, typically upon retirement. A deferred annuity accumulates money. Also, they accumulate interest on the investment.

(b) Immediate Annuity – Here, you begin to receive payments from the insurer immediately. For example, upon retirement, an investor can purchase immediate annuity with his accumulated retirement corpus. Here, a deferred annuity is converted into an immediate annuity.

Within these two basic categories, annuities are further divided into:

(i) fixed annuity – where the pay-out is a fixed sum or fixed amount; and

(ii) variable annuity – where pay-out is tied to underlying investment such as, performance of overall market, a particular investment (e.g. gold), and/or a combination of two. The value depends on performance of underlying product you choose. However, in variable annuities annual expenses are likely to be much higher than the expenses on regular mutual funds.

Other Types of Annuity

1. **Period certain annuity:** Here, investor is guaranteed a specific payment amount for a specific period of time (say, 10 years or 25 years). If the investor passes away (dies) before the end of period, his beneficiary will receive balance annuity payments for the balance period.

2. **Life certain annuity:** Here the investor is guaranteed specific payment for the rest of his life; there is no survivor benefit (i.e., beneficiaries don't get anything). At the time of death, all payments stop. Also, if the investor passes away before receiving any annuity pay-outs, the entire balance in his account will be retained

by the insurer. The annuity provides a guaranteed, regular amount of income for the rest of the investor's life.

3. **Life with period certain annuity** – This annuity is a combination of the above two – life certain annuity and period certain annuity. Here, the investor receives a guaranteed pay-out; either for the rest of his life or until a specified period – whichever is earlier.
4. **Either or survivor annuity** – Here, either partner/spouse will continue to receive pay-outs from the insurer for the rest of his/her life even after the spouse passes away.
5. **Equity-indexed annuity** – It is a combination of fixed and variable annuity. Here, one gets to enjoy the upside of a stock market bull run and also protect oneself against the downside as the investment earns a guaranteed minimum return even if stock prices fall.

24.4 NATIONAL PENSION SYSTEM (NPS)

It is a defined contribution scheme (unlike EPF, PPF where returns are guaranteed by the government) regulated by Pension Fund Regulatory and Development Authority (PFRDA). Investment in NPS is to be maintained until 60 years. Upon retirement, a part of the corpus will be allowed for withdrawal as lump sum, and balance will be mandatorily paid out as pension.

Let us look at the salient features of NPS:

Who is covered?

- An individual who has joined central government service [at present, the equity component is invested such that it replicates a stock market Index] [are expected to component] on or after 1 January 2004;
- Employee of a Central (Civil) Ministry or Departments; or
- Employee of a non-Civil Ministry or Department including railways, posts;
- Telecommunication or Armed Forces (Civil); or
- Employee of an autonomous body, grant-in-aid institution, union territory or any other undertaking whose employees are eligible to a pension from the Consolidated Fund of India.

However following individuals are excluded:

- employees already covered under Provident Fund and Miscellaneous Provisions Act, 1952 and any other special Acts governing these funds; or
- an individual who has joined Central Government service before 1 January 2004; or

- employees of the Indian Armed Forces (Army, Navy and Air Force); or
- an individual employed in a department or at a post under which you are not eligible to receive a pension from the Consolidated Fund of India.

Operational Aspects of New Pension Scheme

Allotment of Account Number

When a person joins government service, he/she is allotted a unique Permanent Retirement Account Number (PRAN). This unique account number will remain the same throughout. The same can be used from any location and can be continued with even after job change. The PPAN will provide you with two personal accounts, namely:

1. a mandatory tier-I pension account, and
2. a voluntary tier-II savings account.

Advantages

- **Cost** - NPS is the cheapest among current retirement products and defined contribution schemes; it is also easy to transact in NPS.
- **Flexibility** – The subscriber is given a PPAN, which will remain with him forever. The account is portable irrespective of change in job/location.
- **Returns** – There is a likely potential of having returns higher than traditional debt investments.

Disadvantages

- **Taxability:** The contributions get tax benefit under Section 80C. However, at the time of withdrawal, only the lump sum would be tax exempt up to 40% of corpus accumulated/generated.
- **Comparison to mutual funds:** Since the NPS is meant for retirement and financial security; it does not permit flexible withdrawals as are possible in the case of mutual funds.
- **Returns:** If an individual is voluntarily investing in NPS, then he/she might as well invest in the stocks or mutual funds (MF).

National Pension System (NPS) is arguably one of the cheapest investment products in the world. On an investment of Rs. 1 lakh, the fund management fee is just Rs. 10 a year, compared to Rs. 1500-2500 charged by a mutual fund or a ULIP. It is also a very tax-friendly product. Besides enjoying tax deduction under Sec 80C, the NPS offers an exclusive window of Rs. 50,000 under Section 80CCD (1) and additional deduction to corporate employees who invest in the scheme under Sec 80CCD (2). Besides, there is no tax incidence if the investor switches from one asset class to another or changes his pension fund manager. Despite these attractive features, the NPS has not taken off as expected. The total assets of all private NPS tier 1 subscribers is less than Rs. 5000 crore (October, 2016). To make the scheme more attractive to subscribers, the Pension Fund Regulatory and Development Authority (PFRDA) has made several changes in the rules governing the scheme.

Increased Equity Exposure

One big grouse against the NPS was that it caps the equity exposure at 50%. This problem has been fixed with the introduction of the new life cycle fund option that allows up to 75% equity exposure. The Aggressive Life Cycle Fund (LC-75) will have 75% exposure to equities till the age of 35 and thereafter start reducing it by 4% every year. "Risk appetite comes down significantly with age. Since the starting equity allocation is kept high at 75%, the rate of reduction also has to be higher," explains PFRDA Chairman, Hemant Contractor.

However, this increased equity exposure is restricted only to the life cycle fund. Active choice investors, who choose their own asset mix, cannot invest more than 50% in equities. Also, the equity limit for government employees is still fixed at 15% (October, 2016).

24.5 CONCEPT OF REVERSE MORTGAGE

Let us understand mortgage first. A *mortgage* is a loan secured by a property and paid in instalments over a set period of time. A mortgage represents a loan or lien on a property to finance the purchase of your home that has to be paid over a specified period of time. If you don't pay debt, the lender has the right to take back the property and sell it to cover the debt.

Reverse Mortgage: A house can generate money by way of rent, which improves one's financial situation, which is why concept of *reverse mortgage* was introduced. Although reverse mortgage is well-known in the western countries, it is a fairly new concept in India. A reverse mortgage is a loan available to senior citizens. Reverse mortgage is so named because the payment stream is reversed, that is instead of the borrower making monthly payments to the lender, the lender (usually bank) makes payments to the borrower.

The process is simple. Once you pledge your house for reverse mortgage with any Housing Finance Company (HFC)/bank, the HFC/bank estimates the value of the house. Then, taking into account the cost of credit, it makes monthly payments to you. The loan is typically settled after the death of the owner/co-owners.

Few important features of reverse mortgage are summarized below:

1. In a typical mortgage, one borrows money in lump sum right at the beginning and then pays it back over a period of time using equated monthly instalments (EMIs). In reverse mortgage, one pledges a property already owned by him/her (with no existing loan outstanding against it). The bank, in turn, gives a person a series of cash-flows for a fixed tenure.

2. The scheme is applicable for the entire country including rural areas. The property should be mortgagable. In some rural areas, agricultural land cannot be mortgaged and hence reverse mortgage loans cannot be considered against a house constructed on such agricultural land.
3. Eligibility Criteria:
   (i) Indian citizen of 60 years or more.
   (ii) Married couples will be eligible as joint borrowers for joint assistance. In such cases, the age criteria for the couple would be at the discretion of the Reverse Mortgage Lender (RML), subject to at least one of them being above 60 years of age and the other not below 55 years of age.
   (iii) Should be the owner of the residential property (house or flat) located in India, with a clear title and indicating the prospective borrower's ownership of the property.
   (iv) The residential property should be free from any encumbrances.
   (v) The residual life of the property should be at least 20 years. There is no minimum period of ownership of property required.
   (vi) The prospective(s) borrower should use that residential property as permanent primary residence.
4. The amount of loan available under RML depends on the age of the borrower, appraised value of the house and the prevalent interest rates of the lending institution.
5. RML cannot be availed against commercial property. The property should be self-acquired, self-occupied and having clear title in favour of the borrower.
6. All receipts under RML shall be exempt from income tax under Section 10(43) of the Income Tax Act, 1961.
7. Any transfer of a capital asset in a transaction of reverse mortgage shall not be regarded as a *transfer*. A borrower, under reverse mortgage scheme, will be liable to income tax (in the nature of tax on capital gains) only at the point of alienation of the property by the mortgagee for the purposes of recovering the loan.
8. The maximum tenure of RML will be 20 years.
9. RML will become due and payable only when last surviving borrower dies or permanently moves out of the house. The loan may, however, be liable to foreclosure on the occurrence of certain events of default.
10. RML will be settled by proceeds obtained from sale of the house (an asset which was mortgaged). After the final settlement, the remaining amount (if any) will be given to the borrower or his/her heirs/beneficiary. However, the borrower or his/her heirs may repay the loan from other sources without bringing the property to sale.
11. RML can be prepaid at any time during the currency of the loan. On clearance of all the dues, all the title deeds will be returned by the lender to owner of the property.

12. The borrower can opt for the frequency of EMI pay out on monthly/quarterly/annual or lump sum payments at any point, as per his/her discretion.
13. The lender will re-value the property mortgaged to it at intervals that may be fixed depending upon the location of the property, its physical state, etc. NHB has advised that such revaluation may be done at least once every five years, and the quantum of loan may undergo revisions based on such revaluation at the discretion of the lender. The frequency of revaluation will be made known to prospective borrowers at the time of sanctioning of the loan.
14. The necessary transaction cost of RML to be paid by the client to the Housing Finance Company (the lender) include loan processing charges, documentation charges, commitment fees on undrawn loan amount, etc.

25 Estate Planning (Succession through Registered Will)

CHAPTER

An estate is the total property, owned by an individual prior to distribution through a trust or will, e.g., real estate, cars, household items, bank accounts and so on. Estate planning distributes real estate and other personal property to investor's heirs.

Estate planning is the process by which an individual or family arranges transfer of assets in anticipation of death or incapacitation. An estate plan aims to preserve the maximum amount of wealth possible for the intended beneficiaries and flexibility for individual prior to death.

Estate planning is an integral part of the process of financial planning. The concept of estate planning is best understood as a process of making proper arrangement for the protection, preservation and provision of a person's total assets for the benefit of his/her family and loved ones. Estate for the purpose of estate planning can be simplified to mean all the property and the property rights that a person owns.

Estate planning acts as a very important tool for an estate owner in an efficient transfer of wealth across generations. Reduction of tax liability is not necessarily the primary goal of estate planning, but effective tax planning is something that the real estate owner should consider in order to reduce tax liabilities on the estate which could take the form of income tax, capital gains tax, stamp duty, etc.

Wills and Trusts are common ways in which individuals dispose of their wealth. Other tools are power of attorney, gifts, partition, succession (when the will is not made), etc. Trusts, unlike Wills, have the benefit of avoiding probate, a lengthy and costly legal process that oversees the transfer of assets.

25.1 OBJECTIVES OF ESTATE PLANNING

1. Transfer of assets to beneficiaries
2. Paying least amount of taxes
3. Planning for incapacity
4. Orderly business succession
5. Who shall receive and when?
6. Selecting executor, trustee, and guardian

Risks Associated with Failing to Plan for Estate Transfers

- Client's property transfer wishes go unfulfilled
- Transfer taxes are excessive
- Transfer costs are excessive
- The client's family is not provided for financially in a proper manner
- Insufficient liquidity to cover client's debts, taxes and costs at death
- Time consuming and expensive probate

25.2 BASIC STEPS IN ESTATE PLANNING PROCESS

1. Establish the client/planner relationship:
   (a) Gather client's information, financial statement
   (b) Transfer of objectives: family and/or charitable
   (c) Intentions and values
2. Determine the client's financial status
3. Develop a comprehensive plan of transfers consistent with all information/objectives
4. Implement the estate plan
5. Review the estate plan periodically

Estate Planning & Hindu Succession Act, 1956

The estate owner who wishes to pass on his/her estate to their legal heirs is called as *testator*. If the testator dies without leaving a valid will behind, he/she is said to have died intestate. The Hindu Succession Act, 1956 (the HS Act) was enacted to reform and codify the Hindu law of intestate succession.

The HS Act defines a person to have died intestate in respect of that property of which he or she has not made a testamentary disposition capable of taking effect. Upon interpretation of this definition, it can be stated that if a will made by a Hindu is found to be invalid, then such a person is also deemed to have died intestate.

25.3 TRUSTS

A trust is created where the absolute owner of property (known as the *settler*) passes the legal title in that property to a person (the *trustee*) to hold in trust for the benefit of another person (the *beneficiary*) in accordance with the terms set out by the settler.

Trusts are often used as vehicles to hold property for present or future needs of dependents and family members, and sometimes also used to reduce the burden of taxes. Common example of a trust is one that provides for accumulation of income and capital for specified children. Retirement trusts are commonly set up by the employers to provide retirement benefits to employees.

Purposes of a Trust

(a) Benefits the settler – frees the settler from managing the trust properly.
(b) Handle and accumulate wealth – settler's wealth is protected from creditors and forms part of the settlor's estate.
(c) Obtain competent professional management of property – investment of the trust property is made with expertise resulting from professional management.
(d) Provides skills which the settler may not possess – settler may lack business acumen to handle the trust property; a trust provides a substitute for this vacuum.
(e) Secure property of beneficiary – trust vehicles not only ensure protection of the trust property but also help in smooth transmission of the same to the beneficiaries.

Trusts in India

Trusts originated at the end of the middle ages as a means of transferring wealth within the family and have remained the characteristic device employed for organizing intergenerational wealth transmission in situations where the transferor has substantial assets or complex family affairs. Modern-day private trusts are used to carry out this function in India. Public trusts, on the other hand, may be used to contribute property towards religious and charitable purposes.

The Indian Trusts Act

Trusts in India are governed by the provisions of the Indian Trusts Act, 1882. A trust as per the Trusts Act is "an obligation annexed to the ownership of property, and arising out of a confidence reposed in and accepted by the owner, or declared and accepted by him for the benefit of another, or of another and the owner."

The person who reposes or declares the confidence is called the "author of the trust" (commonly referred to as a *settler*). The person who accepts the confidence is called the *trustee*. The person for whose benefit the confidence is accepted is called the *beneficiary*. The subject matter of the trust is called *trust property*. The *beneficial interest* or *interest* of the beneficiary is the right against the trustee as owner of the trust property. The instrument, if any, by which the trust is declared is called the "instrument of trust" (commonly known as the *trust deed* or *indenture of trust*).

The concept of ownership in the case of a trust is different under Indian and English law. India does not recognize duality of ownership in the case of a trust, i.e., it recognizes only legal ownership and not equitable ownership as is provided for under English law which recognizes duality of ownership, i.e., legal and equitable. Under Indian law, the trustee is both the legal and beneficial owner of trust property.

The settler must transfer identifiable property under an irrevocable arrangement and totally divest him of the ownership and the beneficial enjoyment of the income from the property.

25.4 TYPES OF TRUSTS

1. Private Trust

A private trust is created for the benefit of specific individuals *i.e.,* individuals who are defined and ascertained or who within a definite time can be definitely ascertained. Private trusts are governed by the Trusts Act. This Act is applicable to the whole of India except Jammu and Kashmir and the Andaman and Nicobar Islands. That apart, the Trusts Act is not applicable to the following:

i. Waqf;
ii. Property of a Hindu Undivided Family; and
iii. Public or private religious and charitable endowments.

A trust can also be created by or on behalf of a minor with the permission of a principal civil court of original jurisdiction. Apart from an individual, a company, firm, society or association of persons is also capable of creating a trust.

However, a trust receiving foreign contribution in India would need approval under the Foreign Contributions Regulations Act, 1976, which is administered by the Ministry of Home Affairs in India. However, such trust can only be a trust, the objects of which are dedicated to cultural, economic, educational, religious or social purposes.

Family (private) trusts may be set up either inter vivo, i.e., during a person's lifetime or under a will, i.e., testamentary trust, either orally or under a written instrument, except where the subject matter of the trust is immovable property, the trust would need to be declared by a registered written instrument such as codicil.

Private trusts may also be used as a collective pooling vehicle for individual retail investors such as.

(a) Mutual funds
(b) REITs (Real Estate Investments Trusts)

2. Public Charitable or Religious Trust

A *public trust* is created for the benefit of an uncertain and fluctuating body of persons who cannot be ascertained at any point of time; for instance, the public at large or a section of the public following a particular religion, profession or faith. A public trust is normally permanent or at least indefinite in duration.

As regards public trusts, there is no Central Act governing formation and administration of such trusts. But various states such as Bihar, Maharashtra, Madhya Pradesh, Orissa, etc., have enacted their own legislations prescribing conditions and procedures for the administration of public trusts. These Acts are more or less similar in nature though there may be certain variations.

A public trust is generally a non-profit venture with charitable purposes and in such cases it is also referred to as a *charitable trust.*

There are four essential requirements for creating a valid religious or charitable trust under Hindu law:

(i) valid religious or charitable purpose of the trust as per the norms of Hindu Law;

(ii) capability of the author of the trust to create such a trust;

(iii) the purpose and property of the trust must be indicated with sufficient precision; and

(iv) the trust must not violate any law of the country.

25.5 WILL

A *will* is explained as a legal declaration made in writing by a person who clearly sets out the manner in which he/she would like his/her property (both movable and/or immovable) wherever situated to be distributed after his/her death. A will therefore is a document which comes into effect the moment its maker dies. Therefore, till the time a will comes into force, it can be cancelled, revoked and varied to suit the maker's circumstances.

Some terms associated with wills are explained below:

- **Codicil** is an instrument made in relation to a will explaining, altering or adding to its dispositions and is deemed to be part of the will.
- **Testator** is the person who makes the will.
- **Testatrix** is used to refer to a female making a will.
- **Probate** is a copy of the will certified under the seal of a competent court.
- **Beneficiary** is a person who inherits the property under a will.
- **Executor** is the legal representative for all purposes of the deceased person and all property under the will vests in him.

Types of Wills

1. **Individual Will:** One of the most common and accepted form of will, where the will is individually written.
2. **Holographic Will:** A will which is wholly in the handwriting of the testator.
3. **Conditional Will:** A will that is expressed to take effect only in the event of happening of some contingency.
4. **Joint Will:** When two or more persons make a joint declaration regarding their properties in one document and the document is executed in accordance with the formalities laid down by the law.
5. **Living Will:** A written statement made by person directing the doctor who may be treating him/her to discontinue treatment if the treatment is only to artificially prolong his life in a terminal illness situation.
6. **Oral Will:** Wills that are not documented and made orally. Such wills are mostly prevalent in the defense services.

(v) parents only (one-half); and

(vi) other ascendants only (one-third).

The remainder is freely disposable.

4. Formalities for Making a Will

Formalities for making a will depend on the religion of the testator. Wills made by persons of all religions including those who marry under the Special Marriage Act, 1954 (except Muslims who marry under customary law) must meet the conditions such as:

- the will must be in writing made by a person who is a major, of sound mind and with free consent;
- the will must be signed by the testator or by some other person in the testator's presence and at his direction;
- the will must be attested by two or more persons;
- the document must be a declaration of intent of the testator with respect to his property;
- the document must specify that his intent should be carried out after the testator's death;
- there must be a disposition of property under the document. The will should clearly set out the properties intended to be transferred and should also set out that the document has been executed without coercion or undue influence.

A will must be dated; otherwise proof of the day on which the will was executed is to be given at the time when the petition for probate is filed. Registration of a will is optional under the provisions of Indian Registration Act and no adverse inference can be drawn against the will in case of no registration.

5. Procedural Aspects

When a person dies, there must be somebody to deal with / administer the estate of the deceased, e.g., sell property, collect debts, repay debts, close bank accounts, etc. Estate and succession laws provide for administrative procedures so that actions taken in relation to the matters of an individual after his death are legally effective. Legal systems broadly divide estate administration procedures into two situations:

(i) where a person has died leaving a will; and

(ii) where a person has died without leaving a will, i.e., intestate.

A person named in the will to administer the estate is called an *executor(s)*. An executor derives the authority to act from the will but this authority must be confirmed by a legal procedure called *probate* which establishes the genuineness of the will. Where a person has died intestate, the court (on an application by an interested party) appoints a person called the *administrator*. An administrator is also appointed (upon application) where the will is invalid or an executor is not named in the will or the executor is unable or unwilling to act. Unlike an executor, an administrator's authority to administer the estate is both conferred by and confirmed under the court-issued document called Letters of Administration (LoA). Executors or administrators are called *personal representatives* of the deceased. A third document important for estate administration is called the *succession certificate* which has limited applications.

Approximately, it takes about 8-10 months to obtain a grant of probate from the court if it is uncontested or between 6-9 years if it is contested. The time limit also depends on whether the matter is before the district court or the High Court. The process for obtaining a LoA or a *succession certificate* is estimated to take between 6-9 months if it is uncontested. If it is contested, the number and location of other parties will also have to be considered. The process may then extend to between 2 to 5 years (or even more).

Importance of a will

What happens when you pass away without a will in place? All your assets and belongings are equally divided and given to your heirs in agreement with succession laws. You might have always wanted to give your most expensive car to your son or preserve your expensive paintings/silverware for your daughter. But if you don't have a will, none of this is possible.

Most importantly, it can lead to disputes in the family and the issue can knock the doors of the court. Money and precious time will be wasted in endless discussions with lawyers and producing various proofs. It is best to save your family from these distressing complications by having a will.

A will also has the power to confer responsibilities. Would you want your child to be raised by a careless relative decided by the court when you are no more? With the help of a will, you can appoint a trusted person as a guardian to take care of your children in your absence.

Now is the Time – Prepare a Will

Will execution is not a difficult task. Any individual above 21 years of age can follow the template of a standard will and state clearly who should get how much. It's best to take the help of a proficient lawyer who can help you draft this document without any errors and moreover, carry out legal formalities such as registration. In case you wish to change the will, it can be amended any time. Nonetheless, whenever you prepare a new will, make sure that you state that it is the newest one and replaces the previous ones. Successful financial planning is not just about creating wealth. You must also have a wealth succession plan ready. And the only way to do so is to have a will so that your finances are distributed in accordance with your desires.

6. Probate

Probate is mandatory where the testator is a Hindu, Sikh, Jain, Buddhist or Parsi and the will is:

(i) executed in certain specified territories; or

(ii) is executed outside those territories but relates to immoveable property located within such territories.

These territories are the cities of Kolkata, Chennai and Mumbai. Probate is not mandatory where the testator is a Muslim or Indian Christian even if conditions (i) and (ii) above are satisfied.

Probate is essential because no right as executor or legatee can be established in any court unless the relevant court has granted probate of the will under which the right is claimed. However, a person who sets up a will which does not mandatorily have to be probated (as per the conditions above) can establish his right without obtaining a probate.

7. To whom can a Probate be Granted?

Probate can only be granted to an executor appointed by will either expressly or by implication. When granted to all those persons who have applied, unless those who do not apply renounce their right as an executor. To obtain a grant of probate, the following procedure is prescribed but there may be some variations depending on the rules of the particular court which has jurisdiction over the matter.

8. Procedure to Apply for a Probate

An application/petition for probate must be filed in court along with the original will in question. The application should be made before the district judge (or High Court depending on the property value and also depending on whether the High Court has original jurisdiction for testamentary matters) in whose jurisdiction the testator at the time of his death had fixed abode or had some property situated.

The application should contain the following facts:

- time of the testator's death;
- a declaration that the will attached is the last will and testament;
- a statement that the will was duly executed;
- value of assets which are likely to be inherited;
- title deeds pertaining to the immovable property mentioned in the will, if any;
- documents pertaining to movable property in the will, if any; and
- a statement that the executor making the application is named in the will.

The executor is thereafter asked to establish the (a) proof of death of the testator; (b) proof that the will has been validly executed by the testator; and (c) proof that the will is the last will and testament of the deceased. Proof of death is usually shown by submission of original death certificate.

9. Practical Issues to be Remembered

The executor must within six months of the grant of probate or letter of administration exhibit inventory and accounts relating to and containing the full and true estimate of all the property in possession and all the credits related to it and also all debts that are owed to the executor in his character. The accounts exhibited must show the assets that have come under the executor's hands and must also depict the manner in which they have been applied or disposed of. Keeping in mind compliances that must be adhered to by an executor, it would be advisable if the executor was an Indian resident.

10. Succession Certificate

A succession certificate has limited effect. The certificate does not give any general powers of administration of the estate of the deceased. The certificate is limited to the collection of debts which existed in the lifetime of the deceased and enables the applicant to have shares transferred in his name if he is otherwise entitled to it.

Further, the grant of the certificate does not establish the title of the grantee as the heir of the deceased. It only confers on the grantee authority for the collection of debts and allows debtors to make payments to the grantee. That said, a succession certificate (together with the death certificate) is usually requested by authorities when a change in title records has to be carried out. Therefore, in terms of practical use, a succession certificate serves as a supporting document. If the certificate granted is with respect to debt or securities for which previously an LoA (letter of administration) has been granted and is in force, the certificate granted after it shall be invalid.

25.6 CURRENT SCENARIO TOWARDS SUCCESSION PLANNING

India has witnessed a steady growth in its high net worth population as a consequence of increasing globalization not only by families and individuals in Tier I cities but also from Tier II and Tier III cities. Although economically the Indian HNI may be a mirror of his/her counterpart in the developed nations, culturally there appears to be a difference in approach. The *Financial Times* reported in 2013 that Asian families in particular suffered from a cultural reluctance to discuss succession. The report stressed on the need for greater awareness of succession planning since a lot of wealth was locked up in family businesses which needed to be effectively devolved to the next generation.

This observation certainly echoes in India where the majority of businesses today are family-run but most Indian business families do not have succession plans in place for personal and/or business wealth. After liberalization of economy in India, a new breed of mobile, highly-skilled, entrepreneurial high net-worth individuals has emerged. Changing social relationships now pose emerging issues such as inter-family relationships between people spread over multiple countries.

Effective estate and wealth planning ensures that families retain control over their businesses and a smooth transition of leadership of businesses between generations of families. It balances the needs of businesses with the interests of family members. Effective planning of wealth of the high net-worth individuals can prevent long and expensive legal disputes between heirs based in multiple jurisdictions. Various structures provide different degrees of control over the purpose for which the wealth can be used and the manner in which it may be used. For instance, the setting up of a trust to manage wealth offers several advantages such as bypassing the probate process, giving heirs the benefit of property without losing control of it and creating a large pool of funds for making investments.

Court systems, legal frameworks and tax laws do not always keep up with socio-economic aspirations and this gap poses challenges to managing the wealth of business families and high net-worth individuals. Future amendments to tax laws may spread the net of the wealth tax wider, which could achieve part of the objective behind levying an inheritance tax. The increase in such a tax could lead to increase of investments abroad in jurisdictions with more favourable tax laws. Laws are also changing to keep pace with new forms of assets such as *intellectual property rights.* With the growth of technology, intellectual property rights are becoming increasingly valuable and complex and also need to be devolved carefully to maximize their value for future generations.

Some challenges that are usually encountered in estate and wealth planning include:

- restrictions imposed by community specific laws;
- limits on transfer of wealth abroad;
- ensuring tax efficiency and flexibility for beneficiaries located in various jurisdictions;
- overcoming compliance issues.

In the light of these complexities in estate and wealth planning, building governance models for management of family businesses and wealth of high net-worth individuals assumes great importance.

"I have not failed. I've just found 10,000 ways that won't work." - Thomas Alva Edison

CHAPTER

26 Tax Aspects Relating to Investments

Taxes have inherently been a complex and confusing subject. To make matter more complicated, the provisions undergo several amendments – both prospectively as well as retrospectively – every financial year making the entire process of understanding the tax laws even more daunting. Even the great physicist, Albert Einstein couldn't help but remark that "the hardest thing in the world to understand is the Income-tax."

This being the case, the common man does not even try to understand fully the nitty-gritty of this baffling subject but prefers to outsource the tax matter to their advisors or chartered accountants. Hence, this subject assumes paramount importance in the service offerings of every investment advisor.

Taxes basically represent the sum of money charged by the government at the prescribed rates in lieu of the various services provided. Taxes form the basic source of revenue to the government. There are mainly two types of taxes in India: direct tax and indirect tax.

26.1 DIRECT TAX

Direct taxes are those which are directly collected from the taxpayer, i.e., the impact and incidence of direct tax fall on the same person. This includes income tax and wealth tax. The Indian Constitution empowers the Central Government to levy and collect direct taxes. The Income Tax law in India comprises the following:

- The **Income Tax Act**, 1961 (ITA): it was enacted in 1961 by the Central Government. It came into force from 1st April, 1962 and extends to the entire country. It contains approximately 400 sections and 12 schedules. The Act incorporates the basic provisions of the Income tax law in India – the chargeability, scope, exemptions, computation mechanism, tax holidays, tax collection, assessments, appeals, etc. However, the Act is amended every financial year through the Finance Act passed by the Parliament (also called the budget provisions).
- The **Income Tax Rules,** 1962 are formulated by the Central Board of Direct Taxes (CBDT) for implementation of the provisions laid down by ITA. The rules are

distinct from the ITA and in case of any difference between the two, the provisions of ITA prevails. The Income Tax Rules can be amended by the CBDT by means of notification in the Official Gazette of Government. Generally, amendments to the Rules are consequential to the amendments to the ITA.

- **Financial Act** or **Annual Budget**: As pointed out above, the Finance Act is passed by the Parliament annually in order to bring about amendments to the ITA. Further, the Finance Act also specifies the rates at which income tax is chargeable.
- **CBDT Circulars**: The CBDT is empowered to issue circulars in order to clarify certain provisions of the law as well as to issue directions/instructions to the income tax authorities for proper administration of the ITA. However, these circulars/directions cannot in any way contradict or defeat the provisions of the law. Further, it may also be noted that the circulars issued by the CBDT are binding only on the income tax department – in other words neither the taxpayers nor the courts are bound by them.
- **Judicial Precedents:** As discussed earlier, the income tax law is a highly complicated subject and a good number of provisions of the ITA are open for multiple interpretations. Therefore, there are constant disputes between the taxpayers and the tax collectors on several issues emanating therefrom. These disputes are ultimately settled by the tax tribunals and the courts and thereafter act as precedents for settling future disputes based on similar issues and facts. Thus, judicial precedents act as a basis for deciding a similar issue arising in future.

Income tax in India is governed by the Income Tax Act, 1961, which lays down provisions with respect to chargeability to tax, determination of residence, computation of income, transfer pricing, etc. Residents are ordinarily subjected to tax on their worldwide income, whereas non-residents are taxed only on their Indian source income, i.e., income that accrues or arises to them in India.

26.2 BASIC CONCEPTS IN INDIAN INCOME TAX

The basic **chargeability of income tax** can be understood as: any person whose total income for the previous year exceeds the basic amount not chargeable to tax is an *assessee* and is liable to tax at the rates of income tax in force for the assessment year. The scope of total income is determined on the basis of the person's residential status.

Person [Section 2(31)]

Under the Income Tax Act (ITA), a *person* is understood as a *unit* liable to pay taxes and includes the following:

(a) an individual;
(b) a Hindu undivided family;
(c) a company;
(d) a firm;

(e) an association of persons or a body of individuals, whether incorporated or not;
(f) a local authority, and
(g) every artificial jurisdical person, not falling any of the preceding sub-clauses.

Income [Section 2(24)]

Income tax is levied as a charge on income, so it is equally important to first understand the meaning of income as defined under the ITA. Here it is of utmost importance to understand the difference between 'receipt of money' and 'income'. All money received by an individual may not be income but every income received is definitely a receipt of money.

Income has been inclusively defined under section 2(24) of the Act to mean and include the following among others:

(a) profits and gains;
(b) dividends;
(c) value of any perquisites or benefits received by an employee;
(d) value of any perquisites or benefits received from any business or profession;
(e) capital gains; and
(f) prize money from lotteries, crossword puzzles, card games, TV shows, races including horse races, etc.

Income may be in cash or kind, and illegal income is also taxable. Income earned by a person should be real, in other words, a person cannot make profit out of its own self by transferring money from one bank account to another.

All income earned by a person need not be taxable. Therefore, if a receipt of money qualifies as income, the next step is to ascertain whether the income is taxable or not.

Total income means the sum total of the taxable income computed in the manner laid down under the Act. The total income is characterized under five different heads of income.

Previous Year [Section 3]

Previous year means the financial year immediately proceeding the Assessment year. The previous year can also be understood as the year in which the income is earned by a person. For instance, the period from April 1, 2013 to March 31, 2014 will be referred to as the previous year for assessment year 2014-15.

Basic Amount not Chargeable to Tax

The prescribed level of income, up to which, a person need not pay any taxes is referred to as the *basic amount not chargeable to tax*. The basic amount of income not chargeable to tax for the previous year 2013-14 is available under the 'rates of tax'.

Assessee [Section 2(7)]

Assessee means a person by whom any tax or any other sum of money is payable under the Act. The term also includes every person in respect of whom any proceeding under this Act has been taken for the assessment of his/her income. In other words, every person who earns taxable income is liable to pay taxes and is called an Assessee.

Rates of Income tax: Tax rates for financial year: 2017-18 (Assessment year: 2018-19) For Individuals/Hindu Undivided Family (HUFs):

Table 26.1

Income (Rs.)	Rate of Tax for Individuals/ HUFs	Rate of Tax for Senior Citizens
Up to Rs. 2,50,000	Nil	Nil (Up to Rs. 3,00,000)
2,50,000 to 5,00,000	5%	5% (300000 – 500000)
5,00,001 to 10,00,000	20%	20%
10,00,001 – 50,00,000	30%	30%
50,00,001 – 1,00,00,000	30% + 10% surcharge on tax	30% + 10% surcharge on tax
1,00,00,000 & Above	30% + 15% surcharge on tax	30% + 15% surcharge on tax

Assessment Year [Section 2(9)]

Assessment year means the period of 12 months commencing on the first day of April every year. All the income earned by a person during the previous year is assessed in the assessment year and taxes thereon are paid during the assessment year itself.

Residential Status and Scope of Income

The scope of the total taxable income for a person for the previous year depends on his residential status – which may be (i) resident; (ii) resident but not ordinarily resident (R & OR), and (iii) Non-Resident (NR).

A resident's total income comprises all his income accrued/received or deemed to accrue/receive within India and outside India. In simple words, a resident's 'global income' is taxable in India.

A non-resident's total income comprises only that income which has accrued/received or is deemed to have accrued/received in India. In other words, a non-resident shall not be liable to pay tax in India for any income accruing or arising outside India.

The total income of a resident but not ordinarily resident is the same as that of a non-resident but with an exception in that his/her foreign income shall be taxable in India if it accrues or arises to him/her outside India from a business controlled in or a profession set up in India. In other words, if foreign income is from a business controlled in or a profession set up outside India and such income accrues and is received outside India, it will not be taxable for a resident but not ordinarily resident person.

Residential Status

Residential status is the principal factor on which the tax liability for an assessee is determined. The rules for determining the residential status for the different categories of persons are different. The foregoing paragraphs emphasize on the rules for calculating the residential status of an individual. Be it noted that the residential status is determined separately for each year and thus an individual may have different residential status in different years.

An individual may either be resident or a non-resident. An individual will be resident in any previous year if he/she satisfies at least one of the following basic conditions:

1. he/she is in India during the previous year for a period of 182 days or more; or
2. he/she is in India during the previous year for a period of 60 days or more and has been in India for 365 days or more during the four years immediately preceding the previous year.

Exception: However, if the individual is an Indian citizen and leaves India in any previous year as a member of the crew of an Indian ship or for the purpose of employment, he/she will have to stay in India for at least 182 days (and not 60 days as in condition 2) to qualify as a resident.

Similarly, if any Indian citizen or a person of Indian origin who is living outside India and comes on a visit to India in the previous year, he/she will have to stay in India for 182 days (and not 60 days as in condition 2) to qualify as a resident.

If an individual doesn't satisfy any of the two conditions as specified above, he/she shall be treated as a 'non-resident'.

A resident could further be categorized as a 'resident and ordinarily resident' or a 'resident but not ordinarily resident'. A resident individual shall be resident and ordinarily resident if he/she satisfies the following two additional conditions:

(a) He/she has been a resident in India for at least two out 10 previous years immediately preceding the relevant previous year; and
(b) He/she has been in India for a period of 730 days or more during 7 years in the immediately preceding relevant previous year.

If any one of the two above additional conditions are not satisfied, then the individual shall be a resident but not ordinarily resident.

26.3 IMPORTANT ASPECTS IN INCOME TAX

Computation of Total Income

Any income that is taxable has to be categorized into any one of the five heads of income that have been notified by the Act. For all purposes of computing the total income or calculating the income-tax, income shall be classified under the following heads of income:

1. Salaries
2. Income from house property
3. Profits and gains of business or profession
4. Capital gains
5. Income from other sources.

Exempt Incomes

The Act has enumerated a list of income under section 10 which are totally exempt from tax. In other words, these incomes are not added to a person's total income.

Gross Total Income

The *gross total income* (GTI) of an assessee is arrived at by aggregating the income computed under the five heads of income and after giving effect to the provisions of clubbing and set-off. The GTI plays a crucial part in the computation of income, as the liability for the assessee to file his/her return of income is determined on the basis of the GTI. As per the provisions of section 139(1) of the Act, if any individual's GTI exceeds the basic limit not chargeable to tax, he/she is liable to file the return of income, even if the tax liability is NIL.

Deductions under Chapter VI-A

In computing the total income of an assessee, deductions specified under section 80C to 80U will be allowed from his/her gross total income. All the deductions under these sections are grouped under Chapter VI-A of the Act. However, the aggregate amount of deductions under this chapter shall not in any case, exceed the gross total income of the assessee.

Tax Payments

The tax liability of an assessee for a previous year has to be discharged during the relevant previous year itself. The Act provides for the following modes for collection of taxes.

1. *Tax Deducted at Source (TDS)*

Certain items of income (namely salary, interest, commission, professional fees, contractor's payment, rent, etc.) are liable for tax deduction at source at the prescribed rates at the time of payment thereof. In other words, the payers of such amount are responsible for deducting tax in respect of such payments and depositing the same in the Government treasury, or while the recipient's avails of the credit for the tax are deducted against his/her tax liability.

2. *Advance Tax*

Every assessee should compute his/her estimated taxable income for the year and discharge the tax liability thereon (after considering the TDS credit, if any) in specified proportions, by way of advance tax payable on specified due dates. The due dates for payment of advance tax in case of both individual and corporate assessee are:

Table 26.2

Due Date	Total amount payable
15 June	Not less than 15% of such advance tax
15 September	Not less than 45% of such advance tax
15 December	Not less than 75% of such advance tax
15 March	Entire tax liability for the year: as reduced by the amount or amounts, if any, paid in the earlier instalment or instalments.

Default in payment of advance tax attracts interest liability.

3. *Self-assessment Tax*

Where any tax is payable by the assessee on the total taxable income after taking into account the TDS and advance tax, the same has to be paid by way of self-assessment, along with interest, if any.

Table 26.3 Effective Return on "Tax Exempt" Investments

Investment return	Effective tax rate 10.30%	Effective tax rate 20.60%	Effective tax rate 30.90%
7%	7.621%	8.442%	9.163%
8%	8.824%	9.648%	10.472%
10%	11.03%	12.06%	13.09%
15%	16.545%	18.09%	19.635%

On the flip side, it is a fact that returns from many investment avenues are fully taxable and therefore the investor's effective rate is much lower, after allowing for tax. Effective rate is presented in the table below:

Table 26.4 Effective Return on "Taxable" Investments

Investment return	Effective tax rate 10.30%	Effective tax rate 20.60%	Effective tax rate 30.90%
7%	6.279%	5.558%	4.837%
8%	7.176%	6.352%	5.528%
10%	8.97%	7.94%	6.91%
15%	13.455%	11.91%	10.365%

26.4 TAXABILITY OF REAL ESTATE INVESTMENTS (INDIAN TAXATION LAWS AND RULES)

Taxability of Income

- Rental income is taxable.
- Certain deductions are permitted from the income in computing taxable income on house property. The permitted deductions are:
  - (i) 30% of rent as a standard deduction
  - (ii) Interest paid on borrowed capital – the limit is Rs. 2,00,000 (over & above of Rs. 1,50,000 applicable for self-occupied property)
  - (iii) Municipal taxes actually paid.

- Repayment of principal amount of housing loan is allowed to be deducted from income u/s. 80C up to a maximum limit of Rs. 1,00,000 p.a. (with other listed items).
- Cost of one residential house is exempt from **wealth tax** liability.

Other Taxation Provisions Relevant to REIT Structure

Taxation on **capital gains** arising to a sponsor on exchange of shares in SPVs with units of the REITs arises only at the point of ultimate transfer of REIT units and the exchange of share with REIT units is not considered a transfer. Holding period and cost of sales of SPV in the hands of a sponsor are available on ultimate transfer of REIT units. The capital gain tax rate will be applicable depending on short-term or long-term in nature.

Interest paid to non-resident lenders in case of monies borrowed by REITs in foreign currency taxable at 5% subject to specified conditions.

26.5 TAXATION OF INDIVIDUAL ANNUITIES

A wide variety of investments have been brought under tax deduction benefit ambit designed to minimize tax implications – Equity-linked saving scheme (ELSS) mutual funds, Public Provident Fund (PPF) and other recognized provident funds, saving schemes of post office.

The tax implication of individual annuities is twofold, as explained below.

During Payment of Premium

Deduction u/s 80CCC of Act is allowed on account of investment to the extent of Rs. 1 lakh p.a. The policy can be taken on self, spouse and children.

On Receipt of Pension (Annuity)

Commutation of pension is capitalization of a fraction of monthly pension. It is a lump sum payment of commuted value of a fraction of pension. Commuted value of pension received from a life insurance plan is tax-free. Uncommuted pension amount received is taxable in the hands of pensioner/investor. Such amount shall be taxed as income in the year in which this is received by the assessee or his nominee, as the case maybe.

Note:

- Annuity received from present employer is taxable as 'income from salary'.
- Annuity received from former employer is taxable as 'profits in lieu of salary'.
- Annuity received from any other source (other than the above), i.e., from an insurance company, mutual funds, is taxable as 'income from other sources'.
- Annuity received by the nominee in any mode as mentioned above is added to nominee's taxable income under the head 'income from other sources'.

25.6 TAXABILITY OF CAPITAL GAINS

We have seen earlier that there are broadly two types of returns that one gets from any investment avenue: (i) cash flow – in the form of interest or dividend, and (ii) capital gains - capital appreciation on selling an asset after holding it for a certain period.

Concept of Capital Asset and Transfer

Capital asset means property of any kind held by an assessee, whether or not connected with his business or profession, but does not include: (i) any stock in trade; (ii) personal effects; and (iii) agricultural land.

It is defined that if a piece of land or house property had been held for a minimum period of 36 months, before selling, then it is **long-term** capital gains and if sold within 36 months, the gains on sale shall be treated as **short-term** capital gains, e.g., Mr. X buys Scrip A for Rs. 1000 and holds it for a couple of years and then sells it for say Rs. 1400.

This sum of Rs. 400 is the capital appreciation or capital gain.

Types of Capital Gains and Applicable Rate of Tax

Tax Reckoner FY: 2017-18

Snapshot of Tax Rates Specific to Mutual Funds

The rates are applicable for the financial year 2017-18 (Assessment Year: 2018-19) and subject to enactment of the Finance Bill, 2017.

Tax implications on Dividend Received by Unit Holders

	Individual/HUF	Domestic Company	NRI
Equity oriented schemes:	Nil	Nil	Nil
Debt oriented schemes:	Nil	Nil	Nil
Equity oriented schemes*:	Nil	Nil	Nil

Money market or liquid schemes /debt schemes (other than infrastructure debt fund)**

(i) Individual/HUF = 25% + 12% surcharge + 3% cess = 28.84%

(ii) Domestic company = 30% + 12% surcharge + 3% cess = 34.608%

(iii) NRI = 25% + 12% surcharge + 3% cess = 28.84%

Infrastructure Debt Fund**

(i) Individual / HUF = 25% + 12% Surcharge + 3% Cess = 28.84%

(ii) Domestic Company = 30% + 12% Surcharge + 3% Cess = 34.608%

(iii) NRI = 5% + 12% Surcharge + 3% Cess = 5.768%

* Securities transaction tax (STT) shall be payable on equity oriented mutual funds schemes at the time of redemption/switch to the other schemes/sale of units.

** For the purpose of determining the tax payable by the scheme, the amount of distributed income has to be increased to such amount as would, after reduction of tax on such increased amount, be equal to the income distributed by the mutual fund. In other words, the amount payable to unit holders is to be grossed up for determining the tax payable and accordingly, the effective tax rate would be higher.

Capital Gains Taxation

	Individual/ HUF	Domestic Company	NRI
Long-term capital gains	Nil	Nil	Nil
Short-term capital gains	15%	15%	15%
Long-term capital gains	20% (listed - 20% and unlisted - 10%)*		
Short-term capital gains	30%^ 30%^^/25%^^^ 30%^		

	Short term capital gains $	Long term capital gains $
Equity oriented schemes	15%	Nil

Other than equity oriented schemes 30%^. 10%* (for unlisted) and 20% and (for listed) $ Surcharge at 15%, is applicable where income of individual/HUF unit holders exceeds Rs. 1 crore.

As per Finance Bill, 2017, surcharge at 10% is to be levied in case of individual/ HUF unit holders where income of such unit holders exceeds Rs. 50 lakh but does not exceed Rs. 1 crore. Further, education cess at 3% will continue to apply on aggregate of tax and surcharge.

Surcharge at 7% is applicable where income of domestic corporate unit holders exceeds Rs. 1 crore but does not exceed Rs. 10 crore and at Rs. 12% where income exceeds Rs. 10 crore. Further, education cess at 3% will continue to apply on aggregate of tax and surcharge.

Short-term/long-term capital gain tax will be deducted at the time of redemption of units in case of NRI investors and after providing for indexation.

* Without indexation.

^ Assuming the investor falls into highest tax bracket.

^^ This rate applies to companies other than companies engaged in manufacturing business who are taxed at lower rate subject to fulfilment of certain conditions.

^^^ If total turnover or gross receipts during the financial year 2015-16 does not exceed remaining Rs. 50 crore.

Further, domestic companies are subject to minimum alternate tax not specified in above tax rates. Transfer of units upon consolidation of mutual fund schemes of two or more schemes of equity oriented fund or two or more schemes of a fund other than equity oriented fund in accordance with SEBI (Mutual Funds) Regulations, 1996 is exempt from capital gains.

Transfer of units upon consolidation of plans within mutual fund schemes in accordance with SEBI (Mutual Funds) Regulations, 1996 is exempt from capital gains.

Relaxation to non-residents from deduction of tax at higher rate in the absence of PAN subject to them providing specified information and documents.

Dividend Stripping: The loss due to sale of units in the schemes (where dividend is tax free) will not be available for setoff to the extent of tax-free dividend declared; if units are: (a) bought within three months prior to the record date fixed for dividend declaration; and (b) sold within nine months after the record date fixed for dividend declaration.

Bonus Stripping: The loss due to sale of original units in the schemes, where bonus units are issued, will not be available for setoff; if original units are: (a) bought within three months prior to the record date fixed for allotment of bonus units; and (b) sold within nine months after the record date fixed for allotment of bonus units. However, the amount of loss so ignored shall be deemed to be the cost of purchase or acquisition of such unsold bonus units.

1. *Short-Term Capital Gains (STCG)*

It is 15% (plus 15% surcharge and 3% cess = 17.7675%) on stock (where Security Transaction Tax (STT) has been deducted)/equity oriented mutual fund from assessment year: 2009-10 onwards (earlier up to assessment year: 2004-05 short-term gains will be added to the total income and taxed at rates applicable to taxpayer). Other capital assets will be as per marginal tax rates applicable in the respective financial year and as per the then budget provisions applicable.

2. *Long-Term Capital Gains (LTCG) taxed at 20% saving tax on LTCG*

It is possible to save tax on LTCG and some of the provisions are:

Sec 54 & 54 B: Sell a house/property and/or agricultural land and buy or construct another house/property and/or agricultural land (one needs to follow certain guidelines under the Act).

Sec 54 EC: It provides that where the capital gain arises from transfer of a long-term capital asset, it will be exempt if the assessee/investor has invested the capital gain in the long-term specified asset subject to fulfilment of conditions provided.

Table 26.5 Capital Gains – Details of Various Exemptions

Particulars	Sec 54	Sec 54B	Sec 54EC	Sec 54F
Kind of asset transferred	House/property used for residential purposes	Land used for agricultural purposes	Any capital asset	Any capital asset other than residential house
Eligible assessee	Individual and HUF	Individual and HUF	All	Individual and HUF

Condition of period of holding original asset	3 years	2 years	1 year for shares; listed securities; units of UTI/mutual fund specified u/s. 10(23D); zero coupon bonds; 3 years for any other asset	1 year for shares; listed securities; units of UTI/mutual fund specified u/s. 10(23D); zero coupon bonds; 3 years for any other asset
Exempt amount	The amount of gain or the cost of new asset whichever is less	Lower than the capital gain or the cost of acquisition	Lower than the capital gain or the amount invested in the bonds subject to maximum of Rs. 50 lakh	
Other requirements	See Notes 1 & 2	Assessee or his/her parents must have used the land for preceding two years for agricultural purpose	See Notes 1 & 2. Deduction u/s. 80C not to be granted for the same investment. New asset must be retained for a period of 3 years	See Notes 2 & 3. Must not own more than one residential house other than the new property on the date of transfer of original asset.

Notes:

1. In case a new asset is transferred before three years from the date of purchase/construction, the capital gains exempted earlier will be chargeable to tax in the year of transfer.
2. In order to avail exemption, gains are to be reinvested, before the date of filing the return of income; if the amount is not invested, it is to be deposited on or before that date in the account of specified bank/institution and it should be utilized within the specified time limit for purchase/construction of new asset.
3. Capital gains u/s. 54F exempted earlier shall be chargeable to tax if:
   (i) the assessee purchases within 2 years or constructs within 3 years any residential house other than the one in which reinvestment is made; and
   (ii) the new asset is transferred within a period of 3 years from the date of its purchase/construction.
4. If the cost of new house is more than the net consideration of original asset, the whole of the gains (Note forming part of 54 EC). If the cost of specified asset is less than net consideration, a proportionate amount of the gains will be exempt.

Indexation Benefit

It is a well-known fact that the prices of goods and services we consume keep moving up over the years. This implies that the value of rupee has eroded or the purchasing power has decreased. This general increase in price level is called *inflation*. The price inflation is measured by the annualized percentage change in the general price index, normally CPI (Consumer Price Index) is used but in India the reference point is the WPI (Wholesale Price Index). The Central Board of Direct Taxes (CBDT) calculates Cost Inflation Index (CII) and declares the same every year.

While calculating capital gains, one needs to deduct cost price from selling price. For example: one had bought a residential house for Rs. 8,00,000 in 2002 and sold the same for Rs. 32,00,000 in 2012. On the face of it, the capital gain would be 32,00,000 – 8,00,000 = Rs. 24,00,000. However, the purchasing power has not remained the same over these years. Therefore, there is need to index the cost based on CII. Indexation is the process of adjusting the cost price by using the CII provided by the income tax department.

Table 26.6 Cost of Inflation Index (Income Tax)

S. No.	Financial Year	Cost Inflation Index	Year on Year Increase %	Sr. No.	Financial Year	Cost Inflation Index	Year on Year Increase %
1.	1981-82	100					
2.	1982-83	109	9.00%	19	1999-2000	389	10.83%
3.	1983-84	116	6.42%	20	2000-01	406	4.37%
4.	1984-85	125	7.76%	21	2001-02	426	4.93%
5.	1985-86	133	6.40%	22	2002-03	447	4.93%
6.	1986-87	140	5.26%	23	2003-04	463	3.58%
7.	1987-88	150	7.14%	24	2004-05	480	3.67%
8.	1988-89	161	7.33%	25	2005-06	497	3.54%
9.	1989-90	172	6.83%	26	2006-07	519	4.43%
10.	1990-91	182	5.81%	27	2007-08	551	6.17%
11.	1991-92	199	9.34%	28	2008-09	582	5.63%
12.	1992-93	223	12.06%	29	2009-10	632	8.59%
13.	1993-94	244	9.42%	30	2010-11	711	12.50%
14.	1994-95	259	6.15%	31	2011-12	785	10.41%
15.	1995-96	281	8.49%	32	2012-13	852	8.54%
16.	1996-97	305	8.54%	33	2013-14	939	10.21%
17.	1997-98	331	8.52%	34	2014-15	1024	9.05%
18.	1998-99	351	6.04%	35	2015-16	1081	5.57%
				36	2016-17	1125	4.07%

Table 26.7 Tax Provisions for Mutual Funds AY: 2018-19 (FY: 2017-18)

Fund Type	Dividend Distribution Tax (DDT)	STCG	LTCG	Security Transaction Tax (STT)
Equity Oriented MFs	NA	15% + 15% surcharge + 3% cess (for all categories)	Exempt	On redemptions @ 0.001%
Debt funds	25% (individuals and HUFs) 30% (others)	Marginal rate of taxation for individual/UF/RI and 30% + 15% surcharge + 3% Cess for others	20% after indexation + 15% surcharge + 3% Cess	Not applicable

26.7 ANALYSIS OF TAX-SHELTERED FIXED INVESTMENT AVENUES

The tax advantages associated with various fixed income avenues widely. At one end of spectrum, we have *provident fund* (as well as public provident fund) contributions that enjoy initial as well as continuing tax advantages and at the other end of the spectrum, we have Indira Vikas Patra, which like the debenture issues of private sector companies, offer no tax advantage.

As an investor, who is analysing these investment avenues, he/she would primarily evaluate them in terms of the post-tax rate of return, which may be calculated as follows.

Step I: Find the net investment made for every hundred rupees of gross investment made.

The net investment is simply: 100 – Tax saving on an investment of Rs. 100

Step II: Calculate the post-tax amount that would be receivable by the investor at the time of maturity or withdrawal after n years on every hundred rupees of gross investment. This is equal to:

$$100\ [1 + \text{Interest rate}]\ \hat{}\,n\ [1 - \text{Tax rate applicable on withdrawal}]$$

Step III: Compute the post-tax rate of return. This is equal to the value of r in the following equation: Net investment $(1 + r)\ \hat{}\,n$ = Post-tax amount receivable at the time of maturity or withdrawal.

26.8 TAX PROVISIONS FOR GRATUITY

Eligibility: As per Section 10 (10) of Income Tax Act, 1961, gratuity is paid when an employee completes 5 or more years of full time service with the employer. Let us understand tax treatment of gratuity.

The gratuity so received by the employee is taxable under the head 'Income from salary'. In case gratuity is received by the nominee/legal heirs of the employee, the same is taxable in their hands under the head 'Income from other sources'. This tax treatment varies for different categories of individual assessees.

For the purpose of calculation of exempt gratuity, employees may be divided into three categories:

(a) Government employees: They are fully exempt from income tax arising from receipt of gratuity.

(b) Non-government employees covered under the Payment of Gratuity Act, 1972 – Maximum exemption from tax is the least of:

(i) Actual gratuity received; or

(ii) Rs. 10,00,000; or

(iii) 15 days' salary for each completed year of service or part thereof.

(c) Non-government employees not covered under the Payment of Gratuity Act, 1972 – Maximum exemption from tax is the least of:

(i) actual gratuity received; or

(ii) Rs. 10,00, 000; or

(iii) half-month's average salary for each completed year of service (no part thereof).

Table 26.8 Tax Benefits/Provisions Applicable for Provident Fund

Item	Statutory Provident Fund	Recognised Provident Fund	Unrecognised Provident Fund	Public Provident Fund (PPF)
1. Employee's contribution	Eligible for deduction under Sec. 80 C of IT Act, 1961	Eligible for deduction under Sec. 80 C of IT Act, 1961	Not eligible for deduction under Sec. 80 C of IT Act, 1961. No exemption.	Eligible for deduction under Sec. 80 C of IT Act, 1961
2. Employer's contribution	Fully tax exempt for employee. Not treated as income in the hands of employee in the year in which contribution is made by employer.	< 12% of salary is tax exempt for employee. > 12% of salary is taxable for employee	Taxable at maturity. Not treated as income in the hands of employee in the year in which contribution is made by employer.	There is no employer contribution in PPF.
3. Interest earned/accrued	Fully tax exempted for employee. Not treated as income in the hands of employee in the year of credit.	< 9.5% is tax exempt for employee. > 9.5 % is taxable for employee.	Taxable at maturity. Not treated as income in the hands of employee in the year of credit.	Fully tax exempted.

4. Maturity proceeds	Fully tax exempted for employee.	Fully tax exempted for employee.	Employee's contribution – (i) Maturity amount fully tax exempted. (ii) Interest earned – Taxable as Income from Other Sources. Employer's contribution – (i) Maturity amount taxable as salaries. (ii) Interest earned – Taxable as income from other sources.	Fully tax exempted.

Table 26.9 Bird's Eye View of Taxability at Various Levels in a REIT Structure

Nature of Income Level	Interest paid to SPV	Rental Income on property held by REIT directly	Dividend on shares of SPV	Capital gains on sale of shares of SPV/sale of properties held by REIT directly	Other income	Capital gains on market transfer of units of REIT by unit holders/ Sponsors *
Unit holder	REIT distributing the interest from SPV subject to WHT at 5% -NRs (No further tax in the hands of unit holder)	Taxable in the hands of the unit holder. Further, REIT to withhold tax @ 10% if distributed to resident unit holder and at the applicable rate in force if distributed to non-resident unit holder (not being a company or a foreign company)	Exempt	Exempt	Exempt	STCG - 15% (held for 36 months or less)

Contd.

	WHT at 10% - R (taxed at applicable rates in the hands of unit holder)					LTCG- The whole amount of gain after 36 months i.e. LTCG is exempted. (held for more than 36 months)
REIT	Exempted	Exempted	Exempted	Tax rate applicable depending on period of holding, etc.	Tax at 30%	N.A.
SPV (in the form of a company)	Tax break available on interest (subject to conditions) no WHT applicable on interest payment	N.A.	DDT at 17.65%	N.A.	N.A.	N.A.

Source: As per Finance Bill, 2015

Note: Above rates are excluding surcharge and education cess

* Sale on stock exchange subject to securities transaction tax

WHT = withholding tax; R = resident; NR = non-resident; STCG = short-term capital gain tax; LTCG = long-term capital gain tax

Note: The latest provision of Budget 2017 are:

Capital gain and pass-through status to Real Estate Investment Trusts (REITs), curbing of black money in the real-estate sector and housing for all, are some highlights for the real estate sector. However, the industry wants to see more on easing the liquidity crunch. Real estate watchers said the pass-through status will help monetise real estate assets and attract new investments in REITs. It will also establish a level-playing field for the domestic and foreign private equity funds.

A *pass-through* status means that the income generated would be taxed in the hands of the investor, and that the fund itself would not have to pay tax on the same. Without this clarification, it was feared that REITs may be subjected to double-taxation; paying tax whenever income was generated at the fund level, and then again in the hands of the investor.

Anshuman Magazine, CMD, and CBRE South Asia, said: "Rental income under the REIT structures has also been given a pass-through status, while a mere presence of a fund manager in India does not indicate permanent residence and not to face adversarial tax consequences."

26.9 TAXATION OF TRUST

1. Private Trust

For the purpose of Indian taxes, a private trust is not regarded as a separate taxable unit. However, a trustee under the ITA acquires the status of the beneficiaries and is taxed in the role of the beneficiaries in a representative capacity. The provisions relating to taxation of trusts are laid out in Section 161-164 of the ITA.

There are three types of private trust:

- **Irrevocable Determinate (Specific) Trust**

  In such a trust, the beneficiaries are identifiable and their shares are determinate; a trustee can be assessed as a representative assessee and tax is levied and recovered from him in a like manner and to the same extent as it would be leviable upon and recoverable from the person represented by him (i.e., the beneficiary). There is no further tax in the hands of the beneficiary on the distribution of income from a trust.

- **Irrevocable Discretionary Trust**

  A trust is regarded as a discretionary trust when a trustee has the power to distribute the income of a trust at its discretion amongst the set of beneficiaries.

  In case of an onshore discretionary trust, with both resident and non-resident beneficiaries, a trustee will be regarded as the representative assessee of the beneficiaries and subject to tax at the maximum marginal rate, i.e., 30%. Moreover, the trustee should not be subject to Indian taxes or reporting obligations. However, if all the beneficiaries of such discretionary trust are Indian residents, then a trustee may be regarded as the representative assessee of the beneficiaries and can be subject to Indian taxes (on behalf of the beneficiaries) at the maximum marginal rate, i.e., 30%.

- **Revocable Trust**

  Under the ITA, a transfer shall be deemed to be revocable if it contains any provision for the re-transfer directly or indirectly of the whole or any part of the income or assets to the transferor or it in any way gives the transferer a right to re-assume power directly or indirectly over the whole or any part of the income or assets. Thus, where a settlement is made in a manner that a settler is entitled to recover the contributions over a specified period, and is entitled to the income from the contributions, the trust is disregarded for the purposes of tax, and the income thereof taxed as though it had directly arisen to the settler. If there are joint settlers to a revocable trust, the income of the trust will be taxed in the hands of each settler to the extent of assets settled by them in the trust.

2. Public Trusts

Subject to conditions, income from property held in trust or other legal obligation, for a religious or charitable purpose is tax exempt.

Charitable purpose as defined in section 2(15) of the Income Tax Act includes relief of the poor, education, medical relief, preservation of environment and preservation of monuments or places or objects of artistic or historic interest, and the advancement of any other object of general public utility.

27 FEMA Guidelines Relating to Investments in India

CHAPTER

- India's new industrial policy in the year 1991 introduced by the P.V. Narsimha Rao government had opened the doors to foreign trade in India. *Foreign trade* means import and export of goods and services and *foreign investments* refers to Foreign Direct Investments (FDI) and portfolio investments and investments in other forms.
- The regulations and provisions under the Foreign Exchange Regulation Act (FERA) did not help to achieve the desired objectives of development of foreign trade, and promotion.
- In 1991, Indian government was forced to open up its economy and since then FERA was liberalised considerably. However, post-South East Asian currency crisis and other developments, the need was felt of more pragmatic and investor-friendly policies and regulations. Therefore, Foreign Exchange Management Act (FEMA), 1999 was enacted with the aim of managing foreign exchange rather than regulating the same as under FERA. FEMA as it stands today may well facilitate more inflow of foreign investments to realize the *make in India* objective.
- Along with FEMA, a new industrial policy was announced. This policy has been revised periodically to suit the need of the economy and investors. FEMA along with new industrial policy have put India on the growth map.
- The potential of huge inflow of foreign funds is seen as heaven of opportunities for both, foreign business entities and foreign residents to invest their money for wealth maximization. This has naturally made India an attractive destination. Keeping in mind the bundle of investment opportunities, let us have a look at the implications under the Indian foreign exchange laws vis-à-vis management of investments both inside and outside India.

27.1 OVERVIEW OF FEMA

FEMA provisions are governed by the Foreign Exchange Management Act, 1999 (amended from time to time), Notifications, Regulations, and Circulars, Master Directions, etc., issued by the Government of India (GOI) and the Reserve Bank of India (RBI) from time to time.

The investments coming from abroad and the investments made abroad should be in accordance with the laws prevailing in the country.

Illustration 1: In order to issue equity shares to an eligible foreign investor, one needs to comply with FEMA provisions issued by RBI and also the Foreign Direct Investment policy guidelines issued by the GOI from time to time.

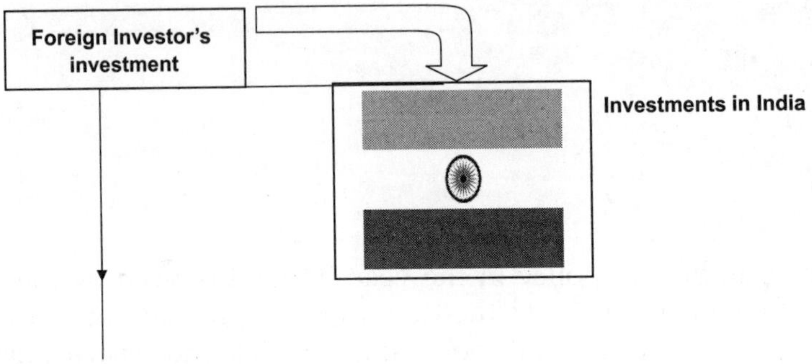

Subjected to and in accordance with

1. Foreign direct investment policy (GOI)
2. Foreign Exchange Management Act, 1999
3. Notifications
4. Rules
5. Regulations
6. Circulars

{ As amended and issued from time to time. } (applies to items 3–4)

Illustration 2: In order to invest or create a wholly owned subsidiary or a joint venture outside India, the eligible investor shall comply with FEMA regulations and such other laws prevailing in India which governs such provisions.

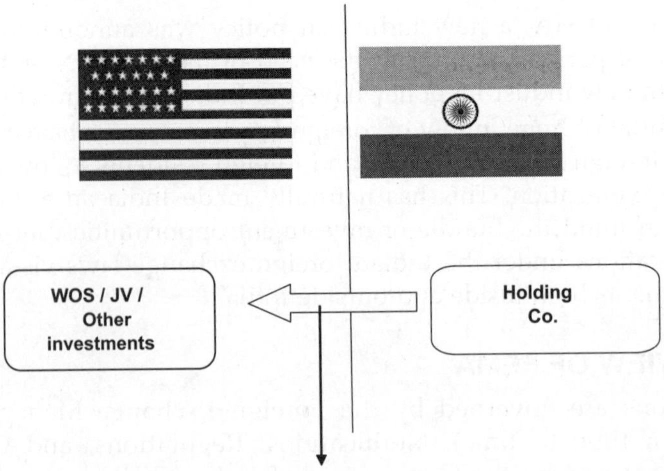

Subject to FEMA regulations and any other relevant laws

- The policies and procedures provided by the authorities regulate the FEMA provisions. These policies and procedures issued provides guidelines for routing investments in and outside India which will further ease foreign trade in India and provide and develop a conducive environment for the Indian domestic markets.
- The following are some of the possible areas for foreigners intending to invest and maximize their wealth:
  1. Investments having fixed income avenues
  2. Securities market
  3. Portfolio investment scheme
  4. Real estate market
  5. Mutual Funds
- It is to be noted that government has eased the norms for investment in India. However, the same is sector-specific and the investment conditions applicable to one type of foreign investor may differ from the conditions applicable to another type of investor.

27.2 FIXED INCOME AVENUES

- While investments that provide fixed income are the obvious preference, it oftentimes takes a backseat in view of the fast paced stock market where these investments are still very attractive to many types of investors. Honestly, given a choice, all investors will chose to be risk averse. However, the retired investor class who or those approaching retirement prefer such investments more since their aim is to preserve capital and ensure a guaranteed income.
- There are various types of instruments which enables the investor to earn fixed incomes. Some of the examples of such investments are fixed deposits, bonds, etc.

➢ **Fixed Deposits**

1. The various schemes available to non-residents along with various facilities provided can be explained with the help of the following table.

Table 27.1

Particulars	Foreign Currency (Non-Resident) Account (Banks) Scheme [FCNR (B) Account]	Non-Resident (External) Rupee Account Scheme [NRE Account]	Non-Resident Ordinary Rupee Account Scheme [NRO Account]
(1)	(2)	(3)	(4)
Eligible persons	NRIs (individuals/ entities of Bangladesh/ Pakistan nationality/ ownerships require prior approval of RBI)	NRIs (individuals/ entities of Bangladesh/ Pakistan nationality/ ownerships require prior approval of RBI)	Any person resident outside India (other than a person resident in Nepal and Bhutan). Individuals/entities of Pakistan nationality/ ownerships, entities of Bangladesh ownership and erstwhile Overseas Corporate Bodies require prior approval of the Reserve Bank.
Suitability	NRIs who wish to keep their overseas savings in India but do not want to convert them in INR.	NRIs who earn income abroad and would like to remit it back to India.	These accounts are generally used by NRIs who earn income in India.
Joint account	In the names of two or more non-resident individuals provided all the account holders are persons of Indian nationality or origins. Resident close relatives (relative as defined in Section 6 of the Companies Act, 1956) on 'former or survivor' basis. The resident close relative shall be eligible to operate the account as a Power of Attorney holder in accordance with extant instructions during the lifetime of the NRI/PIO account holder.	In the names of two or more non-resident individuals provided all the account holders are persons of Indian nationality or origin. Resident close relative (relative as defined in Section 6 of the Companies Act, 1956) on 'former or survivor' basis. The resident's close relative shall be eligible to operate the account as a Power of Attorney holder in accordance with extant instructions during the lifetime of the NRI/ PIO account holder.	May be held jointly with residents.

Nomination	Permitted	Permitted	Permitted
Currency in which account is denominated	Any permitted currency, i.e., a foreign currency which is freely convertible	Indian Rupees	Indian Rupees
Repatriation	Allowed	Allowed	Not allowed except: i. All current income ii. Up to USD 1 (one) million per financial year (April-March), by a NRI/ PIO.
Type of Account	Term Deposit only	Savings, Current, Recurring, Fixed Deposit	Savings, Current, Recurring, Fixed Deposit
Period for fixed deposits	For terms not less than 1 year and not more than 5 years.	From one to three years. However, banks are allowed to accept NRE deposits above three years from their Asset-Liability point of view.	As applicable to resident accounts.
Rate of interest	With effect from March 1, 2014: (i) deposits of 1 year to less than 3 years maturity, interest shall be paid within the ceiling rate of LIBOR/SWAP rates plus 200 basis points; (ii) deposits of 3-5 years maturity, interest shall be paid within the ceiling rate of LIBOR/ SWAP rates plus 300 basis points. On floating rate deposits, interest shall be paid within the ceiling of SWAP rates for the respective currency/maturity plus 200 bps/300 bps as the case may be. For floating rate deposits, the interest reset period shall be six months.	With effect from March 1, 2014, interest rates offered by banks on NRE deposits cannot be higher than those offered by them on comparable domestic rupee deposits.	Banks are free to determine their interest rates on savings deposits under Ordinary Non-Resident (NRO) Accounts. However, interest rates offered by banks on NRO deposits cannot be higher than those offered by them on comparable domestic rupee deposits.

Operations by Power of Attorney in favour of a resident by the non-resident account holder	Operations in the account in terms of Power of Attorney are restricted to withdrawals for permissible local payments or remittance to the account holder himself through normal banking channels.	Operations in the account in terms of Power of Attorney are restricted to withdrawals for permissible local payments or remittance to the account holder himself through normal banking channels.	Operations in the account in terms of Power of Attorney is restricted to withdrawals for permissible local payments in rupees, remittance of current income to the account holder outside India or remittance to the account holder himself through normal banking channels. Remittance to the NRI/PIO account holder is subject to the ceiling of USD 1 (one) million per financial year.
Taxability	Both the principal amount and the interest earned on it is completely tax free.	Both the principal amount and the interest earned on it is completely tax free.	While the principal amount is completely tax free, the interest you earn on that principal is taxed in the hands of the NRI as per the applicable income tax slab rates.

27.3 EQUITY SHARES

Part A Introduction

- It is a general perception that lower the age of the investor, the higher shall be the risk taking appetite of such person.
- When it comes to risk, we are talking about equity shares, intra-day trading, settlements on net basis, high volatility, constant fluctuations in the price, arbitrage opportunities, etc.
- The Indian equity market is also known as the Indian stock market which is the third biggest market for trading in securities after China and Hong Kong in the Asian region.
- A survey suggested that it had a market capitalization of approximately $600 billion. The two major markets for the securities in India are:

  (a) Bombay Stock Exchange

  (b) National Stock Exchange
- The equity participation of investors from abroad including both, individuals and foreign institutional investors has made this sector a very attractive proposition.

- Over a period of years, the Indian markets have become very dynamic. It is one of the largest trading floors attracting millions of investors across the globe. One needs to be careful before investing in any type of securities.

Part B (1) Foreign Investments in Indian Equity Shares

- Be it noted that the equity participation has not been relaxed in all sectors of the Indian economy. These relaxations, in the Foreign Direct Investment Policy as issued by the Department of Industrial Policy and Promotion, Ministry of Commerce and Industry, Government of India, have to be kept in mind by the RBI while providing FEMA guidelines to make sure that the rules, regulations and circulars issued in connection therewith are in line with such policy.
- The FEMA provisions provide that the Foreign Direct Investment (FDI) in India shall be on either of the following ways:
  (a) Automatic Route
  (b) Approval Route (from RBI, GOI, FIPB, other authorities as the case may be)
- Under the automatic route, the company issuing instruments as permitted shall accept investments up to the amount of the permissible ceiling and the payment for such investments shall be as per the permissible modes.
- The following entities have to apply under the Government Route:
  (a) Companies intending to issue the permissible instruments beyond a specified sectoral limit
  (b) Companies engaged in specified activities
- The following are the specified activities where the foreign investments are prohibited **(Notification No. FEMA 20/ 2000 – RB dated 3rd May, 2000):**
  (a) Lottery business including government/private lottery, online lotteries, etc.[1]
  (b) Gambling and betting including casinos, etc.
  (c) Chit funds
  (d) Nidhi company
  (e) Trading in transferable development rights
  (f) Real estate business (as defined under FEMA) or construction of farm houses
  (g) Manufacturing of cigars, cheroots, cigarillos and cigarettes, of tobacco or of tobacco substitutes

(h) Activities/sectors not open to private sector investment, e.g., atomic energy and railway operations (other than specified permitted activities).

---

[1] Foreign technology collaboration in any form including licensing for franchise, trademark, brand name, management contract is also prohibited for lottery business and gambling and betting activities.

Part B (2) Investment in Portfolio Investment Scheme (PIS)

- Foreign portfolio investment is the entry of funds into a country where foreigners deposit money in a country's bank or make purchases in the country's stock and bond markets, sometimes for speculation.
- Portfolio investments typically involve transactions in securities that are highly liquid, i.e., they can be bought and sold quickly. A portfolio investment is an investment made by an investor who is not involved in the management of a company, which is in contrast to direct investment, which allows an investor to exercise a certain degree of managerial control over that entity.
- Equity investments where the owner holds less than 10% of a company's shares are classified as portfolio investment. These transactions are also referred to as *portfolio flows* and are recorded in the financial account of a country's balance of payments. According to the Institute of International Finance, portfolio flows arise through the transfer of ownership of securities from one country to another.
- The FEMA defines the Portfolio Investment Scheme, permitting non-resident Indians and foreign institutional investors to buy and sell shares and convertible debentures of Indian companies, and units of domestic mutual funds at any of the Indian stock exchanges.

Applicability

Non-resident Indians: - NRIs are eligible to purchase shares and convertible debentures issued by Indian companies under Portfolio Investment Scheme provided they are permitted by AD Category-1 Bank.

Application for the PIS

- Banks designated by the RBI can accept applications at branches located close to the nearest stock exchange. An NRI can operate the PIS through only one selected branch. In order to operate from more than one branch, special permission from the RBI is required. The following documents are generally required by designated banks to apply for the PIS:

  (a) PIS application form
  (b) RPI or NRI Form, with details of shares bought from the primary market
  (c) Tariff sheet of the PIS
  (d) Demat Account opening form

Investment in Listed Indian Companies by NRIs

(a) NRIs can invest in shares of a listed Indian company through any recognized stock exchange.

(b) NRIs can invest through the designated AD's on repatriation and non-repatriation basis under the PIS route up to 5 per cent of the paid-up capital/paid-up value of each series of debentures of the company.

(c) The aggregate paid-up value of shares / convertible debentures purchased by all NRIs together cannot exceed 10 per cent of the paid-up capital of the company/ paid-up value of each series of debentures of the company.

(d) The aggregate ceiling of 10 per cent can be raised to 24 per cent by passing of a resolution by its Board of Directors followed by a special resolution to that effect by its General Body which shall necessarily be notified to the Reserve Bank of India.

Sectors Prohibited for Investments by RBI

NRIs are not allowed to invest in any company which is engaged in the following:

(a) Business of chit fund

(b) Nidhi company

(c) Agricultural plantation activities

(d) Real estate business

(e) Construction of farmhouses

(f) Manufacturing of cigars, cheroots, cigarillos and cigarettes of tobacco or of tobacco substitutes

(g) Trading in transferable development rights

Accounts through which NRI's can purchase securities

- NRI can approach a designated bank of any AD Category-1 bank for permission to open a single designated account under PIS for routing investments.
- Payment made on repatriation basis has to be by way of inward remittance of foreign exchange through normal banking channels or out of funds held in NRE/FCNR.
- If shares are purchased on non-repatriation basis, the NRIs can also utilize their NRO account in addition to their other accounts as above.

Sale of Shares

- The PIS allows for sale of shares, bonds and debentures by NRIs to residents through private arrangement with the approval of the RBI. General authorization from the RBI is also available for transfer of shares, bonds and debentures by way of gifts to his close relatives.

  For sale or transfer of shares and debentures of Indian companies to other NRIs, no permission is required from the RBI. The transferee NRI, however, would require permission for purchase of the shares.
- Short-selling or selling the shares bought by NRI investors before delivery is prohibited.

Repatriation of PIS

- Proceeds of sale of stocks purchased under the PIS from NRE or FCNR accounts or from foreign remittances are repatriable. However, investments made in the PIS from NRO accounts are not eligible for repatriation.
- A combination of repatriable and non-repatriable investments under the PIS permitted though these would have to be operated through NRE and NRO accounts respectively. Exclusive NRE and NRO accounts have to be maintained for PIS, which can be held by joint account holders as well.

27.4 INVESTMENTS IN REAL ESTATE

FDI in Real Estate by NRI/PIO

To encourage inflow of funds, RBI has allowed direct investment from foreign residents, companies from outside India to invest in India. NRI/PIO's have been given various options to invest their money in India and the government promotes and attracts investment with the introduction of a liberal and transparent policy for overseas Indians. Most of the sectors are open for investment under the automatic route wherein prior approval of RBI is not required before investments are made in India.

Incentives

- NRIs/PIOs are allowed to purchase immovable properties in India. Housing finance companies and banks have been permitted to offer NRI home loans and also to PIOs.
- Repatriation has been made easy for NRIs as they can approach the authorized dealers of foreign exchange without going through the RBI. The rental income obtained from investment in Indian real estate can also be repatriated every year.
- Sale proceeds of immovable property acquired out of inward remittances or debit to NRE/FCNR (B) account can be repatriated. Also, there is no lock-in period with regard to immovable property that is inherited. The repatriation in the case of residential properties is however restricted to a maximum of two properties.
- NRIs can get home loans and repay it through inward remittance using normal banking channels or by debit to his NRE/FCNR(B)/NRO account or out of rental income derived from renting out such property. Repayment of loan in foreign exchange is treated as equivalent to foreign exchange received for purchase of residential property.
- NRIs are allowed 100% investment in companies engaged in construction, real estate development and funding of housing development.

Investment Options

- NRIs/PIOs can invest in limited companies engaged in real estate development. The aggregate paid-up value of shares/convertible debentures purchased by all NRIs can be raised to 24% of the paid-up capital of the company/paid-up value of series of debentures.
- Foreign direct investment is encouraged and permitted, subject to certain conditions, in the following real estate sectors in India. It includes hotel development, tourism, hospitality, hospitals, and resorts township development, development of commercial real estate, built-up infrastructure, housing and construction projects, building educational institutes, building recreational facilities, infrastructure projects at both regional and local level as well as Special Economic Zones.

Transfer

- NRIs/PIOs are allowed to transfer immovable property to a resident Indian. The sale proceeds of the property received will be credited only to the NRO account.

Restriction

- NRIs/PIOs are restricted from investing in agricultural/plantation/farm land in India.
- PIOs are restricted from transferring of immovable property by way of sale to another PIO residing abroad.

27.5 INVESTMENTS OUTSIDE INDIA

Earlier, during the 1990s purchase of goods or availing of services from abroad was considered a status symbol. Similarly, if someone would have a thought of making an investment outside India, the typically negative minded people would say, "Here comes the next TATA BIRLA." Such was the mindset of the people of India. However, one needs to understand that this is one of the most remarkable developments India has ever achieved. This is one of the reasons for expansion of foreign trade in our country.

Taking it forward, business organizations started developing thoughts of making investments outside India in the form of shares, securities, setting up a wholly owned subsidiary/joint venture outside, etc. The Reserve Bank of India has come up with various provisions[2] governing such activities subject to the net worth of the company intending to make investments, line of activity in which it is engaged, the underlying financial commitment intended, etc.

[2] Notification No. FEMA 120/RB-2004 dated July 7, 2004 and Master Circular No. 11/2015-16 dated 01/07/2015.

27.6 MUTUAL FUNDS

Part – A Introduction

- Mutual funds in India were introduced in the year 1961 when the GOI had launched the Unit Trust of India (UTI). Following the UTI, there were many mutual funds which entered the Indian market sponsored by the banking sector.
- With the advent of the era of reformation post the new industrial policy introduced by the GOI, the Mutual Fund sector was opened up to private players after 1993.
- The Securities and Exchange Board of India (SEBI) introduced the regulatory framework for Mutual Funds in 1996.
- Despite all efforts taken to promote the Mutual Funds sector, the investments, although attractive and provides various benefits including deductions of Income under section 80C of the Income Tax Act, 1961, this sector does not receive the required level of investments.

Part – B Foreign Investment in Indian Mutual Funds

- The FEMA provisions have defined the Portfolio Investment Scheme, permitting the non-resident Indians, persons of Indian origin and the Foreign Institutional Investors (FIIs) to buy and sell units of the domestic mutual funds in the Indian stock exchanges.
- RBI has granted General Permission to SEBI Registered FIIs to invest in India under the Portfolio Investment Scheme.
- Further, investments by NRIs do not require any specific prior approval of the RBI for investing in the units of the mutual funds. Specific prior approval is required to be taken only by FIIs and OCBs.
- The repatriation of sale proceeds of the units of mutual funds invested is allowed only if the non-resident had an NRE or FCNR bank account in India.
- The Mutual Funds are regulated by SEBI. Accordingly, the Mutual Funds are required to comply with the terms and conditions stipulated by SEBI. The amount representing investment should be received by payment modes permitted and accepted. The dividend/interest of units may accordingly be remitted to the investor.

Part – C Investments in Overseas Mutual Funds

- Indian Mutual Funds registered with the SEBI are permitted to invest in units/securities issued by overseas mutual funds or unit trusts registered with overseas regulators and in the specified securities. However, a limited number of Indian Mutual Funds are permitted to invest cumulatively up to USD 1 billion in overseas exchange traded funds as may be permitted by SEBI from time to time.

UNIT-V

28 CHAPTER

Common Errors in Investment Management

"Investing is not gambling and shouldn't be treated as a hit-or-miss proposition."

Investors appear to be prone to the following errors in managing their investments:

- **Ill-defined approach:** Often investors do not spell out clearly their goals *vis-à-vis risk* disposition and investment policy. This creates confusion and impacts decisions. From the outset, every investor should form an investment strategy that serves as a framework to guide future decisions. A well-planned strategy takes into account several important factors, including time horizon, tolerance for risk, amount of investable assets, and planned future contributions. "At the outset, individuals should have a clear sense of what they want to accomplish and the amount of volatility they are willing to bear."
- **Unrealistic goals:** Some (or many) investors have unrealistic and exaggerated expectations from their investments. Many a times, they are misled by factors: (a) false and unjustified claims made publicly, and (b) exceptional performance of some, may be due to fortuitous factors, managed artificially (unethical practice).
- **Investing in individual stocks instead of in a diversified portfolio of securities:** Investing in an individual stock increases risk versus investing in an already-diversified mutual fund or index fund that allows spreading and thus reducing risk. Investors should maintain a broadly diversified portfolio incorporating different asset classes and investment styles. Failing to diversify leaves individuals vulnerable to fluctuations in a particular security or sector.

  Also, never confuse mutual fund diversification with portfolio diversification, said Brian Breidenbach, CFA, CPA, Managing Principal of Breidenbach Capital Consulting, and LLC in Louisville, KY. However, remember that it is also possible to over-diversify and own too many investment products—the best course of action is to seek a delicate balance between the two.

- **Cursory decision making:** Investors base their decisions on partial evidence, hearsay, or casual tips given by brokers, friends and others. "Listening to the media for their sole source of investment thinking rather than pursuing a professional relationship with an advisor is a far too common investor mistake."

  "Believing that information that is new to the investor is not known to anybody else is a real mistake. A useful rule is that if you've heard it, so have many others, hence the information is likely to have been already factored into the market price.

- **Tendency to speculate:** Some investors usually have a short time horizon, willing to assume high risk, resort to a very high and substantial borrowing, *vis-à-vis* their personal resources (leverage). Determining your appetite for risk involves measuring the potential impact of a real monetary loss of assets on both your portfolio and your psyche. However, do not wait until a sudden or near-term drop in the value of your assets to conduct an evaluation of your level of tolerance for risk.

- **Neglect:** Individuals often fail to begin an investment program simply because they lack basic knowledge of where or how to start. Likewise, periods of inactivity are frequently the result of discouragement over previous investment losses or negative growth in the equities markets. To be certain, investors should continue investing in every market—albeit through different investment vehicles—as well as establish a mechanism to make regular contributions to their portfolios. Investors should also regularly review their holdings to ensure they are adhering to their overall strategy.

- **Decision-making by tax avoidance:** While individuals should be aware of the tax implications of their actions, the first objective should always be to make a fundamentally sound investment decision. A wiser move is to simply find a good tax consultant.

- **Churning your investment:** Too frequent trading in investments cut into returns more than anything else. Again, the solution is a long-term *buy-and-hold* strategy, rather than an active trading approach.

- **Basing decisions on emotions:** Making investment decisions based on hope and fear, or even worse, greed and panic, destroys wealth, by causing investors to buy in at a high price and sell cheaply. This is exactly the reverse of the dictates of common sense.

- **Timing the market:** Investors will say, "but I'll come out of the market before bad times, and go back in for good times." That sounds like a sensible plan, except that it is next to impossible to achieve in practice. Missing the best single day or missing best few weeks would impact and can reduce one's potential of earning higher or better returns. Time, not timing, is the secret in investing.

- **Concentration:** The temptation, once one starts down the slippery slope of investing in a particular favoured asset, is to pile more of one's wealth into it than is wise to do. After all, the logic runs, if it's the best asset to be in, why would one invest in anything else? This flies in the face of common sense as stated in the old proverb, 'don't put all your eggs in one basket'. But it can also be demonstrated to be unwise mathematically. Investing in different assets that move up and down in different ways reduces the overall risk in a portfolio without necessarily having a commensurate effect on performance.
- **Ignoring costs:** Costs have a real effect on investment returns, especially compounded over a long term. So, paying high costs is, largely, a waste of money. Better to control costs and drive down the middle of the fairway.
- **Chasing performance:** Studies have shown that good past performance is not a reliable indicator of the future. Better to remove the guesswork and the extra risk by replicating the desired asset class as closely and cost-effectively as possible.
- **Ignoring other risks:** Investors tend to concentrate on the risk to their capital. This is natural and right, but to do so in isolation leaves one prey to other risks. Consider the retired person, with Rs. 10,00,000 in the bank, relying on the income to supplement his pension. If interest rates fall, so too will his income. He may even have to dip into capital to supplement the lost interest, so the interest rate risk becomes a capital risk anyway.

Consider, too, that same Rs. 10,00,000 and think about its purchasing power. Today, there is no risk to the purchasing power – our hypothetical investor can go out and buy Rs. 10,00,000 of goods and services if he chooses. Can he buy the same goods and services for Rs. 10,00,000 next year? No, because inflation will have raised their price. And the longer the time horizon, the greater the risk to purchasing power.

29 Guidelines for Investments

CHAPTER

So far in the foregoing chapters, we have learnt about key issues relating to the process of investment management including the characteristics of various investment avenues available to investors. We will now discuss how to translate the knowledge, skills, insights, and perspectives gained so far into specific guidelines for investment decision making.

It is fair to say that most investors make money when markets are going up but when the bull market ends, and they never last forever, many investors will be wondering where they went wrong.

Proper Planning

Here investors need to ask a few questions such as:

1. What do I want from my investments?
2. How much risk would I like to take?
3. Do I need regular income or just capital growth?

Investing for the Right Reasons

Quite often we see investments based on factors like year-end tax savings, a friendly tip, hot news, surplus of money at a given point of time and so on. Your investment decision should be backed up with proper research or reasoning.

Choose the Right Time Frame

There is no right or wrong way to approach other than look within yourself and define your preferences and what is reasonable for you. Short-term investing or "trading" takes more time and attention. It can also require greater nerves. It also requires more education and information. Short-term trading can be exciting and quite profitable. Long-term investing is ideal for those people who prefer to "set and forget" as they say. Long-term investing involves less of your time and requires less information on an on-going basis. It is more suitable to people that do not have the time or desire to watch the market every single day.

Each of us must approach investing in a way that is compatible to our preferences and personality.

After having gone through the various aspects of the financial plan (a formal, concrete written one), now is the time to implement it. Broadly, guidelines are divided into the following:

- Guidelines for base level investments and fixed income investment avenues.
- General guidelines for equity investment and for aggressive and conservative equity investors.

Assessing your current Wealth

It is always advisable to calculate your net worth first.

1. List all your assets that you own, e.g., cash, bank accounts, all financial investments, jewellery, vehicles, receivables, property, other assets, etc.
2. Then list all your liabilities, amount you owe to others, e.g., credit card dues, bills outstanding, loans outstanding, taxes due, other liabilities, etc.
3. Subtract liabilities from Assets to obtain the **net worth**. This will provide you an indication of your capacity to achieve your financial goals.

Leverage Ratio

This is a measure of the role of debt in the asset build-up of the investor. It is calculated as Total liabilities/Total assets OR 1 – Solvency Ratio.

For example, an investor's total assets on a given date is Rs. 60 lakh and the total liabilities is Rs. 12 lakh, then applying the formula as above, his/her leverage ratio

= 12/60 = 20%

or 1 – 0.80 = 0.20 (20%)

The extent of investor's solvency can be determined by calculating his/her net worth. In the above example, Solvency ratio = 60 – 12 = 48, which is 80% (48/60) of the total assets.

Higher the leverage, riskier it is. Put differently, higher the solvency, better for the investor. Further, investor needs to ensure that a risky investment position is not compounded with high leverage financing it.

Ways to increase net worth:

- Appreciation of assets
- Reduction in liabilities
- Increase in income
- Decrease in expenses.

Liquidity Ratio

Liquidity refers to meeting either near-term liquidity needs or contingency. Normally, the practice followed is to calculate six months of the investor's needs (running and maintenance expenditure) over the following six months (excluding loan repayments). It is calculated as: Liquid assets/Liquidity needs

For example, an investor has liquid assets to the tune of Rs. 5 lakh, being current market value (short-term FD of Rs. 2 lakh and some open-ended MF scheme for Rs. 4 lakh). Over the next six months his/her needs are say, Rs. 4 lakh. Applying the formula as above,

Liquidity ratio = 5/4 = 1.20

This should generally be more than 1. The higher it is, more comfortable for the investor.

Debt Servicing Ratio

We have noted above that the leverage ratio measures the 'extent of debt' in asset acquisition, though it does not directly measure the 'pressure' it has on the investor's finances. Here the debt servicing ratio comes handy.

It is calculated as: Debt servicing commitment/Income. For example, investor's annual income is Rs. 15 lakh, and debt is Rs. 3 lakh. Applying the formula as above, 3/15 = 20%.

Higher the debt servicing ratio, higher is the financial pressure for the investor and there could be more trouble if the situation turns adverse. Debt servicing should ideally be up to 20-25% or may be up to 33% (including investor's mortgage of the first house).

29.1 GUIDELINES FOR BASE LEVEL INVESTMENTS AND FIXED INCOME INVESTMENTS

1. Accord top priority to buying your own residential house.
2. Seek appropriate insurance cover (life, medical, personal accident, mortgage cover, etc.).
3. Avail of tax shelters.
4. Choose fixed income avenues judiciously.
5. Make a modest commitment to equity, gold and a few other commodities.
6. No single investment, regardless of how secure, will allow you to avoid all risk.
7. Stick to your plan. Plan to be based on how much risk one can handle. The goals must be compatible with one's tolerance level of risk. Plan should be risk-return compatible.
8. Periodically review and revise your portfolio; when required rebalancing the portfolio helps lessen the risk in downturns and improve growth in upturns.

Savings Ratio & Expenses Ratio

Savings ratio is the percentage of annual income that a person is able to save. Put differently, Savings Ratio is 1 – Expenses Ratio.

Suppose a family earns annual income of Rs. 5 lakh and annual expenses are Rs. 4.50 lakh, thus saving Rs. 50,000 annually. Applying the formula as above, savings ratio = 50000/500000, i.e., 10% of annual income. Put differently, 500000 – 450000 = 50000

Savings is not limited to money that is retained in savings bank account. Money invested in various assets already, e.g., PPF, shares, fixed deposits, NSC, mutual funds, real estate, gold, etc., are also a part of savings (made and invested in the past).

However, there are some savings which may not be made available to the investor during the year, e.g., the company's contribution to: PF, superannuation fund, gratuity, etc., which are being deposited on behalf of the investor in respective accounts for the defined purpose. These funds although belongs to the investor, but cannot be given in cash before their maturity, and expiry of certain period/years. At the same time, this belongs to the investor and to be included both in his/her income for the year and added to savings.

Higher the savings ratio, more steady is the investor's likely financial future.

29.2 GENERAL GUIDELINES FOR EQUITY INVESTMENTS

- Accord top priority to buying your own residential house
- Seek appropriate insurance cover (life, medical, personal accident, mortgage cover, etc.)
- Avail of tax shelters
- Adopt a suitable formula plan
- Establish value anchors
- Assess market psychology
- Combine fundamental and technical analysis
- Diversify sensibly (across market caps, securities and geographies)
- Periodically review and revise your portfolio

29.3 GUIDELINES FOR AGGRESSIVE EQUITY INVESTORS

In addition to the general guidelines for equity investment, aggressive investors should keep in mind the following being especially relevant:

(a) Monitor the environment with keen insight
(b) Scout for "special" situations in the primary market
(c) Pay heed to growth shares
(d) Beware of the games operators play
(e) Invest selectively in new issues
(f) Anticipate earnings ahead of the market
(g) Leverage your portfolio when you are bullish
(h) Take swift corrective actions

The following guidelines will be helpful to investors interested in "growth stocks".

1. Tuning is not very important, but with appropriate timing, one may be able to pick up shares at the threshold of high growth rate.
2. Choice of stock should not be based on a simple factor alone. Multiple criteria using different appraisal techniques may be employed.
3. It is better to diversify investment in growth stocks, industry-wise. Because different industries grow at different times by eliminating differences.
4. One should not hold the stock for more than 5 years to gain advantage.

29.4 GUIDELINES FOR CONSERVATIVE EQUITY INVESTORS

In addition to the general guidelines for equity investment, conservative investors should bear in mind the following:

- Avoid certain kinds of shares/securities
- Apply stiff screening criteria
- Look for relatively safe opportunities in the primary market
- Participate in the schemes of mutual funds
- Refrain from short-term switch hitting

29.5 STOCK SELECTION PARAMETERS

Financial Parameters

- Profit margins
- Return on capital employed
- Return on equity
- EPS growth
- Turnover growth
- Operating leverage
- Financial leverage

Non-Financial Parameters

- Business dynamics
  - Growth, risks, returns, competitive position, unsustainable factors
- Management quality
  - Fairness to minority investors
  - Competence to run business

    - What do they do with cash?
- Intangible assets
    - Brands, distribution, intellectual property rights (IPR)

Information is the 'King'

- Price sensitivity of information
- Sources of information
    - Annual reports and press releases
    - Analyst and investor meets
    - Company websites
    - Broker research
    - Registrar of Companies (RoC)
    - Credit rating agencies
    - Exchange and regulatory websites
    - Own research and information gathering efforts

1. *Implementation*

For instance, start with systematic investment (on a monthly basis); to buy required insurance cover (life, health, property, and so on) including investment on tax-free instruments, etc.

2. *Review*

In order to cope with changes, periodic review and revision is required:

- The most important factor in a financial plan is "continuous monitoring and review of plan".
- Set a timeframe, annual review is the norm – unless some important event (like birth, death, change in family income, migration to different country, etc.) occurs at the client's end.
- Review must consider whether the plan is on course or else carry out restructuring as appropriate in the relevant circumstances.
- Maintain adequate diversification when relative values of various securities in the portfolio change.
- Incorporate new information relevant for risk-return assessment.
- Expand or contract the size of portfolio to absorb funds or withdraw funds as needs demand.
- Reflect changes in your risk disposition.

29.6 GUIDELINES TO INVESTORS

1. Deal with a registered member of the stock exchange. If you are dealing with a sub-broker, make sure that all bills and contracts are made in the name of a registered broker.
2. Give specific orders to buy or sell within the fixed price limits and/or time periods within which orders have to be executed.
3. Insist on contract notes to be passed on to you on the dates, when the orders are executed.
4. Make sure that your deal is registered with the stock exchange in a trade (*souda*) block book. In the case of a dispute, this will help trace the details of the deal easily.
5. Collect a settlement table from the stock exchange mentioning the pay-in and pay-out days. Each stock exchange has its own trading periods which are called *settlements*. All transactions within this period are settled at the end. All payments for shares bought and their deliveries take place on the pay-in day. An awareness of pay-in and pay-out days is useful when a broker tries to act smart.
6. Insist on delivery. If the company returns your papers and shares with objections, contact your broker immediately.
7. Ensure that shares bought are transferred in your name before the company's book closure date. This is necessary to make sure that you receive benefits like dividend, interest and bonus shares. All companies have a book closure date on which the list of shareholders in the company is finalized.
8. Complain if the broker does not deliver the shares bought in your name. Proceed to contact another broker with the bill/contract given to you by the earlier broker, and the exchange authorities and the latter will purchase the shares on your behalf. In such an event, the first broker will have to pay the difference in price (if any).
9. Do not take delays or harassment. You have to complain to the grievance cell of the stock exchange or the SEBI in case of delay or harassment.

Global investing is useful for diversification across countries.

- Investing in a range of countries allows investors to reduce the general impact of risks inherent in their home markets on their assets and their net worth.
- Certain markets have a negative or low correlation with some other market in the world, e.g., Canada and China.
- In today's global financial village, it is imperative for an investor to take exposure in outside countries as well thus helping realize various financial needs.
- **Currency** plays an important role in international investing; sometimes it allows an investor to cover his/her currency risks as well as have a global asset diversification.
- Additionally, local laws of different countries could be used to the advantage in some specific situation/condition.

Normally, a financial planner will provide advice on:

- Systematic savings
- Cash flow management
- Investment management
- Asset allocation for investments and portfolio diversification
- Managing risk through insurance coverage
- Tax strategies to increase investible surplus and post-tax returns
- Leaving behind legacy for next generation
- Debt management

30 CHAPTER

Presentation of the Investment Financial Plan

It is mandatory for the financial planner to present his plan in writing. Because a written plan allows the investor to go through the plan at his/her convenience/leisure.

- Read the plan as many times as possible to understand it thoroughly
- Raise any doubts that may arise
- Co-relate the different strategies discussed in the plan
- Allow the planner to explain in detail the rationale behind the recommendations
- Allow the planner to clearly state assumptions on the basis of which the plan was created.

Structure of the Financial Plan

The essential components of a typical financial plan are:

Table 30.1

Part	Contents
Current Personal Financial Statements	Statement of net worth, statement of income and expenditure
Financial Objectives	Financial goals and objectives of the clients along with their respective priorities.
Assumptions	Assumptions made by the financial planner in making the plan. These are generally related to: inflation, rate of interest, taxation, etc.
Financial Plan Strategy	The strategy on which the financial plan has been based. This is derived from the client's risk profile and investment preferences.
Recommendations	Specific recommendations in areas like: retirement planning, insurance, emergency fund, tax planning.

Projections	Projections are derived from the recommended strategy. These are based on the assumptions presented above.
Fees and charges	Charges of the financial planner. Fees should be for preparing, implementing, monitoring and periodic review of the plan.
Action plan	Action points derived from the recommendations.
Agreement in writing	Both financial planner and client agree (in total) in writing about the contents of the plan.
Disclosures	Full disclosures of risks following the recommended investment strategy; any other areas of potential conflicts of interest.
Disclaimers	Disclaimer that attempts to restrict responsibility of the financial planner for the events that are outside his control.
Supporting documentation	Financial calculations and analysis to support the recommendations.

30.1 CASE STUDY 1

Personal Profile and Financial Goals
Client Name: Superman

Present Age: 42

Date of Birth: 07-April-1971

Occupation: Service (in IT Company)

Retirement Age: 55

Financial Goals: The following are the personal/financial goals identified.
Client has shared income, expenditure and total investments made with planner.

REQUIREMENTS (as on 7 August, 2011)

Requirement	Present Value	Year Required	Future Value
Tejal's education	Rs. 20,00,000	2022	Rs. 46,63,278
Irfan's education	Rs. 20,00,000	2027	Rs. 68,51,885
Tejal's wedding	Rs. 15,00,000	2026	Rs. 47,58,254
Irfan's wedding	Rs. 15,00,000	2031	Rs. 69,91,436
Family monthly expenses	Rs. 34,669	From 2024	Rs. 88,766

Table 30.2

Calendar Year	Monthly Exp	Home Loan EMI	ICICI child Ins. policy	HDFC policy	Total p.m.	Yearly requirement
2009	30000	20500	6500	2500	59500	714000
2010	32250	20500	6500	2500	61750	741000
2011	34669	35500	6500	2500	79169	950025
2012	37269	35500	6500	2500	81769	981227
2013	40064	35500	6500	2500	84564	1014769
2014	43069	35500	6500	2500	87569	1050827
2015	46299	35500	6500	2500	90799	1089589
2016	49771	35500	6500	2500	94271	1131258
2017	53504	35500	6500	2500	98004	1176052
2018	57517	15000	6500	2500	81517	978206
2019	61831	15000	6500	2500	85831	1029971
2020	66468	15000	6500	2500	90468	1085619
2021	71453	15000	6500	2500	95453	1145441
2022	76812	15000	3000	2500	97312	1167749
2023	82573	15000	3000	2500	103073	1236880
2024	88766	15000	3000	2500	109266	1311196

Table 30.3

Year	Income	Expenses For Children	Expenses For Self & Deb	Total Expenses	Surplus	Surplus + Income	Remarks
2012	800000			0	8,00,000	8,80,000	Current savings of 3,00,000 from 2011 being carried forward to 2012

2013	1380000			0	13,80,000	15,18,000	
2014	2340947			0	23,40,947	25,75,042	Income from policies maturing in 2013 included
2015	3075042			0	30,75,042	33,82,546	
2016	3882546			0	38,82,546	42,70,800	
2017	4770800			0	47,70,800	52,47,881	
2018	5747881			0	57,47,881	63,22,669	
2019	6822669			0	68,22,669	75,04,935	
2020	8004935			0	80,04,935	88,05,429	
2021	10572799			0	1,05,72,799	1,16,30,079	Income from policies maturing in 2020 included
2022	12130079	4663278		4663278	74,66,801	82,13,481	Tejal's education expenses this year
2023	10635484			0	1,06,35,484	1,16,99,032	Income from policies maturing in 2022 included
2024	12656652		1311196	1311196	1,13,45,456	1,24,80,002	Income from policies maturing in 2023 included
2025	14295751		1409536	1409536	1,28,86,215	1,41,74,837	
2026	18274837	4758254	1515251	6273505	1,20,01,332	1,32,01,465	Tejal's wedding this year

Contd.

2027	14159085	6851885	1628895	8480780	56,78,305	62,46,136	Irfan's education expenses this year. Income from policies maturing in 2026 included
2028	6746136		1751062	1751062	49,95,074	54,94,581	
2029	5994581		1561476	1561476	44,33,105	48,76,416	
2030	17226416		1678587	1678587	1,55,47,829	1,71,02,612	
2031	17452612	6991436	1804481	8795917	86,56,695	95,22,364	Irfan's wedding this year
2032	9872364		1939817	1939817	79,32,547	87,25,802	
2033	25725802		2085303	2085303	2,36,40,499	2,60,04,548	
2034	26004548		2241701	2241701	2,37,62,847	2,61,39,132	
2035	26139132		2409829	2409829	2,37,29,304	2,61,02,234	
2036	26102234		2590566	2590566	2,35,11,668	2,58,62,835	
2037	25862835		2784858	2784858	2,30,77,977	2,53,85,774	
2038	25385774		2993723	2993723	2,23,92,052	2,46,31,257	
2039	24631257		3218252	3218252	2,14,13,005	2,35,54,306	
2040	23554306		3459621	3459621	2,00,94,685	2,21,04,154	
2041	22104154		3719092	3719092	1,83,85,062	2,02,23,568	
2042	20223568		3998024	3998024	1,62,25,544	1,78,48,098	
2043	17848098		4297876	4297876	1,35,50,222	1,49,05,245	
2044	14905245		4620217	4620217	1,02,85,028	1,13,13,531	
2045	11313531		4966733	4966733	63,46,798	69,81,478	
2046	6981478		5339238	5339238	16,42,240	18,06,464	

Assumptions:

Yearly savings of Rs. 5 lakh either from Superman's salary or rental from properties
Yearly investment earning on savings assumed at 10%
Yearly inflation of 7.5% is made in the requirements for self.

After detailed discussion regrading Debt and Mutual Funds, two asset classes are selected to achieve financial goals.

Recommendations were made for Term Insurance plan (pure risk) which is bought. However, buying additional (besides medical cover provided by current employer) and health cover (mediclaim plan) is pending yet.

Charges/Fees: Rs. 10,000 yearly fees towards preparation of financial plan, helping implement the plan and to monitor on yearly, regular basis.

Taxation: Though discussed, it would be considered for one financial year and on regular basis.

This financial plan is finalized, agreed in principle by both planner and client. The implementation process has begun and one round of annual review has taken place. Disclosures with respect to investment products and risks thereon have been discussed and matched with client's investment profile.

30.2 CASE STUDY 2

(An approach commonly followed and practised by Certified Financial Planner)

Dear Shaktimaan,

We congratulate you for having taken the right decision to undergo financial planning process for your family. Financial and investments planning indeed are most crucial tasks that any person/family should undergo if he/she/they are serious about achieving their important goals in life.

As a valued customer, we offer a comprehensive financial plan, a solution for investments that will help you plan and execute properly towards achieving stated needs/goals. The plan will also help you keep a regular track of progress, achievement of your investment needs/objectives.

Based on the information being provided, your current financial situation is being analyzed. The report along with action plan outlined will ensure you achieve goals and investments objectives.

Please bear in mind that, as your financial situation may change over time, this report will serve you as a guide, and as a part of an ongoing, long-term planning process, which needs to be fine-tuned accordingly. The changes that may occur in your personal and financial situation, are important, and therefore needs to be incorporated, updated in order to re-evaluate and ensure you remain on track meeting your goals.

This financial report is to be viewed as an investment barometer, which is prepared as per the details furnished by you. We request you to go through this customized plan at your convenience. Please do contact us for any concerns and/or suggestions you would like to be either removed or incorporated or modified in the plan. We will be more than happy to review the plan and carry out necessary changes which suit your financial needs, goals and investment objectives.

We are glad and thankful to you for the opportunity provided by you. We certainly hope that this financial plan would be helpful to you in more ways than one. Please feel free to call us to know more about our various services.

Your trusted Advisor,

Sunil Kapadia

Sun Investments & Financial Services

Personal Profile and Financial Goals

Client Name: Aayushman

Present Age: 43

Date of Birth: 5th May, 1970

Occupation: Service

Retirement Age: 55

Financial Goals: Following are the personal/financial goals identified.

Table 30.4

Goals	Years to maturity	Age at Goal maturity	Present Cost (Rs.)
Child's education	14	57	2500000
Child's marriage	20	63	500000
Retirement	12	55	50000 (p.m.)
Tour exp. post-retirement	12	55	3000000

Total: Rs. 6000000 + Rs. 50000 on a monthly basis (for the retirement)

Note:

(a) The years to maturity represent the number of years (time) remaining before the actual need begins. The corresponding column is your projected age at the time of goal maturity.

(b) Except for retirement, the present cost for the selected goal is the total one time amount required for fulfilling the concerned goal satisfactorily as of today. For retirement goal specifically, the present cost represents the monthly income requirement as of today that you may need to have after retirement, e.g., your need for Rs. 50,000 worth today's value after retirement, every month, till survival.

Future Values Required

The present cost of your goals has been increased at the rate of inflation or the general price rise for the years to maturity. The future cost represents the money that you need in future to meet your stated financial goals/objectives.

Table 30.5

Your Goals	Years to maturity	Your age at goal maturity	Present cost (Rs.)	Future cost (Rs.)
Child's education	14	57	2500000	7342984
Child's marriage	20	63	500000	2330479
Retirement	12	55	50000 (p.m.)	32439836
Tour exp. Post-retirement	12	55	3000000	6884295
			Total:	**48997594**

Future Cost

The *future cost* for retirement is the amount of retirement kitty that you would need at the time of retirement. This amount is estimated to meet all your monthly income needs (at present cost) during your years of retirement.

Earmarking Existing Investments

Here some existing investments are assumed to be earmarked or kept aside for that particular goal. This would grow at a certain rate for the years till goal maturity. The future value of this earmarked investment is estimated to be used for meeting the future goals. The additional amount required is net amount that you will fall short of in meeting your goals, even after adjusting for the future value of earmarked investments. In case your existing investments are more than what you needed, you will find a negative figure for the additional amount required, representing surplus fund remaining after meeting the goals.

Table 30.6

Your Goals	Years to maturity	Future cost (Rs.)	Earmarked	Existing	Investments	Additional amount required
			Existing Inv. Amt.	Expected return %	Future value (Rs.)	
Child's Edu.	14	7342984	750000	10.50 %	3034822	4308162
Child's marriage	20	2330479	0	0	0	2330479
Retirement	12	32439836	2000000	10.5%	6627921	25811915
Post retirement Tour exp	12	6884295	0	0	0	6884295
Total:		**48997594**	**2750000**		**9662743**	**39334851**

Savings Plan

The *savings plan* is the summarized investment plan that you need to undertake immediately in order to meet your financial goals. In case where we have already earmarked some existing investments, the savings plan is in addition to such earmarking. Further, in such cases the savings plan is targeted to meet the shortfall in goals or the additional amount required. In case, where no earmarking is done, the savings plan would be targeted to meet the future cost of the goal.

Table 30.7 New Investments to be Planned

Your Goals	Years to Maturity	Your Age at Goal Maturity	Additional Amount Required	Expected Returns %	Lump sum/One Time Rs.	Saving Years	Yearly Rs.	Monthly Rs.
Child's Edu.	14	57	4308162	10.50	0	14	0	11350
Child's Marriage	20	63	2330479	10.50	0	20	0	6140
Retirement	12	55	25811915	10.50	0	12	0	68000
Post-retirement Tour Exp.	12	55	6884295	10.50	0	12	0	18135
Total:			**39334851**					**103625**

Total yearly investments required: Rs. 12,43,500
Total monthly investments required: Rs. 1,03,625

Monthly savings are capable of meeting your required amount in future.

Further, the investments that you will make is assumed to deliver the expected returns on a consistent basis during savings years.

The *savings years* are the ones, you need to make savings for achieving goals. However, if your retirement comes before the goal maturity, your yearly and monthly saving instalment amount will be calculated for the years remaining till retirement. The accumulated amount at the time of retirement for such goal(s) would then be invested, and would grow at risk-free return, till the time goal matures, and/or to meet the additional amount required. For lump sum investments though, this limit does not apply and the investments would be made till goal maturity.

Note:

1. The required yearly and monthly savings are taken after considering the savings growth rates, if any, assumed over time. Hence, they may increase and/or change in future, depending on the growth rates assumed for the respective periods.
2. For the amount of monthly savings, the calculations have been made such that the monthly SIP remains constant.

Life Insurance: Each one of us faces numerous risks in our lives, the biggest of which is our life. Though an insurance cover cannot protect you against emotional loss arising out of these risks, it softens the economic crisis that usually accompanies these losses. It is thus critical that you have a protective shield against such losses from any untoward event.

In this plan, we have tried to assess the life insurance cover that you require. The life cover takes into consideration all your financial goals, household expense protection, current liabilities and investments made as on date. Return assumed on such insurance amount is risk-free return. Calculation given below explains the total life insurance cover.

Table 30.8

A. Protection needed for investments identified				**3000000**
Your Goals	**Years to Maturity**	**Current Cost**	**Future Cost**	**Current Need**
Child's Edu.	14	2500000	7342984	2500000
Child's Marriage	20	500000	2330479	500000
B. Outstanding Liabilities/Loans				1500000
C. Household Expenses (pm)				3600000
Protecting household expenses of Rs. 50000 per month for next 6 years.				

D. Total required life insurance cover	8100000
E. Existing life insurance cover	6000000
Balance life insurance cover required (D - E)	2100000
Retirement is not considered for calculating insurance.	

Total life insurance cover that you require now is Rs. 21,00,000 as per details provided. We believe this amount would reasonably protect the family, your dreams in case of any uncertainty.

Investment Analysis - Expected Returns: The expected returns are weighted average returns of all existing investments earmarked and new investments planned for your goals. You may observe it as single return for existing and new investments—calculated at 10.50%.

To achieve investments return of 10.50% p.a. following "**asset allocation**" is suggested:

Table 30.9

				Likely return @ 10.48611%	**Per month and 13326**
Asset Class	**% allocation**	**Likely return in %**	**Last column**	**Allocation per month Rs.**	**Allocation Yearly Rs.**
Fixed rate	60	8.75	525.00	**62175**	746100
Equity & Equity MF	28	14.50	406.00	**29015**	348180
Gold	12	10.00	120.00	**12435**	149220
	90		1051.00	**103625**	**1243500**

Asset Allocation: The asset allocation represents the portfolio distribution into equity, debt, gold for existing investments earmarked. The asset allocation can be seen as in line with the expected return from the investments to be made.

Please understand that, both expected return and asset allocation for existing investments would evolve and change over time. Further, returns so generated from new investments would also get added to existing investments for goals identified. Asset allocation and return for new or future investments would continue to remain same, unless any change occurs.

Assumptions

(a) Taxation: Taxation effect is not considered. All returns are assumed to be pre-tax only.

(b) Inflation: The inflation rate at 8% is assumed and used for calculation of future cost.

(c) Life Expectancy (85 Years): Life expectancy is taken as per mutually agreed discussion. A person on retirement will have a retirement kitty which he will invest in some asset with lower risk. He will then survive through the earnings thereon and by making withdrawals from kitty so accumulated. On reaching life expectancy, you will have exhausted this capital/accumulation so generated.

(d) Expected Returns: Equity and Mutual Fund; at 14.5% – Bank Deposit, PPF/EPF; at 8.75%; Gold at 10% and Returns on Retirement Kitty at 10.50%.

Note: The actual results may vary with the estimated results of this calculation. However, one can reasonably be sure of achieving all goals if one follows the recommendations, as suggested by planner/advisor, without any break in investments. Further, a regular monitoring of the portfolio and the goals will help to stay focussed in achieving the same.

Disclosure Statement

This document has been prepared to help you make important decisions regarding your financial future. Before reviewing the financial plan and investments options presented herein, please take proper note of the inherent features and limitations associated with this information. The content of this report is based on data, information provided by you. Financial/investment plan could be erroneous if any material and relevant information remained undisclosed, or partially disclosed, or misrepresented.

However, the future is uncertain and cannot be guaranteed. The assumptions are only estimates, with no assurance of their attainability or ultimate outcome and hence there can be material differences in the actual results and financial projections made. The investments returns mentioned are subject to market fluctuations and other associated risks. Also, changes that may occur in your personal and financial situations which are dynamic in nature and hence can't be visualized/factored completely now.

The financial/investment planning incorporates certain methodology in the calculations and client agrees to study, and understand the same. The appropriateness of the methodology (one of many) used here cannot be guaranteed fully. The statements, projections, strategies, plan, etc., presented here are intended only as a guide. The same is left to the client's best judgement for the appropriateness, completeness, and applicability. The client is at liberty to use his/her prudence/intelligence or seek any expert advice before acting upon the same. It is possible that the principal, partner, advisor, etc., preparing the financial/investment plan is also engaged in the business of financial product distribution and earnings, namely, commission income that may accrue from it. The client/recipient of this plan specifically acknowledges this and that the statements, recommendations, etc., made here may result into sales of the respective company's products consequently.

Your financial planner is not responsible or legally liable for reviewing plan on an ongoing basis or for updating it, unless such service agreements have specifically been entered into, renewed and compensated as mutually agreed. This financial plan does not create any legal obligation or any responsibility either on the part of client, or on principal, partner, advisor who have prepared it and as mentioned in the plan. Although all relevant/important data, information of client shall be treated with utmost confidentiality, however, the client hereby acknowledges and agrees that such financial plan and other information may be shared/referred internally for the purpose of rendering the services.

As a client you are under no obligation to follow, in whole or in part of any of the alternatives presented in this financial/investment plan, or to purchase any financial or non-financial products or services through your planner and/or advisor.

30.3 CASE STUDY 3

Personal Profile and Financial Goals

Client Name: Rambharose

Present Age: 53

Date of Birth: 1st January, 1948

Occupation: Service (in Tyre Company)

Retirement Age: 58

Financial Goals: The following are the personal financial goals identified and investments needed.

Table 30.10 New Investments to be Planned

Your Goals	Years to Maturity	Your Age at Goal Maturity	Additional Amount Required	Expected Returns %	Lump sum /One time Rs.	Monthly Rs.
Children's Marriage	1	54	250000	12.00	250000	0
	4	57	340000	12.00	0	5550
	6	59	800000	12.00	0	7650
Retirement	5	58	6582225	12.00	250000	75050
Post-retirement Medical case	5	58	700000	9.00	0	8550
Total:			**8672225**		**500000**	**96800**

Client has shared income and expenditure, with planner.

Charges/Fees: Rs. 5,000 yearly fees towards preparation of financial plan, helping implement the plan and to monitor yearly on regular basis.

Taxation: Though discussed, it would be considered for a financial year, on regular basis.

This financial plan is finalized, agreed in principle by both planner and client. The implementation process has begun and client has started making monthly investments in part. Disclosures with respect to investment products and risks thereon have been discussed and matched with the client's profile.

"Wit is educated insolence." – Aristotle

31 Research in Investments

CHAPTER

If one looks back one realizes, twenty-five years that the following products were not available then, and have emerged due to catering to investor's needs, the changing environment, availability of lot of information through various media/channels, new regulations, and lot of research that has been carried out.

1. New Pension System (NPS)
2. RGESS (Rajiv Gandhi Equity linked Saving Scheme)
3. Reverse Mortgage (for retirees)
4. Derivative products
5. Arbitrage products
6. Structured instruments
7. Infrastructure bonds
8. Asset allocation products
9. Exchange traded instruments
10. Quant products (based on Algorithm model)
11. Gold scheme in mutual funds
12. ULIP (in life insurance)
13. Family floater (a type of health insurance)
14. REIT (Real Estate Investments Trust for investing into Commercial Properties) and ReInv (Real Investments Trust for investing into Infrastructure Projects), and so on.

31.1 RESEARCH IN SECURITIES MARKET

In order to deepen the understanding and knowledge about Indian capital market, and to assist in policy making, SEBI has been promoting high quality research in capital market. In collaboration with **NCAER**, SEBI brought out a *Survey of Indian Investors*, which estimates investor population in India and their investment preferences. SEBI has also tied up with reputed national and international academic and research institutions for conducting research studies/projects on various issues related to the capital market.

In order to improve market efficiency further and to set international benchmarks in the securities industry, **NSE** administers a scheme called the 'NSE Research Initiative' with a view to developing information base and a better insight into the working of securities market in India. The objective of this initiative is to foster research, which can support and facilitate:

(a) stock exchanges to better design market microstructure,
(b) participants to frame their strategies in the marketplace,
(c) regulators to frame regulations,
(d) policy makers to formulate policies, and
(e) expand the horizon of knowledge.

In pursuance of the announcement made by then Finance Minister in his Budget Speech in February 2005, SEBI has established the **National Institute of Securities Markets** (NISM) in Mumbai to promote securities market education and research. Towards accomplishing the desire of Government of India and vision of SEBI, NISM has established six distinct schools to cater to the educational needs of various constituencies such as investor, issuers, intermediaries, regulatory staff, policy makers, and academia and future professionals of securities markets. NISM is mandated to implement certification examinations for professionals employed in various segments.

31.2 PRIVATE EQUITY

Researchers have used a variety of other more or less satisfactory ways of getting a handle on private equity market volatility. These include examining the volatility of returns earned from private equity funds and using indices of smaller company stocks as a proxy for private equity.

This research highlights the importance of a number of themes emphasized earlier. First, it seems that investors in private equity have not on an average earned a premium reward to compensate them for the extra financial gearing often involved in private equity. Second, the pattern of manager performance persistence is important, as investors need to convince themselves that they can identify better than average managers. Skill is essential. Investors cannot profit from market returns in private equity through a passive, market-matching strategy, so they should not expect to do even averagely well unless they can gain access to skilled managers. Without skilled managers, investors will be condemned to underperform unless, for a period, they happen to get lucky.

An **efficient capital market** is one in which security prices adjust rapidly to the arrival of new information and, therefore, the current prices of securities reflect all information about the security. Some of the most interesting and important academic researches during the past 20 years have analyzed whether our capital markets are efficient or not. This extensive research is important because its results have significant real-world implications for investors and portfolio managers. In addition, the question of whether capital markets are efficient is one of the most controversial areas in investment research.

31.3 RESEARCH FINDINGS

Bing carried out a survey (May-June, 1971) of practitioners' stocks evaluation methods and found that several approaches were in vogue. He found that analysis (1) used time horizon from 1 to 3 years, and (2) preferred to use several techniques in combination. Seventy-five per cent of the analysts followed rules of the thumb to normalize P/E ratio.

(i) The compound current actual P/E with what they considered normal for the stock in question.

(ii) They estimated future earnings (1 to 3 years out) with what they considered normal for the stock in question.

(iii) They compared the multiplier and growth or earnings of individual stocks with industry group multiple and earnings growth.

Michael, Kishore & others ("Earnings announcements are full of surprises", June, 2007) based their study on a number of stocks, and opined that differences in P/E between stocks were due to projected earnings growth, expected dividend payout, and variation in rate of earnings growth or growth risk. Bower and Bower ["Risk and the Valuation of Common Stock" (May-June, 1969)] also came up with a similar conclusion.

The dividend risk in marketability of stock, price variability, and conformity with market behaviour. Malkiel and Cragg ["The consensus and accuracy of some predictions of the growth of corporate earnings", (March, 1968)] found positive effect of earnings growth on P/E. They further found that dividend payout effect was not clear.

Research evolves on a continuous basis either to create some new products, new features, add-on benefits, combination of asset-class, or to cater to ever changing needs/requirements of an investor. The journey of research involves lot of hard work, obtaining and analyzing various information/data of different segment of investors, e.g., income, savings, preferences, age profile, risk appetite, pricing, sticking to current regulatory norms, the overall environment of a particular economy, tax incentives, diversification, and so on.

32 CHAPTER

Six Sigma Approach for Different Investment Models

Goal Statement To help and advise family clients in the matter of monetary investments for need-based financial plan.

Problem Statement To maximise return on investments (in the range of 10-15% p.a. CAGR as per client's need)

Starting Date It differs for each client. Though advisable to save and invest early and for a longer period to reap benefits of compounding (**normally 25 years onwards**)

End Date Usually clients would want to build corpus for their retirement life needs, for children's education and marriage, buying some assets, foreign tour, etc. (age bracket: **55-62** years)

Team members Consultant and client (2 or 3 members)

Resources required Time, money, information/analysis on various relevant products including regulatory laws and economic data

Table 32.1

Tool Used	Important Consideration	Critical to Quality (CTQ)	Key Performance Indicator (KPI)
Define	To achieve family's financial goals	Waiting time and product's cycle time	Healthy growth of savings of a portfolio of different asset classes over a defined period, at 10% to 15% p.a. CAGR
Measure	Realistic expectations	Cost of delay in initiating savings and investments	Transparency on various products' charges and fees

Analyze	Family profile and lifestyle, net income liabilities, present savings, understanding of risk, risk appetite life, health and home insurance	Choosing products not relevant to one's investment plan. Frequent churning of portfolio (which increases costs).	Succession plan and distribution of assets amongst legal heirs.
Improve	Disciplined approach; re-balance the portfolio so as to remain on course		Regular review and desired action to ensure goals are met on time.
Control	Greed and fear	To have patience, not to panic, remain flexible	Usage of corpus as plan to service the retirement and then leave legacy for next generation.

KPIV, KPOV

Y = f (X1, X2, X3, ……., Xn)

where Y is the KPOV

X1, X2,….., Xn are KPIVs. There can be more than one KPOV.

Table 32.2

KPIV (Xs)		C / U	Process	KPOV (Ys)
X1	Fixed rate instruments	C	To make investments in all relevant assets	Goals achieved as per planned rate of growth
X2	Securities market and Mutual Fund	C	Class	
X3	Real estate	C		
X4	Gold	U		

32.1 CAUSE AND EFFECT MATRIX FOR MODERATE INVESTOR

A. (for **moderate growth, say 12%** p.a. CAGR, as per client's need and profile)

Table 32.3

Important Rating for Ys- > (1 to 10)						8	7	9	
					KPOV (Ys)	Corpus (as defined)	@ regular interval	Rate of Growth	TOTAL
X1	Fixed rate Instruments	6	6	3					117
X2	Securities Market and Mutual Fund	9	6	9					195
X3	Real estate	6	3	6					123
X4	Gold	3	6	3					93

Relationship between X & Y can be 1, 3 & 9

32.2 CAUSE AND EFFECT MATRIX FOR AGGRESSIVE INVESTOR

B. (for **aggressive growth, say 15%** p.a. CAGR, as per Client's need and profile)

Table 32.4

Important Rating for Ys- > (1 to 10)					8	7	9	
				KPOV (Ys)	Corpus (as defined)	@ regular interval	Rate of Growth	TOTAL
X1	Fixed rate Instruments	3	6	3				93
X2	Securities Market & Mutual Fund	9	9	9				216
X3	Real estate	6	3	6				123
X4	Gold	3	6	3				93

Relationship between X & Y can be 1, 3 & 9

32.3 CAUSE AND EFFECT MATRIX FOR CONSERVATIVE INVESTOR

C. (for **conservative growth, say 10%** p.a. CAGR, as per client's need and profile)

Table 32.5

Important Rating for Ys- > (1 to 10)						**8**	**7**	**9**	
					KPOV (Ys)	**Corpus (as defined)**	**@ regular interval**	**Rate of Growth**	**TOTAL**
X1	**Fixed rate Instruments**	9	9	9					**216**
X2	**Securities Market and Mutual fund**	6	9	6					**165**
X3	**Real estate**	6	3	3					**96**
X4	**Gold**	3	6	3					**93**

Relationship between X & Y can be 1, 3 & 9

Proverbial Investment Wisdom

1. If you begin with a prayer, (begin with contemplation) you can think clearly and make fewer mistakes.
2. Outperforming the market is a difficult task.
3. Buy value, not market trends or the economic outlook.
4. Buy low – simple in concept, difficult in execution.
5. There's no free lunch.
6. Learn from your mistakes.
7. Devote time and effort.
8. Do your homework or hire experts.
9. Invest in something you know or understand.
10. Invest – don't trade or speculate.
11. Don't rely on experts, sentiments and tips.
12. View risk differently.
13. Keep it simple, concentrate on your defense.
14. Nothing ventured, nothing gained.
15. Beware of "fighting the last war."
16. Money management is 10 per cent inspiration and 90 per cent perspiration.
17. To err is human, to hedge is divine.
18. Buy a business, not a stock.
19. Manage a portfolio of business.
20. Diversify – by company, by industry, by time horizon, by asset classes, by country.
21. No stock is inherently good or bad; it is the price that makes it so.
22. Search for bargains among quality stocks.
23. You never understand a stock unless you are long (or short).
24. Be long-term but watch the ticks.
25. Never throw good money after the bad.
26. Don't panic, do not be fearful or negative too often.
27. Successful money managers have brains, nerve, and luck.
28. Investigate, and invest.
29. Invest for maximum total net return.
30. If you have all answers you probably don't even understand the questions.
31. Open-mindedness, flexiblity and independent thinking about all types of investments will yield big dividends.
32. No money manager can perform successfully in all kinds of markets. There is no man for all seasons.
33. The greatest of all gifts is the power to visualize and estimate things at their true worth.
34. Shallow men believe in luck, the wise and the strong believe in law of cause and effect.

5. The trend is the friend.
7. Diversify and hold.
8. Don't fall in love with a stock.
12. Never look back.
13. Keep tight control on your emotions.
14. No one is smarter than the market.
17. Be an optimist; it helps in investing.
18. Don't chase [illegible].
19. Markets can go [illegible].
20. Markets can remain irrational longer than you can remain solvent.
21. Nobody rings a bell at the top or bottom.
22. Buy the rumour and sell the news.
23. Markets are driven by fear and greed.
24. Don't try to catch a falling knife.
25. The trend is your friend until the end.
26. Bulls make money, bears make money, pigs get slaughtered.
28. Invest, don't gamble.

References and Bibliography

1. Shah, P., Bairathi, R, Amit, & Mantri, S. (2015). Analysis of REIT Regulations in India. (KPMG; Knight Frank India; Hariani & Co.; NAREDCO)
2. Kumar, P. et al. (2015). India's Real Estate Market: Outlook of Structured High Yield Debt. Kushman & Wakefield.
3. Ram, V.P. & Bala S.D. (2014). First Lesson in Strategic Financial Management. 3rd edition (revised).
4. Bansal, N. (2014). Indian Real Estate – Opening Doors. KPMG.
5. Sankaran, S. & Shashikant, U. (2013). Investment Advisor (Level II). Series X-B.
6. Shashikant, U. (2013). Continuing Professional Education (CPE) Program–Mutual Fund. CIEL.
7. Desai, V. (2012). Financial Markets and Financial Services: Ensuring Growth–Enhancing Value.
8. Bhat, S. (2011). Security Analysis & Portfolio Management.
9. Dr. Dharambeer et al. (2011). Indian Commodity Market: Growth & Prospects. IJMT.
10. Pandey, I.M. (2010). Financial Management. 10th edition.
11. Department of Consumer Affairs, Government of India Forward Market Commission, (2010), Do's and Don'ts for dealing in Commodity Futures.
12. Chandra, P. (2008). Investment Analysis and Portfolio Management.
13. IMS Pro School (2008), Introduction to Financial Planning (Concept book).
14. IMS Pro School (2008), Investment Planning–(Professional Development Program).
15. IMS Pro School (2008), Estate Planning (Concept book).
16. Stanyer, P. (2008). Guide to Investment Strategy.
17. Baid, R. (2007). An Easy Reader of AMFI –Mutual Fund Testing Program.
18. BSE Training Institute (2007). Comprehensive Course on Capital Markets. (Powerpoint presentation).
19. Ahuja, N.L. (2006). Commodity Derivatives Market in India: Development, Regulation and Future Prospects.

20. NCFM Workbook (2003), Capital Market (Dealer) Module.
21. Chandra, P. (1992). The Investment Game – How to Win. 3rd edition.
22. Yasaswy, N.J. (1992). Finance and Profits – The Manager's Handbook.
23. RBI's Handbook on Indian Economy. (2014)
24. SEBI's Handbook & Bulletin. Various Issues.
25. Keane, S.M. (1983). Stock Market Efficiency: Theory, Evidence and Implications. Oxford: Philip Allan Publishers.
26. Lo, A.W. & Mackinlay, A.C. (1999). A Non-Random Walk Down Wall Street. N.J.: Princeton University Press.

www.sebi.gov.in
www.bseindia.com
www.rbi.org.in
www.incometaxindia.gov.in
www.finmin.nic.in
www.indiakanoon.org
www.mca.gov.in
www.cfp.net
www.irda.gov.in
www.amfiindia.com
www.pfrda.org.in
www.nism.ac.in
www.mcxindia.com
www.nseindia.com

Index

S